Africa in Global History

Africa in Global History

A Handbook

Edited by Toyin Falola and Mohammed Bashir Salau

ISBN 978-3-11-135333-3
e-ISBN (PDF) 978-3-11-067801-7
e-ISBN (EPUB) 978-3-11-067814-7

Library of Congress Control Number: 2021944282

Bibliographic information published by the Deutsche Nationalbibliothek
The Deutsche Nationalbibliothek lists this publication in the Deutsche Nationalbibliografie;
detailed bibliographic data are available on the Internet at http://dnb.dnb.de.

© 2023 Walter de Gruyter GmbH, Berlin/Boston.
This volume is text- and page-identical with the hardback published in 2022.
Cover credits: shuoshu / DigitalVision Vectors / gettyimages.de
Printing and binding: CPI books GmbH, Leck

www.degruyter.com

Contents

Toyin Falola and Mohammed Bashir Salau
Introduction —— 1

Peter J. Mitchell
Chapter 1
Human Origins, Early Societies and Migration to 1000 CE —— 19

Oyeniyi Bukola Adeyemi
Chapter 2
Africa in the Mediterranean World —— 43

Moses I. Olatunde Ilo
Chapter 3
Tran-Saharan Networks to 1800 —— 65

Pedro Machado
Chapter 4
Africa and the Indian Ocean World to 1800 —— 79

David L. Imbua
Chapter 5
Africa and the Atlantic World, 1400–1860 —— 99

J.A. Oluyitan
Chapter 6
Africa and Europe in the Nineteenth Century: The "Legitimate Trade" Era and Christian Missionaries —— 125

Bala Saho
Chapter 7
The European Conquest of Africa, 1879–1914 —— 141

Aliyu Sakariyau Alabi
Chapter 8
Impact of African Colonial Experience 1914–1940 —— 153

Abdul Kuba
Chapter 9
Africa and the World Wars —— 169

Ajibola A. Abdulrahman
Chapter 10
Nationalism and Decolonization in Africa, 1918–1975 — 185

Sifiso Mxolisi Ndlovu
Chapter 11
South African Apartheid and Resistance: A Global History — 203

Sifiso Mxolisi Ndlovu
Chapter 12
The Geopolitics and Geo-economics of Apartheid South Africa and the Cold War: A Global History — 219

Noah Echa Attah
Chapter 13
Diseases and Medicines in African History — 239

William Ackah
Chapter 14
Africa and the Globalization of Religion in the Contemporary Era — 263

Evelyn Onwaniban
Chapter 15
Africa and the Cold War — 281

Flavia Gasbarri
Chapter 16
Africa and the USA — 297

Jodie Yuzhou Sun
Chapter 17
Africa and China — 315

Nnaoma Hyacinth Iwu
Chapter 18
Foreign Aid to Africa Since 1940 — 335

Idom T. Inyabri
Chapter 19
Globalization, African Popular Culture and Hip Hop: An Embedded History — 355

Toyin Falola
Chapter 20
Contemporary Globalization and Africa —— 373

Select Bibliography —— 391

Notes on Contributors —— 419

Index —— 423

Toyin Falola and Mohammed Bashir Salau
Introduction

One of the most mistaken and tragic stereotypes about African history is that it, in contrast to western history, does not contribute to and benefit from a world history perspective. Although Africa was seen as part of a global world by Europeans and Islamic scholars and travelers prior to the modern era, the idea that history only begins in societies with written records combined with a growing sense of European superiority led Enlightenment European philosophers such as David Hume and G. W. F. Hegel to characterize Africa as having contributed very little to world history.[1] Hegel, in fact, imagined a racial division of Africa and argued that in contrast to North Africa and Egypt, where he believed people were "less black" and possessed history, sub-Saharan Africa was isolated from other parts of the world and contributed minimally to world history. He also described black Africans as "living in barbarism," uncivilized, and childlike.[2] Such negative stereotypes became the bedrock of European justification for their authority in facilitating the Atlantic slave trade and subsequently in the colonization of Africa.

During the first half of the twentieth century, the racial model of world history that emerged from the Enlightenment was replaced by a similar civilizational model. The pioneers of the civilizational model included Oswald Spengler, Arnold Tonybee, and Karl Jaspers, to mention just a few.[3] In their works, these pioneers and their successors stressed their commitment to understanding the meaning of history as well as commitment to understanding "civilizations" and cultural continuities. In addition to being less concerned with nation states than with cultural and racial groups, they had little to say about the lives of ordinary people as well as about general economic and social patterns. They also offered a hierarchical order of civilization in which Europeans were presented at the epitome of civilization and Africans were characterized as lacking civilization entirely. Thus, the civilizational model, as the earlier racial model, presented Africa as having little role in world history, and presented African history as having no depth.

The notions that Africa had only little influence on world history, and that African history lacks depth, had devastating consequences for Africans and for the many peoples of African descent in the diaspora. Unsurprisingly, prior to the first half of

---

[1] David Hume, *Essays and Treatises on Several Subjects in Two Volumes, Volume 1* (London: T. Cadell, 1777); and Georg W. F. Hegel, *Lectures on the Philosophy of World* (Cambridge: Cambridge University Press, 1975).
[2] Hegel, *Lectures*, 174–75.
[3] Examples of works by these writers include: Arnold J. Toynbee, *A Study of World History*, 12 vols. (Oxford: Oxford University Press, 1934–1961); Oswald Spengler, *The Decline of the West*, 2 vols. (New York: Knopf, 1934); and Karl Jaspers, *The Origin and Goal of History*, trans. M. Bullock (London: Routlege and Paul, 1953).

AFRICA
In the World

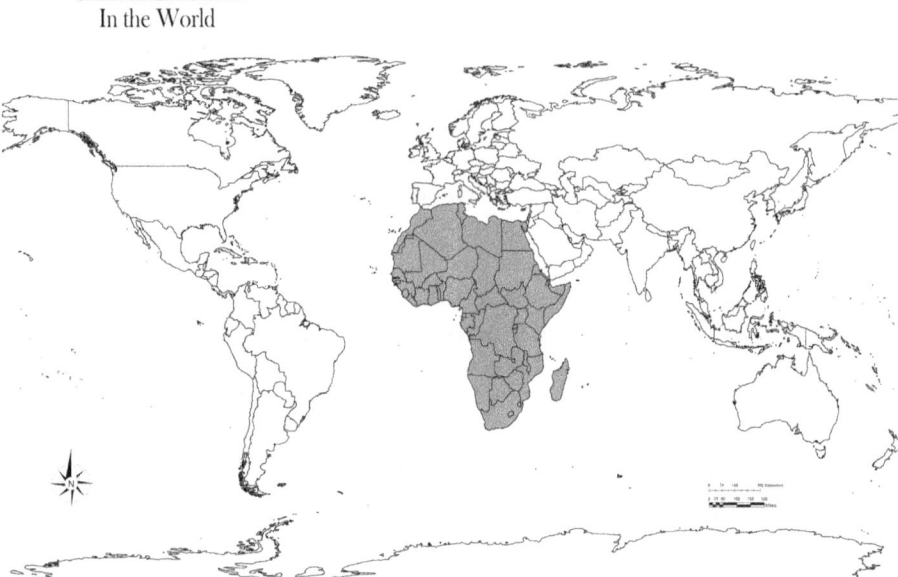

Map 1: Africa in the World. © Toyin Falola.

the twentieth century, African American intellectuals, political activists, and religious leaders not only made connections to Africa, but also asserted Africa's place in world civilization as a means of refusing to consign themselves to being chattel. In the twentieth century, focusing on these negative notions about Africa, or on the earlier concepts of whiteness and civilization, W. E. B. Dubois, an African American scholar, critiqued these stereotypes by stressing that the history of Africa dated back to at least 5000 BC, and that in the course of this long history Africans had actively participated in and shaped the trajectory of world history.[4] In addition to Dubois, other twentieth-century African American scholars including Carter G. Woodson stressed the theme of Africa's contributions to humanity and the theme of Africa's long history in their works.[5] As part of the broad movement to liberate Africans and peoples of African descent in the diaspora, some Africans and African Americans emphasized that black civilization had its root in Egypt, and that Egyptian civilization gave birth to the European civilization. By the 1950s, a Senegalese scientist and historian, Cheikh Anta Diop, was at the forefront of those making such Afrocen-

---

4 W. E. B. Dubois, *The World and Africa: An Inquiry into the Part Which Africa Has played in World History* (New York: Viking, 1946).

5 Examples of Carter G. Woodson's relevant works include *The African Background Outlined* (Washington: ASNLH, 1936) and his *African Heroes and Heroines* (Washington: Associated Publishers, 1939).

tric claims.⁶ However, it is significant to note that Afrocentrism as propounded by Diop and others has been criticized partly on the grounds that it presents African culture as singular and conflates biology and culture.⁷

The study of world history changed significantly after the 1940s, with greater attention paid to Africa's role in the world and to stressing processes and comparisons rather than civilizations and the meaning of history. This change was associated with several factors: the emergence of African history as a valid area of historical research; the increased interaction of nations; the globalization of education in the United States; the proliferation of the writings of non-Western scholars; the emergence of new works that approached world history along a scientific and cultural path; the efforts of the United Nations Educational, Scientific and Cultural Organization (UNESCO) to produce a non-centric history of humankind; the changing definition of community in various parts of the world; and the need to better prepare European and American students for life in a pluralistic world and increasingly multicultural nations.⁸ Out of this intellectual ferment, many non-Africanist scholars championed new models of world history. For example, William McNeill advocated a model that emphasized the processes which transcended regions, and incorporated Tonybee's emphasis on large scale patterns of change. McNeill also stressed that change is a product of contact and collisions between societies.⁹ Marshall Hodgson offered a hemispheric and interregional approach;¹⁰ and Geoffrey Barraclough examined the rise of Europe stressing themes mainly related to the modern period like the impact of the industrial revolution and impact of European rule on Africa and other parts of the world.¹¹ Still, despite these new approaches, Africanist scholars criticized much of this work on world history as being biased or Eurocentric or Americentric. For example, Patrick Manning attacked the world history periodization model proposed by Jerry Bentley as 'Eurocentric' because it stresses the notion of civilization instead of emphasizing the concept of cultural interaction.¹²

In the context of the intellectual ferment of the 1950s and 1960s, research by Africanist historians sought to undermine the view that African history did not contrib-

---

6 Cheikh Anta Diop, *The African Origin of Civilization: Myth or Reality*, ed. Mercer Cook (Chicago: Chicago Review, 1989).
7 Kwame Anthony Appiah, "Europe Upside Down: Fallacies of the New Afrocentrism," in *Perspectives on Africa: A Reader in Culture, History, and Representation*, ed. Roy Richard Grinker and Christopher B. Steiner (Oxford: Blackwell, 1999), 728–31.
8 Patrick Manning, *Navigating World History: Historians Create a Global Past* (New York: Palgrave Macmillan, 2003), 10–13.
9 William McNeill, "A Defence of World History (The Prothero Lecture,)" *Transactions of the Royal Historical Society* 32 (1982): 75–89.
10 Marshall G. S. Hodgson, *Rethinking World History: Essays on Europe, Islam and World History*, ed. Edmund Burke III (Cambridge: Cambridge University Press, 1993).
11 Geoffrey Barraclough, *Turning Points in World History* (London: Thames and Hudson, 1979).
12 Patrick Manning, "The Problem of Interactions in World History," *The American Historical Review* 101, 3 (1996): 771.

ute to and benefit from a world history perspective. Accordingly, this approach has established a few key ideas, such as reframing Africa as the cradle of humankind, as well as demonstrating that Africa is a diverse, complex and dynamic continent with a rich history. This approach has also emphasized that while Africans have shaped their historical destinies, the continent's historical evolution has also been affected by external influences, and, ultimately, that no understanding of world history is complete without African history. In integrating Africa into world history, scholars have employed diverse approaches. For instance, Philip Curtin emphasized the comparative approach and favored focusing on trans-Atlantic interaction;[13] Walter Rodney employed the dependency theory in the context of examining the relationship between Africa and Europe;[14] Edward Alpers places East Africa in the context of the Indian Ocean World;[15] John Lonsdale embraced the globalization approach in his study of ethnicity in Africa;[16] Frederick Cooper advocates examining how the colonial experience impacted societies of both the colonizers and the colonized;[17] Jean Francois Bayart and Stephen Ellis use of the paradigm of extraversion in their study of Africa's relationship with other parts of the world;[18] Donald R. Wright demonstrates how global events shaped people's lives over many centuries in Niumi, a small town located in the Gambia River region of West Africa;[19] and Iris Berger integrates social history and women's history in examining the connections between South Africa and other parts of the world.[20]

As part of his contribution to the literature produced by Africanist historians after the 1940s, Patrick Manning published *Navigating World History: Historians Create a Global Past*.[21] In this study, he defines world history as "the story of connections within the global human community,"[22] reviews world history studies, explores the development of new institutions for world history, and highlights connections and similarities among world's people as well as the major differences that divide

---

[13] Philip Curtin, *Cross-Cultural Trade in World History* (Cambridge: Cambridge University Press, 1984); and Philip Curtin, *The Rise and Fall of the Plantation Complex: Essays in Atlantic History* (Cambridge: Cambridge University Press, 1990).
[14] Walter Rodney, *How Europe Underdeveloped Africa* (Washington, DC: Howard University Press, 1974).
[15] Edward Alpers, *East Africa and the Indian Ocean* (Princeton, NJ: Markus Wiener, 2009); and Edward Alpers, *The Indian Ocean in World History* (Oxford: Oxford University Press, 2013).
[16] John Lonsdale, "Globalization, Ethnicity, and Democracy: A View from 'the Hopeless Continent'" in *Globalization in World History*, ed. Anthony G. Hopkins (New York: Norton, 2002) 202–03.
[17] Frederick Cooper, *Colonialism in Question: Theory, Knowledge, History* (Los Angeles: University of California Press, 2005); and Frederick Cooper, "Conflict and Connection: Rethinking Colonial African History," *The American Historical Review* 99, 5 (1994): 1516–45.
[18] Jean Francois Bayart and Stephen Ellis, "Africa in the World: A History of Extraversion," *African Affairs* 99, 395 (2000): 217–67.
[19] Donald R. Wright, *The World and a Very Small Place in Africa* (Armonk, NY: M. E. Sharpe, 1997).
[20] Iris Berger, *South Africa in World History* (Oxford: Oxford University Press, 2009).
[21] Manning, *Navigating World History*.
[22] Manning, *Navigating World History*, 3.

them. He also, among other things, proposes study programs for graduate studies as well as teaching methods that stress key events and processes of world history.

In the same year in which *Navigating World History* was published, Prentice Hall released the first undergraduate textbook that placed Africa in a global context. The authors, Erik Gilbert and Jonathan T. Reynolds, sought to pay almost equal attention to two periods of history: the period before 1500 and the period since. They also rejected Eurocentric stereotypes about Africa in part by offering African perspectives on world history and in part by emphasizing African diversity and dynamism. In placing Africa in a global context, Gilbert and Reynolds addressed a variety of topics such as Africa and human origins, Africa and the early Christian world, East Africa and the advent of Islam, and slavery and the creation of the Atlantic world. Even as they largely focused on themes that illustrated the important role that Africa has played in world history, they also offered both continental and regional discussions.[23]

The publication of *Navigating World History* and of *Africa in World History*, sparked a flurry of attention on the topic of Africa in global history that translated, over time, into a sustained scholarly project. As Reynolds explains, between 2004 and 2006 alone:

> the African Studies Association Executive Board saw it fit to sponsor two roundtables on the subject of "Globalizing Africa: Placing Africa in World History" and identified them as being of "special interest" to Africanists. In 2004, both H-World and H-Africa listserves saw extensive (and occasionally heated) exchanges on the topic, and the journals *Historically Speaking* and *World History Connected* each hosted special forums on the subject. Also in 2004, the Ohio University Press announced the launching of a series entitled "Africa in World History." In 2005, the World History Association held their annual conference at Al-Akhawayn University, Morocco, with "Africa in World History" sharing the masthead with "the Mediterranean in World History" as the conference theme. Finally, the current year (2006) will see the publication of this focus issue of the *World History Bulletin* on the subject, and the Annual Meeting of the African Studies Association will be built around the theme of "(re)Thinking Africa and the World: Internal Reflections, External Responses."[24]

As a result of the efforts of Africanist scholars like Manning, Gilbert, and Reynolds, as well as the efforts of academic associations and networks, courses on Africa in world history are now offered in universities throughout the United States and the world. More textbooks have also been published as a result of these early efforts. However, of the relevant textbooks designed for undergraduates and published since 2004, only one carries the name "Africa in World History", only one focuses on the ancient period to date, and places the entire African continent in a global context. In this principal textbook, Robert Harms offers accounts that reflect the diver-

---

23 Erik Gilbert and Jonathan T. Reynolds, *Africa in World History: From Prehistory to the Present* (Upper Saddle River, NJ: Pearson, 2004).
24 Jonathan T. Reynolds, "Africa in World History," *World History Bulletin* 22, 1 (2006): 3.

sity of the African continent, stresses the complex ways in which Africans have blended local interests and outside influences in specific historical contexts, and sheds light on specific aspects of Africa's past. It features an introductory chapter that deals with diverse issues including Africa's ecosystems and human origins. Following this introductory chapter, Harms' study is divided into six parts that pay almost equal attention to two periods of history: before 1870 and since 1870. In focusing on these two periods of history, the rest of the study provides a chronological account of history that stresses the connections, similarities, and differences between the four major parts of Africa as well as the differences between Africa and other parts of the world. Although mainly featuring chronological accounts, the chapters also highlight some common themes such as the agricultural revolution, the Bantu migrations, Christianity in North Africa, the scramble for Africa, African resistance to European expansion. It is also significant that each chapter in the book offers relevant images and maps, primary sources, and instructor resources for teaching.[25]

Previous textbooks overviewing the place of Africa in world history (from the ancient to contemporary times) have been periodized in ways that suggested the start of a modern era that inevitably began with the European initiation of the Columbian exchange and the Atlantic slave trade in the sixteenth century or with the imposition of colonial rule in the late nineteenth century. However, many Africanist scholars have noted that such periodization privileges the history of Europeans in Africa. The reasoning goes that the impact of Europe on Africa was marginal by the late eighteenth century, since European forces only touched the African continent at a few coastal points, and because the major transformation of the character of trade between Africa and the capitalist world took place in the early nineteenth century," it can be said that modernity dates not from the imposition of colonial rule, as used to be thought, but from the early nineteenth century".[26] We agree not only because we seek to center Africa on the world historical stage, but also because the robust phases of the industrial revolution that helped consolidate the modern commercially integrated world took place after 1800. Accordingly, unlike previous relevant works, this handbook (except for the chapter that covers the entire Atlantic slave trade era) focuses on two periods: before 1800 and since 1800. However, in focusing on these two periods, unlike previous textbooks on Africa in global history, this book emphasizes the modern period with an eye towards our world today. We take this approach not because the period prior to 1800 is less relevant or less rewarding, but because the pre-modern era informs much of today's happenings and political discussions.

Although this handbook seeks to be part of the literature designed for a one-year African history undergraduate survey, and even though it mainly draws on existing scholarship, it does not cover some of the themes in previous works, and it certainly

---

25 Robert Harms, *Africa in Global History With Sources* (New York: W. W. Norton and Company, 2018).
26 Anthony G. Hopkins, *An Economic History of West Africa* (London, Longman, 1973), 126.

does not cover all the important themes related to pre-modern and modern Africa. For instance, we do not feature any chapter on themes like trans-Saharan networks after 1800, Africa and the Middle East in the modern era, African women in the global economy, and the African impact on China. Despite such gaps, this handbook emphasizes the religious, economic, political, cultural, and social connections between Africa and the rest of the world. It does, however, take a comparative and interdisciplinary approach by drawing on scholarship from diverse disciplinary backgrounds such as sociology, political science, and anthropology.

It is notable that, unlike previous principal textbooks on Africa in global history designed for undergraduate survey courses, this handbook features specially commissioned papers by a range of notable scholars that offer sophisticated and comprehensive overviews of a variety of topics and themes. The extent to which each essay stresses the connection between Africa and the rest of the world varies considerably. This variation is tied to several factors, including the topic of the essay, the available materials related to a topic, and the judgement of authors regarding how best to present the materials that each of them draws upon in their essays. Nevertheless, in stressing the connection between Africa and the rest of the world, this handbook offers continentwide, regional, and localized narratives that illustrate that world history began in Africa, that Africa has been historically dynamic, that North African history is crucial to understanding the history of sub-Saharan Africa, that Africa has never been isolated from the world, and that the impact of Africa on the world since ancient times is far greater than many people think. In terms of impact of Africa on other parts of the world, this volume suggests that within the period before 1800, various societies in North Africa controlled parts of the Middle East and Europe or became core parts of the Islamic world or shaped historical developments in the Mediterranean world. Even before 1800, Africa also contributed to the ideas, culture, wealth, and splendor of other parts of the world. For instance, it was profits derived partly from the Atlantic slave trade that encouraged European monarchies to not only invest in new technologies or to industrialize, but also to become increasingly imperialistic in the seventeenth and eighteenth centuries. After 1800, Africa supplied Europe with important raw materials that allowed for its dominance on the world stage up to the late twentieth century and it continues to supply China, the United States, and other developed countries with such critical resources. Within this same period, Africans played critical roles in shaping developments in Europe and elsewhere, including during the two world wars, and during the contemporary period in which the consolidation of a global village is at the top of the capitalist agenda.

Although some chapters in this handbook represent original contributions to the field while others offer surveys, the analyses in the various chapters allow us to better understand why Africa is underdeveloped despite its relatively large size, relatively large population, and abundant mineral resources. Africa's underdevelopment is due to historical and contemporary factors. In terms of historical factors, Africa's underdevelopment stems from the trans-Saharan trade, to the Atlantic slave trade, to the Indian Ocean trade, to the "legitimate" trade, and to colonial policies. Even though it is difficult to determine whether African societies enjoyed high level of products per capita before the development of the earliest of these trades, the initial and subsequent international commerce of credit systems encouraged African indebtedness to foreign merchants and forced many Africans to attempt to cover their growing trade deficits by enslaving people. This tendency to exchange slaves for commercial goods, which was associated with the trans-Saharan, trans-Atlantic, and Indian Ocean trades, was accompanied by the evolution of states in which African masses were dominated by few African elites who held significant wealth, human capital, and political power. In the nineteenth century, a supposed legitimate trade emerged from the ending of the Atlantic slave trade that encouraged the expansion of trade based on "trust", and it equally encouraged the expansion of slavery or of the use of slaves in most parts of Africa, even in societies like the Sokoto caliphate that withdrew from that trade.[27] During this legitimate trade era, African indebtedness to foreign merchants persisted, and political, economic, and social inequalities intensified, even though more centralized states emerged or were consolidated. It has been argued elsewhere that slavery associated with both the slave trades and legitimate trade was "corruption: it involved theft, bribery, and exercise of brute force as well as ruses. Slavery thus may be seen as one source of precolonial origins for modern corruption."[28] In another study, Mohammed Bashir Salau has shown how a few Sokoto caliphate political and business elites profited from the institution of slavery.[29] Here we do not disagree with the assertion that slavery may be one source of precolonial origins for modern corruption, but we seek to stress that both the slave trades and the legitimate trade era were important sources of precolonial origins for modern inequality and related conflicts. Moreover, while the slave trades and legitimate trade resulted in extraordinary technological and scientific proficiency in various parts of the world, especially in Europe, these benefits were less noticeable in Africa. In the end, the technological backwardness of Africa was one of the major factors which made it possible for the European powers to impose their hegemony on Africa. During the colonial era, European administrators eroded the authority of the old ruling classes, deprived many Africans of their traditional livelihood, and designed economies intended to meet the needs of European manufacturers. Even though colonial rule brought some benefits for some Africans, colonial policies such as those identified above have mainly contributed to Africa's underdevelopment (or have mainly benefitted Europe). Given that colonial policies were not primarily aimed at promoting technological or industrial development or at least at addressing inequality and stereotypical perceptions of the continent, it is not surprising that the response to the imposition of the economic systems includ-

---

[27] Paul E. Lovejoy, *Jihad in West Africa During the Age of Revolutions* (Athens: Ohio University Press, 2016).
[28] Patrick Manning, *Slavery and African Life* (Cambridge: Cambridge University Press, 1990), 124.
[29] Mohammed Bashir Salau, *Plantation Slavery in the Sokoto Caliphate: A Historical and Comparative Study* (Rochester: University of Rochester Press, 2018).

ed an anticolonial movement, neocolonialism, continuing resentment against the West, and political instability in postcolonial Africa. Also, that the inequality, political rivalry, politics of clientelism, and stereotypical perceptions that were in African societies in the precolonial era persisted to a considerable degree through the colonial era into the present encourage many African strongmen to use ethnicity, corruption, nepotism, and the weakening of formal institutions as means of gaining or exercising power. Our argument in this handbook, therefore, is that Africa's history largely explains its current underdevelopment. However, unlike some previous writers who focus on the link between colonial rule and contemporary economic backwardness,[30] we stress that slavery and the slave trades significantly shaped subsequent political and economic developments in Africa.[31]

In terms of contemporary factors, this handbook demonstrates that Africa's underdevelopment is mainly related to neocolonialism and local political fragmentation, political instability, mismanagement and corruption, population explosion, and dependence on one crop or on one commodity, which have emerged in the wake of globalization. Economic liberalization and market reforms embraced by most African countries have increased rather than decreased inequality, and it has not helped to end the indebtedness of Africa to foreign interests, which has historical roots. Despite the economies of many African states having expanded since the 1980s, few elites control Africa's wealth while most people have been left out—in many societies this exclusion has followed ethnic, gender, racial or religious divisions. Any attempt to maintain the growing gap between the rich and the poor can only lead to more conflict and continued underdevelopment.

Because the steps taken by African countries to enhance their place in the world have so far proven ineffective, one of the suggestions in this handbook is that there is a need for the decolonization of African economies and peoples. What should this decolonization process look like? First, because Africa is fragmented and many of the states located in it are not viable economic units and vulnerable to foreign intervention, urgent steps should be taken to strengthen or to ensure the success of the African Economic Community. If Africa wants to enhance its benefits from international trade or from contemporary globalization and to achieve economies of scale, it is in its own interest to ensure the success of this union. To ensure that Africa is less vulnerable to foreign intervention, some have also suggested the establish-

---

30 Examples of such previous works include Englebert Pierre, "Pre-colonial Institutions, Post-colonial States, and Economic Development in Tropical Africa," *Political Research Quarterly*, 53 (2000): 7–35, and Robin M. Grier, "Colonial Legacies and Economic Growth," *Public Choice*, 98 (1999): 317–35.
31 Examples of previous works that offer similar interpretations include Nathan Nunn, "The Long Term Effects of Africa's Slave Trades," *Quarterly Journal of Economics* (2008): 139–76; *New Encyclopedia of Africa*, comp. Joseph Miller (Detroit: Charles Scribner's Sons, 2008) s.v. "History, World: Africa in."; and Miller and Manning, *Slavery and African Life*.

ment of a United States of Africa. However, foreign interests and national rivalries have worked against the formation of such a broadly conceived state.

The nation-state model of political organization that Africans inherited from colonial powers has worked to their disadvantage and ensured that their resources have mainly benefitted developed industrial nations, and that each African state is competing to establish its own industries and currency. Since such trends related to the inherited nation-state model of political organization are illogical and self defeating, African leaders should consider organizing a conference in which an African-centered partition of Africa takes place. Through an African-centered partition (which, of course, cannot be actualized without experiencing considerable challenges), more viable and less vulnerable countries could be established throughout the continent as a means of strengthening African markets and as a means of uplifting Africa from the margins of the capitalist world system. In suggesting that African states should strengthen the African Economic Community, or that they should undertake an African-centered partition of Africa, we are not suggesting that Africa should be a closed society, or that it should be exclusively inward-looking and cut itself off from the rest of the world. Rather, we are suggesting that Africans should use the patterns of viable economic and political unification to renegotiate trade agreements with various parts of the world and to better assert African agency worldwide. Second, African states must end dependence on foreign aid, as this has fostered corruption. Aid also undermines local efforts to develop social services, and it favors accountability to international donors instead of Africans. Accordingly, minimizing foreign aid would promote accountability and compel African governments to look inward for funding through taxation and development.[32] Third, African states need to establish rule of law and strengthen their existing institutions so as to prevent corruption, to foster the operation of free markets, to promote free trade, to allow for the maintenance of low taxation and government spending, and to limit regulations that may hinder business and innovation.[33] Fourth, African states should ensure that education and innovation are given priority. In terms of education and innovation, there are three considerations: creating better citizens by promoting new value systems, producing affordable equipment that could be used widely to boost production especially in agriculture, and producing Green energy equipment that could be used in tackling the climate change problems in the twenty-first century. Fifth, to help reduce poverty, African states should foster women's empowerment, in part by improving healthcare, and in part by increasing investment in female education. In fostering women's empowerment or tackling the problem of poverty, African states should also embrace better population policies.

---

32 See Dambisa Moyo, *Dead Aid: Why Aid is not Working and How There is a Better Way for Africa* (New York: Farrar, Strauss and Giroux, 2009) for further discussion on such issues as the ineffectiveness of foreign aid in Africa.

33 See Peter T. Bauer, *Dissent on Development* (Boston: Harvard University Press, 1972) for relevant in-depth discussion on how to empower underdeveloped societies, including in Africa.

Although there are some themes and topics in this handbook that a reader might be familiar with, there are others that have not been comprehensively addressed in previous textbooks. These include such themes as disease and medicine in African history, Africa and the globalization of religious culture in the contemporary era, Africa and the USA, Africa and China, popular culture, and contemporary globalization and Africa. We hope this handbook will stimulate future research on such topics that would allow us to better understand the place of Africa in world history.

This handbook is structured chronologically, and each chapter focuses on a different topic, so this book can also be read thematically. In chapter 1, Philip Mitchell explores human origins and the major transformations that took place from the earliest evidence of tool use to 1000 CE. In so doing, he draws upon the results of archaeological fieldwork and findings from other disciplines to offer insights on Africa's past and its connections with other parts of the world. Mitchell accepts that Africa is where humans originated but shows that recent research has modified understanding of how modern humans evolved in Africa and when they first left the continent. He also stressed how the earliest ecological societies that emerged in Africa eventually transitioned from hunting and gathering to food production. This transition to food production profoundly affected how people interacted with each other and with the environments in which they lived. Mitchell shows how the development of towns, kingdoms, metal-working, and long-distance networks of trade, emanating from the transitions to food-producing economies within Africa, were important in making the continent an integral part of the larger world. He also shows how historical events that took place outside of Africa, such as the domestication of certain plants and animals in Asia and the efforts of people of Syro-Palestinian origin (the Hyksos) to extend their sphere of influence, contributed to the integration of Africa into the "world system" of that era. Finally, Mitchell's essay highlights the Bantu expansion and the expansion of food production to areas south of the equator.

Drawing on diverse sources and eschewing easy narratives, Bukola Oyeniyi, in chapter 2, examines historical processes and interrelationships, structures and events, to place Africa within the larger context of the Mediterranean world in the period between the eighth century BCE and 1800 CE. While Africa's role in the Mediterranean world has often been overlooked, this essay stresses that Africa was significant to trade and commerce, government and administration, as well as religious exchanges and intellectual production across the Mediterranean before the advent of Islam. In addition, it demonstrates that even though the spread of Islam significantly shaped political, economic, social developments in Africa, and that even though Islam played a more dramatic role in the insertion of Africa into the Mediterranean world than Christianity, it is misleading to describe Muslim conquerors of Egypt and the Maghreb as solely Arab Muslims. Africans were not passive bystanders in the shaping historical developments in Africa and the Mediterranean after the rise of Islam in the seventh century. In rejecting conventional interpretations, Oyeniyi identifies several North Africans who played important roles in the development of Christian theological and philosophical tradition, as well as several African Muslim scholars who shaped relevant developments in the Islamic World.

In chapter 3, Moses Ilo focuses on a long-distance trade, the trans-Saharan trade, that broke the isolation of sub-Saharan Africa from the rest of the world and that ultimately fostered Africa's integration into the world capitalist system by 1800 CE. His analysis considers the factors responsible for the rise and gradual decline of this trade. In so doing, it stresses that African commercial networks were vital in the development of the trade, and that the decline of the trade by 1800 CE was partly due to the rise of the Atlantic trade, which facilitated direct contact between Europeans and Africans. It also demonstrates that while some individuals and societies benefitted from the trans-Saharan trade, it led to the enslavement of a significant number of Africans and other negative consequences.

In chapter 4, Pedro Machado examines the connection between Africa and the Indian Ocean World. Focusing mainly on the period from about 2000 BCE to 1800, his analysis considers the varied ties and actors that bound Africa to the Indian Ocean World. It also considers the processes that structured the historic interaction between Africa and furthest reaches of the ocean in question. In considering such issues, Machado not only suggests that the nature of linkages between Africa and the Indian Ocean World have endured in different ways across vast temporal and spatial scales, but also helps to confirm that Africa and Africans were indispensable in shaping world history.

In chapter 5, David Imbua discusses the initial contact between Africans and Europeans, before examining the longstanding relationship between the two groups between 1400 and 1860 CE. In terms of the initial contact between the two groups, Imbua stresses that even though Africans were already living in Europe and traveling there before the fifteenth century, it was the fifteenth-century Portuguese voyages along the Atlantic coast of Africa that enhanced the movement of Africans to Europe, and that resulted in increasing direct contact between Europeans and Africans in Africa. In terms of the longstanding relationship between the Europeans and Africans in this period, Imbua stresses early diplomatic relationships, the introduction of Christianity to Atlantic Africa, and the initial offshore trade in African agricultural and mineral resources. He also emphasizes the Atlantic slave trade and its impact. In this regard, Imbua finds that trade dramatically transformed Africa and Africans. In contrast to studies that undermine the role of Africa in the construction of Atlantic history and culture, Imbua shows that enslaved Africans were carriers, protagonists, and perpetrators of African cultures in the Americas. Finally, Imbua argues that as the slave trade progressed, the trade in other African commodities in the period examined brought benefits to a few Africans who used these contacts to form marriage alliances with Europeans and acquire wealth, skills, and education.

J. A. Oluyitan, in chapter 6, examines the impact of the "legitimate" trade or the end of the Atlantic slave trade as well as the impact of Christian missionaries in nineteenth-century Africa. His analysis indicates that the development of the legitimate trade coincided with the development of an international illegal slave trade involving

Africa; stresses that the expansion of the legitimate trade was tied to several factors including the expansion of slave use on plantations; and stresses the role of Christian missionaries in religion, commerce, and agriculture as well as in the eventual European conquest of Africa. In contrast to recent revisionist works that argue that the transition or development of the legitimate trade had insignificant impact on Africa, Oluyitan shows that despite some benefits, the development of the legitimate trade mainly fostered cultural imperialism, contributed to the persistence of internal slavery and slave trade in Africa, and reduced the opportunities of Africans to enter capital-intensive and large-scale enterprise.

Bala Saho, in chapter 7, examines the issue of European conquest of Africa. Focusing on the period between 1879 and 1914 CE, he ties the scramble for Africa mainly to the industrialization taking place in Europe and the associated competition among European powers for supremacy. Saho also identifies the major events that took place in Africa, such as Henry Morton Stanley's treaty-making efforts in Congo, that led to the convention of the famous Berlin Conference (1884–1885) and that ultimately precipitated the scramble for Africa. On the question of African responses to European expansion, Saho highlights attention to the works of scholars like Terrence Ranger and Timothy Weiskel to demonstrate that Africans either resisted European conquest or accommodated themselves to European rule mainly based on a careful consideration of their total situations. In addition to stressing that Africans often pursued clear purposes of their own, Saho identifies several types of resistance embraced by Africans between 1879 and 1914. He concludes that despite armed resistance to European expansion, Africans were eventually conquered and dominated by European powers due to several factors, including disunity among African societies, African collaboration with Europeans, and the superior weapons used by the Europeans.

In chapter 8, Saka Aliyu Alabi looks at the issue of colonial legacy, examining not only how colonial rule transformed Africa in the period between 1914 and 1940, but also how Africans shaped historical developments in Europe within the same period. His analysis suggests that colonialism led to dramatic economic, political, and social changes in Africa and it uncovered its limitations. Focusing partly on the issues of empire exhibitions, Libyans in Italy, European modern architecture, and African intellectuals in Europe; Alabi's analysis also shows how Africans in Europe shaped political, architectural, and intellectual developments outside of their continent.

In chapter 9, Abdul Kuba mainly compares two related issues: Africa's roles in the world wars and the consequences of these wars on the continent. He finds that Africa has played a critical role in forging the modern world. Partly thanks to Africa and Africans, the Allied powers won both World War I and World War II, and partly thanks to these two wars, Africans insisted not only upon the reform of the colonial order, but also upon the ending of this order.

In chapter 10, on nationalism and decolonization in Africa, Ajibola Abdulrahman reveals that European/colonial policies, the Great Depression, and the Pan-Africanist movement shaped the development of African resistance and nationalism even before the Second World War. He also draws attention to the fact that, to address their specific grievances, Africans had embarked on gender or rural-based protests, and that they had also formed religious, political, Pan-African, and others such associations even before the Second World War. Although most efforts prior to the Second World War were directed at reforming the colonial system, Africans became committed to ending European rule after the war. Abdulrahman ties this shift in African demand to international and local factors, such as the wartime challenges experienced by Africans, the rise of the United States and the Soviet Union as new superpowers, and the efforts of Pan-Africanists. Overall, his analysis of nationalist activities during and after the Second World War, including of the liberation movements in Portuguese and Spanish colonies in the 1970s and 1980s, shows that African nationalism was shaped by a mix of various factors.

In chapters 11 and 12, Sifiso Ndlovu contributes to the literature that centers the perspectives of Africans in the study of Africa in global history, by featuring the views of Thabo Mbeki and other South Africans in his examination of the history of South African apartheid. Chapter 11 details how the National Party enforced the apartheid policy after it was voted to power in 1948 by whites from all social levels who felt threatened by the African, colored, and Indian working class; stresses the actions the party took to ensure its survival; explains the role of the ANC in the anti-apartheid struggle; and describes the ending of apartheid rule. In explaining the role of the ANC in the anti-apartheid struggle and in describing the ending of apartheid rule, Ndlovu does an excellent job of enhancing our understanding of the views of prominent ANC members about the importance of establishing or consolidating relationships with countries in Africa and elsewhere for their liberation movement, and about the 1980s and 1990s negotiations that helped in the ending of apartheid rule.

In Chapter 12 Ndlovu builds on this discussion by emphasizing how and why Western powers ensured that South Africa emerged as a nuclear power under the apartheid regime during the Cold War era. His analysis indicates that the growing significance of mineral resources in Southern Africa and of the South African coastline for the super powers in question partly motivated them to either establish or to support the relevant African government in establishing significant scientific, technological and military projects in South Africa during the Cold War era. It also suggests that based on the relevant Western support it received, South Africa played a central role in fostering Western influence, especially in the African continent. In addition to highlighting the Western nations support for South Africa during the Cold War era, the chapter sheds light on several other issues such as the views of ANC members regarding South Africa's nuclear program, how the ANC shaped developments in the United Nations, the nature and outcome of the anti-apartheid protests that took place in the 1960s-1980s, the attitude of the Soviet Union and its allies to the ANC, and the benefits that South African revolutionaries derived from attending the Lenin School in Russia.

Noah Echa Attah, in chapter 13, identifies some of the historic diseases that Africa has witnessed and discusses the various initiatives (local and global) adopted overtime to control such diseases. In so doing, he reveals the local or external origins of specific diseases and explains why some diseases are still existing in Africa. In addition, he stresses not only the role of Africans, but also the role of colonial governments, Christian missionaries, non-African philanthropists, and global bodies in controlling relevant diseases. Overall, Attah suggests that the controls and managements of diseases in Africa have been largely dependent on the medical system of the developed world, and he calls for greater attention to the development and incorporation of local solutions.

In chapter 14, William Ackah employs an approach which looks beyond religious labels and follows people and communities to examine the role of Africa in the globalization of religion in the contemporary era. His findings on current religious practices undermines the notion that Africans are incapable of establishing viable organizations, stresses the connections and continuities of African spirituality, and shows the centrality of Africans in the development and globalization of Christianity, Islam, African Traditional religion, and new diasporic religions. Ackah's work is interesting because it reminds scholars and students of religion that interesting insights could come less from looking beyond the religious label and following the people and the communities, but from studying African spirituality and religious tradition in the contemporary era by placing the African at the center of analysis and by doing two other things: doing much more comparative analysis across faith traditions, and making conscious efforts to advance causes of justice for African descendant communities.

In chapter 15, Evelyn Onwaniban breaks down the history of Africa's incorporation into the world capitalist economy into four phases (the age of the Trans-Atlantic slave trade, the age of European rule, the age of decolonization and anti-apartheid struggle, and the age of "new globalization) before considering relevant scholarly debates over the origins of the Cold War within the context of the third phase. Onwaniban also pinpoints some of the key developments that took place globally in the Cold war era and focuses on Africa's involvement in the Cold War. For her, even though the evidence shows that African societies used the Non-Aligned movement as a platform for fostering their interest and shows that such societies benefitted from the Cold War, it mainly supports the conclusion that the Cold War largely had a deleterious impact on Africa.

Flavia Gasbarri's contribution in chapter 16 complements Onwaniban's essay quite neatly in the sense that it mainly deals with the Cold War and its impact. However, here, Gasbarri mainly focuses on relations between Africa and the United States since the mid-1950s, and she demonstrates that as the international scenario changed during the Cold War era, the directives of US foreign policy in Africa and the level in which Africa was able to affect the Cold War and US foreign policy also changed. In demonstrating that the directives of US foreign policy in Africa and the level in which Africa was able to affect the Cold War and US foreign policy changed, Gasbarri ties Africa's eventual downgrading in Washington's priorities and the recent uncoherent US foreign policy in Africa to the disappearance, in 1988, of the Cold War mind-set that had guided US action in the continent since the 1950s

In chapter 17, Jodie Yuzhou Sun, like Onwaniban and Flavia, emphasizes Cold War developments, but mainly contributes to the literature on Chinese relations with Africa. Sun, unlike several writers who focus on Africans in China,[34] traces the history of Chinese-African relations to the 7th century, and shows that even though Chinese migrants were based in several parts of Africa before 1954, China had not adopted any meaningful policy towards Africa by that date. She shows how China sought to win the heart and minds of Africans following its adoption of the "Five Principles of Peaceful Coexistence" that became the underlying basis of Chinese foreign policy from the mid-1950s to 1966. She also shows how China's foreign policy as well as the nature of its relationship with Africa changed from 1966 to date. Moreover, in her analysis, Sun argues against generalizations that African countries have always been manipulated by foreign countries, and she emphasizes how older Afro-Asian solidarity discourse is used to legitimize more recent political, economic and cultural connections between Africa and China.

In chapter 18, Hyacinth Iwu examines some aspects of the history of foreign aid to Africa. His essay spotlights the historiographical debates about the emergence and motive of foreign aid as well as about why Africa continues to demand such aid despite huge assistance already received since the Cold War era from donor countries. It also discusses the origin and growth of foreign aid to Africa, identifies the agencies providing aid to Africa, identifies the different types of aid that donors provide to Africa, and identifies relevant foreign aid disbursement hurdles. By addressing all these issues, Iwu not only establishes that Africa has remained a major aid-receiving continent since the 1940s, but also demonstrates that local corruption and the conflicting agendas of external forces and African leaders undermine foreign aid disbursements in Africa.

Idom T. Inyabri, in chapter 19, contributes to the scholarships on globalization, Hip Hop, and popular culture by reflecting on how hip hop is informed by and responds to globalization in Africa. Focusing mainly on Nigeria, he ties the emergence of Hip Hop among Nigerian youths in the 1990s to their country's implementation of the International Monetary Fund Structural Adjustment Programs policies. He also identifies the range of issues/themes covered by the Nigerian Hip Hop genre and key Nigerian Hip Hop artists. In his analysis, he argues that Hip Hop was important to Nigerian youths. It helped many of them to re-invent and sustain themselves in incredibly challenging times, and has allowed many of them, and the African conti-

---

[34] Examples of works by such writers include Adams Bodoma. "The African Trading Community in Guangzhou: An Emerging Bridge for Africa-China Relations," *The China Quarterly* 203 (2010): 693–707; and Tu Huynh, "A 'Wild West' of Trade? African Women and Men and the Gendering of Globalisation from Below in Guangzhou," *Identities: Global Studies in Culture and Power* (2015): 1–18.

nent in general to shape the historical transformation of the world in contemporary times.

Finally, in chapter 20, Toyin Falola addresses how the world emerged as a 'global village,' and focuses on the place of Africa in contemporary globalization. He argues that even though Africa remains at the periphery of the operationalization of globalization, it has benefitted from new opportunities. Falola also finds that even though Africa has benefitted from contemporary globalization, the development of a globalized world has created not only complacency in Africa, but has also created a space for bad-blood and rivalries that gives the continent no room for a coherent engagement with the outside world. Finally, he suggests that for Africa to emerge out of its current peripheral condition in the globalized world it needs to decolonize its economies and peoples, since the conventional template it has been riding on has proven to be inadequate, and it needs to play a leading role tackling the problem of climate change problems in the twenty-first century.

Peter J. Mitchell
Chapter 1
Human Origins, Early Societies and Migration to 1000 CE

Abstract: Africa has the longest history of any continent. Combining archaeology with other disciplines, notably genetics, linguistics, and the palaeoenvironmental sciences, provides the basis for understanding that history. *H. sapiens* evolved in Africa by 300,000 years ago and the oldest evidence for behaviour signalling complex cognition and symbolic thought is also found there. These innovations likely provided the basis for subsequent human expansion into the rest of the world. Building on millennia of adaptation, African societies successfully survived the climatic challenges of the late Pleistocene and in some parts of the continent began to engage in food production from at least 8000 years ago. Pastoralism based on non-native livestock species spread rapidly across the continent's north, with crops of Middle Eastern origin also introduced to the Nile Valley, the Maghreb, and the highlands of Ethiopia. South of the Sahara, on the other hand, a variety of indigenous agricultural systems developed, expanding in combination with livestock as far as South Africa by early in the Christian era. The processes by which iron-working was invented/adopted in sub-Saharan Africa remain obscure, but knowledge of metallurgy spread rapidly, helping to form the basis on which towns and complex societies began to appear in regions such as Mali and Nigeria by 1500 years ago.

Keywords: Human evolution; hunter-gatherers; food-production; metallurgy; complex societies.

Introduction

Africa is where we began, the continent on which *Homo sapiens* evolved. With the longest history of any landmass, it offers unparalleled insights into the human evolutionary story, but its significance reaches far beyond accounting for our origins in deep time. Home to some of the world's most diverse societies, Africa's populations elaborated rich artistic traditions that they painted and engraved on the continent's rocks or sculpted in clay, stone, and wood. They domesticated an extraordinarily wide range of plants, many of which spread far beyond the continent's shores, while incorporating plants and animals with distant origins of their own into their economies. Additionally, they devised distinctive forms of subsistence, technology, social organisation, urbanism, and interaction that frequently followed uniquely African pathways, distinct from the trajectories pursued in other parts of the world.

This chapter provides a background to these themes, from the earliest evidence for tool use to the close of the first millennium AD, a time when towns and cities had

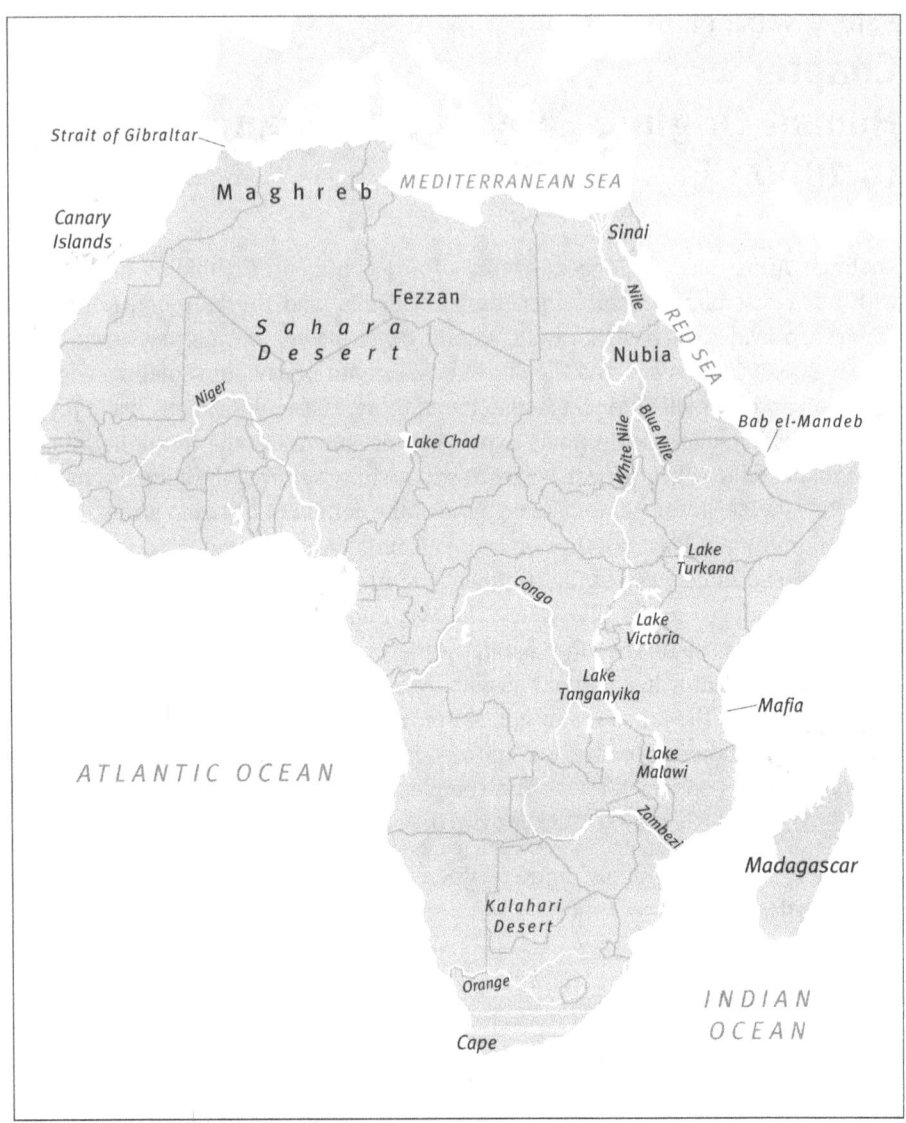

Map 2: Africa. © Peter Palm, Berlin.

already appeared in several regions of the continent and most Africans supported themselves by farming with iron tools, even while stone artefacts and ways of life focused on pastoralism or hunting and gathering remained important for many. This discussion draws primarily upon the results of archaeological fieldwork, complemented by input from other disciplines: palaeoanthropology (especially significant for our knowledge of human evolution); Quaternary science (for reconstructing past environments); historical linguistics (informative on many non-tangible aspects of past societies, but with a much shallower time-depth than archaeology); written historical sources (universally recent in date and largely confined to North and Northeast Africa); and the genetics of people, plants, and animals (still largely inferred from living populations, but including ever more studies based on ancient DNA). Taken together, and enriched in some cases by oral history and comparative ethnography, work in these fields is producing an ever richer, more finely textured view of Africa's past and its connections with other parts of the world.

1 Human origins

Humans form part of a broader hominid family that also includes chimpanzees, bonobos, and – more distantly – gorillas and orang-utans. Comparative studies of human and chimpanzee DNA place the split between these lineages anywhere from 12 to 6 million years ago (henceforth 'mya'), although hybridisation likely continued for some time.[1] By 4.4 mya evidence of bipedal locomotion is found in fossils assigned to *Australopithecus anamensis*, a species that shows strong continuities with later hominins, *i.e.* the narrower group to which modern humans and their immediate ancestors belong. A wide variety of hominin taxa is recognised in the ensuing Plio-Pleistocene period (4.4–1.8 mya), all much more capable of upright walking than any living ape. Two broad trends can be identified. Some species, namely the 'robust' australopithecines of East and South Africa, evolved larger teeth, jaws, and associated muscles and crania, consuming hard, coarser, more fibrous plant foods in the increasingly arid, open environments that emerged ~2.6–1.8 mya. Conversely, from about 2.3 mya other fossils hint at the evolution of larger brains and reduced dentition, traits associated with the emergence of the genus *Homo*, although clear evidence of this is limited before 2.0 mya.[2]

Chimpanzees use and make a wide diversity of tools.[3] Early hominins probably did so too, but most of the organic materials that they may have used have not survived. Artefacts from the site of Lomekwi 3 in northern Kenya, on the other hand, show that by 3.3 mya at least some populations were making tools from flaked stone.[4] Cut-marked bones from highland Ethiopia dating to 2.6 mya indicate that one early use for these artefacts was to access the meat and marrow of animals. However, such bones are rare before 2 mya and stone tools were probably also used to

---

[1] Priya Moorjani *et al.*, "Variation in the molecular clock of primates," *Proceedings of the National Academy of Sciences (USA)* 113 (2016): 10601–12.
[2] Robert A. Foley, "Hominin evolution as the context for African prehistory," in *The Oxford Handbook of African Archaeology*, ed. by Peter J. Mitchell and Paul J. Lane (Oxford: Oxford University Press, 2013), 277.
[3] Bill McGrew, *Chimpanzee Material Culture: Implications for Human Evolution* (Cambridge: Cambridge University Press, 1992).
[4] Sonia Harmand *et al.*, "3.3-million-year-old stone tools from Lomekwi 3, West Turkana, Kenya," *Nature* 521 (2015): 310–15.

pound plant foods and work wood, among other activities.[5] In any event, the capacity to make and use stone artefacts evolved before *Homo* itself, and may even have been practised by more than one hominin line, just as polished bone fragments were probably used as tools in East and South Africa by robust australopithecines and *Homo* alike.[6]

The current understanding, however, is that only the genus *Homo* exited Africa into other parts of the Old World. Often termed 'Out-of-Africa 1', this process had certainly begun by ~1.8 mya, when fossils assigned to the significantly larger-brained and habitually bipedal species *Homo ergaster* occur at Dmanisi, Georgia, although recently excavated stone tools from central China dated to 2.1 mya suggest that it may have started significantly earlier.[7] In any event, by 1.0 mya *H. ergaster* and its close relative *H. erectus* were widely distributed across tropical and sub-tropical regions of the Old World, often – though not always – associated with increased dependence on meat and a long-lasting lithic technology known as the Acheulean, of which bifacially flaked stone handaxes and cleavers are the hallmarks.[8] Within Africa, Acheulean artefacts are widely distributed, with North Africa and today's Sahara Desert strongly represented along with the continent's east and south.[9] Thus far, however, there is little definite sign that hominins were present in the more forested (but poorly researched) regions of the Congo Basin and West Africa before 200,000 years ago (henceforth 'kya').[10]

A scarce fossil record means that most of the African hominin specimens dated to the Middle Pleistocene (780–125 kya) can be viewed as part of a single evolutionary lineage, evolving from *H. erectus* into *H. sapiens*, our own species. The surprising discovery of the significantly smaller-brained, more archaic, and perhaps more arboreally adapted *H. naledi* fossils in South Africa's Cradle of Humankind just west

---

[5] Lawrence H. Keeley and Nicholas Toth, "Microwear polishes on early stone tools from Koobi Fora, Kenya," *Nature* 293 (1981): 464–65; Manuel Domínguez-Rodrigo et al., "Cutmarked bones from Pliocene archaeological sites at Gona, Afar, Ethiopia: implications for the functions of the world's oldest stone tools," *Journal of Human Evolution* 48 (2005): 109–21; Rafael Mora and Ignacio de la Torre, "Percussion tools in Olduvai Bed I and II (Tanzania): implications for early human activities," *Journal of Anthropological Archaeology* 24 (2005): 179–92.
[6] Rhiannon C. Stammers, Matthew V. Caruana, and Andy I. R. Herries, "The first bone tools from Kromdraai and stone tools from Drimolen, and the place of bone tools in the South African Earlier Stone Age," *Quaternary International* 495 (2018): 87–101.
[7] Zhu Zhaoyu et al., "Hominin occupation of the Chinese Loess Plateau since about 2.1 million years ago," *Nature* 559 (2018): 608–12.
[8] Clive S. Gamble, *Settling the Earth: The Archaeology of Deep Human History* (Cambridge: Cambridge University Press, 2013).
[9] Mohamed Sahnouni, Sileshi Semaw, and Michael Rogers, "The African Acheulean: an archaeological summary," in *The Oxford Handbook of African Archaeology*, eds. Peter J. Mitchell and Paul J. Lane (Oxford: Oxford University Press, 2013), 309.
[10] Patrick Roberts, *Tropical Forests in Prehistory, History, and Modernity* (Oxford: Oxford University Press, 2019), 87.

of Johannesburg, now dated to as recently as 335–236 kya,[11] nevertheless underlines how much we still have to learn. At the same time, it is important to remember that a great deal of significant social and cognitive change may lurk behind the relative conservatism and stability of Acheulean stone tool kits; an expanding use of plants as foods and raw materials may be one such development, barely glimpsed at sites where wood is preserved, such as Kalambo Falls in Zambia.[12] The use of fire for cooking, warmth, and self-protection was likely another important adaptation.[13]

Crucial to modern understandings of how the later phases of human evolution unfolded has been the suggestion from analysing the DNA of contemporary populations that all living humans uniquely descend from a relatively small group located somewhere south of the Sahara.[14] This 'Out-of-Africa 2' hypothesis stood in sharp contrast to multi-regional models that posited the convergent evolution of *H. sapiens* in multiple parts of the Old World,[15] and was eagerly tied by some to the advantages thought to stem from the evolution of the cognitive and linguistic capacities that characterise our species today.[16] However, more recent research has offered a more nuanced view of Out-of-Africa 2, in part by identifying genetic inheritances in modern Eurasian, Native American, Australian Aboriginal, and Oceanic populations that reflect interbreeding with Neanderthals somewhere in western Asia. Interbreeding with another archaic population, termed 'Denisovans' after the cave in Siberia where their fossils were first found, contributed further DNA to populations in East Asia, Australasia, and the Americas.[17]

Changes have also been made to how we think modern humans evolved in Africa and when they first left it. Redating of fossils from Jebel Irhoud, Morocco, to ~300 kya makes them the oldest known *H. sapiens* individuals and shows that our species did not, as previously thought, evolve solely south of the Sahara.[18] A much more complex, dynamic pattern of population expansion, contraction, and interbreeding

---

11 Paul H. G. M. Dirks et al., "The age of *Homo naledi* and associated sediments in the Rising Star Cave, South Africa," *eLife* 2017,6 (2017): e24231, accessed April 21, 2020, doi:10.7554/eLife.24231.
12 J. Desmond Clark, *Kalambo Falls Prehistoric Site, Volume III* (Cambridge: Cambridge University Press, 2001).
13 John Gowlett, and Richard W. Wrangham, "Earliest fire in Africa: towards the convergence of archaeological evidence and the cooking hypothesis," *Azania: Archaeological Research in Africa* 48 (2013): 5–30.
14 Rebecca L. Cann, Mark Stoneking, and Allan C. Wilson, "Mitochondrial DNA and human evolution," *Nature* 325 (1987): 31–36.
15 Chris B. Stringer, "Modern human origins – Distinguishing the models," *African Archaeological Review* 18 (2001): 67–75.
16 For example, Paul A. Mellars, "Why did modern human populations disperse from Africa ca. 60,000 years ago? A new model," *Proceedings of the National Academy of Sciences (USA)* 103 (2006): 9381–86.
17 Omer Gokcumen, "Archaic hominin introgression into modern human genomes," *American Journal of Physical Anthropology* 171,S70 (2020): 60–73.
18 Daniel Richter et al., "The age of the hominin fossils from Jebel Irhoud, Morocco, and the origins of the Middle Stone Age," *Nature* 546 (2017): 293–96.

across the whole continent now seems likely,[19] complete with inputs from morphologically archaic hominins within Africa itself.[20] A partial skull from Iwo Eleru, Nigeria, may document one such group as recently as 16–12 kya.[21]

Such a shifting mosaic also fits much better with the episodic and regionally variable evidence for the emergence of forms of behaviour (often termed 'modern') that provide evidence of complex cognition and symbolic thought.[22] Examples include the use of composite technologies (e.g. stone-tipped spears hafted in resin), mechanically projected weapons (e.g. bows and arrows) and similar complex devices for procuring animals (e.g. traps), jewellery, burial of the dead, pigment use, and art.[23] Neanderthal populations in western Eurasia certainly had some of these abilities,[24] but it is in Africa and with *H. sapiens* that they first coalesce as a whole. South African sites such as Blombos, Sibudu, Diepkloof, and Klasies River dating broadly to 125–60 kya show this best,[25] but some are evident much earlier, and it would be unwise to presume that it was specifically in the southern part of the continent that they emerged first; key early evidence also comes from Morocco and Israel.[26] Taken together, the innovation of these behaviours provides the basis for viewing *H. sapiens* as a specialised generalist, a species able to successfully colonise a wide range of environments beyond those settled by earlier hominins. Within Africa, tropical rainforests, montane grasslands, and deserts exemplify such settings, while on a global scale they encompass periglacial, arctic, and high-altitude habitats, as well as the extension of *Homo*'s range into Australia and the Americas.[27]

---

19 Eleanor Scerri, "The North African Middle Stone Age and its place in recent human evolution," *Evolutionary Anthropology* 26 (2017): 119–35.
20 Arun Durvasula, and Sriram Sankararaman, "Recovering signals of ghost archaic introgression in African populations," *Science Advances* 6 (7) (2020): eaax5097, accessed April 21, 2020, doi:10.1126/sciadv.aax5097.
21 Katerina Harvati et al., "The Late Stone Age calvaria from Iwo Eleru, Nigeria: morphology and chronology," *PLoS ONE* 6 (2011): e24024, accessed April 21, 2020, doi:10.1371/journal.pone.0024024.
22 Sally McBrearty, and Alison S. Brooks, "The revolution that wasn't: a new interpretation of the origin of modern human behavior," *Journal of Human Evolution* 39 (2000): 453–563.
23 Marlize Lombard, "Hunter-gatherers in southern Africa before 20,000 years ago," in *The Oxford Handbook of African Archaeology,* eds. Peter J. Mitchell and Paul J. Lane (Oxford: Oxford University Press, 2013), 367–86.
24 Wil Roebroeks, and Marie Soressi, "Neandertals revised," *Proceedings of the National Academy of Sciences (USA)* 113 (2016): 6372–79.
25 Lyn Wadley, "Those marvellous millennia: the Middle Stone Age of southern Africa," *Azania: Archaeological Research in Africa* 50 (2014): 155–226.
26 Abdeljalil Bouzouggar et al., "82,000-year-old shell beads from North Africa and implications for the origins of modern human behavior," *Proceedings of the National Academy of Sciences (USA)* 104: (2007): 9964–69; Erella Hovers et al., "An early case of color symbolism: ochre use by modern humans in Qafzeh Cave," *Current Anthropology* 44 (2003): 491–522.
27 Patrick Roberts, and Brian A. Stewart, "Defining the 'generalist specialist' niche for Pleistocene *Homo sapiens*," *Nature Human Behaviour* 2 (2018): 542–550.

A small but growing set of archaeological and fossil finds and new genetic data suggests that the first successful step in that expansion – the dispersal of *H. sapiens* into the Near East – took place as early as 130–80 kya, and that it likely extended beyond the eastern edge of the Mediterranean, where sites like Qafzeh and Skhul (both in Israel) have long been known,[28] perhaps reaching as far as China and Southeast Asia. That this period, known as Marine Isotope Stage (MIS) 5, saw global climatic conditions at first broadly similar to those of today may have helped people move into new environments. Recent dates from Australia, settlement of which required multiple inter-island voyages and had been effected by ~65 kya,[29] certainly support this more extensive view of early *H. sapiens*' movements out-of-Africa, even if significant further dispersal from the continent is still signalled by genetics ~70–50 kya.[30] As with previous cases, two exit routes are likely: by land across Sinai into Israel and over the narrow channel of the Bab el-Mandeb at the southern end of the Red Sea from Eritrea and Djibouti into Yemen. In contrast, there is no evidence that people crossed into Europe from North Africa, whether via the Strait of Gibraltar or by moving from Tunisia to Malta and onto Italy.

2 Late Pleistocene African hunter-gatherers

Some physically archaic populations clearly persisted in parts of the continent until the end of the Pleistocene, the geological period that terminated 12,000 years ago.[31] Aside from this, however, for at least the last 60,000 years Africa has been home to people cognitively no different from those alive today. In that sense, the variation evident in the archaeological record over this time span – and probably from much earlier too – reflects the history that Africans created and the cultural decisions that they made, not the evolution of novel, biologically based intellectual capacities. Given Africa's size and environmental diversity, the changing nature of its climate, and the many ways in which human societies can constitute themselves, it follows that we should expect those societies to exhibit considerable variety. In this section, I offer a sense of that variety, with an eye to what archaeological, genetic, and linguistic data have to say about the relationships between different human populations and their possible movements and distribution over the African landscape.

Following the ending of the first peak of the last glacial cycle (MIS 4) around 59 kya, Africa – and the rest of the world – experienced a long period of often sharply fluctuating climate (MIS 3) in which conditions were cooler and frequently also

---

[28] Hovers et al., "An early case," 491–522.
[29] Kasih Norman et al., "An early colonisation pathway into northwest Australia 70–60,000 years ago," *Quaternary Science Reviews* 180 (2018): 229–39.
[30] Marc Haber, et al., "A rare deep-rooting D0 African Y-chromosomal haplogroup and its implications for the expansion of modern humans out of Africa." *Genetics* 212 (2019): 1421–28.
[31] Harvati et al., "Iwo Eleru, Nigeria," e24024.

drier (though at some times and in some places wetter) than those of today. This was followed by markedly colder and generally more arid conditions from 29 kya (MIS 2) that were at their most intense ~24–17 kya. During this Last Glacial Maximum (LGM) sea-levels fell some 120 metres, exposing areas of continental shelf around Africa's periphery, vegetation belts moved downslope, ecological communities experienced profound changes in composition, deserts expanded, and tropical rainforests underwent significant reduction with the establishment of more open forest-savannah mosaics. The phrase 'Pleistocene-Holocene transition' captures the shift out of this situation and into broadly contemporary climates and ecosystems, but was far from being a smooth and unilinear process, something most evident in the sustained reversion to near LGM conditions (the Younger Dryas) 13–11.6 kya, after which temperatures rose rapidly to near-modern levels.[32]

In the face of these changes some parts of Africa appear to have been effectively abandoned for long periods. The Sahara, for example, was, if anything, even drier than now, and there is no evidence that people lived there from about 60,000 years ago until almost the end of the Pleistocene.[33] Only along the Nile did human communities survive, but even there evidence is sporadic until after 25 kya.[34] Crucial to their survival was the fact that the water, plants, and animals on which they depended were 'unearned' in the sense of coming not from local rains, but from rainfall in highland regions far to the south, where conditions remained relatively humid. Similar situations were at least intermittently likely elsewhere, for example, in the northwest of southern Africa's Kalahari Desert into which rivers flowed from the distant highlands of Angola.[35] Other areas that may have served as long-term refugia for human populations, supporting the largest, most persistent numbers of people, likely included those close to the Equator, where global changes in rainfall and temperature probably had least effect. Archaeological sequences from East Africa do, indeed, suggest that occupation was more continuous there than in many other parts of the continent.[36] The same may hold for the tropical rainforests, especially if expansion of more open, mosaic environments increased the diversity of resources

---

[32] For a continent-wide summary of how these changes in climate and ecology impacted on human populations, see Sacha C. Jones and Brian A. Stewart, eds., *Africa from MIS 6–2: Population Dynamics and Palaeoenvironments*. Dordrecht: Springer, 2016.

[33] Nick Drake, and Paul Breeze, "Climate change and modern human occupation of the Sahara from MIS 6–2," in *Africa from MIS 6–2: Population Dynamics and Palaeoenvironments*, eds. Sacha C. Jones and Brian A. Stewart (Dordrecht: Springer, 2016), 109.

[34] Angela E. Close, "*Plus ça change:* the Pleistocene-Holocene transition in Northeast Africa." in *Humans at the End of the Ice Age: The Archaeology of the Pleistocene-Holocene Transition*, eds. Lawrence G. Straus et al. (New York: Plenum Press, 1996), 43–60.

[35] Sallie L. Burrough, "Late Quaternary environmental change and human occupation of the southern African interior," in *Africa from MIS 6–2: Population Dynamics and Palaeoenvironments*, eds. Sacha C. Jones and Brian A. Stewart (Dordrecht: Springer, 2016), 164.

[36] Lawrence S. Barham and Peter J. Mitchell, *The First Africans: African Archaeology from Earliest Toolmakers to Most Recent Foragers* (Cambridge: Cambridge University Press, 2008), 269.

on which people could count, but a scarcity of well-dated sequences in Central and West Africa makes it difficult to be sure how far this was so. Conversely, Mediterranean-type ecologies at Africa's northwestern (the Maghreb) and southwestern (South Africa's Cape) extremes offer quite strong occupation signals, especially during MIS 2; in both regions, winter-rainfall regimes may have been more effective at delivering precipitation under cooler conditions than present and landscapes with considerable topographic variation in relatively compact areas offered people readier access to diverse resources, including those from seas and coasts.[37]

This broad overview of some of the ecological variation to which people were exposed is evident archaeologically in what they ate and how they organised themselves socially. In southern Egypt and the far north of Sudan, for example, communities emphasised fishing and wetland plants like nutgrass (*Cyperus rotundus*) and tubers; both the plants and, if smoked or dried, the fish could have been stored for months, giving local economies a strong delayed-returns element, *i.e.* one in which resources are processed and kept for later use. Though probably not settled permanently in any one place, groups were likely strongly territorial judging from the many different stone tool industries found in this relatively small area of Africa, along with multiple instances of interpersonal violence.[38] Fishing was also intensified in parts of the Rift Valley[39] and, at times, in highland Lesotho in Africa's far south, where precipitation remained reliable and colder temperatures simultaneously reduced the availability of plant food and encouraged the growth of local fish stocks.[40]

Africa's plentiful game animals were another mainstay of human diets. In East Africa, for example, a large open-air site at Lukenya Hill, Kenya, was repeatedly used for mass-killing a now extinct antelope related to hartebeest and wildebeest, most likely intercepted during its annual migration.[41] However, the more typical pattern is one in which people harvested a broad range of species, from small to large, territorial to migratory. Exploring how far this involved or necessitated movement

---

[37] Peter J. Mitchell, *The Archaeology of Southern Africa* (Cambridge: Cambridge University Press, 2002), 110–11; Nick Barton, and Abdeljalil Bouzouggar, "Hunter-gatherers of the Maghreb 25,000–6,000 years ago," in *The Oxford Handbook of African Archaeology*, ed. by Peter J. Mitchell and Paul J. Lane (Oxford: Oxford University Press, 2013), 433.
[38] Close, "*Plus ça change*"; Angela E. Close, and Fred Wendorf, "North Africa at 18,000 BP," in *The World at 18,000 BP, Volume II, Low Latitudes*, eds. Clive S. Gamble and Olga Soffer (London: Unwin Hyman, 1990), 41–57.
[39] Katherine M. Stewart, *Fishing Sites of North and East Africa in the Late Pleistocene and Holocene: Environmental Change and Human Adaptation* (Oxford: British Archaeological Reports, 1989).
[40] Brian A. Stewart, and Peter J. Mitchell, "Beyond the shadow of a desert: aquatic resource intensification on the roof of southern Africa," in *Foraging in the Past: Archaeological Studies of Hunter-Gatherer Diversity*, ed. by Ashley Lemke (Boulder: University of Colorado Press, 2018), 159–208.
[41] Curtis W. Marean, "Implications of Late Quaternary mammalian fauna from Lukenya Hill (south-central Kenya) for palaeoenvironmental change and faunal extinction," *Quaternary Research* 10 (1992): 65–128.

from place to place – and the range of social interactions that people maintained – can be approached from multiple angles. In East Africa's Rift Valley one promising source of information comes from identifying the outcrops from which the volcanic glass obsidian was obtained, thereby tracking its movement over the landscape. Thus, at Lukenya Hill, an earlier occupation phase which combined tactical killing of game and consumption of plants within a small foraging radius contrasts with a later one, in which people hunted a wider variety of game and had enhanced access to non-local materials for making their tools.[42] Advances in stable isotope chemistry mean that in favourable circumstances ostrich eggshell beads can also be sourced to the particular geologies in which their parent eggs were laid. In highland Lesotho, for example, such beads came from at least 100–150 km away in the southern African interior, with movements over much longer distances evident in intensely cold, probably more resource-stressed episodes like the Younger Dryas. Whole groups of people are unlikely to have moved so far, leaving the beads as witnesses to long-distance networks of contact between multiple communities that transmitted information, secured access to exotic items, and spread risk by creating the equivalent of a social insurance scheme against ecological downturns among those participating.[43]

Increasing numbers of genetic studies cast further light on the relationships of African hunter-gatherers. For example, southern African Bushmen (San), whose languages include a variety of distinctive click sounds, retain greater genetic diversity than any other living population. Although this does not mean that modern humans originated uniquely in this part of the continent, the ancient DNA of skeletons in Malawi and Tanzania indicates that the genetic ancestry they now represent once extended significantly further north.[44] Rainforest foragers ('Pygmies') also preserve distinct genetic signatures of considerable antiquity, in this case implying two largely isolated populations in the western and eastern halves of the Congo Basin.[45] Linguistic data, on the other hand, do not reach back into the Pleistocene, although Bushman peoples speaking southerly Tuu languages may have a long history of separation from those further north who speak Kxa'a, consistent with some genetic studies, differences in stone tool technology, and the potential barrier effects on movement between northern and southern regions of southern Africa created by cy-

---

[42] Sibel B. Kusimba, "The Early Later Stone Age in East Africa: excavations and lithic assemblages from Lukenya Hill," *African Archaeological Review* 18 (2001): 77–123.
[43] Brian A. Stewart et al., "Ostrich eggshell bead strontium isotopes reveal persistent macroscale social networking across late Quaternary southern Africa," *Proceedings of the National Academy of Sciences (USA)* 117 (2020): 6453–62.
[44] Pontus Skoglund et al., "Reconstructing prehistoric African population structure," *Cell* 171 (2017): 59–71.
[45] Paul Verdu et al., "Origins and genetic diversity of pygmy hunter-gatherers from western Central Africa," *Current Biology* 19 (2009): 312–18.

clical episodes of intensified aridity and the episodic presence of the Kalahari's Makgadikgadi mega-lake.[46]

Separated from the rest of the continent by a hyper-arid Sahara, the Maghreb was also comparatively isolated, although movement was possible along the North African coast at times and the DNA of several skeletons associated with Iberomaurusian tools from Taforalt in northern Morocco suggests that people entered the region from the Near East on at least one occasion during the late Pleistocene. Associations with the appearance across North Africa of stone tool technologies emphasising backed bladelet manufacture are uncertain,[47] but the latter's presence underlines a phenomenon of pan-continental significance that took place 50–20 kya: the replacement of older, Middle Stone Age traditions of tool-making by ones dominated by much smaller tools, including the use of microlithic inserts set into wooden hafts to make a diversity of artefacts, technologies that archaeologists collectively label 'Later Stone Age'. Unlike the substitution of Middle Palaeolithic technology by Upper Palaeolithic toolkits in Europe, however, this change was in no way connected to the displacement of one hominin species by another. Africa's much longer record of behavioural 'modernity' discussed above likewise disassociates it from the emergence of complex language and cognition.[48]

3 Transitions to food-production

Particularly following 13 kya, the many individuals buried at Taforalt and other late Pleistocene sites in Morocco and Algeria, most of whom had had their upper incisors deliberately removed (perhaps as a rite of passage in adolescence), suggest that Iberomaurusian groups there possessed a strongly shared sense of identity and a keen interest in using cemeteries to assert ties to specific points on the landscape. Changes in site use and subsistence, including intensified exploitation of land snails, also happen from this time.[49] These practices underline how the Pleistocene-Holocene transition was a period of major social and economic change, not only in Africa but across the world. Integral to these changes in many regions was a profound shift in how people gained their food: from hunting and gathering wild plants and animals, albeit perhaps using strategies like firing the landscape to manage their productivity, to a situation in which societies increasingly depended upon a much narrower range of species brought under more direct human control. This was not

---

[46] Mitchell, *The Archaeology of Southern Africa*, 125; Joseph K. Pickrell et al., "The genetic prehistory of southern Africa," *Nature Communications* 3 (2012): 1143, accessed April 21, 2020, doi:10.1038/ncomms2140; Robbins, "The Kalahari."
[47] Marieke van de Loosdrecht et al., "Pleistocene North African genomes link Near Eastern and sub-Saharan African human populations," *Science* 360 (2018): 548–52.
[48] Barham and Mitchell, *The First Africans*, 303–04.
[49] Barton, and Bouzouggar, "Hunter-gatherers", 438.

a change that happened everywhere at the same time or in the same way, and some Africans (e.g. the Ju/hoãnsi Bushmen of the Kalahari) largely maintained a hunting and gathering way of life into the 1960s,[50] but it was one that profoundly affected how people interacted with each other and with the environments in which they lived: towns, kingdoms, metal-working, and long-distance networks of trade all emerged on the basis of these transitions to food-producing economies.

People rapidly recolonised the Sahara soon after 12,000 years ago, likely arriving from all possible points of the compass: the Nile Valley, the Maghreb, and West Africa. They took advantage of the region's 'greening' as the expansion of rainfall belts into it from north and south created much lusher, savannah habitats and a network of lakes and rivers that were at least sometimes traversed using boats. Numerous archaeological sites and a rich rock art tradition testify to human presence in what is now desert, while the invention and swift take-up of pottery from Mali to Sudan provided a new means of cooking – and storing – fish, shellfish, and wild cereals that perhaps signals the innovation of sub-Saharan Africa's widespread porridge-based cuisine.[51] Moreover, in Fezzan, human relations with animals took a novel path: dung accumulations from Barbary sheep (*Ammotragus lervia*) suggest that people repeatedly penned them up inside rock-shelters, presumably in an effort to tame them. This experiment was, however, short-lived and, except for the donkey,[52] none of Africa's native mammals were ever domesticated.

Instead, and though the issue has been contested based on a few fragmentary, difficult-to-identify finds from Egypt's Western Desert,[53] livestock-keeping was introduced to Africa from outside. Three species were involved: sheep and goats, both of purely Near Eastern origin, and cattle, which interbred with wild North African aurochsen and formed the key element of the new pastoralist lifestyle.[54] Along with these new resources, wild plant foods, especially grains, also remained important.[55] Herders and herding spread across the Sahara from east to west and north to south

---

[50] Richard B. Lee, *The !Kung San: Men, Women and Work in a Foraging Society* (Cambridge: Cambridge University Press, 1979).
[51] Randi Haaland, "Porridge and pot, bread and oven: food ways and symbolism in Africa and the Near East from the Neolithic to the present," *Cambridge Archaeological Journal* 17 (2002): 165–82.
[52] Peter J. Mitchell, *The Donkey in Human History: An Archaeological Perspective* (Oxford: Oxford University Press, 2018), 29–39.
[53] Michael Brass, "Early North African cattle domestication and its ecological setting: a reassessment," *Journal of World Prehistory* 31(2017): 81–115.
[54] Savino di Lernia, "The emergence and spread of herding in Northern Africa: a critical reappraisal," in *The Oxford Handbook of African Archaeology*, ed. by Peter J. Mitchell and Paul J. Lane (Oxford: Oxford University Press, 2013), 532.
[55] Krystyna Wasylikowa et al., "Exploitation of wild plants by the early Neolithic hunter-gatherers of the Western Desert, Egypt: Nabta Playa as a case study," *Antiquity* 71 (1997): 923–41; Julie Dunne et al., "Earliest direct evidence of plant processing in prehistoric Saharan pottery," *Nature Plants* 3 (2016): 16194, accessed April 21, 2020, doi:10.1038/nplants.2016.194.

between 8.0 and 4.5 kya, pushed and pulled by oscillations in climate.[56] Aptly described as 'cattle-before-crops', this new way of life employed livestock as a dependable, and directly controlled, source of food that could be readily moved around the landscape to best exploit fluctuations in water and grazing.[57] In marked contrast to Eurasia, however, pastoralism was successfully pursued in the Sahara – and later in East and southern Africa too[58] – in the absence of cultivation or of trade with farmers. Analysis of organic residues in 7100-year-old pottery from Fezzan confirms that milk formed part of this distinctively African adaptation from very early on, neatly matching genetic estimates for the antiquity of the mutation for lactase persistence in speakers of the Nilo-Saharan languages that many of these early herder communities likely spoke.[59]

This pastoralist adaptation was seriously compromised when the Sahara experienced its last major dessication around 4,500 years ago, producing conditions similar to those of today. One response was to focus on hardier sheep and goats rather than cattle in those few areas where livestock could still be kept. Another was to move south into areas that retained sufficient rainfall to support pastoralism and now became free of the menace of tsetse fly-borne trypanosomiasis: herders appear in both West Africa's Sahel grasslands and those of Kenya from about 2500 BCE.[60] Finally, some communities intensified use of cereals such as pearl millet (*Penisetum glaucum*) and sorghum (*Sorghum bicolor*) in ways that changed the morphology of their grains and thus attest to domestication, in the process creating mixed farming economies that combined herding with cultivation. This development, crucial to the later history of much of Africa, is first evident in Mali (pearl millet at Karkarichinkat) and Sudan (sorghum at sites of the Butana culture).[61] However, it played out – or was certainly widely adopted – across a broad swathe of the continent between desert

---

[56] Fekri A. Hassan, "Palaeoclimate, food and culture change in Africa: an overview," in *Droughts, Food and Culture: Ecological Change and Food Security in Africa's Later Prehistory*, ed. Fekri A. Hassan (New York: Kluwer Academic/Plenum Publishers, 2002), 11–26.

[57] Fiona B. Marshall, and Elisabeth Hildebrand, "Cattle before crops: the beginning of food production in Africa," *Journal of World Prehistory* 16 (2002): 99–143.

[58] Andrew B. Smith, *African Herders: Emergence of Pastoral Traditions* (Walnut Creek: AltaMira Press, 2005).

[59] Julie Dunne et al., "First dairying in green Saharan Africa in the 5th millennium BC," *Nature* 486 (2012): 390–394; Sarah A. Tishkoff et al., "Convergent adaptation of human lactase persistence in Africa and Europe," *Nature Genetics* 39 (2007): 31–40.

[60] Diane Gifford-Gonzalez and Olivier Hanotte, "Domesticating animals in Africa," in *The Oxford Handbook of African Archaeology*, eds Peter J. Mitchell and Paul J. Lane (Oxford: Oxford University Press, 2013), 497.

[61] Frank Winchell et al., "Evidence for sorghum domestication in fourth millennium BC eastern Sudan: spikelet morphology from ceramic impressions of the Butana Group," *Current Anthropology* 58 (2017): 673–683; Katie Manning et al., "4500-year-old domesticated pearl millet (*Penisetum glaucum*) from the Tilemsi Valley, Mali: new insights into an alternative cereal domestication pathway," *Journal of Archaeological Science* 38 (2011): 312–322.

and rainforest before 1000 BCE, perhaps preceded in areas such as Sudan's Middle Nile by an even longer history of cultivating morphologically wild sorghum.[62]

Along with legumes like cowpeas (*Vigna unguiculata*), sorghum, pearl millet, and other grains (notably African rice [*Oryza glaberrima*]) became the key crops people grew in the savanna regions of Africa north of the equator, later spreading far to its south as well (Section 5). But they were by no means the continent's only crop complex. Cereals and legumes of Near Eastern origin, especially wheat (*Triticum* sp.) and barley (*Hordeum vulgare*), were, for example, grown in Egypt and Nubia (northern Sudan) from at least 4500 BC,[63] becoming the mainstays of the civilisations that later developed there (see Section 4). At a still unknown date, the same two cereals were also introduced into highland Ethiopia and Eritrea, either from the Nile or from across the Red Sea; ancient DNA from a skeleton in southwestern Ethiopia documents movement of people from Eurasia into north-eastern Africa after 4,500 years ago that may be associated with the second of these possibilities.[64] But before Near Eastern crops arrived, Ethiopian/Eritrean communities had likely domesticated several local plants, particularly t'ef (*Eragrostis tef*), the small-grained cereal used to make *injera*, the region's distinctive flatbread, and noog (*Guizinotia abyssinica*), which yields an edible oil. More low-lying areas of southern Ethiopia, on the other hand, are home to a fourth suite of crops: the banana-like enset (*Musa ensete*), finger millet (*Eleusine coracana*), another cereal, and varieties of yam (*Dioscorea* spp.), although once again we still have little idea of the circumstances in which their domestication took place.[65]

Given their location, Ethiopia and Eritrea must have been pivotal to the early movements of African crops beyond the continent. Both sorghum and pearl millet were grown in India and Pakistan by 1500 BCE, likely introduced via southern Arabia rather than directly; other species followed the same path. Moving the other way, broomcorn millet (*Panicum mileaceum*), a crop of ultimately Chinese origin, was grown in Nubia by 1700 BCE.[66] Intercontinental connections are also evident in Africa's far northwest. Here, sixth-millennium BCE dates for wheat and pulses in north-

---

[62] Randi Haaland, "Fish, pots and grain: early and mid-Holocene adaptations in the central Sudan," *African Archaeological Review* 10 (1992): 43–64.
[63] Marco Madella et al., "Microbotanical evidence of domestic cereals in Africa 7000 years ago," *PLoS ONE* 9(10) (2014): e110177, accessed April 21, 2020, doi:10.1371/journal.pone.0110177.
[64] Marcos Gallego Llorente et al., "Ancient Ethiopian genome reveals extensive Eurasian admixture throughout the African continent," *Science* 350 (2015): 820–822.
[65] Dorian Q. Fuller and Elisabeth Hildebrand, "Domesticating plants in Africa," in *The Oxford Handbook of African Archaeology*, eds Peter J. Mitchell and Paul J. Lane (Oxford: Oxford University Press, 2013), 520.
[66] Frank Winchell et al., "On the origins and dissemination of domesticated sorghum and pearl millet across Africa and into India: a view from the Butana Group of the far eastern Sahel," *African Archaeological Review* 35 (2018): 483–503.

ern Morocco[67] are so early as to suggest arrival not via a slow – and unsubstantiated – movement along North Africa's coastal plain, but as part of the broader dispersal of Neolithic farmers across the western Mediterranean, *i.e.* from the European side of that sea. Traces of Italian obsidian in Tunisia and finds of ostrich eggs and ivory at later Neolithic sites in Portugal and southern Spain confirm the value of thinking about the Maghreb in a broader pan-Mediterranean context at this time.[68] Much later, the Middle Eastern-derived crops grown there also reached the Canary Islands, settled from southern Morocco by at least the early first millennium CE.[69]

South of the Sahara the grasslands of the Sahel become increasingly wooded toward the Equator, ultimately giving way to tropical forest. In West Africa, Ghana's Kintampo Complex speaks to a long, drawn-out process whereby crops and livestock of savannah origin were gradually incorporated into subsistence regimes that also exploited a wide range of forest plants and animals.[70] Taking advantage of temporarily drier conditions people grew pearl millet in central Nigeria and southern Cameroon, areas now too wet for this crop, in the mid-first millennium BCE,[71] but subsistence economies in West Africa's forest zone are much better known for their dependence on two other crops. Human consumption of virtually the whole plant, in addition to its lack of seeds, make yam domestication all but invisible archaeologically, but genetic studies identify the forests of the Niger River basin between Ghana and Nigeria as the likely origin point of the main cultivated species, *D. rotundata*.[72] Across West Africa yams are typically eaten with sauces made using the oil from oil palm nuts, the kernels of which survive well when carbonised in fires. Their increase at sites like Bosumpra Cave, Ghana, along with increased frequencies of oil palm (*Elaïs guineensis*) in pollen cores, implies that the oil palm-yam combination was in place no later than 1000 BCE.[73] Before the end of the following millennium small-scale food production was undoubtedly widespread across West Africa.[74]

---

67 Jacob Morales et al., "The introduction of south-western Asian domesticated plants in north-western Africa: an archaeobotanical contribution from Neolithic Morocco," *Quaternary International* 412(B) (2016): 96–109.
68 Cyprian Broodbank, *The Making of the Middle Sea: A History of the Mediterranean from the Beginning to the Emergence of the Classical World* (London: Thames and Hudson, 2013), 318.
69 Rosa Fregel et al., "Mitogenomes illuminate the origin and migratory patterns of the indigenous people of the Canary Islands," *PLoS ONE* 14(3) (2019): e0209125, accessed April 21, 2020, doi:10.1371/journal.pone.0209125.
70 Joanna Casey, "The Stone to Metal Age in West Africa," in *The Oxford Handbook of African Archaeology*, eds Peter J. Mitchell and Paul J. Lane (Oxford: Oxford University Press, 2013), 609.
71 Gabriele Franke, "A chronology of the central Nigerian Nok Culture – 1500 BC to the beginning of the common era," *Journal of African Archaeology* 14 (2016): 257–89; Stefanie Kahlheber, Koen Bostoen, and Katharina Neumann, "Early plant cultivation in the Central African rain forest: first millennium BC pearl millet from south Cameroon," *Journal of African Archaeology* 7 (2009): 253–72.
72 Nora Scarcelli, et al., "Yam genomics supports West Africa as a major cradle of crop domestication," *Science Advances* 5 (2019): eaaw1947, accessed April 21, 2020, doi:10.1126/sciadv.aaw1947.
73 Sarah E. Oas, Catherine A. D'Andrea, and Derek J. Watson, "10,000 year history of plant use at Bosumpra Rockshelter, central Ghana," *Vegetation History and Archaeobotany* 24 (2015): 635–53.

4 The first complex societies and the adoption of metallurgy

Archaeologists often use the term 'complex society' to refer to what are more colloquially described as 'civilisations', but the key elements are the same. One comprises elaborate, specialised decision-making and decision-implementing institutions that integrate large numbers of people, extract resources from the many to support the few via some form of class system, and call upon the supernatural to legitimise this state of affairs, in other words a state form of political organisation. Often, though not always, this is associated with towns and cities: large, dense concentrations of people, many of whom no longer directly produce food for themselves but instead engage in a variety of crafts and other specialised activities, living together in settlements that are hubs of manufacture, trade, administration, and other services for a wider hinterland. As far as we know, economies based on food production to create reliable surpluses for the support of those who do not farm or herd are a pre-condition for these developments, and in Africa they are first found along the Lower Nile.

Egypt has long been recognised as one of the world's oldest civilisations, but the processes of population growth, acquisition of prestigious valuables from afar, craft specialisation, and competition intrinsic to the formation of the state were not restricted to the land of the pharaohs.[75] Emerging from many centuries of farming experience and fuelled by the gift that is the annual flood of the Nile, Egypt was united under the First Dynasty at the end of the fourth millennium BCE. However, expanding exchange and social differentiation are also evident immediately upstream in Lower Nubia, most of which was submerged by the building of the Aswan High Dam. To remove this challenge, one of the first things Egypt's new monarchs did was to abort the development of competing state-level societies to their south.[76] Egypt itself then cycled through repeated periods of centralisation and political unity (the Old, Middle, and New Kingdoms) that alternated with eras of political fragmentation and, on occasion, invasion from outside (the First, Second, and Third Intermediate Periods) until its conquest by Alexander the Great in 332 BCE.[77]

A hallmark of Egypt's 'Kingdoms' was their acquisition of resources from beyond the Nile Valley. In the first instance, this involved copper, stone for statues and other purposes, gold, and turquoise from Sinai and the deserts either side of the river,

---

[74] Andrea U. Kay et al., "Diversification, intensification and specialization: changing land use in western Africa from 1800 BC to AD 1500," *Journal of World Prehistory* 32 (2019): 179–228.
[75] David Wengrow, *The Archaeology of Early Egypt: Social Transformations in North-East Africa* (Cambridge: Cambridge University Press, 2006).
[76] David N. Edwards, *The Nubian Past: An Archaeology of the Sudan* (London: Routledge, 2004), 73.
[77] Ian Shaw, ed., *The Oxford Illustrated History of Ancient Egypt* (London: Thames and Hudson, 2000).

something most spectacularly demonstrated by the chain of donkey trails, already established by 2500 BCE, that lead hundreds of kilometres through the eastern Sahara to a still unconfirmed destination.[78] Egypt's kings also organised expeditions to the southern end of the Red Sea, using ships reassembled on its northern shores that had been made along the Nile and were then carried by people and donkeys through the intervening desert.[79] Their objective was the land of *Pwnt*, the coastlands of southeastern Sudan and Eritrea, from which gold, ivory, myrrh, and frankincense were all obtained.[80]

Surrounded by seas and deserts, Egypt's relative isolation ended abruptly in the mid-second millennium BCE when rulers of Syro-Palestinian origin, the Hyksos, took control of its northern half. Following their expulsion, the kings of the Eighteenth and Nineteenth Dynasties (c. 1550–1069 BCE) established direct control over much of the Levant, becoming leading players in the international politics of the Bronze Age Near East and eastern Mediterranean.[81] The introduction of the horse-drawn chariot as an elite parade vehicle and weapon is perhaps the most obvious consequence of this, the diplomatic correspondence preserved in the ruins of the city of Tell el-Amarna (c. 1350–1335 BC) one of the most detailed and informative.[82] However, the collapse of the Bronze Age powers at the turn of the twelfth/thirteenth centuries BC left Egypt much weaker,[83] and its independence increasingly ebbed away in the millennium that followed.

Upstream of the Nile's First Cataract Egyptian access to metals and other prestige items was for a long time significantly compromised by the emergence of an indigenous civilisation strong enough to cause the Twelfth Dynasty's pharaohs (c. 1985–1795 BCE) to populate Lower Nubia with a series of massive fortresses. Centred on the fortified city of Kerma near the Third Cataract, this independent Sudanese polity flourished along the Middle Nile from the late third millennium BC until its eventual conquest around 1500 BCE. But while adopting some Egyptian influences, its architecture, burial practices (including the sacrifice of both people and hundreds of cattle), and political organisation remained resolutely distinct.[84] Moreover, as

---

[78] Frank Förster, "Beyond Dakhla: the Abu Ballas Trail in the Libyan Desert (SW Egypt)," in *Desert Road Archaeology in Ancient Egypt and Beyond*, eds Frank Förster and Heiko Riemer (Köln: Heinrich-Barth Institut, 2013): 297–338.

[79] Cheryl Ward, "Building pharaoh's ships: cedar, incense and sailing the Great Green," *British Museum Studies in Ancient Egypt and Sudan* 18 (2012): 217–32.

[80] Kenneth A. Kitchen, "The land of Punt," in *The Archaeology of Africa: Food, Metals and Towns*, eds. Thurstan Shaw et al. (London: Routledge, 1993): 586–608.

[81] Ian Shaw, "Egypt and the outside world," in *The Oxford Illustrated History of Ancient Egypt*, ed. Ian Shaw (Oxford: Oxford University Press, 2000): 308–23.

[82] Barry Kemp, *The City of Akhenaten and Nefertiti: Amarna and its People* (London: Thames and Hudson, 2012).

[83] Eric H. Cline, *1177 B.C.: The Year Civilization Collapsed* (Princeton: Princeton University Press, 2014).

[84] Edwards, *The Nubian Past*, 79.

Egypt's control of Nubia ebbed at the end of the Twentieth Dynasty (c. 1069 BCE) an independent state re-emerged further south at Napata. Drawing upon both Egyptian and Kerman traditions, this kingdom of Kush briefly re-united the Lower and Middle Niles in the late eighth/early seventh centuries BCE and survived, focused eventually at Meroë much closer to Khartoum, into the fourth century CE.[85]

Copper was used to make tools in Egypt and Nubia even before the emergence of the First Dynasty and, following the pattern seen in western Eurasia, was later alloyed with tin to make bronze:[86] testifying to the complexity of Bronze Age trade routes, that tin likely came from Afghanistan, although sources in southeastern Turkey were also exploited.[87] Centuries after iron replaced bronze in the Near East, Egypt and Nubia underwent this transition in the mid-first millennium BCE; enormous mounds of slag left from smelting iron ore testify to the extent of production at the later Kushite capital of Meroë.[88]

When, where, and how, metallurgy was adopted south of the Sahara remains one of archaeology's great mysteries, complicated by the fact that iron, not copper or bronze, was the first metal worked there.[89] The technological transition from stone to iron that this signals is unparalleled elsewhere in the world, but understanding it is bedevilled by fluctuations in the atmospheric concentration of the ^{14}C isotope between 800 and 400 BCE that seriously handicap archaeology's most widely used dating tool, radiocarbon dating, at a crucial juncture for understanding what transpired. Accurately identifying metallurgical residues and the possibility that people burnt much older wood to make charcoal for use in smelting (which would result in erroneously old radiocarbon dates) are additional complications.

With these caveats in mind, iron was certainly smelted in central Nigeria by 400 BCE. But was the technology to accomplish this developed locally or was it introduced from outside? If the latter, then two options exist: contact with the Nile Valley, either northeast across the Sahara or in a more easterly direction toward Nubia; or contact with the settlements that the Phoenicians began establishing at Carthage and elsewhere along the coastline of the Maghreb from around 800 BCE.[90] The difficulty with both hypotheses is twofold. In the first place, there is zero archaeological evidence for any cultural connection between West Africa and either the Nile Valley or North Africa, although the long-term survival of pastoralists in the Sahara – and

---

85 Derek A. Welsby, *The Kingdom of Kush. The Napatan and Meroitic Empires* (Princeton: Markus Wiener Publishers, 1996).
86 Bernd Scheel, *Egyptian Metalworking and Tools* (Oxford: Shire Publications, 1989).
87 K. Aslihan Yener et al., "New tin mines and production sites near Kültepe in Turkey: a third-millennium BC highland production model," *Antiquity* 89 (2015): 596–612.
88 Jane Humphris and Thomas Scheibner, "A new radiocarbon chronology for ancient iron production in the Meroe region of Sudan," *African Archaeological Review* 34 (2017): 377–413.
89 Shadreck Chirikure, *Metals in Past Societies: A Global Perspective on Indigenous African Metallurgy* (Cham: Springer, 2015), 17.
90 Terry S. Childs, S. and Eugenia W. Herbert, "Metallurgy and its consequences," in *African Archaeology: A Critical Introduction*, ed. Ann B. Stahl (Oxford: Blackwells, 2005), 280.

the gradual development of oasis farming in Fezzan in the early/mid-first millennium BCE[91] – at least open up a scenario for the second option. On the other hand, short of a remarkably rapid transfer south, neither at Carthage nor along the Nile was the use of iron established early enough to allow these regions to have acted as sources for the emergence of iron smelting in Nigeria.[92]

Could iron smelting therefore have developed independently south of the Sahara in a technological transition of purely local origin? Radiocarbon dates of the second and third millennia BCE associated with iron slag and artefacts at sites in Nigeria, Cameroon, and the Central African Republic would certainly support this,[93] but are widely held to suffer from the 'old wood effect' mentioned above. A recently published iron blade from southern Bénin, immediately west of Nigeria, is less suspect since the relevant radiocarbon dates, of around 1020 BCE, come from closely associated, short-lived oil palm kernels.[94] Nevertheless, the absence of evidence for an older pyrotechnological tradition in non-ferrous metals, glass, pottery, or even baking has left most archaeologists sceptical that any society could go directly from using flaked and polished stone tools to smelting iron.[95] That said, however, it may be unwise to assume that the technological sequences known from Eurasia were necessarily followed elsewhere.[96] What do we know, is that within only a few generations of smelting being unambiguously evident in West Africa both iron technology and food-production were spreading far into the equatorial regions of the continent and, eventually, beyond.

But before turning to these topics, two other West African developments must be noted. First, the advent of iron tools – coupled with a period of drier climate – likely made it easier for farmers to settle and work seasonally flooded areas of central Mali during the middle of the first millennium BCE. Opportunities for population growth and the generation of tradable surpluses in foodstuffs and craft items, as well as the necessity to engage in trade to secure iron and salt unavailable in floodplain environments, saw sites like Dia and Jenné jeno increase in size and eventually take on an urban aspect by the later first millennium CE.[97] Significantly, however, their growth –

---

[91] David Mattingly, ed., *The Archaeology of Fazzan, Volume 1. Synthesis* (London: Society for Libyan Studies).
[92] Chirikure, *Metals*, 25.
[93] Pamela Eze-Uzomaka, "Iron and its influence on the prehistoric site of Leija," in *The World of Iron*, eds. Jane Humphris and Thilo Rehren (London: Archetype, 2013), 3–9; Etienne Zangato, and Augustin F. C. Holl, "On the iron front: new evidence from north-central Africa," *Journal of African Archaeology* 8 (2010): 7–23.
[94] Inga Merkyte, Søren Albek, and Klavs Randsborg, "Urbanizing forest: archaeological evidence from southern Bénin," *Journal of African Archaeology* 17 (2019): 100–101.
[95] Paul T. Craddock, "New paradigms for old iron: thoughts on E. Zangato & A.F.C. Holl's 'On the Iron Front,'" *Journal of African Archaeology* 8 (2010): 29–36.
[96] Chirikure, *Metals*, 27.
[97] Roderick J. McIntosh, *The Peoples of the Middle Niger: The Island of Gold* (Oxford: Blackwells 1998), 173–75.

and that of complex landscapes of settlement around them – seemingly took place in the absence of any trans-Saharan stimulus and without intensifying cultivation of any one crop: subsistence remained diversified, including an important component from wild plant and animal resources,[98] and towns of up to 20,000 people were apparently organised without recourse to the establishment of obvious hierarchies, a heterarchical form of social organisation that represents a distinctively West African pathway to urbanism.[99]

Over 1000 km to the southeast in the rainforests of Bénin and Nigeria other forms of social complexity developed over the same period. Large earthwork systems hint that processes of population growth and urbanisation were underway in southwestern Nigeria by the mid-first millennium CE, founded on the rich potential of rainforest cultivation and eventually linked to the establishment of high-quality craft traditions in metal and glass at royal courts.[100] Demographic growth and nucleation are also evident further west in Ghana and at a much earlier date in Bénin.[101] However, the well-known terracotta sculptures that accompanied human burials in the Nok Culture of central Nigeria do not seem to have been associated with anything other than an essentially egalitarian society.[102]

5 The expansion of food-production beyond the equator

Today, hundreds of millions of people in the southern two-thirds of Africa speak Bantu languages, a sub-group of the larger Niger-Congo family that is spread throughout much of West Africa. Linguists are clear that Bantu languages dispersed relatively recently, perhaps not much more than 3000 years ago, from an area on the extreme northwest of their present distribution, along the border of Nigeria and Cameroon. Genetic research is now providing many new insights into how this took place, while archaeology suggests that over most of equatorial and sub-equatorial Af-

---

[98] Susan K. McIntosh, "Modeling political organization in large-scale settlement clusters: a case study from the Inland Niger Delta," in *Beyond Chiefdoms: Pathways to Complexity in Africa*, ed. Susan K. McIntosh (Cambridge: Cambridge University Press, 1999), 66–79.
[99] McIntosh, *The Peoples of the Middle Niger*, 6–10.
[100] Akinwumi Ogundiran, "Towns and states of the West African forest belt," in *The Oxford Handbook of African Archaeology*, eds. Peter J. Mitchell and Paul J. Lane (Oxford: Oxford University Press, 2013), 861.
[101] Gérard Chouin, and Chris R. DeCorse, "Prelude to the Atlantic trade: new perspectives on southern Ghana's pre-Atlantic history (800–1500)," *Journal of African History* 51 (2010): 123–45; Merkyte, Albek, and Randsborg, "Urbanizing forest."
[102] Peter Breunig, ed., *Nok: African Sculpture in Archaeological Context* (Frankfurt-am-Main: Africa Magna Verlag, 2014).

rica it was intimately connected to the expansion of ways of life that integrated food-production with the use of iron, pottery, and a much more settled existence.[103]

Reconstructions of terms shared by early forms of the Bantu languages now found in much of Central and West-Central Africa imply that their speakers practised a mixed subsistence strategy in which yams and oil palm played a key part, along with goats, dwarf breeds of which are resistant to the trypanosomiasis endemic to Africa's rainforests.[104] The likely archaeological correlate of this lies first in village sites with pottery, ground and polished stone axes/hoes, oil palm kernels and – rarely – caprine bones in Cameroon and Gabon from the middle of the first millennium BC. Finds of pearl millet at some Cameroonian sites suggest that the expansion of food-producing communities was facilitated by drier conditions at this time that allowed a degree of cereal cultivation in what would now be rainforest,[105] but iron metallurgy is almost certainly a more recent phenomenon, scarcely evident before 2000 years ago.[106]

Precisely how the ancestors of people speaking Bantu languages reached the Great Lakes area of East Africa remains in debate, with movement along the rainforest's northern edge or south through it and then back northeast via a temporarily drier savannah corridor both proposed.[107] Distinctive pottery known as Urewe and traces of iron-smelting are certainly present in Uganda, Rwanda, Burundi, and north western Tanzania by the last centuries BC, but direct evidence of food production, though assumed, is frustratingly scarce. Linguistic evidence nevertheless points to Bantu-speakers acquiring both cattle and cereals before entering the Great Lakes region, although how and where are both unknown:[108] prior to 500 BCE, East Africa was, as far as we know home only to hunter-gatherers (some, like those making Kansyore pottery on the shores of Lake Victoria, with a significant delayed return economy based partly on fish and shellfish) and herders (generically dubbed the 'Pastoral Neolithic'), none of whom grew crops.[109] In any event, in the early centuries CE

---

103 Koen Bostoen, "The Bantu expansion," *The Oxford Research Encyclopedia of African History* (2018), accessed April 21, 2020, doi 10.1093/acrefore/9780190277734.013.191
104 Jan Vansina, "A slow revolution: farming in subequatorial Africa," *Azania* 29/30 (1994/95): 17.
105 Stefanie Kahlheber, Koen Bostoen, and Katharina Neumann, "Early plant cultivation in the Central African rain forest: first millennium BC pearl millet from south Cameroon," *Journal of African Archaeology* 7 (2009): 253–72.
106 Pierre de Maret, "Archaeologies of the Bantu expansion," in *The Oxford Handbook of African Archaeology*, ed. by Peter J. Mitchell and Paul J. Lane (Oxford: Oxford University Press, 2013), 634.
107 de Maret, "Archaeologies."; Laurent Bremond et al., "Past tree cover of the Congo Basin recovered by phytoliths and $\delta^{13}C$ along soil profiles," *Quaternary International* 434 (2017): 91–101; Jean Maley et al., "Late Holocene forest contraction and fragmentation in central Africa," *Quaternary Research* 89 (2018): 43–59.
108 de Maret, "Archaeologies," 635–636.
109 Paul J. Lane, "The archaeology of pastoralism and stock-keeping in East Africa," in *The Oxford Handbook of African Archaeology*, edited by Peter J. Mitchell and Paul J. Lane (Oxford: Oxford University Press, 2013), 593.

Bantu-speaking farmers expanded massively to the south, bringing cultivation, pottery manufacture, and metallurgy as far as South Africa's Eastern Cape Province in just a few centuries.[110] The speed with which their archaeological signature – the Chifumbaze complex – spread has long been thought to imply that this expansion was primarily the result of migration, not the adoption of new technologies by indigenous hunter-gatherer populations. An increasing body of genetic studies is now reinforcing this view. They show that hunter-gatherers were rapidly displaced or assimilated in many places, though this was far from universal, especially where farming proved less viable.[111] Movement through both the interior of south-central and southern Africa (in part following the Rift Valley) and along or close to the continent's east coast is indicated, including the first settlement of offshore islands such as Mafia in Tanzania.[112]

The Chifumbaze complex (or 'Early Iron Age' as it is also sometime called) was not, however, the earliest introduction of livestock or pottery into Africa's far south. Sometime in the last few centuries BC Epeople who drew part of their linguistic, genetic and cultural ancestry from Pastoral Neolithic (and perhaps also hunter-gatherer) communities in East Africa moved south[113]. Direct evidence of their presence in central and southern Tanzania, Malawi, and Zambia has yet to be found, but cattle and sheep were being kept in northern Botswana – and sheep at least as far south as the southwestern Cape of South Africa – by the first century CE[114] Movement may have been rapid through the intervening area, perhaps facilitated by drier conditions that reduced the threat endemic diseases posed to livestock, although one domesticate – the donkey – never made it through.[115] Once in southern Africa, incoming herders clearly intermarried with the hunter-gatherers they encountered,[116] some of whom may have actively acquired livestock for themselves as a new resource, one valued both as food and for social and ritual purposes.[117] Another innovation, pottery, was even more widely taken up, employed not just by early herders, but

---

[110] David W. Phillipson, *African Archaeology* (Cambridge: Cambridge University Press), 219.
[111] Skoglund et al., "Reconstructing."
[112] Alison Crowther et al., "Coastal subsistence, maritime trade, and the colonization of small offshore islands in Eastern African prehistory," *Journal of Island and Coastal Archaeology* 11 (2016a): 211–37.
[113] Thembi Russell, and Faye Lander, "'What is consumed is wasted': from foraging to herding in the southern African Later Stone Age," *Azania: Archaeological Research in Africa* 50 (2015): 267–317.
[114] Karim Sadr, "The archaeology of herding in southernmost Africa," in *The Oxford Handbook of African Archaeology*, eds. Peter J. Mitchell and Paul J. Lane (Oxford: Oxford University Press, 2013), 645–55.
[115] Peter J. Mitchell, "Why the donkey didn't go south: constraints on the spread of *Equus asinus* into southern Africa," *African Archaeological Review* 34 (2017): 21–41.
[116] Tom Güldemann, "A linguist's view: Khoe-Kwadi speakers as the earliest food-producers of southern Africa," *Southern African Humanities* 20(1) (2008): 93–132.
[117] Russell, and Lander, "What is consumed."

also by hunter-gatherers as far east as Lesotho and KwaZulu-Natal, centuries before immigrant farmers arrived.[118]

Another of the great unknowns of Africa's early history concerns several crops that ultimately originated in Southeast Asia or even New Guinea. Two kinds of tuber – taro (*Colocasia esculenta*) and further varieties of yams (*Dioscorea* spp.) – are involved here, but also – and more significantly – the banana and plantain (*Musa* spp.). Today, these crops are important to farmers across Africa's humid tropics, with *Musa*, in particular, a staple for millions of people around East Africa's Great Lakes.[119] When and how they were introduced to Africa is, however, deeply unclear, and for neither taro nor yams has any relevant archaeological evidence yet been identified. The once-common assumption that all three taxa were brought to the continent as by-products of Madagascar's settlement by Austronesian-speaking settlers from Indonesia is certainly too simplistic, not least because there is little reason to assume that they formed an integrated package that necessarily dispersed as a whole. The situation is complicated by the recovery of phytoliths identified as *Musa* spp. in mid-first-millennium BCE contexts at Nkang, Cameroon.[120] If accepted – and debate continues – this requires a much earlier introduction to Africa's eastern seaboard and passage through both East Africa and the equatorial rainforest, areas for which we have no evidence of farming activity at the requisite time, potentially powerful arguments against the accuracy of the Nkang evidence or its dates. Later introduction around the northern edge of the Indian Ocean and into Africa via Ethiopia,[121] or as part of the spread of other Asian crops within emerging trans-Indian Ocean trade networks in the second half of the first millennium CE[122], is perhaps more likely; Madagascar itself has no convincing evidence of human settlement before the mid-first millennium CE.[123] When this becomes more plentiful toward the year 1000, it forms part of a much broader engagement of Africa's eastern seaboard and areas further inland with long-distance intercontinental trade networks that contributed to a significant growth in social complexity, processes paralleled at much the same time across the continent in the Sahel and the forests of West Africa.

---

118 Karim Sadr, "An ageless view of first millennium AD southern African ceramics," *Journal of African Archaeology* 6: (2008): 103–30.
119 Robert C. Power et al., "Asian crop dispersal in Africa and late Holocene human adaptation to tropical environments." *Journal of World Prehistory* 32 (2019): 353–92.
120 Christophe Mbida et al., "The initial history of bananas in Africa. A reply to Jan Vansina," *Azania* 40 (2003): 128–35.
121 Power et al., "Asian crop dispersal".
122 Alison Crowther *et al.*, "Ancient crops provide first archaeological signature of the westward Austronesian expansion," *Proceedings of the National Academy of Sciences (USA)* 113 (2016b): 6635–40.
123 Peter J. Mitchell, "Settling Madagascar: when did people first colonize the world's largest island?" *Journal of Island and Coastal Archaeology* 15 (2020): 576–95.

Oyeniyi Bukola Adeyemi
Chapter 2
Africa in the Mediterranean World

Abstract: Using insights gained from analyzing extensive archeological evidence of pre-Islamic rock art images, numerous inscriptions from early eleventh to late-thirteenth century tombstones and Libyco-Berber scripts, this chapter describes the historical processes and interrelationships, structures and events, that placed Africa within the larger context of the Mediterranean world. From the earliest writings of Graeco-Roman and Christian authors and trade records and travel reports kept by Arab Muslims and European traders, travelers, and explorers, the chapter challenges the popular view of Africa south of the Mediterranean Sea as an isolated and static area and reveals the historical contours and interconnections, sub-regional and regional systems, diplomatic and cultural exchanges within Africa and between Africans and the Arab, Europeans and Asians worlds which proved that Mediterranean Africa was more than just a patch of barren land intersecting the Mediterranean littoral and Sahara Desert, but a crossroad of trade and diplomacy, religion and knowledge.

Keywords: Mediterranean Africa; *Bilad al-Sudan*; Islamization; Arabization; Mauri; Almoravids; Berber.

Introduction

While not pretending to be a *tour de horizon* of African history in the Mediterranean world, this chapter uses extensive archeological evidence from more than fifty stone structures and mosques, commercial and housing compounds, and livestock enclosures, as well as inscriptions on remains of early eleventh to late-thirteenth century cemeteries and tombstones, to challenge the view that Africa south of the Mediterranean Sea as an isolated and static area, characterized only by a barren Sahara Desert.

In describing the historical processes and interrelationships, structures, and events that placed Africa within the larger context of the Mediterranean world, this chapter puts early Graeco-Roman and Christian writings into conversation with those of their Muslim counterparts. These, combined with traders and explorers' records are used in weaving a narrative that explores the historical contours and interconnections, sub-regional and regional systems, diplomatic and cultural exchanges within Africa and between Africans and the Arabs, Europeans, and Asians' worlds.

As Fernand Braudel notes, the "Greater Mediterranean" or the "Mediterranean of the historian" or the "Mediterranean of historical dimensions" covers from the southern shores of the Mediterranean Sea to the middle Niger-Basin, encompassing both Upper Nile Valley and the Ethiopian Highlands.[1] In other words, the Mediterranean goes beyond its north pole (which bordered Europe) to include areas occupied by North African peoples and others below the Sahara Desert, as well as across the Red Sea. The Arabs call these parts of Africa the *Bilad al-Sudan* – the Land of Blacks.[2] Previous studies have shown that the *Bilad al-Sudan* (or, effectively, North Africa), the middle Niger-Basin in West Africa, and both the Upper Nile Valley and the Ethiopian Highlands in Central and East Africa can be described as a socio-economic and cultural repository from which regional formations in the Sahara and the middle Niger-Basin, the Nile Valley area and Euro-Arab continents interact and draw their contents.[3] As a melting pot and a crossroad, the greater Mediterranean and *Bilad al-Sudan* serve as a global collective and a formation that enabled African culture and practices to interlink and cross-fertilize with their European and Arabian counterparts.

The chapter focuses on the emerging patterns of local, trans-local, and global interactions and integrations, long-term and short-term trajectories of social-cultural developments and intellectual production, inter-cultural identities and socio-economic linkages, shared artistic traditions and practices, diplomatic and economic exchanges and interactions that define this area between the eighth century BCE and the eighteenth century CE.

Without a doubt, the various events that characterized this period shaped and continue to reshape Mediterranean Africa. A few examples of these include the bringing of Africans in Mediterranean Africa under Islam or under Islamic rule (Islamization), the linguistic shift that made the Arabic language and culture the dominant language and culture in these areas (Arabization), the establishment of literacy, especially in Mathematics and Algebra, the adoption of mortuary culture and megalithic funerary architecture, and the ceremonial complexes tied to astronomical rituals and rock art imagery. The chapter focuses primarily on analyzing these events and the processes that produced contemporary Mediterranean Africa.

Islam in Africa: A Brief Odyssey

Islam came to Africa in two distinct ways. In 614 CE, the Prophet Muhammed sent 124 of his followers across the Red Sea into Aksum, Abyssinia (now Ethiopia).[4] These refugees, moving in two batches of 23 and 101, crossed Djibouti (Eritrea) and Somalia

---

[1] F. Braudel, *The Mediterranean and the Mediterranean World in the Age of Philip II* (London: Collins, 1972), 3.
[2] Ousmane O Kane, *Beyond Timbuktu: An Intellectual History of Muslim West Africa* (Cambridge, USA: Harvard University Press, 2016), 12.
[3] Kane, *Beyond Timbuktu*, 24.
[4] John L. Esposito, *Islam: The Straight Path* (Oxford: Oxford University Press, 1998), 3–36.

into Ethiopia in their bid to escape persecution from the inhabitants of Mecca. King Armah An-Najashi of the Kingdom of Aksum, a Christian kingdom, received them.[5] This forced migration is known in Islam as the first *hijra*, Arabic for flight or migration. Before returning to Mecca in 628 CE, these Muslim refugees had spread Islam from Ethiopia into Somalia. Their most significant achievement was not only the conversion of King An-Najashi to Islam, but also the building of the first and oldest African mosque (Masjid al-Qiblatayn) in Zeila, Somaliland in 627 CE.[6]

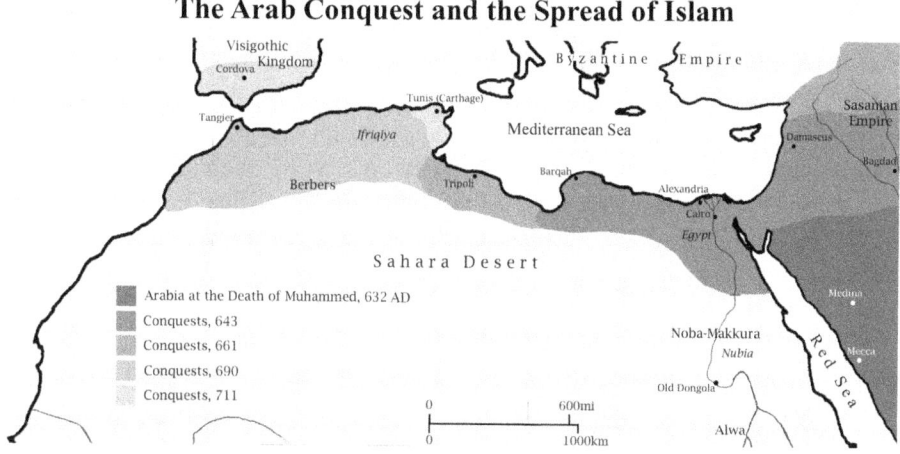

Map 3: The Arab Conquest and the Spread of Islam. © Toyin Falola.

Unlike the first arrival of Islam, which was peaceful, the second arrival came through wars and conquests. Between 639 CE and 641 CE, at the command of Caliph Umar ibn al-Khattab Muslim troops from Saudi Arabia invaded and conquered Egypt.[7] From Egypt, Caliph Muawiyah I sent Arab military expeditions to Libya, which was conquered in 642 CE. Five years after the conquest of Libya, Caliph Uthman Ibn Affan ordered the conquest of Tunisia.[8] Under the Umayyad caliphs, the Byzantine who had ruled Algeria, Morocco, and most parts of North Africa were dislodged and by 709 CE, the entire North Africa had been brought under the banner of Islam.

Before the Arab conquest, Christianity tried to replace African indigenous system in Egypt and much of North Africa. At the height of its powers, Christianity success-

---

5 William Montgomery Watt, *Muhammad: Prophet and Statesman* (Oxford University Press, 1961), 66.
6 Holzer, Georg-Sebastian, "Political Islam in Somalia: A Fertile Ground for Radical Islamic Groups?" in *Geopolitics of the Middle East*, vol. 1, 2008: 23.
7 Betts B. Robert, *Christians in the Arab East: A Political Study* (Athens: Lycabettus Press, 1978), 35.
8 Moshe Perlmann, *History of the Prophets and Kings: The Ancient Kingdoms*, Vol. 04, (Cairo: Dar al-Ma'arif, 1969). 183.

fully established itself in Alexandria, Libya, Nubia, and Ethiopia where it imposed the Coptic system.⁹ Despite its successes, it existed side-by-side with African indigenous systems. However, with the Arab conquest came Islamic religion and legal system, Arabic language and learning, and artistic tradition, etc. The Arab conquest therefore brought another layer of socio-cultural and political change that dramatically altered cultural, economic, and political traditions across Mediterranean Africa.

Shortly after conquering Egypt, the Fatimid established the Al-Azhar University in Cairo, the Mongol invaded and conquered all centers of Islam in Asia. Egypt, consequently, emerged as the new center of Islamic religion, intellectual production, and power.¹⁰ The emergence of Egypt as Islam's primus center of religion and Arab culture led to a precipitous decline in Christian population in Egypt. Just as Islam replaced Christianity, Islamic jurisprudence effectively replaced Euro-Christian legal systems in much the same way as Arabic literature and science replaced Euro-Christian learning. This stagnation in Graeco-Roman Christian traditions, legal system, and spirituality spread across North Africa. With Islamic religion and culture firmly entrenched in North Africa, Egyptian Muslim leaders, now predominantly African, not only took a commanding position within the Islamic world, but also on all sides of the Mediterranean.

Under Uqbah ibn Nafi (Sidi Uqbah) in 682 CE, Arab Muslims raided the Berber (Amazigh) whose territories stretched from south of the Mediterranean Sea to the Niger River bends and from the Atlantic Ocean to the Siwa Oases in Egypt.¹¹ The Umayyad caliphs, from around 661 CE to about 750 CE, ruled the Maghreb as part of their Muslim Empire from their abode in Damascus.

Following the conquests of Egypt in the seventh century and the entire North of Africa in the eighth century, Arab Muslims also invaded the Sahelian region of Africa. Unlike in Egypt and its North African neighboring states, the spread of Islam into the Sahel entailed both military conquests and peaceful trade relations.¹² With Egypt and North Africa under their control, Muslim traders led trading expeditions into Nubia in the seventh century where they encountered the ancient Kingdom of Makuria, located on the east bank of the Nile opposite the Wadi Howar.¹³ Makuria, an Old Nubian Kingdom with Old Dongola as its capital, was one of the most important entry and departure point for caravans, bringing trade items, including slaves,

---

9 Thomas C. Oden, *Early Libyan Christianity: Uncovering a North African Tradition* (Westmont, IL: InterVarsity Press, 2011), 32.
10 Nicholson Reynold Alleyne, *A Literary History of the Arabs* (Cambridge: Cambridge University Press, 1907), 84.
11 Ray A. Kea, "The Mediterranean and Africa" in *A Companion to Mediterranean History*, ed. by Peregrine Horden and Sharon Kinoshita (USA: Wiley Blackwell, 2014), 437.
12 Ousmane Oumar Kane, *Beyond Timbuktu: An Intellectual History of the Muslim West Africa* (Cambridge: Harvard University Press, 2016), 10–13.
13 Mariusz Drzewiecki, "The Southern Border of the Kingdom of Makuria in the Nile Valley" in *Institut Des Cultures Mediterraneennes et Orientales De L'academie Polonaise Des Science, Études et Travaux*, XXIV, 2011: 95–7.

from West Africa through Darfur and Kordofan and, invariably, into the rest of the Old World through Egypt and across the Red Sea to Asia.

Christianity spread from Egypt to Makuria in the sixth century, but unlike Egypt and North Africa, Makuria fought and repelled the Muslims. Unable to defeat Makuria, the invaders signed the Baqt Treaty in 651 CE, which ensured peaceful diplomatic and trade relations, with Makuria. This peace treaty served to preserve Makuria's independence from the Muslims' intrusion, which helped Makuria's development. Makuria, at the height of its power invaded and annexed Nobatia to the north. Rather than attacking the Kingdom of Alodia, also known as Alwa, to the south, it entered into dynastic relationships with this medieval Nubian kingdom.[14]

Territorial expansion and peaceful relations with its neighbors brought dramatic changes to Makuria. New and imposing architectural masterpieces, ranging from pyramids to mastabas, finely crafted wall-paintings and elaborately decorated potteries were built.[15] During this time, the Nubian language become the prevalent written language across the African Sahel. Makuria's prosperity cannot be dissociated from its strategic location as an international commercial and cultural highway linking North Africa with other sub-Saharan African states, and Asia across the Red Sea.

Things however turned awry for Makuria between the thirteenth and fourteenth centuries, when the Muslims who were originally trading with Makuria, resorted to warfare. Makuria's resistance collapsed when a civil war broke out in 1365 CE.[16] The outcomes of the civil war were not just a loss of territories on the kingdom's southern flanks, but also the Muslims' occupation of Old Dongola.[17] By the 1560s CE, the invaders had established full control from Lower Nubia to as far upstream as Al Dabbah and Kordofan, Islamizing and Arabizing them all.

Besides the Makuria kingdom, there was also the Soninke Empire, which was established in the eighth century. The Soninke Empire, sometimes called Ghana Empire, was the first major state to develop in the Sahel.[18] The Soninke Empire ranged from the upper Senegal river and along northwestern Mali and Fouta Djalon in Guinea, to the Gambia and southern Mauretania. Its inhabitants were essentially West African Mande, Wolof, Tukur, and Malinke ethnic groups. Other parts of the Soninke Empire included the Songhai in the center and Gao to the east.

From the eighth century to the thirteenth century, the Soninkes derived great wealth from crop production and trade, most importantly the Trans-Saharan trade. They controlled trade routes across the Sahara Desert, using camels and horses.

---

14 Mohamed Babiker Ibrahima and Omer Abdalla Omer, "Evolution and Changes in the Morphologies of Sudanese Cities" in *Urban Geography*, vol. 35, No. 5, 2014: 735–756.
15 Godlewski Wlodzimierz, "Introduction to the Golden Age of Makuria" in *Africana Bulletin*, vol. 50, 2002, 75–98.
16 R. S. O'Fahey and Jay Spaulding, *Kingdoms of Sudan* (London: Methuen Young Books, 1974), 17.
17 O'Fahey and Spaulding, 1974: 20.
18 Nehemia Levtzion and Jay Spaulding, *Medieval West Africa: Views from Arab Scholars and Merchants* (Princeton: Markus Wiener, 2003), 27.

These pack animals, especially camels, were useful in transporting different items of trade while horses were used in warfare. One of the key reasons for the development of centralized and non-centralized polities in the Sahel was the use of horses in warfare.

The expansion of Islam into West Africa started with African Berber traders and scholars who, as masters of the desert, spread Islam in the course of their trading activities.[19] Berber traders travelled in stages, bearing and exchanging desert salt and dates, Euro-Arab and Asian fabrics and drinks, etc. for sub-Saharan African gold and leather, kolanuts and other food items from the forest regions. The most significant item of trade were enslaved people.

From the fifth century, caravans of camel facilitated exchanges between the Soninke traders and their North African trading partners. The Garamantes and other Berber groups made a successful career out of navigating and supervising this international trade networks.[20] As Al Bakri, a Spanish scholar who witnessed the development, describes Basi, the king of the Soninke in the eleventh century CE, the king

> led a praiseworthy life on account of his love of justice and friendship for the Moslems. The city of Ghana consists of two towns situated on a plain. One of these towns, inhabited by Moslems, is large and possesses twelve mosques, in one of which they assemble for the Friday prayer. There are salaried imams and muezzins, as well as jurists and scholars.[21]

North African Muslim traders also forged trade links from Zawila in today's Southern Libya to Bornu and Kanem around both Lake Chad and Northern Nigeria. Bakri described Zawila as a

> town without walls and situated in the midst of the desert. It is the first point of the land of the Sudan. It has a cathedral mosque, a bath, and markets. Caravans meet there from all directions and from there the ways of those setting out radiate. There are palm groves and cultivated areas which are irrigated by means of camels.[22]

Between the ninth and fourteenth centuries, the Kingdoms of Bornu and Kanem flourished as commercial centers. Kanem was the first of the two to accept Islam, with the Kingdom of Bornu to follow suit later. From the description above, one can submit that Zawila, Bornu, and Kanem were important commercial centers that not only played significant role in the Trans-Saharan trade system, but also in the spread of Islam.

---

[19] James Kritzeck and William H. Lewis, *Islam in Africa* (New York: Van Nostran-Reinhold Co, 1969), 287–327.
[20] Bukola A. Oyeniyi, *The History of Libya* (Santa Barbara: ABC-CLIO, 2019), 15–16.
[21] Al-Bakri, from the Book of Routes and Realms, as cited in N. Levtzion. and J. F. P. Hopkins, *Corpus of Early Arabic sources for West African History* (New Jersey, USA: Markus Wiener, 2000), 62.
[22] Levtzion and Hopkins, *Corpus of Early Arabic Sources*, 62.

After the collapse of the Soninke Empire, Mali, one of Sonnike's outlying states, gained prominence. By the fourteenth century, under the leadership of its leader, Sundiata Keita, Mali Empire emerged as the most powerful kingdom in West Africa.[23] Under Mansa Musa, Mali's most popular leader, Mali was not only a prosperous center of trade, but also a great seat of Islamic education and learning, jurisprudence and philosophy.

Lying next to the Atlantic Ocean on the western edge of the Sahara Desert were groups of proto-Berber peoples such as the Bafour, Pharusii, Perorsi, Toucouleur, and Wolof of Mauretania.[24] These were the descendants of earliest coastal *Imraguen* Berbers who were predominantly hunters, pastoralists, and fishermen.[25] Due to climate change, overgrazing, overcultivation, and desiccation of the Sahara forced the Pharusii, Perorsi, Toucouleur, and Wolof, to leave the area. Between the third and fourth centuries CE, Berber immigrants from southern Libya who were searching for pasturage joined the Bafour. This first wave of immigrant Berbers subjugated the Bafour, introduced the use of horses and camels, while, between the seventh and eighth century, the second wave of immigrant Berbers changed Mauretania's ethnic composition.[26]

Although research on the history of pre-Islamic religious universe of Mauretania is still developing, available Arabic and archaeological sources on the introduction and spread of Islam in Mauretania however showed that North African Muslim traders and explorers, mostly Kharijite and Ibadi Muslims, were responsible for the spread of Islam into Mauretania. From the above, it can be argued that from Egypt and the Maghreb in North Africa, to Mauretania and Mali in West Africa and Nubia in East Africa, Islam in Africa has multilayered histories.

The Place of Africans in the Spread of Islam

Africans featured prominently in the life of Prophet Mohammed and in the history of Islam. Following his mother's death, little Muhammed was left in the care of Barakah Um Ayman, an Egyptian who was described in Islamic history as a wet-nurse.[27] The Prophet Muhammed described Barakah as 'my mother after my mother'.[28] As an

---

[23] J. D. Fage, *The Cambridge History of Africa: From c. 1050 to c. 1600* in J. D. Fage, Roland Anthony Oliver (eds.) Cambridge: Cambridge University Press, 1977), 390.
[24] Contemporary Mauretania now encompassed the old territories of ancient and present Mauretania.
[25] J.D. Fage, *The Cambridge History of Africa*, Vol. 5. (Cambridge: Cambridge University Press, 1976), 338–339.
[26] Titus Burckhardt, *Moorish Culture in Spain* (Pakistan: Suhail Academy, 1997), 7.
[27] Halime Demiresik, *The Mothers of the Believers* (Istanbul: Sultantepe Publications, 2012), 48.
[28] Adib Rashad, *Islam, Black Nationalism and Slavery: A Detailed History* (USA: Writers Inc. International, 1995), 17.

adult, Prophet Muhammed married Habibat and Maryam, both of whom were Egyptians and Coptic Christians.[29] As Margoliouth noted, Prophet Muhammed's grandfather, Abd al-Muttalib, was married to African women who bore him ten sons, "all of whom were black."[30] Prophet Muhammed also adopted Zayd bin Harith, an African, who rose to prominence as a general in the Prophet's army.[31]

After receiving the Quran and the establishment of Islam in 670 CE, many of the earliest converts to Islam were ex-slaves.[32] A few examples of earliest African converts to Islam whose names and activities survived are Bilal Ibn Rabah and Abu Anjashah al-Habashi.[33] Bilal Ibn Rabah, an Abyssinian slave who was bought by Abu Bakr, was the first Mu'adhdhin, the officer responsible for calling the faithful to prayer, in Islamic history. As was reported, following Muhammed's victory over the inhabitants of Mecca in 630 CE, he, Bilal Ibn Rabah, climbed the minaret of Kaaba, and issued the first call on all Muslims to prayer. Bilal Ibn Rabah later became the treasurer of the early Islamic State under Prophet Muhammed's leadership. He later became the Governor of Syria when Muslim invaders conquered Syria.[34] Many of these early converts were bought by either Prophet Muhammed himself or by Abu Bakr, the first Caliph and successor to Muhammed.[35]

Abu Anjashah al-Habashi, also an African, was bought by Prophet Muhammed and, prior to his death, Prophet Muhammed left his family in Abu Anjashah al-Habashi's care, a step that ostensibly showed how much trust Prophet had in Abu Anjashah al-Habashi.[36]

As already noted, Prophet Muhammed sent some of his followers to Ethiopia in 615 CE to escape persecution. The initiative to send these Muslims to a Christian king in a Christian kingdom showed the kind of respect Islam enjoyed amongst Africans and the trust and admiration the Muslims had for Africa and Africans. It is on record that after accepting Islam, King al-Najashi also sent a delegation, which includes the King's son, to Prophet Muhammed.[37]

Given the above, describing Muslim invaders and conquerors of Egypt and the Maghreb as solely Arab Muslims stands logic on its head. By 690 CE, many of the

---

29 Demiresik, *The Mothers of the Believers*, 48.
30 David Samuel Margoliouth, *Mohammed and the Rise of Islam* (Wood Dale, IL: Alpha Editions, 2019), 57.
31 David S. Powers, *Zayd* (USA: University of Pennsylvania Press, 2014), 18.
32 Daniel Pipes, "Mawlas: Freed Slaves and Converts in Early Islam" in *Slavery & Abolition: A Journal of Slave and Post-Slave Studies*, vol. 1, (2), 1980, 132–177.
33 Muham Taqra, *The Story of Bilal Ibn Rabah (580–640): Great Muslim Warrior from Africa* (USA: Jannah Media Publishing, 2015), 34–45.
34 Muham Taqra, *The Story of Bilal Ibn Rabah*, 45.
35 Habeeb Akande, *Illuminating the Darkness: Blacks and North Africans in Islam* (London: Ta-Ha Publishers, 1872), 12–56.
36 Habeeb Akande, *Illuminating the Darkness*, 65.
37 Martin Lings, *Muhammad: His Life Based on the Earliest Sources* (London: Inner Traditions, 2006), 81–84.

so-called Arab Muslims were either Africans who converted to Islam or their descendants. Another important development of this period that is hardly mentioned in the literature is the fact that many of the pure Arabs married African women and raised families. Their descendants, who knew no other place of birth other than Africa, were erroneously referred to as Arabs, a description that persists even today.

Between the 1492 and 1775 CE, many Europeans relocated to the Americas. They and their descendants are today referred to as Americans and not Europeans. Why then were descendants of Arab Muslim invaders, many of whom were originally Africans, who returned back to Africa, married African women, and raised African children still being referred to as Arabs? What are the implications of this on the general history of Islam, especially in politics, administration and knowledge production? A cursory look at the history of the Moors would help in answering these questions.

With Egypt and the entire Maghreb fully under the control of the Muslims by 690 CE, the Iberian Peninsula was the next frontiers before these Muslims. At the forefront of this development were the Berbers.

Thousands of Berbers served as warriors, fighting in wars and propagating Islam. Janina Safran, citing Ibn al-Qutiyya, noted that African Berber Muslims under their leader, Tariq Ibn Ziyad, who served as a military commander under the Umayyad leader, Musa ibn Nusayr, orchestrated the conquest of the Iberian Peninsula.[38] Michael Barry described the conquerors of the Iberian Peninsula as "Arab invaders". Notwithstanding this misleading description, he also admitted that Tariq's army composed of mainly African Berbers, and that Musa ibn Nusayr was an ex-slave of North African origin.[39]

Maria Rosa Menocal detailed the longstanding efforts to deny Africans' achievements in the conquest of Visigothic Hispania. As she noted, "The Almoravids were Berber tribesmen who had been building a considerable empire in North Africa". She then went on to describe them as a "fanatic group of North African Muslims" who, "for the next 150 years," took over "Christian states" and ruled it in ways alien to "al-Andalus and its ways".[40]

Many have argued that since the word Berber has been used to describe peoples from the Atlantic Coast in West Africa to the Red Sea in East Africa as well as others across North Africa and Western Asia.[41] Therefore, they argued that is difficult to say

---

[38] Janina Safran, *Defining Boundaries in al-Andalus: Muslims, Christians, and Jews in Islamic Iberia* (Ithaca: Cornell University Press, 2013), 21.
[39] Michael Barry, *Homage to Al-Andalus: The Rise and Fall of Islamic Spain* (Dublin: Andalus Press, 2016), 21–22.
[40] Maria Rosa Menocal, *Ornament of the World: How Muslims, Jews, and Christians Created a Culture of Tolerance in Medieval Spain* (New York: Back Bay Books, 2002), 43.
[41] See, for instance, Michael Russell, *History and Present Condition of the Barbary States* (New-York: Harper & Brothers, 1837) and Mordecai Manuel Noah, *Travels in England, France, Spain, and the Barbary States* (New-York: Kirk and Mercein, 1819).

concretely that the conquerors of Visigothic Hispania – modern day Spain and Portugal, were truly North Africans Muslims.[42] The fact that a North African Berber, Tariq Ibn Ziyad, led an army of seven thousand African Berber warriors and a few Arab troops against a hundred thousand Iberian troops and conquered Visigothic Hispania between 711 and 718 CE rendered such argument infantile. Tariq and his men defeated the European troops and captured Cordoba, Granada, Toledo, Guadalajara, and Astorga. Following his conquest of Visigothic Hispania, Tariq was appointed governor of Hispania. He was later recalled to Damascus in 714 CE and decorated, as the 'Rock of Gilbratar' – Spanish derivation of the Arabic 'Jabal Tariq' (meaning "Mountain of Tariq").

It must be noted that in Arab and Islamic history, not only were there unambiguous claim that the conquerors of Visigothic Hispania were North African Muslims, but also that they were predominantly Mauris (Moors in English).

Knowledge Production and Exchanges up to the Eighteenth Century CE

Africa's roles in knowledge production and dissemination predated the emergence of Islam. The continent, most especially areas bordering the Mediterranean Sea, had always played significant roles in the philosophical and intellectual traditions of the pre-Islamic world.

Prior to the coming of Islam, Egypt and North Africa were significant in the Roman and Christian political and military, religious and scholastic universe. Africans not only played roles in the administration of the Roman Empire, but also were leading lights in the Western philosophical and religious traditions.

At the height of its power, Rome invaded and conquered many foreign nations. Under Julius Caesar and, later Augustus Caesar, Egypt and North Africa – conquered and colonized – became parts of the Roman Empire.[43] Consequently, increasing numbers of Romans arrived in Egypt and North Africa. In the same vein, the number of Egyptians and other Africans such as Carthaginians (Tunisians), Libyans, Numidians (Algerians), Mauris (Mauretanians) and other Berbers also increased in Rome.[44] As David Noy noted, immigrant population in Rome rose to about 5 percent of the total population, while some of these foreigners were slaves, others were skilled workers and soldiers.[45]

---

42 Abia Afsar Siddiqui, *The Book of Islamic Dynasties: A Celebration of Islamic History and Culture* (London: Ta-Ha Publishers, 2008), 12.
43 Wickham Chris, *The Inheritance of Rome: A History of Europe from 400 to 1000* (London: Penguin, 2009) 15.
44 Roger S. Bagnall and Bruce W Frier, *The Demography of Roman Egypt* (Cambridge: Cambridge University Press, 2006), 16.
45 David Noy, *Foreigners at Rome: Citizens and Strangers* (UK: Classical Press of Wales, 2000).

Foreigners in Rome had Roman citizenship, enjoying such rights as protection from expulsion. Many of these foreigners became important figures in Roman, Christian, and Western religious, literary and philosophical traditions. While one rose to become a Roman emperor, others become authors and philosophers, bishops and popes.

The only Roman emperor of North African origin was Emperor Septimius Severus, a Libyan from Leptis Magna, who brought North Africa, Britain, and Iran under Roman rule, ruled the Roman Empire for eighteen years in the second century CE.[46] Besides warfare, he was known in Roman history for his military reforms and the constructions of monumental architectural works.

Two of the most significant Roman writers of African origin are Apuleius and Publius Terentius Afer, popularly known as Terence. Apuleius, the author of *The Golden Ass*, was from Madauros, Numidia (Algeria).[47] Terence, also of North African origin, was a playwright. During the Middle Ages and Renaissance, Terence's works were used in most monasteries and convents to teach Latin, moral lessons, and Christian ethics. His comic plays continued to have a long-lasting impact on Western drama till this day.[48]

A number of other North Africans also played important roles in the development of Christian theological and philosophical tradition. Quintus Septimus Florens Tertullianus, popularly known as Tertullian, was a Roman theologian from Carthage (in Tunisia) whose most famous work is *Apologeticus*.[49] Three Roman popes were of North African origin. The first is Victor who, like Tertullian, was born in Leptis Magna, was made a pope during the time of Emperor Marcus Aurelius Commodus Antoninus Augustus in the second century.[50] The second was Pope Miltiades who was also the Bishop of Rome at the end of the fourth century. The last was Pope Gelasius I, who was a prolific writer of letters and treatises, all of which survived. His best known and most famous letter was the *Duo Sunt*, which he addressed to Emperor Anastasius I.[51]

In this famous letter, the pope established the distinction between the "holy authority of bishops" and "royal powers". This was in response to the emperor's claim that Constantinople was a "new Rome", a claim the pope challenged.[52]

---

[46] Simon Elliott, *Septimius Severus in Scotland: The Northern Campaigns of the First Hammer of the Scots* (London: Greenhill Books, 2018).
[47] The Editors of Encyclopaedia Britannica, "Lucius Apuleius", in *Encyclopedia Britannica*, accessed May 4, 2021 at https://www.britannica.com/biography/Lucius-Apuleius.
[48] St. Augustine of Hippo referred to *The Golden Ass* as 'The Metamorphoses of Apuleius'. The *Golden Ass* remains the only ancient Roman novel written in Latin that survived in its entirety.
[49] R. L. Wilken, "Tertullian" in *Encyclopedia Britannica*, accessed 4 May 2021 at https://www.britannica.com/biography/Tertullian.
[50] Raymond D. Davis, *The Book of Pontiffs* (Liverpool: University Press, 1989), 6.
[51] Raymond D. Davis, *The Book of Pontiffs*, 96.
[52] Chris Wickham, *The Inheritance of Rome: Illuminating the Dark Ages, 400–1000*. Vol. 2 (New York: Penguin, 2009), 34–45.

Numerous other Africans featured in the history of the Church during this period. It was on record that in 180 CE, Emperor Marcus Aurelius Commodus Antoninus Augustus of Rome ordered the assassination of twelve Christians of African origin in Sicilli (Sicily).[53] These African Christian fathers were martyred for their refusal to worship Emperor Commodus. In March 203 CE, Emperor Septimus Severus also ordered the killing of a twenty-two-year-old Carthaginian noble, Perpetua.[54] Perpetua, and Felicity, another African Christian believed to have been enslaved by Perpetua, were both martyred in the town of their birth, Carthage (near Tunis, capital of modern Tunisia).[55]

An important African Christian father was Titus Flavius Clemens (from 150 CE to 215 CE), popularly known as Clement of Alexandria. Clemens was a Hellenistic theologian and the first president of the Catechetical School of Alexandria.[56] He was from Alexandria, Egypt. Oregenes Adamantius, who was popularly known as Origen, was also from Alexandria, and, besides succeeding Clemens as the principal of the Catechetical School of Alexandria, he was widely known for his book, *The Hexapla* – a synopsis of six different versions of the old testament.[57] In 231 CE, Origen wrote *De Principiis*, which dealt with Christians' obedience to the rule of faith such as God, as the Creator; the incarnation of Jesus, as the preexistent Lord; the Holy Spirit, as one of the divine triads.[58]

Perhaps the most famous Christian theologian of African origin was Augustinus Hipponensis (Augustine of Hippo or Saint Augustine). Saint Augustine was a theologian and a philosopher who served as the Bishop of Hippo Regius in Numidia. He was born on November 13, 354 CE at Thagaste and died at Annaba, both in Algeria.[59]

St. Augustine, formally recognized in Roman Catholicism as a Doctor of the Church, was perhaps the most significant Christian thinker after St. Paul. St. Augustine adapted classical thoughts into Christian teachings and created a theological system that made the concept of Trinity an important part of Christianity as we have it today. In addition, St. Augustine, through his numerous writings, most especially *Confessions* and *The City of God*, shaped the practice of biblical exegesis. Just as he was remarkable for his writings, St. Augustine was also remarkable for what he did for and on behalf of Christianity.

In 410 CE, a ragtag army led by Alaric, a military General of Germanic origin, attacked and seized the city of Rome. The attack was blamed on the Christians

---

53 W. H. C. Frend, "The Christian Period in Mediterranean Africa" in J.D. Fage (ed.) *Cambridge History of Africa, Vol. 2*, (Cambridge: Cambridge University Press, 1979), 410.
54 Frend, "The Christian Period in Mediterranean Africa", 416.
55 Frend, "The Christian Period in Mediterranean Africa", 435.
56 Frend, "The Christian Period in Mediterranean Africa", 443
57 Frend, "The Christian Period in Mediterranean Africa", 456
58 Frend, "The Christian Period in Mediterranean Africa", 489.
59 J. O'Donnell, "St. Augustine" in *Encyclopedia Britannica*, accessed 4 May 2021 at https://www.britannica.com/biography/Saint-Augustine.

and Rome's acceptance of Christianity was considered as evidence that the Roman Empire had mistaken its way with the gods.[60] Many openly declared that the old Roman gods did a better job of protecting Rome than the Christian God.

For the next fifteen year, St. Augustine took the defense of Christianity upon himself. In his *City of God*, he made a splendid argument in support of God's ways, outlining a new way to understand human society – the City of Man, and the ways of the divine – the City of God.[61] He argued that the sack of the city of Rome was of no spiritual importance compared to the true home of Christians and source of citizenship for all Christians – the heavenly Jerusalem. As he boldly argued, Rome – the City of Man was doomed to be conquered; hence, any wise person must keep their faith in the Christian God, as a passport into the City above, paradise.

Another important contribution of St. Augustine to Christianity was his resolution of unarguably the most controversial and longest-lasting theological debates of the fourth century – the Christian doctrine of the Trinity.[62] The Trinity holds that God is but a three coeternal and consubstantial entity; hence, God, the Father, God, the Son (also known as Jesus Christ), and God, the Holy Spirit. In order words, "one God in three Divine persons".[63]

In the fourth century, no small controversies existed over this issue. From Trinitarianism and Arianism to Binitarianists and Monarchianists, different subsets of Christianity shared the view of a one God in whom there is no plurality. For a fact, there is no explicit doctrine of the Trinity in the Bible, however, there are many verses that served as pedestals for a "triadic" concept of God. For example, in all the gospels, Jesus was quoted as saying "I and my father are one" (Matthew 17:4 and Luke 9:33). Similarly, St. John quoted Jesus also as saying: "The Father is greater than I" (John 14:28).

St. Augustine, in laying the argument to rest and cementing the concept of Trinity, made references to Jesus' last few days with the twelve disciples, after a vision where "they saw Jesus' glory and two men" – Moses and Elijah – standing with Jesus (see Luke 9:28–36). As Moses and Elijah were leaving, Peter said to Jesus, "Master, it is good for us to be here. Let us put up three shelters: one for You, one for Moses, and one for Elijah" (Matthew 17:4). Making references to similar spiritual allusion, St. Augustine argued that three visitors visited Abraham and were symbolic

---

[60] Peter Heather, *The Fall of the Roman Empire: A New History of Rome and the Barbarians*, (Oxford University Press, 2006), 84–100.

[61] The Editors of Encyclopaedia Britannica, "The City of God" in *Encyclopedia Britannica*, accessed 4 May 2021 at https://https://www.britannica.com/topic/The-City-of-God.

[62] Saint Augustine, *The Trinity (Works of Saint Augustine: A Translation for the 21st Century)*, (trans. Edmund Hill and John E. Rotelle (editor), (USA: New City Press, 2012).

[63] Daley E. Brian, "The Persons in God and the Person of Christ in Patristic Theology: An Argument for Parallel Development", in *God in Early Christian Thought: Essays in Memory of Lloyd G. Patterson*, ed. by Andrew B. McGowan, Brian E. Daley and Timothy J. Gaden (Leiden-Boston: Brill, 2009), 323–350.

of the three persons of the Trinity. As he argued, there were no indications in the Bible about whether these visitors were unequal or not, hence, St. Augustine argued, the 'threeness' of God is represented in the Father, Son, and Holy Spirit.[64]

With the coming of Islam, development in Christian faith not only stagnated, but Islam also upstaged and replaced it. As it was the case with Christianity, Africans were not passive bystanders in the spread and development of Islam.

In Timbuktu, Jenne and Walata in the Sahelian region and in Tangier, Fez, Cairo and at various centers in North Africa, African Muslims, many of whom were scholars and jurists, philosophers and artists, poets and dramatists, using Arabic, Ajami, Swahili, and other African languages as languages of intellectual engagements, formed associations and established universities where scientific knowledge in Astronomy and Chemistry, Physics and Mathematics, Geography and Philology, were carried out.[65] These African Muslims proved themselves as masters and trailblazers in knowledge production and dissemination in Africa before transferring their intellectual culture to Muslim Spain, which was to become the fountain of knowledge for others in Christian Europe.

In most literature, those African Muslims were described as primarily traders, but recent studies have shown that trade, which used to be their most popular activity, was of little significance compared to their activities in knowledge production and dissemination.[66] The process of transforming from merchants and traders to generators and disseminators of knowledge, under African Muslims leadership, not only entrenched the place of Africa in the Mediterranean world, but also cemented Islam as a philosophical and intellectual tradition.

From Egypt and Sudan to Morocco and Algeria as well as from Tunisia and Mauritania to the Soninke Empire and Mali, Arabic literary production developed at different times and differs in quality. While in Egypt and Algeria, Arabic creative writing flourished early in the beginning of the Arab invasion, in others, for instance, the Soninke and Mali empires, it was delayed. Unlike Egypt, which had a flourishing literary culture even before the Roman times, writing tradition in Mali cannot be dissociated from the Islamization and Arabization process after the 8th Century. Notwithstanding how and when writing began in Mediterranean Africa, some of the earliest historical and literary works on Africa were written in Arabic by Islamic scholars.[67] Their works, excellent and respectable, not only attracted attention from within Africa, but also from the rest of the Arab world and outside it.

---

[64] Gilles Emery, *The Trinity: An Introduction to Catholic Doctrine on the Triune God* (USA: The Catholic University of America Press, 2011), 123.
[65] John O. Hunwick, *Timbuktu and the Songhay Empire: Al-Sadi's Tarikh al-Sudan Down to 1613 and Other Contemporary Documents* (Leiden: Brill, 2003).
[66] Shamil Jeppie and Souleymane Bachir Diagne (eds.), *The Meanings of Timbuktu* (Cape Town: HSRC Press, 2008), 34.
[67] Alexandra Huddleston, *Divine Learning: The Traditional Islamic Scholarship of Timbuktu, Mali*, vol. 11, (2), 2009, 129–135.

As noted earlier, African Muslims established universities in Al-Azhar and Ibn Rashiq universities – both in Cairo, Egypt, Al-Qayrawan, Al-Qarawiyyin and Qurtuba, Timbuktu and in other places in both Egypt and the Maghreb. Students from within the African continent, Europe, Damascus, and other places across the Muslim world trooped to these institutions, where notable African Muslim professors taught. Notable African Muslim scholars who taught in these institutions and whose works survived include Abbas Ibn Firnas (an inventor), Al-Jahiz (a zoologist), Al-Idrisi (a geographer), al-Hasan ibn Muhammad al-Wazzan al-Fasi (later known as Johannes Leo Africanus) (a geographer), and Labana of Cordoba (a mathematician). Besides Labana, other Muslim mathematicians of African origin are Muhammed ibn Muhammed al-Fulani al-Kishnawi, Abu Kamil Shuja ibn Aslam, al-Qurashi, al-Hassar, Ibn al-Yasamin and Ibn Mun'im. In the case of Ibn Mun'im, he was also the founder of the University of al-Qarawiyyin, Fez, Morocco. Ahmad Baba Al-Massufi, popularly known as Ahmad Baba was a well-known teacher and professor, Islamic philosopher and Arabic grammarian who authored over forty books.[68]

In Alexandria, Fez, and Timbuktu, millions of manuscripts from different parts of Africa and the Muslim world formed a single Islamic scholarly heritage. These manuscripts not only revealed the core curricula used in these universities, but also the broad range of disciplines – ranging from religious exegesis to Quranic expositions, law and philosophy, architecture and history, botany and biology, chemistry and physics, mathematics and algebra, medicine and nursing, occultism and music, tailoring and fashion, among others.

There have been attempts at different times to compile the list of earliest Arab/Muslim writers of African descent. These efforts have yielded a number of studies, two of which are most significant – *Corpus or Early Arabic Sources for West African History*[69] and *Cuoq Recueil des Sources Arabes Concernant L'Afrique Occidentale du VIII au XVI Siecle*,[70] which was written in French. It must be noted that while the *Corpus* did not contain the entire works of these earliest African Muslim writers, it offers a bird-eye view to each of the books, quoting extensively from them to illustrate their contents. As these works showed, African Arabic writings – from poetry to prose and drama – ranged from religious treatises and philosophical essays, to dramas and novels. A huge volume of short stories of didactic nature were also included.

In the *Corpus*, Hopkins and Levtzion compiled a list of earliest Arabic sources on African history. On this list, there were sixty-five known Arabic writers who wrote about Mediterranean Africa between the ninth and fifteenth centuries. Of these sixty-five writers, three – Al-Ya'qubi, Al-Umari, and Ibn Khaldun – wrote two differ-

---

[68] For details about these individuals, see P. Bearman,; Th. Bianquis; C. E. Bosworth; E. van Donzel; W.P. Heinrichs (eds.), *Encyclopaedia of Islam*. I (2nd ed.) (Leiden: Brill publishers, 1986).
[69] Levtzion and Hopkins, *Corpus of Early Arabic Sources*, 492.
[70] Pere Joseph, *Cuoq Recueil des Sources Arabes Concernant L'Afrique Occidentale du VIII au XVI Siecle, (Bilad al-Sudan)*, traduction et notes per Joseph M. Cuomo, preface de R. Mauny, Coll. Sources d'historie médiévale, Institut de recherche et d'historie des textes (Paris, Ed. Du C. N. R. S., 1975), 490.

ent books while Al-Mqrizi wrote three different books. Roland Oliver, commenting on the *Corpus*, noted:

> Here, in 372 pages of clear English translations, is the sum of what Islamic scholars wrote about West Africa between the ninth and fifteenth centuries. Notes necessary to its evaluation and detailed indexes and glossaries facilitate comparative use... The work has been supremely well done, and will never need to be done again.[71]

In addition to those already mentioned, other early African Muslim scholars include Ibn Hawqal (961 CE) who wrote about Arab merchants in Awdaghast,[72] Umme Jilmi who studied the Quran under Muhammad Mani and converted to Islam, Al-Qalqashandi who compiled an encyclopedia on government and administration for bureaucrats in fourteenth-century Egypt (Subh al-A'sha), Al-'Umari who wrote Masalik al-Absar and Abu Ishaq Ibrahim al-Kanemi, a renowned poet and man of letters from Bornu.[73]

During this ostensibly golden age of Islam in Africa, books were in fact costlier than gold. The University of Sankore, Timbuktu, Mali was famous not only because it had three campuses in Timbuktu, Djinguereber, and Jingereber, but because of its enormous collection of manuscripts.[74] Its international reputation also rested on the fact that courses such as the study of Arabic grammar and syntax, astronomy and logic, rhetoric and prosody were on offer. Other courses taught include astronomy and astrology, botany and biology, dogma and geography, Islamic law and literary analysis, mathematics (including calculus and geometry) and algebra, medicine and nursing, mysticism and morphology, music and rhetoric, philosophy and geomancy, architecture and astronomy, history and politics, and poetry and drama. Writing about Timbuktu, Mahmud Kati, a seventeenth-century African Muslim author, noted in the *Tarikh al- Fettash*, a chronicle of the reign of Sonni Ali of Songhay Empire, that the city had no equal among the cities of the blacks, and was known for its solid institutions, political liberties, purity of morals, security of its people and their goods, compassion towards the poor and strangers, as well as courtesy and generosity towards students and scholars.[75] Corroborating Kati, Leo Africanus, a Berber and Andalusi diplomat and author who was a household name among European literati, wrote in *A History and Description of Africa*, which was published at about 1526 that:

---

[71] See Levtzion and Hopkins, *Corpus of Early Arabic sources*, vii.
[72] Ludwig W. Adamec, *Historical Dictionary of Islam* (Scarecrow Press, 2009),137.
[73] For more, see Achebe Nwando, Samuel Adu-Gyamfi, Joe Alie, Hassoum Ceesay, Toby Green, Vincent Hiribarren, and Ben Kye-Ampadu, *History Textbook: West African Senior School Certificate Examination*, accessed May 4, 2021 at https://wasscehistorytextbook.com/
[74] Ki-Zerbo, J. (ed). *UNESCO General History of Africa, vol. IV*, (USA: University of California Press, 1998).
[75] The *Tarikh* was his most famous work. Andreas W. Massing, "Baghayogho: A Soninke Muslim Diaspora in the Mande World", in *Cahiers d'Etudes Africaines*, XLIV (4), 176, 2004, 887–922.

> The people of Timbuktu have a light-hearted nature. It is their habit to wander into town at night between 10pm and 1am, playing instruments and dancing ... There you will find many judges, professors and devout men, all handsomely maintained by the king, who holds scholars in much honour. There, too, they sell many handwritten North African books, and more profit is to be made there from the sale of books than from any other branch of trade.[76]

As Ahmed Baba noted, although goods ranging from gold and textiles to tea and tobacco reached Timbuktu, the most profitable trade items in Timbuktu were books.[77] Both Baba and Kati confirmed that buying books was not only a socially acceptable way of displaying wealth and of prestige, but also that the rich, nobles and kings invested heavily in buying and collecting books. Although many of its library holdings perished through raids, wars, and vagaries of nature, tens of thousands of books and manuscripts survive till today.[78]

This development in scholarship and intellectual pursuits was not limited to North and West Africa, as similar development occurred in the medieval Sudanese empire of Makuria and Ethiopia. The cases of Makuria and Ethiopia were quite interesting. Approximately 250,000 old manuscripts written in eight different languages still survive in Makuria and modern Ethiopia.[79]

Not minding the dangers posed by warfare and raids, fire and floods, insects and pillaging, tens of millions of manuscripts and books have survived from Mediterranean Africa, with Timbuktu alone yielding up over 700,000 manuscripts.[80] Other areas where enormous number of manuscripts and books have been found are the West African cities of Chinguetti, Walata, Oudane, Kano and Agadez.[81]

As Sertima noted, North African Muslims brought the light of learning to "... Europe during the Dark Ages."[82] Cordoba under the Moors, was also described as "the wonderful city of the tenth century" whose streets were

---

[76] Johannes Leo Africanus, *A History and Description of Africa* (Whitefish, MO: Kessinger Publishing, LLC, 2007).
[77] Jacqueline Passon, Klaus Braun, Said HamidSalih al-Mahdi Khalifa, Najmiya as-Sadeq at-Tellisi, Mansour El Nayedh and Joschua Metzger, "Places of Trade, Communication and Religion—Important Oases", in Braun K., Passon J. (eds.) *Across the Sahara* (Cham, Switzerland: Springer, 2020), 165–247.
[78] See the UNESCO's Timbuktu Manuscripts Project at
https://archive.is/20120715204006/http://portal.unesco.org/ci/en/ev.php-URL_ID=17480&URL_DO=DO_TOPIC&URL_SECTION=201.html#selection-361.0-366.0. See also the Library of Congress "Ancient Manuscripts from the Desert Libraries of Timbuktu" compilation at https://www.loc.gov/exhibits/mali/mali-checklist.html
[79] William Y. Adams, "The United Kingdom of Makouria and Nobadia: A Medieval Nubian Anomaly" in *Egypt and Africa: Nubia from Prehistory to Islam*, ed. by W.V. Davies (London: British Museum Press, 1977), 257.
[80] Adams, "The United Kingdom of Makouria and Nobadia", 250.
[81] Fallou Ngom, "West African Manuscripts in Arabic and African Languages and Digital Preservation" in *Oxford Research Encyclopedia of African History*, (USA: Oxford University Press, 2016).
[82] Ivan Van Sertima, *The Golden Age of the Moors* (USA: Transaction Publishers, 1992), 143.

well paved and there were raised sidewalks for pedestrians. At night one could walk for ten miles by light of lamps, flanked by uninterrupted extent of buildings. All this was hundreds of years before there was a paved street in Paris or a streetlamp in London. Its public baths numbered into the hundreds, when bathing in the rest of Europe was frowned upon as a diabolical custom, avoided by all good Christians. Moorish monarchs dwelt in sumptuous palaces, while the crowned heads in England, France and Germany lived in big barns, lacking both windows and chimneys and with only a hole in the roof for the exit of smoke. Education was universal in Muslim Spain, being given to the humblest, while in Christian Europe 99 percent of the populace was illiterate, and even kings could neither read nor write. In the tenth and eleventh centuries, public libraries in Christian Europe were conspicuous by their absence, while Muslim Spain could boast of more than seventy, of which the one in Cordoba housed 600,000 manuscripts.[83]

Sertima, cited above, noted that at the height of their powers, the Moors established more than seventy public libraries and universities in Almeria and Cordoba, Granada and Jaen, Malaga, Servile, and Toledo. Across the whole of Christian Europe however, there were only two universities of consequence.

There is no gainsaying the fact that Christian Europe would find it extremely difficult to concede any of the above unparallel achievements to Africa and Africans. It is certainly too much to concede. Hence, one can understand why books written even in the twenty-first century continue to deny Africans' conquest and administration of Visigothic Hispania between 690 CE and 1490s CE.

Just as intellectual culture, orchestrated by Islam, developed widely across Mediterranean Africa, so too were technological and cultural exchanges. The Garamantes, for example, adopted irrigation from Egypt and through their own invention, adapted their desert environment in ways not seen before in the area.[84]

Besides oral accounts, earliest known record of the Garamantes' existence dates to the works of Herodotus of Halicarnassus in the fifth century BCE. Herodotus, like other Roman authors, described them as Berbers while other Roman writers likened them to other dark-skinned people from sub-Saharan Africa.[85] Contemporary evidence, most especially the remains of Homo sapiens found in caves at Jebel Irhoud, Morocco, has shown that they were Berbers and were one of the earliest inhabitants of Mediterranean Africa.[86] The Garamantes, based on contemporary archaeological evidence, were mostly from Libya. They were brilliant farmers and resourceful engineers, who constructed pyramids and tombs, invented irrigation, which they used for

---

[83] Stanley Lane-Poole, *The Story of the Moors in Spain* (South Carolina: CreateSpace Independent Publishing Platform, 2016), 87.
[84] R. C. C. Law, "The Garamantes and Trans-Saharan Enterprise in Classical Times" in *The Journal of African History*, Vol. 8, No. 2, 1967: 181–200.
[85] Daniel F. McCall, "Herodotus on the Garamantes: A Problem in Protohistory" in *History in Africa*, Vol. 26, 1999: 197–217.
[86] Ian Sample, "Oldest Homo Sapiens Bones ever found shake Foundations of the Human Story" in *The Guardian*, accessed May 4, 2021 at https://www.theguardian.com/science/2017/jun/07/oldest-homo-sapiens-bones-ever-found-shake-foundations-of-the-human-story

agricultural purposes. Garamantians' success cannot be dissociated from three key things – trade, agriculture, and warfare.

Herodotus described Garamantian kingdom as "a very great nation" of great traders whose inhabitants also herded cattle, and farmed dates.[87] On their war-readiness, he noted that Garamantians, using chariots driven by four horses, hunted their fellow desert-based Ethiopian cave-dwellers. Much of Garamantians' wealth came from control of the Trans-Saharan caravan trade routes. As middlemen, the Garamantians exchanged products of both the Saharan and sub-Saharan Africa with the Roman along the Mediterranean coasts. Chief amongst products of this exchange system were salt and natron, a naturally occurring mixture of sodium carbonate decahydrate that was used for embalming and glassmaking, gold and other semi-precious stones. Others included ivory, wild animals, and hides.

As archaeologists have found, Garamantians were renowned for their dexterity in making tools of iron, bronze, gold, and silver. Besides finding metalworking hearths, furnaces where translucent red carnelian and other semi-precious stones were turned into jewelry have also been found, evidence supports the idea that that the Garamantians traded victims of their warfare as slaves.[88]

The Garamantians also combined great engineering techniques with local knowledge to tame their unfriendly desert environment. Dotting the desert landscape were spots, marked by their white crusts of calcium carbonate and other mineral deposits, showing areas that were originally lake beds. Thanks to local knowledge, the Garamantians understood that beneath these patches of land and at the base of the rock plateau of Wadi Ajal were fossil water locked in underground water-chambers and rock formations, commonly called aquifers.

With the diffusion of irrigation methods from Egypt, Garamantian engineers invented the *foggaras* – an underground water-extraction mechanism that depended on extensive networks of regularly-spaced vertical shafts, which drained the water in the aquifers for irrigation.[89] Using these foggaras, the Garamantians cultivated dates and grapes, olives and figs, sorghum and millet, barley and wheat, which were supplemented with livestock such as cattle and pigs, sheep and goats.

By about 800 BCE, Garamantes' foggara technology had replaced the shaduf water-raising system of Egypt and became the most widely used device across North Africa in the production of wheat and barley, figs and grapes, sorghum and millet, dates and cotton. Besides its use in agricultural production, foggaras were also widely used in large-scale salt production. From this, it could be argued that the Garamantes were pivotal in the diffusion of water-management technology. At the height of its power, it was a preferred destination for caravans from Wargla

---
87 Herodotus, *History of Herodotus* (transl. George Rawlinson) (Digireads.com, 2016), 183.
88 Nikita Efthymia, "Activity Patterns in the Sahara Desert: An Interpretation Based on Cross-Sectional Geometric Properties" in *American Journal of Physical Anthropology*, vol. 146, 2011: 423–434.
89 Ali Mostafaeipour, "Historical Background, Productivity and Technical Issues of Qanats" in *Water History*, vol. 2, 2010: 61–80.

and Ghadames, Qayrawan and Jabal Nafusa. By the ninth century, it also become a major center of Islamic scholarship.

The Makurian trade network stretched from India in the east to al-Andalus, from North Africa to the Sahel, and Ethiopia and east Africa to Byzantium.[90] Interactions and exchanges with these different parts of the Mediterranean world allowed for the spread of Makuria's distinctive lithic technologies and ceramic traditions.[91] Its megalithic funerary architecture, which diffused from Egypt, and ceremonial complexes were tied to astronomical rituals.

Prior to the eighth century, Makuria was essentially a Christian kingdom. Its legal system was a marriage of indigenous African system and the Greco–Roman system. Greek, combined with Sahidic, Coptic, and Old Nubian were its languages of education and learning. Between the eighth and fifteenth centuries, Arabic combined with Sahidic Coptic and Old Nubian linguistic tradition to foster a unique cultural and social life, ecclesiastical and philosophical traditions. Archaeologists working at Qasr Ibrim and other cities in northern Makuria, have discovered five multilingual archival materials. As Burstein noted, from Old Dogoma to Faras and Qasr Ibrim, the cathedrals and temples were filled with bibles and homilies, hymnals and liturgical texts, records of saint lives and magical texts, administrative and legal documents, diplomatic texts and royal proclamations, property inventories and commercial contracts, records of land sales and personal correspondences.[92]

By Way of Conclusion

Africa and the Mediterranean witnessed dramatic changes from the advent of Islam and, most significantly, from the eighth century. Whether as invaders and crusaders or as merchants and explorers, Arab Muslims were not only missionaries spreading Islamic religion and culture but also suppliers of Arab and European goods, including fabrics and other exotic items from Asia. In addition, they were also producers and generators of knowledge.

Through exchanges and networks, Sahelian Africa negotiated gold and copper, salt and slaves with North Africa. In turn, technical knowledge and inventions such as shaduf and pyramids, mastabas and tombs, writing and art, belief and mortuary culture, political tradition of divine kingship and religious beliefs diffused from Egypt and North Africa into the Sahel. These exchanges created knowledge structure that was based on human reason and not divine revelation. It also created different historical trajectories along the Mediterranean. With the highway of rationality paved by both North Africa and the Sahelian kingdoms, Africa beamed the light of knowl-

---

90 Kea, "The Mediterranean and Africa", 437.
91 Kea, "The Mediterranean and Africa", 426.
92 S. M. Burstein, "When Greek was an African Language: The Role of Greek Culture in Ancient and Medieval Nubia", in *Journal of World History* 19, no. 1, 2008: 41–61.

edge and invention, intellectual and philosophical advancement to Europe and the Arab worlds in a distribution and exchange system that provided framework of communication for both mercantile accumulation by traders and intellectual engagements of the literati. This development in and around the Mediterranean fostered multiple and layered identities that were based on interconnectedness of these sundry parts.

Moses I. Olatunde Ilo
Chapter 3
Tran-Saharan Networks to 1800

Abstract: This chapter focuses on the development of a long-distance trade that linked sub-Saharan Africa with North Africa and other parts of the world. The trans-Saharan trade, from earliest times to 1800 identifies important trade routes, articles of trade, markets networks, and commercial networks. The chapter also demonstrates that despite the significance of the relevant commercial networks and the trans-Saharan trade in general, the trade in question gradually declined from the late sixteenth century due to several factors including the rise of the Atlantic trade.

Keywords: Commercial networks, trans-Saharan trade, Islam, slavery, ethnicity.

Introduction

South of both the Mediterranean Sea and Mediterranean northern Africa lays the Sahara Desert. This desert is greater than the whole of Europe, and it is by far the largest desert in the world. Even though the Sahara Desert is largely characterized by dry sand, it also has mountains and oases that allow for agriculture and sedentary living in several places. Even though the desert presents many obstacles, it could be crossed. Indeed, right from the premodern times, the Sahara Desert became home to major trade routes associated with the famous trans-Saharan trade.[1]

The trans-Saharan trade was mainly characterized by interactions between sub-Saharan Africa and North Africa, but it also fostered connections between Africa and other parts of the world. The trade reached its height in the sixteenth century before experiencing a gradual decline. This chapter examines the factors responsible for the growth and expansion of the trans-Saharan trade. It also discusses the effects of trans-Saharan exchanges and the factors responsible for the decline of the trade. In examining these issues, this chapter demonstrates the importance of the use of camels for transportation, the rise of Islam, and of the development of market and commercial networks as key factors in the expansion of the trade between sub-Saharan Africa and North Africa. In addition, the chapter stresses that the trans-Saharan trade left a complicated legacy and that its decline resulted from several factors including political insecurity as well as the rise of the alternative trade across the Atlantic.

---

[1] J. D. Omer-Cooper et al., *The Growth of African Civilization: The Making of Modern Africa Vol. 1* (London, Longman, 1968), 1–3.

The Origins and Growth of the Trans-Saharan Trade

Trans-Saharan trade dates back to as early as circa 1000 BCE.[2] Mutual needs for goods led to the development of the first trade routes that linked societies south of the Sahara to that north of the desert. To cross the desert, the first means of transport included wheeled chariot and pack animal. Right from the start, those who participated in the trade encountered numerous challenges such as scarcity of water and food as well as attack by bandits and animal predators. Early Arabic writers left behind accounts that shed light on the pains which traders encountered in the process of crossing Sahara. For instance, according to one of them:

> At Sijilmasa he purchased ... food for his camel. ...it was ten days of discomfort... water there bitter and the place is plagued with flies. Crossing of the desert attracted ten days night journey with absence of water ... the long stretched of the tedious journey made groups to miss the actual route of crossing the Sahara. While many brave men died on ... trading journey.[3]

Despite these difficulties, the trans-Saharan trade involved the exchange of significant amounts of goods. It also ultimately became famous in Africa, Europe, and beyond. Available evidence indicates that even European, Middle Eastern, Indian and Chinese goods and services were gradually integrated into the trade over time. The phenomenal development of this desert traffic from about the fifth century was tied to the use of the camel as a principal means of transportation. The camel had many advantages over the pack animals that were initially used to cross the Sahara. For instance, the camel's splayed feet could move faster and enjoy a distinct transport cost advantage over donkey, oxen, and head porterage. Similarly, the camel could carry much load than a donkey, and it could survive longer without fresh water than such pack animals.[4] Recognizing such advantages, the Berbers made the camel the principal means of transportation across the Sahara. Following the introduction of the camel, trade across the Sahara was broken into fewer stages, and it became more regular and voluminous.[5]

Even though the trade became more regular and voluminous, the commodities of the trade were constrained by the fact that the journey across the desert took approximately three months. In view of this, highly perishable commodities were not suit-

---

[2] Toyin Falola and A. Adeniran, *A New History of Nigeria for Colleges Book 1* (Lagos: John West Publication, 1986), 194.
[3] Basil Davidson, *A History of West Africa 1800–1800*, (London: Longman, 1965), 31–32.
[4] Sebastian R. Prange, "Trust in God, but tie your Camel First: The Economic Organization of the Trans-Saharan Slave Trade between the Fourteenth and Nineteenth Centuries," *Journal of Global History* 1 (2006): 227. Also, see J. D. Omer-Cooper, et al. *The Growth of Modern Africa Vol 1: The Nineteenth Century to the Partition* (London: Longman, 1968), 110.
[5] Falola and Adeniran, *New History of Nigeria*,194.

able for such a trade and had to be left out.⁶ Equally, West Africa was the leading supplier of gold to the international economy accounting for about sixty percent of the global production. African gold not only contributed to the smooth and efficient functioning of the domestic economy of Europe but also sped up the settlement of international debt and, subsequently, indebtedness.⁷ Within African itself, the importance of the gold trade was evident. It contributed to the wealth and political power of the great state of western Sudan and the rise of some north African ports. Other prime commodities of trans-Saharan trade were slaves and salt. The former was needed by the Arabs to serve as soldiers, laborers, and servants. The latter was a scarce commodity in most parts of Africa. The desperate need for salt made it possible for north African merchants to exchange this salt for an equivalent weight in gold.⁸

Islam also shaped the development of the trans-Saharan trade. Soon after the rise of Islam in Arabia in the seventh century, Muslim forces conquered and converted many societies in Arabia and elsewhere thereby establishing an extraordinarily expansive commercial and cultural system. The establishment of this commercial and cultural system helped the expansion of the trans-Saharan trade by creating new markets for African goods in Muslim societies. In addition, Islam offered other benefits to the trans-Saharan trade. First, it provided a common language for merchants as well as for ubiquitous trading *marabous* (cleric) and *talibe* (disciples) who dominated the relevant trade routes and entrepots.⁹ Second, Islam equally a common bond based on trust.¹⁰ Chapters of the Quran extolled the virtues of competition, just profit-making, honesty, and civilizing influence of trade while the hadith promised salvation to 'honest' merchants and condemned speculation or unjust profit making.¹¹ Influenced by such religious stipulations, merchants developed a notable credit system. The whole system depended on mutual trust, and there is evidence that many merchants sought to not betray such trust. For example, according to one source, when a Northern African trader died in the Mali Empire, his goods were kept intact until his relatives could claim them.¹²

Islamic traditions also provided a uniform system of weights, measures, currencies, and relatively stable exchange rates. Islam therefore provided a model for trading procedures, acceptable commercial practices and means to enforce them includ-

---

6 Paul K. N. Ugboajah, "Traditional African Economic System," in *African Culture and Civilization*, ed. by S. Ademola Ajayi (Ibadan: Atlantis Books, 2005), 105–06. Also see G. T. Stride and Caroline Ifeka, *Peoples and Empires of West Africa, 1000–1800* (Nairobi: Thomas and Nelson, 1970).164–66.
7 Ugboajah,"Traditional African Economy," 106.
8 Ugboajah, "Traditional African Economy," 106.
9 Marie Perinbam, "Social Relations in the Trans-Saharan and Western Sudanese Trade: An Overview" *Comparative Studies in Society and History* 15, 4 (1973): 426.
10 Perinbam, "Social Relations in the Trans-Saharan," 426.
11 Perinbam, "Social Relations in the Trans-Saharan," 426.
12 G. T. Stride and Caroline Ifeka, *Peoples and Empires of West Africa 1000–1800* (Nairobi: Thomas Nelson, 1971), 170.

ing a code for interpersonal relationship within mercantile communities.[13] Islam also played a role in the protection offered to merchants and clerics during long hazardous journeys across the desert. Often inspired by religious factors, many Muslim states that emerged in various parts of Africa following the rise of Islam were given official protection and that such protection was equally extended to itinerant merchants, especially those who had links with such states.[14] Even though Muslim states offered protection to merchants and clerics or provided security along trans-Saharan routes before 1800, the practice continued well into the nineteenth century. For instance, by the early nineteenth century, the Sanusi brotherhood established its lodges at suitable resting points along the Wadai-Benghazi trans-Saharan trade route, which improved travelling conditions and security.[15] To further enhance security along these trade routes, deep wells were dug under Sanusi supervision at Bishara, 150 kilometers from Kufra while the rebellious non-Muslim Zuwaya people were brought under Muslim control.[16]

Throughout the history of the trans-Saharan trade, many trade routes went from West Africa to North Africa. It is difficult to establish precisely how many of such routes existed.[17] Nevertheless, of the known trade routes, the following three stood out: the western route that linked West Africa through Mauretania to the rich Muslim states in Morocco, Adar, al Andalus (Southern Spain) en-route the cities of Western Europe; the central route which linked the great markets of the Middle Niger, en-route Tuat, Algeria, other markets of the central Maghreb, Ghadames, Agades, Tunisia and Morocco; and the eastern routes which linked Tripoli, through Murzuk in Fezzan, Ghat, to Hausa land in Bornu Kanem.[18] The importance of various the trans-Saharan trade routes varied partly according to political developments over time. Trading along each route was often complex and was not single directional partly because many routes crisscrossed.

The trans-Saharan trade routes were often controlled by states or ethnic groups that either occupied or dominated areas in which trade routes and oases or in which camel, food, water and other requirements were located. The most important of these included Agades, Ghat in Salah, Tagbaza, Chadames and Sijilmasa.[19] In most cases, merchants from dominant ethnic groups formed networks with corporate economic

---

13 Perinbam, "Social Relations in the Trans-Saharan," 426.
14 Perinbam, "Social Relations in the Trans-Saharan," 420.
15 John Wright, "The Wadai-Benghazi Slave Route"*Slavery and Abolition* 13, 1 (1992): 176.
16 Wright, "The Wadai-Benghazi Slave Route,"176.
17 There are divergent views. Some claimed three main routes while others claimed four routes. This work aligns with three main routes. See C. C. Ifemesia, "The Peoples of West Africa Around A.D. 1000" in *A Thousand Years of West African History*, ed. by J. F. Ade Ajayi and Ian Espie (Lagos, Thomas Nelson, 1965), 46. Also, see Basil Davidson, *A History of West Africa 1000–1800* (London: Longman, 1965), 191; and G. T. Stride and Caroline Ifeka eds., *Peoples and Empires of West Africa, 1000–1800* (Lagos: Nelson, 1971), 164–66.
18 Davidson, *A History of West Africa*, 191.
19 Ugboajah,"Traditional African Economy," 106.

interests and institutions. Members of such commercial networks often exercised constraints on individual behavior thereby ensuring not only loyalty, but also those verbal agreements are based on socially accepted standard.[20] Market networks, within each ethnically controlled area, coordinated vast trading areas along each trade route through personal ties. Thus, wholesale trade was often administered by merchants and their representatives who collaborated on the basis of ethnic ties. Frequently, ethnic ties were reinforced by lineage and marriage ties while sometimes, lineage and family ties co-existed with clientelistic relationships.[21]

In the context of the state and ethnically controlled trans-Saharan trade routes, Berber merchants along with Arabs and Jewish merchants either sold goods to foreign traders along the Mediterranean coasts or traveled to sub-Saharan African markets, mainly in the northern savanna, to purchase goods. Those that travelled to sub-Saharan markets sometimes dealt directly with government suppliers and by so doing often advanced goods on credit to important state officials. They were also a source of credit for local merchants in the sub-Saharan region. To facilitate trade, North African merchants who visited the northern savanna area of West Africa either acted through brokers or maintained houses locally. Whichever of these options they embraced, North African merchants often passed on their goods to indigenous Muslim merchants who plied the savanna routes.[22]

The indigenous Muslim merchant groups that plied the savanna routes include the Juula (Dyula), Hausa, and Beriberi, just to mention a few. Typically, merchants in each of these groups advanced goods on credit in lieu of future payment and acted as suppliers to both the trans-Saharan and trans-Atlantic markets. It is also interesting that most of the merchants typically identified with their place of origin or city of residence, or both.[23]

In terms of commodities or articles of trade, North African merchants brought goods like salt, beads, cowries, copper, guns, silks, sword, pots, paper, Arabic books, brass vessels, and mirror to West Africa[24] in exchange for gold, slaves, wax, honey, ivory, ebony, textiles and leather goods.[25] These commodities were generally moved from one part of Africa to the other part by camel caravans. These caravans differed in size. Thus, caravans of 1,000 and 12,000 have been recorded before 1800.[26]

---

[20] Perinbam, "Social Relations in the Trans-Saharan," 419.
[21] Perinbam, "Social Relations in the Trans-Saharan," 424.
[22] Paul E. Lovejoy, *Transformations in Slavery: A History of Slavery in Africa* (Cambridge: Cambridge University Press, 2011), 89.
[23] Lovejoy, *Transformations in Slavery*, 90–91.
[24] Davidson: *A History of West Africa*, 30.
[25] K. P. Moseley, "Caravel and Caravan: West Africa and the World Economies c. 900–1900 AD" *Reviews Fernand Brandel* 15, 3 (1992): 528.
[26] For reference to the latter size, see Robert Collins, *Africa: A Short History* (Princeton: Markus Wiener Publishers, 2005), 59.

The Impact of the Trans-Saharan Trade

The trans-Saharan trade affected the fortunes of many African peoples and societies. It enhanced prosperity of many societies located in both North Africa and West Africa. For instance, even before 400 CE many North African societies were under the rule of Phoenicians and Roman, the trade helped to build the comfort and splendor of large North African cities such as Carthage, Laptis and Sabratha[27]. Similarly, it led to the establishment of cities in the Sahara region as well as in the Western and Central Sudan, especially after the eighth century. The development of such cities followed a similar pattern.[28] Typically, they began as small trading settlements, but they grew bigger as more traders patronized them. Overtime, such settlements became centers of craft production. In recognition of the need for governments to maintain law and order for the safety of the traders and citizens the rulers of these cities often extended their power over wider regions. Partly due to such expansionist activities, these cities grew into states and these states grew into empires.[29] For example, Agades, Gnat, Walata, Tichitt and Murzuk were all Berber cities that emerged in the Sahara area.[30] Some of these cities like Walata, and Tichitt still exist even though they have lost their wealth and importance. In contrast, other cities like Audoghat and Sijilmasa have entirely disappeared.

Examples of cities and states that emerged in Western and Central Sudan include Bouna, Boundoukou in Ivory Coast, and Salaga in Ghana, among others. As in the Sahara area, some of the old cities of the Western and Central Sudan have disappeared, while others, like Timbuktu, Gao, Jenne are still in existence.[31] Timbuku and places like Kano were deserts that became important centers for the production of clothing materials including cotton, which were in great demand in Europe and Arab world.[32] In terms of Gao, it became one of the leading centers of trans-Saharan trade before 1000 CE following the arrival of Lemtuna (Berber) traders there. After establishing itself as an important center of the trans-Saharan trade, Gao began to expand its power beyond the lands immediately around the city. Nevertheless, it was increasingly envied by rival powers, and at a point the great Mali ruler Mansa Musa sent out his generals and armies to annex it.[33] Following the decline of the Mali empire, Gao was also incorporated into the Songhai empire.

In all, the cities and states that developed in Western Sudan and elsewhere partly as a result of the trans-Saharan trade, rulers and state functionaries valued long distance trade not only because it contributed to the wealth of their local merchants,

---

27 Davidson, *A History of West Africa*, 29.
28 Davidson, *A History of West Africa*, 30.
29 Davidson, *A History of West Africa*, 30.
30 Davidson, *A History of West Africa*, 31.
31 Davidson, *A History of West Africa*, 31.
32 Ugboajah, "Traditional African Economy System,'" 107.
33 Davidson, *A History of West Africa*, 69–71.

but also because it allowed for the collection of customs dues and tolls that enhanced the power of the state.[34] Moreover, participation in this long-distance trade facilitated access to Muslim scholars and clerics who helped many local rulers to administer their societies.

In addition to fostering the growth and prosperity of cities and states, the trans-Saharan trade promoted the spread of Islam and Arab culture. Following the rise of Islam in Arabia, Muslim forces conquered many North African communities by the seventh century.[35] As Islam became an important religion in Egypt and elsewhere in North Africa, Arabic also became the language of daily life in many of these societies. Eventually, even societies in Western and Central Sudan that did not embrace the use of Arabic for the conduct of their daily affairs encouraged many of their citizens to adopt Arabic writing. Thus, Arabic writing was in use at Gao/Kwakaw by the early eleventh century as evidenced by rock inscription and epitaphs that bear calendar dates.[36] The spread of Islam from North Africa to sub-Saharan African societies was made possible by Muslim clerics and merchants associated with the trans-Saharan trade.[37] These Islamic clerics and merchants converted many local rulers who, in turn, encouraged their subjects to embrace Islam.[38] Following the acceptance of Islam in sub-Saharan Africa, pilgrimages to Mecca, the building of mosques and schools, and working with Muslim or Arab scholars such as Ibn Batutta, Leo Africanus, El Mashudi, El Idiris also became increasingly common.

The trans-Saharan trade also promoted the expansion of farming partly by allowing for the introduction of new agricultural technologies and new crops to many African societies. For instance, maize and wheat were introduced to sub-Saharan Africa from North Africa through trans-Saharan routes. Similarly, through this trade route African rice cultivated by early farmers in the region of the Middle Niger lakes from about 1500 BCE, as distinct from Asian rice brought in much later was introduced to farmers in other regions like Senegambia.[39] The introduction of such crops enabled significant population growth in many communities, and the expan-

---

34 Perinbam, "Social Relations in the Trans-Saharan," 433.
35 Davidson, *A History of West Africa*, 136.
36 Sonja Magnavita, "Sahara and West Africa," in *A Companion to the Global Early Middle Ages* ed. by Hermans Erik (Arc Humanities Press), 343.
37 For detailed discussion on the role of the trans-Saharan trade in the spread of Islam in sub-Saharan Africa see, for instance, Nehemia Levtzion, "Islam in the Bilad al-Sudan to 1800," in Nehemia Levtzion and Randall Pouwels, *History of Islam in Africa* (Athens, OH: Ohio University Press, 2000), 63–92.
38 It should be stressed, however, that the presence of Muslim merchants and the conversion of local dynasties did normally not mean a mass conversion to Islam. Indeed, mass conversion was subsequently fostered by the jihad wars that took place between the seventeenth century and nineteenth century as well as by European colonialism. For more discussion on the role of jihads and European colonialism on the spread of Islam, see, for instance, Austen, *Trans-Saharan Africa*, 91–93 and 138.
39 Davidson, *A History of West Africa*, 10–11.

sion of farming further helped to support people involved in craft production and in other such non-agricultural activities.[40]

Apart from new food crops, many livestock, some of which were used for transportation, were introduced to sub-Saharan Africa from North Africa through the trans-Saharan trade routes. Domesticated beasts of burden like horses, donkeys and camels were introduced into sub-Saharan Africa through the trans-Saharan trade.[41] Also, the use of horses for commercial, social, and military purposes was also introduced into West Africa through these same routes.

The trans-Saharan trade stimulated craft production in many parts of Africa. To satisfy demand for relevant products by merchants, an increasing number of Africans specialized in leatherwork, textile craft, and gold or jewelry making.[42] In a related way, the trans-Saharan trade also encouraged technical progress in West African mines that supplied merchants with gold and other products.[43] In turn, the enhancement of mining and precious metals trade facilitated the development of monetary systems in Africa. The major monetary systems that it helped to develop were based on the use of currencies like cowries and mithgals.[44] Cowries enjoyed wider acceptability until the early twentieth century before it lost it value as a medium of exchange.

Although the trans-Saharan trade benefitted many peoples and societies in Africa and elsewhere, it had negative impacts. Prominent among these deleterious impacts was the devastation of many societies as a result of the increasing supply of arms and weapons like muzzle loading guns. In sub-Saharan Africa, the increasing availability of firearms after the sixteenth century encouraged many warriors to carry a rifle as a symbol of manhood, and encouraged many Sudanese rulers to use such weapons as a means of enforcing their political authority and/or of expanding their societies. It was in this context that many African rulers amassed significant number of arms. For instance, Sabun, a ruler based somewhere along the Wadai-Benghazi trade route, bought guns from North African traders and had his slaves trained in their use.[45] Beyond the period of this paper, large quantities of surplus muzzle loaders became available for shipment to Africa, Middle East, and elsewhere. Sultan Muhammaal Sharif owned 300 guns, his successor Sultan Ali had 4,000 of good quality, while Sultan Dudmurra had an arsenal of 10,000 rifles.[46] It was also in this context

---

40 Davidson, *A History of West Africa*, 11.
41 C. C. Ifemesia, "The Peoples of West Africa around A.D.1000," in *A Thousand Years of West African History: A Handbook for Teachers and Students* ed. by J. F. Ajayi and Ian Espie (Ibadan: Ibadan University Press, 1965), 45.
42 C. C. Ifemesia, 'The Peoples of the West Africa around A.D. 1000' 46. See also Magnavita, "Sahara and West Africa," 343.
43 Davidson, *A History of West Africa*, 29.
44 Magnavita, "Sahara and West Africa," 343.
45 Wright, "The Wadai- Benghazi Slave Route," 177.
46 Wright, "TheWadai-Benghazi Slave Route, 177–178.

that many societies fought each other over the control of trans-Saharan routes. In North Africa, bitter Mediterranean clashes between the Christians of southern Europe and Muslim Turks advancing through North Africa from Egypt were partly over the control of the trans-Saharan trade in the sense that each side was trying not only to control sections of the North African coastline, but also to acquire mastery of the trade with West Africa. As part of such classes, in 1517, a famous sea battle was fought between the Christians and the Muslims of Greece. The Christians won this battle, but they were unable to extend their influence over the Turkish province of Tunisia or the Turkish ruled state of Algeria.[47]

In addition to the Mediterranean clashes between European Christians and Turkish Muslims and Berbers societies in Northern Africa often fought each other for control of the trans-Saharan trade. For example, during the early part of the second millennium CE, most of the Sahaja-Zanata (Berber) conflicts in the Western Sahara involved struggle for control of trade routes and commercial entrepôts. A specific conflict relevant to this analysis erupted in 1053–1057 between the Sanhaja and Zanata over the control of Sijilmasa-a commercial entrepôt situated close to the Moroccan-Algerian border.[48] It is interesting that an early Arab writer Ibn Khaldun, in one of his famous works, *Histories des Berbers* comments on such 'Berber desert wars' which were inspired as much by political as by commercial objectives.[49] It is also significant that apart from Berber communities fighting each other over the trans-Saharan trade, some sought to extend their influence to sub-Saharan Africa for similar reasons. For instance, the Sanhaja Berbers and their supporters sought to colonize the Sonninke of Ghana, in order to control the important southwestern Saharan trading town of Awadaghost.

Another major struggle over the control Tagbaza, an important salt mining area, was between Morocco and Songhai. In 1578, the Portuguese invaded Morocco, but were defeated at Al Ksar–al-Kabir thereby ending European occupation before the 1590s.[50] Subsequently to this military prowess, Moroccans turned their attention southwards. Mulay Ahmed (aged twenty-nine) succeeded the Sultan of Morocco who died shortly after defeating the Portuguese, launched an attack against Songhai, which was then under Askia Dawud in 1591. Shortly after this attack, Songhai was defeated at the famous battle of Tondibi in March 1591. From Tondibi, Morocco pushed into Timbuktu and Gao. In the course of this Moroccan expansion many people died, and Moroccan forces acquired much valuable loot.[51] However, Songhai did not give up. It embarked on guerilla tactics and finally attacked and expelled the Moroccans from its territories. In the end, however, the Moroccan invasion undermined Songhai's influence and resulted in further conflict over the control of the relevant

---

47 Davidson, *A History of West Africa*, 193.
48 Perinbam, "Social Relations in the Trans Saharan," 420.
49 Perinbam, "Social Relations in the Trans Saharan," 419.
50 Davidson, *A History of West Africa*, 83.
51 Davidson, *A History of West Africa*, 83.

trans-Saharan trade routes.[52] In addition to shaping the collapse of the Songhai empire, the trans-Saharan trade also influenced the collapse of other Western Sudan states like Ghana, Mali, and Kanem Bornu.[53]

In addition to devastation of communities caused by major rival states competing over trade routes, bandits, mercenaries and even ambitious professional soldiers often wreaked havoc on many people and societies on their own account.[54] For instance, in about 1680, a section of the Tuareg called Wulliminden seized Gao and made a camp there. Similarly, in 1737, the Wulliminden actually captured Timbuktu for a time and made the local pashas to pay tribute.[55]

Another deleterious impact of the trans-Saharan networks is that it encouraged slave raiding and slave trading. Slave trading across the Sahara existed since the beginning of the trans-Saharan trade. However, following the rise of Islam in the seventh century, there was an increased demand for slaves in the Sahara, North Africa, and other parts of the Mediterranean. This demand encouraged the enslavement of many people from the Sahel, a forested region of sub-Saharan Africa. Those enslaved were mainly acquired through warfare, although kidnapping and self-enslavement due to the negative impact of drought were among other factors that resulted in enslavement. Once enslaved and moved across the Sahara, sub-Saharan Africans were employed in various ways. Some served as wives and concubines of their masters, some served as eunuchs who helped in running the household, some served on agricultural enterprises, some served in mines, some served in the palace bureaucracy, and some served as slave soldiers in armies.[56] Even though some slave soldiers and other relatively few slaves could acquire considerable power, the largely violent manner in which all slaves were acquired resulted in the destruction of many societies as well as to death and other forms of human sufferings especially in sub-Saharan Africa. Moreover, many slaves died in the course of their movement across the Sahara while others died due to appalling conditions of mines or farms in their final destinations.[57] Despite the human sufferings and deaths associated with the trans-Saharan slave trade, slaves remained important trade items by 1800 and were clearly used as currency during the nineteenth century. As Prange notes;

> Slaves were widely used as currency with important implications for transaction cost and credit arrangements. For instance, some Sudanese rulers refused to pay merchants by any other means

---

52 Davidson, *A History of West Africa*, 85.
53 Davidson, *A History of West Africa*, 207.
54 Davidson, *A History of West Africa*, 261.
55 Davidson, *A History of West Africa*, 264.
56 For more details on the use of slaves in North Africa and Arab lands see, for instance, Ralph Austen, *Trans-Saharan Africa in World History* (New York, Oxford University Press, 2010), 31–32.
57 Sebastian R. Prange, "'Trust in God, But Tie Your Camel First.' The Economic Organization of the Trans-Saharan Slave Trade between the Fourteenth and Nineteenth Centuries," *Journal of Global History* 1 (2006):221

than slaves. While in 19th century Moroccan merchants continued to insist on payment in slaves to the dismay of French colonial Administrators.[58]

It is important to stress here that in total over six million slaves were moved across the Sahara desert between 650 and 1800[59] and that, at a point, merchants involved in the movement of these slaves from sub-Saharan Africa were concerned about the legitimacy of the enslavement process.

Furthermore, in helping to spread Islam and Arab culture, the trans-Saharan trade also helped to undermine many indigenous African religions and cultures. Indeed, with the expansion of the trade, some completely abandoned their local religious practices like *Bori* for Islam. Other people simply incorporated their local religions and culture into Islam while others refused to embrace the religion. Whatever option any individual in sub-Saharan African took, however, in the end indigenous religions and cultures were undermined in this part of the world.[60]

Finally, the trans-Saharan trade facilitated the spread of epidemic diseases such as plague. According to one source, the spread of such diseases might have been associated with two factors. First, it was likely made worse by physical contact between merchants, travelers and peoples of diverse background who participated in the trade. Second, disease was often introduced through infested commodities such as imported textiles that had insects transmitting relevant pathogens or that had viruses, bacterium and micro-organisms.[61]

The Decline of the Trans-Saharan Trade

The trans-Saharan trade expanded and reached its peak between 1490 and 1590. Thereafter, it gradually declined. Why? First, the increasing exhaustion of the gold mines located in the Western Sudan undermined the trans-Saharan trade, as many North African traders were discouraged from venturing into West Africa because the region was increasingly unable to supply their major need.

Second, the decline of the trade was related to Moroccan-Songhai War of 1591–92 (discussed above), and to other related changes in sub-Saharan Africa especially along the coastal cities.[62] Following the decline of Songhai, a political vacuum developed in Western and Central Sudan. This political vacuum resulted in incessant warfare between numerous states. This recurring warfare affected trade in many market towns as well as the western routes. Thus, these routes, which were previously the

---

58 Prange, "'Trust in God, But Tie Your Camel First,'" 221.
59 Lovejoy, *Transformations in Slavery,* 26 61.
60 Magnavita,"Sahara and West Africa," 343.
61 Magnavita,"Sahara and West Africa" 343.
62 Perinbam, "Social Relations in the Trans-Saharan," 424.

most important in West Africa, became less used after 1590s than before.[63] Contemporary European travelers who visited West Africa after the 1590s noted the declining importance of the western routes or that they were not regularly used. One such European traveler, a Frenchman known as Venture De Paradis specifically informs us that there was, "only one caravan along the main Western route every two or three years. While many other routes were often out of action."[64]

Given that the western routes were not extensively used after the 1590s, it is not surprising that previously prosperous Sijilmasa as well as other old Saharan oasis towns and market cities located along the western routes or in western Sudan suffered monumental setbacks. They all lost wealth, fame, and power. The increasing impoverishment of such cities in turn had a spillover effect on other neighboring societies and states. Thus, many societies in the Senegambia, Middle Niger, and Central Sudan witnessed different forms of setbacks. In terms of the development of Islam, for instance, with the decline of the Songhai, the unity of Muslims and the spread of Islam in the region were relatively undermined.[65] As a result, some non-Muslim societies like Mossi increasingly sought to undermine the Muslim states in Western Sudan. It is significant to stress, however, that while the western routes suffered monumental setbacks, the Central Saharan routes was less negatively affected by the decline of Songhai. Indeed, trade in the central and eastern routes expanded considerably after the 1590s. Nevertheless, the activities of Tuareg bandits caused increasing anarchy and insecurity which further undermined the trans-Saharan trade even in the central and eastern routes by 1800.

Third, the decline of the trans-Saharan trade was related to the development of the Atlantic trade. From the fifteenth century onwards, following the development of better ships in Europe, a new system of trade involving Europeans and Africans located along the Atlantic Ocean and Indian Ocean coasts gradually developed. By 1800, the Europeans involved in this trade brought goods like cloth, iron, brass, knives, hatchets, metal dishes, cheap jewelry, mirrors, alcohol and guns directly to West Africa, in exchange for items like gold, ivory, and, most importantly, slaves. Because West Africans traded directly with the Europeans, instead of through the Muslim Arab and Berber middlemen who dominated the trans-Saharan trade, African merchants recorded better trade profit.[66] The result was that increasing amounts of goods were diverted from the trans-Saharan routes towards the Atlantic coast. By 1800, therefore, while West African merchants were obtaining better prices for their goods along the Atlantic coasts, the trans-Saharan trade had already considerably declined in volume.[67]

---

[63] Davidson, *A History of West Africa*, 207.
[64] Davidson, *A History of West Africa*, 207.
[65] Davidson, *A History of West Africa*, 208.
[66] G. T. Stride and Caroline Ifeka, *Peoples and Empires of West Africa 1000–1800* (Nairobi: Thomas Nelson, 1971), 171.
[67] Davidson, *A History of West Africa*, 208.

The final reason for the decline of the trans-Saharan trade was tied to the European conquest of Africa. The European conquest of Africa took place in the late nineteenth and early twentieth centuries, and not within the period before 1800, which is the focus of this chapter. Nevertheless, it is permissible to state that following European conquest, the European power further undermined the trans-Saharan trade was in part by promoting the export of West African products primarily to European markets and by introducing new boundaries and policies that help to undermine regional exchanges in Africa.[68]

Conclusion

This chapter examined the trans-Saharan trade and networks up to 1800. It suggests that the trans-Saharan trade networks helped broke the isolation of many parts of Africa and subsequently helped ensure that the continent became integrated into the global capitalist economy.[69] It was generally true that the longer the distance, the more trade was confined to the commodities with high value-to-bulk ratios.[70] Thus, trade in such goods was more profitable than local or regional commerce. The Berbers of the desert were key actors in the development of the trans-Saharan trade, and the trade has survived for more than 2,500 years. In the course of its existence, the introduction of camel revolutionized the trans-Saharan trade. Following the introduction of the camel, the trade reached its zenith in about 1500, before it gradually started to decline. The decline of this trade was partly related to the rise of the Atlantic trade that fostered direct interaction between Europeans and West Africans.[71]

The trans-Saharan trade was characterized by long distance travel, lack of reliable communication, trading risks, wars, conflicts and sandstorm, hot sun, cold nights, shortage of water among others. Nonetheless, the participants held market networks together through personal, ethnic and clientelist ties and homogenous religion that further enhanced the prosperity of the networks. Mosely rightly captures significance of these networks as the quoted Perlin and Curtin that:

> The world system remained a network of inter societal links, arranged in multiple clusters or subsystems with competing cores ...Trans Saharan trade can be said to have produced 'local structure' and 'external contact' as demonstrated in the above analysis of networks leading to different evolutionary trajectories of the international level till present.[72]

---

68 K. P. Moseley, "Caravel and Caravan: West Africa and World Economics c. 900–1900 AD," *Review Fernand Braidel Centre* 15, 3 (1992): 545. For similar discussion on European colonialism and trans-Saharan trade see, for instance, Austen, *Trans-Saharan Africa*, 118–138.
69 Ugboajah,"Traditional African Economy," 107.
70 Prange,"Trust in God But Tie Your Camel First," 219.
71 Davidson, *A History of West Africa*, 33.
72 Moseley, "Caravel and Caravan," 549.

Consequently, the trans-Saharan networks were based on high degree of flexibility and adaptability. This was characterized by an integrated network of ethnics, slaves, cultural, religious, exchange, production, social, and most importantly, commerce of pre-modern times linking West Africa, to North Africa, Europe and Mediterranean world. It would be wrong to comment on the right disappearance of trans-Saharan networks owing to its gargantuan challenges. Traders still found ways of carrying on their business. In 1635, for instance, some English merchants in Morocco were able to tell their partners in London that they were sending many English goods by camel to Timbuktu, Gao, and other parts of West Africa and were exchanging with West Africa gold.[73] Finally, with the arrival of Europeans in West Africa and growing competition between caravel and caravan, the trans-Saharan networks lost its economic centrality and role in Africa's destiny in 1920s.[74]

---

[73] Davidson, *A History of West Africa*, 264.
[74] Wright, "The Wadai-Benghazi Trade Route," 175.

Pedro Machado
Chapter 4
Africa and the Indian Ocean World to 1800

Abstract: Africa has been integral to the histories of the Indian Ocean. The movements of goods, people, ideas, and texts braided communities along its coasts and interiors with those across the ocean in bonds forged by a range of commercial, social, and political imperatives. This chapter describes key aspects of the historical relationship between Africa and the broader Indian Ocean lands over two millennia of complex and multilayered commercial, social, religious, and cultural intercourse. While it will identify the processes that structured the far-flung interactions between Africans and the furthest reaches of the ocean, its focus of necessity will be on the western Indian Ocean where these interactions were most pronounced and enduring, and where Africans established dynamic and sophisticated connections with the Red Sea, the Gulf and South Asia as they forged wide-ranging connections with the worlds around them and helped shape them in fundamental ways.

Keywords: Trade; Egypt; Red Sea; Gulf; South Asia; East Africa; Swahili coast; Islam; Slavery; Cloth.

Introduction

Africa has always been integral to the worlds of the Indian Ocean. Although the intensity of its connections to this broader oceanic space have varied across time and chartered different social and cultural geographies as delineated by the movements of people, things, ideas, texts and even legal idioms that have travelled between coasts and interiors, Africa and Africans have been indispensable in shaping its many histories. Caravan and trade routes linked interior exchange with coastal mercantile interests and, in turn, to the broader transoceanic shipping routes that together shaped the contours of the Indian Ocean as a space of multilayered interactivity over many centuries. The African continent's connections to and intercourse with the Indian Ocean, therefore, spanned vast distances of braided terrestrial and maritime linkages that assumed varying degrees of importance for commercial activity over short, medium, and long distances.

Yet African connectivity to the Indian Ocean was not defined only by the economic realm or mercantile interests, as important as these were to the establishment and maintenance of relationships between different parts of the continent and the further reaches of the ocean. Rather, the ties that bound Africa to the Indian Ocean world were various and involved a variety of actors, from the botanical and food exchanges that brought bananas, yams, and other comestible items to the continent; and the Arab and Muslim travelers in the ninth and tenth centuries who sailed from southern Arabia to Mogadishu, Kilwa, and elsewhere; to the musical influences that have spread from the continent to offshore islands such as the Comoros and Reunion and are maintained by particular diasporic formations; as well as African sailors who laboured on coastal and transoceanic vessels as they chartered maritime itineraries of varying length and complexity. These wide-ranging experiences and movements reflect the myriad ways in which Africans both engaged with and shaped the historical currents of the Indian Ocean, creating vital sinews of connection that were constitutive of the ocean's mutable social geographies.

This chapter describes key aspects of the historical relationship between Africa and the broader Indian Ocean world over two millennia of complex and multilayered commercial, social, religious and cultural intercourse. While it will identify the processes that structured the far-flung interactions between Africans and the furthest reaches of the ocean, its focus of necessity will be on the western Indian Ocean where these interactions were most pronounced and enduring, and where Africans established dynamic and sophisticated connections with the Red Sea, the Gulf, and South Asia, forging wide-ranging connections with the worlds around them and helping to shape them in fundamental ways.

Worlds of Exchange

Trade and commercial exchange have long existed across the African continent, with overland routes extending to maritime commerce through the intricate linkages that structured elements of the Indian Ocean global economy. While details in many instances are not available for early periods, fragmented and partial evidence points nonetheless to active exchange. Plant and animal exchanges between Africa, Arabia, and South Asia appear to have become established no later than 2000 BCE, likely through the small-scale trade of fishing communities. Domesticated crops from the northern savannah regions of Africa – among them sorghum, pearl millet and hyacinth bean – were taken to India along routes skirting the northern coastline of the Arabian Sea, while the zebu cow was transported in the opposite direction in one of the many animal exchanges that took place.[1] In the ancient Red Sea, trade existed between Egypt and the land called Punt on the African coast near the southern end of the sea, identified today as the coast of Sudan and Eritrea. In a connection that dated to the middle of the third millennium BCE, Egyptian texts and scenes especially from the fifteenth century BCE onward make clear the regular trade that existed to and from Punt. Goods such as ivory, gold, and incense were supplied to Egypt, and in the tenth century BCE it was even recorded that King Solomon of Israel

---

[1] Edward A. Alpers, *The Indian Ocean in World History* (New York: Oxford University Press, 2014), 24–25. See also Haripriya Rangan, Edward A. Alpers, Tim Denham, Christian Arthur Kull and Judith Carney, "Food Traditions and Landscape Histories of the Indian Ocean World: Theoretical and Methodological Reflections," *Environment and History*, 21, 1 (2015): 135–57.

sent fleets every three years to Ophir below the mouth of the Red Sea for similar African goods, including gold in vast quantities.[2] During the reign of Ptolemaic Egypt, the port of Berenike was established on the western coast of the Red Sea and served as a conduit through which great numbers of goods were transported, among them African war elephants, glass beads from India, and spices and Chinese textiles. Berenike remained vital even after the conquest of Ptolemaic Egypt by the Romans in 30 BCE, with archaeological finds confirming its stature as a trading port linking Africa with the eastern Mediterranean and Arabian Sea.[3]

By this time, linkages were also firmly articulated in a vertical dimension, along a north-south axis, with Eastern Africa seemingly a regular destination on maritime itineraries. This is suggested by the *Periplus of the Ærythrean Sea*, a first-century CE commercial guide written by an unknown Alexandrian Greek that identified major ports of trade (such as "Rhapta", located to the far south of the Horn) and goods (ivory was noted as a major export) traded between the Red Sea, Africa, and South Asia.[4] But broader lateral connections are also suggested by Austronesian voyages to and settlement in Madagascar sometime between 100 BCE and 300–400 CE that shaped the island's language in unique ways, setting it apart linguistically from other African languages – such as Swahili – that developed from the expansion of Bantu-speaking people along coastal East Africa and across to the Comoros.[5]

With the rise and spread of Islam in the eighth and ninth centuries CE (discussed in the next section), a process for which trade was an important catalyst but also one through which trade expanded in subsequent centuries, the place of Africa in commercial engagement flourished in the Indian Ocean. Persian merchants, sailing from Siraf, voyaged to the coast and islands of East Africa (and elsewhere) in the tenth century, while Arab and Gulf merchants dispatched vessels to the coast from Sharma on the coast of Hadramawt between about 980 and 1140 for cargoes of copal resins used as incense.[6] When Ibn Battuta (the Moroccan jurist and traveler whose itineraries took him to many different lands of the Dar al-Islam) visited Mombasa in the fourteenth century, he noted the ivory trade that animated coastal commerce, as it had done for some time before he arrived on the coast.[7] Ivory was taken to multiple

---

2 David O'Connor, "Egypt, 1552–664 BC," in *Cambridge History of Africa*, vol. 1, *From Earliest Times to c.500 B.C.*, ed. J. Desmond Clark (Cambridge, UK: Cambridge University Press, 1982), 917–18. 935–40; 1 Kings 9:26–28, 10:11–12, 22.
3 Steven Sidebotham, *Berenike and the Ancient Maritime Spice Route* (Berkeley: University of California Press, 2011); idem, "Overview of Fieldwork at Berenike (Red Sea Coast), Egypt, and in the Eastern Desert, 2011–2015," in *Stories of Globalisation: The Red Sea and the Persian Gulf from Late Prehistory to Early Modernity. Selected Papers of Red Sea Project VII*, ed. by A. Manzo, C. Zazzaro and D. J. de Falco (Leiden: Brill, 2019): 183–224.
4 Lionel Casson, *The Periplus Maris Erythraei* (Princeton, NJ: Princeton University Press, 1989).
5 Uniquely, Malagasy forms part of the Western Malayo Polynesian subfamily, with links to Borneo in Indonesia.
6 Alpers, *Indian Ocean in World History*, 48–49.
7 *The Travels of Ibn Battuta*, trans. Reverend Samuel Lee (London: John Murray, 1829).

destinations in the western Indian Ocean, with Mogadishu a key transit port that also maintained overland connections with the Horn and Ethiopia. One of these destinations, Aden, imported large cargoes of ivory, along with animal skins, ambergris, rice, and mangrove poles used in house construction, in return for which merchants shipped goods such as southern Arabian pottery, glassware and paper. By this time, gold exports from the East African coast at Kilwa, channeled through Sofala to its south but sourced from the deep interior of the high plateau of today's Zimbabwe, sustained the rulers of the city-state and helped fuel its and the coast's trade with the larger region.[8]

A critically important staple of Indian Ocean commerce was cloth, especially South Asian textiles that constituted the most widely accepted medium of exchange in the region and were in high demand among African populations.[9] They were highly valued and utilized in a variety of ways expressing cultural and social meaning, and conveying political authority. Africans thus sought particular types of cloth with distinctive patterns, reflecting sophisticated consumer preferences that served as the connective sinews between coastal and interior peoples, traders, merchants, rulers and producers. Already by the fourth century BCE there is evidence of Gujarati textiles in particular being present on Socotra Island, and the *Periplus of the Ærythrean Sea* includes references to the commercial exchange of cottons with the Gulf of Aden and Red Sea coast of Africa. Other evidence, such as the fifth century CE archaeological materials uncovered on the Egyptian side of the Red Sea at Berenike of patterned textiles, as well as the cloth fragments collected in Egypt dating to the late ninth and tenth centuries CE, suggests the continuity of this textile commerce. By the twelfth and thirteenth centuries, correspondence making reference to cotton cloths from north-western India being trade in Aden and Fustat, hints at an expansion in trade, a process that was well underway by the fifteenth and sixteenth centuries.[10]

---

[8] M.N. Pearson, *Port Cities and Intruders: The Swahili Coast, India, and Portugal in the Early Modern Era* (Baltimore: Johns Hopkins University Press, 1998).

[9] It is important to underscore that the generic category of "South Asian," "Indian" cloth used in this essay is of necessity vague as to the particularities of the cloths that entered East and Southeast Africa because space constraints do not permit elaboration. Cloths varied significantly in serving different markets and have to be distinguished according to their distinct materiality which reflected key aspects of their production such as market tastes, artisan innovation and the application of vibrant colors in the manufacturing process by expert dyers and printers. For the rich variety of textiles being imported into the region in the eighteenth and nineteenth centuries, see Machado, *Ocean of Trade: South Asian Merchants, Africa and the Indian Ocean, c. 1750–1850* (Cambridge: Cambridge University Press, 2014); and Sarah Fee, "Filling Hearts with Joy: Handcrafted 'Indian Textiles' Exports to Central Eastern Africa in the Nineteenth Century," in *Transregional Trade and Traders: Situating Gujarat in the Indian Ocean from Early Times to 1900*, ed. by Edward A. Alpers & Chaya Goswami (New Delhi: Oxford University Press, 2019), 163–217.

[10] Further details can be found in Pedro Machado, "Cloth's Many Waterways: Indian Ocean Textiles and the Deep Histories of Exchange," in *World on the Horizon: Swahili Arts Across the Indian Ocean,*

By this time, Gujarati cottons had been arriving on the East African coast for several centuries. Although they were traded in the Horn by the first century CE, they became more widely available from the twelfth to fourteenth centuries due likely to the spread of Muslim commercial networks. Certainly, Gujarati cottons were dominant in the Horn and along the Swahili coast by the fifteenth century, with Massawa, Berbera and Mogadishu maintaining links with this productive western Indian region. A well-established trade in Gujarati textiles was evident further along the southern coast at Malindi and Mombasa (from which textiles were also sent onto places such as Zanzibar and Mafia), while the Pate ruler, Mwana Mkuu, sent ships expressly to Gujarat to purchase cloths.[11]

The entrenched and seemingly growing commerce in Gujarati cottons at the coast is confirmed by Portuguese records from the late fifteenth and early sixteenth centuries that make clear that trade stretching from Barawa (in contemporary Somalia) to Inhambane on the southern shore of the Mozambique coast was reliant on their importation in considerable quantities, styles, colours and shapes.[12] The bulk were transported into the interior where markets were increasingly being established throughout the Zambesi Valley among African traders and rulers, who sought "Indian cotton goods with which they were familiar and which were in demand."[13] This was reflected, among other ways, by the volume of cloths that were arriving on the coast – for instance, in the early years of the sixteenth century, 100,000 Indian cloths were brought to Angoche from Malindi while approximately 83,000 were imported directly into Mozambique Island from India. In the 1650s, more than 250 tons of mostly Gujarati cottons entered East Africa annually, some of which seems to have been sent onto the Comores and Madagascar.[14]

Indian specialization in African production became further entrenched in Gujarat as African consumers stimulated its manufacturing capacities, with certain textile centres producing particular textiles in hundreds of thousands of pieces per year in the eighteenth century and into the nineteenth. In Mozambique, for instance, annual imports regularly reached between 300,000 and 500,000 pieces (or close to two million metres of cloth) by the 1750s, reflecting the extremely large and varied nature of demand across the northern, central and southern reaches of the territory and its

---

ed. by Prita Meier and Allyson Purpura (Champaign, IL: Krannert Art Museum and Kinkead Pavilion, 2018).

11 Jeremy Prestholdt, "As Artistry Permits and Custom May Ordain: The Social Fabric of Material Consumption in the Swahili World, c. 1450–1600," Program of African Studies Working Papers, 3. Evanston: Program of African Studies, Northwestern University, 1998.

12 For details, see Machado, "Awash in a Sea of Cloth: Gujarat, Africa and the Western Indian Ocean, 1300–1800," in *The Spinning World: A Global History of Cotton Textiles, 1200–1850*, ed. by Giorgio Riello and Prasannan Parthasarathi (Oxford: Oxford University Press, 2009).

13 Justus Strandes, *The Portuguese Period in East Africa* (Nairobi: East African Literature Bureau, 1961), 92 and 50; Alexandre Lobato, *A expansão portuguêsa em Moçambique de 1498 a 1530*, I(Lisbon: Agência Geral do Ultramar, 1960), 57.

14 Machado, "Awash in a Sea of Cloth."

vast interior lands. East and Southeast Africa were thus firmly enmeshed in a Gujarati cloth nexus that brought cotton growers, yarn spinners and weavers in the Indian interior into close relation with African traders and cloth consumers throughout East and Southeast Africa. In return, large quantities of ivory and in many instances slaves (especially from the 1760s) were brought to the coast and shipped across the ocean by South Asian merchants.[15] Cloths operated as exchange media through which equivalencies of value could be established, but through their incorporation into particular cultural, social and political practices exhibited also a crucial use value that transcended the commercial, and would take on new valences in the nineteenth century.[16] Cloth never operated in a singular economic register precisely because it was embedded within larger contingent spheres of signification and meaning.

Ocean of Islam

The rise and spread of Islam from Arabia in 622 CE spurred a remarkable period of growth in oceanic commerce and marked a transformative moment for the social, religious and cultural worlds of the Indian Ocean. Africa and Africans played critical roles in its spread and establishment throughout the lands, coasts and islands of the continent, forging dense and enduring entanglements that would produce profound changes among its peoples. In its early years, the expansion of Islam would connect southwest Asia and North Africa to form a vast market for luxury as well as everyday commodities.[17] Following early conquests of Egypt and Persia, Islam became the dominant faith of the Red Sea, Gulf, and Arabian Sea coasts, reaching coastal East Africa by the eighth century. Gulf merchants sailed down the coast from ports such as Mogadishu to Zanzibar to explore trading opportunities and brought new religious ideas as well as trading commodities with them. Among them were religious refugees escaping the enforcement of Islamic orthodoxy of the Umayyads who had begun to assert their control over the Gulf.[18] The spread of Islam, as elsewhere, was thus indelibly associated with trade and commercial exchange, even while the

---

15 For further details of how exchange operated and was mediated by different actors, see Machado, *Ocean of Trade*.

16 One of these changes was the entry of American cottons into East Africa from the 1830s, a process that was nonetheless responsive to African consumer preferences, with significant repercussions for manufacturing in New England, for which see Jeremy Prestholdt, *Domesticating the World: African Consumerism and the Genealogies of Globalization* (Berkeley: University of California Press, 2008).

17 Abdul Sheriff, *Dhow Cultures of the Indian Ocean: Cosmopolitanism, Commerce and Islam* (London: C. Hurst & Co, 2010), 171.

18 Sheriff, *Dhow Cultures*, 276; Mark Horton and John Middleton, *The Swahili: The Social Landscape of a Mercantile Society* (Oxford: Blackwell, 2000). A recently published collection showcases the most current interpretations of various aspects of Swahili history: Stephanie Wynne-Jones and Adria LaViolette (eds.), *The Swahili World* (London: Routledge, 2018).

arrival of religious leaders and scholars over time cemented it among coastal society and would spur its expansion into the interior in later centuries as well as bring different Islamic traditions to the coast.[19]

As Islam was adopted into local belief systems through a process of syncretic assimilation by local peoples over time, particular forms emerged on the East African coast that reflected a mixing of local with universal practices. Practices among coastal Islam continued to include non-Muslim origins through to the fifteenth and sixteenth centuries at least, after which they appear to have become less visible in devotional practice. The earliest evidence of an Islamic presence on the coast dates to the period 780–850 CE and comes from archaeological excavations at Shanga in the Lamu archipelago.[20] While early mosques were small and constructed from natural local materials such as coral, with growing converts from among the African population, a large Friday mosque was already present around the tenth century at what may have been Ras Mkumbuu on Pemba island. At least one mosque was present in more than thirty communities by the fourteenth century, with Islam having extended to the Comoros and Madagascar possibly a few centuries earlier. [21]

In these early centuries, the prominence of Gulf influence along the coast and its offshore islands was clear, both in claims by ruling dynasties to Shirazi origin and by the dominance of Shia Muslims among the populations of the most important towns at the time; these were all located along the northern reaches of the coast because it was there that voyagers from the Gulf had made landfall on their African voyages. By the eighth or ninth centuries, however, an Ibadi presence was already established on the coast, possibly at Tumbatu and, as Ibadis migrated south, also at Kilwa Kisiwani that emerged as the dominant city-state on the coast by the twelfth century due to its connection to the gold trade discussed above. While the earliest mosque at Kilwa dates to the thirteenth century, it underwent continual expansion and subsequent renovation in the following decades and centuries.[22] In the period between 1000

---

[19] While Islam endured overwhelmingly at coastal and island sites in East Africa, a relatively small Muslim presence developed around the fifteenth century on the Zimbabwe plateau from which gold that was channeled through Kilwa and Sofala was extracted; these Muslim traders encompassed Arabs, Swahili and Islamized Shona. See Edward A. Alpers, "East Central Africa," in *The History of Islam in Africa*, ed. by Nehemia Levtzion and Randall L. Pouwels (Athens, OH/Oxford/Cape Town: Ohio University Pres/James Currey/David Philip, 2000). One Islamic tradition, Sufism, developed particularly broadly in the nineteenth century, for which see Anne Bang, *Sufis and Scholars of the Sea: Family Networks in East Africa, 1860–1925* (Abingdon: Routledge, 2003); and A. H. Nimtz, *Islam and Politics in East Africa: The Sufi Order in Tanzania* (Minneapolis: University of Minnesota Press, 1980).
[20] Mark Horton, *Shanga: The Archaeology of a Muslim Trading Community on the Coast of East Africa* (Nairobi: British Institute in Eastern Africa, 1996).
[21] Mark Horton, "Primitive Islam and Architecture in East Africa," *Muquaramas*, 8 (1991), 103–118; Randall L. Pouwels, "The East African Coast, c. 780 to 1900 C.E.," in *History of Islam in Africa*, ed. by Levtzion and Pouwels, 252.
[22] See Neville Chittick, *Kilwa: An Islamic Trading City on the East African Coast* (Nairobi: British Institute in Eastern Africa, 1974), as cited in Pouwels, "East African Coast."

and 1500 CE, "Islamization" on the coast contributed to the emergence of key features of Swahili society and economy that combined maritime activities with cultivation, braided together coastal and translocal trade, and a city-state form of organization, immigration and settlement of foreign merchants who increasingly became integrated into coastal communities through intermarriage with local women.[23]

Over these centuries, several important changes reflected the continued dynamism of the Swahili coast as a constitutive element of the trading currents of the Indian Ocean and its merchant networks. One of these, as observed by Ibn Battuta, was the dominance of Shafi'i Sunni Islam at Mogadishu, Mombasa, and Kilwa, whose leaders had family origins in Yemen in southern Arabia.[24] Migrations from Hadramawt, occurring in the second half of the thirteenth century as well as in the sixteenth and seventeenth centuries (the nineteenth century also saw important Hadrami tariqas spread from Zanzibar and the Comoros to the interior and further along the coast to Mozambique Island and inland), were significant for they married locally and created family lineages scattered widely along the East African coast and its islands, including Madagascar. This created networks of branches connected by family ties which further underpinned the commercial intercourse locally and transregionally. Amid vibrant commercial exchange involving significant trades in gold, ivory and slaves – for which the Swahili were lynchpins connecting the interior with the coast and ultimately with lands across the ocean – growing urbanization also became an established feature of the coast as settlements grew into large port towns with the built environment also signaling growing social stratification among populations.[25]

When the Portuguese entered this world at the end of the fifteenth century, they inserted themselves into its myriad networks, while also pursuing aggressive campaigns (at times through strategic alliances) against Islam and Muslim rulers along the coast and elsewhere in the western Indian Ocean.[26] Most emphatically, they established a fortified presence in Sofala, Mozambique, and Kilwa early in the century in an effort to profit from the gold trade, and became embroiled in struggles with the Ottomans who had captured Egypt and launched a counteroffensive in the Red Sea and Indian Ocean; towards the end of the century, they would also attempt to take Pate and Mombasa but were rebuffed by Portuguese forces. Yet, even as the Portuguese drove Muslims out of places such as Sofala, reorienting the gold trade away from the southern plateau of Zimbabwe and towards the Zambezi Valley which became accessible from towns under their control such as Mozambique Island and

---

23 Sheriff, *Dhow Cultures*, 242–243.
24 For a useful discussion of Ibn Battuta and the broader contexts of his travels, see Ross E. Dunn, *The Adventures of Ibn Battuta: A Muslim Traveler of the Fourteenth Century*, 3rd edition (Berkeley: University of California Press, 2012).
25 Sheriff, *Dhow Cultures*; see also essays in Wynne-Jones and LaViolette, *Swahili World*.
26 There is a large literature detailing Portuguese engagement with East Africa and the western Indian Ocean but a good overview is offered by Pearson, *Port Cities*.

Angoche, Islamic communities survived. Muslim-Swahili were prominent in coastal northern Mozambique while there appears to have been a gradual increase in the Muslim presence in the eighteenth century.[27] Elsewhere on the coast, commercial expansion in East Africa for which the rise of the Busaidi sultanate of Zanzibar was a catalyst – deeply connected to Oman and financially underwritten predominantly by Kachchhi merchants – would rejuvenate Sunni Islam, expand trading linkages with the African interior and entangle Nyamwezi, Swahili, Arab, Omani, South Asian, American, and European trading interests (among others) amidst widespread commercial efflorescence in the region spurred by regional and global demand for such commodities as ivory, pearls and dates. But this is a story that unfolded over the nineteenth century and does not concern us here.[28]

Africa Across the Ocean

Africans established a presence in the Indian Ocean over many centuries through diasporic formations that spread from the continent to the Arabian peninsula and western India, and east to the Bay of Bengal and the South China Sea. While the movements of Africans across this ocean remains less studied than that of the Atlantic, its neglect as an aspect of the global diaspora of African peoples is not quite as marked as it once was. Increasingly, there is interest in exploring the manifold itineraries and experiences of Africans as they traversed the waters of the ocean and became dispersed across many of its lands. These movements had ancient roots and followed different migratory patterns, including for trade and commercial settlement as appears to have been the case with Bava Gor, a widely revered African Muslim *pir* (saint) who is today remembered as an Abyssinian trader who travelled to Gujarat in the fourteenth or sixteenth century.[29] Yet, in many instances, these movements involved the forced migrations of Africans as they were incorporated into different slavery and unfree regimes under the control of a range of political systems, and that were shaped by varying social and cultural contexts.[30]

---

27 Alpers, "East Central Africa," 305–306.
28 Several aspects of this history are well known but others have been insightfully and innovatively examined in such recent works as Johan Mathew, *Margins of the Market: Trafficking and Capitalism across the Arabian Sea* (Oakland: University of California Press, 2016); and Thomas F. McDow, *Buying Time: Debt and Mobility in the Western Indian Ocean* (Athens, OH: Ohio University Press, 2018).
29 See, inter alia, Helene Basu, "Drumming and Praying: Sidi at the Interface of Spirit Possession and Islam," in *Struggling with History: Islam and Cosmopolitanism in the Western Indian Ocean*, ed. by Edward Simpson and Kai Kresse (New York: Columbia University Press, 2008), 291–322; idem, "Redefining Boundaries: Twenty Years at the Shrine of Gori Pir," in *Sidis and Scholars: Essays on African Indians,* eds. Amy Catlin-Jairazbhoy and Edward Alpers (Trenton, NJ: Rainbow Publishers, 2004), 62–85.
30 Interest in the presence of Africans in India has been especially vibrant, for which see, for example, Kenneth X. Robbins and John McLeod (eds.), *African Elites in India: Habshi Amarat* (Ahmedabad:

Slaves and unfree peoples were traded for thousands of years in the Indian Ocean. Africa and Africans are often seen to be synonymous with slavery, a product of the weight that the trans-Atlantic slave trade and its models of chattel slavery carry in shaping understandings of the African diaspora.[31] However, in the Indian Ocean, especially when considered over a broad time frame, Africans may actually have constituted a minority of the slaves who were traded across this oceanic space. Rather, Indian and Southeast Asian slaves were trafficked in significant numbers along regional networks that shipped slaves over short, medium, and long distances, and through complementary overland and maritime routes.[32] While the lack of sources makes it difficult to establish this trade's overall magnitude, there is little doubt that it was significant.[33]

Despite the equally challenging scenario of establishing the volume of African slaves sent into the Indian Ocean, its centuries-long duration and widespread nature suggest it involved high numbers of captives, with trades assuming different intensities and trajectories depending on the period. Slaves from areas throughout northeast Africa – including today's Djibouti, Eritrea, Ethiopia, Somalia and Sudan – were trafficked regularly to ancient Egypt. In *Periplus of the Ærythraen Sea*, slaves are listed as one of the cargoes traded along the ocean's northwest littoral. This took place during one of the peak periods in the long history of Indian Ocean slaving.[34] By the beginning of the ninth century CE, slaves were also being shipped from

---

Mapin Publishing, 2006); Shihan de Silva Jayasuriya and Richard Pankhurst (eds.), *The African Diaspora in the Indian Ocean* (Trenton, NJ: Africa World Press, 2003); Shihan de Silva Jayasuriya and Jean-Pierre Angenot (eds.), *Uncovering the History of Africans in Asia* (Leiden: Brill, 2008); Pashington Obeng, *Shaping Membership, Defining Nation: The Cultural Politics of African Indians in South Asia* (Plymouth, UK: Lexington Books, 2007); and Beheroze Shroff, "Voices of the Sidis: Indians of African Descent," in *Knowledge and the Indian Ocean: Intangible Networks of Western India and Beyond*, ed. S. Keller (New York: Palgrave Macmillan, 2018).

31 For useful surveys of the African diaspora, ones that nonetheless reflect an overly determined focus on the Atlantic, see for example, Michael A. Gomez, *Reversing Sail: A History of the African Diaspora* (Cambridge: Cambridge University Press, 2005); and Sean Stillwell, *Slavery and Slaving in African History* (Cambridge: Cambridge University Press, 2014).

32 Pedro Machado, "Slavery and Histories of Unfreedom in the Indian Ocean," in *Indian Ocean Current: Six Artistic Narratives*, ed. by Prasannan Parthasarathi (Boston/Chicago: McMullen Museum of Art & University of Chicago Press, 2020).

33 Overviews of slave trading in the Indian Ocean and works that capture its multidirectionality and diverse social makeup include, for instance, Gwyn Campbell (ed.), *The Structure of Slavery in Indian Ocean Africa and Asia* (London: Frank Cass/Routledge, 2004); Kerry Ward, *Networks of Empire: Forced Migration in the Dutch East India Company* (New York: Cambridge University Press, 2009); and Richard Allen, *European Slave Trading in the Indian Ocean, 1500–1850* (Athens, OH: Ohio University Press, 2014).

34 Gwyn Campbell, "Introduction: Slavery and Other Forms of Unfree Labour in the Indian Ocean World," in *Structure of Slavery* ; Gwyn Campbell, "Slavery in the Indian Ocean World," in *The Routledge History of Slavery*, ed. by Gad Heuman and Trevor Burnard (London: Routledge, 2011), 52–63.

the East African coast south of the Horn in a trade that was well established and increasingly drawing in large numbers of Africans.

A sense of the scale of this trade is suggested by the dense concentrations of East Africans on agricultural estates in southern Mesopotamia where rulers of the Abbasid Caliphate sought to utilize so-called Zanj slaves (Zanj was the term used by Arab geographers to refer to the Swahili coast) to satisfy the enormous labour demands of converting the saline marshes of southern Iraq into land suitable for agriculture in the eighth and ninth centuries CE. Along with slaves from northeast Africa (the Sudan and Ethiopia) who were shipped through Red Sea ports, slaves from the Swahili coast were transported in their thousands over this period, many of whom also served as palace slaves and in the military. Severe conditions and exploitation of slaves, following several minor uprisings, resulted in a large-scale revolt against the Abbasids that lasted for over a decade from 869 to the early 880s. The Zanj Revolt severely weakened Baghdad and its empire as the movement consolidated control over the southern reaches of the caliphate before eventually capitulating to a heavy armed response from the state, among other factors.[35]

Over the following centuries, slavery and slave trading remained key components of Indian Ocean exchange and an important mechanism fueling the development of a widespread African diaspora throughout this oceanic region. The rapid expansion of Islam around the coastlines of the Arabian Sea after the seventh century CE inaugurated a second significant period of slaving from approximately 800 to 1300, and enabled Muslim mercantile groups to create far-flung commercial networks that moved not only commodities such as Indian textiles – as well as ideas – but also bonded peoples. These networks facilitated the transoceanic shipment of slaves from the Horn and eastern Africa to the Arabian Peninsula, Persian Gulf, and South Asia.[36]

By the thirteenth century, enslaved Africans from the highlands of Ethiopia were found in the Ilyas Shahi sultanate of Delhi, and the Muslim jurist Ibn Battuta encountered slaves (known as *habashi* in late medieval and early modern sources) working as sailors and soldiers. He may have encountered other Africans who were not slaves, however, for between this period and the fifteenth century, many travelled to South Asia as religious leaders and jurists, for instance, and it would be a misconception therefore to reduce the African presence in this region to the singular category of slavery. Nonetheless, there is no denying that the role of African

---

35 Daniel Pipes, *Slave Soldiers and Islam* (New Haven: Yale University Press, 1981); Sheriff, *Dhow Cultures*, 222–226; Alpers, *Indian Ocean in World History*; Pier M. Larson, "African Slave Trades in Global Perspective," in *The Oxford Handbook of Modern African History*, ed. by John Parker and Richard Reid (Oxford, UK :Oxford University Press, 2013), 67; T. M. Ricks, "Slave Trade: Islamic World," in *Macmillan Encyclopedia of World Slavery*, v. 2, ed. by P. Finkelman and J. C. Miller (London: Simon & Schuster and Prentice Hall International, 1998).
36 Edward A. Alpers, "India and Africa," *Oxford Research Encyclopedia of Asian History*, Sept. 2018, https://doi.org/10.1093/acrefore/9780190277727.013.26

slaves in the subcontinent was significant, with some occupying positions of political authority and from the late fifteenth and sixteenth centuries were powerful figures in the political and military life of India. Along with *habashi* military leaders usurping power in Bengal sultanate and, for a short time, establishing an independent state before being ousted and fleeing to the Deccan, African slaves also worked as concubines and bodyguards at the court of the Bahmani sultanate where they exerted considerable influence over local politics.[37]

None attained greater prominence than Malik 'Ambar, born with the Oromo name Chapu in the Horn of Africa around 1548 and sold into slavery at the slave-market of Mokha. After a short time in Baghdad, he was sold to an important *amir* in the Deccan kingdom of Ahmadnagar in the early 1570s, followed sometime later by political and military service under Abhang Khan Habashi where he came to command 150 horsemen. He rose to dominant political authority under the Nizam Shahi dynasty and emerged in 1600 as *peshwa* of Ahmadnagar, a post he would hold until his death in 1626. Apart from managing to expel Mughal forces from Ahmadnagar, he maintained maritime interests and with associates sent regular vessels to the Red Sea and Hadramawt. After Malik Ambar's death, other *habashis* – including his son, Fath Khan – continued to play significant political roles in Ahmadnagar as also in the Bijapur Sultanate.[38] Over the course of the seventeenth century, *Sidis* (a term used in Gujarat and elsewhere in South Asia to refer to people of African origin but applied historically indiscriminately to African slaves) would come to control Janjira (a fortified island off Rajapuri) from which they entered into open conflict in the 1660s with the expanding Maratha state of Shivaji for commercial control of the Konkan.[39] African captives continued to be encountered on the Deccan plateau and in Gujarat where they also served prominently in the armies of domestic rulers and in Indian navies. Further afield, there is evidence that African slaves were used in Bengal in military service in the third quarter of the fifteenth century and also served as eunuchs.[40]

As highly effective political actors, these figures were a testament to the longstanding slave trading linkages that existed between Africa, the Middle East, and South Asia. Yet, while their lives offer us a window into some of the ways in which they affected political, military and naval activity particularly in India, it is extremely difficult to get a precise sense of the magnitude of the broader slave trades of

---

37 Alpers, "India and Africa."
38 Richard Eaton provides a useful account of Malik Ambar's life in *A Social History of the Deccan, 1300–1761: Eight Indian Lives* (Cambridge, UK:Cambridge University Press, 2005), 105–28.
39 Sanjay Subrahmanyam, "Between Eastern Africa and Western India, 1500–1650: Slavery, Commerce and Elite Formation," *Comparative Studies in Society and History*, 61, 4 (2019): 805–834. In addition to previous references to scholarship on the African diaspora in South Asia, see also Jazmin Graves, "Mai Misra's Khicari: Remembrance and Ritual, Re-Presentation in the Sidi (African-Indian) Sufi Tradition of Western India," *Symposia*, 9 (2018):1–13.
40 Machado, *Ocean of Trade*, 213.

which they were a part. Organized predominantly by Muslim, Arab, and Swahili merchants, these trades undoubtedly encompassed large numbers of individuals. East Africans were often shipped first to Sur and Muscat before being taken onto final destinations. By the 1580s and 1590s, Islamic trading networks extended as far south as Sofala and possibly even to Inhambane on the far southern coast of Mozambique, and involved the resident Swahili community of Madagascar, Swahili merchants primarily from Lamu and Pate, and Muslim merchants from the Comoros as well as Hadrami and Yemeni Arabs. Slaves from Madagascar were shipped to the East African coast and Comoro islands, and from there were sent on to destinations in the Arabian Peninsula and lands bordering the Persian Gulf, and likely also to South Asia. This trade seems to have resulted in over 100,000 slaves being exported from Madagascar in the seventeenth century alone.[41]

Overall, despite the limitations of the available sources, recent estimates place average annual exports of African slaves from the Red Sea and East African coasts to the Middle East and South Asia at between 2,000 and 3,000 in the period from 800 to 1700, rising to 2,000–4,000 in the eighteenth century and possibly reaching as many as 5,500 once we include Madagascar.[42] Combining the numbers trafficked in the trans-Saharan with those for the western Indian Ocean slave commerce puts exports of Africans to the Mediterranean, Middle East, South and Southeast Asia at between 10.9 and 11.6 million over the period from 650 to 1900.[43] These captives, at least until the nineteenth century, were made up predominantly of female slaves in shipments to the Arabian Peninsula and Persian Gulf, while the flow of East African slaves to South Asia was heavily weighted towards men.[44] The ratios would change

---

41 Machado, *Ocean of Trade*, 213; Pier Larson, *Ocean of Letters: Language and Creolization in an Indian Ocean Diaspora* (New York: Cambridge University Press, 2009), Table 1.2. While according to Paul Lovejoy, *Transformations in Slavery: A History of Slavery in Africa*, 3rd edition (Cambridge: Cambridge University Press, 2012), as many as 1,000 slaves may have been shipped annually by Arab traders just to Oman from northwestern Madagascar in the late seventeenth century, Thomas Vernet rather sees the Swahili trade from the great island as amounting to 2,000–3,000 slaves per year in this period. He notes that "[I]f we add to these figures the direct trade run by Arabs and Comorians in the Antalaotra port towns, we can suppose that the whole Malagasy slave trade amounted to around 2000 to 5000 slaves per year, not counting the European slave trade in the region….show[ing] that slave trading was one of the main activities of the major port towns of northwestern Madagascar and the Comoros in the seventeenth century as well as between the Swahili coast and southern Arabia," See Vernet, "Slave Trade and Slavery on the Swahili Coast (1500–1750)," in *Slavery, Islam and Diaspora*, ed. by B. A. Mirzai, I. M. Montana and P. Lovejoy (Trenton, NJ: African World Press, 2009), 60. I should note, however, that his estimates have been challenged recently by Gwyn Campbell, *Africa and the Indian Ocean World from Early Times to circa 1900* (Cambridge: Cambridge University Press, 2019).
42 Larson, *Ocean of Letters*, Table 1.2.; idem, "African Slave Trades in Global Perspective," Table 3.1; Richard B. Allen, "Ending the History of Silence: Reconstructing European Slave Trading in the Indian Ocean," *Revista Tempo*, 23, 2 (May–August 2017), 296.
43 Lovejoy, *Transformations in Slavery*.
44 Larson, "African Slave Trades in Global Perspective."

in the nineteenth century amidst an intensification in slave trafficking as a result of particular dynamics related to an efflorescence in regional and global commerce.[45]

European entry into the Indian Ocean added a further dimension to the histories of African forced migrations from the continent. In many European settlements, slavery became a defining feature of social life, and Africans were trafficked as part of broader trades in Asian captives that defined the ocean as a sea of global slavery with connections to the Pacific and Atlantic trades.[46] Inserting themselves into commercial environments in which slavery and trading was already often widespread, European labour demands resulted in an expansion of slaving throughout the ocean, with at least over half a million slaves being shipped throughout the waters of the ocean over a period of roughly 350 years between 1500 and 1850.[47]

Soon after their arrival on the Swahili coast in the 1490s, Portuguese merchants began transporting slaves from northern Mozambique, Mombasa, Madagascar, and other areas across the western Indian Ocean to their possessions in South Asia and the rest of the *Estado da Índia* stretching as far as Macau in China and Nagasaki in Japan, as they came to rely on captive labour to meet a variety of labour and military needs. While it was noted by the end of the sixteenth century that "great numbers" of slaves were being shipped from Mozambique to India, it was rare for the trade to reach one thousand slaves in any given year and on average around 200–250 slaves left the African coast for South and East Asia between the early sixteenth century and the mid-1830s.[48] From the late eighteenth and especially over the course of the first half of the nineteenth century, in a context of increased African slaving connected to particular regional and global dynamics, Portuguese slavers deepened their involvement in shipping African captives to the islands of the western Indian Ocean and – with the participation of Brazilian interests – sent significant numbers of captives to southern Atlantic destinations such as Rio de Janeiro and Bahia. These dispersals broadened the scope of the African diaspora and, as an element of broader forced migrations of Asian unfree people, underscored the global nature of slaving

---

45 For a sense of these changes in the commercial worlds of the western Indian Ocean in the nineteenth century, and repercussions for African slave trafficking, see, among others, Frederick Cooper, *Plantation Slavery on the East Coast of Africa* (New Haven/London: Yale University Press, 1977); Abdul Sheriff, *Slaves, Spices & Ivory in Zanzibar: Integration of an East African Commercial Empire into the World Economy, 1770–1873* (London: James Currey, 1987); Matthew S. Hopper, *Slaves of One Master: Globalization and Slavery in Arabia in the Age of Empire* (New Haven: Yale University Press, 2015).
46 The widespread nature of the multi-directional and pan-regional slave traffic that was carried out by Europeans in the Indian Ocean (predominant among them were Portuguese, British, French and Dutch traders) is reflected in the 450,000–565,000 slaves that were shipped to European factories and colonial centres from eastern Africa, Madagascar, India and Southeast Asia between 1500 and 1850. See Richard Allen, "Slave, Convict and Indentured Labor and the Tyranny of the Particular," *Joseph C. Miller Memorial Lecture* (Berlin: EB Verlag, 2020).
47 Richard Allen, *European Slave Trading in the Indian Ocean, 1500–1850* (Athens, OH: Ohio University Press, 2014).
48 Machado, *Ocean of Trade*; Allen, "Ending the History of Silence."

that is obscured when we treat oceanic worlds as discrete units of historical analysis. Africa and Africans participated in regimes of captive labour that also saw Chinese slaves shipped by Portuguese vessels from Macau to Mozambique, albeit in small numbers.[49]

The entry of Dutch and later French traders into the waters of the Indian Ocean led to even greater European involvements in the commercial exchange of unfree peoples. With its commercial networks that spanned southern and eastern Africa, as well as India, Sri Lanka and Southeast Asia, the VOC (Vereenigde Oostindische Compagnie or Dutch East India Company), and private merchants purchased slaves in a number of areas. In the seventeenth century, Dutch shipped several thousand Africans to the areas of South and Southeast Asia where the VOC had established a presence, from its administrative centre at Batavia to commercial emporia such as Malacca, spice plantations in the Moluccas, and settlements in Ceylon. Africans were used to fulfill a variety of labour needs, for instance to construct a fortress at Colombo in the 1670s. The VOC also purchased slaves in large numbers in Madagascar and along the coast of Mozambique for their settlement at the Cape, where the slave population – including Muslim captives brought from today's Indonesia that would establish Islam in the country[50] – reflected the Company's wide-ranging involvement in slaving and further demonstrates that Africa could be both destination and source for the chattel labour trades of the Indian Ocean.[51]

Labor demands in the Mascarene islands, located to the east of Madagascar, spurred French interests in exploiting supplies of African slaves. French slave trading was a notable feature of the Indian Ocean world especially in the eighteenth and early nineteenth centuries. Colonization of the Mascarene Island of Île de Bourbon (Réunion; 1663) and the Île de France (Mauritius; 1721) by the Compagnie des Indes provided the catalyst for the development of a substantial trade in captives that, like other European interests that drew also on South Asian sources of supply,

---

49 I note that, through alliances with local traders and rulers, Portuguese slavers became extensively involved in the shipment of Asian slaves around the Indian Ocean, notably from coastal South India, Bengal, Burma, Java and elsewhere to the Philippines; and were among the merchants sending Asian slaves across the Pacific to Mexico during the union of the Spanish and Portuguese Crowns between 1580 and 1640. See Tatiana Seijas, *Asian Slaves in Colonial Mexico: From Chinos to Indians* (Cambridge: Cambridge University Press, 2014); Allen, "Ending the History of Silence."
50 See Ward, *Networks of Empire*; idem, "Southeast Asian Migrants," in *Cape Town Between East and West: Social Identities in a Dutch Colonial Town*, ed. by Nigel Worden (Johannesburg/Hilversum: Jacana and Verloren, 2012).
51 Allen, "Slave, Convict and Indentured Labour." For details of VOC slavery at the Cape, see for instance, Robert Shell, *Children of Bondage: A Social History of Slave Society at the Cape of Good Hope, 1652–1838* (Hanover: Wesleyan University Press, 1994); Nigel Worden, *Slavery in Dutch South Africa* (Cambridge: Cambridge University Press, 1985); Worden, "Indian Ocean Slaves in Cape Town, 1695–1807," *Journal of Southern African Studies* 42, 3 (2016): 389–408; and Patrick Harries, "Mozambique Island, Cape Town and the Organization of the Slave Trade in the South-West Indian Ocean, c. 1797–1807," *Journal of Southern African Studies*, 42, 3 (2016): 409–27

primarily involved African – overwhelmingly from East Africa and Mozambique – and Malagasy slaves. French interest in establishing coffee and sugar plantation agriculture in the Mascarenes drove the demands in these highly labor-intensive industries, first in Réunion in the 1720s for coffee and more significantly from the late 1790s and early 1800s for sugar production in Mauritius.[52] While already between 1670 and 1714 approximately 1,000 slaves from Madagascar had been sent to the Mascarene Islands by French traders, it was the passing of a royal decree in 1769 liberalizing trade in the Mascarenes and, in 1787, the opening of Madagascar's trade to all foreign nationals that saw slave trading increase dramatically, both from long-standing sources of chattel labor such as Madagascar and with others along the East African coast, particularly Mozambique.[53] The slave population consequently grew from just under 40,000 in the mid-1760s to almost 133,000 by the first decade of the nineteenth century, with slaves providing critical labor services at port facilities, and growing foodstuffs needed by naval squadrons and other vessels sailing in the region. After the islands came under British control in 1810, a clandestine trade in captives saw at least 107,000 enslaved Africans, Malagasy (and also Southeast Asians) arrive in the Mascarenes until the trade ended around 1827 for Mauritius and in the early 1830s in Réunion.[54]

British traders conducted a smaller but nonetheless important trade. Reflecting further the global nature of Indian Ocean slaving of which Africa was an integral part, English commercial interests financed at least forty slaving voyages that carried slaves (along with other cargo) from Madagascar to the Americas between 1675 and 1700. East India Company (EIC) ships also trafficked Malagasy, Comorian and Mozambican slaves – together with West African slaves – to British settlements in India and trading factories in Java and Sumatra from the 1620s to the early 1770s.[55] When considered together, African captives shipped by Europeans represented rising proportions of ever-increasing slave exports from eastern Africa. As Richard Allen has noted, British, Portuguese, Dutch and French slavers took 25–39 per cent of approximately 133,000–165,000 exports during the seventeenth century, rising to as much as 52 per cent of projected exports of 637,000–833,000 in the eighteenth century, and ranging between 58 and 66 per cent of the 810,000–1,000,000 Africans

---

52 Machado, *Ocean of Trade*, 216.
53 Markus Vink, "World's Oldest Trade: Dutch Slavery and Slave Trade in the Indian Ocean in the Seventeenth Century," *Journal of World History* 14, 2 (2003), 145.
54 Richard B. Allen, *Slaves, Freedmen and Indentured Laborers in Colonial Mauritius* (New York: Cambridge University Press, 1999); idem, "Suppressing a Nefarious Traffic: Britain and the Abolition of Slave Trading in India and the Indian Ocean, 1770–1830," *The William and Mary Quarterly*, Third Series, 66, 4 (Oct. 2009), 888.
55 The numbers of slaves that were taken from these areas on EIC vessels to Asian settlements and factories totaled, in one estimate, a "minimum" of 3,100. See Richard Allen, "Human Trafficking in Asia before 1900: A Preliminary Census," *International Institute for Asian Studies Newsletter*, 87 (October 2020): 33.

traded primarily in the western reaches of the ocean in the period between 1800 and 1873.[56]

The thousands of Africans who were sent from the shores of eastern Africa into the slave trades of the western Indian Ocean (some reached more distant locations such as China but never in significant numbers) in most instances had already traveled great distances to the coast before they were loaded onto sailing vessels. They had, in many instances, entered enslavement through violent capture in raids or as a result of kidnapping, and included children. Captives were drawn from the vast internal slave trades in Africa that fed all of the continent's external trades but are often overlooked in considerations of Indian Ocean slavery and this ocean's African diaspora.[57] The broad range of source areas from which slaves were drawn reflect the intricacies of this commerce and its multi-directional nature, with captives brought from wide-ranging geographies that stretched from northeast Africa and supplied the export markets of the Red Sea, Hadramaut, Gulf, South Asia and even as far south as Zanzibar; the hinterland of the East African coast and far into the interior to the west of Lake Tanganyika from which slaves were taken to Zanzibar, southern Somalia, Hadramaut, Gulf, South Asia and the Seychelles; to East Central and South Central Africa where slaves were drawn from areas such as northern and southern Mozambique, Malawi, Zambia and the Zimbabwean plateau where in addition to being sent to the same markets as East African slaves were sent to the Comoros, western Madagascar, the Mascarenes, Seychelles, western India and the Cape.[58]

Africa's diasporic histories created by these vast movements of slaves in the Indian Ocean has left a rich and complex legacy. Its traces are identifiable, for instance, in the musical and dance traditions that have endured in different parts of the ocean and became integral elements of the cultural expression of different host societies. Additionally, as noted by Edward Alpers, "these two cultural forms are very often intimately associated with popular religion, spirit possession, and

---

[56] Allen, *European Slave Trading*, 22–24; and Allen, "Slave, Convict and Indentured Labor." Factors driving up demand in the eighteenth and nineteenth centuries for African slave labor – apart from the coffee and sugar plantation economies of the Mascarenes mentioned previously – included the labor needs of the clove and coconut plantations at Zanzibar and Pemba; expansion in regional ivory trading for Asian as well as European and American markets (amidst robust demand among Africans for commodities such as Indian textiles and from the 1820s and 1830s American cottons) that required greater use of slave porters to carry tusks from the far interior to the coast; date farming in the Gulf; pearl diving in the latter and Red Sea; and grain cultivation by slave villages in Madagascar and riverine Somalia. For details, see, for example, Stephen J. Rockel, *Carriers of Culture: Labor on the Road in Nineteenth-Century East Africa* (Portsmouth, NH: Heinemann, 2006); Sheriff, *Slaves, Spices & Ivory*; Cooper, *Plantation Slavery*; Jonathon Glassman, *Feasts and Riot: Revelry, Rebellion, and Popular Consciousness on the Swahili Coast, 1856–1888* (Portsmouth, NH: Heinemann, 1995); Hopper, *Slaves of One Master*; McDow, *Buying Time*.
[57] Pier M. Larson, "Horrid Journeying: Narratives of Enslavement and the Global African Diaspora," *Journal of World History* 19, 4 (December 2008): 431–64.
[58] Edward A. Alpers, "Recollecting Africa: Diasporic Memory in the Indian Ocean World," *African Studies Review* 43, 1 (April 2000): 85.

healing." African language use has persisted too, in a variety of forms, as in Madagascar where traces of Emakhuwa – a language of northern Mozambique – are evident today among Makoa who were brought to the island as slaves generations ago.[59]

However, communities of African descent have often struggled with marginalization by mainstream society and the suppression of cultural memories associated with the stigma of slavery as a status undesirable and inimical to the social and cultural politics of belonging and social mobility. In certain places, such as the Arabian peninsula, African slaves assumed the tribal identity of their masters as slave pasts were effaced from memory. In Oman, even presentations of music and dance widely regarded as African in origin (Al-Laiwa) are vague with respect to how this form came to the country.[60] The particular complexities of how race and genealogy figure in the construction of identities in the Gulf, where remembrances of slave pasts have been forgotten in ways that are not dissimilar to some other cases in the Indian Ocean but that nonetheless have distinctive features, together with a variety of recent political, social, and economic factors (such as the extension by Gulf states of national citizenship to descendants of slaves) have made recovering histories of servile ancestry of little to no interest. This is a function, in large part, of the success of their cooption into the project of nation-building.[61]

In others places, such as India, processes of assimilation over time have resulted in an occlusion of slave pasts, even as communities of African descent have continued overwhelmingly to exist in poverty and at the lower rungs of the social scale.[62] Still in others, the presence of Africans has been actively forgotten, for instance in Mauritius, where shifts especially in the nineteenth century as a result of the large influx of indentured labourers from South Asia transformed the demographic make-up of the island. This resulted in the "Hinduization" of society and contributed to the marginalization of Creoles.[63] There have been moments, nonetheless, when slavery was recognized, for instance, during the 150th anniversary of its abolition in 1985. However, the continued social, economic and political exclusion of many slave descendants mobilized oppositional politics in the 1990s to redress stark inequalities and have continued to seek recognition of their past in shaping Mauritian history.[64]

---

59 Alpers, "Recollecting Africa," 90, 94.
60 As a result, one scholar has concluded that one is thus left with "the impression that Omani traders witnessed the dances from the safe distances of their ships rather than the truth – that they carried back thousands of young Africans to labor on their shores." See Hopper, *Slaves of One Master*, 214.
61 Hopper, *Slaves of One Master*.
62 Alpers, "Recollecting Africa," 87, where the author discusses further the challenges that African-descended people have faced in India and elsewhere in regions of the western Indian Ocean.
63 Alpers, "Recollecting Africa."
64 I discuss aspects of this struggle of Creoles for recognition of their history and the politics of memorialization in Mauritius further in Machado, "Memory, Memorialization, and 'Heritage' in the Indian Ocean," in *Reimagining Indian Ocean Worlds* ed. by Smriti Srinivas, Bettina Ng'weno and Neelima Jeychandran (London: Routledge, 2020), 149–164.

African histories, in their myriad cultural manifestations, are present throughout the Indian Ocean and those communities from the continent who shaped their contours have left us a rich and complex archive of its practices and folkways.

Conclusion

No one experience or history defines how Africa and Africans have been part of the Indian Ocean, nor of how the ocean was shaped by the presence of those from the continent. The diversity of forms of engagement by Africans across this oceanic region were too broad and entrenched to defy easy categorization. Equally, this engagement has characterized many of the ocean's most significant periods as the continent's peoples forged relationships and chartered trajectories that brought them into close and sustained contact with a range of areas. This intercourse was critical in shaping the social, commercial and cultural contours of the ocean, and contributed vitally to its dynamism as a space of plural and intersecting histories. In this essay, I have been able to explore only some aspects of these intersections to suggest the nature of linkages that have endured in different ways across vast temporal and spatial scales. The two – Africa and the ocean – are entangled and their histories cannot be fully understood without reference to each other.

David L. Imbua
Chapter 5
Africa and the Atlantic World, 1400–1860

Abstract: Before the arrival of the Europeans on the west coast of Africa, the Atlantic Ocean played little role in the lives of the people there, who were astounded by arrival of Europeans to their domain. This began to change from the middle of the fifteenth century when a coalition of interests pulled the coastal regions of Africa into the Atlantic world. Before long a large infrastructure mobilized and exported animal, plant, and mineral products, as well as slaves across the Atlantic to Europe and later the Americas. By the nineteenth century, the interactions between European merchants and their African counterparts had moved Africa from the margins of the Atlantic economy to a central position, and by so doing bound the continent's material and human resources to Western exploitation. This study examines the character of that interaction from the fifteenth to the mid-nineteenth century to argue that though some individuals and export centers on the African coast realized short-term benefits from facilitating the Atlantic trade, Africans were by and large more important to the Atlantic world than the Atlantic world was to Africans.

Keywords: Atlantic world, Christianity, Diaspora, Diplomacy, Europeans, trade.

Introduction

Comprising the western littorals of Africa and Europe and the eastern coastal rim of the Americas, the post-Columbian Atlantic world, arguably the most important geographical milieu of modern history, has been an organizing concept for the historical study of the Atlantic Ocean rim from about the fifteenth century to the present. Atlantic history presents a broad range of topics on the historical relationships and linkages between different sub-regions of the Atlantic world. Some of the most exciting contemporary research focuses on themes such as migration and Diasporas; scientific and technological diffusion; conquest, colonization, imperialism, and race relations, among other engaging discourses. These have deepened scholars' interest world over, stressing the significance of the Atlantic throughout human history. The beginning of extensive Atlantic contacts between Europe, Africa, and the Americas had telling implications for the histories of all the regions involved.

Despite its strategic position in the Atlantic world economy, some scholars have undermined the role of Africa in the construction of Atlantic history and culture. Bernard Bailyn, who equates Atlantic history with European civilization, is among such scholars. Robin Law and Kristin Mann write that "although Bailyn brings Africa into the discussion briefly through a treatment of the Atlantic slave trade, his references are primarily to works that equate Atlantic history with European civilization. In his conception, Africa has played a very limited role in shaping the history and culture of the Atlantic basin."[1] Unlike Bailyn, Paul Gilroy treats the Atlantic as "one single, complex unit of analysis," in which both blacks and whites are "perceived as agents" of change and development.[2] He conceives the Atlantic as "continually crisscrossed by the movements of black people- not only as commodities but engaged in various struggles towards emancipation, autonomy, and citizenship." Though Gilroy's study is commendable, his perspective leaves much to be desired. He approaches the Atlantic community from the perspective of the North Atlantic diaspora (and, more especially, of its intellectuals), in which Africa figures as an object of retrospective rediscovery rather than as an active agent of change.[3] It is rare to find studies that center Africa in the phenomenal dramas that took place in the Atlantic world. Such perspectivization gives credence to the prevailing stereotypes of African incapacity and passivity in global relationships. The exposure of Africa to the Atlantic Ocean generated the spontaneous distillation of a complex crossing of forces that merged with local constellations to change the course of Africa's Atlantic history in decisive ways. More than this, the great borrowings and exchanges that took place in the Atlantic world among a population that was radically different in language, culture, and physique indicate that the influence of the interactions did not flow in only one direction. Indeed, as diplomats, students, settlers, sailors, slaves among other designations, Africans who migrated – both voluntarily and involuntarily – to the Atlantic world played a more profound role in shaping the culture of the Atlantic world than often realized.[4] This chapter examines the intermingling between Africa and the Atlantic world from the fifteenth to the mid-nineteenth century.

Early Religious and Diplomatic Relations

Christianity in Northern Africa is nearly as old as when it was established in Palestine. It was introduced into Mediterranean Africa and by the fourth century CE Monasteries had been established in Egypt, and thousands of churches founded in present day Maghreb. In fact, many Africans of the Maghreb became important churchmen, namely St. Augustine, Cyprian, and Tertullian. In Egypt, Christianity became so strongly rooted that the Egyptian Christians evolved their new brand of Christianity known as Monophysitism.[5] From Egypt, the Christian faith spread to

---

[1] Robin Law and Kristin Mann, "West Africa in the Atlantic Community: The Case of the Slave Coast," *William and Mary Quarterly* LVI, 2 (1999): 308.
[2] Paul Gilroy, *The Black Atlantic: Modernity and Double Consciousness* (London: Verso, 1993), 6.
[3] Law and Mann, "West Africa in the Atlantic Community," 309–10.
[4] John K. Thornton, *Africa and Africans in the Making of the Atlantic World, 1400–1800* (Cambridge: Cambridge University Press, 1998), 129–131.
[5] J. C. Anene, ed., *Essays in African History: 19th and 20th Centuries* (Ibadan: Onibonoje Press, 1977), 11.

the Eastern Sudan kingdoms of Marqurra and Alwa, and Ethiopia in the fourth century.

The situation was different in Atlantic Africa where Christianity came with the arrival of the Portuguese in the fifteenth century. European sailors first reached sub-Saharan Africa in 1442, when Portuguese ships arrived at the Senegal River. Given Portuguese concerns to find Christian allies in Africa or convert rulers to Christianity, the Portuguese preached the gospel in the areas where they traded. Whether it was in Jolof, Benin, Kongo, Ndongo, Akan, Warri or elsewhere, the Portuguese aimed at religious conversion. In Benin, the Oba and the royal household embraced Christianity. And by the sixteenth century, there was exchange of ambassadors between Benin and Lisbon. From 1483, the Portuguese were also in the kingdom of the Kongo. At the beginning they found it necessary and desirable to respect the sovereignty of the kingdom of Kongo as well as enter into partnership with the people. Hence, they presented themselves as allies just as they had done along the coast of Senegal, The Gambia, Ghana, and Benin.[6] Consequently, these kings willingly traded with the Portuguese, exchanged ambassadors with Lisbon, and received Christian missionaries, masons, carpenters, and other skilled artisans.

After the Portuguese made contact with the powerful and expanding kingdom of Benin in 1486, the Oba (King) of Benin dispatched a trusted official to Lisbon to investigate the strange visitors' country firsthand. Described in Portuguese accounts as "a man of good speech and natural wisdom," the Benin ambassador was received with great hospitality and fanfare: "great feasts were held in his honour, and he was shown many of the good things of these kingdoms" and given presents of "rich clothes for himself and his wife" at his departure.[7] He also brought back fancy gifts for the Oba of Benin, along with missionaries to persuade him to adopt Christianity, and traders to buy additional quantities of pepper and other goods that Benin had been selling to the Portuguese. The ambassador's report was evidently positive, since the king of Benin permitted the Portuguese to establish a coastal "factory" or trading post for the pepper trade.[8] Oba Ozolua sent new emissaries to Lisbon in 1514 and again in 1515 to discuss trade, conversion to Christianity, and the sale of firearms. A Portuguese chronicler notes, "the delight of the king of Benin was so great that I do not know how to describe it, and likewise that of all his people." The subsequent action of the king validates this report. By the end of August 1516, the king decided to give "his son and some of his noblemen- the greatest

---

6 Basil Davidson, *Africa in History* (New York: Macmillan, 1969), 136.
7 David Northrup, *Africa's Discovery of Europe, 1450–1850* (New York: Oxford University Press, 2009), 15.
8 Northrup, *Africa's Discovery of Europe*, 16.

in his kingdom- so that they might become Christians" and in his order for a church to be built in his capital.[9]

Elsewhere in the Senegalese kingdom of Jolof, Bumi Jeleen who had ruled according to Muslim principles, changed direction when they encountered the Portuguese in 1487–88. Juleen enjoyed a mutually beneficial trade with the Portuguese, from whom he obtained horses "and other needful goods," treated the Portuguese traders well to encourage their return, and sent presents by them to King Joao II (1481–1495) of Portugal. In return, King Joao sent rich gifts to Jeleen, along with agents to persuade him to join the Christian faith. At first, Jeleen did no more than listen respectfully to the request to convert from Islam to Christianity, but the attempt by his half-brother to seize the Jolof throne from him made him seek a closer alliance with Portugal. In 1487, he sent his son to Lisbon to plead for horses, arms, and soldiers from King Joao to enable him hold on to his throne. Though King Joao was sympathetic, he only sent horses, with a declaration that other aids would only be sent if Jeleen agreed to become a Christian. Driven out of his kingdom by his rivals in 1488, Jeleen himself was in Portugal with some of his followers, pleading for aid and expressing willingness to become a Christian. In Lisbon, the King Joao II received Jeleen in style, provided him and his followers with clothing, silver and attendants. At the Portuguese court, Jeleen is said to have cut a splendid figure, and he impressed with his dignified comportment and the speech he made about his dethronement. He was also admired for his superb horsemanship. He renewed his request for arms and pledged to convert to Christianity. The Portuguese monarch received his word with great pleasure and provided him with detailed instructions in the Christian faith which left him convicted.

On November 3, 1488, Jeleen and six of his chief followers were baptized as Christians, with the Portuguese king, queen, other members of the royal family, a papal commissioner, and the Bishop of Tangier serving as their godparents. Jeleen was knighted and renamed Dom Joao in his patron's honor. Subsequently, he was furnished with twenty caravels, well-armed and carrying priests and religious articles in preparation for the conversion of the entire kingdom after his restoration to the throne. The vessels were also loaded with materials for building a Portuguese trading fort at the mouth of the Senegal River, for, in aiding Jeleen, King Joao was also strongly motivated by the desire to establish contact with the fabled inland city of Timbuktu, "where are the richest trades and markets of gold in the world."[10] Northrup informs us that none of these plans materialized because:

> Soon after arriving in Senegal, the captain of the fleet, fearful of dying of a tropical disease, killed King Jeleen and sailed straight back to Portugal without completing the building of the for-

---

[9] David Northrup, "Africans, Early European Contacts, and the Emergent Diaspora," in *The Oxford Handbook on the Atlantic World, C. 1450- C. 1820*, eds. Philip Morgan and Nicholas Canny (London: Oxford University Press, 2013), 40.
[10] Quoted in Northrup, *Africa's Discovery of Europe*, 33.

tress or making contact with Timbuktu. The kingdom remained in the hands of the rebels and the plans for its conversion to Christianity were abandoned.[11]

In West Central Africa, the powerful kingdom of Kongo on the lower Congo River became most adept at mastering European diplomatic culture and at the same time greatly inclined to political and Christian influences from Portugal. The people of Kongo first learned of the Portuguese in 1484 when a small fleet of ships led by Diogo Cao arrived at the mouth of the Kongo River. Soon after their arrival, Cao sent four Franciscan monks to meet with the Manikongo (the Kongo ruler) at his distant capital while the fleet explored the coast in an effort to find an all-water route to India. Done with the exploration, Cao took four Kongolese noblemen, including Prince Kasuta, back to Portugal with him, promising to bring them back on his next expedition. The Kongolese were welcomed as lavishly as the embassies from Benin and Jolof when they reached Lisbon.[12] For fifteen months Kasuta and his companions studied the Portuguese language and received religious instructions.

When they returned to Kongo in 1487, Manikongo Nzinga a Nkuwu joyfully received them and the presents they brought to him from King Joao. The ruler sent back his own royal gifts of colourful palm-cloth and carved ivory, along with a delegation to seek craftsmen, agricultural specialists, and women for instruction in home economics, as well as missionaries."[13] In response, Kongo received three Portuguese ships in 1491 bringing priests and religious objects, carpenters, masons, and their tools. Meanwhile, the Kongolese ambassadors learned Portugal's language and customs and adopted Christianity, as Kongo's ruler was soon converted and christened King Afonso of Kongo. King Afonso dispatched another delegation to Lisbon headed by his cousin and his son. Henrique (Henry) who studied in Lisbon and was ordained a priest and consecrated as Kongo's first Catholic bishop in December 1520. Henry and his uncle also gained an audience with Pope Leo X, and part of the skill displayed in subsequent diplomacy involved appeals to the papacy when direct relations with Lisbon were unsatisfactory.[14] In 1521, Bishop Henry and four other new African priests returned to Kongo to take up their duties under the watchful eye of King Afonso. The first sub-Saharan African to become a Catholic bishop, Henry was also the last for over 250 years. During the 1540s and 1550s Kongo kept a resident ambassador in Lisbon.

The royal family in Kongo undertook a series of steps to Christianize Kongo and to Africanize Christianity. With the assistance of the priests, carpenters and masons they had brought from Portugal, the capital was rebuilt in stone and renamed San Salvador, and many Congolese were sent to Europe for education. This state of affairs endured for a while before their Christian activities were greeted with hostility occa-

---

[11] Northrup, *Africa's Discovery of Europe*, 27.
[12] Northrup, *Africa's Discovery of Europe*, 27.
[13] Northrup, *Africa's Discovery of Europe*, 37.
[14] Northrup, "Africans, Early European Contacts," 41.

sioned by the arrogance of Portuguese who unceremoniously threw the "idols and fetishes" of the old religion into bonfires as well as the Portuguese extension of the slave trade to the Kongo in an attempt to meet the demand for slaves in the rapidly expanding Portuguese sugar plantations on the island of Sao Tome to the north. By the mid-1520s, a poignant series of letters from Afonso to the King of Portugal, and to the Pope testified to the expanding slave trade's destructive effects. A coalition of factors dealt a devastating blow on the prospects of the Portuguese-Christian enterprise in Atlantic Africa, and so the "network of catholic rulers spread all across Africa" in the seventeenth century faded. As Adrian Hastings notes, by 1700 the "likelihood of any Catholic presence in black Africa of more than minuscule size had become extremely slight"[15] making, the Portuguese attempt to institute a Christian state in Africa a failure.

The modern era of the missionary expansion of the Christian church dates from the late eighteenth and early nineteenth century as part of Christians' responsibility for the regeneration of Africans. Anti-slave trade and slavery concerns played a vital role in stimulating European interest in Africa, providing an impetus to mission work. In their attempt to spread the Christian faith, win converts and transform African societies, Christian missions of all denominations invaded Atlantic Africa with the gospel of the so-called legitimate commerce and Christianity as a key to civilization and eventual colonization. Abolitionists, humanitarians, philanthropists all supported the missionaries in the new dispensation.

Offshore Commercial Relations and Exchanges

The principal element of Africa's connection with the Atlantic world was trade. This trade was made possible as well as facilitated by various seaports which linked Atlantic Africa and the outside world.[16] Indigenous African rulers did not allow European traders to erect substantial shore facilities on the coast, so the trading process was largely kept offshore, on small islands or trading hulks or aboard transient ships. Because of this, the local political authorities usually regulated European trading activities and Europeans depended heavily on their African hosts for security and the extensive labor force they needed to load and offload their ships. Morgan avers, "the only exception to the marginality of the European presence in Africa was Portuguese Angola, but in truth its territory was confined to a small area near Luanda, a few outposts in the interior, and a small trading post at Benguela."[17] Consequently, some African rulers appointed officials to oversee the commercial relations with Eu-

---
15 Adrian Hastings, *The Church in Africa 1450–1950* (Oxford: Clarendon Press, 1994), 127.
16 David Imbua, *Intercourse and Crosscurrents in the Atlantic World: Calabar-British Experience, 17th-20th Centuries* (Durham: Carolina Academic Press, 2012), 52.
17 Philip D. Morgan, "Africa and the Atlantic, C. 1450 to C. 1820," in *Atlantic History: A Critical Appraisal*, ed. by Jack P. Green and Philip D. Morgan (Oxford: Oxford University Press, 2009), 225.

ropeans. By the 1720s, for example, the post of *Yevogan*, or "Chief of the White Men" at the important port of Whydah, had evolved into three separate offices: one for the French, one for the English, and for the Portuguese. In time there would be six such "Captains of Trade."[18] Before a ship could begin to trade in any of the ports, European merchants had to pay elaborate customs fees or 'comey' as well as make expensive gifts to the ruler and to his chief commercial agents.

It should be recalled that Africa, and West Africa in particular, was called the White Man's Grave because of the very high mortality of Europeans there. Before quinine came into use as an antimalaria drug in the mid-nineteenth century, most Europeans were susceptible to the virulent African disease environment such that only few survived on the coast even for a short period of time. Despite the high mortality rate of Europeans in Africa due to the tropical climate, disease, and sanitation, they were not discouraged from trading in West Africa because it was highly profitable. Aside from taking full responsibility for their coming, Europeans paid rent, customs and excise duties, as well as other tributes and fees for the privilege of trading in Africa. As tenants, Europeans depended completely on their African landlords who controlled the areas of trade. The term "subordinate symbiosis" as coined by scholars describes Europeans' dependence on Africans in routine commercial relationship. European merchants cultivated friendly relations with the local agents and respected indigenous authority whom they depended on for the establishment of trading posts and forts. The so-called European factories and forts were in reality "joint African-European ventures" rather than "outposts of European power." Europeans fortified and ran the forts, but Africans dominated their personnel and regulated both the price of goods and the quality of gifts, which were essential social courtesy. Willen Bosman, Chief factor at Elmina in the 1690s and William Davenant, an English MP charged with assessing the African trade in 1708, considered gifts to be the primary means by which access to trade on the Gold Coast was established and maintained. The practice of offering gifts to African rulers started as an inducement. Over time, it became mandatory and necessary for the smooth conduct of the coastal trade.[19] In many African ports, the refusal to render gifts and comey meant that the trader was unserious with the business.

Experience had taught the Europeans to pay their comey and other forms of homage to the chiefs, who in turn ensured their safety and smooth trade dealings. African rulers had made it clear who held the upper hand on the coast. For example, when some Portuguese trespassed on sacred ground while building the Mina fort, local residents forced the Portuguese to pay compensation. In retaliation for an offence in 1570, two coastal communities massacred over 300 Portuguese at Mina, decorating the grave of an African king with the skulls of fifty of them. A few years later

---

18 Northrup, "West Africans and the Atlantic," 43.
19 David L. Imbua, "Old Calabar Merchants and the Off-Shore British Community, 1650–1750," *Paideuma: Mitteilungen Zur Kulturkunde* 59 (2013): 68.

another community took vengeance by razing the Portuguese outpost at Accra and slaying its inhabitants.[20] Both Africans and Europeans had learned the benefits of mutual respect and cooperation. One scholar has described the relationship between African traders and rulers and European merchants and ship captains as a voluntary partnership. African and European traders formed "a moral community" which was held together by economic ties and cross-cultural links, all of which enhanced the creation of a climate of understanding.

Because of its pioneering effort, the Portuguese crown claimed exclusive control over all trade with Atlantic Africa, a right that was acknowledged by a papal decree in 1455. Irrespective of how merchant communities outside of Portugal felt, the crown attempted to enforce its monopoly as much as possible and restricted interlopers and competitions from trading on the Guinea Coast of Africa. To provide secure depots from which to trade, the Portuguese had colonized the uninhabited Cape Verde Island from the 1460s and the islands of Sao Tome and Principe in the Gulf of Guinea from the 1480s. Nevertheless, Elmina, established on the Gold Coast in 1482, was the most important fort in West Africa. Here, African gold, ivory, foodstuffs and slaves were exchanged for iron ware, firearms, textiles and foodstuffs. As a result, Portuguese merchants were well established on the coasts of West and Central Africa, with trading outposts and rudimentary settlements.

In the second half of the sixteenth century, the English, the French, the Dutch and the freebooting Portuguese began to break into the Portuguese monopoly. A British pirate, John Hawkins, had intruded and sailed away with slaves from the Liberian Coast in 1530. In 1553, another British sailor, Captain Windham, visited the Benin River. British interests in the West African trade were represented by state-chartered companies. The earliest of the British African companies was chartered by Queen Elizabeth in 1558. This company was superseded by another called the Adventurers to Guinea and Benin, which was given a charter by King James I in 1618. The Adventurers built Fort James on a small island in the Gambia River. Following 1660, a bigger company came into being, which founded trading posts at Sierra Leone and the Gold Coast where they built the Cape Coast Castle. The Danes, who also traded on the coast, built a stone fort known as Fort Christiansburg (meaning Christians' Fortress) in 1659.[21]

The main area of the French activity was in the Senegal-Gambia region. They penetrated Senegal from the middle of the seventeenth century and established ports such as St. Louis, Goree and Rufisque. The intentions, as elsewhere, along the coast was to protect the trade from European rivals and hostile African neighbours. The French were also active in Madagascar. Meanwhile, the Dutch were not to be outdone by the British or the French. In 1621 they founded the Dutch West Indian Com-

---

20 Northrup, "Africans, Early European Contacts," 43.
21 J. C. Anene and G. N. Brown, *Africa in the 19th and 20th Centuries* (Ibadan: Ibadan University Press, 1966), 10.

pany for West African trade and set up forts, particularly on the Gold Coast, in order to challenge the position of other rivals.

The initial interest of the Europeans was to trade minerals and in the agricultural resources of Africa such as ivory, malaguetta, timber, dye wood, gum, hides, bees wax, leather, sugar and spices, notably peppers. Though the Portuguese agent of Gomez Company carried 200 African captives to Lisbon where they were sold into slavery, the buying and selling of slaves was not the primary objective of the pioneer Europeans in Africa. Despite John Hawkins' piratical activities which involved slaves, the English were particularly averse to the slave trade. As late as 1620, Richard Johnson could still reject a Gambian's offer of slaves, affirming that the English "were a people who did not deale in any such commodities, neither did wee buy or sell one another, or any that had our owne shapes."[22] Unfortunately, this aversion eroded after 1650 because of the rapid development of plantation economies in the Americas which depended on Black slavery. To this matter, we shall return shortly.

From the onset, the Portuguese were eager to divert some of the gold trade, which for centuries had crossed the Sahara to Morocco and other parts of North Africa, into the Atlantic. Their efforts had little success in Upper Guinea but hit the jackpot on the appropriately named Gold Coast. In 1502, apparently one ship (of the 12 or 15 King Manuel normally sent there each year) carried away 2,000 ounces of gold from Mina (later renamed Elmina, from the Arabic *al-minah*, meaning the port). The Portuguese found the Gold Coast so rich in gold that they immediately built a great fortress to deter other European seafarers following in their wake. The fortification effort did not work out as other European nations quickly made their presence known on the Gold Coast. In their first year (1553), the English managed to obtain 2,400 ounces of gold. Dutch trade grew to involve some twenty ships a year in the early seventeenth century, with gold as the major export. West Africa in this period was the principal source of gold for Western Europe, exports averaging between 25,000 and 27,000 ounces a year from 1471 to 1600 and over 32,000 ounces a year in the first half of the seventeenth century.[23] For the first 250 years of African-European commercial relations, gold formed the main basis of exchange, and not until the beginning of the eighteenth century did the value of slaves begin to exceed that of gold and other goods.

Sugar was another early African export that later became an important feature of the larger Atlantic economy. As they occupied uninhabited Atlantic islands, the Portuguese introduced sugar cane plantations and the system of African slave labor they had learned from Mediterranean Muslims. The Cape Verde exported sugar, indigo, and American tobacco, but the centre of sugar production in the sixteenth century was the island of Sao Tome. Canes were introduced to the island from Madeira,

---

[22] P. E. H. Hair and Robin Law, "The English in Western Africa to 1700," in *The Oxford History of the British Empire, vol. 1. The Origins of Empire*, ed. by Nicholas Canny (London: Oxford University Press, 1998), 250–55.
[23] Northrup, "Africans, Early European Contacts," 42.

along with Portuguese and Italians familiar with sugar production. Settlers, including exiled Jews and convicts, were licensed to buy slaves from the mainland to grow and harvest the sugarcane. In addition to their backbreaking work in the fields, slaves were expected to supply all their own food.[24]

During the same period free Africans in the mainland were cultivating spices for export to Europe. The Benin Kingdom was a major supplier of a pungent indigenous pepper (*Piper guineense*), which was far superior to the malagetta pepper (*Amomum melegueta*) that came from the Winward Coast (later Ivory Coast) west of the Gold Coast and which held its own against the pepper (*piper nigrum*) arriving in Europe in great quantities from India. Indeed, in 1506, the Portuguese king tried to ban further purchase of Benin pepper lest it compete with Indian pepper, but an illegal Portuguese trade from Benin continued for some time. It was this pepper that lured the first English ship to Benin in 1553.[25] The Oba of Benin was pleased with the prospect of opening trade with a second European country (the Portuguese having traded there since 1486) that he offered to sell pepper on credit to be repaid on the next voyage, should the English lack sufficient trade goods. The English were pleased with the value of the eighty barrels of pepper loaded aboard their ships anchored offshore.

Africans exported several other commodities including forest and wild animal products: elephant tusks, civet oil, vegetable gums, animal hides, dyewoods, and beeswax. Africans bartered these goods for textiles, metal wares, alcoholic spirits, tobacco, firearms, and currencies. Following the development of the South Atlantic System in the New World by European capitalists, the traffic in slaves came to dwarf all other items from Africa. The shift was necessitated by the fact that Black slave labor was crucial for the exploitation of the enormous natural resources of the Americas which made the European colonization enterprises in those Amerindian lands attractive and profitable. The transatlantic slave trade first became significant at the end of the sixteenth century, tripled in volume over the course of the seventeenth century, and then doubled again during the eighteenth century. The 1780s was the acme of the trade and slaves comprised over ninety percent of the value of all African exports during this period.

Africa and the Atlantic Slave Trade

In any discussion of Africa and the Atlantic world, the transatlantic slave trade, which marked a significant turning point in the historical development of Africa, especially in her relations with Europe and the Americas, looms large. Walter Rodney contends that "to discuss trade between Africans and Europeans in the four centu-

---

24 Northrup, "Africans, Early European Contacts," 42.
25 Northrup, "Africans, Early European Contacts," 43.

ries before colonial rule is virtually to discuss slave trade."[26] The export of slaves featured significantly in Africa's engagement with the Atlantic world during the two centuries after 1650. John Thornton has pointed out a twofold impact of the African slaves in the making of the Atlantic world. On the one hand, slaves made up a permanent work force and thus were especially useful for the continuous activities required by some agricultural and most stock raising, as well as the majority of artisanal, skilled, and domestic employment. As workers and servants, African slaves and their descendants made a significant contribution to the Atlantic economy. On the other hand, enslaved Africans brought with them a cultural heritage in language, aesthetics, and philosophy that helped to form the newly developing culture of the Atlantic world.[27]

The starting point is to question why Africans were recruited, packed in the way horses or dogs would not be allowed to be packed today, and transported in the most horrific conditions through the Middle Passage to the Americas to serve as the main providers of long-term labor in areas of America where there were large and conquered populations of Native Americans. Though slavery was an ancient global institution deeply rooted in the cultural imagination of many societies around the world, the enslavement of Black people in Africa and peoples of African descent in the Americas from the sixteenth through much of the nineteenth centuries was to enhance the exploitation of the enormous natural resources of the Americas, which in turn made colonization of Amerindian lands profitable for Europeans. After a thorough examination of the growth of Atlantic slavery, Eric Williams concludes, "its origin can be expressed in three words: in the Caribbean, Sugar; on the Mainland, Tobacco and Cotton." It cannot be stretched too far that sugar, tobacco, cotton, and rice required large plantations and hordes of cheap labor to which Africans were most suited. The Black slaves were not only the strength and sinews of plantation agriculture, but also of the mining, cleaning and transportation of minerals, and herding of cattle, all of which were labor-intensive occupations.

Though some African residents of Iberia had accompanied Europeans to the Americas earlier, the first slaves shipped directly from Africa to the Americas departed from the islands under the control of the Portuguese. As early as 1503, a few Africans were exported from the Portuguese settlements to America, and under Ferdinand V sanction was given to this traffic. In 1525 the *Santa Maria de Bogona* left Sao Tome with a cargo of 300 slaves, of whom 213 survived the voyage to Santo Domingo. The next year two smaller ships left Cape Verde for Cuba with a total of 162 slaves. In 1532 three ships from Sao Tome with a total of 692 slaves sailed for the Spanish Caribbean. These islands acted as bulking centers for these early voyages, most of the slaves having been purchased in small groups from neighbouring mainland areas. The first recorded slave passage from the African mainland to the

---

26 Walter Rodney, *How Europe Underdeveloped Africa* (London: Bogle-L'Ouverture, 1990), 103.
27 Thornton, *Africa and Africans in the Making of the Atlantic World*, 130 and 138.

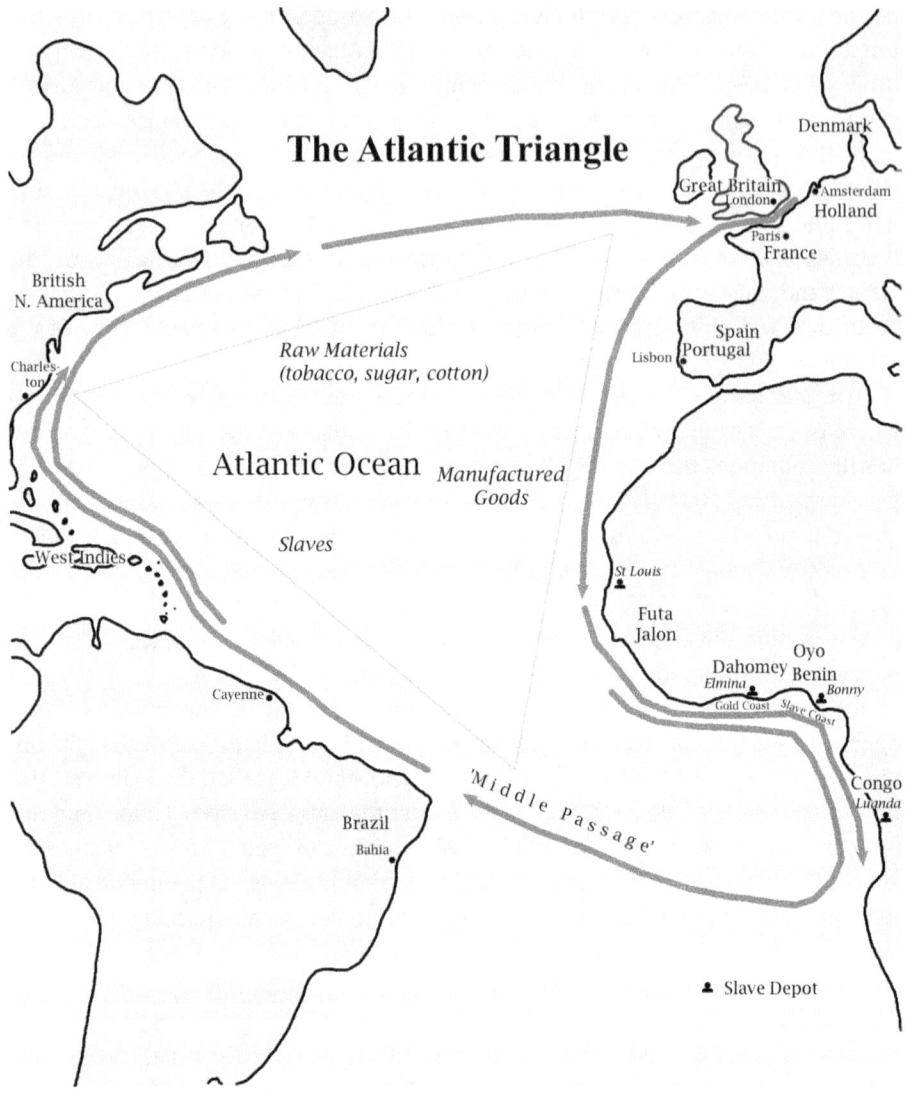

Map 4: The Atlantic Triangle. © Toyin Falola.

Americas was the 1534 voyage of the *Conceicao* from the Congo River to Santo Domingo and Jamaica. Senegambia had a fairly trans-Atlantic slave trade totaling over 200,000 by 1650, the greater part going to the Spanish Caribbean colonies up to the 1560s and thereafter to Spanish Central America. After 1550 slaves came primarily from West Central Africa, which in the first half of the seventeenth century accounted for 84 percent of the entire trans-Atlantic slave trade.[28]

---

28 Rodney, *How Europe Underdeveloped Africa*, 46.

The trade which began at first in hundreds and then thousands soon involved the forced migration of millions of Africans because slaves rarely reproduced themselves. There were several chartered companies formed in the seventeenth century to carry on the slave trade. In 1662, for instance, a company was formed, chartered by Charles II, and headed by the Duke of York, to supply the British West Indies with 30,000 slaves annually and Britain's share in the traffic gradually increased, until after securing what was called The Assiento Contract, which made over to her the privilege of supplying the Spanish West Indies with slaves; 192 ships left British shores annually for Africa.[29] This monopoly of supplying the Spanish West Indies was formerly possessed by France, but was secured to Britain by the treaty of Utrecht, as its gain from the victories of the great Marlborough. Apart from chartered companies, individuals were also involved in the slave trade and in some cases, shipped many more slaves than the companies. The collapse of the Royal African Company's monopoly was important to the expansion of the British slave trade. William Pettigrew argues that: "The separate traders benefited from undoubted economic advantages over the company.... They traded faster, beat the company's ships across the Atlantic, and received higher prices for their slaves."[30] For both the chartered companies and individual traders, until circumstances began to change during the first half of the nineteenth century, trade with West Africa was essentially based on the exportation of slaves for service on American plantations growing tropical produce for sale in Western Europe. Villages that had once served as bases for fishing or salt production expanded to become ports, where trade became centered. Luanda, Cabinda, and Benguela on the West-Central African Coast, Bonny and Old Calabar in the Bight of Biafra, Ouidah (a lagoon side port) in the Bight of Benin, Anomabu and Cape Coast on the Gold Coast, and James Fort and St. Louis in Senegambia dominated Africa's Atlantic trade.[31] The slave trade did not only lead to the rise and fall of cities, but changed the nomenclature of some regions. The Gold Coast, for instance, declined in relative importance as the slave trade shifted eastward, while the Bight of Benin became known as the Slave Coast because of its prominence in the trade during the first half of the eighteenth century, becoming dominant in West African coastal trade during the second half of the century.

Slaves were obtained through a variety of means, including: *panyarring* or the act of taking free persons when they were offered passage between ports by Europeans; boating, a very dangerous system in which some Europeans were killed by those they tried to forcefully steal from their boats; kidnapping; raiding for slaves by both European and African merchants; theft of children; buying and selling by slave agents, both European and African in several slave markets and on the coasts, punishment for crimes, especially crimes against social norms that threatened the wellbeing of

---

[29] Hugh Goldie, *Calabar and its Mission* (Edinburgh: Oliphant Anderson & Ferrier, 1901), 57.
[30] William A. Pettigrew, "Free to Enslave: Politics and the Escalation of Britain's Transatlantic Slave Trade, 1688–1714", *William and Mary Quarterly* LXIV, 1 (2007): 6.
[31] Morgan, "Africa and the Atlantic," 224.

the community; the manipulation of the many oracles and shrines that existed in the various regions, robbery and slave catching expeditions *inter alia*.[32] The relative role of warfare *vis-à-vis* other methods of recruitment has been a subject of debate. However, extant records support Paul Lovejoy's position that warfare, kidnapping, and raiding were the major sources of slaves from Africa.[33]

The use of people as pawns to underpin credit was widespread in western Africa during the era of the transatlantic slave trade. Known by various local names along the West African coast, including but not limited to *awona* in Akan, *awubame* in Ewe, *awoba* in Ga, *iwofa* in Yoruba, *iyoha* in Edo (Benin), *abrofa* in Akwamu, *ubion* in Efik/Ibibio, *igbaibe* in Igbo, *pagi* in Ijaw, and *gbanu* in Fon,[34] pawns were people used as collateral for credit in the export slave trade. In contrast to Benin's offer of credit to the first English traders, seventeenth and eighteenth- century African traders often insisted on receiving goods on credit and, as European accounts show, there were default cases on some of the credit advancements. To curtail their losses, European traders keyed into the West African custom of pawning. African merchants receiving goods on credit handed over human pawns to European slavers in pledge of repayment. The incidence of pawning in western Africa probably grew in tandem with the growth of slave exports to the Americas. The abolitionist Thomas Clarkson noted in 1788 that African merchants received goods on credit from the slave ships "for the purpose of slaving those ships, on which account they travel," noting that that the merchants were "obliged to leave a pledge or security for their return," the pledge consisting of "their own relations, who are detained till they come back."[35] If the debt was not repaid before the ship sailed, the pawn became a part of the slave cargo, hence:

> Pawning arrangements shifted some of the risk associated with credit advance by Europeans to African merchants because; in the event of default, unredeemed pawns could be shipped to America for sale... pawnship gave shipmasters some insurance against default by slave suppliers.[36]

Lovejoy and Richardson have concluded that "without mechanisms such as pawnship to secure credit, the number of slaves purchased by Europeans in Western Africa

---

[32] Joseph A. Ushie and David L. Imbua, *Essays on the History, Language and Culture of Bendi* (Ibadan: Kraft Books Limited, 2011), 65–67.
[33] Paul E. Lovejoy, "Miller's Vision of Meillassoux," *The International Journal of African Historical Studies* 24, 1 (1991): 136.
[34] Paul E. Lovejoy and David Richardson, "The Business of Slaving: Pawnship in Western Africa, C.1600–1810." *The International Journal of African Historical Studies* 42, 1 (2001): 87.
[35] Thomas Clarkson, *An Essay on the Slavery and Commerce of the Human Species & Particularly the African* (London: J. Phillips, 2nd edn., 1788), 27–28.
[36] Lovejoy and Richardson, "The Business of Slaving," 87.

would have been considerably less ... pawning helped therefore to underpin the expansion of the Atlantic economy."[37]

Black slavery in the Americas was, first and foremost, an economic system in which the master, usually white, tried to maximally exploit the labor of the slave for his economic benefits and wellbeing. On this, David Eltis posits that "of the many post-Neolithic slave societies, those of the European-dominated Americas appear to have had the most obvious economic foundation."[38] Robin Blackburn puts it more poignantly: "The slaves of the New World were economic property, and the main motive for slaveholding was economic exploitation."[39] Simply put, people from one continent forced those from a second continent to produce a narrow range of consumer goods in a third- having first found the third's native population inadequate to their purpose.[40] In sugar cane, tobacco, and cotton plantations, in the mines and in the cities, the African slave was the hand and foot of a ruling class that would not degrade itself with manual work. To maximally exploit the slave, they were regarded as a tool, a chattel, a thing, the possession of another, a legal non-person and a socially dead person without any entitlement to the fruits of their labor. On a general note, enslavers made life extremely difficult and miserable for enslaved Africans and their descendants. The Inquisition archives hold many documents that provide detailed discussion of mistreatment of slaves by their masters, sometimes driving them to suicide and often causing them to run away, plot their master's death, or blaspheme.[41] Combining all these elements, sociologist Orlando Patterson defines American slavery as "a relation of domination, a brutal system of exploitation and human degradation; and a special form of human parasitism."[42]

Despite the controversy surrounding a host of issues relating to the Atlantic slave trade, scholars are quite agreed that the trade impaired Africa's potential to develop economically and maintain its social and political stability. The demand for slaves and the struggle to meet that demand impacted all economic, political, social, and religious activities, especially in the coastal and forest regions of Africa. The ubiquity of this impact led Adiele Afigbo to conclude that: "no theme, not even that of the evolution of states, big and small, in early African history, can rival the significance of the slave trade and its abolition in the history of any region of Africa or the continent as a whole."[43]

---

[37] Lovejoy and Richardson, "The Business of Slaving," 89.
[38] David Eltis, "Europeans and the Rise and Fall of African Slavery in the Americas: An Interpretation." *American Historical Review* 98.5 (Dec. 1993): 1399.
[39] Robin Blackburn, *The Overthrow of Colonial Slavery: 1776–1848* (London: Verso, 1988), 7.
[40] Eltis, "Europeans and the Rise and Fall of African Slavery," 1399.
[41] Thornton, *Africa and Africans in the Making of the Atlantic World*, 179.
[42] Orlando Patterson, *Slavery and Social Death: A Comparative Study* (Cambridge: Harvard University Press), 12.
[43] Adiele E. Afigbo, "Africa and the Abolition of the Slave Trade." *William and Mary Quarterly* LXVI, 4 (2009): 706.

The negative impact of the Atlantic slave trade on Africa can be seen on the personal, family, communal, and continental levels. The incessant raids for slaves led to insecurity, suffering and the destruction of life and property in Africa. As Africa became disorganized, and vulnerable to European manipulation, the peace and comfort associated with African communalism was disrupted by forceful separation of families and communities. In total disregard to the groans and tears from victims, the slavers tore husbands from wives and children from parents. No consideration was given to family, friendship, or geographical ties, and this continued to the New World where they were subjected to absolute separations.

The European demand for slaves caused political upheavals and wars in Africa. Walter Rodney notes that the process by which captives were obtained on African soil was not trade at all. It was through warfare, trickery, banditry and kidnapping. He insists that "[w]hen one tries to measure the effect of European slave trading on the African continent, it is very essential to realize that one is measuring the effect of social violence rather than trade in any normal sense of the word."[44] Across swathes of western and central Africa between the fifteenth and eighteenth centuries, militarized warrior-states arose as imported firearms flooded the region. These centralized warrior-states became deeply involved in slave-raiding violence, which continued well into the nineteenth century.[45] Many communities relocated as far from the slavers' route as possible, which hindered their technological and economic development as they devoted their energy to hiding and defending themselves. To date, the deep wounds sustained in the process of recruiting slaves are yet to be healed and have continued to breed unhealthy relations among African states in the slave trade corridor.

In his "The Import of Firearms in West Africa" (1977), Joseph Inikori discusses the devastating impact of the proliferation of firearms in Atlantic Africa during the period of the slave trade. Following the large-scale introduction of guns and gunpowder from the 1650s onwards and the subsequent proliferation of numerous wars aimed at acquiring slaves, West Africa became highly unsecured and disorganized. Because guns became important for both predation and defense, it was impossible to control their use. The politics and lessons of the time compelled states to accept weapons and do the bidding of European slavers or bear the grave consequences of refusing to do so, since: "if a particular state refused to participate, it soon found itself a target of raids by others who had acquired European guns."[46] The continuous supply of firearms to West Africa resulted in a great surge of slave exportation from Africa, "both fueled by and fueling wars and banditry that often led to enslave-

---

44 Rodney, *How Europe Underdeveloped Africa*, 104.
45 Richard J. Reid, *A History of Modern Africa 1800 to the Present* (West Sussex: John Wiley and Son Limited, 2012), 26.
46 Okon E. Uya, *African Diaspora and the Black Experience in New World Slavery* (Calabar: Clear Lines Publishers, 2010), 68.

ment."⁴⁷ The tragic history of the Kongo civil wars that supplied America with so many people in the eighteenth century is an excellent example of the complexity of enslavement.⁴⁸

Because millions of Africans were displaced, killed and transported to the New World, the slave trade affected the demographic balance in Africa and contributed significantly to its population decrease. The massive loss of population affected economic productions and social systems of most communities. The enslavement of the virile young men and women, "the flower of their society," negatively altered the population structure in many areas. The massive loss of the African labour force was made more critical because it was composed of able-bodied young men and women. Slave buyers preferred their victims between the ages of fifteen and thirty-five, and preferably in the early twenties.⁴⁹ It is virtually impossible to make any assessment of how this monstrous rape of African manpower affected the population of sub-Saharan Africa as a whole, given that one of Africa's core themes has been the attempt to build up its population.⁵⁰

Depopulation stunted economic growth and brought about food insecurity. The slave trade era was a period of endemic famine in Africa. During the bad years people often sold their children or themselves, and slavers had difficulty feeding the slaves they bought. During the famine of 1757–58, the French Commander turned about 500 slaves out of the fort to fend for themselves because he could no longer feed them. Eyo Honesty testified that he saw famine in a Calabar neighboring community, when people sold themselves and children for a few yams or few coppers.⁵¹ While in some areas these famines were caused by drought and locusts, the slave trade eroded traditional mechanisms for dealing with such natural disaster. As slave-raiding warriors pillaged and burned granaries, people moved to safer, but less productive, areas.

The slave trade connected Africa to the world economy and in the process, transferred to the New World part of Africa's relative advantage in the production of commodities for the evolving global market. Apart from retarding the growth and development of commodity production for international trade in Africa, the slave trade delayed the development of market institutions and the general commercialization of economic activities. In return for their role in creating the capital that made industrialization possible, Africans received frivolous, phony, and meretricious goods that did not promote economic development. In many ways, the slave trade helped to structure African societies in ways that were inimical to capitalist development. As

---

47 Thornton, *Africa and Africans in the Making of the Atlantic World*, 334.
48 Thornton, *Africa and Africans in the Making of the Atlantic World*, 306.
49 Rodney, *How Europe Underdeveloped Africa*, 105.
50 Reid, *A History of Modern Africa*, 26.
51 David Northrup, *Trade Without Rulers: Pre-Colonial Economic Developments in South-Eastern Nigeria* (London: Clarendon, 1978),74.

a result, European nations became richer and Africa was confined to the depths of poverty and deprivation, a legacy that is still being felt today.

Aside from hampering development and prosperity in Africa, the slave trade retarded the growth of local crafts, many of which gradually died out. Walter Rodney refers to what happened to Africa's local industries in the face of European cannibalism as "technological arrest or stagnation and regression which made people forget even the simple technique of their forefathers."[52] Economic development and technological advancement require the judicious use of the country's human capital and natural resources under peaceful atmosphere. The slave trade denied Africa of all this.

One of the fundamental misjudgments made by European politicians, humanitarians, intellectuals, and philanthropists alike was the notion that slavery and 'legitimate' commerce were mutually exclusive. The struggle to suppress the slave trade and to spread the gospel of 'legitimate' production promoted indigenous slavery in many parts of Africa. As aptly stated by Afigbo, "legitimate trade emerged in the interior as the twin brother of the 'illegitimate trade' in slaves; indeed, the two developed sort of as Siamese twins. They were carried on along the same routes, and their wares were displayed and sold in the same markets."[53] Clearly, the transition from the slave trade to the so-called legitimate trade did not represent any major break in the patterns established in the slave trade period. The promotion and expansion of legitimate trade, which Europeans avidly believed would squeeze out the 'illegitimate' trade would not have been achieved with the exclusive use of free labour. E. S. D. Fomin asserts that slavery did not exist in most non-centralised societies in Africa until after the abolition of the external slave trade and thus concluded that "slavery was externally introduced from the 'trans'-systems."[54]

A significant impact of the slave trade is its role in the creation of the African diaspora. Africans were forced to migrate to various parts of the world, mostly to the New World in the Americas and the Caribbean, but also to India, Indonesia, Philippines, and the Far East generally. They were also taken to Europe in appreciable numbers. Wherever enslaved Africans were ultimately placed in the Americas and the Caribbean to serve the labor needs of the New World, they established vibrant enclaves of African cultures and institutions that have today become more important than the inhumanity of slavery. We now turn briefly to this theme.

---

[52] Rodney, *How Europe Underdeveloped Africa*, 114.
[53] Afigbo, "Africa and the Abolition of the Slave Trade," 709.
[54] E. S. D. Fomin, *A Comparative Study of Societal Influence on Indigenous Slavery in Two Types of Societies in Africa* (New York: The Edwin Mellen Press, 2002), 2.

Black Slaves and their African Cultural Roots

We begin this brief section with the assertion that "the slave-ships carried not only men, women and children, but also their gods, beliefs, and traditional folklore."[55] Existing evidence supports the assertion that "no matter how exploitative the institution of slavery was, or how traumatic the Middle Passage and subsequent enslavement were, the condition itself… did not necessarily prevent the development of an African-oriented culture."[56] The claim by scholars such as Franklin Frazier and Stanley Elkins that the dynamics of the slave trade and the harsh conditions of labor in the Atlantic world had the effect of traumatizing and marginalizing enslaved people, so that they became cultural receptacles rather than donors, has been rejected by many modern scholars.[57] In an effort to make sense of the world which denied them dignity and the fruits of their labor, enslaved Africans fashioned out institutions that enabled them cope with the exigencies of their most unfortunate condition. In doing this, they utilized their African cultural roots. For want of space, we will use only religion and popular culture to demonstrate that, despite their chains, enslaved Africans were carriers, protagonists and perpetrators of African cultures in the Americas.

Religion

Throughout the period of enslavement and much after, Blacks in the New World adhered primarily to traditional African derived religions and beliefs. At various places, they rejected the process of religious assimilation, and 're-Africanized' themselves instead. Because of this, we find a large body of African religions in the New World to this day. Described variously as *Santeria* (Cuba), *Voodoo* (Haiti and Southern United States), *Myalism* and *Obeah* (Jamaica), *Shango* (Trinidad) and *Candomble* and *Mbanda* (Brazil, Uruguay and Argentina), these religious manifestations had a common base in the traditional African concept of *magara* (fulfilment) and the explanations as to why the achievement of *magara* eludes man and society.[58]

Magara refers to the ultimate purpose of life for an individual and their community which aims at perfect happiness and fulfillment. To live robustly and be esteemed by the community, was basic to African thinking.[59] According to this African cosmology, fulfilment eludes individuals and communities because of the machina-

---

55 Roger Bastide, *African Civilizations in the New World* (London: C. Hurst & Company 1967), 23.
56 Thornton, *Africa and Africans in the Making of the Atlantic World*, 182.
57 Thornton, *Africa and Africans in the Making of the Atlantic World*, 152.
58 Okon Uya, *Contemporary Issues on Slavery and the Black World* (Calabar: Clear Lines, 2003), 18.
59 Margaret W. Creel, *A Peculiar People: Slave Religion and Community-Culture among the Gullahs* (New York: University Press, 1988), 73.

tion of malevolent forces working through persons who delight in causing suffering by placing "evil spirits" on them through their ritual powers of magic and sorcery.[60] Community and individual progress, according to this system of thought, depended largely on the ability of the groups to rally round benevolent spirits through the invocation of the traditional priests who, through rituals, could identify and exorcise the evil spirits from both individuals and community. Denounced as superstition and pagan worship by slave masters, these Africans derived religious thought, held sway in the slave communities and appropriate institutions were created to sustain it. Because of this, the traditional priests served Black communities as sorcerers, fortune tellers, philosophers, and root doctors.[61]

Religious worldviews from different parts of Africa have been firmly established in various corners of the New World. Even in the United States where efforts were made to strenuously deny enslaved Africans the opportunity of practicing their ancestral religion through the banning of their drums and other ritual objects, there is the persistence of African-based religious attitudes and practices, especially the Sea Island areas of South Carolina and Georgia. The religion of the Gullah, as the inhabitants of the region are called, are based on a synthesis of religious traditions derived from the Akan of present-day Ghana, the Kongo/Angola region, and white Christianity.[62] Features of African religion in the Americas, including the tendency to view spirituality as a means of "communal harmony, solidarity and accountability"; the tendency to regard death as a door between two worlds rather than as the end of life; the belief in, and veneration of, ancestors; belief in spirit possession which could occur only in an appropriate atmosphere of ceremony; belief in magic, charms, dreams, witchcraft, conjurors, root and charm doctors, and so on led Bastide to conclude that: "The American Negro lives in two worlds, each with its own separate rules: while adapting to his social environment, he still in another sphere of existence maintains his ancestral religion."[63]

Significantly, too, when Blacks began to join the Christian denominations in their various societies, they tended to "Africanize" and assimilate the major symbols and images of their Christian churches. Thus, among the Black Catholics in Brazil and Cuba, *Xango* (*orisha* of lightning and thunder) became St. Jeronymo (in Brazil) and Saint Barbara (Cuba); *Oxossi* (*orisha* of the hunter) became St. George; *Yemanja* (*orisha* of the sea) became Our Lady of Mercy and of Rosary; *Ogun* (*orisha* of war and blacksmith) became Saint Peter, to whom Ogun gave the keys to Paradise. Others were: *Yansans* (orisha of wind and storm) became St. Barbara; *Omolu* (orisha of pestilence and disease) became St. Sebastian, *Iroco* became St. Francis, *inter alia*. Far from being a reflection of the much-heralded tolerance of the Catholic religion in

---

60 Uya, *Contemporary Issues on Slavery*, 19.
61 David Imbua, *Slavery, Slave Trade and the African Diaspora* (Makurdi: Aboki Publishers, 2018), 147–48.
62 Uya, *Contemporary Issues on Slavery*, 22–23.
63 Bastide, *African Civilizations in the New World*, 123–24.

the Americas towards Africans, African-Catholic syncretism was a technique used by Blacks to mask, protect and preserve their religions against destruction by White Masters.

Popular Culture: Music and Dance

The contributions of Blacks in the area of popular culture – aesthetics, music, songs, dance, arts, and folklore were enormous. Few scholars today could seriously doubt that African music and dance lay at the root of Afro-American music and dance and, moreover, that this part of the African aesthetic sense is the one that is most appreciated and appropriated by European and American culture.[64] That African music crossed the Atlantic is confirmed by Hans Sloane's record of both words and music of seventeenth-century Afro-Jamaican songs. The African patrimony of such musical and dance forms as the "Negro Spirituals," Gospel, Blues, the Charleston, and Jazz of the United States of America; the Calypso and Reggae of the Caribbean Island; the *rumba, Conga, mambo* and *Mozambique* of Cuba; the *Candombe* of Brazil, Uruguay and Argentina; the *Samba* of Brazil; *Quaquey* of Chile; the *Tango* and *Milonga of* Argentina; and the *Merenada* of Bolivia, is no longer in doubt. As Robert Farris Thompson has aptly observed: "Kongo influence contributed to the rise of the national music of Brazil, the Samba; to the fundamental dance of Cuba, the rumba and the most sophisticated and important North American music, Jazz."[65]

The art of African Americans reached its greatest height in the area of music. Musicologists have continued to admire the beauty as well as the lyrics of the musical forms created by enslaved Africans which some regard as the omnibus which carried forward their African beliefs, customs and legends. Apart from their arresting styles and forms, the spirituals, Blues, Jazz, Calypso, and Soul were impressive commentaries on the human condition. Jazz, for example, has been described by one of its greatest protagonists, Dizzy Gillespie, as a creation in America "not through any great educational force, but from the souls of the people who were brought here under protest." The "Negro Spirituals," on their own, capture the full range of human emotions – loneliness, challenge, commitment, patience, tragedies, triumphs, failure, success, trails, frustration, and faith. Enslaved Africans' songs were messages – loaded and expressed protest, frustrations, hope, survival, triumphs, vitality, and endurance. It is one of the ironies of slavery that, from the depths of suffering of that most inhuman institution, there have sprung these beautiful songs of hope and inspiration that are still being rendered in churches.

---

[64] Thornton, *Africa and Africans in the Making of the Atlantic World*, 221.
[65] Quoted in Joseph Halloway, *Africanisms in American Culture* (Bloomington: Indiana University, 1991), 148.

Black dance has had a national profile in the New York area with companies led by leading African American choreographers: Alvin Aileyi, Arthur Mitchel, Eleoi Pomare, and Peari Primus.⁶⁶ The philosophy of African dance gave slaves the ability to accept and tolerate a harsh world where masters and overseers were capricious. David Northrup attests that the enslaved African folk-song "reminds the race of the 'rock whence it was hewn,' it fosters race pride, and in the days of slavery it furnished an outlet for the anguish of smitten hearts. The plantation song in America, although an outgrowth of oppression and bondage, contains surprisingly few references to slavery. No race has ever sung so sweetly or with such perfect charity, while looking forward to the year of Jubilee."⁶⁷ Music-making and dance symbolize vitality and a sense of aliveness expressed through visual, physical, and musical modes which are inextricable. African Americans musical forms have impacted greatly on the mainstream musical tradition of Indo and Furo-Americans. Bastide's comment on music is insightful: "The Negro has, indeed, been exposed to the influence of a white musical environmental; but he has only borrowed what suited him, and his choice has been dictated by his traditional African attitudes."⁶⁸

Beyond Commodity and Slave Trade

Interaction between African and European merchants from the fifteenth to the nineteenth century involved much more than trade of produce and people. The economic and commercial ties had a significant impact on the social and cultural relationship, which were inseparable from the smooth conduct of trade.⁶⁹ The imperative to stay on good terms required that the European merchant investors interacted with local agents to work out mutually advantageous conditions for trade and social life. With reference to the British, Christopher Brown indicates that: "British traders placed a priority on cultivating peaceful relations with local merchants and sovereigns in the hope of keeping commerce open and on favorable terms."⁷⁰ The need to stay on good terms was mutual.

Relations between African and European merchants on the coast enhanced the process of using European languages in Africa. Once Africans saw what they might gain, they were quick to seize the initiative in learning European languages. A large number of coastal African rulers and traders became conversant in Portuguese and

---

66 Abdul A. Alkalimat, "The Contribution of African-Americans to the Development of the United States of America." In *African Today*, ed. Ralph Uwechue (London: African Books, 2000), 383.
67 David Northrup, *Crosscurrents in the Black Atlantic, 1770–1965: A Brief History with Documents* (Boston and New York: Bedford/St. Martins, 2008), 116.
68 Bastide, *African Civilizations in the New World*, 42.
69 Imbua, "Old Calabar Merchants," 66.
70 Christopher L. Brown, *Moral Capital: Foundations of British Abolitionism* (Chapel Hill: University of North Carolina Press, 2006), 304.

then in other European languages. The first English to reach Benin in 1553 were surprised when the King of Benin welcomed them in Portuguese, which he "had learned as a child." Many of the Kongolese elite learned to read and write Portuguese in the sixteenth century as did some Africans elsewhere. Initially, English, Dutch, and French traders also used Portuguese as a lingua franca, but it was not long before some Africans mastered their languages as well. In 1614 the African ruler at Cape Mount on the Upper Guinea coast was able to speak French, while his wife "spoke good Dutch," which she had learnt while the companion to a Dutch factor."[71] A ruler in Sierra Leone in 1666 entertained a French explorer in Portuguese. Later, after the visitor proposed a toast to the health of one of his son's wives, the lady answered in French, "*Monsieur, je vous remercie*" and told him afterwards, in Portuguese, that from experience she could easily pick out the French members of his party by their manners.[72] Writing with particular reference to the Old Calabar experience, Hugh Goldie posits that:

> It was the custom of the principal traders to put their sons on board the vessels while they lay in the river, to acquire a smattering of English, and some of them learned to write it, while they could not write a word of their own language.[73]

Corroborating this view, Okon Uya writes, "the Efik took advantage of their early contact with the Europeans to acquire skills in the speaking and writing of English and accounting which stood them extremely well in the expanding European trade."[74] Paul Lovejoy and David Richardson found that "the leading traders in Old Calabar were literate and relatively fluent in English as early as the 1750s."[75] The twelve letters written by Old Calabar merchants in the eighteenth century and published by Lovejoy and Richardson in 2001 testified to the fact that writing and reading in English was popular among the people of Calabar. It is thus hardly surprising that the most extensive surviving text from pre-colonial Africa with great insight into the organization of the slave trade in the eighteenth century is Antera Duke's Diary.[76] Across Atlantic Africa, competent speakers of Portuguese, English, French and Dutch were highly valued and appreciated for facilitating commercial exchanges and navigating cross-cultural relations. Northrup informs us that:

---

[71] Northrup, *Africa's Discovery of Europe*, 65.
[72] Northrup, *Africa's Discovery of Europe*, 65.
[73] Hugh Goldie, *Calabar and Its Mission* (Edinburgh: Olipant Anderson and Ferrier, 1901), 92.
[74] Okon Uya, "Slave Routes of the Lower Cross River Region." Paper Presented at the Old Residency Museum, Calabar (18 May 2001), 6.
[75] Paul E. Lovejoy and David Richardson, "Trust, Pawnship, and Atlantic History: The Institutional Foundations of the Old Calabar Slave Trade," *American Historical Review* 104, 2 (1999): 341.
[76] Stephen D. Behrendt, A. J. H. Latham and David Northrup, *The Diary of Antera Duke, an Eighteenth-century African Slave Trader* (Oxford: Oxford University Press, 2010), 3.

> Linguists [interpreters] conducted delicate negotiation with African rulers and merchants on behalf of the Europeans and were accordingly well-compensated. For example, quacounoe Abracon (as the English spelled his name) functioned as the RAC's chief broker at their Little Komenda 'factory' from 1681 to about 1683 and represented the RAC in its dealings with the settlement's political leaders. In addition to profits from his personal trading, commissions on sales for the RAC that may have garnered him 40 ounces a year- enough to make him a wealthy man locally.[77]

Some of the coastal people who acquired proficient skills in literacy and numeracy went ahead to establish schools where the natives were given elementary education. Monday Noah asserts, "even before the arrival of the missionaries in Calabar, the Efik had set up their own schools run by the local educated elites."[78] Ekei Oku dates western education in Calabar back several decades before the seventeenth century, noting that "there is today an ancient writing school slate in the form of a folio which dates back to the 17th century and belonged to Ebrero Nonam."[79] Because the pre-missionary schools in Calabar were established when the lucrative slave trade was going on, teachers in such schools received slaves as their remuneration.[80] Waddell reports that "Eyamba's brother and secretary, commonly called Mr. Young, taught young men in Calabar at the rate of a slave each."[81]

Apart from those who were educated on the West African coast, children of some rulers and merchants were taken overseas for education and training. Whether it was in Kongo, Benin, Gold Coast or elsewhere, the Portuguese had taken some young people to Portugal where they were trained as translators. John Lok had followed the early Portuguese practice of taking a few Africans back to Europe when he carried five African men to England in 1555 from the Portuguese outpost of Shama at the western end of the Gold Coast so that they might learn English and serve future English merchants as interpreters. At least three of them later returned and became brokers and intermediaries in the trade.[82] In Old Calabar, it was not uncommon for British merchants to place children of their local agents in British schools. Archibald Dalzel informed the African Association that "there is rarely a period that there are not at Liverpool, Calabar Negroes sent there expressly to learn English."[83] As I have argued elsewhere, "the education of prominent youths in trading families [in Old

---

[77] Northrup, "West Africans and the Atlantic," 50.
[78] Monday Noah, *Old Calabar: The City States and the Europeans, 1800–1885* (Uyo: Scholar Press, 1980), 102. See also John Adams, *Remarks on the Country Extending from Cape, Palmas to the River Congo* (London: Frank Cass, 1966), 14.
[79] Ekei E. Oku, *The Kings and Chiefs of Old Calabar, 1785–1925* (Calabar: Glad Tidings, 1989), 12.
[80] David L. Imbua, "British Colonial Education in Calabar: Hedge School Policy as Standard for Education in Contemporary Nigeria," *Ubuntu Journal of Conflict and Social Transformation* 5, 1 (2016): 82.
[81] Hope M. Waddell, *Twenty-Nine Years in the West Indies and Central Africa: A Review of Missionary Work and Adventure, 1829–1858* (London: T. Nelson & Sons, 1963), 259.
[82] Northrup, "West Africans and the Atlantic," 38.
[83] Robin Hallet, ed., *Records of the African Association: 1788–1831* (London: Thomas Nelson and Sons, 1904), 195.

Calabar] was suggested, encouraged and financed by British traders."[84] John Currantee, the chief Caboceer (headman) at the English fort of Anomabu, sent his son William Ansah to Britain to study in the late 1740s." During the decade Ansah spent there, the English lavishly entertained and lionized him. King George II sent him back in 1750 in the British warship, *HMS Surprise*, richly clothed as an English gentleman. William Ansah readapted to coastal life and worked as a clerk and linguist at the Anomabu fort.[85]

Commercial relations generated other kinds of intimate relationships that deepened acculturation and brought the parties involved closer than one would ever have thought. Some Europeans whose commercial duties kept them in Africa for years took African women and raised Eurafrican families. This became necessary because the Portuguese women who had accompanied their husbands to the Gold Coast soon became miserable and often died. Documents indicate that European husbands maintained these African wives "in grand style", dressed them "in splendid clothes" with abundant jewelry. Prominent African men arranged marriages between female family members and resident European traders as part of a "landlord-stranger" relationship, a way to welcome the foreigner into the family. On the commercial side of the marriage, the European husband provided trading capital and access to overseas trading networks, while his wife served as an interpreter of language and customs and provided an *entrée* to the inland families and trading networks that were also linked to the local chief by marriages.[86] Prominent African men sometimes promoted ties between female family members and resident European traders as a way of gaining better access to foreign goods.

In Angola, the Portuguese soldiers brought from Sao Tome in 1571 and from Luanda after 1575 to defend the Kongo Kingdom from invaders "took Kongo concubines, and they and their *mulatto* children formed a distinct trading community" known as *Pombeiro*. Their ability to communicate easily and effectively with both sides enabled the *Pombeiros* to dominate trade routes into the interior by the early seventeenth century. In Calabar, the sexual relationship between a British merchant and Willy Tom's daughter produced a female child whom the English tried in vain to take to England for education.[87] Circumstances were similar on the Gold Coast, where the Director-General of Cape Coast Castle in the early eighteenth century had four children from a local wife. The head of the English factory at Tantumkweri in about 1770, John Cockburn, had several children by his African wife, Ambah.[88] The daughters of such marriages were preferred as wives by new European residents, while the sons were often successful culture brokers. There were often long-term fi-

---

[84] Imbua, *Intercourse and Crosscurrents*, 48.
[85] Northrup, "West Africans and the Atlantic," 51.
[86] Northrup, *Africa's Discovery of Europe*, 71.
[87] Waddell, *Twenty-Nine Years*, 488.
[88] Northrup, "West Africans and the Atlantic," 53.

nancial advantages for the women, since they might inherit considerable sums in the likely event that tropical diseases made them widows.

Conclusion

In this wide-ranging historical discussion, I have attempted to reconstruct the character and dynamics of interaction between Africa and the Atlantic world from the fifteenth to the nineteenth century to demonstrate how the growth of Atlantic exports from the 1400s affected coastal societies, which were more fully integrated into the Atlantic world than the hinterlands. In exchange for the goods that the European shipped across the Atlantic to Africa, Africans exported gold, ivory, forest products, and slaves. Due to demand in the Americas, the volume of the trade expanded, with human captives becoming the principal export from the mid-seventeenth century. Despite the controversy surrounding the number game, the Atlantic slave trade was unarguably the greatest population movements in history, and certainly the largest migration by sea. In contrast to the Americas, there was no widespread European conquest, no decimation of the population by unfamiliar diseases, and little subordination of native peoples to alien authority. Though some local rulers and merchants gained from the opportunities provided by the Atlantic, many people and communities entered the Atlantic as victims of exploitation and oppression. However one looks at it, the social costs of the Atlantic trade for Africa completely dwarfed the private gains of a few members of the African elites.

Importantly, the interaction and exchanges between Africans and Europeans from the fifteenth to the nineteenth century facilitated the Atlantic diaspora, which is responsible for the growing emphasis on the African diaspora. Wherever they were taken to in the Americas and the Caribbean, Africans created vibrant living communities whose culture and social institutions were discernibly African. In fashioning out their cultural universes in the New World, the slaves utilized their African cultural roots. They sometimes borrowed mannerisms and forms from the Euro-American and Amerindian environments to express their fundamental African cosmologies. Today, all attest to the great significance of African contributions to religion, music, dance, sport and entertainment in various corners of the Atlantic world.

J.A. Oluyitan
Chapter 6
Africa and Europe in the Nineteenth Century: The "Legitimate Trade" Era and Christian Missionaries

Abstract: The study examines the "legitimate trade," one of the significant historical developments in nineteenth-century Africa, which had repercussions on the African continent. The article, relying heavily on secondary source materials, analyses the development of this trade. In so doing, it demonstrates the paradox associated with the development of the "legitimate trade" partly by stressing that contrary to the basis of the trade; it actually promoted illegal slave trading and the expansion of slavery in many parts of Africa. The paper also considers two other things: the factors that aided illicit slave trading in Africa up till 1896 and the interface between the Christian Missionaries and the development of the "legitimate trade." Overall, it concludes that the trade was both beneficial and harmful to Africa in many ways.

Keywords: Slavery, labor, "legitimate trade," plantations, Christian missionaries.

Introduction

"Legitimate" trade refers to the nineteenth century international trade in which Africans exchanged agricultural produce for products supplied mainly by European powers. This trade replaced the Atlantic slave trade. This chapter examines the development of the legitimate trade, with a focus on factors that led to the expansion of the trade. It describes the illegal slave trade that developed during the legitimate trade era as well as the activities of relevant Christian missionaries. Further, it summarizes the impact of the legitimate trade on Africa. Overall, the chapter concludes that the "legitimate" trade was both beneficial and harmful to Africa in many ways.

The Development of the "Legitimate" Trade

With the passage of the act abolishing the Atlantic slave trade in 1807, British authorities hoped or expected that the nefarious trade would be eradicated in various parts of the world. However, the contrary was the case. Millions of enslaved Africans entered the Americas during the first half of the nineteenth century. Consequently, Britain came under pressure to establish an anti-slavery patrol on the West Coast to capture slaving ships. Yet, the recalcitrant slave traders did not give up as they continued their business. Given this situation and other challenges which confronted the naval squadron around the West African coast, including the persistence of the slave trade, abolitionist humanitarian organizations came to the realization that the steps hitherto taken to prohibit the slave trade were totally inefficient and inadequate. British humanitarians argued that elimination of the slave trade could be more effectively carried out by attacking the issue at its economic root. This could be accomplished by showing Africans an alternative method of obtaining money with which to buy European goods, which they thought would be a better option to implement in the quest to end the Atlantic slave trade. Indeed, abolitionists advocated for trade in natural products and not in human beings as the basis of exchange. The ideas of many abolitionists were based largely on the theory of "the Bible and the Plough" put forward by Sir Thomas Fowell Buxton.[1] The concept of "the Bible and the Plough", which implied Christianity and application of labor to agriculture, was criticized and condemned by many non-abolitionists, but the British adopted the idea in their efforts to curb the slave trade. It was in this context that the "legitimate" trade developed. In terms of participation in the legitimate trade, not all African societies were involved since, for instance, some former slave supplying societies were unable to produce required agricultural produce while others that were insignificant players in the Atlantic slave trade became major forces in the "legitimate commerce."

Palm oil, among other commodities, attracted high demand in Europe in the nineteenth century. Europe's industrial revolution brought about the demand for oil and fat. It served as a lubricant to oil the machinery and for the production of soap and candles. The working population needed candles for lighting and soap for washing. Besides the demand for oil, there were other commodities such as ivory, cotton, camwood, beeswax, available in West, East and Central Africa that attracted Europeans.

One of the areas in West Africa rich in palm trees indispensable for the production of palm oil was Niger Delta. The area had navigable waterways and many tributaries. It would eventually become known as the oil rivers due to the high level of palm oil production in the area.[2] The richest port in terms of oil production was Bonny. The oil was prepared in the markets of the interior by boiling the husks in water and skimming off the resultant oil. Subsequently, it would be transported to Lagos or the Delta ports. In 1810, a thousand tons of palm oil were exported to England. By 1855, it increased to 40,000 tons.[3] But the actual work of buying the oil and paddling the canoes of this supposed legitimate trade was carried out by slaves known as pullaboys. Slaves were still employed in the thousands in agricultural pursuits and palm oil trade during the nineteenth century. Big states such as Ibadan and

---

1 Kristin Mann, *Slavery and the Birth of an African City. Lagos, 1760–1900* (Bloomington: Indiana University Press, 2007), 87.

[2] Toyin Falola "Trade with the Europeans in the 19th Century" in *An Economic History of West Africa Since 1750*, ed. by G. O. Ogunremi and E. K. Faluyi (Apapa: First Academic Publishers, 1996), 101.

3 Isichei, *History of West Africa since 1800* (London: Macmillan Education Limited, 1977), 152.

Calabar were surrounded by slave plantations. Despite the elimination of Atlantic slave trade, slavery did not end within Africa. Slaves were purchased and sold in Guinea, where they worked in groundnut fields. Such farms became the basis for a buoyant and prosperous industry in Senegambia. Vegetable oil could be obtained from groundnut, Senegambia exported an average of 29,000 tons of vegetable oil a year.[4] The development of the steamship in the second half of the nineteenth century made the dramatic increase achievable.

In terms of exchange, the Europeans would bring their goods such as guns, cloths, beads, lead, and copper rods and sold to middlemen who would then take these goods into the interior markets to get African products. Exchange of products generally in West Africa was based on trust system. It was the most popular form of exchange between the European merchants and their African counterparts. This trust system was arranged whereby European shoddily produced goods were exchanged with agricultural commodities and natural minerals (such as gold) available in Africa through the barter system. The European merchants would make available their products to their agents on credit and they would sell the commodities in their custody; money realized would be utilized to purchase African products.

Europeans supplied junk such as second-hand clothes, old sheets, cast-off uniforms, spirits, and technologically outdated firearms during the "legitimate" trade era that cannot be compared, in terms of value, to African precious materials such as palm products, ivory, timber, rubber and gold. It is also clear that Europeans not only failed to introduce new technologies, but also undermined African efforts to enhance the prices of commodities they sold to Europeans. With regards to new technology, for instance, moves by African merchants at Calabar at the beginning of the nineteenth century to acquire sugar-making equipment from England failed. British authorities refused to sell the equipment in question that sugar that would be produced in Calabar and would compete with Britain's West Indian interests. In the same vein, steps taken by African middlemen at Calabar to ship their palm oil directly to England to obtain higher prices were frustrated by the British consul.[5] This was the emblematic of trade relations throughout Africa during this supposed era or legitimate trade. This unequal trading system ensured that Africa's agricultural products, minerals, and the labor of Africans primarily serviced Europe's economic interests and needs, with little return for African trading partners.

The development of illegal slave trading across the Atlantic and Indian oceans coincided with the development of the "legitimate" trade. Whereas the export of slaves from Africa to the United States of America during the previous century was permissible; it became outlawed after 1807. Measures to suppress Atlantic slave trading included patrolling of a British naval squadron. To reinforce the

---

4 Isichei, *History of West.*
5 Chinweizu, *The West and the Rest of us: White Predators, Black slavers and the African Elite*, (New York: Vintage Books, 1975), 39.

above steps; another British bill materialized in 1833 abolished slavery in most British colonies. Ironically, the trade continued up till the 1860 in West Africa and other areas on the continent. Indeed, the trade assumed a gigantic proportion in the aftermath of 1807 abolition law. If the slave export of the eighteenth century (7.8 m) is compared with that of the nineteenth century (6.2 million); it would be realized that the gap (1.6 million) was not too wide.[6]

Illegal slave trading occurred primarily in the regions known as the Bights of Benin and Biafra. In the 1820s, approximately 163,000 left Bight of Benin and between 1830s and 1840s, another 182,000 slaves were exported.[7] Lagos and Dahomey were the leading slave ports in this area.[8] Lagos continued exportation of slaves at record levels exceeding 100,000 slaves until British intervention in 1851. By the end of the nineteenth century, approximately 445,000 slaves representing 11.5 percent of the illegal Atlantic trade left for the Americas and Europe.[9]

The Bight of Biafra produced less than 14 percent of trans-Atlantic slave shipments between 1800 and 1850. In fact, the British navy liberated 17,622 slaves in this area.[10] This was not the case with areas covered by many rivers of upper Guinea where the naval squadron could not operate effectively. The far western coast produced about 5,600 slaves per year in the decade that followed 1807. It subsequently fluctuated in the range of between 5,000–6,400 annually until around 1840.

Slave trading did not become illegal in East and Central Africa until 1836 when Portugal abolished the slave trade. It would be naïve to assume that slave trading ended with the passage of European legislation, however, as we have seen in the case of Britain. Between 1801 and 1866, West Central African exported 2,077,000 slaves; this accounted for more than half of all people shipped to the Americas in the period. West-Central Africa supplied the Americas with almost half a million more slaves (1,920,000) between 1801–1850 than they sold in the second half of the eighteenth century (1,447,000 slaves).[11] Madagascar was another hub in East Africa where illegal slave trading persisted. Madagascar was traditionally an exporter of slaves but a market for imported African slaves developed in the nineteenth century in the Merina empire which covered almost one third of the Island.[12]

With the Britanno-Merina Treaty of 1868, the prohibition of slave exports from Madagascar became a reality. However, the agreement remained a dead document until 1877 when Rainilaiarivony proclaimed the freedom of all "Mozambiques" im-

---

6 Paul E. Lovejoy, *Transformations in Slavery: A History of Slavery in Africa* (New York: Cambridge University Press, 2011), 137.
7 Lovejoy, *Transformations in Slavery*, 143
8 Lovejoy, *Transformations in Slavery*, 137.
9 Lovejoy, *Transformations in Slavery*, 142
10 Lovejoy, *Transformations in Slavery*, 144.
11 Lovejoy, *Transformations in Slavery*, 144.
12 Gwyn Campbell, "The East African Slave Trade, 1861–1895: The 'Southern' Complex," *The International Journal of African Historical Studies*, 22 (I) (1989): 6.

ported since 1868.¹³ The above steps notwithstanding, the structure of the slave trade in Madagascar did not change until 1882. There was a clear regional division between the west coast of Madagascar where East African slaves were exported at ports north of the River Mansmbolo, and ports to the South of that river where Malagasy slaves were shipped out. It is evident that more than 13 percent of East African slaves that arrived in Madagascar in the early 1870s entered through Maintirano. This number increased to 30 percent in the 1880s. Another important slave entrepot, apart from Maintirano, was the Tsiribihina delta. It was equally significant as a center for slaves. It is on record that 2,000 departed from the center in 1870 while about 2,373 were exported through Toliara, another important center for illicit slave trading in Madagascar. ¹⁴ It is important to note that slave trading after the Britenno-Merina treaty did not come to an end until 1896, when slavery was abolished in Madagascar.

Besides, certain region of Zambesia and Malawi supplied slaves to the island of western India Ocean between 1870s and 1880s. Equally, east and west of Lake Malawi notably around Lake Chilwa, Chiuta and Amarambi met substantial demand for slaves by the French island and Merina empire in the 1880s. In addition, a combination of wars and famine in the interior followed general failure of crops in East and Central Africa in 1885 compelled many families to sell their children into slavery.¹⁵ Evidently, the supply area affected by illicit slave trade to the western India Ocean islands was considerable, as "slaves are brought down from the whole country between the lakes and the coast, a distinct measuring from west to east 200 to 500 miles and from north to south about 700 miles."¹⁶ It is also important to mention that most Malawi chiefs participated actively in illegal slave trading in the area under examination. They raided particularly east of the M'lela River, among the Lomwe (Mekua) and later in Jumbe, Angoni, Magwangwara, Makanjile and Mpenda regions around Lake Malawi. Slaves captured in these areas were sold to Arab and Swahili traders. Another important area for illegal slave trading in the period was Mozambique. Slaves from Mozambique were sold to Madagascar. An international blockade of the northern Mozambique formed by Britain and Portugal in 1888 failed to hinder clandestine trade in either slave exports or arms imports.

Additionally, slaves in the late nineteenth century were increasingly diverted from the northern routes to the Swahili coast and the less closely supervised German and Portuguese territories. The managing director of the Imperial British East Africa Company, George Mackenzie, indicated in 1892 that there existed nine main slave routes from interior of East Africa to the coast. Four of these routes crossed German Tanganyika to reach Lindi, Kilwa and Mikindani. Slave trading in these areas was ex-

---

13 Campbell, "The 'Southern' Complex," 6.
14 Campbell, "The 'Southern' Complex," 8.
15 Campbell, "The 'Southern' Complex," 13.
16 Campbell, "The 'Southern' Complex," 14

ceptional. It is little wonder that one observer claimed that "the slave coast of Africa is the coast of German East Africa from Mikindani up to Targa."[17]

Another revelation made in 1892 by the governor general of German East Africa that large caravans converged regularly on the coast south of the Rufiji River at Kilwa and Lindi, where the slaves were transported in French vessels to Madagascar and the Comoros. The two vessels crossed Portuguese East Africa ended in the region of Ibo and Quelimane. The other routes were dominated by Arab traders. These included routes from Lake Malawi to the Swahili coast; the first connected the south end of the Lake Mikindani; the second which crossed the center of the lake ended at Lindi and the third, with Kilwa as the terminus started from the northern end of the lake.[18]

Of course, a discussion of locations in East and Central Africa where illicit slave trading occurred would be incomplete without mentioning Zanzibar. It is worthy of note that an increase in slave trading occurred at a period when Zanzibar entered into a treaty with England to eliminate the trade. Obviously, profit associated with the illegal slave trading promoted the trade. It stands logic on its head if the trade continued after 1807, even after 1833 in West Africa, and in East Africa after the 1836 abolition law, without profit. Without considerable gains, the trade would have died naturally.

The East African coast saw a 500 percent increase in in the sale of slaves bought in the interior. Prior to the operations of a British naval squadron along the East African coast, the price of slaves in the Malawi region was $3.83.[19] In any case, slaves were hardly ever purchased through cash, as cotton pieces of British or American origin, ammunition, and gunpowder were utilized as articles of exchange. Sometimes, articles such as hoes, beads, and iron bars were used. Besides, the trans-Mozambique Channel run attracted profits as high as 1,000 percent. This encouraged many of the dhows that formerly specialized in coasting to change to the slave trade making multiple crossings in the same season. This situation was tied closely to demand. For example, in Imerino, the average price of a slave doubled from around $30 in 1860 to $62 in the early 1870s. This increase was not unique. Slave trading in West Africa was so lucrative that the trade continued in spite of the British naval squadron along the West African coast. Lagos alone, in the Bight of Benin, exported no less than 30,000 slaves between 1826 and 1830. By the second half of the 1830s, Lagos produced 100,000 slaves. Were it not for the British intervention in 1851, Lagos would have continued the illegal trade. Bonny, like Lagos, also continued in the trade. In 1826, twelve slaves and twelve British merchantmen were reported in Bonny.[20] By 1830s, Bonny was the chief slaving state in the Niger Delta. It should

---

17 Campbell, "The 'Southern' Complex," 17.
18 Campbell, "The 'Southern' Complex," 17.
19 Campbell, "The 'Southern' Complex," 18.
20 Michael Crowder, *The Story of Nigeria* (London: Faber and Faber, 1975), 128.

be noted that tasks associated with slave trading were more adventurous, which could not be compared with the legitimate trade which involved a lot of farming.

Another factor which sustained illegal slave trading for several years was the reactions of the Africans. Obviously, slave trading, legal or illicit, could not be carried out by recalcitrant slave merchants without the cooperation and active connivance of the local people in Africa: one depends on the other. Steps taken by Britain from 1807, and subsequent measures to suppress the slave trade came as a rude shock to many African chiefs that regarded Britain as their best customer. To better appreciate this idea, consider the conversation between King Opobo Pepple and Captain Hugh Crow during his last visit to Bonny. In response by Pepple to Crow that Britain had decided to abolish slave trade was direct and spontaneous: "We think trade no stop, for all the Ju-Ju men tell we so, for demn say you country can niber pass God Almighty."[21] In the same vein, as late as 1842, Lieutenant Levinge of the West African naval squadron indicated that Africans in the Delta often asked him whether England was at war with the other nations of Europe. "They cannot understand why we take [the slavers]. We carried on the slave trade so shortly before ourselves, that I do not think they clearly understand why we should be so anxious to suppress it now."[22] It is obvious that legitimate traders did not find it easy in their interaction with Africans in the period that followed abolition of slave trade. The recalcitrant slave merchants, on the other hand, enjoyed the friendship and cooperation of the chiefs and local population. This scenario often played out in Calabar which by the "twenties had largely devoted itself to trade in palm oil and timber everyone rushed to meet the slavers" requirements.[23]

The above idea is equally germane when we consider the level of slave exports in East and Central Africa between 1836 and 1899. The role of the local rulers and their people in providing support for the Arabs and Portuguese slave traders was very relevant. In fact, it is doubtful whether the Arabs and Portuguese would be successful in getting large numbers of slaves without the cooperation and friendship of the local political elite. It is evident that the powerful Yao Chiefs raided the poorly organized and defenseless populations of the eastern lakeshore of Nyasa to provide slaves for the Arabs.[24]

The Bemba and the Ngoni in the west carried out the same sort of atrocities. The Nyamwezi were equally supportive, as they were great buyers of slaves. The interior bands referred to as ruga-ruga in Nyamwezi countryside were also notorious. The Maviti and Magwangmana raided and pillaged the countryside for slaves to be sold to the Arab traders. One of the notorious Nyamwezi Chiefs, Mirambo, was so skillful and ruthless that by 1800, he had secured the control of the Ujiji route. With his sup-

---

21 Crowder, *The Story*, 128.
22 Crowder, *The Story*, 128.
23 Crowder, *The Story*, 128
24 Roland Oliver and Anthony Atmore, *Africa Since 1800* (London: Cambridge University press, 1972), 72.

port and alliance, Tippu Tib exploited the eastern Congo for human resources and materials.²⁵ There were 6,020 slaves in Luanda in 1850 while most of the slaves that arrived in Zanzibar, about 15,000 (out of 19,000) came from the area of Lake Malawi.²⁶ The other 4000 came from Mrima coast, opposite Zanzibar.

One other relevant factor in this discussion was the nature of slave trade *vis-à-vis* legitimate commerce. Whether legal or illicit, the slave trade involved destructive means such as kidnapping, raiding and pillaging. Through these approaches, men and women became enslaved. They could either be exported elsewhere or retained in Africa. Unlike the above, "legitimate" trade was largely agricultural ,which involved a lot of work and stress. Tasks such as cropping and harvesting required many hands and large up-front investments. On the other hand, raiding and kidnapping produced immediate dividends and appeared popular compared to the laborious work associated with farming and the legitimate trade. However, it would be naïve to assume that Africans prior to the nineteenth century were less industrious, lazy and indolent. That idea canvassed by some scholars is completely invalid, erroneous, and untenable.²⁷

There is no doubt that slave trade, whether legal or illegal had an impact on Africa. In fact, categorization of slave trading into legal and illicit is merely for analysis. It is not meant to lessen the atrocities connected with slave trading on the continent. It is clear that trade in human beings forced the exodus of a significant number of young, robust, and able-bodied Africans who died *en route* to the Americas and Europe. Without taking the mortality figures of such slaves into cognizance, as well as those that died through natural hazards, smallpox, and dysentery; about thirteen million slaves were exported during the Atlantic slave trade. It brought about a lot of destruction, devastation, and death, especially in East and Central Africa. The loss of most of active and vibrant productive labor force had great implications on economic growth, development, and future history of African societies.

While the development of illegal slave trading coincided with the development of the "legitimate" trade, the expansion of the legitimate trade was tied to several factors including the efforts of African-based smallhold farmers and the expansion of slave use on plantations. There is no doubt that slaves were in use in Africa prior to the nineteenth century. For instance, prior to this date, the Portuguese had large plantations of sugar, coffee, coconut and palm oil in the offshore islands of Fernando Po, Sao Tome, and Principe. Of course, these plantations relied on slave labor. However, despite the use of slaves in such plantations between the fifteenth and sixteenth centuries, the number of slaves retained in Africa between the fifteenth and sixteenth centuries was of no consequence to the ones exported overseas.

---

25 Oliver and Atmore, *Africa Since 1800*,72,
26 Lovejoy, *Transformation in Slavery*, 230.
27 The above is in consonance with what Hopkins called "Merrie Africa" school of thought. See A.G. Hopkins, *Economic History of West Africa*, London, 1973, p. 10.

Table 1:1. Slave departures from Africa: The Atlantic trade.

Period	Number of Slaves	Percent
1450–1500	81,000<dy>	0.6
1501–1600	338,000<dy>	2.6
1601–1700	1,876,000<dy>	14.6
1701–1800	6,495,000<dy>	50.7
1801–1900	4,027,000<dy>	31.4
TOTAL	12,817,000	

Source: Cited in Paul E. Lovejoy, *Transformations in slavery: A history of slavery in Africa* (New York: Cambridge University Press, 2011), 19.

During the nineteenth century, slaves retained in Africa were in considerable proportion. As the industrial revolution became consolidated in Britain and other European countries, demand for raw materials such as palm oil, palm kernel, peanuts, coffee and rubber increased. But this could not have been the only factor which brought expansion in the use of slaves in this period. Although the expansion in the use of slaves was related to other factors not directly related to the ending of the Atlantic slave trade (such as the Sokoto caliphate jihad wars), the abolition of Atlantic slave trade was equally germane since enslaved Africans who could not be shipped across the Atlantic due to the abolition of the Atlantic slave trade were retained and used in many parts of Africa. In any case, since the abolitionists wanted to foster Africa's trading relationship with Europe so as to undermine the slave trade, they decided to develop settlements and agricultural plantations in several parts of West Africa. Some of the earliest plantations they established were based in Sierra Leone and Liberia. In Sierra Leone, palm oil and palm kernels were ultimately grown abundantly in the southern hinterland of this broader society.[28]

As nineteenth century progressed, Africa witnessed the opening of a number of farmlands and plantations for the cultivation and growth of agricultural products. Unlike Atlantic slave trade, agricultural production required more lands for planting and harvesting. There was also the need for processing of crops and transportation of materials to the ports. In the 1840s there were many plantations around the port towns of Quidah and Porto Novo, and near the Dahomey capital of Abomey.[29] These plantations were owned by Dahomey monarch, local merchants, and officials as well as Brazilian traders. Kuenum, a prosperous businessman at Dahomey, owned thousands of slaves. In the same vein, there were royal plantations of palms, and corn called lefftle-foo on the outskirts of Abomey.[30] The Sherbro equally had large plantation to produce palm oil and food crops. These plantations relied heavily on

---

[28] Patrick S. Caulker, "Legitimate Commerce and Statecraft: A Study of the Hinterland Adjacent to Nineteenth Century Sierra Leone," *Journal of Black Studies*, 11, 4, (1981): 409.
[29] Lovejoy, *Transformation in Slavery*. 172.
[30] Lovejoy, *Transformation in Slavery*.

slave labor. In the Gold Coast, the transition to palm oil cultivation in such areas as the Akwapem Hills encouraged plantation development.[31]

In the 1850s, Kurunmi of Ijaye owned farmlands where hundreds of slaves engaged in agricultural work. Warlords in other parts of Yorubaland also employed slave labor in their farmlands. Among these was Oluyole, the Basorun of Ibadan (1837–1847) and Ogunmola. Both of them had thousands of slaves; some served as soldiers while others attended to farm work. The former had large and separate plantation for food items where these slaves worked. The more the Africans adjusted their attitude in favor of the "legitimate" trade, the more the need for laborers to gather the palm-nuts; porters to carry oil to the coast. This was confirmed by Sir Richard Burton when he informed the British Parliamentary Select Committee on Africa in 1864 that legitimate trade had led to an increased demand for slaves as porters. During the 1860s, Lagos exported an average of almost 600,000 bales of cotton annually. This feat could not have been feasible without increase in the use of slaves given the fact that between 1820 and 1830, Lagos exported 30,000 slaves.[32] And as indicated earlier, Lagos was the leading slave port in the Bight of Benin in the first quarter of nineteenth century.[33] This same picture was obtainable in Asante, where slaves worked in gold mining and harvesting of kola nuts. In the same vein, the Aro, the Efik of Old Calabar, the Igbo of Aboh and the Ijaw of the Niger Delta, employed slaves as porters and canoe men. Slaves were equally used in the palm oil plantations near old Calabar, Aboh and the Aro settlements. It should be noted that the bulk of the export crops was not plantation based; it was through family and lineage farms.[34]

This picture is similar to the Igbo and Ibibio groups from the Cross River. Their region was well known for the production of palm oil and kernels, but this did not depend much on plantations. In the Ngwa region of the palm belt, men harvested the palm kernels while their women cracked the nuts and extracted the oil. Lineage members were also at liberty to harvest produce on the communal land of the village. Once the process was concluded, the women would carry the oil to market. However, Yellow Duke of Old Calabar possessed of not less than 3,000 slaves in the late nineteenth century.[35] Those slaves worked in the palm tree plantations of their master and conveyed palm oil to designated markets in old Calabar.

The expansion of slave use equally prevailed in other parts of Africa. In the West-Central Africa, the Ambakistas had coffee plantations where slaves were used extensively. In the same vein, several large-scale European plantations in this area utilised slaves. In fact, between 1880s and 1890s, twenty-eight coffee plantations existed in

---

[31] Ray Kea, "Plantations and Labour in the South-East Gold Coast from the Late Eighteenth to the Mid-Nineteenth Century," in *From Slave Trade to 'Legitimate Commerce*, ed. by Robin Law 119–130.
[32] Mann, *Lagos, 1760–1900*, 39.
[33] Mann, *Lagos, 1760–1900*, 40.
[34] Lovejoy, *Transformation in Slavery*, 177.
[35] Lovejoy, *Transformation in Slavery*, 179.

the area with not less than 3,798 slaves.[36] At Mocamedes, slaves with numbers between 2,000–4,000 worked from sunrise to sunset, with a two-hour break in the middle of the day and Sundays off.[37] Sugar cane attracted much attention in the 1840s, but was almost completely replaced by cotton between 1860s and 1870s. Slaves also provided useful assistance in fishing. Furthermore, the Portuguese employed slaves extensively in their coffee, cotton, and sugar cane plantations in Angola.[38] Similarly, the Luso-Africans invested in the establishment of plantations in the hinterland between the 1830s and 1870s, they equally depended on slave labor. Overall, there is no doubt that industrial revolution in Europe as well as abolition of slave trade brought about a massive increase in the use of slave labor in Africa. This development, one way or the other, affected economic growth in Africa.

Christian Missionaries and "legitimate" Trade in Africa

The relationship between the Christian missionaries and legitimate trade in Africa was very strong. One cannot be isolated from the other. In the first place, the whole idea of "legitimate" trade rested largely on the concept of the Bible and the plough, an idea that the conversion of a heathen African to Christianity should be accomplished through agricultural production. Accordingly, the missionaries made use of every available opportunity to preach and condemned slave trade. They regarded slave trade as nefarious, evil, and unacceptable to God. They went beyond the pulpit to encourage Africans to produce legitimate trade crops. Some of the missionaries donated seedlings of crops to African farmers, and also enlisted European firms to come to Africa and set up their business. In 1841, the collaboration between missionaries and businessmen resulted in the famous expedition up the River Niger. The purpose of the expedition included promotion of trade in the interior and establishment of a model farm. The model farm was meant to serve as an exhibition center for the surrounding population. Two missionaries, Rev. J. F. Schon and Samuel Crowther were on the board of the Niger expedition. This Niger expedition was organized by the Society for the Extinction of the Slave Trade and for the Civilization of Africa. Regardless of the laudable objectives of the expedition in question, it achieved no tangible results. Most of the members of the expedition died due to malaria. The model farm they purchased at Lokoja was a failure; treaties signed with the Obi

---

36 Lovejoy, *Transformation in Slavery,* 230.
37 Lovejoy, *Transformation in Slavery,* 231.
38 Patrick U. Mbajekwe, "East and Central Africa in the Nineteenth Century" in *Africa: African History before 1885,* vol. 1. ed. by Toyin Falola (Durham: Carolina Academic Press, 2000), 350.

of Aboh and the Atta of Igala were not ratified.³⁹ However, the British missionaries (especially the Church Missionary Society) did not consider the expedition as a total failure. They believed that it would provide some lessons for subsequent arrangement to the interior of Nigeria and other parts of Africa. And, in their opinion, as industrial revolution spread all over Europe; it became important for the Africans to cooperate with the Europeans by supplying required commodities to the industrialized world.

By 1842, Birch Freeman had successfully opened a station for the Methodist Mission at Badagry. The same year witnessed resettlement of liberated slaves in Abeokuta. With this development, Yoruba Mission came into existence. In 1846, Hope Waddell arrived in Calabar with some Christian Jamaicans to start the Church of Scotland Mission. Between 1850 and 1865, the Church of Scotland had established stations up the Cross River. In the same vein, the Yoruba Mission had successfully opened stations at Oyo, Iseyin, Saki, Ogbomosho, Ijaye, Ilaro and Isaga.

The purpose of the Christian missionaries in Africa in this period was clear. They had a dual objective to promote "legitimate" trade and to convert Africans regarded as idolatrous and heathen. Both goals were pursued with passion, but the latter was subsumed by the former. Immediately after the inception of the Yoruba mission, the missionaries invited Thomas Hutton and Co., to establish a trading store.⁴⁰ Subsequently, factories opened at Abeokuta and Badagry. These factories further added to the visibility of Abeokuta as a center of "legitimate" commerce.

In addition, through the encouragement and persuasion of Henry Venn; and Ajayi Crowther; Thomas Clegg, an industrialist and one of those laymen of the Church of England, agreed to start cotton production for European market in Abeokuta. As a matter of fact, Ajayi Crowther and his son had shares in the Thomas Clegg Company based in Abeokuta. The missionary also encouraged palm oil production in Egbaland and Lagos. In 1856 alone, 15,000 tons of oil were exported from Egbaland. Besides, West African companies which operated with dominance on the upper Niger enjoyed the support of Samuel and Josiah Crowther. In 1873, Josiah Crowther served the company as Company Agent General.⁴¹ Besides, the missionaries acted as pathfinders for British firms on the Niger. It was the assistance of clerics like Ajayi Crowther that allowed British companies to dominate the trade of the Niger Delta area. They collaborated with traders from time to time and worked in alliance against political elites perceived as enemies of legitimate trade. In 1852, the British Authorities humiliated and deposed Kosoko due to the pressures of Christian missionaries.⁴² The latter believed strongly that Kosoko's interest was in tandem with the slave trad-

---

39 J. F. Ade Ajayi, *Christian Missions in Nigeria 1841–1891: The Making of a New Elite*. (London: Longman Group Ltd, 1969), 12.
40 Ajayi, *Christian Missions*, 12.
41 Crowder, *The Story*, 167.
42 Crowder, *The Story*, 156.

ers and consequently should not be allowed to rule a strategic trade port such as Lagos.

Of course, promotion of legitimate trade by Christian missionaries in this period should not be regarded as narrow and restrictive. It covered other areas on the African continent. Christian missionaries in West and East Africa also supported and encouraged the growth and development of legitimate commerce. Admittedly missionary enterprise in East Africa begun in 1844 with the arrival of Johann Krapf, a German, in Mombasa.[43] However, legitimate trade started to receive required attention and support during the activities of David Livingstone. He regarded the spread of Christianity and promotion of legitimate trade as intertwined and inseparable. He went in search of navigable rivers which he called the "Open Path to Commerce and Christianity."[44] His crusade against slavery and support for the legitimate trade was unparalleled. He was the driving force behind the elimination of the East African Arab-Swahili slave trade. His appeal in favour of legitimate trade in 1857 culminated in the formation of the Universities Mission to Central Africa (UMCA) by a group of English Churchmen.[45] Besides, James Stevenson of Glasgow incorporated the Living Stone Central African Trading Company. The organization had the objective of supplying the mission stations in East and Central Africa with necessities and exporting ivory at a price favorable to the people of East and Central Africa. Besides, other missionaries came to East Africa. By 1864, the Holy Ghost Fathers were already in Zanzibar and in 1868, they founded a resettlement center for freed slaves at Bagamoyo.[46] In the same vein, the Church Missionary Society established a similar center in Freetown on the outskirts of Mombasa.

As indicated above, the missionaries contributed significantly to the growth and development of legitimate trade. However, their roles in some instances appeared narrow. They failed to stand against the exploitation of Africans by European traders and countries. The fact that the missionaries occasionally obtained financial assistance from the slave merchants made it difficult, if not impossible for them to condemn atrocities associated with the structure of legitimate trade.

Admittedly, Samuel Ajayi Crowther had an altercation with some European traders on the Niger, but this disagreement was as a result of the moral laxity on the part of the latter. The missionaries were quick to identify local rulers in favour of slave trade who eventually were dealt with by the British authorities. This same attitude was not adopted to put pressure on the European firms and government to assist in the development of local communities involved in the "legitimate" trade. The establishment of churches during this period was accompanied by founding of schools. However, the objective of such education was far from the vocational and technical

---

43 Mbajekwe, "East and Central Africa," 347.
44 Mbajekwe, "East and Central Africa," 347.
45 Mbajekwe, "East and Central Africa," 347.
46 Mbajekwe, "East and Central Africa," 347.

needs of Africans. In short, missionaries failed to identify ways through which Europe could help Africa in terms of science and technology.

Impact of "Legitimate" Trade and Christian Missionaries on Africa

There is no doubt that "legitimate" trade and Christian missionaries fostered the relationship between Africa and Europe and allowed more Africans to participate in international trade. Indeed, the "legitimate" trade accommodated the participation of not only the "haves" and "have-nots." Production of palm oil in Bonny or Calabar and other areas in the West, East and Central Africa involved the participation of thousands of smallholder farmers and other workers—a far cry from the domination of powerful rulers and merchants that characterized the Atlantic slave trade. Even though more smallholders participated in the "legitimate" trade and even though the trade created problems for major players in the slave trade such as the Aro, the impact of the nineteenth century commercial transition was not uniform throughout West Africa. As Chima Korieh writes "Some societies underwent a crisis; others did not. Moreover, the impact of the commercial transition on particular societies depended on the nature of each society's relationship to the Atlantic system, as well as on environmental factors."[47]

With the abolition of the Atlantic slave trade and the development of the "legitimate" trade, pawnship became more common in many parts of West Africa.[48] It is evident that in the context of the "legitimate" trade, creditors did not only force debtors to provide them human pawns to work as interest, but they also embraced alternative means of recouping loans and punishing crimes. For instance, in the Gold Coast, instead of accepting pawns, many creditors preferred seizing debtors' kin and holding them hostage in squalid dungeons, physically reminiscent of slavery. As Sarah Balakrishnan has shown merchants imprisoned debtors' female relatives because women's sexual violation in prison incentivized kin to repay loans, and they generally resorted to the practice of imprisoning those loved by their debtors mainly because the needed more cash rather than more bodily labor to "conduct cash-heavy middleman operations between hinterland plantations and the seaboard

---

[47] Chima Korieh, "The Nineteenth Century Commercial Transition in West Africa: The Case of the Biafra Hinterland," *Canadian Journal of African Studies* 34, 3 (2000): 608.
[48] For more details on pawnship in nineteenth-century West Africa see, for instance, Toyin Falola, "Slavery and Pawnship in the Yoruba Economy of the Nineteenth Century," *Slavery and Abolition* 15, 2 (1994): 221–245; E. Adeniyi Oroge, "Iwofa: An Historical Survey of the Yoruba Institution of Indenture," *African Economic History* 14 (1985): 75–106; and Paul E. Lovejoy and Toyin Falola, eds., *Pawnship, Slavery and Colonialism in Africa* (Asmara, Africa World Press, 2003).

– and at a time when local currencies were undergoing rapid inflation."[49] It is interesting that in addition to fostering the emergence of prisons, the development of the "legitimate" trade spurred other transformation in practices of trade and credit in the Gold Coast and elsewhere in Africa.[50]

The "legitimate" trade was promoted with the support and encouragement of missionaries. These missionaries, who often formed alliance with Europeans traders, became involved in local politics of some coastal African societies. For instance, in the case of Lagos, the humiliation and overthrow of Kosoko in Lagos was largely due to the pressure put on the British authorities by the missionaries. In addition to shaping political developments in coastal regions of Africa, the missionaries helped to expand European influence into the interior of Africa through several means including participation in shipping expeditions and the spreading of Christianity. In spreading Christianity, missionaries also helped to educate many Africans through the establishment of mission schools and vocational centers. The former produced the first set of Western educated Africans, many of whom trained as clerks, teachers and priests. Some of these people in their determination to help spread Christianity translated the bible into various African languages.[51] The efforts of Bishop Ajayi Crowther in this regard is well known. He translated the bible stories into the Yoruba language, and, as several other Western educated Africans, he helped to bridge ethnic and linguistic differences.[52] Unlike mission schools, the vocational schools trained adult converts in industrial arts such as carpentry and brick making. It is interesting that Bishop Crowther also opened one such vocational center, the Preparandi Industrial Institute, at Lokoja in 1879. Initially, this Lokoja based institute had about twelve students (boys), and they were taught carpentry, brick making, and the like.[53] However, despite the benefits they brought, Christian missionaries embraced the assumption of European and Christian superiority. In the end, their efforts represented a new form of cultural imperialism and laid the ground for the formal European conquest of Africa.

Internal slavery and slave trade in Africa persisted throughout the nineteenth century mainly because of the recurring demand for labor that was used in the production of "legitimate" trade products. Both African elites and Europeans, including Christian missionaries viewed slavery as an important institution in Africa that was

---

49 Sarah Balakrishnan, "Of Debt and Bondage: From Slavery to Prisons in the Gold Coast, c. 1807–1957," *Journal of African History* 61, 1, (2020): 7.
50 For further discussion on such changes see, for instance, Rebecca Shumway and other scholars Rebecca Shumway, *The Fante and the Transatlantic Slave Trade* (Rochester, NY: University of Rochester Press, 2014); and Raymond E. Dumett, *El Dorado in West Africa: The Gold-Mining Frontier, African Labour and Colonial Capitalism in the Gold Coast, 1875–1900* (Athens; Ohio University Press, 1999).
51 Adebayo Oyebade, "Euro-African Relations to 1885," in *Africa: African History Before 1885*,vol.1, ed. by Toyin Falola (Durham: Carolina Academic Press, 2000), 426.
52 Duke Akamisoko, *Samuel Ajayi Crowther in the Lokoja Area* (Ibadan: Safer Books Ltd., 2002), 43.
53 C.M.S CA3/033/1, Simon B. Priddy to Crowther, 1860.

essential for economic development. Towards the end of the nineteenth century, however, the attitude of Europeans towards internal African slavery and slave trading changed due to exclusion of Europeans from specific markets. Accordingly, by the end of the nineteenth century the Europeans used the persistence of slavery and slave trading as a justification for their conquest of Africa.

Despite the fact that missionaries helped to educate many Africans and to bridge their ethnic and linguistic differences during the "legitimate" trade era, the trade reduced the opportunities of Africans to enter capital-intensive and large-scale enterprise.[54] As Christopher Chamberlain has shown, Europeans gained control of the regulated first tier in the three tiers system of trade that evolved during the "Legitimate trade" era while African commercial enterprise was forced to operate within the limits of the second and third tier trade in which the unregulated pattern involved a "multiplicity of intermediaries", intense competition, low profits and a high rate of turnover.[55] As he has further shown, given that their relegation to the second and third tier trade ensured that Africans were unable to amass commercial capital required to finance large-scale enterprise that could have consolidated the gains associated with legitimate trade, it is misleading to tie the origins of the commercial underdevelopment of African traders to colonial policies.[56]

Conclusion

Undoubtedly, the nineteenth century was a critical period in the history of the relations between Africa and Europe. Through the "legitimate" trade, the relations between the two continents became closer. It led to the commercialization of land and labor. It also encouraged individualism as could be seen in the Niger Delta and other areas on the continent. The missionaries equally played important roles in the development of the legitimate trade. However, the period aggravated the predicament of Africa. The slave merchants in alliance with the missionaries provided a platform for spurious treaties which eventually led to colonization. While the missionaries shaped the colonization of Africa during the era of the "legitimate" trade, the trade itself was, to reiterate, both beneficial and harmful to Africa in many ways.

---

[54] Christopher Chamberlin, "Bulk Exports, Trade Tiers, Regulation, and Development: An Economic Approach to the Study of West Africa's Legitimate Trade," *The Journal of Economic History*, 39, 2 (1979), 438.
[55] Chamberlin, "Bulk Exports, Trade Tiers," 436.
[56] Chamberlin, "Bulk Exports, Trade Tiers," 438.

Bala Saho
Chapter 7
The European Conquest of Africa, 1879–1914

Abstract: European colonization and the eventual balkanization of Africa followed decline of the Atlantic slave trade occurred from the mid-nineteenth to the early-twentieth century. This chapter examines a number of factors both in Europe and in Africa that enabled the European conquest of Africa. This chapter also discusses some of the ways in which the conquest and subjugation of Africa was carried, out as well as the manner in which Africans resisted these colonial intrusions.

Keywords: Colonialism, Berlin Conference, Partition, Resistance, Subjugation, Religion.

The history of the European conquest of Africa represents the most tumultuous and consequential period of African history. As many scholars of Africa have suggested, between 1879–1914, Africa witnessed the unexpected and sudden rise of colonialism across the continent. Before this period, and in spite of the Atlantic slave trade that had plagued the continent since the middle of the fifteenth century, the continent enjoyed a large degree of sovereignty, where African rulers controlled various political states and territories. Beyond a few limited European stations on the African coasts, the European presence on the continent was quite limited in the early nineteenth century.[1] However, within just a few decades, the Europeans expanded from these few outposts to controlling almost the entire continent and in the words of Adu Boahen, Africans were converted from citizens of their own continent into dependent colonial subjects.[2]

The manner in which the conquest and subjugation of the African continent was carried out requires an understanding of what had occurred both in Europe and in Africa during the preceding 150 years. In Europe, technical, social, and political revolutions (the Age of Enlightenment, 1715–1789; the French Revolution, 1789–1799; the Industrial Revolution, 1760–1840) transformed the continent and the rest of the world in ways never witnessed before. European presence was felt in nearly all the corners of the world. Even faraway places such as China were not spared from European influence, as witnessed in the Opium Wars (1839–1860), prompted by Great Britain's imposition of the opium trade on China.

In addition, the Industrial Revolution led to tremendous technological innovation, which facilitated the European colonization of Africa and other parts of the

---

[1] For a thorough examination of the effects of colonialism, see A. Adu Boahen, *African Perspectives on Colonialism* (Baltimore: Johns Hopkins University Press, 1987).
[2] Boahen, *African Perspectives on Colonialism*, 27.

world. Chiefly, the invention of the Maxim gun and new transportation technologies such as the steamship, railway, and the telegraph gave the Europeans a huge advantage over Africans in spite of the latter's fierce resistance. Added to these were advances in medical technology that aided in the fight against malaria and other diseases, which improved the survival rates of Europeans on the continent. These new technologies enabled expeditions and missionary activities into the interior of Africa and also increased demands for natural resources such as gold, palm oil, cotton, iron, and rubber. Therefore, the Industrial Revolution provided a new impetus in Africa's colonization.[3]

In Africa, change and development were experienced in many areas. One of the most important changes was the suppression of the slave trade, which came as a surprise to some African middlemen who had been running the trade. However, the slave trade was quickly replaced by the trade of natural products including ivory, copal, beeswax, honey, wild coffee, peanuts, cotton, and above all, rubber. It was no wonder that Africans soon began to develop a "gathering-based economy," which allowed any person, not just local rulers and middlemen, to indulge in these new, "legitimate" trading opportunities. As a result, a certain level of wealth spread across much of the continent. This wealth led to the emergence of what some scholars have called a "nouveau riche," both male and female, in rural areas, along with a great increase in the number of entrepreneurs in urban market centers.[4]

Another change that occurred in Africa was in religion, especially Islam. In the second half of the nineteenth century, West and North Africa witnessed the rise of militant Islam, encouraged by Islamic leaders who attempted to impose theocratic states as European colonization was also spreading in these areas. For example, the religious wars of 'Usmān dan Fodio (1754–1817), who established the Sokoto Caliphate came to be one of the most successful revolts at the time. After his death in 1817, supporters of the jihad (Holy War) expanded the caliphate with a strong adherence to religious teaching and practice until early 1900. Another example was 'Umar Taal who developed his jihād in the westernmost part towards the Atlantic and in the forest regions against those he saw as enemies of Islam.[5]

These developments put European nations on a collision course with each other, especially between Britain and France but also including the rise of Germany as a colonial power. The relationships between European nations encouraged the emergence of neomercantilism, which led to the abandonment of free trade and the erection of tariff barriers to protect the young industries of Europe. It also increased demand for raw materials and territories where the surplus capital generated by the

---

[3] For Europe's industrial transformation and its impact on Africa, see Erik Gilbert and Jonathan T. Reynolds, *Africa in World History: From Prehistory to the Present*, 3rd ed. (Boston: Pearson, 2012).
[4] Boahen, *African Perspectives on Colonialism*, 2–4. See also Frederick Cooper, *Africa since 1940: The Past of the Present* (Cambridge: Cambridge University Press, 2012).
[5] Jean-Louis Triaud, "Islam in Africa under French Colonial Rule," in *The History of Islam in Africa*, ed. Nehemia Levtzion and Randall L. Pouwels (Athens: Ohio University Press, 2000), 171.

Industrial Revolution could be transferred. To Africa's disadvantage, Europe also needed places where the unemployed and vagrants, by-products of the Industrial Revolution, could be moved, factors that led to the creation of settler colonies in some parts of the African continent.

The Conquest and Partitioning of Africa after the Berlin Conference

The European conquest of Africa became more profound in the second half of the nineteenth century, which saw a renewed interest on the part of Europeans to access Africa's natural resources as well as to spread Christianity. Historians have come to characterize these European incursions as the three C's (Civilization, Christianity, and Commerce). In the name of their civilizing crusade, Europeans ventured beyond the coastal areas into the interior of the continent. For example, by the 1840s, David Livingstone began Christianizing parts of southern Africa as the Dutch, Germans, and British conquered, colonized, and planted seeds of segregation. In West Africa, the French established a colony in Senegal in the 1860s and began building a railway line from Dakar, the capital of Senegal, through Mali to Niger in the late 1870s with the aim of pushing French interest to inland Africa. Though the construction of the railway did not finish until 1924, parts of it were in operation by 1904; a development that facilitated French influence in the region.

Also noteworthy was the dispatch of Henry Morton Stanley (1841–1904) to Africa under the direction of King Leopold II of Belgium in 1879 to explore and to conclude treaties with rulers of Congo. Stanley had in the 1860s been to Africa in search of Livingstone. This move by Belgium seemed to have alerted the other European powers who had also increased their presence in the region. For example, during the same period, the British dealt a heavy blow to the Asante city of Kumasi, then the Gold Coast by imposing their rule on it. By the early 1880s, the French completed their annexation of most parts of North Africa: Algeria, Tunisia, and Morocco. In Egypt, colonial interference was much more complicated. By the time of the construction of the Suez Canal in 1859, England and France had already established economic and financial interest in Egypt. The building of the canal, ports, and railroads increased Egypt's national debt and brought the country further under foreign control. However, in 1881, Egypt experienced financial and political turmoil and Britain used the crisis to destroy the city of Alexandria and to occupy Egypt and to safeguard their commercial interest.[6] In the early parts of 1884, Germany also joined the foray and claimed a few areas, namely what are today the countries of Togo, Cameroon, Tanzania, and Namibia.

---

6 Robert T. Harrison, *Gladstone imperialism in Egypt: Techniques of domination*. (Westport, CT: Greenwood Press, 1995).

As a result of these territorial conquests, Otto von Bismarck, chancellor of Germany, called the key European powers in Africa to Berlin for the infamous Berlin Conference, which ran from late 1884 to early 1885. Although more than a dozen European powers took part in the conference, Britain, France, Belgium, and Portugal were the key players who gained the most land and had the largest impact on Africa.[7] However, the conference in many ways put the nail in the coffin with regard to the final colonization of Africa. Many scholars suggest that by 1884, the continent was already firmly under European control, and the conference sought to prevent European powers from fighting among themselves over their possessions in Africa. In other words, the representatives at the Berlin Conference were laying in print the partitioning of Africa to avoid political crisis in Europe. Since there was no African representation, the European powers had assumed their conquest as a fait accompli.

The conference ended with a treaty known as the Berlin Act, which set forth the rules of engagement to complete colonial occupation. One of the rules specified that treaties signed with African rulers were to be considered as legitimate titles, meaning that the European power could claim authority over the designated space. Another resolution from the conference specified that when any European power laid claim to any part of the continent, that power should inform other signatory powers. This was essential, as it removed the possibility of the European powers clashing over the same geographical space. Also instrumental was the declaration of effective occupation. This rule, by all measures, meant that conquest would be followed by settlement. In other words, Europeans would assume responsibility in the physical management of these territories. An equally important outcome of the conference was the point that each European power could extend its coastal possessions inland to a certain extent and claim spheres of influence. Hence, the European powers made the extraction of the continent's resources easier from territories that were far from navigable waters. It should be noted that by this time navigable waters were the highways of transportation. Added to these proclamations was the freedom of navigation on the Congo and Niger Rivers. With this rule, European powers settled among themselves ways and means of keeping the African continent as a source of wealth extraction and also a place where they could spread the gospel.[8]

Consequently, by the time the conference was over, some of the European powers had not only solidified their territorial gains but also claimed new areas of influence. The haste to lay claims to the continent has been coined "the Scramble for Africa." The desire to gain a colonial stronghold led Jules Ferry, a French statesman, to remark in 1885: "A policy of containment and abstinence would set France on a road

---

[7] George Shepperson, "The Centennial of the West African Conference of Berlin, 1884–1885," *Phylon* 46, 1 (1985): 37.

[8] L. H. Gann and Peter Duignan, eds., *Colonialism in Africa, 1870–1960* (Cambridge: Cambridge University Press, 1970).

to decadence and initiate its decline into a third- or fourth-rate power."[9] Such a statement underscores the nature of the scramble. One way this scramble was carried out was to embark on signing treaties with African rulers with promises of protection against their rivals and to prevent them from signing treaties with other European powers. For example, "between 1880 and 1895, the British concluded treaties with many rulers in northern Ghana, Yorubaland, Benin and in Nigeria."[10] The scramble also produced treaties between the European powers that distinctively separated the colonies of each. For instance, "by the Anglo-German Treaty of 1890, Germany recognized British claims to Zanzibar, Kenya, Uganda, Northern Rhodesia, Bechuanaland, and eastern Nigeria."[11] Most importantly, the European powers often flexed their muscles to subdue local resistance and forced African leaders to accept their domination.

For example, by the late 1890s, Britain had seized control of Yorubaland and Benin. Under the leadership of Frederick Lugard (1858–1945), the sphere of influence inherited from Royal Niger Company was brought under effective British control and made into a viable territory. In this vein, Lugard, commanding the West African Frontier Force, assaulted the powerful Fulani emirates and subdued them, imposing British sovereignty by the early twentieth century, finalizing their occupation of British West Africa.[12]

From the late 1880s, in southern Africa, especially in South Africa, huge economic and social transformations were taking place. The discovery of diamond and gold fields in the region led to rapid industrialization and urbanization. In a short period, the British gained control over even those colonies controlled by the Boers. These dramatic developments led to a massive migration of Africans from throughout southern Africa to work in the mines and other areas. It also led to the creation of huge social and economic divide between Europeans and Africans. For example, the whites by this time had conquered the indigenous inhabitants and reinforced a comprehensive program of racial segregation and discrimination. Laws such as the Natives Land Act of 1913 prohibited Africans from purchasing or leasing land outside the reserves from people who were not Africans. These laws limited land ownership by Africans to demarcate reserves and transformed blacks into wage or tenant

---

[9] William J. Duiker and Jackson J. Spielvogel, *The Essential World History*, 9th ed. (Boston: Cengage, 2019).
[10] Boahen, *African Perspectives on Colonialism*, 33. For more on colonialism, see Ronald Robinson and John Gallagher, *Africa and the Victorians: The Climax of Imperialism in the Dark Continent* (New York: St. Martin's Press, 1961).
[11] Boahen, *African Perspectives on Colonialism*, 34.
[12] For more on the scramble, see Robin Brooke-Smith, ed., *The Scramble for Africa* (London: Macmillan, 1987); Ieuan Griffiths, "The Scramble for Africa: Inherited Political Boundaries," *Geographical Journal* 152, 2 (July 1986), 204–16; and Thomas Pakenham, *The Scramble for Africa, 1876–1912* (New York: Random House, 1991); and Frederick Lugard, *The Political Memoranda: revision of Instructions to Political officers on Subjects Chiefly Political and Administrative* (London: Frank Cass and Co. Ltd, 1970).

laborers for white farmers, ensuring white domination in the industrial cities and rural townships.[13] Moreover, in many parts of the country, particularly in the Orange Free State (OFS), whites imposed a reign of terror, and most of "these sentiments expressed the growing African conviction that the courts and laws were instruments of oppression favoring the European propertied classes."[14] In fact, in 1913 the OFS was the only province in South Africa to require urban residential passes for female Africans and coloreds, where women first protested against these passes in 1898. At a meeting held on May 29, 1913, women pledged to refuse to carry passes any longer and expressed their willingness to endure imprisonment.[15]

It should be stressed that because economic factors were the basis for colonial impulse, most of the earlier economic activities in Africa were ran and managed by concession and trading companies. These ventures played important roles in the exploitation of Africans and their resources. Some of the glaring examples of atrocities committed by such ventures were recorded in the Congo Free State, a state that was regarded as a "safety valve" on the Belgian kettle, in both a social and an economic sense. Here, concession companies shaped the subjugation of Africans and used brutal methods to force Africans to harvest natural products.[16]

Another example was the United Africa Company that was chartered by the British in 1886 with a mandate to operate in all the territory of the Niger Basin. Similar activities were done by the German East Africa Company, which operated in parts of East Africa until it was taken over by the government of Germany in the early 1890s. However, Germany continued to claim territories in the area which saw them in collision with many of the ethnic groups living in the area.

John Iliffe characterizes the 1905 Maji Maji uprising as an organized revolt that took the Germans by surprise. The revolt, compounded by regional drought in the neglected southeastern region of the colony, demonstrated the willingness of Africans to resist foreign domination. The revolt was directed against the Arabs, Indians, and Europeans who lived in this region. As news of the war spread, groups such as the Mbunga, Pogoro, Ngoni, Matumbi and Ndingo joined the revolt and attacked foreign interests as far away as the northern tip of Lake Malawi. For two years, the war

---

13 Leonard Thompson, *A History of South Africa* (New Haven, CT: Yale University Press, 2001); and K. K. Virmani, *Nelson Mandela and Apartheid in South Africa* (Delhi: Kalinga Publications, 1991).
14 See Martin J. Murray, "'The Natives Are Always Stealing': White Vigilantes and the 'Reign of Terror' in the Orange Free State, 1918–1924," *Journal of African History* 30, 1 (1989): 107–23. The quotation implies that grievances by Africans usually fell on deaf ears, as the laws did not favor them.
15 Julia Wells describes how these revolts by women against passes gained results in 1923 by the relaxation of pass law enforcement and the exclusion of women from pass laws. See Julia C. Wells, *We Now Demand! The History of Women's Resistance to Pass Laws in South Africa* (Johannesburg: Witwatersrand University Press, 1993).
16 Vincent Viaene, "King Leopold's Imperialism and the Origins of the Belgian Colonial Party, 1860–1905," *The Journal of Modern History*, 80, 4, (December 2008):741–790, 741; Herman Obdeijn, "The New Africa Trading Company and the Struggle for Import Duties in the Congo Free State, 1886–1894," *African Economic History* 12, (1983): 195–212.

spread until it was quelled in 1907. Iliffe shows that the Germans also met with resistance among the Hehe, whom they had previously defeated with assistance from soldiers from the Sudan.[17]

It should be stressed that the European conquest of the African continent was complex and arduous and sometimes involved the recruitment of African allies and soldiers. A pertinent case was the 1901 British onslaught on Fode Kaba (1818–1901), an Islamic militant who waged wars in parts of The Gambia and Senegal. The British force comprised half a battalion of the Third West India Regiment from Sierra Leone and half a battalion of the Second Central African Regiment, and with the cooperation of Musa Molloh Baldeh (d.1931), another local Islamic militant.[18]

Hence, by 1914, the partition of the continent was completed except for Ethiopia and Liberia. The case of Ethiopia was quite interesting because it was the only African country that scored a decisive victory over a European army. In 1896, at the famous battle of Adowa, the Italian army was militarily and technologically humiliated. Liberia enjoyed a special protection from the United States of America and was therefore left untouched by the European powers. as European powers aggressively sought to control the continent's peoples, territories, and resources. It is therefore safe to note that the Berlin Conference solidified the scramble for Africa. The European incursions and the conflicts between some African states or empires exposed weaknesses in relations between various African rulers. Some of these rulers were forced to collaborate with the European invaders against their local rivals. Finally, Europe's superiority in guns further hastened this conquest and sealed the fate of the African continent.

Resistance to Colonialism

One of the most intriguing aspects of the European colonization of Africa is the response of Africans to these incursions. According to many scholars, the trajectory of African resistance and collaboration followed a wide of spectrum of responses, ranging from direct confrontation as early as the sixteenth century to accommodation in the nineteenth century. For example, with respect to the Kingdom of Kongo, Basil Davidson points to King Afonso I's collaboration with and opposition to Portuguese slavers in 1526, and the collaboration of King Jaja of Opobo, in what is today Rivers State in Nigeria, in the second half of the nineteenth century.[19] In the same vein,

---

[17] John Iliffe, *Tanganyika under German Colonial Rule* (Cambridge: Cambridge University Press, 1969).
[18] J. M. Gray, *A History of the Gambia* (London: Frank Cass & Co. Ltd, 1966), 471.
[19] Basil Davidson, "African Resistance and Rebellion against the Imposition of Colonial Rule," in *Emerging Themes of African History: Proceedings of the International Congress of African Historians, Dar es Salaam, October 1965*, ed. T. O. Ranger (London: Heinemann, 1968). For information on resis-

Allen Isaacman and Barbara Isaacman portray Chikunda resistance and collaboration as one of adaptation to changing political, economic, social, and cultural realities that took hold of the Zambezi Valley in Mozambique after colonialization of the region.[20] J. D. Hargreaves maintains that while some African rulers were manipulated by Europeans into collaboration, more often than not Africans pursued clear purposes of their own.[21]

Whatever the reaction, it is clear that the period from the mid-nineteenth century to the early twentieth century saw more forms of resistance manifest against colonialism. For example, in the historiography of resistance in South Africa, the Anglo-Zulu War of 1879 has gained currency as the greatest African resistance against colonial forces. At the Battle of Isandhlwana, the British lost over a thousand men when the Zulu warriors overran their main staging camp. What gave currency to this defeat was the fact that the Africans were armed only with lances and spears.[22]

In many cases, African states sought the protection of European powers. The Ndebele/Shona clashes of 1893 and uprisings of 1896–1897 in Zimbabwe are other examples of resistance and collaboration that gave European settlers an opportunity to trade off one group against another in establishing themselves, and to cement control over labor. In another example, the Portuguese and the British were caught up in the wars between the Sena and the Barue people of the Malawi-Mozambique borderlands in 1902, when these European powers each supported one side against the other.[23]

In the early twentieth century, other forms of resistance common in the eastern, central and southern African regions were directed against the imposition of capitalism. In some cases, Africans organized broad-based strikes or armed insurrections, but in most cases, opposition arose in the form of small-scale, atomized actions. During this period, direct confrontation began to abate, and Africans expressed their hostility in a number of indirect ways such as tax evasion, social banditry, work slowdowns, and the destruction of European property. Terrence Ranger, for example, reports that in southern and central Africa, "just before the arrival of tax collectors, all

---

tance during the slave trade, see Sylviane A. Diouf, ed., *Fighting the Slave Trade: West African Strategies* (Athens: Ohio University Press, 2003).

20 Allen F. Isaacman and Barbara S. Isaacman, *Slavery and Beyond: The Making of Men and Chikunda Ethnic Identities in the Unstable World of South-Central Africa, 1750–1920* (Portsmouth, NH: Heinemann, 2004); Jon Abbink, Mirjam de Bruijn, and Klaas van Walraven, eds., *Rethinking Resistance: Revolt and Violence in African History* (Leiden: Brill, 2003); and Michael Crowder, *West African Resistance: The Military Response to Colonial Occupation* (London: Hutchinson, 1971).

21 J. D. Hargreaves, "Towards a History of the Partition of Africa," *Journal of African History* 1, 1 (1960), 108.

22 Thompson, *A History of South Africa*; Nelson Mandela, *Long Walk to Freedom: The Autobiography of Nelson Mandela* (Boston: Little, Brown, 1994); and William J. Pomeroy, *Apartheid, Imperialism and African Freedom* (New York: International Publishers, 1986).

23 Allen F. Isaacman and Barbara S. Isaacman, "Resistance and Collaboration in Southern and Central Africa, c. 1850–1920," *International Journal of African Historical Studies* 10, 1 (1977): 31–62.

or most of the villagers would flee into an inaccessible region and stay there until the officials left." Another class of opposition regarded as social bandits adopted an aggressive stance toward the colonial regimes. The bandits periodically returned to their homeland and attacked symbols of rural oppression—the plantation overseers, labor recruiters, tax collectors, and African police—in an effort to protect their kin. Mapondera, the best-known social bandit of south-central Africa, for more than a decade led a band that protected the local peasantry from exploitative company officials and abusive Rhodesian and Portuguese administrators.[24]

In a case study of France's imperial conquest of the western Sudan, Timothy Weiskel describes how one ethnic group of the Ivory Coast reacted with violence to colonial administration during the 1889–1911 period, with vigorous resistance to the compulsory growing of agricultural exports. This led to the French launching a full-scale military expedition, which inflicted devastating results on the population.[25]

In their study of the Volta-Bani anticolonial war, Mahir Şaul and Patrick Royer present both an important discourse in the trajectory of resistance and collaboration as well as a classic case of an anticolonial struggle based on clear calculations of the weak and patchy nature of colonial control, which gave the impression that colonialism could be ended. The war began as an opposition to forced military conscription for World War I and to protest heavy taxation. The leaders of the movement and most of the local population were thus convinced that, with organization, determination, and effective warfare techniques, they could secure victory over the colonial regime.[26] In fact, World War I ushered in a wave of recruitment for Africans' participation in the war. Thousands of Africans were conscripted voluntarily or by force to join the war as soldiers, couriers, and as builders of the war infrastructure. Many people were recruited through chiefs who were expected to deliver up the numbers required of them by the political officers. A good example of successful recruitment during World War I is France's mobilization of the African troops known as *tirailleurs sénégalais*.[27]

In a similar examination of Africans adapting to new environments, Charles van Onselen suggests that the growth of industrial mining in the early twentieth century

---

[24] Terrence O. Ranger, *Peasant Consciousness and Guerrilla War in Zimbabwe: A Comparative Study* (Berkeley: University of California Press, 1985); and Terrence O. Ranger, *Revolt in Southern Rhodesia, 1896–1897: A Study in African Resistance* (Evanston, IL: Northwestern University Press, 1967).
[25] Timothy C. Weiskel, *French Colonial Rule and the Baule Peoples: Resistance and Collaboration, 1889–1911* (Oxford: Clarendon Press, 1980).
[26] Mahir Şaul and Patrick Royer, *West African Challenge to Empire: Culture and History in the Volta-Bani Anticolonial War* (Athens: Ohio University Press, 2001).
[27] Richard S. Fogarty and David Killingray, "Demobilization in British and French Africa at the End of the First World War," *Journal of Contemporary History*, 50, 1, (2015): 100–123; Christian Koller, "The Recruitment of Colonial Troops in Africa and Asia and their Deployment in Europe during the First World War," *Immigrants & Minorities*, 26, 1/2, (2008):111–133; G.W.T. Hodges, "African manpower statistics for the British Forces in East Africa, 1914–1918," *Journal of African History*, 19, 1 (1978): 101–116.

created an environment in which Africans struggled to fight against the social, cultural, and economic conditions created by the mining industry. Van Onselen chronicles the struggles of Africans with wage labor, the system of recruitment, and conditions in the mines and mine compounds as strategies of survival against an impending capitalist system.[28]

To fully understand the dynamics of resistance and collaboration, one needs to look at the Maji Maji uprisings of 1905 in German East Africa. John Iliffe characterizes Maji Maji as an organized revolt that took the Germans by surprise. The revolt, compounded by regional drought, began in July 1905 in the neglected southeastern region of the German colony, demonstrated the willingness of Africans to resist foreign domination. The revolt was directed against Arabs, Indians, and Europeans who lived in this region. For two years, the war spread until it was quelled in 1907. Iliffe shows that the Germans also met with resistance among the Hehe, whom they had previously defeated with assistance from soldiers from the Sudan.[29]

Religion and religious leadership also played an important part in accommodating or opposing colonial advancement. Nowhere was this more visible than in North and West Africa during the nineteenth and early twentieth centuries. In West Africa, David Robinson underscores that Muslim societies accommodated the French colonial regime. The accommodation permitted the Marabouts (Islamic scholars) and brotherhoods to develop considerable autonomy in religious, economic, and social spheres while surrendering the political and administrative domain to the French.[30]

In a similar study, of Mahdism and resistance to colonial rule in the Sokoto Caliphate, Paul Lovejoy and J. S. Hogendorn argue that the Mahdists were revolutionaries who sought to overthrow all established authority, including the colonial regimes and local officials who collaborated with the Europeans. They further show that in order to crush the Mahdist resistance at Satiru, the British collaborated with the Sokoto aristocracy, while the French secured similar aristocratic support in overcoming the Mahdists at Kobkitanda and Karma.[31]

In 1898, a compelling example of an attempt to resist European domination was the Battle of Omdurman, where a small number of well-armed Anglo-Egyptian soldiers with maxim and mounting guns confronted a Sudanese army of forty thousand. Despite a determined and valiant effort, eleven thousand of the Sudanese perished before Sudan was brought under European rule. It is reasonable to conclude that in addition to division between African kingdoms and the collaboration of African

---

28 Charles van Onselen, *Chibaro: African Mine Labour in Southern Rhodesia, 1900–1933* (London: Pluto Press, 1976).
29 Iliffe, *Tanganyika under German Colonial Rule*.
30 Robinson, *Paths of Accommodation*; and David Robinson, "The Murids: Surveillance and Collaboration," *Journal of African History* 40, 2 (1999): 193–213.
31 Paul E. Lovejoy and J. S. Hogendorn, "Revolutionary Mahdism and Resistance to Colonial Rule in the Sokoto Caliphate, 1905–6," *Journal of African History* 31, 2 (1990): 217–44.

leaders and Europeans, newly invented weapons greatly enhanced European military ventures in Africa and secured the eventual domination of the continent.

Conclusion

Between 1870 and 1914, almost all of Africa was carved up and occupied by European powers such as Great Britain, France, Portugal, Belgium, Italy, Spain, and Germany. During this rapid period of colonization, Africans were converted from sovereign and royal citizens of their own polities into colonial and dependent subjects. European powers preoccupied themselves with practical issues of not only how to extract Africa's raw materials to feed their booming industrial economies but also how to rule Africans in such a way that could benefit Europe. To achieve these goals, European powers introduced systems of administration for each individual colony, as the British and the Germans did, or for a group of colonies, as the French did. It should be stressed that these colonies were administered by colonial officials who were appointed by the European colonial powers and were therefore more concerned with what favored Europe than Africa.

While the varieties of colonial administrations established in the European colonies of Africa shared many features in common, they also differed significantly. Historians have over the past few decades distinguished these systems by classifying them as either direct rule or indirect rule. Direct systems of administration were generally associated with the French and Portuguese colonies, whereas indirect rule is generally associated with the British extensions or overseas colonies in Asia and Africa. Finally, it can be argued that the experience of colonialism largely shaped postcolonial African states and the colonization of Africa needs to be evaluated not only by the history of Europeans in Africa but also by the responses of Africans to adverse circumstances imposed on the continent as a result of the actions of Europeans.

Aliyu Sakariyau Alabi

Chapter 8
Impact of African Colonial Experience 1914 – 1940

Abstract: African history cannot be reduced to binaries such as coloniser/colonised, colonies/metropoles and imperial/subaltern but must be understood through multiple contexts. Since the last half of the twentieth century, Africanist scholars have asserted the agency of Africans not only in the history of Africa but also of the world. In addition to expanding our understanding of African experience with colonialism, scholars have also examined ways in which Europe was shaped by its colonies. This chapter explores African experiences in the first half of the twentieth century as they relate to not only the major world events of the century such as both World Wars and the Great Depression, but also the consolidation of colonial administrations, indirect rule and assimilation, the emergence of anticolonial movements and Pan Africanism, and the dynamics and encounters surrounding the empire exhibitions, subversion of power relations in the movement of prisoners from Libya to Europe, sexuality of power relations, architectural inspirations from Africa to Europe, progress of Islam and Christianity and African intellectual response to European intellectual intervention on Africa. This discussion of such a wide range of topics illuminates the influence of Africans on Africa itself and on Europe's socio-economic and political milieu, despite the limitations imposed by imperialism. Thus, Africa impacted global history even from its subaltern contexts.

Keywords: African Impact, Colonialism, African Agency, Inter-war years, Pan-Africanism.

Introduction

Since the last half of the twentieth century, Africanist scholars have asserted the agency of Africans not only in the history of Africa, but also of the world. Although under the hegemony of the colonising European imperialists, Africans engaged with their colonial experience in ways that impacted not only Africa but also Europe. As Frederick Cooper argued, writing on the colonial past serves to teach a lesson to the present: the hypocrisy of European claim as model of democracy and progress. Scholars have also revealed ways in which Europe was made from its colonies.[1] When examined through the lens of key events in the twentieth century, we are

---

[1] Frederick Cooper, *Colonialism in Question Theory, knowledge, History* (Berkeley: University of California Press, 2005), 3,6.

able to see the dynamic experiences and impacts of Africans on Africa itself and also on Europe's socio-economic and political milieu, despite the limitations imposed by imperialism.

Africa's contact with Europe and the rest of the world did not begin with colonialism; rather colonialism was the culmination of a relationship dating back to the fifteenth century. Economic considerations have been the major impulse of Europe's centuries long relationship with Africa.[2] Although missionary and political incursions into the African territories had been attempted earlier, they were not successful as shown in the experience of the Portuguese in Benin kingdom and South African kingdoms.[3] Political and missionary incursions were not successful until the nineteenth century, as detailed in the previous chapter. It was the economic relations that have had the most enduring influence.

The relationship began with European explorers exchanging goods with coastal African communities, stretched in the transatlantic slave trade with its devastating socioeconomic and political consequences on Africa on one hand, and on other hand, the slave trade facilitated the development of the western world over a period of four centuries. This trajectory culminated in the colonialism from the nineteenth century which lasted until the mid-twentieth century. Walter Rodney has argued about the dialectical relationship of development and underdevelopment in his seminal work *How Europe Underdeveloped Africa*, in which he argued that Africa helped Europe to develop proportionate to how Europe underdeveloped Africa. Until the nineteenth century, Africans had little knowledge of the internationalization of trade which Europe was in full control of, hence the dependency which has characterised the relationship between Europe and Africa.[4]

However, dependency is not the only way to explain the experience of Africans. Scholars like Fredrick Cooper advocate for scholarship which explores how the colonial experience impacted both the colonisers and the colonised. More than this binary, he encouraged scholars of this history to search for ways in which power was deployed by Europeans, and the way in which power was engaged, contested, deflected, and appropriated by Africans.[5] This is particularly important in examining the history of Africa from the beginning of the First World War one to the beginning of the Second World War, a period marking the height of colonialism. The subsequent events that led to the decolonisation and eventual granting of independence to most African countries had their roots in this period. As Europeans impacted Africans, Africans too, even though subaltern, impacted Europeans.

This chapter intends to show the dyadic impact of colonialism on Africa on the one hand, and Europe on the other, despite being the hegemonic other, and by ex-

---

[2] A.G. Hopkins, *An Economic History of West Africa* (London: Longman Group Limited, 1973), 164.
[3] Kevin Shillington, *History of Africa* (New York: St. Martin's Press, 1995), 289.
[4] Walter Rodney, *How Europe Underdeveloped Africa* (Abuja: Panaf Publishing, 2009), 86–87.
[5] Fredrick Cooper, "Conflict and Connection: 'Rethinking Colonial African History," *American Historical Review* 99, 5 (Dec. 1994): 15–17.

tension, such impacts on the rest of the globe from the beginning of the first World War to the beginning of the second World War. As Hopkins noted some four decades ago, Africans occupy a central place in the history of their continent.[6] There was a multiplicity of engagements and at different levels and these cannot be understood through simple binaries of the colonizer and the colonized. More than being a passive recipient of European hegemony, Africans had agency, and this affected how Europe thought and related with Africa during this high period of colonialism.[7]

The Colonial Experience in Africa 1914–1940

By 1914, after defeating or occupying most African societies, Belgium, Britain, France, Germany, Italy, Portugal and Spain had established colonial empires on the continent. These European powers, who determined the political geography of Africa based on imperial interests, implemented policies aimed at not only consolidating their rule, but also at enhancing their place in the world. To help enhance their place in the world, they also ensured that Africa participated in World War I.[8] Although the war was also fought on African soil, World War I battles fought in Africa had little effect on the general course of the war in Europe; however they had important implications for Africa. Indeed, in the course of World War I, more than a million African soldiers were involved, while many more men, women and children, often forcibly recruited, served as carriers and in such other capacities for the soldiers.[9] Also during the war, the British joined their French allies and easily overran the German territories of Togo and Kamerun.[10] The destruction caused by these campaigns led to severe hardship among the rural people of these regions. Villages were burnt and their foodstuffs and labour requisitioned indiscriminately.[11] The effects of the war were further compounded by famine and the influenza pandemic that followed the war in 1918–1919, which led to the death of tens of thousands of people. The post-war pandemic in fact killed more people than the war, made possible in no small way by the movements of people during and after the war.[12]

---

6 Hopkins, *An Economic History*, 1.
7 John D. Hargreaves, *Decolonization in Africa* (New York: Addison Wesley Longman Limited, 1996), 13.
8 Michael Crowder, "First World War and its Consequences in Africa," in *UNESCO General History of Africa VII Africa Under Colonial Domination 1885–1935* ed. A. Adu Boahen (Paris: Heinemann Educational Books, 1985), 283.
9 Richard S. Fogarty and David Killingray, "Demobilization in British and French West Africa at the end of the First World War," *Journal of Contemporary History* 50, 1 (2015): 100–123; Shillington, *History of Africa*. 345–346.
10 Shillington, *History of Africa*, 343.
11 Shillington, *History of Africa*, 345.
12 Shillington, *History of Africa*, 346.

Apart from causing severe hardship and death, the war led to a resurgence of resistance from Africans who were dissatisfied with colonial rule, especially their forced recruitment into service as soldiers and carriers. Though such resistance was ruthlessly put down, this resistance shows that Africans were not passive to European hegemony.[13] While World War I affected the lives of many Africans in significant ways, it also ensured that Germany lost its African colonies, and that only six colonial systems remained in Africa throughout the interwar years. As noted elsewhere, because Germany lost its African colonies due to the war, it can be argued that World War I was responsible for the humiliation that set the ground for the Second World War and subsequent relevant developments in Africa.[14]

Besides the changes brought by World War I, the period between 1914 and 1940 witnessed several other developments. Economically, an increasing number of Africans were offered employment in the expanding colonial civil service after World War I so as to help the European powers consolidate their colonial empires; physical infrastructure such as railways, roads, and ports were constructed or expanded to meet the increasing need and adaptation of Africans to modernity and to foster the exploitation of African resources;[15] and new technologies such as the automobile, aeroplane, railway, telephone, radio and print technology were introduced.[16]

The European powers were not interested in promoting industrialization in Africa even though they provided new employment opportunities, developed physical infrastructure, and introduced new technologies. Instead, they encouraged the production of cash crops. The production of cash crops partly served to feed the industry and the economy of the metropoles. During this period, West African farmers had to accept the prices dictated by a world economy in the hands of Europeans, even though they produced a considerable proportion of the cocoa, palm produce, and groundnut on offer in the international market. Generally the prices of all West African agricultural exports were influenced by changes in the level of income in the industrial metropoles. A large proportion of incomes from exports in turn were to be spent on imported consumer goods.[17] By the 1930s, agricultural exports of West Africa had grown exponentially from less than a hundred tonnes at the turn of the nineteenth century to hundreds of tonnes.[18]

To foster cash crop production in settler colonies like Kenya, Southern Rhodesia, and Algeria, colonial administrators seized land from Africans and gave them to

---

13 Crowder, "First World War,"296–99.
14 "Africa's Role in WWI a Forgotten Chapter," Wednesday, 28 July 2004, *The Washington Times*, Wednesday, 28 July 2004. Accessed 11/05/2020.
15 Claude Ake, *African Political Economy* (New York: Longman Ltd, 1981), 43–45;Nasson, "More Than,"163;
16 B. O. Oloruntimehin, "African Politics and Nationalism, 1919–1935," in *Unesco General History*. ed. Boahen, 579.
17 Hopkins, *An Economic*, 169.
18 Hopkins, *An Economic*, 174.

small groups of European settlers. They also implemented many other policies, such as excluding Africans from tea cultivation, that forced many Africans to work for European planters, further subordinating Africans to Europeans on the continent. Unlike in settler colonies, attempts to establish European plantations in West Africa were unsuccessful. As Hopkins argues, these unsuccessful attempts were not due to climatic or humanitarian concerns but due to other factors such as the opposition from African traders who were afraid that European owned plantations would undercut them.[19] In West Africa, therefore, cash crop production was dominated by African farmers. Although the colonial governments provided little or no technological support for these farmers, they adapted quickly to colonial situations. The history of cocoa in Ghana is a testimony to the agency and adaptability of Africans in new situations. Although the cocoa crop was alien to the region, within two decades the production had resulted in export figures of some 40,000 tonnes per annum, from some four million acres and employing millions of people. Although the colonial government played some roles in providing seeds and plants, neither government officials nor the expatriate firms had much influence on the activities taking place in the interior as the industry was established. The credit should go to the migrant farmers from the south eastern part of the Gold Coast who began to move to the virgin lands of Akim Abuakwa.[20]

It is notable that many of the actions that African farmers took to promote their interests impacted the ways Europeans dealt with them. For instance, the decision of cocoa farmers in Ghana to hold up their produce until the price was raised in 1921, 1930–31, and 1937[21] led to the British government decision to set up the marketing board to purchase the produce from the farmers instead of the big corporations which had until then been playing that role. This marketing board, the West African Cocoa Control Board, was established in 1938. Another notable instance of African agency in the context of economic relations between colonial subjects and their masters involved an individual known as Tete Ansa.[22] Between 1925 and 1935, this Ghanaian founded producer cooperatives in Ghana and Nigeria in order to strengthen the bargaining positions of farmers and lower their cost. He also founded the Industrial and Commercial Bank in Nigeria to finance African's participation in external trade, a trade that colonial powers ensured was dominated by Europeans throughout the colonial era.[23] Although his ventures later ran into trouble, it nevertheless was an in-

---

19 Hopkins, *An Economic*, 214.
20 Hopkins, *An Economic*, 216–17.
21 Hopkins, *An Economic*, 256.
22 Rodney, *How Europe*, 202.
23 For further details on external trade see, for instance, Vanderlaan H. Laureens, "Marketing West Africa's Export Crops: Modern Boards and Colonial Trading Companies," *Journal of Modern African Studies* 25, 1 (1987), 1–24.

dication of the possibility of African agency even in a context not particularly favourable to the Africans.²⁴

In colonial Africa, slavery and other forms of forced labor were used in agriculture and in public projects like building roads and railroads.²⁵ Even though the European powers used slavery as a justification for the conquest of Africa, they favored the use of slave labor mainly because they wanted to prevent social dislocation. Thus, in places like Northern Nigeria it was only in the late 1930s that slavery was eventually ended. In terms of the use of forced labor, practices varied from region to region. Nevertheless, in all regions, Africans spent a great deal of their time evading forced labour. In the end, even though the use of forced labor had not been abolished by 1940, relevant African resistance had brought to the fore the importance of unforced labour as catalyst for economic growth.

One of the consequences of the use of forced labor and/or of the colonial labor demand was migration. The evidence indicates that during the period migrants often moved to cities and that they were largely men. It also shows that European employers preferred employing male laborers. In the colonial economies, therefore, women were marginalized while an increasing number of young male laborers acquired wealth to do several things including to challenge established hierarchies in rural societies.²⁶

Overall, while colonialism may have had mixed economic impact on Africa, colonial economic policies implemented between 1914 and 1940 mainly ensured that African economies were geared towards cash crop production and more generally towards generating surplus value that was partly transferred to Europe. The fact that surplus value was transferred to Europe is significant for several reasons. For instance, it suggests that profits from colonising Africa and other sources worked together to finance scientific research which further increased the socio-economic disparity between Europe and Africa.²⁷

In the period under study, previous rulers had lost their sovereignty and independence because of the perfection of racist colonial administrative systems. The racist administrative systems embraced by the Europeans powers varied, but they were all shaped by the commitment to save cost, and they all involved the use of considerable African manpower. In the imperial ideology of the time, Africa was seen as a responsibility or trust by the Europeans for the sake of Africa as well as for the

---

24 Hopkins, *An Economic*, 256.
25 For interesting discussion on the connection between slavery and cash crop production see, for instance, Gareth Austen, "Cash Crops and Freedom: Export Agriculture and the Decline of Slavery in Colonial West Africa," *International Review of Social History* 54, 1 (2009): 1–37.
26 That women were marginalized does not mean that many of them did not defy the conventional notion of women as sedentary dependents of migrant husbands. See Mudeka Ireen, "Gendered Exclusion and Contestation: Malawian Women's Migration and Work in Colonial Harare, Zimbabwe, 1930s to 1963," *African Economic History* 44 (2016): 18–43.
27 Rodney, *How Europe*, 209.

world.²⁸ The British administrative system is known as "Indirect Rule." It embraced the indigenous administrative systems and the use of African customary laws. In implementing Indirect Rule, the British ensured that Europeans were dominant forces in administration, and that they imposed their interpretation of customary practices and traditional authorities on Africans in their various colonies like Nigeria, Malawi and Uganda. However, as Spear noted, when Europeans sought to appropriate tradition, they became subject to a discourse which they had little knowledge or control of.²⁹ For instance, in eastern Nigeria where there were no socio-political formations, they imposed a hierarchical chieftaincy structure known as the "warrant system."- Frederick Lugard, who introduced the Indirect Rule system into Northern Nigeria and elsewhere, considered this system of administration as the cheapest and most effective method to rule over large territories and populations.³⁰ However, partly by imposing its interpretation of customary practices and traditional authorities, the British had divorced the chiefs or traditional leaders from their peoples and they had reshaped social or ethnic identities by 1940.³¹ Thus they risked its appropriation to challenge their own authority as the African people find in this European invention an opportunity to challenge colonial authority.³²

In the case of the French, prior to 1917, they had adopted an assimilation policy that sought to turn their African subjects into French citizens This policy was subsequently abandoned in part because France was not truly ready to give citizenship to its African subjects and in part because most Africans were not willing to change their African identity, personality, and culture. Following the abandonment of the policy of assimilation in 1917, the French embraced the policy of "association." Association stood for a type of indirect administration with preservation and improved governance of local institutions and respect for their past.³³ Under this policy, the French employed sections of the African political elite as intermediaries between themselves and local people. As junior partners in the colonial administrative system, they sought to respect African language, customs, and institutions. In the end, therefore, the policy of association was not much different from Indirect Rule, and it also contributed to divorcing the relevant African political elite from their peoples and to reshaping social or ethnic identities. As Konklin argues, the policy was more tied to the need to contain the *evolues* (Europeanized Africans) in par-

---

28 R. F. Betts (Revised by M. Asiwaju), "Methods and Institutions of European Domination," in Boahen (Ed.)*UNESCO General History of Africa VII*, 312.
29 Thomas Spear, "Neo-Traditionalism and the Limits of Invention in British Colonial Africa," *Journal of African History* 44 (2003), 6.
30 Shillington, *History of Africa*, 354–55.
31 Betts (Revised by M. Asiwaju), "Methods and Institutions,"315.
32 Spear, "Neo-Traditionalism,", 7.
33 Betts (Revised by M. Asiwaju), "Methods and Institutions,"319.

ticular, and to re-establish discipline among the populace in general than to any civilizing motive.[34]

Colonial rule also encouraged the spread of Christianity and Islam. Between 1914 and 1940, Christian missionaries were viewed as important allies by colonial governments, mainly because the latter considered Christianity as an important tool for social control. As a result, colonial governments often ensured a favorable environment for the work of missionaries in many parts of Africa, especially in areas where there were no large Muslim populations. Although Christian missionaries effectively spread Christianity to various parts of Africa, they were unable to completely undermine the indigenous African religions. As a matter of fact, by 1940 many Christian missionaries and churches had incorporated aspects of indigenous African religions into their rituals. While most African attended churches that were led by European preachers, some of them embraced the teachings of African preachers who founded their own African Christian movements or churches. In many cases, African Christians who founded their own independent churches, such as John Chilembwe in Nyasaland and Simon Kibangu in Belgian Congo,[35] had, because of their radical teachings, become sources of concern for the colonial government.[36]

In terms of western education, Christian missionaries monopolized it before the end of World War I. However, after the war colonial governments became involved in providing education, in part by offering grants-in-aid to the churches, and in part by establishing secular elementary and secondary schools. The decision of the colonial governments to establish secular elementary and secondary schools or to become involved in providing education was tied to the criticism of missionary education which was more bent on emphasizing prayers than on emphasizing reading, writing, and arithmetic. It was also tied to the demands of an increasingly number of African elites who gradually recognized that western education was a means for social and political advancement. While the schools established by 1940 were attended by a relatively few African children, they helped to train independent African leaders like Obafemi Awolowo and Julius Nyerere.

In areas where Muslims predominated, European powers often recognized and supported Muslim leaders in order to not cause social dislocation. The support for these Muslims allowed them to use state resources to help promote the spread of Islam. It is also evident that other factors such as the local perception that Islam was an "African" religion favored its expansion during the period. Moreover, available evidence indicate that an unintended consequence of colonial rule was the spread of Islam into new areas such as the Christian dominated forest and coastal

---

34 Alice L. Conklin, *A Mission to Civilize: Republican Idea of Empire in France and West Africa, 1895 – 1930* (Carlifornia: Stanford University Press, 1997) 175.
35 Opoku, "Religion in Africa," 530 – 31.
36 Bengt Sundkler and Christopher Steed, *A History of the Church in Africa* (Cambridge: Cambridge University press, 2004),637, 643; K. Asare Opoku, "Religion in Africa During Colonial Era," in *Unesco General History,* ed.A. A. Boahen,526.

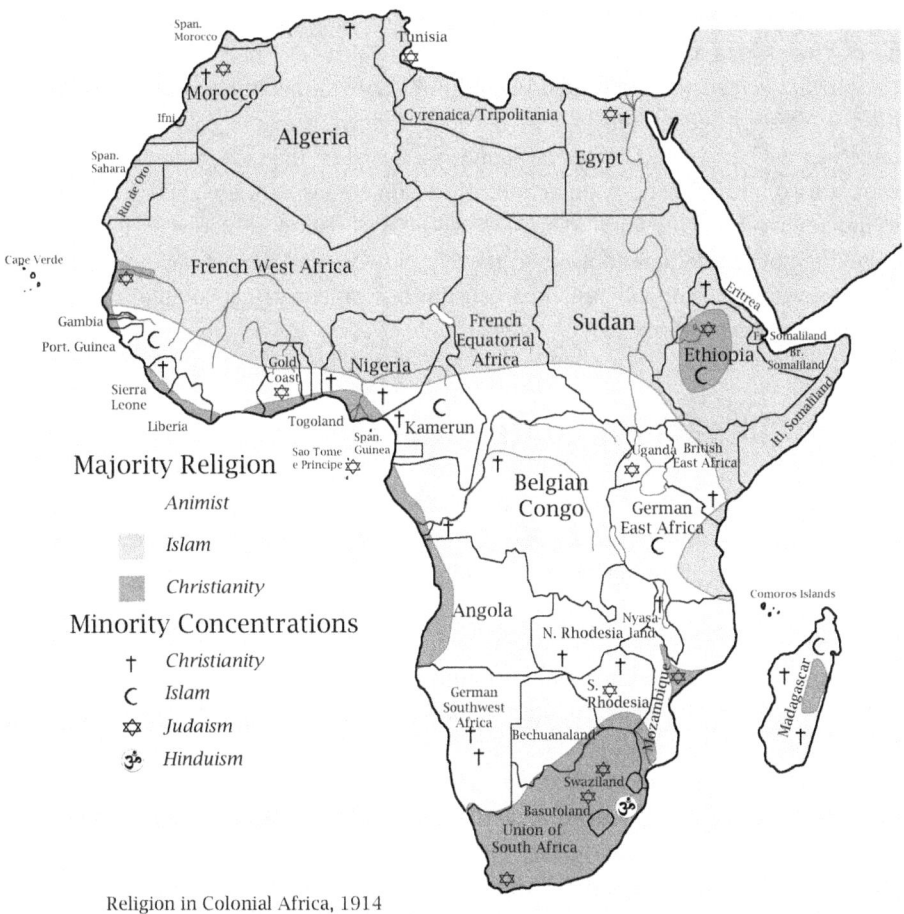

Map 5: Religion in Colonial Africa, 1914. © Toyin Falola.

regions of West Africa. The spread of Islam to these regions is partly tied to the reorientation of trade from the Sahara to the coast and the efforts of Muslim preachers who took advantage of this reorientation to penetrate into areas hitherto unexplored. That the Muslims were Africans, without the superiority complex of the Christian missionaries helped the spread of Islam. For example, the Ilorins played important roles in deepening Islam among the Yoruba and around the Niger Benue confluence partly because of their favorable attitude towards indigenous social and cultural practices like polygamy.[37] In similar ways were the Dyula and Hausa traders influential in the spread of Islam into hitherto unreached areas, often disregarding colonial

---

[37] Aliyu Sakariyau Alabi, "Transmission of Learning in Modern Ilorin: A History of Islamic Education 1897–2012," (PhD thesis Universiteit Leiden, 2015), 3.

boundaries.³⁸ In Senegal, the Sufi brotherhood flourished, their influence reaching all of West Africa and beyond.³⁹

Muslim societies often lagged behind their Christian counterparts in the acquisition of western education, in part because education in the colonial period was largely in the hands of Christian missionaries. Based on the recognition that Muslims were wary of Christianity, colonial authorities sometimes partnered with key Muslims to provide western education to Muslims without Christian influence.⁴⁰ However, despite attempts by colonial powers to partner with Muslims, most Muslims were dissatisfied with colonial policies. Thus, Muslim resistance against colonial rule spread in several parts of Africa.

African Impact on Continental Europe

While Europe influenced Africa's political and economic fortunes, subaltern Africa also had visible influence on Europe. For example, Africa shaped the development of modern European architecture in a subtle yet important way. At the beginning of the twentieth century the modern movement in architecture in Europe was characterised by a formal code, incorporating various technological advances from the industrial revolution. The movement found new solutions to stylistic debates that had bothered art critics and architects alike. The modern movement meant a retreat from established historical styles, and it involved a sort of boredom with formality. A desire of the promoters of this movement was to engender a global phenomenon, thus, as Pedro Jiménex-Vicario *et al* have shown, they incorporated architectural ideas from Africa, particularly vernacular architectural styles of North Africa and Middle East.⁴¹ Vernacular architecture thus played an important role in the new language the architects developed partly as solutions to the problems European shave brought on Europe through the belligerency of war..

In a similar, if obtuse way, the practice of deportation embraced by the Italians in colonial Africa also allowed Africans to shape developments in parts of Europe. From 1911 to 1943 when its colonial empire in Africa ended, Italy was the only colo-

---

38 Sundkler and Steed, *A History of the Church*. 649.
39 For the spread of Islam among the Yoruba see G.T.O Gbadamosi, *The Growth of Islam Among the Yorubas 1841–1908* (London: Longman Group Limited, 1978) and Alabi, "Transmission of Learning" for the spread of Islam around the Niger Benue confluence see, Ahmed Rufai Mohammed, *History of the Spread of Islam in the Niger-Benue Confluence Area: Igalaland, Ebiraland and Lokoja c.1900–1960* (Ibadan: University Press,2014) and on the Tijjaniyya in Senegal see Rüdiger Seesemann, *The Divine Flood Ibrahim Niasse and the Roots of a Twentieth-Century Sufi Revival* (Oxford: Oxford University Press, 2011).
40 Sundkler and Steed, *A History of the Church*. 644, 647, 651–54.
41 Pedro Miguel Jiménez-Vicario, Pedro García-Martínez & Manuel Alejandro Ródenas-López "The Influence of North African and Middle Eastern Architectures in the Birth and Development of Modern Architecture in Central Europe (1898–1937),"*Mediterranean Historical Review* 33, 2 (2018): 179–198.

nial power that was deporting in large numbers of its colonial subjects to its metropole as a punitive measure against resistance to colonialism by Libyans. The Libyans organized resistance in coalition with the Turks as soon as the Italians occupied their land. Undoubtedly, deportation was intended to intimidate the colonial population, but it was also an indication of its weakness as a colonial power. During World War I deportation to Italy increased, and, in this context, Libyans were mostly taken to prisons and penal colonies in Sicily and the province of Syracuse. The presence of Libyans in Italy in some respect shaped the Italian condition. Indeed, their presence resulted in sexual relationships between deported Africans and Italians. At a point the presence of *askaris* in Italy caused conflict with the local population especially as the social norms in Italy between the coloniser and colonised was different with those of the colony; particularly, in relations between 'black' men and 'white' women. As a result of such conflict, the Italian authorities decided on bringing the *askaris* and their family to Italy rather than bringing them as single persons.[42]

It is evident that the Italian authority of the fascist regime had greater regard of the Libyan nobles exiled in Italy, particularly the *zawia* chiefs, who were allowed to come with their families. A notable example is Hassan Reda es-Sanussi who was exiled to Ustica in 1930 but had to be transferred to Tremiti in 1931 because of his excessive familiarity with many families in Ustica. In particular, a notable of Ustica had promised him his daughter upon payment of half a million lira as dowry. Whether or not es-Sanussi ultimately married an Italian, the encounter of Libyans and Italians, particularly interracial sexual relationships, disrupted the social norms that were supposed to govern Italy and its relations with its colonial subjects. However, for Africans in Italy, it allowed them to doubt the superiority claims of Europeans.[43]

In addition to architecture and immigration platforms, empire exhibitions were other platforms through which Africans shaped developments in Europe. African personalities featured in such imperial exhibitions as objects of study and intellectuals especially in Britain and France. Accordingly, in focusing on empire exhibitions in these two European countries, what follows stresses that whether as objects of study or intellectuals, Africans made conversations about such issues as empire, Pan-Africanism, and Garveyism possible in Europe and they also participated in framing relevant conversations.

After World War I, both Britain and France, the two major colonial powers, sought to inculcate a feeling of imperial citizenship and camaraderie in their colonies, and one of the ways they did this was through organizing empire exhibitions. The British held its empire exhibition in 1924–25 in north London suburb of Wembley. It was held to celebrate imperial contributions to the British war efforts and display the promises of an imperial future. The organisers also hoped the exhibition

---

42 Francesca de Pasquale, "The 'other' at Home: Deportation and Transportation of Libyans to Italy During the Colonial Era (1911–1943),"*IRSH 63 Special Issue* (2018):211–31.
43 Pasquale, "The 'other' at Home." 229.

would help address the problems of Britain and its empire in the post-war years. These problems were variously conceived as the loss of European markets, the "uneven distribution of the white population among the territories of the British Empire," industrial and commercial competition from Japan and the United States, raw material shortages, the "imbalance of the sexes" resulting in Britain from the war, "obstructionism," in India, the "yellow peril," and new military rivalries.[44] The exhibition favored the expression of ideas on relevant exhibition themes by African participants. Moreover, with strong West African representations, the exhibition showed the irreconcilable contradictions of power relations in a period of accelerating change and globalisations.[45] Intended to promote imperial loyalty, many educated Africans who visited the exhibition interpreted it differently from the organisers and began making contact with the international movements of Pan Africanism and Garveyism, with consequences for the future relations between Britain and her colonies.[46]

Many African participants who attended the exhibition faced problems of accommodation due to hotel colour bar rules. Thus, as the exhibition progressed, British claims to liberality, imperial citizenship, and capacity to modernise its colonies would be challenged by journalists and public audiences who visited the West African pavilion.[47] African intellectuals were not happy at the absence of Africans in the planning of an event they were to be exhibited. Some argued that Africans are past the age they would be exhibited as curios. After sometime, West African craft workers in the exhibition rebelled and refused to be photographed. The exhibition itself was part of the series of event that inspired the formation of West African Student Union (WASU) in 1925, the students having met many West African notables who came for the exhibition and together with the students held discussions about the future of West Africa.[48] In trying to create a 'United Empire' the exhibition projected ideas of white racial superiority and masculine power, but these sparked reactions from colonised West Africans that eventually led to the break of the Empire through anti-colonial independence movement.

In 1930, the French held their own Paris Colonial Exposition for metropolitan, imperial, and international audiences. It attracted millions of visitors and roused public interest in the colonies. It also led to wide debates about French colonialism and counter demonstrations by colonial subjects in the metropole. The French Communist party organised a parallel exhibition, tagged "The truth of the colonies." Migrations after World War One and the growing passion for black culture transformed

---

44 Daniel Mark Stephen, "'White Man's' Grave: British West Africa and the British Empire Exhibition of 1924–1925,"*Journal of British Studies*, 48, 1 (Jan., 2009): 103.
45 Stephen, "'White man's' Grave," 103.
46 Hakim Adi, *Pan Africanism A History* (London: Bloomsbury Academic, 2018), 28–29; Stephen, "'White man's' Grave," 106.
47 Stephen, "'White man's' Grave," 118.
48 Stephen, "'White man's' Grave," 126.

the imperial metropolis into a centre of global anti-imperialism.[49] The relative freedom enjoyed by the subjects in the metropole and the racism they experienced shaped the development of anti-colonial politics. Sexual relations across racial lines became part of the engine of such anti-colonial politics.[50]

As Africans who travelled from their continent exclusively to attend these empire exhibitions, Africans scholars who were based in Europe were not just passive subjects. They also contributed to anti-colonial activities in Europe as well as to their disciplines, even if their voices were not given prominence due to the power imbalances embedded within the colonial system.[51] African scholars produced groundbreaking scholarship and criticised prominent scholars of the day on political and intellectual grounds. In the 1930s, many Africans and Caribbeans came to Britain as self-conscious British intellectuals, but soon realised their roles as representatives of blacks all over the world in the struggle for colonial reform.[52] They founded platforms such as the West African Student Union (WASU) and League of Coloured People (LCP); centers for cultural and intellectual exchange, and new means for social commentary and political dissent.[53] Their voices were stifled in the face of scepticism by European professionals at best, or hostility at worst. Excluded from mainstream academic publishing, they found outlet in journals and other publications of black organisations. In the correspondences, memoirs, and biographies they produced, we see the contours of a vibrant intellectual counterculture at the heart of the British Empire. Intellectuals such as Eric Williams, Jomo Kenyatta, Alex Atta Yaw Kyerematen, some of whom became leaders of their independent countries in African and the Caribbean were all writing in this context. They wrote within and against the colonial historiography. Taking advantage of their proximity to seat of government and cultural power, they sought to intervene in public and academic discourse on the future of the colonies. Intellectual discourse based on set values and protocols offered a model of relations of reciprocity and co-operations and by which progressive change might be achieved in the Empire.[54]

From the 1930s Africans began to go in the fields of economics, history, anthropology, law, and medicine. Among such Africans were future independent leaders of Africa like Jomo Kenyatta and Nnamdi Azikiwe. Kenyatta received grants to work on his book *Facing Mount Kenya* in the 1930s, supported by Bronislaw Malinowski, the

---

49 Adi, Pan Africanism. 4.
50 Marc Matera, "Introduction: Metropolitan Cultures of Empire and the Long Moment of Decolonisation Cultures of Colonialism in the Metropole," in *Brave New World: Imperial and Democratic Nation-Building in Britain between the Wars* (School of Advanced Study, University of London, Institute of Historical Research 2011),1435–1437.
51 Marc Matera, "Black Intellectuals and the Development of Colonial Studies in Britain," *Journal of British Studies*, 49, 2 (April 2010):388–418.
52 Hakeem Adi, 'Pan-Africanism and West African Nationalism in Britain,' *African Studies Review* 43,1 (2000): 69–82.
53 Matera, "Black Intellectuals,"389.
54 Matera, "Black Intellectuals," 390.

prominent Chair of anthropology at the London school of Economics. In their writings on West African history, Azikiwe and Ladipo Solanke challenged the notion of intractable racial difference.[55] The importance of the African scholars began to felt in the academia as acknowledged by Malinowski, who said that "the literature produced by the educated Africans…constitute a body of evidence on which scientific work by a White anthropologist must sooner or later be undertaken."[56] Malinowski acknowledged that European racism, not the reputedly primitive mind of backward races represented the greatest obstacle to cultural exchange and mixture. Kenyatta and A. A. Y. Kyerematen emphasised the objectivity of their scholarship with the added advantage of insider knowledge.[57]

An important influence on educated Africans was the Pan African movement that was rousing a new confidence and identity among blacks in the America and in the Caribbean. It sought to promote the idea of a united Africa. The influence of Marcus Garvey was important, particularly his call for 'Africa for Africans' and the expulsion of all Europeans, inspired many young educated Africans, many of whom would play important roles in the nationalist movements of the 1940 and 1950s. Around this period French-speaking writers from West Africa and the Caribbean developed a new sense of black respect known as *negritude*, a clear rejection of the French policy of assimilation. Senegalese poet, Leopold Senghor was an important figure in this movement.[58] Importantly, Pan Africanism provided the rallying point for Africans all over the word against colonialism and its impact went beyond attainment of independence by the nation states created by colonialism.[59]

Conclusion

The period from the beginning of World War I to the beginning of World War II can be regarded as the high period of colonialism when European powers were consolidating their hold on their colonies; a time when granting of independence to the colonies was not on the agenda. Administrative policies of indirect rule and assimilation/association were put to the test in this period with varying degrees of success. European economic policies with their mixed impact were largely geared towards appropriation of surplus from African resources for the benefit of the metropoles, which further increased the socio-economic disparity between Europe and Africa. Martial resistance largely over and despite being the subaltern, the agency of Africans

---

55 Matera, "Black Intellectuals," 393.
56 Bronislaw Malinowski, *The Dynamics of Culture Change: An Inquiry into Race Relations in Africa*. Ed. Phyllis M. Kaberry, (New Haven: Yale University Press, 1946), 58–59.
57 Matera, "Black Intellectuals," 402.
58 Shillington, *History of Africa*, 359.
59 Mark Malisa and Philippa Nhengeze, "Pan Africanism: A Quest for Liberation and the Pursuit of a United Africa," MDPI *Genealogy* 2018.

could be discerned not only in their impacts on the colony but also on the metropoles and the colonial authorities such as their interventions in economic realities in the colonies and intellectual contributions to the study of Africa dominated by European intellectuals. African participation in World War I became part of the demystification of the Europeans. The two major religions of Christianity and Islam expanded in this period, contrary to European design and also impacted Africa, particularly in the field of education.

Africa and Africans made holding empire exhibitions possible in Europe and though Africans were subjects, they were not passive about European hegemony and in a variety of ways challenged and impacted Europe and the world such as can be seen in the appropriation of vernacular architecture from North Africa and as well as interracial sexual relations that subverted colonial assumption of superiority and power relations. Pan Africanism was also an important ways Africans impacted not only Africa but also the world; organising and demanding for better relations between the colonialists and their subjects; the seed of the nationalist movements that won independence for most of Africa were sown in this era. Beyond the dependency lens, this chapter shows ways in which Africa impacted the world from its subaltern position through the agency of Africans.

Abdul Kuba
Chapter 9
Africa and the World Wars

Abstract: This study examines Africa's participation in both the First and the Second World Wars. It compares the war campaigns, African contributions, and the impact of both wars on Africa. This chapter argues that the roles of Africa in the world wars were decisive factors in determining the outcomes and that the course and the outcome of the wars also affected and shaped Africa's social, economic, and political contexts. The chapter draws archival records, mostly kept by the British national archives, military records, and other secondary data that discusses aspects of the world wars.

Keywords: First World War, Second World War, Allied forces, Axis powers, labor.

Introduction

Following the Berlin Conference of 1884/85, Africa was partitioned among major European powers. By the outbreak of the Great War, as World War I was known, the entire continent, except for Liberia and Ethiopia, was practically under the domination of six European powers: Britain, France, Belgium, Portugal, Spain, and Italy. Britain controlled over three million square miles of territories and claimed over fifty million Africans as colonial subjects. France ruled over four million square miles of African territory with over forty million people. The vast territory of Congo was under the domination of tiny Belgium. East and West Africa were under Portuguese control, while the vast majority of Northeast Africa fell under the Italians.[1] Though colonial policies and administration differed from country to country, the primary thrust of acquisition of colonies by the various European powers was to satisfy the metropole's economic interests. In most cases, colonies were often viewed as appendages of the metropolitan country. Therefore, in this context, each African country had no choice but to support its colonizer when rival Europeans waged war against each other beginning in November 1914.[2]

The First and Second World Wars had a tremendous impact on the world and left behind an immense historical memory and an indelible mark on humanity. Although

---

[1] Max Yergan, *Africa in the War*, (New York: Broadway,1900), 1, Anne Samson, *World War I in Africa: The Forgotten Conflict among the European Powers*, International Library of Twentieth Century History (New York: I.B. Tauris & Co. Ltd, 2013), 5.
[2] M. Crowder, "The First World War and Its Consequences in Africa," A. Adu Boahen, ed., *UNESCO General History of Africa, Vol. VII, Abridged Edition: Africa Under Colonial Domination 1880–1935*, Abridged Edition (London: University of California Press, 1990), 283.

https://doi.org/10.1515/9783110678017-010

the root of the wars was in Europe, Africa and Asia were both drawn into the wars by their colonial masters. In spite of the growing literature on the two world wars, none of the works provides a comparative analysis of the two world wars. There have been great deal of works that provide account on the experiences of African soldiers, European soldiers, ordinary Africans, and the general impact of the two wars on the continent.[3] Works like *Africa and the First World War; Fighting for Britain; World War I in Africa: The Forgotten Conflict*, and *Black Shame: African Soldiers in Europe, 1914–1922*, by Melvin E. Page and David Killingray, Anne Samson, and Dick Van Galen Last, respectively, rely heavily on oral interviews to provide account on the experience of Africa in the First World War and how it impacted Africans who served in the military both at home and abroad.[4] Page, for instance, provides case studies of British, German, French, and Belgian colonies. Complementing David Killingray and Richard Rathbone's work, Judith Byfield, Carolyn Brown, Timothy Parsons, and Ahmad Alawad Sikainga's edited work, *Africa and World War II* addressed the significant roles Africans played in the Second World War. Their work reinvigorates and provides a balance to the general history of the Second World War.[5]

Despite the great contributions made by the works discussed above, none of them provide a comparative study of the wars. The purpose of the current work is to study Africa's involvement in both wars by comparing similarities and differences in war campaigns, African contributions to both wars, and the impact of both wars on Africa. Comparing such issues provides insight into how Africa was affected by both wars and Africa's role in the world during the colonial era. Hence, part of the argument of this chapter is that both wars shaped the political, economic and the social dynamics of the African continent.

Africa and the First World War

During World War I, Africa became a major hotspot where European imperialists interests clashed. There were two phases of campaigns in Africa during the war. The

---

[3] David Killingray and Martin Plaut, *Fighting for Britain: African Soldiers in the Second World War*, Reprint edition (Woodbridge: James Currey, 2012), 2. It is notable that examples of such works that focus on the First World War include Hew Strachan, *The First World War in Africa* (New York: Oxford University Press, 2004); and Robert Gaudi, *African Kaiser: General Paul von Lettow-Vorbeck and the Great War in Africa, 1814–1918* (New York, Dutton Caliber, 2017).

[4] Melvin E Page, *Africa and the First World War* (New York: St. Martin's Press, 1987), 2.; David Killingray and Richard Rathbone, eds., *Africa and the Second World War* (Palgrave Macmillan UK, 1986), 1. Anne Samson, *World War I in Africa: The Forgotten Conflict among the European Powers*, International Library of Twentieth Century History (New York: I.B. Tauris & Co. Ltd, 2013), 1. Dick van Galen Last, *Black Shame: African Soldiers in Europe, 1914–1922*, ed. Ralf Futselaar, trans. Marjolijn de Jager, Reprint edition (London: Bloomsbury Publishing, 2016), 1.

[5] Judith Byfield and Carolyn Brown, eds., *Africa and World War II* (New York: Cambridge University Press, 2015), ii.

first phase was short-lived and only lasted for a few weeks as Allied powers made all efforts to ensure that Germany could not utilize its African ports. Immediately after the outbreak of war, the Allied forces occupied Lome in Togo, Duala in Cameroon, and Swakopmund and Luderitz Bay in South West Africa.[6] The campaign in Togoland was the shortest, but it was also one of the essential expeditions embarked by the Allied powers. In Togoland, German's wireless station at Kamina also became the main target of Britain and France. The station served as a medium for which the Germans disseminated information to South America.[7] To end German control of the station or Togoland, the French attacked Kamina from Dahomey, while the British entered Togo's German colony from the Gold Coast. Unable to resist the onslaught from the Allied powers, Major Von Doring, the acting German governor in Togoland, surrendered to the Allied forces on August 26, 1914. This major victory recorded by the Allied forces in Togoland inspired them to attack several other German territories in Africa. Thus, after seizing Togoland, the Allied forces launched a devasting attack against Cameroon on August 15, 1914. By September of that same year, they had destroyed Douala, the German commercial center, and trading port. This center also served as the colonial capital and a powerful wireless station. Moreover, Douala served as a haven for German settlers in the colony.[8] Following the conquest of Douala, the Germans surrendered in another part of Cameroon; Mora, in February 1916.

In southern Africa, Britain's ability to quashed the Boer rebellion played a decisive role in Britain's success over the German South-West African colony. The Boers and the British army had engaged in several confrontations from 1899 to 1902 over the recognition of British imperialism in South Africa. This fracas was finally brought to an end on 31 May 1902 through the signing of the treaty of Vereeniging. The Boers pledged their allegiance to Britain and recognized Britain's annexation of the Transvaal and the Orange Free state.[9] The allegiance of the Boers to the British proved valuable during the First and the Second World Wars, allowing the British to recruit armies from South Africa. These were the troops the British used to attack the German colony in South-West Africa. In this attack, Britain advanced from the coast through the Orange River and Bechuanaland before capturing Windhoek, the German colonial capital, in May 1915. By July 1915, Britain had taken full control of the entire German South-West African colony.

In East and Central Africa, significant battles were fought in German East Africa, Portuguese Mozambique, Northern Rhodesia, British East Africa, the Ugandan Protectorate, and the Belgian Congo. Even though German hostilities with the British

---

[6] Richard Rathbone, "World War I and Africa: Introduction," *Journal of African History* 19, 1 (1978): 408.
[7] Hew Strachan, *The First World War: A New History*, Reissue edition (London: Simon &Schuster, 2014), 13–14.
[8] Strachan, *The First World War*, 16.
[9] Alan Farmer, *Access to History: The Experience of Warfare in Britain: Crimea, Boer and the First World War 1854–1929*, 1st edition (London: Hodder Education Publishers, 2011), 99.

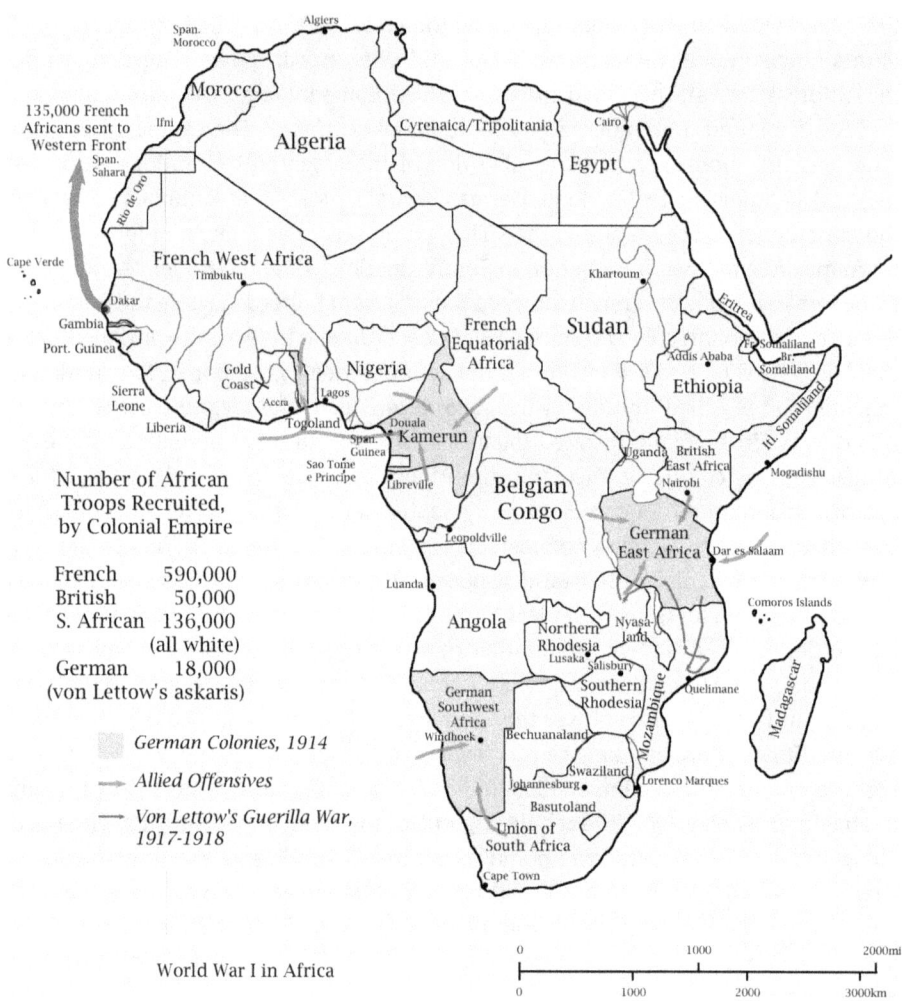

Map 6: World War 1 in Africa. © Toyin Falola.

and the French forces in German East Africa formally ceased after the British bombarded the port of Dar es Salaam in 1916, World War I campaign persisted in East Africa beyond that year. This was partly due to the outstanding leadership of a German Colonel, Paul Emil von Lettow-Vorbeck, who only accepted to surrender in November 1918.[10]

---

10 Crowder, "The First World War and Its Consequences in Africa," 289. Michelle Moyd, "Ordeal and Opportunity: Ending the First World War in Africa," *The Fletcher Forum of World Affairs* 43, 1 (2019): 148.

During the First World War, the French relied heavily on the services of indigenous African soldiers. These soldiers included West African troops, popularly known as Tirailleurs Sénégalais (Senegalese riflemen), Algerians, also known as Turcos and Spahis, Tunisians, Moroccans, Malagasies, and Somalis. Of the estimated two hundred thousand West African soldiers who fought in the war, one hundred and ninety-two thousand were Tirailleurs Sénégalais. Some Africans voluntarily joined the Tirailleurs Sénégalais, while most of them were conscripted into the army. The Tirailleurs Sénégalais were armed by the French to fight against their white enemies in Europe, particularly on the Western Front.[11]

The English, on the other hand, were skeptical of recruiting large numbers of African troops to fight in Europe, but ultimately recruited African forces to fight in African and Middle Eastern campaigns.[12] During the battle of Kamina, Britain relied heavily on the West African Frontier Force (WAFF). This force consisted of people from diverse ethnic groups, including Hausa, Fulani, Yoruba, and Akan from the Northern Territories of the Asante confederacy in the Gold Coast. On August 3, 1914, Major General Dobell, a commander of the West African Frontier Force, drew up brief estimates to deploy the West African Frontier Force in the event of war. General Dobell's main objective was to launch an offensive attack on Lome and Kamina in Togoland and Duala, Buea, and Victoria in the Cameroons.[13] At the outbreak of the war, the commanders (Lt. Col. R. A. De B. Rose, and Mr. W. C. F. Robertson) of the Gold Coast Regiment of the WAFF mobilized forces from Kintampo, Sunyani, Gambaga, Kumasi, Krachi, Zuarungu, and Accra. Most of the forces were camped at Ada. On the morning of August 5, 1914, a telegram was sent from the colonial office announcing the declaration of war. Major General Von Doering, the acting Governor of Togoland, sent the following message to Mr. Robertson:

> As I understand from home, war has broken out between Great Britain and the German Empire. Regarding the insecurity of native tribes, it is in the interest of Togoland and the Gold Coast to omit warlike enterprises likely to have no bearing on decisions arrived at in Europe. Propose further that we remain neutral and would be glad to receive an early reply.[14]

After instructions from London on August 6, Mr. Robertson felt that the Togoland proposal of neutrality could not be honored and thus approved the wireless station's

---

11 Melvin E. Page, "Introduction: Black Man in a Whiteman's War," in, *Africa and the First World War,* ed. Melvin E. Page, (New York: St. Martin's Press, 1987), 4; see also, Dick van Galen Last, *Black Shame*, 1.
12 Colonel A. Clarke Brigadier F. A.S. Haywood, *The History of the Royal West African Frontier Force*, 1st edition (Aldershot: Gale and Polden Ltd, 1964), 104.
13 Haywood, *The History of the Royal West African Frontier Force*, 12; and Bill Nasson, "More Than Just von Lettow-Vorbeck: Sub-Saharan Africa in the First World War," *Geschichte Und Gesellschaft* 40, 2 (2014): 161.
14 De-Valera N. Y. M Botchway, and K. Osei Kwarteng, *Africa and the First World War: Remembrance, Memories and Representations after 100 Years*, (New Castle: Cambridge Scholars Publishing, 2018), 5.

capture at Kamina. The West African Frontier Force (WAFF) fought gallantly to ensure the Allied forces' victory in Kamina.[15] Italy's decision to deploy troops from Libya to fight in Europe, however, proved disastrous. The colonial troops recruited from Libya did not get to the frontline because most troops died from pneumonia in Europe. Those who survived the disease were sent back to Libya. As for Belgium, it also recruited troops from Congo, and it is evident that many of them fought in the Western Front.[16]

In addition to enjoying the support of African troops, European powers obtained funds and resources in support of the war effort from many African societies. For instance, the Gold Coast colony raised funds to assist the Allied forces to meet their expenses during the wars. In one case, J. E. Casely Hayford (founder of the National Congress of British West Africa) helped set up the Sekondi Gold Coast Imperial War Fund. Through this initiative, the Gold Coast people and chiefs successfully raised over G.B. £3700 in December 1914. This amount was eventually transferred to London. In 1915, another G.B. £1500 was raised to purchase an aeroplane to support the British. The Gold Coast alone supported the British government with eleven aeroplanes during the First World War.[17]

While European powers benefitted from Africa's support during the war, the war's impact on the continent was, to a considerable extent, devastating. To be sure, available evidence indicates that villages, farms, and other properties were destroyed in the various battles fought on the continent. Many Africans lost their lives during the war in the midst of combat or due to other factors such as famine (which affected many communities due to the plundering and destruction of farms by soldiers) and diseases.[18] For instance, eighty-three percent of the five thousand soldiers dispatched by Britain, which included battalions from Nigeria and East African troops from the King's African Rifles, who took part in the battle of Mahiwa-Nyangoa during the Eastern Campaign in October 1917, lost their lives. The official death toll of the Allied forces in East Africa (dominantly African troops and civilians) exceeded a hundred and five thousand people. More than forty-five thousand men were obliterated in British East Africa alone. This number constituted almost one-eighth of the adult population of Kenya, Uganda and Zanzibar put together.[19] Casualties in the wars were not limited to the Allied forces and their African troops. The Axis forces also had their share of relevant casualties. For instance, in German East Africa, the plundering of farms by the German colonial troops brought hardship to the Africans and resulted in famine and the death of one-fifth of the population of German

---

15 Botchway and Kwarteng, *Africa and the First World War*, 6.
16 Richard S. Fogarty and David Killingray, "Demobilization in British and French Africa at the End of the First World War," *Journal of Contemporary History* 50, 1 (January 1, 2015): 102.
17 David Kimble, *A Political History of Ghana: The Rise of Gold Coast Nationalism, 1850–1928*, (Oxford: Oxford University Press, 1997), 376.
18 Botchway and Kwarteng, *Africa and the First World War*, xvii.
19 The British Library, "The First World War in East Africa," Accessed September 22, 2020.

East Africa in 1916. Overall, throughout the First World War, civilians were the most endangered group in Africa.[20]

As the war wreaked havoc or led to the death of many in various African societies, a considerable number of European administrative and commercial personnel moved to join the army in the Western Front or enlisted in locally-based regiments for campaigns elsewhere in Africa. This European exodus resulted in administrative and trading vacuums filled by Africans in most parts of Africa, except in Egypt, where the European population expanded due to an influx of British troops using it as a base for the Allied offensive in the Middle East.[21]

Following the commencement of World War I, Africa experienced severe economic disruption. In terms of trade, initially, prices paid for Africa's exports declined while prices of imports rose due to supply shortages. Germany's trading and business interests in Africa were also undermined by the Allied powers, and eventually, Germany ceased to be Africa's major overseas trading partner. Although Africa initially experienced economic depression during the war, the demand for products needed to boost Allied war efforts such as cotton soon led to a boom, which did not necessarily entail increased prices for such items. The prices of exports did not always reflect the increased demand for them. Even the demand was not always reflected in increased wages, as the colonial states often intervened to keep wages low in the economies of African colonies. Such state intervention took different forms, including price control, compulsory cultivation of crops, requisition of food crops, and labor recruitment for essential projects. Such intervention mainly benefitted European establishments.[22]

Wartime demand for African products included the demand for subsistence crops for the feeding of soldiers. In most cases, subsistence crops were either requisitioned or paid at prices below the market price, and this means that many subsistence farmers suffered during the war. In terms of imports, even though relevant shortages undermined agricultural production in places like Egypt, such shortages also fostered the growth of import substation industries in other African societies like South Africa, where European markets' prospects for local products became increasingly recognized.[23] During the war, government revenue diminished considerably. This decline in revenue forced colonial administrators to halt most public works and put aside development plans until after the war. Nevertheless, because of the need to solve the problems associated with moving war supplies, many mines, motorable roads, and ports were either constructed or established. For instance, mines

---

20 Rathbone, "World War I and Africa," 3.
21 M. Crowder, "The First World War and Its Consequences in Africa" in *UNESCO General History of Africa, Vol. VII, Abridged Edition: Africa Under Colonial Domination 1880–1935*, (London: University of California Press, 1990), 289.
22 Crowder, "The First World War and Its Consequences in Africa," 302.
23 Crowder, "The First World War and Its Consequences in Africa," 303.

were opened in the Enugu area of Nigeria during the war to make a local fuel source available for the railways.

The war exposed the Europeans' weaknesses and broke the myth of white supremacy. This gave a boost to nationalist activity and the development of a more critical approach by African educated elites towards their colonial masters. The shared experience of African and European soldiers impacted the lives of ordinary Africans. During the war, African soldiers discovered the strength and weakness of the Europeans, who were initially regarded by majority of Africans as superhumans. African soldiers instructed Europeans on the technique of modern warfare. This was evident that the Europeans were not omniscient. This new knowledge of the Europeans was spread by returning African soldiers and porters. This saw the rise of Africans the demand of their lost sovereignty and increase participation in governance. It was in line with this that the President of the United States, Woodrow Wilson, proposed a fourteen-point program for world peace.[24]

These developments inspired demands for immediate independence in places like Tunisia and Egypt, which encouraged an increasing number of sub-Saharan Africans to demand a more significant say in their affairs. Another factor that encouraged many Africans to demand reforms after the end of the First World War is that many Africans believed that the European powers should reward their loyalty during the war. This neglect on the by the Europeans sparked the sense of nationalism among returning soldiers. While the war inspired African nationalism, it also inspired white nationalism and imperialism.[25] Unlike the Second World War, European powers firmly established their control over their colonies, and even went further to gain more colonial possessions during and after the First World War. Following the defeat of the Germans by the close of 1916, their possession of South-West Africa was taken over by the British, Togoland and Cameroon went to an Anglo-French contingent, and German East Africa fell under the control of British and Belgian troops.[26]

With their control over East Africa, the English secured the right to elect representatives to the Legislative Council in Kenya. By 1918 they formed the majority in government and introduced legislations such as the Crown Lands Ordinance, which made racial segregation in the White Highlands possible, the Native Registration Ordinance, which introduced a pseudo-pass law for Africans, and the Soldier Settlement Scheme which allocated large portions of the Nandi reserve for settlement of white soldiers after the war. These privileges granted to the white community stimulated nationalism among Kenyans.[27]

---

[24] Bethwell A. Ogot, Chapter 13, "Kenya Under the British, 1895 to 1963,' in B. A. Ogot and J. A. Kieran, eds., *Zamani: A Survey of East African History* (Nairobi, Longmans, 1974), 268.
[25] Crowder, "The First World War and Its Consequences in Africa," 305.
[26] W. M. Roger Louis, *Great Britain and Germany's Lost Colonies 1914–1919*, First edition (Oxford, Clarendon Press, 1967), 5.
[27] Crowder, "The First World War and Its Consequences in Africa," 307.

Apart from reactions against the white community's privileges in Kenya, there were numerous revolts and protest movements that took place during the war. Some of these protest movements were directly connected with the war itself. For instance, due to maltreatment they experienced, an army of about fifteen thousand to twenty thousand from the Volta-Bani region (now Burkina Faso) staged an uprising against the French administration between 1915 and 1916.[28] Aside from the resistance staged by African troops, other African societies saw the war as an opportunity to fight for their liberation and express their displeasure against the colonial authorities. Series of protests were staged by both women and religious leaders during the outbreak of World War I. In East Africa, the Giriama led by Mekatilili wa Menza revolted on the early days of the war.[29] The reason behind the Giriama revolt was the unlawful exploitation of their labor and undermining their culture.[30] Although revolts of this nature started in East Africa, they soon spread throughout Zimbabwe, Mozambique, Democratic Republic of Congo, and Uganda.

Africa and the Second World War

Africans' involvement in World War II has also received little scholarly attention. Works like George Howe's *the Mediterranean Theater of Operations* and Gerhard L. Weinberg's *A World at Arms* which incorporate Africa into the grand narrative tend to focus more attention on the activities of the Allied and Axis forces in North and Northwest Africa, than to their war-related activities in other parts of the continent. This is understandable, given that these two regions were sites of campaigns during the war.[31] Good examples of such campaigns took place in Egypt and the Horn of Africa in the mid-1940s. In the early campaigns, Italian forces were the first to launch attacks against Allied nations and their African colonies. Outside of Egypt and the Horn of Africa, an extensive campaign took place in Northwest Africa between 1940 and 1943.

By November 8, 1942, Allied forces were still unable to contain the Axis forces in North Africa. In this context, over a million American soldiers were dispatched to Northwest Africa. These troops from America were part of the Allied expeditionary forces, which consisted of ground, air, and sea units from both the United States

---

28 The British Library, "The First World War in East Africa." Accessed September 22, 2020.
29 Cynthia Brantley, *The Giriama and Colonial Resistance in Kenya, 1800–1920* (Berkley: University of California Press, 1981), 60.
30 A.J. Temu, "The Giriama War, 1914–1915," in *War and Society in Africa*, 1st Edition ed. Bethwell A. Ogot (London: Routledge, 1970), 215–36.
31 Gerhard L. Weinberg, *A World at Arms: A Global History of World War II*, 2nd edition (Cambridge, Cambridge University Press, 2005), 431; George F. Howe, *The Mediterranean Theater of Operations Northwest Africa: Seizing the Initiative in The West* (Office of the Chief of Military History Department of the Army, 1970), 3.

and the British Commonwealth. This was the first large-scale offensive operation embarked by the Allies in North Africa. With 107,000 troops, the Allied powers first invaded Casablanca, Oran, and Algiers. From Algiers, they move eastward to take on the German Africa corps under the command of General Erwin Rommel.[32] After a series of confrontation and battles between the Allied led British-American forces and the Axis forces, the Germans surrendered in May 1943. The outcome of this campaign, which is known as Operation Torch, had a huge psychological boost among the Allies. Ernie Pyle, an American war correspondent in his words, recounted the mood of the Allied forces after the campaign:

> This immense surrender of the Germans had a tremendous boost in the Americans' morale than anything that could have happen to them. Victory in battle is like winning at poker or catching lots of fish...As a result; the hundreds of thousands of Americans in North Africa now are happy men.[33]

The occupation of important parts of French North Africa by Allied forces was well planned and executed. Success from that operation proved to have far more extensive outcome than intended, and it shaped the course of the war in the Mediterranean. After defeating their enemies in Algeria and Morocco, the Allied forces turned their attention to Tunisia. During this time, the disgruntled Rommel, who had been defeated in Operation Torch, gathered enough momentum to attack the Allied line's central station in Tunisia.[34] In this attack, the Axis and Rommel's primary mission was to disintegrate Eisenhower's forces in Western Tunisia. A counterattack from the Allied forces suffered massive loss and was pushed by Rommel and General von Arnim's joint forces to the Kasserine Pass in February 1943. After a series of intense battles, the Axis forces finally surrendered in May 1943.[35] This victory solidified Allied control of the Mediterranean Sea and important coastal regions. The victory in North Africa also provided the Allies forces air and sea supremacy throughout the southern Mediterranean, and it gave them access to the Suez Canal.[36]

Aside from North Africa, other campaigns took place in Africa during the Second World War. In the course of their Horn of Africa or Mediterranean campaign, the Italian troops stationed in Ethiopia invaded British Somaliland in August 1940. Next, they moved westward into Sudan to capture the upper Nile valley. From there, Italian forces moved further southward to seize the British colony of Kenya. In the context of this Italian expansion, the Allied forces, under the command of Lieutenant General

---

[32] Trevor Nevitt Dupuy, *Land Battles, North Africa, Sicily, And Italy: Military History of World War II V3* (Kila: Kessinger Publishing, L.L.C., 2007), 30.
[33] Dupuy, *Land Battles, North Africa, Sicily*, 100.
[34] Daniel R. Mortensen, *A Pattern for Joint Operations: World War II Close Air Support, North Africa* (CreateSpace Independent Publishing Platform, 2015), 70.
[35] "The Naval, Military and Air Situation from noon January 30, to noon February 6, 1941," War Cabinet Weekly Resume (75), The National Archives, February 6, 1941, cab/66/14/48
[36] Howe, *The Mediterranean Theater of Operations Northwest Africa*, 4.

Alan Cunningham engaged the axis forces from Ethiopia. This was despite the fact the Allied forces were numerically disadvantaged, having less than one-third of the strength of Italian forces in East Africa. Altogether, the struggle between the Allied and Axis forces in East Africa was protracted. Even though it started in June 1940, the British successfully brought the East African campaign to an end by November 1941.[37]

Madagascar, located off the coast of East Africa, was also an important theatre of the Second World War. Indeed, largely because it possessed critically important harbors, Allied and Axis forces fought for hegemony over Malagasy in 1942. This 1942 engagements drew South African troops to the battlefield. They supported the Allied powers against the Vichy French, who, in turn, were allies of the Nazi Germans. At the conclusion of the war, the Allied forces and the South Africans succeeded in seizing Madagascar from the Japanese on May 4, 1942.[38]

World War II campaigns in Africa and various parts of the world involved troops from different parts of Africa. Indeed, about two million African soldiers were conscripted into the European armies during the war, with nearly four hundred thousand drafted into the British army by the end of 1945. The Tirailleurs Sénégalais fought again in the Second World War. They played a crucial role in the liberation of the French from German control. African soldiers were the decisive factor in most important battles between the Axis and the Allied powers, especially battles in northern Africa, particularly Libya, Tunisia and Egypt, and East Africa. Similarly, African troops fought in the liberation and seizure of Malagasy from Vichy France in 1943.[39]

Many South Africans provided military service during the Second World War. The Union of South Africa was involved in battles in north Africa against Erwin Rommel and the Afrika Korps. The South African 1st Infantry Division also took part in the Battle of El Alamein before they were withdrawn to South Africa in 1942 to be re-constituted as an armored division.[40] Other South African pilots also joined the Royal Air Force and fought against the Axis forces in the European theatre. They played a significant role in the defeat of Benito Mussolini and his Italian forces during the East African Campaign of 1940–41. The South Africa Air Force, in conjunction with the converted Junkers Ju 86s of 12 Squadron, carried out the first bombing attack at Moyale on June 11, 1940, immediately after Italy's declaration of war.[41] Throughout

---

[37] Howe, *The Mediterranean Theater of Operations Northwest Africa*, 10.
[38] The British National Archives, "Japan Surrenders," (The National Archives, Kew, Surrey TW9 4DU), accessed September 13, 2020.
[39] The Island of Malagasy (now Madagascar) during the Second World War outbreak was under the control of the Vichy French, who were allies of the Nazi Germans. See David Brock Katz, *South Africans versus Rommel: The Untold Story of the Desert War in World War II* (Guilford, Connecticut: Stackpole Books, 2017), 5.
[40] David Killingray and Martin Plaut, *Fighting for Britain: African Soldiers in the Second World War*, Reprint edition (Woodbridge, James Currey, 2012), 130.
[41] Lieutenant Colonel David E., "Early North African Campaigns 1940–1942: A Case Study," USAWC class of 1992, 37.

the various campaigns of the Second World War, the contribution of South Africans consisted of troops, airmen, and material resources.[42]

In Europe and elsewhere, thousands of African soldiers were captured as prisoners of war. In the mid-1945 alone, the British, French and Italians employed over 400,000 African troops. "Overall, Africa contributed nearly one million men to the war, drawn from the British, French, Italian and the Belgian colonies, and South Africa; the total death toll probably exceeds 50,000."[43]

The imperatives of World Wars II led to the increasing demand for African goods and resources. As a result, European powers were forced to intensify their intervention in the lives of ordinary Africans. Colonial intervention included food rationing, price controls, and labor requisition. Requisitioned laborers were used in various sectors deemed essential to the war effort, such as coal mining and rubber production. Ordinary men and women were also mobilized to produce food crops and raw materials such as rice, groundnut, rubber, uranium, and palm oil. It is evident that Allied powers could not have adequately fed their populations and protected their national economies or even successfully prosecuted the war without mobilizing ordinary Africans to produce such goods.[44] On the part of the Axis powers, they also pressured Africans to produce goods and pressed not less than three hundred and fifty thousand Africans into unpaid carrier services. It is notable that even Allied powers employed Africans in such non-combatant capacities during the war. For example, the Senegalese writer and director Ousmane Sembene was conscripted into the French army to serve as a truck driver and later as a chauffeur in Charles de Gaulle's Free French forces.[45]

Aside from the exploitation of African labor to provide food for European soldiers, Africans were also forced to bore their colonial masters' financial burden. Many African countries were made to raise funds to support the course of the war. For instance, through the Nigerian War Fund, Nigerians also raised GB£ 210,999 and purchased aeroplanes to support the Allied forces in 1942.[46]

The Second World War saw a rapid increase in urbanization and a dramatic expansion of cities in many parts of Africa. The expansion of many cities like Freetown was tied to the dramatic increase in the number of goods, soldiers, military equipment, and supplies transported during the war. The expansion of cities in such a context, therefore, created employment opportunities for thousands of Africans. Over time, the number of African city dwellers almost doubled, and by 1946, there were

---

42 Katz, *South Africans versus Rommel*, 10.
43 Timothy Parsons, "Introduction: The Military Experiences of Ordinary Africans in World War II," in *Africa and World War II* Judith eds. Byfield and Carolyn Brown (New York: Cambridge University Press, 2015), 8, David Killingray and Richard Rathbone, eds., *Africa and the Second World War* (Palgrave Macmillan UK, 1986), 14.
44 Botchway and Kwarteng, *Africa and the First World War*, xix–xx.
45 Dennis Laumann, *Colonial Africa: 1884–1994* (New York, Oxford University Press, 2012), 63.
46 Byfield and Brown, *Africa and World War II*, xx.

more African towns and cities compared to white towns and cities. The increasing urbanization experienced during the war, as with the recruitment of African soldiers, disintegrated many families. Millions of those separated from their families were young men and women. Urbanization enabled many of these young people to break away from the gender and age discrimination that was common in rural settings, and it also allowed many of them to evade the authority and control of husbands and elders.[47] However, it is notable that many Africans who moved to the cities during the war lived in squatter communities established on the outskirts of cities such as Johannesburg and Cape Town.

The Second World War fostered sex trade and interracial interaction. While African men who fought outside their homeland developed romantic relationships with non-African women, a considerable number of European, American, and African soldiers in Africa had no option but to embrace commercial sex. This commercial sex was financially rewarding, and it attracted a significant number of women from a diverse background who engaged in prostitution in cities like Accra and Sekondi. The booming sex trade that such women were involved in had social and health repercussions, which, in turn, prompted colonial authority to adopt strict anti-prostitution laws and to check the traffic of women and children across colonial boundaries.

In addition to promoting sex trade and interracial interaction, the war led to the introduction of mass media, particularly radio broadcast, in Africa. This mass media developed due to the need to win colonial subjects' support or the need to disseminate information about the war and military recruitment. Examples of the radio stations that emerged during the Second World War include Radio Omdurman in Sudan and the Abeokuta radio station in Nigeria.[48]

During the war, participation in military campaigns and many colonial policies resulted in hardship for most Africans. For instance, at the end of the war, the delay in repatriating many African troops from Asia, which was caused by a shortage of shipping and racism, inflicted hardship and suffering on such troops. Similarly, the mobilization of African communities to provide labor, food, and other resources contributed to food shortages, flight from villages, and other problems. There was a general increase in the standard of living for all Africans due to the massive increase in consumer goods. Costs of foodstuffs rocketed in both rural and urban markets in West Africa due to the war and its associated environmental problems.[49]

The hardship experienced by most Africans generated resistance, social unrest, and strikes against the colonial governments. Some of the important strikes were carried out in South Africa. For instance, the ones by ports workers. In Johannesburg, urban Black workers demanded better working conditions. They also formed trading

---

[47] Ahmad A. Sikainga, "Conclusion: Consequences of the War," in *Africa and World War II*, ed. by Byfield and Brown, 503.
[48] Sikainga, "Conclusion," 506.
[49] David Killingray & Richard Rathbone, "Introduction" in *Africa and the Second World War* eds. David Killingray and Richard Rathbone (London, Palgrave Macmillan, 1986), 8.

unions that engaged in a series of strikes throughout the 1940s. In 1941 the Council of Non-European Trade Unions (CNETU) was formed. By 1946 with a total number of hundred and fifty-eight thousand members, the CNETU organized one hundred and nineteen unions. The African Mineworkers Union (AMWU) was the most important union among these new trade unions. In 1946 the AMWU agitated for an increase in their wages in the gold mines and succeeded in getting sixty thousand workers to boycott work in the mines. The colonial police crushed the strike that left twelve dead, but it demonstrated the potential strength of organized black workers in challenging the labor system.[50]

The experience of the war and its aftermath encouraged not only strikes but also encouraged countless African men and women who served in various capacities in the war, like Ousmane Sembene, to participate in anti-colonial politics.[51] In general, soldiers who fought on the sides of the Allied and the Axis powers in the two wars were ill-treated. They were kept separate from their white comrades, except when they operated in mixed regiments for united actions at the front. The *Tirailleurs Sénégalais* who fought on the side of the French in both the First and Second World Wars were often humiliated by inexperienced white officers who assumed that the only way to instill discipline in black soldiers was beating. Black soldiers who fought for the British were also tormented and humiliated to uphold the color divide. This experience left permanent scars in the minds of the many soldiers.[52] Indeed, it was such war experiences of Sembene and other African troops that shaped their perspective in a significant manner and that encouraged them to embrace the anti-colonial struggle.

Even though the war experience and its aftermath also urged the European powers to implement various measures aimed at stabilizing their African economies, it did not allow for self-determination or the ending of colonial rule. Thus, European powers worked hard to preserve their empires during and immediately after the war. To preserve their empire, the French sought to enhance the unity of its empire by offering some responsibilities to educated Africans while the British sought to integrate Africans into local governments before gradually allowing some form of self-government within the commonwealth.[53] Interestingly, such attempts to preserve the empires at the same time facilitated interactions between Africans and Africans in the diaspora as well as interaction among Africans. Capitalizing on increasing cross-cultural exchanges and connections, African nationalists, labor movements, peasants, and other social forces increasingly demanded full rights and self-determi-

---

50 Louis Grundlingh, "The Recruitment of South African Blacks for Participation in the Second World War," in *Africa and the Second World War* eds. David Killingray and Richard Rathbone (London, Palgrave Macmillan, 1986), 192–194.
51 Byfield and Brown, *Africa and World War II*, xx.
52 Dick van Galen Last, *Black Shame*, 75–77.
53 Sikainga, "Conclusion," 507.

nation.⁵⁴ The drive to end colonial rule was heightened following the end of the Second World War, and it was championed by "broad-based, better-organized, and politically sophisticated movements."⁵⁵ These movements ultimately ensured that European powers relinquished power beginning in the 1950s.⁵⁶

Conclusion

This chapter has explored the pivotal role of Africa in the two world wars. Though the roots of the wars were in Europe, Africans involvement in the wars was unprecedented. As colonies of European powers, Africa and its ordinary population were directly and indirectly drawn into the war. The continent provided both military and nonmilitary services in the wars and acted as life-support for both the Allied and the Axis powers by producing food to feed both sides. The continent was also tasked with providing financial support and other war logistics, such as airplanes, in both conflicts. Africa's involvement in the war was crucial in shaping the outcome of the two major conflicts in the twentieth century.⁵⁷

Despite the importance of the European powers, for the most part, the wars had a devastating effect on Africans. The uprooting of men and women to provide services in the wars disintegrated African families and communities and placing the burden of family sustainability on one member of the family. This impacted productivity, which led to famine and the eventual loss of lives in the continent. Aside from economic hardship, the wars had a severe demographic impact on Africa. More than thousands of Africans lost their lives in various war campaigns. Epidemiologically, more than one hundred thousand Africans lost their lives through the 1918 influenza pandemic.⁵⁸ The wars also increased vices in African societies. World War II, for instance, fostered prostitution in urban centers in Africa and Europe due to the massive movement of Africans from rural areas to the urban centers and abroad.

Through the hardship experienced by Africans due to their participation in the wars, nationalistic fervor was rekindled starting from the beginning of the First World War to the aftermath of the Second World War. Africans resisted the inhumane treatment and the unfulfilled promises of the Europeans. There was also the break of the white supremacy myth through the interaction between African soldiers and their European counterparts at the war front. The wars encouraged a sense of self-deter-

---

54 Sikainga, "Conclusion," 506–507.
55 Sikainga, "Conclusion," 508.
56 The National Archives, "Protectorate and Trusteeship" (The National Archives, Kew, Surrey), accessed September 10, 2020.
57 Judith Byfield and Carolyn Brown, eds., *Africa and World War II*, (New York: Cambridge University Press, 2015), xix–xx.
58 Kwame O. Kwarteng and Stephen Osei-Owusu, "The Influenza Pandemic in the Gold Coast and Asante, 1918–1919," cited in Botchway and Kwarteng, *Africa and the First World War*, 145–46.

mination and the desire for self-rule among Africans. Although most of the resistance after the First World War was geared toward achieving some political, economic, and social reforms, they served as foundations for those after the Second World War, eventually leading to Africans' liberation from colonial rule beginning from the 1950s.

The effect and the impact of the wars on Africa reveals how the wars were as much an African war as a European war. The period of the First and the Second World War should not be considered "a Eurocentric time capsule," which were artificially introduced to the African context, but rather, they were fundamental in shaping the history of Africa.[59]

---

[59] Rathbone, "World War I and Africa," 1–9.

Ajibola A. Abdulrahman
Chapter 10
Nationalism and Decolonization in Africa, 1918–1975

Abstract: This chapter focuses on anti-colonial activities in Africa between 1918–1975. It demonstrates that nationalism grew significantly from the interwar years and became extremely militant between 1945 and 1975. In addition to emphasizing that the extreme militant nature of African nationalism after the Second World War was partly tied to the anti-colonial attitudes or activities of the United Nations, the United States of America, the USSR and other global forces, this chapter stresses the grievances of Africans from diverse backgrounds and the colonial policies that helped shaped the development and nature of African nationalism in the study period.

Keywords: Colonialism, Nationalism, Pan-Africanism, Decolonization, African Independence.

Introduction

Nationalism is not a simple word. Its meaning is not always clear. For instance, earliest scholars viewed nationalism as all strategies aimed at homogenizing a population in order to create a common identity attached to an autonomous nation state; Marxist writers define nationalism as a struggle against feudalism or imperialism, and other scholars associate nationalism with ethnicism.[1] While the different definitions of nationalism offered by non-Africanist scholars are important, some Africanist scholars argue that the meaning of nationalism can best be seen in terms that are relative to the African context and culture. For such scholars, nationalism is an ideology embraced by Africans for the attainment of a political objective that could be state/nation-centered, ethnic, pan-Africanist, anti-colonial, and the like.[2] As Freder-

---

1 For different definitions of nationalism see, for instance, E. Gellner, *Nations and Nationalism* (Oxford, Basil Blackwell Ltd., 1983); Anthony D. Smith, *Theories of Nationalism* (London, Duckworth, 1983); Louis L. Snyder, *Dynamics of Nationalism* (Princeton, NJ: Van Nostrand, 1964); and Paul R. Brass, *Ethnicity and Nationalsim: Theory and Practice* (New Delhi, Sage, 1994);
2 Important works by Africanist scholars that have shaped my thinking on the meaning and nature of nationalism include T. O. Ranger, "African Reactions to the Imposition of Colonial Rule in East and Central Africa," in *Colonialism in Africa, 1870–1960* vol. 1, edited by L. H. Gann and P. Duignan (Cambridge, Cambridge University Press, 1969), 293–324; T. O. Ranger, "Connexions between 'Primary Resistance' Movements and Modern Mass Nationalism in East and Central Africa," *Journal of African History* 9, 3 and 4 (1968); 437–453, 631–641; Ali Mazrui and Michael Tidy, *Nationalism and New States*

ick Cooper has pointed out, "the objectives of African political activists were not limited to creating independent states as expressions of a particular national sentiment ... some sought a pan-African nation embracing oppressed people of color wherever they lived, others thought they could transform colonial rule into a Euro-African community stripped of inequality and exploitation."[3] I am convinced that nationalism is constructed and that the objectives that have aroused nationalistic aspirations in Africa, in the period between 1918 and 1975, are diverse. Based on such convictions, I will follow these Africanist scholars and include in my definition and analysis all forms of nationalisms that were evident in the context of this period.

Although nationalism emerged in Africa in the late nineteenth century in response to European expansion and conquest, it grew significantly during the interwar years and became militant between 1945 and 1975. The scholarly literature on this period of nationalism has been a metanarrative of the nationalist triumph, focusing on the nationalists, most of whom were educated elites who challenged the colonial state and became leaders of their countries after securing independence. This narrative privileges the educated elite as the drivers behind the mass movements, as the "geniuses" who "mobilized the masses" from trade unions, war veterans, market women associations, and rural peasants to launch attacks against the "common enemies," *racist* and *exploitative* tendencies of the *European* colonial state. The nationalist triumph narrative ignores the individuals and groups who comprised the masses, framing them as passive recipients of nationalist and anti-colonial messages directed by the educated elites. Although the revolutionary narrative articulated by Frantz Fanon rejects the "anti-colonialism of western-educated intellectuals," scholarly literature continues to ignore the role of peasants, wage workers, and women as *performers* of African nationalism with specific grievances, distinct from those elites who emerged as the faces of liberation.[4]

One of the scholars who pays little attention to the role of women in organising anti-colonial activities in Africa or who ignored the roles of several grassroot movements in the organization of anti-colonial activities in his analysis, Frederick Cooper, also provides a social meaning of decolonization in the sense that he insists that independence was granted to African societies only after post-war development strategies failed or only after the European powers realized that the cost of social improvement outweighed any particular benefit.[5] While this chapter does not dispute that decision making in Europe shaped decolonization in Africa, it does not seek to emphasize the primacy of such European decision making in African decoloniza-

---

in Africa: From 1935 to the Present (Nairobi, Heinemann, 1984); and Frederick Cooper, *Decolonization and African Society* (New York, Cambridge University Press, 1996).
3 Fredrick Cooper, "Decolonization in Tropical Africa," in *The Oxford Handbook of the Ends of Empire* edited by Martin Thomas and Andrew S. Thompson (Oxford, Oxford University Press, 2018), 317.
4 See Elizabeth Schmidt, *Mobilizing the Masses: Gender, Ethnicity and Class in the Nationalist Movement in Guinea, 1939–1958* (Portsmouth, NH: Heinemann, 2005), 1–10.
5 Cooper, *Decolonization and African Society*, 451–453.

tion. Rather, in response to the aforementioned omission, this chapter emphasizes the role of many anti-colonial groups in the development of African nationalism.[6] The chapter is divided into three sections. The first section focuses on nationalism during the interwar period, the second section deals with African Nationalism in the period between 1939–1960s, and the third section focuses on the liberation movements that took place in 1960–1970s.[7]

Nationalism during the Interwar Period

The interwar period was one in which the European powers consolidated their rule in Africa. By this time, Africa had been divided into clearly identified colonies by the European powers. However, within each colony, nationalism developed even before the Second World War. The development of nationalism in Africa during the interwar period was shaped by European colonial policies and by the global Pan-Africanist movement.

Colonial policies were influenced by many factors including local economic conditions, local political activities, European interests, and other international factors. By 1918, policies regarding land, labor, taxation, European immigration, and such other issues were established in most, if not all, African societies. Since the colonial powers insisted that the costs of development and administration in Africa should be met out of local revenues derived from taxation, forced labor, and duties on trade, these colonial policies resulted in land alienation and such other oppressive experiences for most Africans. As a result of land alienation, taxation, and other colonial policies including labor, there were series of labor related strike actions, protest and riots in Africa.[8] In Nigeria in particular, the planned imposition of the direct taxation on women provoked serious protests that culminated in the popular 1929 Aba Women riot.

Even though African resistance was a factor after the First World War, new forms of African resistance had developed by the 1930s. One key influence on African resistance and nationalism was the Great Depression, which crippled the world economy after 1929. In addition to undermining many European economies, the Great Depression also reduced international demand for African products, which in turn forced African farmers to increase production, and this led to the fall in the price

---

[6] A good example of works that stress such a perspective is Fredrick Cooper, "Decolonization in Tropical Africa," *The Oxford Handbook of the Ends of Empire* (2018): 1–20.

[7] Some scholars have extended the decolonization period to 1994 when the Apartheid ended in South Africa. For this interpretation see, for instance, Cooper, "Decolonization in Tropical Africa," 1–20.

[8] Frankema, Ewout, "Colonial Taxation and Government Spending in British Africa, 1880–1940: Maximizing Revenue or Minimizing Effort?, *Explorations in Economic History*, 48, Iss 1, (2011): 136–149.

of goods produced within Africa. Given that falling prices greatly reduced the taxation revenue of colonial governments, colonial administrators were forced to cut down on developmental projects, salaries, and manpower.[9] They also increased direct taxation. In this context, the conditions of most Africans worsened, and they resorted to new forms of resistance including forming associations and political organizations to address specific grievances and embarking on gender-based or rural-based protests.

For instance, educated African elites formed the National Congress for British West Africa (NCBWA) to challenge discriminations and injustices in British West Africa. Among other demands, NCBWA called for access to higher education, "more and better effective representation of [Africans]," and end of the discrimination against Africans in the civil service. NCBWA collaborated with diasporic pan-African organizations such as the West African Students Union (WASU) to challenge colonial injustices in Africa. Although these movements were more pan-West-African, NCBWA encouraged the formation of nationalist political parties, and it was connected to such parties in many colonies. For instance, Herbert Macaulay's Nigerian National Democratic Party (NNDP) shared "some connection in co-operation, programme and ultimate objective" with the NCBWA, particularly the call for Africanization of the civil service. More significantly, NCBWA inspired the later brand of radical nationalism after World War II.[10]

Although most political parties formed before 1945 were established by men, women also formed political movements. For instance, led by Funmilayo Ransome-Kuti, women established the Federation of Nigerian Women's Societies (FNWS] in 1953. FNSW had its origins in the Abeokuta Ladies Club (ALC) which was formed in 1932. In order to accommodate the market women who were mostly illiterate and improvised but exploited by the colonial authorities, ALC changed its names to Abeokuta Women's Union in 1946, Nigerian Women's Union in 1949 and eventually FNWS in 1953.[11] Like several women's organizations in different colonies in Africa, FNWS was formed in the context of nationalism, as an independent womens organization

---

9 See Moses Ochonu, *Colonial Meltdown, Northern Nigeria in the Great Depression* (Athens: Ohio University Press, 2009); O. N. Njoku, "Trading with the Metropolis: an Unequal Exchange" in *Britain and Nigeria, Exploitation or Development?* ed. by Toyin Falola (London: Zed Books, 1987), 124–41; See Sara S. Berry, *Cocoa Custom and Socio-economic Changes in Rural Western Nigeria* (Oxford: Clarendon Press, 1975).
10 G.I.C. Eluwa, "The National Congress of British West Africa: a Study in African Nationalism," *Présence Africaine, Nouvelle Série* 77 1er TRIMESTRE (1971): 140–148; G. O. Olusanya, "The Lagos Branch of the National Congress of British West Africa," *Journal of the Historical Society of Nigeria*, 4, 2 (June 1968), 321–333.
11 The Editors of Encyclopaedia Britannica, "Funmilayo Ransome-Kuti Nigerian Feminist and Political Leader" https://www.britannica.com/biography/Funmilayo-Ransome-Kuti#ref1197020

"ready to co-operate and support any political party that works for the uplift and progress of womanhood and for the happiness of Nigerian citizens as a whole."[12]

Similarly, Africans used newspapers and independent African churches to express their grievances. African-owned Newspapers such as *Kwetu* in Tanganyika, Nnamdi Azikiwe's *West Africa Pilot* in Nigeria, *Sekanyolya,* and *Munyonyozi* in Kenya, among others, all disseminated the grievances against colonial rule. They played a significant role in cultivating African resistance to European rule since they served as the "most potent instrument used in the propagation of nationalist ideas and racial consciousness."[13] Independent African Churches also shaped the development of African nationalism. The Kimbanguist Church, which emerged in response to European missionaries' sense of superiority and reluctance to serve under African bishops in Belgian Congo, is a good example.[14] Named after its founder Simon Kimbangu, Kimbanguist church was partly inspired by global garveyism.[15] In resisting the colonial rule, the Kimbanguists not only declined to grow export crops for colonial government, they also refused to pay taxes to the government. Together, political parties and newspapers as well as African independent churches provided platforms for Africans to challenge racial discrimination and to express other grievances against the colonial rule, even as this served as a background to radical nationalism after World War II.

It is significant that many Africans who formed religious and such other associations that sought to address specific grievances during the interwar years benefitted from colonial educational and such other policies, and they probably would not have had much influence in the development of African nationalism without enjoying such benefits. In a sense, therefore, African nationalism did not only develop as a reaction to the aforementioned colonial policies but also because of them.[16]

Other roots of nationalism or African resistance in the interwar years can be traced to the Pan-Africanist movement. Pan-Africanism as an ideology and a cultural or racial movement ironically originated not from continental Africa, but from among

---

12 Joyce M. Chadya "Mother Politics: Anti-colonial Nationalism and the Woman Question in Africa," *Journal of Women's History* 15, 3 (2003):153–57; Also See Cheryl Johnson-Odim and N. E. Mba, *For Women and the Nation: Funmilayo Ransome Kuti of Nigeria* (Chicago: University of Illinois Press, 1977).
13 James S. Coleman, "Nationalism in Tropical Africa," *The American Political Science Review*, 48, 2, (June 1954): 404–26; James F. Scotton, "The First African Press in East Africa: Protest and Nationalism in Uganda in the 1920s," *The International Journal of African Historical Studies*, 6, 2 (1973): 211–28; Emma Hunter, *Political Thought and the Public Sphere in Tanzania: Freedom, Democracy and Citizenship in the Era of Decolonization.* (Cambridge: Cambridge University Press, 2015), 37.
14 See Robert W. July, *The Origins of Modern African Thought: Its Development in West Africa during the Nineteenth and Twentieth Centuries* (New York: Fredrick A. Praeger, 1967).
15 Adam Ewing, "Kimbanguism, Garveyism, and Rebellious Rumor Making in Post-World War I Africa," *A Critical Journal of Black Politics, Culture, and Society*, 20, no. 2, (2018): 149–177.
16 See Toyin Falola, *Nationalism and African Intellectuals* (Rochester: University of Rochester Press, 2004).

people of African descent in the Caribbean and North America. The goals of pan-Africanism included the unity of the people of African descents all over the world to improve their lives. The first Pan-Africanists included people like Marcus Garvey who founded the Universal Negro Improvement Association (UNIA), a Black Nationalist organization that organized people of African descent in the diaspora prior to World War I. After its emergence, the Pan-African movement influenced continental Africans that sought education in the United Kingdom and the United States. In these western societies, various Pan-African organizations were formed during the interwar years including the Ethiopia Association (EA), Ethiopian Progressive Association (EPA), Nigerian Progress Union (NPU), and the West African Student Union (WASU). WASU also incorporated students from other colonies in Africa and the Caribbean studying in the United Kingdom. Although WASU was formed to address various challenges facing West African Students in the United Kingdom such as hostels and accommodations, WASU was an avenue for the promotion of African nationalism.[17]

Another vibrant Pan-African organization established in the United States in the 1930s was the Universal Ethiopian Students Association (UESA). Like those before it, UESA attracted African and African American members, the majority of these members, including Nnamdi Azikiwe, were former Garveyites. Through the UESA journal *The African: the Journal of African Affairs*, Pan-Africanists and African activists all over the World found a platform to articulate ideas, address common concerns, and challenge global racism and colonialism in Africa.[18] UESA developed in the context of the Italian invasion of Ethiopia and the failures of the League of Nations and western powers to prevent the invasion. This invasion of Ethiopia, which took place from 1935 to 1936, mobilized pan-African sentiments which, in turn, encouraged the formation of another major organization known as the Pan-African Federation (PAF). As the UESA, PAF became committed not only to the total liberation of Ethiopia but also to the ending of colonialism in Africa.

Even though PAF and UESA eventually became committed to the ending of colonial rule in Africa, earlier Pan-Africanists were less concerned with actualizing this goal than with the reform of the colonial system. Indeed, those who attended the first Pan-Africanist conference organized in 1910 by Henry Sylvester-Williams and the subsequent ones organized by W. E. B. Du Bois in 1919 and 1927 were not committed to ending colonial rule in Africa. Overall, partly based on this fact, African resistance had a limited impact before the Second World War.

---

17 WASU collaborated with African nationalists such as Casely Hayford.
18 Keisha N Blain, *Set the World on Fire, Black Nationalist Women and the Global Struggle for Freedom* (Philadelphia: University of Pennsylvania Press, 2018), 161; Hillina Seife, "A New Generation of Ethiopianists: The Universal Ethiopian Students Association and The African: Journal of African Affairs, 1937–1948," *African and Black Diaspora: An International Journal* 3, no. 2 (2010): 197–209.

African Nationalism in the Period Between 1939 – 1960s

During World War II, Ethiopia and North Africa became theatres of war. A significant number of African troops were recruited to fight in the global conflict. Most of them either died or experienced extensive physical suffering. The war also increased the demand for more African commodities. This increased demand and other related factors led to increased reliance on forced labor, the establishment of marketing boards, intensified unequal exchanges between Africa and Europe, and heavier demands on Africans than ever before. For many Africans, these demands and related wartime government policies meant the destruction of families and social structures, increased suffering in workplaces, lower living standards, forced migration to cities, and a host of other challenges. The hardships of war encouraged many Africans to seek political reform.[19] This section will highlight the significant roles played by Africans in nationalist movements during and after the Second World War. However, before doing that we must first consider how related global factors shaped the development of African nationalism during this same period.

Outside of Africa, the war weakened the colonial resolve of France, and as Ali Mazrui argues, "impoverished Britain and weakened her capacity to maintain the largest empire in human history."[20] Put differently, the war had a negative impact on the economies of European nations and this forced their policymakers to consider changes to imperial governance, including abandoning African colonies, for stimulating the economies of the metropolis. Moreover, weakened economies undermined the prestige of the colonial powers in Africa and this, in turn, encouraged African nationalists to demand the total liberation of their countries.

During the Second World War, the United States and USSR emerged as the new global superpowers. These new superpowers were against colonial rule and placed relevant European "colonies under international scrutiny and eventually out of [their] control."[21] Playing a leading role in international politics after World War II, the United States and USSR condemned empires and demonstrated their willingness to support nationalists in Africa fighting for self-government. The United States and Britain signed the Atlantic Charter in 1941, with a particular emphasis on "human

---

[19] See, Judith A. Bayfield, Carolyn A. Brown, Timothy Pearsons, and Ahmad Alawad Sikainga, *Africa and World War II* (New York: Cambridge University Press, 2015); Michael Crowder, "World War II and Africa: Introduction," *Journal of African History*, 26, no. 4 (Oct. 1985): 287–288.

[20] Ali A. Mazrui, "Africa Between Nationalism And Nationhood," *Journal of Black Studies* 13, no. 1, (Sept. 1982): 34.

[21] Cheikh Anta Babou, "Decolonization or National Liberation: Debating the End of British Colonial Rule in Africa," *The Annals of the American Academy of Political and Social Science*, 632, no.1, (Sept. 2010): 43.

rights and the rights of self-determination for all nations."[22] For Britain, the self-determination clause in this charter referred exclusively to the European societies conquered or occupied by Germany during the war. However, the United States insisted that it should refer to colonial peoples in Africa and elsewhere as well. This American position inspired nationalists in Africa to demand independence.

Following the end of World War II, the then newly established United Nations took several steps that encouraged Africans to seek independence. For instance, it proclaimed the right of all nations including the colonies in Africa to self-determination. This right to self-determination was enshrined in the United Nations' Atlantic Charter. Clause Three of the U. N. Charter required the colonial powers to "…respect the right of all peoples to choose the form of government under which they will live; and sovereign rights and self-government [be] restored to those who have been forcibly deprived of them." As mentioned above, this proclamation greatly influenced the nationalist movement, and also accelerated the process of decolonization in Africa. Indeed, since its establishment, the decolonization of Africa remains one of the greatest successes of the United Nations.[23]

During and after World War II, racial discrimination intensified in the Caribbean and North America. The period between 1940s and 1960s was not only an era of decolonization but it also "witnessed the civil rights movement in the United States,"[24] in response to Jim Crow laws and other forms of racial injustices. Civil Rights organizations in the United States such as Southern Negro Youth Congress (SNYC), the Council on African Affairs (CAA), and the National Association for the Advancement of Colored People (NAACP) confronted segregation and racial injustice. Members of these civil rights groups, including Pan-Africanists such as W.E.B. Du Bois and Paul Robeson, drew strong connections between the civil rights in the United States and the global struggle for racial equality and self-determination in Africa. African Americans maintained that they not only shared the oppression of colonized peoples in Africa, "but that their fate in the United States was intertwined with the struggles of those peoples [in Africa]."[25]

Consequently, World II renewed Pan-African alliances and solidarity between continental Africans and those in the diaspora. Immediately after the war, Kwame Nkrumah and other activists convened the fifth Pan-African Congress in Manchester.

---

22 Babou, "Decolonization or National Liberation," 43.
23 Mamadou Hebie, "Was There Something Missing in the Decolonization Process in Africa?: The Territorial Dimension," *Leiden Journal of International Law*, 28, no. 3 (Sept, 2015): 529–30.
24 Mohammed Bashir Salau, "African Diasporas: History and Historiography," *Oxford Encyclopedia of African Historiography: Methods and Sources*, 1, (March, 2019) Online version, accessed February 6, 2020. https://www-oxfordreference-com.umiss.idm.oclc.org/view/10.1093/acref/9780190698706.001.0001/acref-9780190698706-e-354
25 Thomas J. Noer, "Penny M. Von Eschen Race against Empire: Black Americans and Anticolonialism, 1937–1957," review of *Race against Empire: Black Americans and Anticolonialism, 1937–1957*, by Penny M. Von Eschen. *The American Historical Review*, 104, no. 3, (June 1999): 931–932.

The Manchester Pan-African Congress has been considered the most significant of all the congresses both for its theme and attendance. For the first time, the Congress had in attendance many delegates from Africa, including important leaders of national movements in various colonies in Africa such as Nkrumah from Gold Coast, Obafemi Awolowo from Nigeria, and Jomo Kenyatta among others. The central theme of the congress was decolonization in Africa, as the delegates condemned imperialism and called for the end of colonial rule in Africa. The Manchester Pan-African Congress provided an avenue for African descended people all over the world to debate the strategies to end colonialism in Africa and to combat global racism. The fifth Pan-African Congress significantly influenced the activists from Africa, as they mobilized and led national movements that accelerated the decolonization process throughout the continent.

Given that the fifth Pan-African Congress helped to transform the Pan-Africanism from a protest movement to a tool of African nationalist movements, it is unsurprising that by late 1940s, diaspora activists had conceded that continental Africans, only with the supports of their diaspora brothers, should be at the forefront of anti-colonial liberation and pan-African politics.[26] Pan-Africanist leaders in the diaspora were satisfied with the popularity and assertiveness of continental African activists studying in the United States and the United Kingdom in the anti-colonial Pan-African politics.[27] One foremost pan-Africanist, Du Bois, was impressed with the large delegation from West Africa that he met at the meeting of the Bureau of the Partisans of Peace in Prague in 1949. Du Bois declared that Africans more and more were "stepping to the front in leadership of African world."[28]

For their part, African activists acknowledged the role of the diaspora activists in the 1950s. Dr. J.B. Danquah, an elected member of the Gold Coast Legislative Council, wrote to one of the civil rights organizations in the United States, "I have watched your movement from strength to strength...[i]t is good for the [African] race that

---

26 By the late 1940s, beginning from 1947, Diaspora leaders and activists had come to terms with Cold War anticommunism and began to sever existing links with Africans and Asians to focus on racial segregation in the United States. See Penny M. Von Eschen *Race against Empire: Black Americans and Anticolonialism, 1937–1957* (Ithaca, NY: Cornell University Press, 1997).
27 Carol Anderson's *Bourgeois Radicals: The NAACP and the Struggle for Colonial Liberation, 1941–1960* (New York: Cambridge University Press, 2015); Robert Trent Vinson, Carol Anderson, "Bourgeois Radicals: The NAACP and the Struggle for Colonial Liberation, 1941–1960," a review of *Bourgeois Radicals: The NAACP and the Struggle for Colonial Liberation, 1941–1960* by Carol Anderson, *The American Historical Review* 121, no. 1, (February 2016), 266–267, https://doi-org.umiss.idm.oclc.org/10.1093/ahr/121.1.266.
28 W. E. B. Du Bois, "African Youth at Prague," *New Africa*, September, 1950, 8. Reproduced from the Collections of the Manuscript Division, Library of Congress, by the Council for African Affairs, accessed January 10, 2020 https://hv-proquest-com.umiss.idm.oclc.org/pdfs/001439/001439_011_0246/001439_011_0246_From_1_to_203.pdf

you in the United States have taken up our cause to let the World see our sores."²⁹ Similarly, A. A. Adio-Moses, the Secretary-General of the Trades Union Congress of Nigeria, also expressed pleasure that "the knowledge that we have friends at the other end of the Atlantic is comforting and inspiring in our struggle for freedom from want and heartless exploitation."³⁰

Following the Manchester Conference, Nkrumah organized two pan-Africanist conferences in 1958 shortly after Ghana became independent in 1957. Nkrumah and many other African political elites continued to pursue pan-Africanist goals even after 1958. By 1960, they organized the second All African People's Conference and the second Conference of Independent African States in Tunis and Addis Ababa, respectively.³¹ Such subsequent pan-Africanist activities helped to ensure the total liberation of many African countries.

Although international factors, including the Pan-Africanist movement, shaped the development of nationalism in Africa, without mass support the ending of colonial rule in Africa would have been more difficult if not impossible. As noted above, the conditions of many Africans worsened during the war. Africans were conscripted into the European armies, and their experience fighting along European counterparts had the impact of neutralizing the myth of European invisibility. The effect of World War II at home was also crucial as colonial administrations forced farmers and mine workers to produce and sustain the European war efforts. The hardship at home and war experience of African soldiers helped to stimulate national consciousness among Africans and helped to encourage them to join mass political movements that eventually sought self-government.

Those who led the mass political movement that developed of this era were the educated elites. By the end of World War II, Africa could boast of prominent educated elites such as Nigeria's Nnamdi Azikiwe and Obafemi Awolowo, Ghana's Kwame Nkrumah, Kenya's Jomo Kenyatta, Guinea's Sekou Toure, Tanzania's Julius Nyerere among others who championed the movement that accelerated the decolonization of Africa. This class of educated elites commanded "high prestige in the African community and [were] confident to exercise political power."³² One of them, Azikwe, was described as a messiah around whom "the merchants rally; the school teachers talk

---

29 "What Leaders in Africa Say About the Council's Work," a Publication of Council for African Affairs, accessed January 10, 2020, https://hv-proquest-com.umiss.idm.oclc.org/pdfs/001439/001439_011_0246/001439_011_0246_From_1_to_203.pdf
30 Ibid.
31 "All-African People's Conferences," *International Organization* 16, no. 2, (1962): 429–434. http://www.jstor.org/stable/2705395; Omorigho O. Eruteya, "The Significance of The All-African Peoples' Conference in the Development of African Nationalism," (Thesis, University of Southern California, 1960); "12 African States will Meet Tuesday," *New York Times*, June 12, 1960, 21.
32 James S. Coleman, "The Politics of Sub-Saharan Africa," in *The Politics of the Developing Areas*, ed. by Gabriel A. Almond and James S. Coleman (Princeton University Press, 1960), 281.

his language; the farmers pray for him; civil servants draw inspiration from his words; musicians echo his name."[33]

Using newspapers, political parties, and other platforms, African nationalist leaders like Azikwe, attacked colonial policies and led political movements for independence. They continued to use African-owned newspapers to criticize colonial policies that worsened or threatened the conditions of Africans. For instance, after World War II, the *West Africa Pilot* criticized Britain's attempt to renege on the principles of clause three of the U. N. charter that promised self-government in Africa.[34]

The nationalist political parties that emerged during the decolonization era included the Convention People's Party in Ghana under Kwame Nkrumah; the National Council of Nigeria and the Cameroons[35] and the Action Group in Nigeria under Nnamdi Azikiwe and Awolowo respectively; the Rassemblement Democratique Africain in Guinea under Sekou Toure and also in Ivory Coast under Felix Houphouet-Boigny; the Union Progressiste Senegalaise in Senegal under Leopold Senghor; the Union Soudanaise in the French Soudan under Modibo Keita.[36] Although these nationalist parties were built around strong personalities and educated nationalist leaders, they drew support from masses including wage workers, middle-class traders and cocoa farmers as well as market women.[37] As Aristide Zolberg has pointed out, African political parties "were more like brokers that assembled different constituencies, working through intermediaries."[38] It is important to note that the pattern of decolonization varied from a colony to another. For instance, while decolonization in Nigeria was peaceful, there was massive violent resistance especially in settler colonies such as those in Algeria, Kenya, Angola, and Mozambique.[39]

Contrary to the traditional literature of nationalism that maintained that masses including "peasants had little interest in politics until awakened by their leaders," peasants, women, wage worker were as much conscious and were also concerned with what freedom and democracy meant during the age of decolonization.[40] After

---

[33] James Stern, "Warning from Africa: Without Bitterness by A. A. Nwafor Orizu," *The New York Times*, October 15, 1944, 395. https://search-proquest-com.umiss.idm.oclc.org/hnpnewyorktimes/docview/106923528/C419E026D72042BCPQ/1?accountid=14588

[34] Yaw Twumasi, "Press Freedom and Nationalism under Colonial Rule in the Gold Coast (Ghana)," *Journal of the Historical Society of Nigeria* 7, no. 3 (1974): 499–520; Also see James S. Coleman, *Nigeria: Background to Nationalism* (Berkeley, 1963).

[35] NCNC later changed its name from National Council for Nigerian and Cameroons to National Council of Nigerian Citizens (still NCNC).

[36] Coleman, "The Politics of Sub-Saharan Africa," 296; H. S. Wilson, *African Decolonization*. (London: British Library, 1994), 94.

[37] Schmidt, *Mobilizing the Masses*, 1–10.

[38] Cited in Frederick Cooper, The Politics of Decolonization in French and British West Africa," *Oxford Research Encyclopedias*, (Jan. 2018): 18 https://doi.org/10.1093/acrefore/9780190277734.013.111.

[39] For patterns of decolonization in Africa, see David Birmingham, *Decolonization of Africa*. (Ohio: Ohio University Press, 1995).

[40] See Steven Feierman, *Peasant Intellectuals: Anthropology and History in Tanzania* (Madison, Wisconsin: The University of Wisconsin Press, 1990) and Hunter, *Political Thought*.

World War II, peasants and other marginal groups such as ex-soldiers, trade unions, and women continued to express grievances against the colonial regimes. For instance, the ex-servicemen who claimed to have paid "blood tax" saw their demands for rights citizenship rights being pushed back. Africans who fought with Allied powers in the name of freedom were disappointed that they would not benefit from the freedom they *fought* for. Wage workers continued to make demands such as living wages/family wages, even as peasants continued to protest colonial agricultural policies.[41]

Because the disparate groups had different aspirations and lacked a national platform, the educated elites using political parties were able to reconcile the various resistance groups around some common ground. For instance in the 1950s when the British tried to draw African agriculture into a capitalist economy, the peasants revolted and "joined proto-nationalist organizations, ultimately leading to the triumph of TANU, and to national independence in 1961."[42] Consequently, national anti-colonial movements including armed guerrilla movement tried "to cooperate with or co-opt peasant movements into overthrowing colonial rule in Africa."[43] Although the educated elites were able to harness different grievances into a national movement, the success of nationalist movements in various colonies lied in the grassroots mobilizers who were capable of dictating and determining the directions of the nationalist movement in Africa.

Women, as Elizabeth Schmidt has pointed out, played significant roles in nationalism and decolonization in Africa. Women in Africa became very involved in the anti-colonial nationalism, participating in nationalist political parties as uneducated rank-and-file members and as party leaders and strategists. Although largely illiterate, women were "a major force in constructing, embodying and performing nationalism," mobilizing for and spreading party ideologies and programs. In what Schmidt called "women bush telegraph," the grassroots women nationalists developed strategies such as dance, songs, and other local symbols to pass the nationalist messages across.[44] Largely because of their ability to mobilize, organize, and even shape nationalist parties, some of these women became central figures in nationalist movements. In Tanzania, for instance, Bibi Titi Muhammed was a prominent woman in the nationalist movement, and she was second only to Julius Nyerere.[45]

---

41 Cooper, "Decolonization in Tropical Africa," 3; Cooper, "Politics of Decolonization," 18; Also see Fredrick Cooper, *Decolonization and African Societies: The Labor Question in French and British Africa.* (New York: Cambridge University Press, 1996).
42 Feierman, *Peasant Intellectuals*, 9.
43 Michael Collins, "Nation, State and Agency: Evolving Historiographies of African decolonization," in *Britain, France and the Decolonization of Africa: Future Imperfect?* ed. by Andrew W.M. Smith and Chris Jeppesen, (UCL Press, 2017), 28–29. Accessed February 6, 2020. https://doi.org/10.2307/j.ctt1mtz521.6
44 Schmidt, *Mobilizing the Masses*, 1–10.
45 Susan Geiger, *TANU Women: Gender and Culture in the Making of Tanganyikan Nationalism, 1955–1965* (Portsmouth, NH: Heinemann, 1997), 14–15.

Women were also involved in guerilla wars such as the Mau Mau revolt.[46] Again, there were also prominent women political strategists such as Hannah Kudjoe in Ghana. Popularly known as "Convention Hannah," Kudjoe was "a high-profile, formidable, and well-connected nationalist leader" who single-handedly mobilized rallies up and down the country. When Nkrumah and other nationalist leaders in Ghana were arrested, it was Kudjoe who "led the massive petition drive for the release" of those leaders.[47] Like Kudjoe in Ghana and Muhammed in Tanzania, women nationalists across Africa worked side by side their male counterparts in the anti-colonial movement.

Indeed, by the 1960s, nationalist movements had achieved the political goal of independence in most African countries. However, as Fredrick Cooper has observed, African political elites who helped to end European rule in their countries were not necessarily committed to maintaining inherited colonial borders or to actualizing nation-state goals. Indeed, some "sought a pan-African nation embracing all oppressed people of color; others saw colonial rule becoming a Euro-African community stripped of inequality and exploitation."[48] Unsurprisingly, Nkrumah pursued Pan-African unity after Ghana's independence in 1957 while Toure of Guinea, Senghor of Senegal, and Houphouet-Boigny of Cote d'Ivoire vigorously debated between "franco-African community" and francophone African federation before they eventually settled for nation-states.

In Ghana, Tanzania, Nigeria, Kenya, Guinea, and British Togoland, regional and ethnic nationalisms competed with broader nation-state nationalism.[49] Ablode and Asante nationalism were good examples of ethnic/regional nationalism during decolonization. While Ablode was a movement that sought to reclaim and protect the special status of former British Togoland, Asante nationalism through National Liberation Movement (NLM) demanded autonomy for Asante people, in contrast to Nkrumah's call for Ghana's independence and the eventual creation of a United States of Africa.[50] As scholars have concluded, nationalism was a battle that went

---

[46] See Cora Ann Presley, "The Mau Mau Rebellion, Kikuyu Women, and Social Change." *Canadian Journal of African Studies / Revue Canadienne Des Études Africaines* 22, no. 3 (1988): 502–527.
[47] Jean Allman, "The Disappearing of Hannah Kudjoe: Nationalism, Feminism and Tyrannies of History," *Journal of Women's History* 21, no. 3, (2009), 13–35.
[48] Cooper, "Decolonization in Tropical Africa," 1.
   See Presley, "The Mau Mau Rebellion," 502–27.
[49] Jonathan Glassman, "Slower than a Massacre: The Multiple Sources of Racial Thought in Colonial Africa." *The American Historical Review*, 109, no. 3, (June 2004): 720–754; Kate Skinner, *The Fruits of Freedom in British Togoland: Literacy, Politics and Nationalism, 1914–2014* (New York: Cambridge University Press, 2015); Jean Marie Allman, *The Quills of the Porcupine; Asante Nationalism in an Emergent Ghana* (Madison: University of Wisconsin Press, 1993).
[50] Skinner, *The Fruits of Freedom*; Allman, *The Quills of the Porcupine*.

beyond colonial vs. anti-colonial, as "possibilities for political change grew and shrank in the decades after 1945."[51]

Second Liberation Movement, 1960–1970s

Scholars of African democracy have referred to the wave of democratization in Africa after the Cold War as the second liberation movement. In this section, however, I deployed the second liberation movement in the same way Michael Colin does, to explain the unfinished liberation movement in Africa, particularly in the Portuguese and Spanish colonies.[52] Although the majority of the African colonies under Britain and France gained independence in the early 1960s, the Portuguese would remain in Africa until 1975. Until the late 1950s, the Portuguese and Spanish colonies did not witness the kind of political activism that had earlier started in West Africa.[53] As Britain and France granted independence to their colonies in Africa, Portugal renamed her colonies as "overseas provinces."[54] Portugal remained obstinate in defending its empire, even as international and local pressure for decolonization mounted. The first international challenge by a world body to Portuguese and Spanish colonial rule came from the United Nations. As early as 1955, the United Nations began to question Spain and Portugal about their colonies. When African territories under Britain and France attained independence and joined the UN in the early 1960s, the pressures on Portugal and Spain increased. By December 1960, the United Nations passed resolution 1514 (xv) on the *Declaration on The Granting of Independence to Colonial Countries and Peoples*. This resolution aimed to check "the unyielding stance of Portugal and Spain."[55]

Apart from the UN, the Organization of African Unity also contributed to the second liberation movement in Africa. Kwame Nkrumah, a prominent founding father of AOU, declared after Ghana's independence in 1957 that independence of Ghana would not be complete without freedom of other African countries. Since its creation in 1963, the central focus of the OAU was the "unconditional attainment of national independence by *all* African territories still under foreign domination." [56] OAU supported and assisted the liberation movement in Portuguese colonies by coordinating

---

51 See Cooper, "Politics of Decolonization," 1–20; Cooper, "Decolonization in Tropical Africa;" Frederick Cooper, *Colonialism in Question: Theory, Knowledge, History* (Berkeley, CA: University of California Press, 2005); Smith and Jeppesen, *Britain, France and the Decolonization of Africa*, 1.
52 Collins, "Nation, State and Agency," 28–29.
53 Alicia Campos, "The Decolonization of Equatorial Guinea: The Relevance of the International Factor," *Journal of African History*, 44, no. 1 (2003): 96.
54 Norrie MacQueen, *The Decolonization of Portuguese Africa: Metropolitan Revolution and the Dissolution of Empire* (London: Longman, 1997), 434.
55 Campos, "The Decolonization of Equatorial Guinea," 99.
56 Elwood Dunn, "The OAU and the Mozambique Revolution," *A Journal of Opinion*, 3, no. 1 (Spring, 1973): 29–30.

material aids from the member states and "fighting the battle in the diplomatic arena." Most importantly, OAU gave legitimacy to the political groups and leaders of the liberation movement in the Portuguese and Spanish colonies.[57]

The most important challenge to the Portuguese empires in Africa came from within the colonies. Following the international anti-colonial movement championed by the UN and OAU, the Portuguese began to witness organized political movements calling for independence.[58] As early as the 1960s, the liberation movement had engulfed the Portuguese colonies in Africa. The Popular Movement for Liberation of Angola (MPLA) and the Union of People of Angola (UPA) were formed to lead the liberation movement in Angola. In Mozambique, there emerged political parties such as Makonde National Union (MANU), National African Union of Independent Mozambique, (UNAMI), and National Democratic Union of Mozambique (UDENAMO), each had relied on ethnic and regional supports. The challenge for the nationalist leaders in Portuguese colonies particularly in Mozambique was how to unite these ethnic/regional based parties into a more coherent front. Julius Nyerere and Kwame Nkrumah facilitated the merger of these parties, as the nationalists were able to "build a united front that challenged Portuguese colonial rule."[59] Just like their counterparts in other colonies in Africa, nationalists in Mozambique, Angola, and Guinea-Bissau adopted strategies such as boycott, strike and demonstrations to challenge Portuguese and Spanish colonial rule. However, these strategies proved very ineffective particularly in Portuguese settler colonies, the Portuguese were so determined to cling on.[60]

The unreformable nature of settler colonialism became the main factor that encouraged violent resistance in Mozambique and Angola.[61] In relevant guerrilla wars, nationalists in these two Portuguese colonies, as well as in Guinea Bissau, relied on the cooperation and assistance of independent neighboring countries. As more African countries became independent, "there was every chance of winning some material assistance as well as the offer of safe havens."[62] The wars of independence in Angola, Mozambique, and Guinea-Bissau were an important factor in the 1974 coup in Portugal.[63] As Paul Nugent has argued, guerrilla warfare in Portuguese colonies was successful in that by 1974 the same soldiers who were burdened with fight-

---

57 Ibid.
58 Liberation movements had begun in these territories before the formation of OAU.
59 Andreas Stucki *Violence and Gender in Africa's Iberian Colonies: Feminizing the Portuguese and Spanish Empire, 1950s–1970s*. (Basingstoke: Palgrave Macmillan, 2019), 258.
60 Paul Nugent, *Africa since Independence*. (New York; Palgrave Macmillan, 2004), 262–263.
61 For further discussion on wars of independence in Portuguese colonies see, for instance, Peter Abbott and Manuel Ribeiro Rodrigues, *Modern African Wars (2): Angola and Mozambique, 1961–74* (Oxford, UK: Osprey, 2013); and Filipe Riberio de Meneses and Robert McNamara, *The White Redoubt, the Great Powers and the Struggle for Southern Africa, 1960–1980* (London, Palgrave Macmillan, 2018).
62 Nugent, *Africa since Independence*, 262–270.
63 Mazrui, "Africa between Nationalism and Nationhood," 33–34.

ing the colonial war in Africa participated in the overthrow of the regime in Portugal. As the freedom fighters in the colonies intensified their military campaign, the Armed Forces Movement (MFA) that took over power in Portugal finally "accepted the right of self-determination up to and including independence."[64]

Women also contributed to the anti-colonial nationalist project in Portuguese colonies in Africa. Although they had imagined women as pawns for countering antic-olonial movement, colonial administrators were shocked to find women committed to organizing anti-colonial demonstrations and "formulating political slogans." Women were also actively involved in armed struggle. Women collaborated with revolutionary organizations FRELIMO. Women did not only join the political branch of FRELIMO, they actively collaborated with the military wing since the outbreak of the anti-colonial war in 1964.[65] Just like the Mau Mau's women in Kenya, women's involvement in the liberation movement in Portuguese colonies was not only limited to "transports of weapons and provisions of food for the freedom fighters."[66] They were saddled with "the crucial task of revolutionary indoctrination and "mobilization of the populations." FRELIMO leadership acknowledged women's key roles and contributions that helped to sustain and transform the political and social landscape in Mozambique.[67]

Conclusion

External factors played an important role in challenging European empires in Africa. However, the nationalist movement in Africa helped to accelerate the process of decolonization of Africa. Educated elite championed the nationalist movement leading to independence, but they did not do it alone. Ex-soldiers, women, wage workers, and peasants all had genuine grievances against colonial states as they joined the national movements that challenged the colonial state and called for independence. The fact that these groups had their particular grievances complicated the meaning of African nationalism. There were many forms of nationalism which in some cases went beyond the dichotomy of colonial versus anti-colonial. These forms of nationalism were sometimes in co-operation, sometimes in competition, and even in some other times in "repressive antagonism" with each other.[68] In the name of building

---

[64] Paul Nugent, *Africa since Independence*, 271.
[65] Stucki, *Violence and Gender*, 39–68.
[66] Jennifer Leigh Disney, *Women's Activism and Feminist Agency in Mozambique and Nicaragua* (Philadelphia, PA: Temple University Press, 2008), 51–52; Stucki, *Violence and Gender*, 257–262.
[67] Stucki *Violence and Gender*, 39–68.
[68] Glassman, "Slower than a Massacre" 720–754; Hunter, *Political Thought and the Public Sphere in Tanzania*; John Straussberger, "Storming the Citadel: Decolonization and Political Contestation in Guinea's Futa Jallon, 1945–1961" *Journal of African History* 2, (2016): 57; Skinner, *The Fruits of Freedom in British Togoland*; Jeremy Prestholdt, "Politics of The Soil: Separatism, Autochthony, And De-

peaceful nations, the educated elite that emerged as leaders in post-independence African countries repressed ethnic nationalism, labor, and women movement that had joined and contributed to the national movement for independence during the era of decolonization.

---

colonization at The Kenyan Coast," *Journal of African History*, 55, no. 2, (2014); Paul Bjerk, *Building a Peaceful Nation: Julius Nyerere and the Establishment of Sovereignty in Tanzania, 1960–1964* (Boydell & Brewer, University of Rochester Press, 2015).

Sifiso Mxolisi Ndlovu
Chapter 11
South African Apartheid and Resistance: A Global History

Abstract: The oppressed African majority, together with the liberation movement, was fighting for the destruction of a violent and anti-human regime in South Africa, whose history was one of aggression and oppression not only against indigenous South Africans, but also against neighbouring states. Their commendable resistance to white minority rule exposed the role of western powers who worked to provoke aggression against those who fought for peace, democracy, majority rule, and the end of apartheid. Though the liberation movement promoted progressive internationalism and supported the worldwide anti-apartheid movement, it was of the view that a political settlement and substantive negotiations in South Africa should be an inclusive internal affair, free of external influence.

Keywords: African nationalism, Afrikaner nationalism, apartheid, national liberation struggle, substantive negotiations, political settlement.

Introduction

This chapter examines the emergence of the resistance to apartheid and follows it through the demise of the apartheid government of South Africa. It also uses, as primary sources, oral history testimonies and interviews conducted with, among others, former president Thabo Mbeki and former cabinet ministers of the apartheid regime. Therefore, this chapter is based on collective memories and viewpoints of participants during the apartheid era. This is because voices and experiences of those who participated, even considering the limitations reflected by these collective memories, come much closer to the "truth" than history and political science books that lack such voices, however skillfully written.

Afrikaner power in South Africa rested on three pillars: language, religion and race. The language distinguished Afrikaners from the hated English conquerors; and Calvinism sanctioned the belief that they were chosen by God to reign over the uncivilised masses, the 'savages', namely, the indigenous Africans. Once in power, the Afrikaner-controlled Nationalist Party (NP) set about achieving two main aims in order to buttress its position. The first was to exclude all blacks – or 80 percent of the total population – from the centers of power. The second was to consolidate the Afrikaner – 60 percent of the minority white population – into a single voting bloc. The NP came to power in the 1948 general election and ruled until 1994 which is the longest period by a single political party in the history of South Africa. Afrikaners were still smarting from the defeat suffered at the hands of the

British in the war of 1899–1902, so British imperialism was one of its hated targets. Another was Africans, who were regarded as rivals in the labour market for jobs held by whites. Furthermore, their sheer numbers, threatened to 'swamp' the privileged white minority. Finally, the NP had added communism to its list of dreaded foes; virtually any ill that befell the state was seen as 'communist inspired'. Daniel F. Malan, the first NP prime minister (1948–1954) chose to fight the 1948 election on a platform of anti-communism and crude appeals to racism, which played on the fear of a takeover by the African majority. The NP's Transvaal leader, J.G. Strijdom, put it very bluntly: the NP wanted was nothing less than *baasskap*, or white supremacy. It was this naked racism that secured the party's victory in 1948, and ushered in more than fifty years of apartheid. The NP was voted into power in 1948 by whites from all social levels who felt threatened by the African, coloured and Indian working class. Understandably then, among the most avid NP supporters were those who had the most to lose if the oppressed African majority were given any opportunity to improve their socio-economic status. In other words; the mine owners, the struggling Afrikaner lower classes, the farmers, and the white workers. Indeed, it was the agricultural and labour sectors that felt most threatened and it was their votes that catapulted the NP so unexpectedly into power.

The NP wasted no time. Once in power it piled one draconian law on another until it had a battery of legislation to keep blacks (a term used here to denote all people of colour, including Africans, Coloured people and those of Indian descent) 'in their place'. The election victory in 1948 was followed closely by its post-Second World War policy that ethnic groups and sub-groups should be segregated in their own areas. Here, they argued, each sub-group would develop into a 'self-sufficient unit'. Africans in urban areas would then simply become 'visitors' rather than residents. They would, in other words, be 'migratory citizens, not entitled to political and social rights equal to those of whites' in so-called 'white areas'. This eventually led to the creation of Bantustans or Homelands.[1]

The NP came to power armed with the policy of 'apartheid' which was a term coined by Afrikaner historian Van Biljon as far back as 1935, but the maintenance of 'separate' geographical areas for the conquered indigenous population was by no means new. It had been a cornerstone of colonialism and had become an integral element of the exploitation of African labour in the Union of South Africa after 1910. Furthermore, it was institutionalised by the Land Act of 1913 and the Native (Urban Areas) Act of 1923. As abhorrent as the NP's policies and pass laws were to Africans, the roots of oppression and exploitation can be traced back much further, to colonial conquest and land dispossession. Racial discrimination, dispossession of the land of the indigenous peoples, control of their labour and political domination by a white

---

[1] B. Magubane, "Introduction: The Political Context' in South African Democracy Education Trust (hereafter SADET), *The Road to Democracy in South Africa, Volume 1 [1960–1970]*, 2nd edition (Pretoria: Unisa Press, 2010), 2.

minority were all legacies dating back to the earliest settler period. The hated pass laws that led directly to the Sharpeville massacre in 1960 and the decision by the liberation movements such as the ANC and the PAC to wage an armed struggle against oppression thus have a long history, and it is fitting that we examine the evolution of the pass system.

Regulations to govern the free movement of African people had their origin in the laws controlling slave labour, dating back to the 1760s, when slaves in the Cape Colony were required to carry passes signed by their owners before they travelled anywhere. Vagrancy laws and ordinances were also passed to control the movement of indigenous people. The first pass law was introduced by the British in 1809 to help Afrikaner farmers keep track of their labour. Named the Hottentot Code, it decreed that every Khoikhoi person had to have a fixed 'place of abode' and a pass from his or her master (or from a local official) was required before moving away. This law, and numerous others like it, remained on the statute books in South Africa until 1988 – a grim reminder of the country's slave-owning past and a sharp instrument of racial oppression and discrimination. Ordinances 28 and 49 of 1828 introduced the first pass laws, *per se*, and decreed that all Africans living beyond the frontier had to have a pass to enter the Cape Colony. Penalties for failure to produce a pass included arrest and imprisonment with forced labour for up to a year.[2]

To ensure its survival, the NP gerrymandered parliamentary representation. In 1952 it began a series of unscrupulous efforts to bypass the entrenched clauses of the constitution that protected the coloured franchise. This was eventually achieved in the NP's second term of office, when legislation was passed allowing the senate to be increased from 48 to 89 members, thus giving the new prime minister (1954–1958), Johannes G. Strijdom, the opportunity to pack it with NP representatives. This secured the majority in both houses that was needed to change the constitution. The apartheid regime also expended enormous effort during its first three terms in office on shoring up support among Afrikaner workers so as to tighten its grip on power. Shortly after its victory it launched a systematic purge of the civil service, replacing English-speakers with NP supporters, many of whom were Afrikaner Broederbond members. Three strategic departments in particular bore the initial brunt of this onslaught: the police, the military, and native affairs. The number of Afrikaners employed in public administration rose by 98.5 percent between 1946 and 1960, and English-speaking recruits all but vanished from the civil service. Reserving jobs in the civil service and parastatal organisations for Afrikaners was also a way of rewarding loyal supporters. Afrikaners in white-collar employment rocketed from 29 percent in 1946 to 43.4 percent in 1960. In the ten years between 1948 and 1958, the size of the civil service mushroomed until 30 percent of the economically active white population was on the government payroll. With a view to ensuring that an adequate flow of

---

2 Magubane, "Introduction," 19.

appropriately qualified Afrikaners was available for such positions, there was a massive increase in state subsidies for Afrikaans universities.³

Legislation designed to lay down boundaries between the races was piloted through parliament without delay: the Mixed Marriages Act of 1949 was followed within a year by the Immorality Act, Population Registration Act, the initially unworkable Group Areas Act, and the draconian Suppression of Communism Act. The political threat posed by a burgeoning urban population of 'detribalised' and insurgent African workers alarmed many white South Africans. By deliberately labelling this rising class 'communist' the NP felt it could justify its policy of repression, both to its own supporters and to foreign capitalists, especially the Americans. The Suppression of Communism Act of 1950 was carefully tailored to fit this bill. These provisions virtually gave the authorities a free hand to ban or harass any political organisation they wished. 'Communism' was defined so broadly that it included any initiative which aimed at 'unlawful' social change.

Hendrik F. Verwoerd, South African prime minister (1958–1966), was not really the 'architect of apartheid' as he is often referred to, but he intellectualised apartheid and elevated it to a quasi-religious ideology more than anyone before or after him. As David Welsh says, "In terms of cohesiveness Afrikaner nationalism reached its zenith in the 1960s under Verwoerd's premiership; all of its component spheres were locked into a bureaucracy, headed by the National Party, that coordinated and controlled their activities."⁴ After Verwoerd's assassination on 6 September 1966, and with the fairly rapid movement of Afrikaners into the middle classes, Afrikaner unity slowly started unravelling. Cohesion was further undermined, and space for dissension created, by urbanisation and a much larger number of Afrikaners going to universities and travelling overseas. The primary instinct to maintain and refine apartheid above all else, gradually began to fade. Verwoerd's successor, B. J. Vorster (1966–1978), was a more acceptable leader to many English-speaking whites and South Africa's increasing international isolation after the Sharpeville massacre of 1960 was weakening the harsh English/Afrikaans divide. From the mid-1960s onwards more and more English-speakers started voting for the NP and that had to have an influence on the nature of Afrikaner nationalism, which was initially fuelled by an anti-British and anti-English sentiment.⁵

---

3 Magubane, "Introduction," 12.
4 D. Welsh, *The Rise and Fall of Apartheid* (Cape Town: Jonathan Ball, 2009), 172.
5 M. du Preez, "The National Party and the Changing of the Minds: The 1970s and the 1980s' in SADET, *The Road to Democracy in South Africa, Volume 6 [1990–1994], Part 1*, (Pretoria: Unisa Press, 2013), 36.

Resistance to Apartheid: A Snapshot

When the Convention for a Democratic South Africa (CODESA) formally met in Johannesburg on 20–21 December 1991, among those present were members of both the ANC, representing the majority of the oppressed people in South Africa and the NP, representing white minority rule. This meeting represented a continuation of the traditional intellectual battle of minds that commenced in the early twentieth century between the South African National Native Congress (SANNC, later renamed the ANC) founded in 1912 and the whites-only Union of South Africa government which implemented the racist Act of Union in 1909 passed by the British colonisers and which lead to the formation of the Union of South Africa in 1910. This battle of the minds was fuelled by the fact that by 1909 two conventions about the future of a non-racial, united, and democratic South Africa took place. The first was a racist, whites-only convention that presaged the 1902 Treaty of Vereeniging. The second took place in 1909 and was organised by the founders of the ANC who opposed the establishment of the racist governed Union of South Africa. In essence, this 1909 convention epitomised the struggle for racial justice, dignity, human rights, and a new role for Africans in the international world. Hence their preference for a peaceful, diplomatic solution of the national question in South Africa exemplified by sending various delegations to meet colonial authorities in England.[6] This goal was realised in 1994 and issue which will be discussed as part of the conclusion of this chapter.

In order to meet the apartheid onslaught, attempts were made to unite the main African political organisations, that is, the ANC and the All African Convention (AAC) in December 1948 and early 1949. The unity efforts, however, did not succeed. Meanwhile the ANC began a series of countrywide consultations seeking practical ways to confront the apartheid regime. The famous Programme of Action was adopted by the annual ANC conference in Bloemfontein on 17 December 1949. It was not merely a declaration of principles but also a formulation of resistance methods and how to implement them. Immediately after the adoption of the Programme of Action, the ANC Executive appointed a Council of Action comprising Dr. James. S. Moroka (chairman), Gaur Radebe, Godfrey M. Pitje, Oliver R. Tambo, and C.S. Ramohanoe. The immediate task of the council was to ensure the launching of a boycott and a one-day national strike which took place on 1 May 1950. The strike and stay-away was a big success with 80 percent of African workers remaining at home. The industries in the Witwatersrand, the economic centre of the country, came to a standstill. But the security police resorted to a brutal reprisal and forcibly broke up every gathering of more than twelve-people. By the time the evening came at least eighteen people

---

[6] F. Meli, *South Africa Belongs to Us: A History of the African National Congress* (Harare: Zimbabwean Publishing House, 1987).

were killed and over thirty were injured. As a result of this brutal action by the apartheid regime, a wave of anger spread throughout the country.

This new consciousness was promoted partially by the realisation that Africans had to unite in order to be emancipated, and gain strength to fight more effectively for freedom. As a result, African national freedom meant:
- Redistribution of political power.
- Redistribution of land.
- Redistribution of the social forces of production. The idea of white domination must be banished forever. In a free and independent South Africa in which the African majority leads, the racial difference will not count and will not constitute a stigma. White South Africa, will, under conditions of freedom and equality, be free to contribute to the democratic South Africa in common with the peace-loving African majority.

The basic assumption of African nationalism is that the oppressed African majority can regain their lost birth rights only by dint of group organisation and group solidarity. This presupposes:
- A clear liberation policy outlook and a clear objective.
- A policy based on sound Africanist principles and;
- A suitable programme, capable of harnessing the energy of the oppressed people, and mobilising their resources in the interest of developing emancipatory struggles.

The struggle for national liberation in South Africa was both an anti-colonial and a Pan-Africanist struggle. The ANC's commitment to non-violence was initially deep-seated and long lasting. It took a great deal of shock and outrage before a decision was finally taken to engage in a relatively restrained form of armed struggle in the second half of 1961. Pressure to move in that direction had been mounting since the Sharpeville massacre and the banning of the ANC and the PAC in April 1960. In June 1961, the balance was tipped in favour of violent resistance by the bloody repression of ANC-led stayaways. After banishment of the both liberation movements most of the ANC leaders went into exile including O. R. Tambo, the deputy president, who settled in Tanzania and later in Zambia.

Discussion of a possible turn towards armed struggle made those for whom non-violence had long been axiomatic aware of the existence of an alternative political tradition that stretched back to independent African kingdoms and the wars of resistance they fought against colonial incursions and land-grabbing. Africans might have been stripped of their firearms after 1900, but a military capacity and ethos had not been entirely extinguished. In many areas young men continued to emphasise the military arts, the formation of regiments and the defence of communities. Rural people, previously regarded as an uncertain support base, now presented themselves as a significant reservoir of militant anti-apartheid struggle. Following the banning of the ANC and PAC in 1960, large numbers of their members and supporters – would-be freedom fighters – left South Africa to receive military training in friendly African states and Eastern Europe, particularly the German Democratic Republic and the Soviet Union. There were also those who hoped to pursue their education abroad such as Thabo Mbeki. Many ANC and PAC leaders went into exile at the same time, usually via South Africa's neighbouring states, and eventually established bases in newly independent states such as Tanganyika (Tanzania) and Northern Rhodesia (Zambia). Others settled in Europe (mainly Britain) and the United States. Some also went to, or spent time in the Soviet Union, China, and countries in Eastern Europe.[7] The PAC was working with the Chinese.

In terms of international solidarity, the exiled leadership of the ANC had to take both strategic and tactical decisions which were articulated by Joe Matthews, one of its senior members. We are focusing on the ANC in this chapter not the PAC and the Black Consciousness Movement (BCM) because the ANC was forty-eight years old when it was banned in 1960, the PAC was hardly a year old and the BCM was not yet established. Then ANC had an advantage because it was already operating within the UN system by using international network and similarly, it also operated with African countries within the League of Nations fighting for the liberation of South West Africa (Namibia).[8] Therefore, regarding establishing relationship with the Soviet Union as one of the global superpowers, Matthews elaborates:

> The exiled leadership recognised that historically, any liberation movement faced with a difficult struggle, had to have either a middle or a world power supporter, we looked at the United States war of independence and you said would these colonists have won against Britain without the support of France, and France was a feudal state, completely different from the people they were supporting. But France was supporting them because of its rivalry with the British and they backed the independence movement. So, we said, it's not a question of ideology, it's a question of practicality, which power will support a struggle such as this, or which powers will support us. We knew that the African states generally speaking were too weak... So, we took a decision, it might look like an obvious decision that now look we have got the Soviet Union as the other superpower, the western powers are the trading partners of our country, they are not going to be involved in supporting any armed struggle. So, we have to establish a relationship with Russians.[9]

In addition, the liberation movement also has to establish relationships and consolidate solidarity with countries in Africa, Asia and Eastern Europe:

---

7 S.M. Ndlovu, "The ANC in Exile, 1960–1970," in SADET, *The Road to Democracy in South Africa, Volume 1 [1960–1970]*, (Pretoria: Unisa Press, 2004), chapter 11.
8 S. M. Ndlovu, "African Leaders and the National Liberation Struggle in Namibia' in SADET, *The Road to Democracy in South Africa, Volume 5, African Solidarity, Part 2* (Pretoria: Unisa Press, 2014), chapter 16.
9 Interview with Joe Gaobakwe Matthews conducted by S.M. Ndlovu and B.M. Magubane, 18 July 2001, SADET Oral History Project (SOHP). See also V. Shubin and M. Traikova, "There is No Threat from the Eastern Bloc," chapter 12 in SADET, *The Road to Democracy, Volume 3, International Solidarity, Part 2* (Pretoria: Unisa Press, 2008).

> Then we had to take other decisions. As I say we looked at the historical analogies and so on, we were convinced that you must have some power which is backing you, otherwise you won't be able fight the struggle for national liberation on your own. Alright we said Africa as a continent can be our base…. we need military training facilities or anything like that, countries in the African would be ready to do it, but the equipment and so on will have to come from somewhere else. Then we also had to look at who are our strategic partners in the national liberation struggle. The Algerian struggle had just been won, France pulled out of Algeria, they gained their independence in 1962, and we thought because of their experience and because of the good relations we had with them which we established during the meeting convened by the Non-Aligned Movement during the Bandung Conference in 1955, we had to establish fraternal relations with them. We thought that Algeria will be our Arab centre in North Africa because they had the necessary prestige in the Arab world because of their liberation struggle and they would have a positive attitude to a liberation movement which is fighting an armed struggle and so we decided on Algeria as our main base in North Africa.[10]

The jigsaw puzzle was still incomplete, the liberation movement still had to establish a strategic relationship with countries in Eastern Europe because of the Cold War:

> We decided also that, a country which was very committed to our struggle was the German Democratic Republic, because of the history of Germany, and also because we had their nemesis, West Germany, which had become a main ally of the apartheid regime and so to link up with East Germany seemed a logical thing for us to do. We did not forget that India had a historical link with South Africa, was also a big power, may not be able to participate in supporting us with arms and so on but there were many other things which India could do and one of them was supplying us with medicine, India could provide us with all the drugs and if you look at the history of liberation movements, you still find that our movement never ran short of things like drugs and medicines and so on. Then there were other countries, like Bulgaria which supplied us with food and textiles, that was a country which did a lot for us, Bulgaria.[11]

But then to complete the cycle, humanitarian support was needed, Matthews elaborated:

> We looked at the Scandinavian countries and said right they rejected supporting our armed struggle but they are prepared to give humanitarian assistance. So, we said right, let's strengthen the humanitarian support we receive from International Defence and Aid Fund under Canon Collins and urge these countries to support that fund. We never got money for the armed struggle from the International Defence and Aid, their job was to particularly to support the legal struggle inside South Africa. So almost the entire legal struggle inside the country was finances by International Defence and Aid Fund… We had a very big network which was kept alive until about

---

[10] Interview with Joe Gaobakwe Matthews. See also S. Debeche, "Algeria and the Struggle Against Apartheid in South Africa, 1955–1994," in SADET, *The Road to Democracy in South Africa, Volume 5, African Solidarity, Part 1* (Pretoria: Unisa Press, 2013), chapter 4.

[11] Interview with Joe Gaobakwe Matthews. See also H. Schleicher, "The German Democratic Republic and the South African Liberation Struggle," in SADET, *The Road to Democracy, Volume 3, International Solidarity, Part 2*, chapter 13; V. Gupta, "Solidarity: India and South Africa," in SADET, *The Road to Democracy, Volume 3, International Solidarity, Part 2*, chapter 16; and Shubin and Traikova, "There is No Threat from the Eastern Bloc."

1993/94 when we closed down the Defence and aid Fund and it was also during this period when Scandinavian countries cut their humanitarian support.[12]

On the enemy's side, from 1948 to 1990, there had been a seamless succession of NP prime ministers. Yet, when the P. W. Botha era began in 1978 after the demise of B. J. Vorster (1966–1978), the confidence that had characterised NP hegemony up to the Vorster era had been shattered. In the Botha years, despite its bravado, the NP lacked the confidence that it could suppress the people's aspiration for freedom by force alone. The apartheid regime's relentless detentions, torture and killings; its aggression against the frontline states; and the destabilisation of neighbouring governments, had all failed to bring it the security it sought. Furthermore, the 1983 tri-cameral reforms, a hoax of 'reform' that included whites, Indians and Coloureds, had no takers. From then on the apartheid state suffered paralysis of initiative in the face of mounting struggles from the masses at home and from the international community.[13] Faced with this correlation of forces, which P. W. Botha characterised as 'total onslaught', he formulated the 'total strategy' to defend the ill-gotten gains of years of white supremacy. But when all is said and done, Botha's 'reform' simply amounted to 'change without change'. As Congressman William H. Grey of Philadelphia put it:

> Cursed by nearly all humanity and unnerved by the mounting restiveness of the non-white majority that they oppress; white South Africa today are struggling to find a way to give up *most* of apartheid without relinquishing any of their power.[14]

To defend a system that the UN had described as a crime against humanity in 1973, the South African government's defence budget grew by leaps and bounds – from R120 million in 1960 to more than R140 billion in 1983–84.[15] In the first half of the 1980s, there was increased talk of the grave threat that faced the apartheid regime. This, it was felt, called for nothing less than putting the white population on a war footing, which necessitated closer cooperation between the apartheid state and capital and new initiatives geared to taking 'into account the aspirations of our different population groups' in order to gain 'their trust'.[16] In the process, a 'state within the state', a largely secretive system with a web of interlocking structures was formed, comprising the State Security Council (SCC), National Security

---

12 Interview with Joe Gaobakwe Matthews. See also T. Sellstrom, 'Sweden and the Nordic Countries: Official Solidarity and Assistance from the West', in SADET, *The Road to Democracy, Volume 3, International Solidarity, Part 2*, chapter 6; and A. Cook, "The International Defence and Aid Fund for Southern Africa," in SADET, *The Road to Democracy, Volume 3, International Solidarity, Part 1*, chapter 3.
13 Editorial notes, "Making South Africa Ungovernable," *African Communist*, 101 (1985), 24.
14 W.H. Grey, "US/South Africa: Standing for Sanctions," *Africa Report*, March/April 1986, 27
15 *Southern Africa Report*, 8 April, 1983.
16 General Magnus Malan, cited in D. O'Meara, *Volkskapitalisme: Class, Capital and Ideology in the Development of Afrikaner Nationalism, 1934–1948* (Johannesburg: Ravan Press, 1983), 253.

Council (NSC), Defence Manpower Committee (DMPC) and Regional Security Councils (RSC).

South Africa's war in Angola delivered its own turning point of sorts that had an influence on the thinking inside the military and political establishments in South Africa and brought Namibia's independence closer: the Battle of Cuito Cuanavale. The Angolan army (FAPLA) launched a huge initiative late in 1987 to finally defeat the UNITA rebels in south-east Angola and to destroy their main base at Jamba. The SADF came to UNITA's rescue again and heavily defeated FAPLA at the Lomba River. FAPLA then retreated to Cuito Cuanavale, from where they requested, and received, Cuban military assistance. A series of battles ensued, with about 60,000 troops involved and at the end of March 1988 the SADF withdrew from Angola. Negotiations to end all foreign military presence in Angola began in June 1988 and at the end of that year agreements were signed that meant the end of South Africa's – and Cuba's – military presence in Angola, which started in 1975. South Africa's star negotiator was Foreign Minister Pik Botha. His director-general, Neil van Heerden, said P. W. Botha's negotiating efforts on Namibia 'prepared us to do drastic things in South Africa – such as to free Nelson Mandela. Pik Botha paved the way for the New South Africa.'[17] Chester Crocker, as US assistant secretary of state for African Affairs, who was very involved with the issue and supported the apartheid regime, and in support of the South African Defence Force (SADF) writes the following about Cuito Cuanavale:

> The legend of Cuito Cuanavale is that the SADF was pushed around, defeated, surrounded by hostile forces, and barely able to extricate itself. The reality is that two forces of moderate size tested and checked each other for nine months. The Cubans forestalled the further destruction of FAPLA. The SADF and UNITA consolidated their victory and pushed hard to clear the east bank of the Cuito River, but they pulled back when they realized the price would be too high. The two forces endured a nasty and prolonged engagement in horrible conditions. How, then, did the fighting at Cuito become a heroic Cuban legend? By proclaiming to a credulous world that the town of Cuito Cuanavale – a town under MPLA control since 1976 – was the 'prize' over which the entire campaign was fought, and then by crowing when you have managed not to lose it.[18]

Debunking Crocker's view, Jakkie Celliers who was at the time a senior SADF artillery officer emphasised the following salient points about the battle:

> Cuito Cuanavale was an extremely important strategic turning point, because the SADF was shown to have serious limitations. The significance goes beyond the true events of the day. The SADF didn't take Cuito Cuanavale because they were not prepared to pay the high price of many dead conscripts and other soldiers [Conscription was becoming increasingly unpopular with ordinary white families as the death toll in Namibia and Angola mounted.] That was a stra-

---

17 T. Papenfus, *Pik Botha and his Times* (Pretoria: Litera, 2010); 584. See also M. du Preez, "The Nationalist Party and the Changing of Minds".
18 C. Crocker, *High Noon in Southern Africa: Making Peace in a Rough Neighbourhood* (Johannesburg: Jonathan Ball, 1992), 370–71.

tegic turning point, because it showed the limits of white military might in southern Africa – the government and the SADF for the first time really realised the extent of their military limitations. The South African military strategy around Cuito Cuanavale was uninformed and naïve and they bungled their approach. If it came to a straight battle, the South Africans would have walked over the Cubans, there's no doubt about that. They could definitely have taken Cuito Cuanavale, but they weren't prepared to take the casualties. The point I'm making is that that in itself was a defeat. That was a decision they made. The end result was that they withdrew, all the way to the border of Namibia. Now in strategic terms you have been defeated, and that is more important in reality than the facts on the ground over which the opposing military men will argue until the cows come home.'[19]

While the elaborate security system was being created and unleashed on the township residents by the South African government, the number of those who resisted apartheid rose, which was indicative of the growing crisis facing apartheid rule.[20] Former NP cabinet minister, Stoffel van der Merwe, believes the fear of socialism was as strong as the fear of communism, suggesting again an economic consideration rather than a purely ideological one:

> The ANC reinforced our view that they were communists. The basic tenets of communism were there in all the publications of the ANC. It was difficult to distinguish between communism and socialism. The way in which the ANC received support from the East Bloc, the communist bloc, left you with little doubt that if they came into power, they would try a socialist experiment, which we thought would lead to a Mozambique-type situation. And the evidence was there that many of the African states opted for socialism after they gained their independence.[21]

The African townships were in turmoil and this was not because of communist East Bloc or Soviet Union influence. In 1984, the self-serving black local authorities were elected throughout the country with the lowest ever African voter turnout. Desperate to survive, the discredited councils increased the price of rent, water and electricity sharply. Many residents stopped paying house rents and their water and utility bills – the main source of revenue for local councils. In the meantime, some councillors voted themselves handsome salaries, houses, cars and council chambers. All hell was let loose! In September 1984 riots broke out in the Vaal Triangle, southeast of Johannesburg. The local mayor and deputy mayor of Sebokeng were among the first to be killed. Clergy, students, teachers, lecturers, business people, women's groups, and workers tore down one of the pillars of apartheid. On 20 July 1985 a state of emergency was declared in thirty-eight magisterial districts (this was extended countrywide in 1986). Two days later, O.R. Tambo responded with a call to make

---

19 Interview with Jakkie Celliers by Du Preez conducted by Max du Preez, Pretoria, October 2007, SOHP. On this issue see also H. Lopez Blanch, "Cuba: The Little Giant Against Apartheid', in SADET, *The Road to Democracy in South Africa, Volume 3, International Solidarity* (Pretoria: Unisa Press, 2008), 1156–212.
20 On these issues see SADET, *The Road to Democracy in South Africa, Volume 4, Part 1 and Part 2 [1980–1990]*, (Pretoria: Unisa Press, 2010).
21 Interview with Van der Merwe by Max du Preez, Pretoria, July 2007, SOHP.

the country ungovernable. In the opening weeks of 1986, both the apartheid regime and the ANC publicly confirmed their military strategy and pledged their readiness to escalate their campaigns. A political impasse had been reached.

The continued strife in the African townships pointed to yet more conflict. According to the South African Institute of Race Relations (SAIRR), between February 1984 and January 1986, at least 1,205 people had been killed.[22] Despite the regime's efforts to shore up its military and web of security systems, the levels of resistance increased steadily and reached crisis proportions.[23] The year 1988 was the bloodiest in South Africa's history in terms of guerrilla-related incidents. According to Adriaan Vlok, minister of law and order, there were 291 'terrorist' incidents in 1988 compared to 235 in 1987; 231 in 1986; and 136 in 1985. He also said there were sixty-four 'acts of terrorism' between 1 November 1988 and 12 February 1989. In June 1989 the police reported that security forces had killed 94 and arrested 393 insurgents over the past two years. In the first five months of 1989 some 200 percent more acts of terror had been launched on 'soft' rather than on 'hard' targets.[24]

But the military loss in Angola was an unexpected event, unrelated to the military realities or the dynamics in Afrikanerdom that triggered a new urgency in the NP and the government to make the politics of negotiation a reality. P. W. Botha had a light stroke in July 1987 and a more serious one in January 1989. This signalled the emergence of F. W. de Klerk, the man who was to finally end more than 350 years of white rule.

Conclusion: The End of Apartheid

This final section is based on interviews conducted with Thabo Mbeki, which are cited at length because they lead us to have a better understanding of how apartheid ended. During the early 1990s the liberation movement had many issues to address. These included the aims and objectives of substantive negotiations; the preconditions; the nature and mechanism (such as who would sit at the negotiating table); the cessation of hostilities by both sides; the possibility of the formation of a transitional government; the duration of the negotiations; and the role of the international community in any negotiated resolution of the South African question. The central argument articulated by the ANC was that substantive negotiations were another form of struggle for the fundamental transformation of South Africa by other means.[25] They were always open to the fact that at a certain point the enemy

---

22 SAIRR, *Race Relations Survey, 1988/1989* (Johannesburg: SAIRR, 1990), xxx.
23 See SADET, *The Road to Democracy in South Africa, Volume 4 [1980–1990]* (Pretoria: Unisa Press, 2010), especially chapters 4, 6, 10, and 20.
24 SAIRR, *Race Relations Survey, 1988/1889*, xxx.
25 S.M. Ndlovu, "African National Congress and Negotiations' in SADET, *The Road to Democracy in South Africa, Volume 4*, chapter 2.

might decide that it was ready to talk seriously. It was therefore not surprising that in 1987 Consolidated Goldfields, a South African mining group, funded a project to bring together ANC and Afrikaner establishment figures. Thabo Mbeki recalls the following about these meetings with 'big business' and the Progressive Federal Party (PFP) in Zambia:

> The first interaction [began] in 1985 and went on until we came back [in 1990] ... [in 1987] a British businessman in London, Michael Young, who worked for Goldfields ... says to OR Tambo who was in London, that he thinks that he at Goldfields can arrange for us to meet some of these prominent Afrikaner people. It was in the context of these movements of people from home coming to meet the ANC so he [Young] could make a contribution in that regard. So O.R. Tambo agreed and says go ahead and see what you can do which Michael Young then indeed did do. [26]

After Young's intervention, Professor Willie Esterhuysen of Stellenbosch University coordinated the Afrikaner establishment's delegation that regularly met with the ANC's representatives. He also worked closely with the NIS in this regard. The first meeting took place in October 1987 and the twelfth meeting in 1990. Again, Mbeki remembered:

> This resulted in meetings for a number of years with a group led by Professor Willie Esterhuysen and together with him were other senior personalities in the Afrikaner community – not necessarily politicians and you also had F.W. de Klerk's brother, Wimpie de Klerk and Marinus Dalling, the chief of Sanlam, and Marinus Wiechers who was the head of UNISA. So, it would be people like that and Sampie Terblanche for some time attended these meetings. These were people who were in the upper echelons of Afrikaner society but are not necessary politicians. We started to meet regularly it was not secret either to the ANC or the regime as Esterhuysen would be briefed by national intelligence about questions they wanted answers from us. [27]

As these deliberations continued it became clear to Mbeki that one of the main factors (among others) propelling the apartheid regime to enter into substantive negotiations with the ANC was economic pressure:

> It is during the course of those conversations that they said to us that the then Minister of Finance, Barend du in Plessis, had said ... publicly that apartheid had become unaffordable financially ... It was also a question of what to do with Angola that apartheid had become unaffordable. They had to pull out the SADF forces from Angola. They could no longer afford to sustain that war financially and therefore once they took that decision that SADF must be pulled out of Angola ... [this] meant that a kind of domino effect will take place that they [apartheid regime] would also have to do something about leaving Namibia eventually ... This was said in our meetings. As ANC we immediately came to a conclusion that this is an important report ... you had

---

[26] Interview with Thabo Mbeki conducted by S. M. Ndlovu, Pretoria, 23 February 2011, SADET Oral History Project (hereafter SOHP)

[27] Interview with Thabo Mbeki conducted by S.M. Ndlovu, Pretoria, 23 February 2011, SOHP. See also W. Esterhuysen, "Intelligence at Work: Curtain Raisers to 2 February 1990," *The Thinker*, 13 (March 2010), 24.

that domino effect right along the line. What this report was indicating was that in fact the apartheid regime had become significantly weak and therefore it was most likely to say let us negotiate the resolution of the South African question. So that was one indication that told us this issue of negotiation is bound to arise.[28]

A chance meeting with the chairperson of the Broederbond in New York in 1986 also convinced Mbeki that substantive negotiations would take place soon in South Africa:

And then I think it was again 1986 when I met the then chairman of the Broederbond, Professor Pieter de Lange, who was the principal of Rand Afrikaans University. There was some education meeting in New York organised by I think the Ford Foundation about education in South Africa. He came to that conference as an educationist and so we also attended. I was part of the ANC delegation. I then met him for a number of hours just the two of us in New York. He said to me there are certain things that we must do in South Africa. For instance, we must get rid of the Group Areas Act and we must get rid of the Immorality Act. He said I know that in terms of your thinking these are not significant things, these laws I have mentioned are not significant and therefore they will not form your point of view that reflects readiness to change. But I want you to understand that they are very important for the Afrikaners because what has driven the Afrikaners for many centuries is a fear that here they are surrounded by millions of Africans and therefore they stand the danger at all times to be swamped by these millions and eventually they will disappear as a group and that is why we introduced apartheid ... If you take the Group Areas Act, we say this area is ours as white people – this was a protective measure to avoid us getting swamped by these millions ... Take, for example, the Mixed Marriages Act, Immorality Act and all these things, they are about the same things if we do not do all those things, we the Afrikaners will vanish because we are surrounded by these millions. So, he says, you see these apartheid laws I am talking about, they are a protective wall around us as Afrikaners but that is why we are saying the first thing we must do is to get rid of the Group Areas Act.

Furthermore, according to Mbeki, de Lange reasoned that if the racist laws were expunged, Afrikaners would soon understand that apartheid policies were unnecessary:

Afrikaners will be very worried [if we discard these laws] but they will wake up the following morning and say nothing has happened to us and wake up the next week and say again still nothing has happened to us. Then eventually they will begin to say to themselves it is quite clear we have never needed this Group Areas Act in the first place. Indeed, why do we need a white government? So that is the importance of removing these laws. It will change the mentality among the whites to such a point they will say in fact we do not need apartheid. We thought it was protecting us but this apartheid thing is now becoming a threat. So, I said now I understand and he says in reply, 'Can you please tell Mr Tambo that is what I am saying as chairman of the Broederbond. What I am going to do from now onwards I am going to disappear from the public because Broederbond is organised in chapters around the country. I am going to disappear in order to engage the Broederbond right across the country so that as an organisation, we, all of us, say let us take this step leading to the conclusion which Afrikaners must arrive at [that] we do not need apartheid.' So I said professor, I will certainly report, which I did ... but

---

28 Interview with T. Mbeki conducted by S. M. Ndlovu.

then I said Professor de Lange, there are people among the Afrikaner community who are going to oppose what you are saying, take for instance Eugene Terblanche; he will oppose you and I suspect he will be ready to take up arms to preserve the status quo, what will you do? He says 'we will shoot him'. I was very shocked ... it is coming from another Afrikaner they will shoot another one who is opposing change. He says we will shoot him. I said ok, I understand.[29]

Substantial political changes began on 2 February 1990 in a landmark parliamentary speech when President F.W. de Klerk announced the unbanning of the ANC along with a number of other organisations. He also lifted some of the state of emergency restrictions and announced a new dispensation that would include a democratic constitution based on a racially inclusive universal franchise in South Africa. On 11 February 1990 after the unbanning of the ANC, and on the day when Rolihlahla Nelson Mandela was released from prison, the ANC's Politico-Military Committee (PMC) issued a two-page document titled 'Unbanning of ANC: Some Strategic Considerations'. This document argued that De Klerk wanted to initiate negotiating procedures whilst the balance of political forces was still in his side. His strategy, though it complied with the Harare Declaration demand for substantive negotiations to take place, also highlighted the apartheid regime's tactical endeavours to gain international legitimacy and end decades of isolation. In addition, the ANC pointed out, De Klerk also wanted to restructure apartheid policies, safeguard the faltering economy and guarantee white power and privilege. Despite the unbanning the ANC, the PMC was of the view that De Klerk had failed to meet the ANC's conditions for substantive negotiations because he did not release *all* political prisoners. He had also failed to define and elaborate on the government's conditions for the return of exiles. Furthermore, De Klerk was advised by the PMC to lift the partial state of emergency that was still in place.[30]

After the adoption of the Harare Declaration of 1989 by the international community, calls for an interim government and election of a constituent assembly were raised repeatedly by the ANC. For example, on 3 May 1990, Mandela called for national elections to form a constituent assembly; and in December 1990 an ANC document, 'Programme of Mass Action to Destroy Apartheid and Transfer Power to the People', repeated this call; it was also reiterated at the ANC's December 1990 national consultative conference, which provided a medium for self-criticism and proper planning. Whilst these political skirmishes continued, on 13 December 1990, O. R. Tambo triumphantly returned to South Africa after thirty years in exile. His arrival was in time to attend the first ANC consultative conference held inside South Africa for thirty-one years. It took place in Johannesburg on 14–16 December 1990. Notwithstanding the fact that low intensity warfare and violence continued unabated in var-

---

[29] Interview with T. Mbeki conducted by S. M. Ndlovu.
[30] University of Cape Town Manuscripts and Archives, BC1081, P25.7, Negotiations, 1990–1995, "Common Society: Another Rethink by the PMC on unbanning of the ANC. Some Strategic Considerations."

ious parts of the country, the national conference was a success. The adoption of the theme '1991, the year of mass action for the transfer of power', was an ANC attempt to bring mass struggle into the theatre of negotiations. All these issues were emphasised in the 8 January 1991 annual statement released by Mandela. The same call was endorsed by the ANC's national conference in July 1991.[31]

The long and tortuous road to democracy in South Africa was littered with countless potholes and turning points in the early 1990s. These were defined by the Harare Declaration agreed upon by the regional leaders in southern Africa which was subsequently approved by both the Organisation of African Unity and UN, paving the way for political settlement in South Africa; the unbanning of the liberation movements; the release of political prisoners; the return of exiled South Africans; the establishment of the Convention of Democratic South Africa (CODESA); the scrapping of apartheid legislation; rolling mass action; and state sponsored violence. But the millions of South Africans who queued patiently to cast their votes for the first time on 26–27 April 1994, the fruits of victory and emancipation from white minority rule and oppression, were sweet indeed. But this was political emancipation, now the struggle is set for economic emancipation.

---

[31] See R. Rantete, "Room for Compromise: The African National Congress and the Transitional Mechanism," Centre for Policy Studies, Johannesburg, February 1992, 3.

Sifiso Mxolisi Ndlovu
Chapter 12
The Geopolitics and Geo-economics of Apartheid South Africa and the Cold War: A Global History

Abstract: Whilst white regimes in southern Africa such as apartheid South Africa might have been repugnant to western democratic ideals, these regimes supported the interests of western governments. Western powers were expected by those who supported white minority rule to separate ideological yearnings from the realities of the Cold War and either maintain the apartheid regime in power as a bastion of anti-communism, or at least, assure a slow and peaceful transition to African majority rule that would protect the rights of the white minority in South Africa and in the process perpetuate western imperialism. Western powers claimed that continued white supremacy would drive Africans to communism as the only means of their liberation. Therefore, western powers were expected by anti-communists to support a rapid shift to African majority rule for ideological reasons but also to protect their own long-range interests. The political control exercised by the apartheid regime was doomed because of the action of the liberation movement and support garnered through international solidarity, particularly from the Soviet Union. As a result, the western governments were expected by the international anti-apartheid movements and socialist countries to assist in the downfall of the racist South African government or face the prospect of racial war and a continent totally alienated from the West.

Keywords: Cold war, geopolitics, geopolitics, apartheid, international solidarity, liberation movements, communism, third communist international.

South Africa as a Nuclear Power in the African Continent

This chapter is divided into two sections: the first explores South Africa as a nuclear power during the Cold War and the second examines the international solidarity against the apartheid regime. It will also include an important case study that highlights memories of a committed South African revolutionary in the Soviet Union. Controlling South Africa during the Cold War era was a geostrategic priority for the Western super powers because of its 1,900-mile coastline with harbours at Durban, East London, Port Elizabeth, Cape Town and Walvis Bay (a seaport in the then South West Africa, now Namibia). Being the southernmost country on the African continent, South Africa abuts both the Indian and the Atlantic Oceans and its fascist leaders vociferously pledged to 'defend the free world from the communist threat' during the Cold War era.[1] Thus, apartheid South Africa played a vital role in the global strategy and geo-economics of western imperialism led by the US and UK. The western powers wanted to make the Indian Ocean area a region for their dominance and control, and they regarded South Africa as a 'second Gibraltar' or 'gatekeeper' to the this region. For example, during the closure of the Suez Canal, the volume of world shipping passing the Cape of Good Hope was estimated at seventy ships per day and no less than 25,450 ships a year. The UK alone accounted for 20 percent of the traffic and the major commodity shipped along this route was oil; half a million tons a day. Producing about 77 percent of the gold in the western world and with more diamonds than any country, South Africa was a prized possession of western powers, for it was among the richest countries in the world. The continued exploitation of mineral resources in Africa was also crucial in terms of implementing the Marshall Plan and the European Recovery Plan (ERP) after World War II. South Africa therefore played a central role in maintaining western imperialism, especially in relation to the African continent. This country was a base from which western imperialism could consolidate and extend its hold on the continent. Historically, South Africa has always been closely associated with the West. The country fought as a member of the British Commonwealth alongside western allies in both world wars, occupied a special place in western defence plans, and received a steady flow of arms from western countries. Thus, in the post-war years. After the end of World War II, the US and the UK feared the spread of communism and the Cold War began. The ANC was criticised for their links with the Soviet Union, a point that will be elaborated upon later. The western allies argued that they had to prevent a possible onslaught from the Soviet Union on strategic areas and economic opportunities in Africa.[2]

To consolidate control of southern Africa, western powers held a conference in 1951 on defence strategy in Africa. It was convened in Nairobi by the British and South African governments, and it was emphasised at the conference that South Africa was expected to play a strategic role in containing the Soviet Union. For example, as part of the defence strategy in southern Africa, the UK would rely on the docking and refitting facilities at Simonstown, Durban, and Cape Town. The Simonstown

---

[1] The section is based on S. M. Ndlovu, "The Geopolitics of Apartheid South Africa in the African continent: 1948–1994," in SADET, *The Road to Democracy in South Africa, Volume 5, African Solidarity, Part 1* (Pretoria: Unisa Press, 2013), chapter 1; S. M. Ndlovu, "The Western Super-Powers and the Liberation Struggle in Africa: The Politics of Imperialism, Domination and Resistance, 1948–1980s' in *Afrika Zamani*, 17 (2009), 145–84.

[2] F. Meli, "South Africa Joins Imperialist Bloc in Indian Ocean Offensive," *The African Communist*, 61, Second Quarter (1975), 56; A.K. Ray, "Geopolitics of the Indian Ocean," *Peace and Solidarity: Journal of All-Indian Peace and Solidarity Organisations*, 5, 11 (November 1974); N. K. Krishnan, "Pentagon War Base in the Indian Ocean," *Peace and Solidarity*, 5, 11 (1974); M. Moola, "South Africa: A Threat to Peace in Africa and the Indian Ocean," *Peace and Solidarity*, 5, 11 (1974).

Agreement, a military agreement between Britain and South Africa was signed in 1955 and renewed in 1961, allowed Britain to use the Simonstown base.³ Simonstown was established in 1946 to augment the then existing Royal Navy in defending sea lanes. This agreement between South Africa and the UK was then South Africa's only known military pact. The two countries agreed on cooperation in naval planning for the protection of the Cape sea route. British-built warships costing $50 million were brought to South Africa and political agreements were reached. Both countries undertook what was called a 'joint seaward defence' system. The naval vessels included seaward defence ships, coastal minesweepers, and four frigates. Britain also re-equipped the South African Air Force by supplying it with eight Avro Shackleton maritime reconnaissance aircrafts redesigned for use also as tactical bombers and transports. France, which supplied South Africa with Daphne submarines, was also involved.⁴

To consolidate their strategy of containing the Soviet Union, the western powers concluded that one of the main support areas needed would be southern Africa, the area in which the Union of South Africa, a British dominion at the time, was a key country, until 1961 when the country became a republic. Their argument was based on the fact that most important sources of mineral resources in southern Africa (outside the Union itself) were located in the Belgian Congo (Democratic Republic of the Congo) and Southern and Northern Rhodesia (Zimbabwe and Zambia). Raw materials from these colonies included uranium, platinum, copper, cobalt, gold, chrome, vanadium, and manganese.⁵ Southern Africa – South Africa in particular – was referred to as the 'Persian Gulf of minerals'. Minerals formed the cornerstone of the US foreign policy towards Africa and the West was reliant upon these reserves for supplies strategically important minerals. For example, the US was particularly dependent upon South Africa for reserves of chromium, manganese, vanadium, and the platinum group metals. It was calculated that during the 1980s, South Africa possessed 66.4 percent of the world's reserve of chromium, a mineral that was vital for the manufacture of automobile and computer components in the US. Chromium is also used in the production of stainless steel and in the chemical industry. There is no substitute for manganese in the manufacture of wrought steel – and the platinum group metals, of which South Africa had about 73.2 percent of the world's reserves, are vital for many industrial applications. The United States foreign policy towards Africa was also closely linked to its need for strategic minerals such as chromium, manganese, vanadium and the platinum group metals, which South Africa provided.

---

3 M. Moola, "South Africa: A Threat to Peace in Africa and the Indian Ocean," *Peace and Solidarity*, 5, 11 (1974). See also Bunting, *The Rise of the South African Reich*, (London: IDAF, 1986), chapter 15; J. Maote and T. Temba, "The Outward Drive: South Africa's Military Machine," in *Apartheid*, ed. by A. La Guma (Berlin: Seven Seas, 1971), 123–36; "NATO and South Africa," *Sechaba*, 9, 3(1975).
4 "The Simonstown Agreement," *Sechaba*, 4, 10 (1970).
5 S.M. Ndlovu, "The geopolitics of Apartheid South Africa in the African continent;" S. M. Ndlovu, "The Western Super-Powers and the Liberation Struggle in Africa."

As argued above, the Cape sea route was also of great strategic value in conventional war planning 'east of Suez' because Simonstown was used not only for patrol observation but also for gathering intelligence. This was made possible by a $21 million communication complex that had the capability of charting ship movements in an operational area ranging from the Atlantic to North Africa and from South America to Bangladesh. The sophisticated electronics gear at this installation in Silvermine, near Cape Town, could flash information to war rooms in the US and UK in seconds.[6] The South Africa-Indian Ocean-Middle East axis played a vital role in the growing alliance between the apartheid regime and the western powers. By 1965, about 127 licences were acquired by the apartheid regime for local manufacture of foreign designed military equipment. This was part of a ten-year defence programme for 'modernisation' and 'standardisation' announced by the minister of Defence, P.W. Botha in 1970. According to the US Arms Control and Disarmament Agency, South Africa received in the decade from 1965–1974, military equipment from western powers equivalent to the value of $358 million.[7]

The US maintained an ambiguous position towards the apartheid regime during the period immediately after World War II. Some officials in the US government opposed the regime's racist policies because of an ideological desire to secure African support for the US's Cold War policies in the UN and elsewhere. Thus, the hardening of US policy during the course of 1965. This was in preparation for the outcome of the South West Africa (Namibia) case before the International Court of Justice and also in expectation of the Security Council debate that had arisen from the examination by the Committee of Experts on the feasibility of sanctions against the apartheid regime. To maintain its ambivalent position towards the apartheid regime, the US refused a visa to General R.C. Hiemstra, general chief of staff of the South African Defence Force (SADF) to pay a routine inspection visit to the office of the military attaché located in the South African Embassy in Washington. This contrasted starkly with the full facilities made available to officers of the US armed forces visiting South Africa, including one particular visit in May 1962 by the deputy chief of staff of Intelligence (US Army), who undertook a routine visit to US Army attaché posts in Africa. This visit to various African countries was a direct parallel with the proposed visit to the US by Hiemstra.[8]

Another example of this ambivalence adopted by the US, can be seen in the US opposition to attempts by other countries to exclude South Africa from scientific and technical agencies. By virtue of the agreement establishing the missile tracking station at Grootfontein near Pretoria, the US aircraft and senior personnel enjoyed ex-

---

6 *Armed Forces Journal*, June 1973.
7 US Arms Control and Disarmament Agency, *World Military Expenditures and Arms Transfers, 1965–1974* (Washington: US Arms Control and Disarmament Agency, 1976), 250–51.
8 South African National Defence Force Department (hereafter SANDFD) archives, Pretoria, File MV-B, vol. 2, section 216, "Relations between South Africa and the United States: Summarised Balance Sheet," 21 January 1965, 1–3.

tensive facilities, which in the event of major difficulties arising between South Africa and the US would have provided extremely valuable intelligence. The US also requested additional missile tracking facilities at Walvis Bay and this request was approved in principle by John Vorster. In addition, the Pentagon offered naval and air force courses to their South African counterparts. In terms of space research, South Africa's Hartbeeshoek station near Pretoria played a vital role in US space research and gave the apartheid regime outstanding prestige in this field, but the decision to build an additional station in Spain on roughly the same longitude, meant that Hartbeeshoek could no longer be used by the apartheid regime as a bargaining tool. However, it was of immense importance to South African technology in the field of advanced electronics. Over one hundred white South African personnel received what was described as 'a major free advanced technical education'[9] in a research field of supreme value to the apartheid regime in the event of war or similar national emergency. The pool of electronically-based knowledge systems (including computers) and experience developed at the research station exceeded what was made available to the South African Broadcasting Corporation, the South African Defence Force (SADF) and the Post Office combined.[10]

In terms of development in nuclear based technology and armaments, the apartheid regime decided to purchase a nuclear reactor of American design for Pelindaba nuclear station. This decision made South Africa completely dependent on the US with respect to nuclear fuel and related research on nuclear technology. The US was by far the most advanced country in terms of atomic energy research, and the facilities which the apartheid regime's scientists enjoyed for both contact and training in the US were invaluable to the development of nuclear research – including nuclear power projects – in South Africa. This dependence was successfully exploited by the US State Department to pressure South Africa to accept the International Atomic Energy Agency safeguards. Thereafter, there were no difficulties with the United States Atomic Energy Commission on any aspect of atomic energy cooperation. The US Commission supported apartheid South Africa to the hilt, resulting in a reciprocal aid package offered by South Africa to the US when rich uranium was in a very short supply internationally.[11]

As the Cold War intensified, vast quantities of South African uranium were being used to arm nuclear weapons produced by the US and the UK and it became apparent that apartheid South Africa was a loyal ally of the Western super powers. A great deal went on at places like Pelindaba in Pretoria and Valindaba in Hartbeeshoek – nuclear facilities only a short distance from Pretoria – and at various installations in the Cape Province (including the Koeberg reactor) where South Africa had developed

---

9 *Ibid.*
10 SANDFD archives, Pretoria, File MV-B, vol. 2, section 216, "Relations between South Africa and the United States: Summarised Balance Sheet," 21 January 1965, 8.
11 SANDFD archives, Pretoria, File MV-B, vol. 2, section 216, "Relations between South Africa and the United States: Summarised Balance Sheet," 21 January 1965, 9.

several prototypes of an advanced missile delivery system for more compact versions of the atom bomb. It was therefore not surprising that apartheid South Africa was a founding member of the International Atomic Energy Agency (IAEA) set up in 1957, and was one of the states to draft its statutes. The regime's international status as the most advanced nuclear power on the African continent granted it a permanent seat on the IAEA's board of governors. In 1958, the Atomic Energy Board (AEB) of South Africa established the first nuclear research programme in the African continent that included research on a power reactor concept appropriate to South Africa. At its head was Abraham Roux who had a doctorate in mechanical engineering from the University of the Witwatersrand. He became the chairperson of the AEB in 1967.[12]

By the early 1960s, the South African government had made the decision to build an atom bomb and other nuclear weapons. The targets were, for obvious reasons, Tanzania, Zambia and Angola – countries that provided bases and offices to both the ANC and PAC. The liberation movement in Angola challenged white minority rule enforced by the Portuguese, a member of an unholy alliance with both South Africa and Rhodesia. In August 1968, after the Wankie and Sipolilo campaigns waged by the MK and the Zimbabwe People's Revolutionary Army,[13] General Hiemstra of the SADF told a gathering in Stellenbosch that "terrorist attacks on Rhodesia could gradually develop into full scale war" and he doubted "if Russia would supply nuclear arms to Zambia (where the ANC was based) for use against South Africa."[14] In parliament, P. W. Botha, the then minister of defence, issued a warning that the apartheid regime regarded "facilitating terrorism as an act of provocation, and that any country that incited terrorism and guerrilla warfare must realise that provocation can lead to hard retaliation in the interests of self-respect and peace." Both was referring particularly to Zambia and Tanzania. He asserted that the danger facing South Africa was greater than ever before because "the communists want to pocket South Africa and use it against the free world."[15] Magnus Malan, who was appointed chief of the SADF in 1976 and Minister of Defence in 1980, and then served in P.W. Botha's cabinet, explained that the Atomic Energy Board had started to develop a nuclear explosive ability in the 1960s with a view to use it in mining operations. But this changed in the 1970s:

> Because of the escalation of the physical military threat to South Africa, the Government was compelled to re-evaluate the need for and production of nuclear devices. At the same time incisive action was paid to the active Soviet presence on the African continent. The initial purpose

---

[12] A.J. Venter, *How South Africa Built Six Atom Bombs: And then Abandoned its Nuclear Weapons Program* (Johannesburg: Ashanti Publishing, 2008), chapter 2; See also the special issue of *Sechaba* entitled "The Nuclear Conspiracy: FRG Collaborates to Strengthen Apartheid," No. 9, November-December (1975).
[13] See M. Ralinala *et al.*, "The Wankie and Sipolilo Campaigns," in SADET, *The Road to Democracy, Volume 1*, chapter 12.
[14] *The Star*, 10 August 1968.
[15] *The Rand Daily Mail*, 2 and 4 April 1968.

of the development of a non-military nuclear capability had to be re-evaluated in view of the increasing hostile threat. It was realised that it was necessary to possess nuclear explosive devices, and their development was approved at the highest Governmental level.[16]

Abdul Minty noted that in 1957 under the 'Atoms for Peace' programme the United States and South Africa signed a 50-year agreement for nuclear co-operation. In 1961, South Africa purchased the Safari 1 research reactor from the United States and received extensive technical assistance in the nuclear field from the US, Britain, West Germany, and France. South Africa also collaborated with Israel in solidifying its nuclear programme. In 1976, Roux confirmed that:

> we can ascribe our degree of advancement today in large measure to the training and the assistance so willingly provided by the US during the early years of our nuclear programme, when several Western world's nuclear nations co-operated in initiating our scientist and engineers into nuclear science ... even our nuclear philosophy, unmistakably our own, owes so much to the thinking of American nuclear scientists.[17]

The ANC concluded that that the uranium enrichment plant which was officially announced by Vorster in 1970, was developed with the co-operation of the West German-based Society for Nuclear Research in Karlsruhe and another state-controlled company, STEAG in Essen, and with the agreement and active participation of the Federal Government in Bonn. At first there were several denials from Bonn but in April 1975, Prime Minister Vorster confirmed the existence of a pilot enrichment plant at Valindaba.[18] It was only after South Africa gained independence in 1994 that the international world claimed to have officially 'discovered' that the apartheid regime had built six atom bombs as part of its defence strategy against the liberation movements and African countries that supported them.[19] However, through *Sechaba*, the mouthpiece of the ANC, exposed critical aspects of the apartheid regime's nuclear weapons programme.

From the outset, the ANC took an uncompromising stand on the issue of South Africa's nuclear capability, declaring that the regime intended to use it for purposes of war. In 1979, Leslie Harriman, Nigerian ambassador to the UN, accused the British government of collaboration in South African nuclear projects. Later, a retired nuclear engineer named J. Vogt wrote a letter to the South African minister of mines and energy, questioning the secrecy surrounding activities in the Koeberg nuclear plant if

---

[16] M. Malan, *My Life with the SA Defence Force* (Pretoria: Protea, 2006), 214.
[17] Cited in A. Minty, "South Africa's Nuclear Capability: The Apartheid Bomb," in *Destructive Engagement: Southern Africa at War* eds. P. Johnson and D. Martin (Harare: Zimbabwe Publishing House, 1986), 208–09.
[18] Minty, "South Africa's Nuclear Capability."
[19] A.Venter, *How South Africa Built Six Atom Bombs*; D. Albright, *South Africa's Secret Nuclear Weapons* (Washington: Institute for Science and International Security, May 1994); M. Marder and D. Oberdorfer, "'How the West, Soviets Acted to Defuse South African A-Test," *Washington Post*, 28 August 1977; *Sechaba* special edition on the nuclear conspiracy, 9, November-December, 1975.

indeed there were no secrets about nuclear power plants and their sole intention was to produce energy. Furthermore, when a representative of the conservationist organisation, Friends of the Earth, visited Koeberg in July 1981, he maintained that the 'tenuous political situation' in South Africa made the use of nuclear energy 'inherently risky'.[20]

The world first became aware of South Africa's nuclear ambitions when a Soviet spy satellite took pictures of preparations for an underground explosion at a place called Vastrap in the remote Northern Cape on 7 August 1977. In April 1979 the South African government revealed that the US ambassador's plane had been used to take clandestine photographs of the Valindaba nuclear plant. On 22 September 1979 a US Vela satellite detected a double flash over the southern oceans in the vicinity of Prince Edward and Marion Islands, the tell-tale double flash of a nuclear explosion. The CIA added to the picture by establishing that the South African Navy had been conducting secret exercises in the same area during the time of the explosion, and on 14 July 1980 the US Defence Intelligence Agency declared that its investigations had shown that the double flash was 'probably a clandestine nuclear explosion'.[21] The South African government never admitted that it was indeed a South African nuclear bomb that was exploded.

With the ANC's policies on consolidating their international solidarity struggle against the apartheid regime enmeshed in the Cold War, the western powers could not afford to lose apartheid South Africa to communism.[22] The war scenarios and defence strategies formulated during 1949–50 with western powers were still relevant in B. J. Vorster and P. W. Botha's time, particularly so because the Soviet Union and Cuba were involved in the war in Angola; those early plans influenced the constructive engagement doctrine that defined US foreign policy in South Africa in the 1970s and 80s.[23] It was obvious to the ANC that Richard Nixon and Ronald Reagan's policy made the US an ally of the apartheid regime. The roots of the US's pro-apartheid position go back to the policies of both Henry Kissinger and Chester Crocker.[24] The Rea-

---

20 "Koeberg: Power House for War," *Sechaba* (February 1983), 20; and A. Minty, "South Africa's Nuclear Capability," 208.
21 M. du Preez, *Of Warriors, Lovers and Prophets* (Cape Town: Zebra, 2004), 214.
22 See V. Shubin and M. Traikova, "There is No Threat from the Eastern Bloc," chapter 12; Zhong Weiyun and Xu Sujiang, "China's Support for and Solidarity with South Africa's Liberation Struggle," chapter 15, in SADET, *The Road to Democracy, Volume 3, International Solidarity, Part 2*.
23 University of Fort Hare, (hereafter UFH), O.R. Tambo Papers (hereafter ORT Papers), Folder A 17.1.4, Box 17, Statement of the president of the ANC, Oliver Tambo, to the Council of Foreign Relations, New York, 8 November 1982; Lopez Blanch, H., 'Cuba: The Little Giant against Apartheid', in SADET, *The Road to Democracy in South Africa, Volume 3, International Solidarity* (Pretoria: Unisa Press, 2008).
24 M. El-Khawas and B. Cohen, eds., *National Security Memorandum 39: The Kissinger Study of Southern Africa (secret)* (Westport: Lawrence Hill, 1976); W. Minter, "Destructive Engagement: The United States and South Africa in the Reagan Era," in *Destructive Engagement: Southern Africa at war*, ed. by P. Johnson and D. Martin (Harare: Zimbabwe Publishing House, 1986), chapter 10. See also B. Ma-

gan administration's consolidation of ties with the apartheid regime was linked to its pro-apartheid foreign policy on southern Africa. For instance, in June 1980, addressing the Foreign Affairs sub-Committee on Africa, Crocker, then director of African Studies at Georgetown Centre for Strategic and International Studies, expressed his undying support for the apartheid regime during the sub-committee hearing on US policy towards South Africa: "We [the US] have important interests there [in South Africa] that relate to our global concerns, our economic health and our military flexibility, which we would not want to see lost during this transition, this process of political change in South Africa."[25]

Moreover, another strategic and economic consideration reflected by the US policy towards South Africa was the country's geographical importance. In testimony to Congress in 1980, Crocker stated: "To me there is no debate, that the security of the Cape route is by far the most important Western interest in the African region".[26] By 1979, the US was the world's largest oil consumer (about 19 million barrels a day). Every month about 2,300 ships, including 600 oil tankers used the Cape route, making it the main access route to the West for oil tankers coming from the Persian Gulf. The Suez Canal was too narrow for ultra large crude-oil carriers, levied higher tolls and was unreliable due to political instability in the region. Approximately 65 percent of western Europe's oil imports were transported via the Cape route. South Africa was the only country on the east African coast with the necessary economic infrastructure, military potential, ports, airports and dry docks to support western defence in the area. These factors were enough to convince many in the Reagan administration that protection of the Cape route, and prevention of its falling into the hands of the USSR was vital enough to warrant the support of the pro western government in Pretoria. Crocker himself pointed out: "It is clearly more than a convenience that South Africa's excellent port and air facilities should not be in the hands of a potential adversary."[27] Key elements of the constructive engagement policy included quiet

---

gubane, 'From Détente to the Rise of the Garrison State', in SADET, *Road to Democracy*, Volume 2, Chapter 2.

25 UFH, ORT Papers, Folder A 17.1.4, Box 17, Statement of the president of ANC to Council of Foreign Relations, New York, 8 November 1982, 3. See also C. Crocker, "South Africa: Strategy for Change," *Foreign Affairs*, Winter, 1980/81; C. Crocker, M. Greznes and R. Henderson, "US Policy for the 80s'" *Africa Report*, January–February 1981, 7–14; C. Crocker, "The United States and Africa," *Africa Report*, September–October 1981, 6–8; H. F. Jackson, "Reagan's Policy Rupture," *Africa Report*, September–October 1981, 9–13.

26 C. Crocker, "The United States and Africa".

27 J. E. Davies, *Constructive Engagement? Chester Crocker and the American Policy in South Africa, Namibia and Angola*, (Athens: Ohio University Press, 2007), 58; Crocker, "South Africa: Strategy for Change," 346; Crocker, "US Policy for the 80s"; Crocker, "The United States and Africa;" W. Minter, "'Destructive Engagement'; B. Magubane, 'From Détente to the Rise of the Garrison State."

diplomacy pursued by the US government to persuade the frontline states in southern Africa to open dialogue with the apartheid regime.[28]

In 1981, Crocker, Mario Greznes, and Robert Herderson, re-hashed most of the late 1940s and 1950s arguments discussed in the earlier in this chapter. They co-authored an article entitled, "US Policy for the 80s'" in which they stated that in military and geostrategic terms, the Cape route, an import conduit for the majority of Western imports of petroleum and non-fuel minerals, was not vulnerable to imminent disruption in any credibly foreseeable *peacetime* scenario. In fact, they expressed the view that because of the struggles for national liberation in southern Africa, the potential threat to western oil and mineral supplies was greater on land than on sea. However, there were two worrisome contingencies, and these were important. First, at a time of general war or even limited conflict that could break out elsewhere, the supplies remained vital. It was clearly more than a mere convenience that South Africa's excellent port and air facilities were not in the hands of a potential adversary, the USSR, at such a time. They argued that the Soviet Union was unlikely to begin a war by disrupting western shipping, because they believed there were far more convenient places from which the USSR might seek to disrupt oil traffic. But they were of the view that the USSR would have major advantages once war occurred if political forces hostile to the West, such as the ANC, were in control of South Africa. This concern was applicable both to a wartime scenario in Europe and a large- scale Middle East conflict in which the western powers were involved. For these reasons, the authors suggested that it was clearly not in the US interest that change in South Africa should lead towards a government that was dependent for its existence and survival on Soviet military power, as was the case in Angola. In such a case, the very presence of Soviet forces at Africa's sensitive southern tip would constitute a powerful basis for intimidation of western nations.[29] To counter the 'communist threat' and publicly confirm the strategic importance of southern Africa, in 1981 Crocker affirmed the following arguments articulated previously in the late 1940s and 1950s:

> Our concerns with southern Africa, from Zaire to the Cape, are born out of recognition of the strategic, political, and economic importance of this region to the United States and the Western world. Southern African nations play an important role in meeting US, European and Japanese requirements for critical minerals such as chrome ore, cobalt, industrial diamonds, manganese, platinum, vanadium, copper, tin and asbestos. The Western world must remain engaged in this geopolitically important region during a period of strife and uncertainty. Southern African states form the littoral to one of the vital lifelines of the industrial democracies. We must work actively and play our proper role – diplomatic, strategic, commercial and economic – in this key area to

---

[28] W. Minter and S. Hill, "Anti-apartheid Solidarity in the United States-South African Relations: From the Margins to the Mainstream' in SADET, *The Road to Democracy in South Africa, Volume 3, International Solidarity* (Pretoria: Unisa Press, 2008).
[29] Crocker *et al.*, "US Policy for the 80s," 12; W. Minter, "'Destructive Engagement'; Minter and S. Hill, 'Anti-apartheid Solidarity in the United States-South African Relations."

prevent destabilization and economic decline, and to foster a secure and prosperous regional order.[30]

On the supposed communist threat, Crocker elaborated:

> Failure to be an active participant in the affairs of southern Africa can only lead to heightened regional tension, polarization, and Soviet backed adventurism. That is why we have not shied away from the difficult negotiations in Namibia; why we have not abandoned South Africans of all races who are seeking constructive changes ... and why we have not been dissuaded from pursuing an end to the internationalized strife in Angola. The stakes are too high, the threats to our mutual interests too great. [31]

International Solidarity and the Apartheid Regime

South Africa's racial policies were on the agenda of the UN General Assembly from its very first session in 1946 until the dawn of non-racial democracy in 1994, hence the UN's contribution to the liberation struggle in South Africa. In the 1940s the ANC recognised the value of the UN to the liberation cause; it set up a committee of eminent Africans to interpret the UN Charter as it related to Africa; and to prepare a bill of rights. This action had a dual purpose: to inform the South African regime about the full aspirations of the African people; and to make it clear to the UN member states that Africans had an undisputed claim to full citizenship. The report of the committee, adopted by the ANC in December 1943, became an important ANC policy document. In effect, the ANC had extended its vision to all nations of the world.

The catalyst was in 1946 in the form of a complaint by India on the treatment of Indians in South Africa. The government of India requested that the matter be placed on the agenda of the General Assembly. New discriminatory legislation had been introduced against Indians and was likely to impair friendly relations between the two countries. A. B. Xuma, president-general of the ANC, led a multiracial delegation to lobby at the UN. He presented a memorandum on the discriminatory nature of the government, the oppression of the Black people of South Africa and their demand for full equality. The Assembly rejected the contention of the prime minister of the Union of South Africa, that the treatment of Indians was a domestic matter and argued that the treatment of Indians should be in line with the international agreement reached by the two governments. At the same session the South African government asked for approval of its plan to annex South West Africa (later Namibia), but this was refused and the territory was placed under UN trusteeship. African leaders in South Africa were elated by the defeat of the government on both issues, a decided victory against the policy of white domination. The Assembly discussed the treatment

---

30 Crocker, "The United States and Africa," 7.
31 Crocker, "The United States and Africa," 7.

of Indians in South Africa annually from 1946. The South African government simply ignored these appeals and proceeded to enact other discriminatory laws such as the Group Areas Act, but importantly, the discussions and resolutions of the Assembly led to greater awareness of apartheid and its evils.[32]

Both Sharpeville Massacre of 1960 and Soweto Uprisings of 1976 strengthened the UN's role in fighting against apartheid in South Africa. The Sharpeville Massacre took place when the apartheid regime viciously ended a peaceful protest, as it did with all protest campaigns organised by the Pan-Africanist Congress (PAC) and ANC. State violence and injustices in South Africa attracted international attention because of this incident. The regime's strategy of violent suppression of all discontent and calls for change intensified after 1960 with a considerable number of the anticolonial struggle leaders thrown into jail. In the decade of wanton violence, those leaders who were spared were given long jail terms, as was the case for Dorothy Nyembe, Winnie Mandela, Ratshivhanda Ndou, Rita Ndzanga, and others. These were key activists in the underground struggle that ensued when open political activity came under attack during the 1960s. The ANC's underground struggle intensified and exiled liberation movements now promoted international solidarity campaigns outside the country. This led to the arrest of some 240 peaceful underground activists in 1969 for all manner of violations against what they considered to be illegal laws such as those on internal security, unlawful political gatherings and the suppression of communism.[33] One of the leaders recounted his experiences, telling how they appeared in court on charges of violence and military training, but lacking sufficient evidence the state withdrew the case. The activists were later re-arrested on communism charges, but this case was also thrown out by the court in 1970. They were subsequently banned when the court could not find any satisfactory evidence on which to jail them because their struggle was non-violent.[34]

It was in this climate with all legal channels closed, liberation struggle leaders in jail, and activists banned, that the youth took up the mantle of leading the mass-based, non-violent struggle in the country with increased militancy and energy. The Black Consciousness Movement (BCM) emerged as a result of the mobilisation and agitation of students against the brutality of apartheid by teaching new philosophical weapons against apartheid: pride, self-worth, and Black solidarity in the face of white anti-Black racism. Predictably, the apartheid regime also met this resistance with wanton violence resulting in the cold-blooded murder of the leading BCM acti-

---

[32] A. Reddy, "The United Nations and the Struggle for Liberation in South Africa', SADET, *Volume 3, International Solidarity, Part 1*, chapter 2.
[33] S. Zondi, "Through the Shadow of Death: The ANC's Underground Struggle," in *The Future We Chose: Emerging Perspectives on the Centenary of the ANC*, ed. by B. Ngcaweni (Pretoria: Africa Institute, 2013), 124–37.
[34] According to S.R. Ndou, corroborated by fellow accused, Rita Ndzanga. Both oral history testimonies appear in SADET, *The Road to Democracy in South Africa: South Africans Telling their Stories* (Houghton: Mutloatse Arts Heritage, 2008), 383–94.

vist, Steven Bantu Biko in 1977. His death was the epitome of the brutal violence of the period pushing further away the dream of peaceful pursuit of freedom that Luthuli had.

Before then, primary and high school students had taken to the streets to protest against the imposition of the oppressor's language, Afrikaans, as a language of instruction in all schools as well as an inferior education and curriculum for Africans, the so-called Bantu Education. The 1976 uprisings that began in Soweto, the biggest black township, ended tragically when the police opened fire on students in Soweto and then in other provinces where similar uprisings followed. This left a long trail of blood, the loss of many lives, the disappearance of hundreds of young activists and irreparable tragedy in the soul of South Africa. The world responded with shock. Salim Salim, a member of the Africa Group, a formal negotiation platform and lobby group representing African countries in the UN, accentuated the fact that the Soweto uprising demonstrated the extent of criminality of the apartheid regime.[35] Pik Botha, who was then the apartheid regime's UN ambassador remembers the following about the pressure exerted by the Africa Group and others at the UN:

> Yes, I remember it was very hard, I found there's a time difference between Europe and South Africa, 7/8 hours on the time of the year. And now when you go to bed here in South Africa then it is still early afternoon there. And when you get up there in the morning, then it's already quite late here in the afternoon, that sort of thing. I just remember when I phoned MC Botha, he was minister of Bantu Affairs first and later Bantu Administration–I can't completely remember. A human being tends to forget the unpleasant things in one's life. I remember I called him and told him that the UN Security Council will be meeting in few hours. I have instructions, I must go and speak, I asked the minister what must I say, I need facts, why did the police do what they did... I could clearly see that there was no way I could defend on any rational grounds what happened. I phoned three times and I asked them "are you sure about this because at the UN in New York everybody believes that was the last straw that broke the camel's back sort of and then led the youngsters to erupt, they couldn't take it any longer, it was too much for them". I concentrated more; you can almost say on an educational factor because there was no way the South African government could really morally defend what happened. You couldn't defend it morally but at last you could offer just some explanation on the educational side. Though it was not convincing.[36]

In the context of the Cold War, the ANC's relationship with the Soviet Union changed dramatically after the shooting of peaceful demonstrators in Sharpeville on 21 March 1960. When Oliver Tambo and Yusuf Dadoo left South Africa in April 1960, they had no idea how long they would remain abroad or what their tasks would be. The original intention was merely to establish an external mission, but after the Rivonia arrests and the state's successful destruction of the underground network in South Af-

---

35 Interview with Salim Salim conducted for the Thabo Mbeki Foundation by S.M. Ndlovu and Miranda Strydom, Dar es Salaam, August 2015.
36 Interview with 'Pik' Botha conducted by S.M. Ndlovu and Bernard Magubane, Johannesburg, 3 August 2001. SOHP. Pik Botha later became the minister of Foreign Affairs.

rica, it became necessary to transform the ANC and South African Communist Party (SACP) in exile. In July 1960, Dadoo, SACP leader, visited Moscow, accompanied by the SACP representative in Western Europe, Vella Pillay, to forge fraternal relations. In April 1963, O.R. Tambo, the president of the ANC, paid his first visit to the USSR. Training of MK cadres in the USSR and direct financial assistance followed, which until then had been provided through SACP channels. The first allocation of $300,000 (US) to the ANC was made in 1963. Soviet political and material assistance was an important factor in the ANC's survival in exile. Its significance became especially manifest when the ANC faced tremendous difficulties after the signing of the Lusaka Manifesto calling for dialogue with South Africa. Tanzania and Zambia started to feel increasingly isolated and this affected the activity of the liberation movements based there. The Soviet Union had been skeptical of the Lusaka Manifesto from the beginning; its delegation to the UN registered a number of reservations about the Lusaka Manifesto. In its opinion, the eradication of the colonial and racist regimes in Southern Africa required, not talks and persuasion but, concrete and effective action. Tambo reported at the Kabwe Conference: "In 1969 as a result of complications that our movement faced in this region, we had to evacuate [most of] our army to the Soviet Union at very short notice". [37] MK fighters relocated on special flights from Dar es Salaam mostly to Simferopol and elsewhere in the USSR. Initially it was planned that they would stay in the USSR for a short 'retraining' course, but it soon became apparent that there was still nowhere for them to go and the course had to be extended. The decision 'to prolong to June 1, 1971 the training of the South African cadets who are in the Soviet Union' was taken on 20 July 1970.[38]

The Soviet attitude to the ANC influenced other East European countries. At the end of 1972 an ANC delegation visited Czechoslovakia, the GDR, Hungary, Rumania and Bulgaria and contacts between the ANC and these countries resulted "in a tremendous increase in assistance".[39] As earlier shown, fraternal relations with the Soviet bloc continued throughout the 1970s. In 1921 the Communist Party of the Soviet Union opened the University of the Toilers of the East (KUTV) in Moscow, which was also known as the Lenin School, to train party cadres from the Soviet Union's eastern areas. Several years later the school was placed under the control of the Comintern and began admitting party members from the African continent and from the US. Africans who went study at the Lenin school during the early twentieth century included Albert Nzula, Moses Kotane, JB. Marks and Thabo Mofutsanyana to name but a few. In 1968–69, Thabo Mbeki, then a member of both the ANC and the South African Communist Party went to study at the Lenin School.

On progressive internationalism and solidarity, Thabo Mbeki remembers that the first time he visited the Soviet Union, and Moscow, was in 1964, barely two years after

---

37 *Sechaba*, August 1985.
38 Shubin and Traikova, "There is No Threat from the Eastern Bloc."
39 Ibid.

he arrived in exile and settled in England. That year the USSR Afro-Asian Solidarity Committee hosted a public *'international (mock) trial against apartheid'!* The ANC sent Mbeki to Moscow from London to appear as a 'witness' at this mock trial. The Soviet hosts first allocated to Mbeki a young woman member of the Soviet Komsomol (the CPSU Youth League), who would serve as his guide and interpreter. During their work together she told him enough about opinions among the members of the Komsomol to convince Mbeki that something wrong was taking place in the USSR, which was resulting in a certain level of disaffection among even the Soviet youth who were members of the Komsomol. Unfortunately, some time before the end of the *'mock trial'*, Mbeki's Soviet hosts replaced his Komsomol guide and interpreter. They replaced her with a relatively young man who would only interact with Mbeki strictly on matters which had to do with the *'mock trial'* and his stay in the USSR.[40]

Up to the time Mbeki was at the Lenin School, the School admitted as students only people who were chosen by some of the fellow Communist Parties of the CPSU from the rest of the world. There were no students at this particular school from the national liberation movements such as the ANC. There were also no students at this particular School from the USSR or any of the other socialist countries. The reason for this was that the Lenin School focused on the training of Communist cadres in countries which still had to struggle for the victories, alternatively but dialectically interlinked, of the national liberation, democratic and socialist revolutions. Accordingly, the Lenin School (syllabus) taught:

> the theory and evolution of Marxism-Leninism (dialectical and historical materialism;
> the history of revolutionary practice relating to the national liberation, democratic and socialist revolutions;
> the Soviet (CPSU) experience from before 1917 to date; and,
> practical skills in the conduct of struggle in the conditions prevalent in the countries of the particular students at the School.

In the South African case, the school gave practical training in (i) the functioning and operations of an underground organisation; and (ii) printing propaganda material in conditions of illegality. The latter included hand compositing of the texts which would be printed on the underground printing presses. The Lenin School Library contained books and magazines which covered not only the areas but also much more. For instance, it had novels, poetry books, scholarly on literary criticism, translations of major articles from such major Soviet publications as the CPSU newspaper Pravda, and other material. Relying on this Library, Mbeki had the opportunity to to read:

> a vast amount of literature about the then 'Sino-Soviet dispute', as it was called at that time: [our syllabus did not provide for any formal teaching on this geopolitical matter;

---

40 Interview with Thabo Mbeki conducted by S.M. Ndlovu, 23 March 2020, SADET Oral History Project (SOHP).

> the views of Soviet literary critics about such matters as the Shakespeare plays; and,
> the then eight hundred (800) year old epic poem by the Georgian poet, Shota Rustaveli, entitled *A Tigre in a Knight's Skin*, translated into English by Soviet translation professionals.

Thabo Mbeki elaborated the point that it was during his studies at the Lenin School that he came to understand the critical importance of the role of the translation of books from one language to another, including in such challenging areas as poetry and drama, thus fundamentally to help weld humanity into one interdependent whole, across political and other boundaries. The immaculate professional translations by the Soviet translators helped immensely to ensure, for instance, that Soviet citizens would feel as moved by the English Shakespeare's *Hamlet* as they would, though being far away in the Soviet Union.

Another benefit of the Lenin School was that it helped to expose South African revolutionaries to the situations in other countries, and thus further empowered them in terms of understanding their internationalist responsibilities. Among fellow students were Communists from such countries as Brazil, Paraguay, Canada, India, Palestine, Iraq, among many others, all of whom enriched their understanding of the situation in terms of the international struggle against imperialism. This gives an indication of the enriching experience which would derive from the fact of the presence in the School, at the same time, of revolutionary cadres drawn from what came to be known as the Three Continents, with additions of Communist Parties from within the 'imperialist countries'.[41]

The School used the SACP comrades' presence in Moscow to introduce them to various parts of the Soviet Union. It was in this context that the South Africans gained familiarity with such distinctly Russian and Soviet treasures as the Moscow Red Square, the Tretiakov Gallery, the Bolshoi Theatre, the Hermitage Museum in Leningrad (St Petersburg), the architectural and other treasures of Uzbekistan and other former Soviet Republics, such phenomena as the Casbah in Baku in Azerbaijan, and the sites for the launch of space rockets from Kazakhstan. Mbeki did not have a sense that the School did anything to obstruct interaction between South African comrades and the ordinary Soviet citizens, thus to stop the latter from telling them their honest views about their own country. He elaborated:

> In this regard I am not suggesting, in any way, that our hosts sought to manage our interaction with the Soviet public in such a way as to produce a predetermined outcome, invariably a positive view of the USSR. However, I am arguing that my own 'unguided' excursions at least into Moscow communicated the same message to me that the Soviet population had complaints about their country, but supported the social system it represented.[42]

---

41 Interview with Thabo Mbeki conducted by S.M. Ndlovu, 23 March 2020, SADET Oral History Project (SOHP). See also interview with Essop Pahad conducted by S. M. Ndlovu and T. Nzo, 2019, SOHP.
42 Interview with Thabo Mbeki conducted by S.M. Ndlovu, 23 March 2020, SADET Oral History Project (SOHP). See also interview with Essop Pahad conducted by S. M. Ndlovu and T. Nzo, 2019, SOHP.

According to Mbeki, what the Lenin School communicated to him and others was the central message that as Communist revolutionaries they had a responsibility:

> honestly to communicate to the masses of our people the message that they have a responsibility to liberate themselves;
> to conduct ourselves, as leaders of the struggle in a manner befitting the leaders of our national democratic revolution; and,
> to help provide the direction to the national liberation movement what had to be done to ensure the victory of the national democratic revolution!

In the final analysis, Thabo Mbeki's viewpoint is that the Lenin School worked very well in terms of its parameters as the Political School it was. It worked well within these parameters because;

> it had a clearly defined mission and purpose;
> it attracted students chosen specifically to access the defined syllabus of the School;
> it had the necessary complement of teachers effectively to address the syllabus of the School;
> it had a library which contained academic texts which would support the syllabus, in all languages;
> it had sufficient flexibility to help empower each of the students at the School to confront the challenges in their own countries;
> it encouraged its students to understand that the most effective exercise of leadership required that the leaders must generally be well educated, and open minded enough to understand the imperative to act in a manner consistent with available human knowledge, outside the parameters of ideological belief![43]

Finally, Mbeki emphasised that in the end you could only assess the then Lenin School in the context of the pursuit of a global socialist outcome by the two left tendencies described as:

> \# the 'Third International of Social Democracy', ultimately represented by the then (Bolshevik) Russian Communist Party; and the opposed;
> \# 'Second International of Social Democracy', represented for instance by the then Swedish Social Democratic Party,

The main international issues over which the two trends clashed were those of colonialism and war. The revolutionaries such Lenin and Rosa Luxemburg fought hard to move the Second International to adopt consistent socialist policies towards millions oppressed people of the world enslaved by colonialism and imperialism and to demand independence for the colonies. But the reformist right-wing opportunists constantly evaded this question and betrayed their duty assist the oppressed people of the world. Vladimir Illich Lenin, in his essay *Imperialism; the Highest Stage of Cap-*

---

[43] Interview with Thabo Mbeki conducted by S. M. Ndlovu, 23 March 2020. See also interview with Essop Pahad.

italism, exposed the roots of their thinking and conduct. When the First World War was about to commence both Vladimir Lenin and Rosa Luxemburg pressurised the Congress of the Second International held in Basle to oppose the war and adopt a strong resolution, urging the workers to fight to prevent the outbreak of the war, and should it nevertheless break out, to fight for the overthrow of their respective governments and destroy the ruling capitalist class. It was only a victory on paper. As soon as the war broke out, the big socialist parties in all main capitalist countries ignored the resolution of the Second International. The German Social-Democratic Party, the British Labour Party, the French Socialist Party and other each decided to support its own capitalist government, and called on their workers to shoot down fellow workers in other countries. This betrayal was a death blow to the Second International as an expression of working class, socialist internationalism. After the war, the leaders of the socialist parties came together to 're-establish' the Second International, and indeed some sort of Committee was established.[44]

But in Russia, the Bolshevik Party, did not support the war, it stood by the Basle Resolution and called for the overthrow of the Russian monarchy. In South Africa, the chairman of the Labour Party, Bill Andrews opposed the war in parliament. Right-wing, jingo elements began a witch-hunt against him and his supporters and hounded him out of the leadership. Undeterred, Andrews, Ivon Jones, Sydney Bunting and other militants formed the International Socialist League which continued with the struggle. After the war it was necessary to make a clean break with the Second International. This also was after historic victory of the workers and of the oppressed people in Great October Socialist Revolution in 1917, the revolutionary Marxist parties of all countries came together to form The Third International or Comintern.

The 1974 Portuguese revolution, which expedited the independence of Angola and Mozambique brought prospects for liberation in South Africa closer. The needs of the liberation movement drastically grew as well, even before the 'exodus' of the youth from South Africa that followed the 1976 Soweto uprising. The growing demands for material assistance, including military hardware, in a situation where the political changes in Angola and in Mozambique were favourable to the ANC, were expressed by an ANC delegation, headed by Alfred Nzo in Moscow in January-February 1976. Its purpose was not just 'to discuss inter-party relations', as used to be the case, but also to seek military assistance. After Pretoria's ill-fated intervention in Angola, most African countries took a more positive view of the ANC's co-operation with the USSR. Extremely favourable was the position of the Angolan government. It became clear that Angola could become a reliable rear base; the ANC decided that most MK fighters would be trained in Angola and that only specialised and advanced courses would be organised in the USSR and other friendly

---

44 T. Africanus (pseudonym), "The First International: 100 Years After," *The African Communist* 18 (July-September 1964), 77.

countries. Supplies from the USSR, previously sent Tanzania and Mozambique, were re-routed to Angola. The ANC also appealed to the Soviet Afro-Asian Solidarity Committee to urgently send to Angola for 400 trainees. Two years later, in 1978 the ANC leadership forwarded another request for goods and equipment for the camps in Angola for 10,000 people. The importance of assistance rendered by the Soviet Union and other socialist countries was vividly demonstrated during the conference in support of Angola in February 1976. The journey of the ANC delegation consisting of Johnny Makathini and Cassius Make was a lesson in 'political geography': they had to go from Lusaka to Dar es Salaam, then to Moscow by Aeroflot, the Soviet Airlines, then to Berlin and further to Luanda by Interflug plane, chartered by the GDR Solidarity Committee.

Noah Echa Attah
Chapter 13
Diseases and Medicines in African History

Abstract: Diseases and medicines have been critical in Africa as in the developed world; however, they have not been given the same attention as trade and politics in historical discourse. This is despite the fact that every twelve seconds, according to the World Health Organization (WHO), people die from diseases such as malaria. Africa has experienced diseases that have caused more deaths than major national wars and conflicts, yet they are not given equal attention as the latter. At best, most works on diseases and medicines in African history are subsumed under social history without clear historical context. This chapter will examine aspects of this history, and place some national cases within historical context. It is difficult to cover the history of all diseases in Africa within this chapter; however, diseases such as malaria, HIV/AIDS, and Ebola will be discussed. It is hoped that the etiology of some of these diseases and their controls can be used to understand contemporary challenges, thereby generating greater interest in their histories in Africa.

Keywords: Africa, Disease, Medicine, Missionaries, Pandemic.

Introduction

Africa, like other continents of the world, has experienced diseases and epidemics throughout its history. In the past, global histories, especially from western perspective, have characterized Africa as a 'dark continent' not only in the aspect of developmental indices, compared to other continents, but also as a place where forces of nature make life more difficult.[1] Among these forces, diseases have played significant role, a situation that made early European explorers and missionaries regard Africa as the white man's grave because so many of them died from tropical diseases. Since the above claim by early European and missionaries, some diseases have plagued the continent with devastating effect, including HIV/AIDs, malaria, sleeping sickness, and smallpox.

    Wherever outbreaks have occurred, Africans have endeavored to control these diseases. The history of disease and medicine has often been downplayed in preference for political and economic histories over the years as evident in the existing body of literature. It is therefore important to examine the nature and character of these diseases and how African societies have controlled them over time. This is against the background of Africa's colonial experience, which defined the trajectories of government's responses to diseases in Africa. In addition, the place and experi-

---
[1] Mark Mazower, *Dark Continent: Europe's twentieth century* (London, Vintage 2009).

ence of Africa in global pandemics is critical to this chapter as the continent has always been at the receiving end of global politics of diseases and medicines. This chapter will, therefore, examine diseases and medicines in Africa within the context of global historical discourse, drawing on a few national cases. In order to accomplish this, the subsequent sections will examine, among other issues, African worldviews on diseases and medicines, diseases and the mechanisms used to control them, and missionaries' activities as they relate to disease outbreaks.

African Worldview of Diseases and Medicines

In most African societies, diseases are divided into three major categories, namely, natural, preternatural, and supernatural. Diseases or sicknesses related to infections, food, family factors, and accidents are usually the result of natural causes. Preternatural diseases are linked to witchcraft and sorcery, while supernatural diseases are caused by the gods or ancestors, often due to transgressions.[2] African worldviews of disease and medicine are anchored to traditional medical science based on the appropriate knowledge. The knowledge of African traditional medicine does not require formal education but is instead rooted in apprenticeship under the traditional doctor master (herbalist). The apprentice acquires medicinal knowledge by accompanying the master to the forest to collect recipes. Through this he learns to combine different herbs and the use of mystic forces to treat and address all categories of diseases.

Traditional healers are trained in general medicine, but this does not preclude specialization as many are known for their specialties. Some are known for obstetrics and gynecology – pre-natal and post-natal medicine. Some specialize in psychiatry, while others in pediatrics, where they handle child-related sicknesses such as convulsion. There are also healers who have established reputations in orthopedics. Traditional treatment also involves surgery, which mostly serve socio-cultural ends. The cicatrization of the body, mainly the face, is widespread among people with ethnic facial and body marks such as the Igala and Yoruba of Nigeria. In most cases, incision lines of geometric symmetry and beauty are made on the face. Traditional surgeons, using special knives produced by blacksmiths, make incisions. Medical substances produced from leaves, roots, and bark of trees are applied to incision wounds to sterilize the cuts and prevent hemorrhaging. Other forms of surgery include the extraction of bullets from the human body. This is done through incantations by traditional surgeon who literally calls out bullets from the body of a gun wound victim.

---

[2] Alexander Rödlach, Witches, *Westerners, and HIV: AIDS and Cultures of Blame in Africa* (Left Coast Press, 2006).

Circumcision of both the male and female organs is also expertly done in a way that does not impair the reproductive capability of the person.[3]

In most rural communities of Africa, traditional medicine is often the only source of health care and about 80 percent of the population depend on it.[4] The commonest use of medicine in Africa is to cure illness, with most medicines prepared by cooking the recipes. The cooked liquid is then drunk, or used to wash at intervals. Medicines are also used in other contexts to bring good luck, guarantee good harvests, and protection from, or even harm to a perceived enemy. The wide range of uses for medicine appears in the concept that surrounds African indigenous science, based on the appropriate knowledge of medical and even psychic and cosmic properties of herbs and plants. Medical plants or parts such as roots, stems, stem barks, flowers, leaves, fruits, and seeds are used for medicinal preparations. The use of plants to treat diseases rests partly on the idea that natural vegetation is a storehouse of medical power and properties.

The concepts of illness and disease in the perspective of African tradition are anchored on certain belief systems. In his study of "therapy as a system-in-action," Feierman provided five categories of diseases as exemplified in north-eastern Tanzania.[5] The first is caused by God as against the one caused by man. Sicknesses from God are traceable to natural agencies, while those by man are mostly traceable to sorcery. The natural causation of illness is based on the general principles of the behaviour of things such as infections or deficiencies in body requirements, contrary to the intervention of man. A second category of illness is traceable to accident or neglect and not ill-will or sorcery. However, some accidents could be caused by the instrumentality of witchcraft. A third category is sorcery or witches, and those ensorcelled could sometimes identify them. The fourth is associated to different spirits, which may include nature spirits and the spirits of sorcery. A fifth category consists the moral actions of man as exemplified in oaths falsely taken or evils committed. Aside from these five categorizations, disease may be associated with fate such as found in children who die at infancy and are believed to reincarnate, each time dying as infant from children-related diseases. In Nigeria, such children are known as *abiku* among Yoruba and Igala speaking people, while the Igbos call them *ogbanje*, and the Ibibios *eyin uyio*.[6]

---

3 Simon George Sandeep, "Evaluation of Methanolic Extract of Hypericum Mysorense Ointment for its Wound Healing Activity," (PhD diss., KMCH College of Pharmacy, Coimbatore, Tamil Nadu, India, 2014).
4 World Health Organization. "A Global Brief on Vector-borne Diseases", No. WHO/DCO/WHD/2014.1. World Health Organization, 2014.
5 Steven Feierman, "Therapy as a system-in-action in northeastern Tanzania", *Social Science & Medicine. Part B: Medical Anthropology* 15, 3 (1981), 353–360.
6 Daniel A. Offiong, "Traditional healers in the Nigerian health care delivery system and the debate over integrating traditional and scientific medicine", *Anthropological Quarterly* (1999), 118–30.

Despite these categorizations, in most cases, sicknesses and misfortunes are attributed to human antagonists. In other words, witchcraft or sorcery is blamed for sicknesses and misfortunes. Witchcraft and sorcery are usually associated with unresolved stresses and strains in life, especially when there are tensions between people.[7] In African traditional beliefs, there is hardly distinction between sickness and misfortune as they are mostly seen as two sides of the same coin.[8] Invariably, sicknesses and misfortunes are explained in terms of supernatural rather than natural. It is noted along this line of thought that, there is little or no difference between illness and misfortune among Ethiopians.[9]

The issues of health and sickness in Africa are generally viewed with supernatural or spiritual concerns. Lambo noted that "African concepts of health and illness, like those of life and death, are intertwined."[10] The African, he writes, "does not regard health as an isolated phenomenon, but reflects the integration of the community." Sicknesses are therefore attributed to supernatural forces; hence, they are treated through spiritual forces. It is in this sense that traditional healers mediate between the living and their ancestors. They ensured that people attacked by witches and sorcerers are delivered through the use of higher mythical powers. They also ensured that the ancestors are appeased through sacrifices on behalf of those that have transgressed.

Belief in the power of medicine is fundamental to African thought, which Bostonin discussion on Igala observed that "belief rests partly on the idea that the natural vegetation, which grows so abundantly in the area is a storehouse of medicinal power."[11] This belief is equally shared by the Yoruba, Igbo, Ewe, and other African tribes. The power of medicine is made possible by the combination of the right recipes in conjunction with spiritual or mystical forces, sometimes through invocations. The power of African medicine is such that sometimes, a sick person believed to be dying, and taken away from orthodox hospitals to traditional medical homes became well after treatment.[12] Similarly, sick people are sometimes secretly taken away from hospitals for traditional treatment by relatives because the illness could not be treat-

---

[7] Gerry Campbell, Karl A. Roberts, and Neelam Sarkaria, "Witchcraft, Spirit Possession and Belief-Based Abuse," in *Harmful Traditional Practices* (London: Palgrave Macmillan, 2020), 101–17.
[8] Jacqueline H. Mgumia, "Chuma Ulete: Business and Discourses of Witchcraft in Neoliberal Tanzania," *Journal for the Study of Religion* 33, 1 (2020), 1–26.
[9] Kasahun Girma Tareke, Yohannes Kebede Lemu, Shifera Asfaw Yidenekal, and Garumma Tolu Feyissa, "Community's Perception, Experiences and Health Seeking Behavior Towards Newborn Illnesses in Debre Libanos District, North Shoa, Oromia, Ethiopia: Qualitative study," *Plos one* 15, 1 (2020), e0227542.
[10] Thomas Adeoye Lambo, "Psychotherapy in Africa", *Human Nature* 1, 3 (1978), 32–39.
[11] John Boston, "Medicines and Fetishes in Igala" *Africa: Journal of the International African Institute*, 41, 3, (1971), 200–07.
[12] Raimi O. Olaoye and Noah Echa Attah, "Orthopaedics in the Traditional Medical System of Igala" in *Africa's Indigenous Science and Knowledge System*, ed. by D. O. Akinwumi, et al (Abuja: Roots Books, 2007), 368–77.

ed with "white man's medicine." However, there are instances where people do not get healing through African traditional medicine and only to be successfully treated trough western medication.

In African belief, health issues cannot be separated from the environment and how people relate with themselves. Turner noted among the Ndembu people of Central Africa that those who are sick may not be well until their relationships with others have been investigated and subjected to ritual cleansing.[13] Bishaw also observed in the case of Ethiopia that traditional medicine goes beyond the issue of sickness.[14] According to him, traditional medicine involves the protection and promotion of man's physical, spiritual, and material happiness. He further notes that since sickness and other misfortunes are often conceived as natural and supernatural, the diagnostic and therapeutic methods are usually subjected to spiritual process.

Once a sick person is taken to a traditional healer, at least in contemporary Yoruba society, the first task is finding the cause of the sickness, especially through the instrumentality of *Ifa* divination. This is imperative to the course of treatment. Sometimes, even when a person finally dies as a result of a sickness, the traditional healer still finds it necessary to carry out autopsy through divination so as to find out the cause of the death. For example, when a person dies due to snake bite, the death would be medically attributed to the poison from the snake. But within relevant African belief, the snake may be merely an agent of some evil forces such as witches that must have killed the victim. Similarly, when a person suddenly collapses and dies, it may be medically stated that they died of cardiac arrest, but in relevant African medical thought, the death could be linked with mysterious forces. It is therefore the duty of the traditional healer to discover through divination the cause, sometimes for the purpose of avenging the death.

Diseases are an integral part of African medical science. Sometimes sickness may be as a result of filial impiety, which may have attracted punishment from the ancestors. Sacrifice and appeasement therefore become imperative in the healing process in such circumstance. For example, in treating a wide range of psychiatric disorders, ranging from schizophrenia to neurotic syndromes, priests are sometimes employed in the healing processes, which may include elaborate form of ritual and sacrifice, targeted at the spiritual or magical cause of the illness in a designated shrine.[15]

Also important in African concept of medicine is the prevention against spiritual attacks, especially by enemies through witchcraft. There is a wide range of preventive medicines against automobile accidents, gun shots, snake bite, food poison, etc. Some Africans strongly believe in protection against all forms of illness, including

---

[13] Thomas Adeoye Lambo, "Psychotherapy in Africa", *Human Nature* 1, 3 (1978), 32–39.
[14] Makonnen Bishaw, "Promoting Traditional Medicine in Ethiopia: a Brief Historical Review of Government Policy", *Social Science & Medicine* 33, 2 (1991), 193–200.
[15] Marlene Cabrera, "Mujerista Psychology: A Case Study Centering Latinx Empowerment in Treatment," (PhD diss., Pepperdine University, 2020).

malign contingencies of fate. People with this belief acquire charms from spiritualists for protection against perceived enemies or misfortunes. It is also important to note that this belief system encourages families to immunize their members traditionally against malicious attacks by enemies. Such immunization prevents witches from excising the souls as well prevents other supernatural forces from harming the inoculated.

African Traditional Medicine is characterised by a holistic approach to the spirit–mind–body concept of health. It embraces people, animals, plants, and inanimate objects in an inseparable manner, which all beings derive healing forces. In many poor African countries, a majority of people living with HIV/AIDS continue to depend on traditional healers and herbal treatments.[16] This is not only because healers and herbs are more available and accessible to their communities than orthodox doctors and drugs, but also because majority of Africans believe in the efficacy and power of traditional medicine. African traditional medicine has remained resilient despite the distrust from some conventional health workers that traditional healers have little information about diseases such as AIDS and the lack of standardised training and practices.[17] It is further argued that herbal treatments have often not been rigorously evaluated and prepared or standardized, thereby limiting their qualities.[18] Despite the observable shortcomings concerning African traditional medicine, it has held sway among many people, especially those who are unable to afford western medicine.

However, the place and importance of traditional medical science in tackling the AIDS plague has been recognized by notable bodies in Africa. For example, the idea of the Regional Initiative on Traditional Medicine and AIDS in Eastern and Southern Africa was spearheaded by the Traditional and Modern Health Practitioners Together Against AIDS and Other Diseases (TMHPTAD), in Kampala in 2001.[19] The body was set up to promote a concerted, systematic, and sustained effort at both local and re-

---

[16] G. Anywar, E. Kakudidi, R. Byamukama, J. Mukonzo, A. Schubert, and H. Oryem-Origa. "Indigenous Traditional Knowledge of Medicinal Plants used by Herbalists in Treating Opportunistic Infections Among People Living with HIV/AIDS in Uganda", *Journal of Ethnopharmacology* 246 (2020), 112–20.

[17] Vincent Mabvurira, "Influence of African Traditional Religion and Spirituality in Understanding Chronic Illnesses and its Implications for Social Work Practice: A case of Chiweshe Communal Lands in Zimbabwe" (PhD diss., University of Limpopo, 2016).

[18] Stuart Ainsworth, Stefanie K. Menzies, Nicholas R. Casewell, and Robert A. Harrison, "An Analysis of Preclinical Efficacy Testing of Antivenoms for sub-Saharan Africa: Inadequate Independent Scrutiny and Poor-quality Reporting are Barriers to Improving Snakebite Treatment and Management" *PLoS Neglected Tropical Diseases* 14, 8 (2020), e0008579.

[19] R. King, D. Balaba, B. Kaboru, D. Kabatesi, A. Pharris, and J. Homsye, "The Role of Traditional Healers in Comprehensive HIV," *AIDS Prevention and Care in Africa: Untapped Opportunities Community Based Care* (2004).

gional levels in support of and validation of African Traditional Medicine in relation to HIV/AIDS.[20]

Mapping some Diseases and Controls

Sleeping Sickness

The historiography of diseases and medicines in Africa cannot be complete without the discussion on trypanosomiasis (sleeping sickness), not only because of the mortality rate or the demographic spread of the disease, but also due to the historical scholarly attention given to it over the years. Caused by a parasite, Trypanosome, the carrier of sleeping sickness is a mosquito vector of the Glossina species known as Tsetse fly. Due to the nature and characteristics of its cause, it was referred to as African disease and thus, dominating the history of medicine in Africa in the twentieth century by cross-cultural researchers. Ibn Khaldun, in the fourteenth century, was the first to document the case of sleeping sickness in Africa when writing on one Sultan Djata of the Mali Kingdom, who was killed by the disease.[21] However, the disease never had much recognition until the twentieth century, when it began to spread rapidly in Africa. The disease began to spread at a higher rate throughout Africa, due to the increasing level of migration and integration among various groups as a result of trade and social revolutions on the continent. The spread of sleeping sickness in Africa was also driven by European exploration and exploitation of Africa, especially during the last quarter of the nineteenth century.

The spread of sleeping sickness epidemic differs across time and space. For example, the Central African region initially had the highest rate of spread and mortality compared to other regions in Africa. Between 1896 and 1906 for instance, the mortality rate in the Congo Basin stood at over 500,000 people.[22] In the East African region, the mortality rate as represented by Uganda stood at 250,000 during the epidemics of 1896–1910. In the West African region, the record of the disease came up later as the first case starting with Gambia was recorded in 1901.[23]

---

[20] J. Homsy and R. King, "The Role of Traditional Healers in HIV/AIDS Counselling in Kampala, Uganda. Key Issues and Debates: Traditional Healers", *Societes d'Afrique & SIDA: Newsletter of the Societes d'Afrique & SIDA Network* 13 (1996), 2.
[21] Maureen Malowany, "Unfinished Agendas: Writing the History of Medicine of Sub-Saharan Africa", *African Affairs* 99, 395 (2000), 340–8.
[22] Maryinez Lyons, *The Colonial Disease: a Social History of Sleeping Sickness in Northern Zaire, 1900–1940* (Cambridge: Cambridge University Press, 2002).
[23] Eric M. Fèvre, P. G. Coleman, M. Odiit, J. W. Magona, S. C. Welburn, and M. E. J. Woolhouse, "The Origins of a new Trypanosoma Brucei Rhodesiense Sleeping Sickness Outbreak in Eastern Uganda", *The Lancet* 358, 9282 (2001), 625–28.

Proactive measures were taken during the colonial period by the colonial authorities to mitigate the spread of the disease in Africa. It was thought within the colonial circle that if nothing was done to stop the disease, it could hinder the pursuance of colonial exploitation in Africa.[24] To this effect, the government restricted the movements of people in the Belgian Congo so as to safeguard the reservoir of labor needed for mining activities. In 1916, surveillance method was adopted in the French colonies by the government; using organized campaigns through mobile team that fetched out those infected with the disease, for the purpose of treatment. The colonial army was mandated to enforce this policy, which yielded positive results.

It was a difficult assignment on the part of the colonial authorities to control the spread and effects of sleeping sickness epidemic. From the perspective of the people, the disease could be avoided by keeping away from the areas that were prone to high concentration of Tsetse fly, which was the carrier of the disease. However, most of the colonial authorities in Africa ignored this warning and chose to spend greater portion of public fund in controlling the flies. The situation not only worsened, but public health became synonymous with sleeping sickness epidemic in Africa until sustained surveillance and other measures practically defeated it in 1965. However, in 2000, the disease resurged, largely due to population movement, ecological diversification, wars and population displacements across the continent. The mortality rate of the resurgence in Zaire, for instance, was above that recorded in the earlier phase.[25] The implication of this was that, unlike other diseases in Africa, which have been successfully eradicated over the years, sleeping sickness persisted, as WHO estimated that in the new phase, about 55–60 million people were at the risk of exposure to the disease, especially in Africa.[26]

Smallpox

The history of medicine shows that smallpox was one of the infectious diseases that had wrecked havoc on humanity all over the world. The origin of the disease on the continent of Africa is uncertain, however, some scholars claimed that it can be traced to a smallpox-like rash found on three Egyptian's mummies that were excavated and

---

24 W. Amanfu, "Contagious Bovine Pleuropneumonia (Lungsickness) in Africa", *Onderstepoort Journal of Veterinary Research* 76, 1 (2009), 13–17.
25 Mosiana Ekwanzala, Jacques Pépin, Nzambi Khonde, Sadi Molisho, Herman Bruneel, and Philippe De Wals, "In the Heart of Darkness: Sleeping Sickness in Zaire", *The Lancet* 348, 9039 (1996), 1427–30.
26 Maureen Malowany, "Unfinished Agendas: Writing the History of Medicine of Sub-Saharan Africa," *African Affairs* 99, 395 (2000), 340–8.

dated back to the third century BCE.[27] However, this assertion may be far from the fact as the disease was never noticed in Africa prior to contact with Europeans, especially, the Portuguese. It is, therefore, more persuasive to point to the Portuguese as the ones that brought the disease to Africa during their exploration in the fifteenth century.[28] By fifteenth century, smallpox was already affecting Europe, thus, the Portuguese likely spread it to the continent through their early contacts with the coastal people of Africa. Smallpox disease underwent a community level spread across the continent likely as a result of trade links between the European traders, coastal people, and those at the hinterlands.

The treatment of smallpox in Africa, similar to other diseases, took various methods, but the most popular was the practice of smallpox inoculation.[29] Common in the control of smallpox in Africa was that people were inoculated against possible infection.[30] In the Western region of the continent, the Jukuns, in modern-day central Nigeria, took the lymph on a wisp of straw from pustules of a person who had been ill for eight or nine days and applied it with a razor to the left forearm of the infected person. In the Gold Coast (Ghana), the process of inoculating children against smallpox infection began a few days prior the main exercise. They were to "abstain from all flesh meat, and drink plenty of water acidulated with the juice of limes" for its effectiveness. The practice of inoculation also existed elsewhere in north-eastern region of the continent, especially, a 'pseudo-inoculation'. In Central Africa, inoculation was a regular and reliable practice against smallpox infection, as the people inoculated one another with the substance derived from pustules of the least severe cases. This unconventional method continued until the smallpox vaccination was discovered in 1798.[31]

While the smallpox vaccine was developed with worldwide acceptance, Africans who were already familiar with inoculation resented it. The poor response to the smallpox vaccination made the WHO to commence a campaign for its acceptance in 1959 in Africa. However, the campaign took different approaches across the continent. For example, the French colonial authorities used mobile clinics to reach people, while the British authorities focused on the development of clinics/dispensaries and hospitals in strategic centers that could serve both the urban and rural areas.

---

27 Andrea M. McCollum, Yu Li, Kimberly Wilkins, Kevin L. Karem, Whitni B. Davidson, Christopher D. Paddock, Mary G. Reynolds, and Inger K. Damon, "Poxvirus Viability and Signatures in Historical Relics", *Emerging Infectious Diseases* 20, 2 (2014), 177.
28 Frank Fenner, "Smallpox: Emergence, Global Spread, and Eradication", *History and Philosophy of the Life Sciences* (1993), 397–420.
29 Eugenia W. Herbert, "Smallpox Inoculation in Africa", *Journal of African History* 16, 4 (1975), 539–59.
30 Herbert, "Smallpox inoculation in Africa".
31 Kara N. Durski, Andrea M. McCollum, Yoshinori Nakazawa, Brett W. Petersen, Mary G. Reynolds, Sylvie Briand, Mamoudou Harouna Djingarey, Victoria Olson, Inger K. Damon, and Asheena Khalakdina, "Emergence of Monkeypox—West and Central Africa, 1970–2017", *Morbidity and Mortality Weekly Report* 67, 10 (2018), 306.

While some countries responded positively to the campaign by making available necessary equipment and support, the Eastern African governments failed to allocate funds to support the eradication program.[32] This made the campaign in the region more difficult, as WHO was made to bear the burden of the exercise in the region. However, the success of the campaign made the WHO to officially declare the world free of from smallpox in 1980.[33]

Malaria

Malaria spreads through the female *Anopheles* mosquitoes. Globally, the disease afflicts between 300 million and 500 million people annually, and 90 percent of the cases occur in tropical Africa.[34] In terms of mortality, children under age five are the most vulnerable group, with some 700,000 dying in Africa each year.[35] The first success story on malaria control strategies was in South Africa. Prior to the proposal by WHO to use DDT (dichlorodiphenyltrichloroethane) for hut spraying, Park Ross instituted the first hut spraying malaria control strategy in South Africa in 1905. This early successful hut spraying campaign became the model for similar program in other parts of Africa.

By 1921, malaria control strategies included the introduction of quinine (particularly as prophylaxis for African laborers) and personal protection with the use of bednets and protective clothing. By the late 1920s, larvicidal oiling to prevent anopheline breeding was also utilized.[36] A similar investigation into the development of malaria control strategies in East Africa supports this path of enquiry. Following malaria epidemic crises of 1926 and 1928, priority was given to economic development so as to improve health conditions, which would indirectly reduce malaria incidence. The development of synthetic anti-malarials, particularly chloroquine in the late 1930s, also improved malaria control through a combination of spraying and prophylaxis/treatment.[37]

---

32 Jean-Marie Okwo-Bele, and Thomas Cherian, "The Expanded Programme on Immunization: a Lasting Legacy of Smallpox Eradication", *Vaccine* 29 (2011), D74-D79.
33 Geoffrey L. Smith, and Grant McFadden, "Smallpox: Anything to Declare?", *Nature Reviews Immunology* 2, 7 (2002), 521–27.
34 Sean C. Murphy and Joel G. Breman, "Gaps in the Childhood Malaria Burden in Africa: Cerebral Malaria, Neurological Sequelae, Anemia, Respiratory Distress, Hypoglycemia, and Complications of Pregnancy", *The American Journal of Tropical Medicine and Hygiene* 64, 1_suppl (2001), 57–67.
35 B. Carme, J. C. Bouquety, and H. Plassart, "Mortality and Sequelae due to Cerebral Malaria in African Children in Brazzaville, Congo", The *American Journal of Tropical Medicine and Hygiene* 48, 2 (1993), 216–21.
36 Frank M. Snowden and Richard Bucala, eds., *Global Challenge of Malaria, The: Past Lessons And Future Prospects* (World Scientific, 2014).
37 John Luke Gallup and Jeffrey D. Sachs, "The Economic Burden of Malaria", *The American Journal of Tropical Medicine and Hygiene* 64,1_suppl (2001), 85–96.

Continuities in scientific research and field applications emerged in institutional form in the late 1940s in East Africa. Massive investment in a variety of research institutes in East and West Africa stimulated and supported clinical and laboratory studies of vector-borne disease. However, when the WHO launched its global eradication program at its Eighth World Assembly in 1955, it explicitly excluded sub-Saharan Africa. The peculiarities of this decision are all the more puzzling considering that the 1950 Kampala Conference on Malaria Control in Equatorial Africa had announced the decision to control malaria "by modern methods as soon as possible without awaiting the outcome of further experiments."[38] While the rest of the world was caught up in the euphoria of eradication, Africa was left out of the campaign.[39]

The WHO began malaria control programs in 1948 by spraying mosquito-breeding sites with insecticides and administering anti-malarial drugs. For a time, it appeared that the disease would be eliminated, or at least reduced, but since the late 1970s malaria has resurged. Mosquitoes have developed resistance to insecticides, as have the malaria parasites to traditional chloroquine-based anti-malarial drugs.[40] Malaria is still spreading in urban areas, largely due to the growth of squalid shantytowns, which provide pools of stagnant water where mosquitoes breed. Natural disasters such as floods are other contributors to the spread of malaria. The seriousness of the problem led the WHO and other international groups to launch Operation Roll Back Malaria in 1998 aimed at eradicating malaria through the development of an anti-malarial vaccine.[41] Furthermore, insecticide-treated bed nets have proven to be one of the most effective malaria prevention strategies. The WHO distributed bed nets to families with children under age five in several African countries such as Nigeria and Ghana, and it was discovered that the death rate dropped by 50 to 60 percent among children in these countries.[42]

---

[38] Mary J. Dobson, Maureen Malowany, and Robert W. Snow, "Malaria Control in East Africa: the Kampala Conference and the Pare-Taveta Scheme: a Meeting of Common and High Ground", *Parassitologia* 42, 1/2 (2000), 149–66.
[39] Makama M. Sunday, "Organization Structure and Participation of the Evangelical Church of West Africa in the Delivery of Primary Health Care Services in Kafanchan And Kaduna Districts in Kaduna State, Nigeria" (PhD diss., Mzumbe University, 2011).
[40] Hokey Min, "Mapping the Supply Chain of Anti-Malarial Drugs in Sub-Saharan African Countries," *International Journal of Logistics Systems and Management* 11, 1 (2012), 1–23.
[41] Jose G. Montalvo, and Marta Reynal-Querol, "Fighting Against Malaria: Prevent Wars While Waiting for the "Miraculous" Vaccine," *The Review of Economics and Statistics* 89, 1 (2007), 165–77.
[42] A. S. Obacha, "Malaria Transmission Dynamics and Insecticide Resistance Status of Anopheles Funestus (Diptera: Culicidae) During Four Years of Indoor Residual Spraying in Northern Ghana" (PhD diss., University of Ghana, 2016).

Missionaries, Diseases, and Medicines

Missionary activities operated side by side with colonial administration, especially, on healthcare issues in Africa. Colonial state-provided healthcare systems were complemented by those offered by different missions across the colonies.[43] These complementarities focused on curative care rooted and reflected in missionary medicine's strategic interest in utilizing healing as a route to Christian conversion. However, the role of missionaries in healthcare was partly due to the inadequacy of the colonial state in providing adequate and accessible health infrastructure. Prior to the end of the Second World War, colonial hospitals and dispensaries in Africa were situated mostly in urban areas, thereby serving only a fraction of the total population. This was due to paucity of funding, which also accounted for indirect rule in colonies like Nigeria. Rural communities were, therefore, marginal in colonial thinking regarding healthcare provisions; hence, missionaries provided most of the healthcare services in rural settlements.

Malaria was one of the notable diseases that missionaries paid attention to, especially in the early stage of colonialism in Africa. The fight against malaria in Africa by missionaries was prompted by the experience in the nineteenth century that "Malaria once turned Africa into the missionaries' graveyard."[44] For example, the average life expectancy of missionaries due to malaria was eight years in Central Africa and two years in West Africa.[45] The experience of the missionaries was so bad that some of them died within three months of arriving on the soil of Africa.[46] The experience of the missionaries precipitated the introduction of the famous quinine by the Jesuit Missionaries (an exercise which commenced in Europe) to treat malaria. It was used in Africa for over three centuries for the treatment of severe falciparum malaria.[47]

Most of the early hospitals in Africa were established by missionaries to tackle tropical diseases. For example, Reverend Tommy and his wife, through the Serving in Mission (SIM) built the Egbe ECWA Hospital in old Kabba Province in present Kogi state in 1926. They also made concerted effort to recruit and train medical staff through the establishment of a Nursing Training School (NTS) in 1955, now

---

43 Michael Jennings, "Cooperation and Competition: Missions, the Colonial State and Constructing a Health System in Colonial Tanganyika", in *Beyond the State: The Colonial Medical Service in British Africa*, ed. by Anna Greenwood (Manchester: University Press, 2016), 153–173.
44 Benjamin C. Diara, Johnson C. Diara, and Nche George Christian, "The 19th Century European Missionaries and the Fight Against Malaria in Africa", *Mediterranean Journal of Social Sciences* 4, 16 (2013), 89.
45 Diara, Diara, and Christian, "The 19th Century European Missionaries", 89.
46 Diara, Diara, and Christian, "The 19th Century European Missionaries", 89.
47 Lana Dvorkin-Camiel and Julia S. Whelan, "Tropical American Plants in the Treatment of Infectious Diseases", *Journal of Dietary Supplements* 5, 4 (2008), 349–72.

ECWA School of Nursing. The establishment of such hospitals, though, did not eliminate malaria completely, brought succor to the victims of the plague in Africa.[48]

Missionaries were also active in the area of maternal and child healthcare, which reduced mother and child mortality rate across African countries. For example, missionaries began training indigenous women as midwives and nurses as early as 1918 in Uganda. By 1932, the Church Missionary Society alone had established twenty-three maternity and child welfare centers, mostly in Central Uganda. It is estimated that approximately a fifth of Ugandan women as in other African countries attended a mission clinic for pre-natal and post-natal advice by the 1950s. The Catholic and Protestant clinics were common with their effective activities in most part of Uganda. They operated impressive referral system and transferred high risk cases to the major maternity hospitals in Kampala for intensive investigation. They were so professional to the extent that by 1930s, the maternal and child mortality rates were at similar levels with those in England and Wales.[49] The Catholic Church and a small group of protestant denominations built and managed about forty-seven hospitals in Uganda, a situation that was replicated in most countries of Africa.

The Mission Africa Christian group has also been active in healthcare services by taking up responsibilities in medical programs and institutions in Africa. For example, the mission has partnership with two hospitals in Nigeria, namely, Holley Memorial Hospital (established in Africa in 1950 in response to the need of those suffering from leprosy and tuberculosis) and Ekpene Obom (established to fight against HIV/AIDS). The Mission Africa has been actively running HIV/AIDS clinics and prevention education campaigns. Their efforts toward combating diseases in Africa also manifested in the provision of relief materials to disadvantaged groups, such as people with leprosy and those with physical disabilities.

European and American Protestant missionaries of various denominations such as Adventist, Lutheran, Pentecostal, and Baptist have been active in providing quality healthcare services since the 1930s, especially in East, West, Central and Southern Africa. They successfully combined evangelism with healing centers where converts could be treated for diverse diseases. Hawariate Bete Christian in Ethiopia is one of such healing centers, founded by Marqosi Danghe, a charismatic healer in 1983. Most of the patients were worshippers from among the local Sidamo people in need of treatment and help. Mental illness also figures prominently among the numerous cases they attended to.[50]

---

[48] A. T. Ekundayo, "Settlements Relocation in Northern Nigeria: A Historical Analysis of the Colonial Resettlement Scheme in Yagbaland, 1900–1950", *African Nebula* 4 (2011).

[49] James Hammond, "Evangelization, Injections, and the Baganda: Mengo Hospital and Biomedicine in Uganda" (BA with Honors Thesis, Department of History, University of Michigan, 2013).

[50] Norbert L. Vecchiato, "Illness, Therapy, and Change in Ethiopian possession cults", *Africa* 63, 2 (1993), 176–96.

Africa and Global Pandemics

Historically, the world has witnessed about twenty major global pandemics, including the Black Death of 1346–1353, the Flu Pandemic of 1889–1890, the Spanish Flu 1918–1920, the Asian Flu of 1957–1958, the Acquired Immune Deficiency Syndrome (AIDS) pandemic from 1981 to date, the West Africa Ebola of 2014–2016, and recently the coronavirus (COVID-19) epidemic.[51] This work will however focus on COVID-19, AIDS, Spanish Flu and Ebola, because of their relevance to Africa.

Spanish influenza pandemic of 1918–19

Until the outbreak of coronavirus pandemic, the Spanish influenza pandemic of 1918–19 was the worst disease in global history, ranked deadlier than the Justinian Plague of the sixteenth century and the fourteenth century Black Death.[52] Although the first known case of the 'Spanish' Flu was reported on 11th March, 1918 at a military base in Kansas, United States, scientists have suggested that it must have originated from Britain, China and France and not Spain as assumed.[53] Like in most parts of the world, the pandemic had its consequences on African colonies in terms of spread, duration, and morbidity. The First World War was identified as a major conduit in spreading the virus around the world. It has been strongly suggested that warships with about 150,000 African troops and 1.4 million laborers onboard to the continent from Europe were the first to import the influenza.[54]

The influenza pandemic had three different but related waves, namely, the first mild wave in March-July 1918, the August-December 1918 second virulent wave, and the third wave in 1919. The first wave swept through Europe, America, and Asia, but only North and Southeast Africa were moderately affected on the continent.[55] However, almost the whole of Africa was hit by the virulent second wave, except the Maghreb and southeastern Africa that probably have developed modicum of immunity from the experience of the first wave. The second wave was imported into Africa between mid-August and late-September 1918 through three seaports, namely, Free-

---

[51] O. Jarus, "20 of the Worst Epidemics and Pandemics in History", *LiveScience*. (2020), https://www.livescience.com/worst-epidemics-and-pandemics-in-history.html, 14 July, 2020.
[52] Mary J. Dobson, *Murderous Contagion: a Human History of Disease* (Quercus Publishing, 2015).
[53] Tom Dicke, "Waiting for the flu: cognitive inertia and the Spanish influenza pandemic of 1918–19", *Journal of the History of Medicine and Allied Sciences* 70, No. 2 (2015): 195–217.
[54] Kelley Lee, *Globalization and Health: An Introduction* (Springer, 2003); Stefan Elbe, "Security and Global Health," *Polity*, 2010.
[55] Howard Phillips and David Killingray, eds., *The Spanish Influenza Pandemic of 1918–1919: New Perspectives* (London: Routledge, 2002); Niall P. Johnson, and Juergen Mueller, "Updating the accounts: global mortality of the 1918–1920 'Spanish' influenza pandemic", *Bulletin of the History of Medicine* (2002): 105–15

town, Cape Town and Mombasa.[56] This was made possible through the movements of First World War personnel. For example, the influenza entered Freetown through infected 124 crew members on board the Royal Navy warship from England on 14 August 1918. The virus quickly spread to the general population due to lack of strict restriction on board the ship, as colliers, medical staff from other warships, and dock laborers, as well as sailors onboard other warships became infected.[57]

The virus got to Cape Town from Freetown through the military ships that stopped over in Freetown to refuel. The ships were carrying Native Labur Corps troops to South Africa from Europe, but the troops contracted the disease, as cases began to be reported onboard as soon as the ships left Freetown. The health authorities hospitalized soldiers that showed signs of sickness immediately the ships berthed in Cape Town in September 1918. The remaining soldiers were restricted to a military camp for two days, while those that did not show symptoms of the virus were demobilized and allowed to continue their journeys home by trains. However, the military camp staff, transport unit staff and medical staff, among others, was reported to have contracted the virus the next day. The pandemic got to Durban in South Africa in September 1918, and, by October of the same year, spread to Bechuanaland, Southern Rhodesia, and Nyasaland (Malawi).[58]

A ship from India likely brought the influenza to Mombasa in late September 1918 and became prevalent among demobilized Kenyan Carrier Corps who came through ports across the country. These demobilized soldiers became carriers of the virus to different parts of the country as they travelled to the hinterland by rails, roads, and rivers.[59] In fact, the coasts of East Africa were affected in September 1918, and spread to the hinterland of Uganda. In early September 1918, there were reported cases in Dakar, the capital of Senegal. The disease moved along the Rivers Senegal and Niger before crossing to Upper Volta (Burkina Faso). In late September 1918, the disease reached the Ivory Coast, Dahomey (Benin Republic), and Nigeria. Due to the relatively poor transportation system in Africa, compared to Europe and North America, the spread of the influenza was slow.[60]

The influenza spread through this pattern across the sub-Saharan Africa in the last quarter of 1918.[61] In the space of three months of the importation of the virus through the sea, it caused death and disruption of socio-economic activities through-

---

56 Howard Phillips, "Influenza Pandemic (Africa)" *International Encyclopedia of the First World War* (2017).
57 Phillips, "Influenza Pandemic (Africa)".
58 Johnson and Mueller, "Updating the Accounts: Global Mortality of the 1918–1920 'Spanish' Influenza Pandemic", 105–15.
59 George O. Ndege, *Health, State, and Society in Kenya* (Rochester: University of Rochester Press, 2001).
60 George C. Kohn, *Encyclopedia of Plague and Pestilence: From Ancient Times to the Present* (Infobase Publishing, 2007).
61 Johnson and Mueller, "Updating the Accounts: Global Mortality of the 1918–1920 'Spanish' Influenza Pandemic", 105–15.

out west, central, southern and eastern Africa, a situation made possible by the relatively improved colonial transportation network.[62] The 1918 pandemic infected about 500 million people globally, representing one-third of the world population and killing between 20 and 50 million people.[63] Although the statistics for the mortality rate of the influenza in Africa appears to be inaccurate and unreliable like the global figure, it is estimated that more than 2.5 million out of about 130 million Africans died.[64]

HIV/AIDS

HIV/AIDS, which became a global pandemic after the virus was identified in the 1980s, has been a subject of debate, especially its origin. Although it became a global concern in the 1980s, earlier cases show that the first transmission in humans was recorded at about 1920 in Kinshasa, in the Democratic Republic of Congo (DR Congo), and was verified in 1959 from a blood sample of a man in Kinshasa.[65] It is suggested that sex workers may have been responsible for the high rate of transmission, especially in the urban centers. For example, 85 percent of sex workers was said to have been infected by 1986 in Nairobi, Kenya.[66] The disease spread further into Western Equatorial Africa – Gabon, Congo-Brazzaville and by the end of the 1980s, it had reached most of the West African states. Some occupational groups such as truck drivers, soldiers, traders, miners, among others were the early drivers of the virus through patronage of sex workers, thereby spreading it along transport and trade routes.[67] For example, 35 percent of truck drivers and 30 percent of soldiers in Uganda tested positive in the 1980s. Although HIV got to Malawi, Zambia, Mozam-

---

[62] Andrew J. Tatem, David J. Rogers, and Simon I. Hay, "Global Transport Networks and Infectious Disease Spread", *Advances in Parasitology* 62 (2006), 293–343.
[63] Matthew Heaton, and Toyin Falola, "Global Explanations Versus Local Interpretations: The historiography of the Influenza Pandemic of 1918–19 in Africa", *History in Africa* 33 (2006), 205–230; K. David Patterson, "The Influenza Epidemic of 1918–19 in the Gold Coast", *Journal of African History* 24, 4 (1983), 485–502.
[64] Douglas Almond and Bhashkar Mazumder, "The 1918 Influenza Pandemic and Subsequent Health Outcomes: An Analysis of SIPP Data", *American Economic Review* 95, 2 (2005), 258–62.
[65] Faria, Nuno R., Andrew Rambaut, Marc A. Suchard, Guy Baele, Trevor Bedford, Melissa J. Ward, Andrew J. Tatem, et al., "The Early Spread and Epidemic Ignition of HIV-1 in Human Populations", *Science* 346, 6205 (2014): 56–61.
[66] Emily Oster, "Sexually Transmitted Infections, Sexual Behavior, and the HIV/AIDS Epidemic", *The Quarterly Journal of Economics* 120, 2 (2005), 467–515; Mirjam Van Donk, "'Positive' Urban Futures in Sub-Saharan Africa: HIV/AIDS and the Need for ABC (A Broader Conceptualization)", *Environment and Urbanization* 18, 1 (2006), 155–75.
[67] John Iliffe, *Honour in African History*. Vol. 107 (Cambridge: Cambridge University Press, 2005).

bique, Zimbabwe, and Botswana relatively late, the reported cases at the end of 1980 were almost more than East Africa comparatively.[68]

In the 1990s, there was a surge in new HIV infection rates, probably due to series of wars in countries such as Rwanda, Liberia, and Sierra Leone, among others. Many soldiers drawn from other African countries, as well as rebels in these wars, became infected because of unprotected sex.[69] The situation was compounded by lack of ideas on how to deal with the pandemic in the midst of slim prospect of effective treatment against the background of poor medical facilities in Africa. This was the period that the international community had not mobilized concrete response to deal with the virus. Similarly, African governments were too preoccupied with political crises and were ill-equipped to deal with the disease. It is estimated that out of 14 million HIV patients globally in 1993, sub-Saharan Africa accounted for 19 million and by 1998, Africa had 70 percent of people living with HIV/AIDS. It is equally estimated that one out of seven of people infected during this period came from South Africa.[70] As the disease spread through Africa, people living with it became stigmatized. For example, a South African AIDS activist named Gugu Dlamini was killed by her neighbors after revealing she was HIV positive in 1998.[71] It has been estimated that 15 million Africans have died of the disease as of 2007, showing how it had affected families, communities and development in Africa.[72]

In 1996, a combination of therapies known as HAART was produced for the treatment of people living with HIV, but only the rich countries could afford it. The new drugs led to the drop of the rate of death from HIV by 84 per cent in the developed countries.[73] It also gave hope that the disease could be controlled; however, such expensive antiviral drugs were out of the reach of poor countries in Africa. It is estimated that the drugs cost between $10,000 and $15,000 per person annually, an amount that was between 9 per cent and 67 per cent GDP of sub-Saharan Africa.[74] The situa-

---

[68] Mike Mathambo Mtika, "Political Economy, Labor Migration, and the AIDS Epidemic in Rural Malawi", *Social Science and Medicine* 64, 12 (2007), 2454–63.
[69] Colin McInnes, "Conflict, HIV and AIDS: a New Dynamic in Warfare?", *Global Change, Peace and Security* 21, 1 (2009), 99–114.
[70] Leickness C. Simbayi, Anna Strebel, Allanise Cloete, Nomvo Henda, and Ayanda Mqeketo, "Internalized Stigma, Discrimination, and Depression among Men and Women Living with HIV/AIDS in Cape Town, South Africa", *Social Science and Medicine* 64, 9 (2007), 1823.
[71] Robert Morrell, "Silence, Sexuality and HIV/AIDS in South African Schools", *The Australian Educational Researcher* 30, 1 (2003), 41–62.
[72] Donald Skinner and Sakhumzi Mfecane, "Stigma, Discrimination and the Implications for People Living with HIV/AIDS in South Africa", *Journal of Social Aspects of HIV/AIDS* 1, 3 (2004), 157–64.
[73] Geoff Foster, and John Williamson, "A Review of Current Literature on the Impact of HIV/AIDS on Children in Sub-Saharan Africa", *AIDS-London-Current Science Then Rapid Science Publishers Then Lippincott Raven-* 14 (2000), S275-S284.
[74] Arin Dutta, Andrea Wirtz, Anderson Stanciole, Robert Oelrichs, Iris Semini, and Farley Cleghorn, "The Global HIV Epidemics Among People who Inject Drugs", *The World Bank*, 2012; Colleen V. Chien, "HIV/AIDS Drugs for Sub-Saharan Africa: How do Brand and Generic Supply Compare?", *PLoS One* 2, 3 (2007), e278.

tion temporarily left majority of African nations out of the treatment equation. In 1999, hope came the way of Africa when the United States became flexible in the local production or importation of cheap HIV drugs in Africa, provided the drugs had intellectual property right protection.[75] However, most African countries neither had the industries to manufacture the drugs locally, nor the resources to import them. Similarly, many countries lacked the healthcare infrastructure necessary for large-scale treatment against the background of the near absence of social security or health insurance.

Five pharmaceutical companies agreed to price reductions for HIV drugs in 2000 so as to make them more accessible to people in Africa and other poor countries.[76] Furthermore, the world's biggest drug manufacturers agreed to frequent price cut of patented AIDS drugs until they were relatively affordable. The price cuts and the production of generic drugs were good steps toward expanding access to HIV treatments.[77] The impact of this development is that there was an increase from 100,000 to 810,000 in the number of people that accessed HIV/AIDS treatment in sub-Saharan Africa, between 2003 and 2005. Following the precarious effect of HIV/AIDS, the Botswana government launched a national antiretroviral treatment project, jointly financed by the government, the Gates Foundation, and Merck Drugs Company in 2002. Although, treatment was initially hindered by shortage of health workers and poor health system, it picked up by 2007 with about 95 percent of HIV positive people treated.[78] The success of the treatment program raised the hope for antiretroviral treatment for Africans in need. Countries such as Rwanda, Namibia, Uganda, Kenya, Malawi, and Swaziland have also been relatively successful at rolling out antiretroviral treatment. Despite increased access to treatment in sub-Saharan Africa at the dawn of the twenty-first century, some countries remained less successful. Some of these countries are Sudan and Somalia, due to conflicts, and Nigeria, due to its very poor healthcare system.[79]

---

[75] Nitsan Chorev, "Changing Global Norms Through Reactive Diffusion: The Case of Intellectual Property Protection of AIDS Drugs", *American Sociological Review* 77, 5 (2012), 831–53.
[76] Amir Attaran and Lee Gillespie-White, "Do Patents for Antiretroviral Drugs Constrain Access to AIDS Treatment in Africa?", *JAMA* 286, 5 (2001), 1886–92.
[77] Nathan Ford, David Wilson, Gabriela Costa Chaves, Michel Lotrowska, and Kannikar Kijtiwatchakul, "Sustaining Access to Antiretroviral Therapy in the Less-Develope World: Lessons from Brazil and Thailand", *AIDS* 21 (2007), S21-S29.
[78] Catherine Campbell, Yugi Nair, Sbongile Maimane, and Jillian Nicholson, "'Dying Twice' A Multilevel Model of the Roots of AIDS Stigma in Two South African Communities", *Journal of Health Psychology* 12, 3 (2007), 403–16.
[79] Nweze Justus Amuche, Ifeanyichukwu Emmanuel, Eke and Emeka Innocent Nweze "HIV/AIDS in sub-Saharan Africa: Current status, challenges and prospects", (2017).

The 2014–2016 Ebola Outbreak

Although Ebola was discovered in 1976, it was not until its outbreak in the forested rural area of southeastern Guinea that the World Health Organization (WHO) declared it as a global pandemic on 23 March, 2014.[80] The 2014–2016 Ebola pandemic began with the reported index case in December, 2013, of an 18-month-old patient in southeastern Guinea, suspected to have been infected by bats.[81] The virus spread to Conakry, capital of Guinea, after additional reported cases from the rural area, a situation that forced state health officials to raise alert of a strange deadly disease on 13 March, 2014. It was, however, the Pasteur Institute in France that confirmed it as EVD caused by *Zaire ebolavirus* and by 23 March 2014, the disease had already killed twenty-nine people from forty-nine reported cases.[82] By July 2014, the virus had spread from Guinea to neighboring countries such as Liberia and Sierra Leone, due to the absence of strong health infrastructure.

The potential risk of international spread of the virus further made WHO to declare the deteriorating situation a Public Health Emergency of International Concern (PHEIC) on 8 August 2014. Meanwhile, it had spread to more countries such as Nigeria, Mali, Senegal, Spain, Italy, the United Kingdom, and the United States. Cases of secondary infection were reported in Nigeria, Mali, Italy, and the United States. Most of the secondary cases occurred in health care centers, one of which claimed the life of Dr. Ameyo Stella Adadevoh, who put her life on the line in July 2014 to contain Nigeria's first-ever Ebola patient and prevent the spread.

As part of the efforts to control the Ebola disease, the CDC (Center for Disease Control) put up its Emergency Operations Center in July 2014 to coordinate technical assistance and disease control with partner groups. It therefore deployed personnel to West Africa for the purpose of contact tracing, management of cases, laboratory testing, surveillance, and health education.[83] In order to prevent international cross-border transmissions, travelers were screened at entry and exit points at airports. The screening helped to identify those at risk of the disease and prevent the spread. Furthermore, travelers entering the United States from countries such as Guinea, Liberia, Sierra Leone, and Mali were specifically screened by rerouting

---

[80] Cordelia E. M. Coltart, Benjamin Lindsey, Isaac Ghinai, Anne M. Johnson, and David L. Heymann, "The Ebola Outbreak, 2013–2016: Old Lessons for New Epidemics", *Philosophical Transactions of the Royal Society B: Biological Sciences* 372, 1721 (2017), 20160297.

[81] Annika Brundyn, "A Mathematical Modelling Approach for Understanding the 2014–2016 Ebola Virus Outbreak in Sierra Leone and Liberia", BSc. Thesis, Department of Statistics, University of Cape Town (2018).

[82] Augustine Goba, S. Humarr Khan, Mbalu Fonnie, Mohamed Fullah, Alex Moigboi, Alice Kovoma, Vandi Sinnah, et al., "An outbreak of Ebola virus disease in the Lassa Fever Zone", *The Journal of Infectious Diseases* 214, 3 (2016), S110-S121.

[83] Beth P. Bell, "Overview, Control Strategies, and Lessons Learned in the CDC Response to the 2014–2016 Ebola Epidemic", *MMWR Supplements* 65 (2016).

them to designated airports for better risk assessment.[84] As part of the responses to the disease, 24,655 healthcare workers were trained by CDC on prevention and control in West Africa. In addition, twenty-four laboratories were established in Guinea, Liberia, and Sierra Leone to test suspect patients by the end of 2015.[85]

The pandemic, like others before it, put Africa in particular and the world in general in panicked situation. However, the WHO lifted its PHEIC status on 29 March 2016 after the three major countries, namely, Guinea, Liberia, and Sierra Leone that were affected were declared free of the disease.[86] As indicated in Table 1, a total of 28,616 cases and 11,310 deaths were reported in Guinea, Liberia, and Sierra Leone. An additional thirty-six cases and fifteen deaths were reported in other countries.

Table 1: Countries with Widespread Transmission and other Countries Affected During the Epidemic

Country	Total Cases (Suspected, Probable, Confirmed)	Laboratory Confirmed Cases	Total Deaths
Countries with widespread Transmission			
Guinea	3,814	3,358	2,544
Liberia	10,678	3,163	4,810
Sierra Leone	14,124	8,706	3,956
Affected Countries			
Italy	1	1	0
Mali	8	7	6
Nigeria	20	19	8
Senegal	1	1	0
Spain	1	1	0
United Kingdom	1	1	0
United States	4	4	1
Total	**28,652**	**15,261**	**11,325**

Source: CDC (2019)
COVID-19 Pandemic

---

[84] Varvara A. Mouchtouri, Eleni P. Christoforidou, Cinthia Menel Lemos, Margherita Fanos, Ute Rexroth, Ulrike Grote, Evelien Belfroid, Corien Swaan, and Christos Hadjichristodoulou, "Exit and Entry Screening Practices for Infectious Diseases Among Travelers at Points of Entry: Looking for Evidence on Public Health Impact", *International Journal of Environmental Research and Public Health* 16, 23 (2019), 4638.
[85] Jeffrey C. Hageman, "Infection Prevention and Control for Ebola in Health Care Settings—West Africa and United States", *MMWR Supplements* 65 (2016).
[86] Paul Richards, *Ebola: how a people's science helped end an epidemic* (London: Zed Books Ltd., 2016).

The COVID-19 pandemic is a global pestilence that became pervasive in nature and character. The virus emanated from China in December 2019 and quickly spread to other parts of the world. The virus, which is causes difficulty in breathing, transmits through direct or close contact with the carrier. Although, it is not an airborne disease so far, the level of interaction in contemporary world is making the virus easier to spread than the previous global pandemics.[87] It has been suggested that COVID-19 and the 1918 influenza are respiratory diseases, characterized by coughing or sneezing, but they are different in some ways. For example, while the Spanish Flu had incubation period of between one and two days, COVID-19 has up to two weeks, and the spread is facilitated by asymptomatic carriers.[88] Furthermore, the influenza of a century ago overwhelmingly attacked the young and healthy, but COVID-19's victims are the aged and those with weak immune systems, as well as underlying diseases.[89] Despite these differences, both pandemics have similar socio-economic effects and patterns of morbidity.

Although, accurate figures are difficult to come by, as of 13 July 2020 reported global cases stood at 13,107,962; 572,831 deaths; 7,632,663 recovered cases and 4,902,468 active cases.[90] Reports indicate that the United States of America is the most affected and followed by Brazil. As at the time of writing this paper, update of the virus globally reveals that the following countries are having the highest cases.

African countries were not affected until two reported cases were confirmed in February 2020. However, as of 13 July, 2020, almost all African countries have confirmed cases.[91] African cases as at 13 July, 2020 indicate 594,955 infections, 13,246 deaths and 295,242 recoveries.[92] The top 10 African countries with the highest confirmed cases are presented below.

The World Health Organization (WHO) observed that the confirmed cases in Africa might be higher than officially reported due to low level of tests carried out and shortage of equipment.

---

[87] L. Wang, Y. Wang, D., Ye, and Q. Liu, "A Review of the 2019 Novel Coronavirus (COVID-19) Based on Current Evidence", *International Journal of Antimicrobial Agents* (2020), https://doi.org/10.1016/j.ijantimicag.2020.105948, 14 July, 2020.

[88] Rafael Ballester-Arnal, and Maria Dolores Gil-Llario, "The Virus that Changed Spain: Impact of COVID-19 on People with HIV", *AIDS and Behavior* 24, 8 (2020), 2253–57.

[89] Steffen Roth, Lars Clausen, and Soeren Mueller, "COVID-19. Scenarios of a superfluous crisis", *Scenarios of a Superfluous Crisis* (March 30, 2020), SSRN: 10.2139/ssrn.3564920 (2020).

[90] Saverio Caini, Peter Spreeuwenberg, Gabriela F. Kusznierz, Juan Manuel Rudi, Rhonda Owen, Kate Pennington, Sonam Wangchuk, et al., "Distribution of Influenza Virus Types by Age Using Case-Based Global Surveillance Data from Twenty-Nine Countries, 1999–2014", *BMC Infectious Diseases* 18, 1 (2018), 1–10.

[91] World Health Organisation. *African Countries Move from COVID 19 Readiness to Response as Many Confirm Cases.* WHO Africa, https://www.afro.who.int/health-topics/coronavirus-covid-19, 14 July, 2020.

[92] World Health Organization. *African Countries Move from COVID 19 Readiness to Response as Many Confirm Cases.* WHO Africa, https://www.afro.who.int/health-topics/coronavirus-covid-19, 14 July, 2020.

Table 2: Top Ten Countries with the Highest Cases of COVID-19

S/No.	Country	Total Cases	Total Deaths	Active Cases	Population
1.	USA	3,430,726	137,839	1,774,633	331,065 797
2.	Brazil	1,866,176	72,151	580 513	212 607,642
3.	India	898,680	23,569	308 447	1,380,418,989
4.	Russia	733,699	11,439	218 239	145,936,664
5.	Peru	326,326	11,870	97 345	32 984,938
6.	Chile	315,041	6,979	24 160	19 121,318
7.	Spain	300,988	28,403	N/A	46 755,416
8.	Mexico	299,750	35,006	79 980	128 973,689
9.	UK	289,603	44,819	N/A	67 897,720
10.	South Africa	276,242	4,079	137 289	59,330,493

Source: Worldometer 2020.

Table 3: Top Ten African Countries with the Highest Confirmed Cases

S/No.	Country	Total Cases	Region
1.	South Africa	276,242	South Africa
2.	Egypt	82,070	North Africa
3.	Nigeria	32,558	West Africa
4.	Ghana	24,518	West Africa
5.	Algeria	19,195	North Africa
6.	Morocco	15,745	North Africa
7.	Cameroon	15,173	Central Africa
8.	Ivory Coast	12,766	West Africa
9.	Sudan	10,250	Central Africa
10.	Kenya	10,105	East Africa

Source: Shaban, A.A. (2020). "Africa COVID 19 Stats"

Conclusion

From the foregoing, it is evident that Africa has witnessed the outbreak of one disease or the other. These include malaria, smallpox, sleeping sickness, HIV/AIDs, Ebola and Corona Virus, among others. The continent has employed several means to prevent and control the effects of these diseases over the years. Disease control system as examined within African worldview was largely based on the appropriate knowledge on the disease and the flora within the community. A combination of herbs and mystic forces were used to prevent and limit the damaging effects of all the categories of diseases in Africa. The analysis of diseases and control system showed that over 80 percent of the people in Africa were dependent on the traditional control method irrespective of the existence of the western methods over the years.

There is no doubt that diseases have constituted major challenges to the medical systems in Africa, though with varying degrees of effects and mortality rates across the countries of the continent. The colonial authorities took over the challenges by establishing dispensaries/clinics/hospitals, sometimes with the support of missionaries in order to mitigate the threat of diseases to their colonial enterprises that were majorly economical in nature. Besides, control measures such as sanitation, vaccination and sometimes restriction movements in the case of epidemics were employed by the colonial authorities to ensure healthy colonies.

Pandemics such as the Spanish influenza, HIV/AIDS, Ebola, and COVID-19 have wreaked havoc on the continent as in other regions of the world. However, their control and managements have largely dependent on the medical systems of the developed world. The few case studies examined reveal that disease control in African had combined both the traditional and western methods to prevent and limit the effects of major diseases and pandemics over the years. However, there is urgent need to pay greater attention to the development and incorporation of local solutions into western methods as a better approach to the control of diseases on the continent.

William Ackah
Chapter 14
Africa and the Globalization of Religion in the Contemporary Era

Abstract: This chapter explores the role of religion in Africa and the African diaspora in the contemporary era. It argues that in order to understand and explain contemporary developments, students need to understand that expressions of African spirituality are connected to the spiritual expressions of African descendants. This chapter provides overviews of Christianity, Islam, African traditional religion, and new diasporic African religions, and argues that these traditions in the lived experience of African descendants need to be studied comparatively with African people at the center of such studies. The work concludes by arguing that we should not just study contemporary expressions of African spirituality for academic reasons, but we should study and research in order to advance and elevate the African personality in the twenty-first century.

Keywords: African Personality, African descendants, Christianity, Islam, African Traditional Religion.

Africans in the twenty-first century are a mobile people. Africa has a young population and that populace has been spreading its influence geographically, politically, economically, and socially all over the globe.[1] As they move, the spirituality of their lived experiences moves with them, shaping and influencing as it did for their foremothers and forefathers before them. To grasp the contemporary significance of this dynamic spirituality, our study of the subject also has to move in order to better understand and reflect this complex cosmology as it unfolds. The starting point for this understanding is that the African spiritual present is connected to its ancestral past, what is being witnessed and analysed in the twenty-first century is a continuum of the creativity, resilience, and complex intersectional relationship of African spiritualities in the development of African identities in the world today.[2] This work is not intended to be generic survey of the field of global African religion in the ordinary sense. Rather, the chapter should be read as a series of pointers and provocations that invite the reader to debate, challenge, and further explore and research the wonders of global African religion in its historic and contemporary

---

[1] Paul T. Zeleza, "Rewriting the African Diaspora: Beyond the Black Atlantic," *African Affairs* 104:414 (2005): 58–62.
[2] William Ackah "Mapping the Religious Expressions and Spirituality of African Descendant Communities," in *Religion, Culture and Spirituality in Africa and the African Diaspora*, ed. byWilliam Ackah *et al.* (New York: Routledge, 2018) 6–7.

unfolding. The chapter argues that the study of African spirituality and religious tradition in the contemporary era should be centered around African people. From the abstract to the lived experience, African peoples have always been stretching out their hands, minds, and hearts towards the spiritual realm to make sense of the past, present, and future. As scholars and students of the African experience our research, teaching, and learning should place Africans at the centre of our analysis and follow them around the globe.

African Spirituality in Academic and Cultural Context

All recorded human societies have a conception of a spiritual world. If all human societies emanate from the African continent, then all human understandings of spirituality have an African imprint in their DNA. If we focus on the three major monotheistic faiths that have been the focus of attention of much of the world, they have a discernible African influence according to their own traditions. According to the Hebrew bible, the religion of Judaism was incubated and born in Egypt, with its first leader maintaining his African name even as he received the commandments from his God and developed the rules that would govern the practice of the faith.[3] The call to prayer in Islam that is at the centre of its religious expression, and which is heard around the world today as the clear symbol of its voice emanates from the tongue of an African Bilal ibn Rabah.[4] And according to the New Testament, one of the first converts to Christianity was an Ethiopian Jew who had travelled to Jerusalem to worship, and upon hearing about the new faith on his way home, decided to adopt it as his own.[5] In ancient or classical times, the movement of people in and out of Africa and the movement of African peoples themselves reveals the dynamism of the African spiritual pulse. Its beat may not be heard so clearly in the development of these monotheistic traditions because of the shrill noise of contemporary anti-black racism that denies African contribution to 'civilisation', but it is undeniably there.[6] Its presence demonstrates that contemporary expressions of African Judaism, Islam, and Christianity have deep-seated roots in the continental soil comparable to any

---

[3] See book of Exodus in the Biblical Old Testament. For wider discussion of Judaism and Africa, see Edith Bruder and Tudor Parfitt, eds. *African Zion: Studies in Black Judaism* (Newcastle upon Tyne: Cambridge Scholars, 2012).

[4] Edward E. Curtis IV, *The Call of Bilal: Islam in the African Diaspora* (Chapel Hill: University of North Carolina, 2003), 6.

[5] See book of Acts, Biblical New Testament; see also Gifford C.A. Rhamie *Whiteness, Conviviality and Agency: The Ethiopian Eunuch (Acts 8:26–40) and Conceptuality in the Imperial Imagination of Biblical Studies* (PhD Thesis, Canterbury Christchurch University 2019).

[6] St Clair Drake *Black Folk Here and There: An Essay in History and Anthropology Volume 2* (Los Angeles: Center for Afro-American Studies, University of California, 1990).

ethnic, racialised, or geographically defined community connected to these religious traditions. This may cause a reconsideration as to what are categorised as indigenous religions more broadly. Traditionally the tendency has been to ascribe indigeneity to African religion based on historical origins and geographic location. Emphasis has been placed on a linear model, whereby African religons were practised on the continent (indigenous) and that Islam and Christianity were later imports (transplanted faiths).[7] From the vantage point of the twenty-first century, this linear historical model has limitations, it does not capture the cyclical and changing dimensions of material and spiritual existences where African expressions of religious devotion are multiple and dynamic. And where African descendants have innovated, adapted, and adopted ways of knowing and being both inside and outside of rationalised understandings of time and space.[8] In order to better grasp this, we need to follow the people who are utilising the religious tradition and to understand the how and why certain forms are proving attractive and gaining adherents and what impact this has on African-descendant communities in their local and global settings. We start this exploration with a discussion of twenty-first century African Christianity.

Twenty-first Century African Christianity

Christianity across Africa and its diaspora in the contemporary era is a multi-dimensional expression of religious devotion with many facets ranging from global institutional denominations with significant numbers of African adherents, to small independent worshipping communities in parts of the world with marginal African presence.[9] In between, there are denominations and organisations with millions of followers started by Africans and led by Africans, which are repositioning the faith as an African, as opposed to European, religion. A well-known example of a contemporary African denomination that has mushroomed from its founding in the latter part of the twentieth century in Nigeria to having a global footprint in the twenty-first century is the Redeemed Christian Church of God (RCCG).[10] Started by Pa Josiah Akindayomi in 1952 with a handful of members, the denomination experienced a major transformation under its successor leader Pastor Adeboye. The former mathematics lecturer instituted several structural and organisational changes that made

---

[7] James V. Spickard and Afe Adogame, " Introduction: Africa, The New African Diaspora and Religious Transnationalism in a Global World," in *Religion Crossing Boundaries: Transnational Religious and Social Dynamics in Africa and the New African Diaspora*, ed. by James V. Spickard et al. (New York: Brill, 2010), 1.
[8] Jacob K. Olupona and Terry Rey "Introduction," in *Òrìṣà Devotion as World Religion: The Globalisation of Yoruba Religious Culture*, ed. by Jacob K. Olopuna et al. (Madison: University of Wisconsin Press, 2008), 6–7.
[9] Ogbu Kalu, ed., *African Christianity: An African Story* (Trenton, Africa World Press 2007)
[10] https://www.rccg.org/mission-and-vision/ (accessed 4th December 2020).

the church more outward focused. Its mission template was to plant a church within five miles driving distance in the Global North and five minutes walking distance in the Global South, has resulted in burgeoning membership and influence in Nigeria and an international presence in the Americas, Europe, Asia and across the African continent.[11] The emergence of RCCG and similar churches such as Deeper Christian Life Ministry and Christ Embassy amongst many others speaks to the dynamism and enterprise of these contemporary African churches. They have been able to impose themselves in a crowded religious marketplace on the African continent and become a transnational phenomenon.[12] They have established presence in the diaspora, creating spaces of faith and identity in sometimes hostile environments for migrants.[13]

These newer manifestations of African Pentecostal Christianity also belie notions of Africans as victims of circumstance, unable to create and develop organisations. These African-led denominations are in some instances multi-million-dollar enterprises, engaged in transnational economic activity, global media enterprise and international community engagement and development.[14] They are not the only ones to display this multi-dimensional spirit and ethos.

The latter part of the twentieth century also saw the birth of African Christian Churches in the diasporic space. Students, teachers, engineers, factory workers, traders going to Europe, the US, and Asia in search of opportunities and establishing their own congregations while in those places. The most successful of these use the diaspora platform to then branch back and establish congregations in Africa and other parts of the world.[15] Matthew Ashimolowu's Kingsway International Christian Center is an often-cited example of this phenomenon. With his church from its initial base in London in the 1980s now in this century has branches in Ghana, Nigeria, and South Africa, amongst others, and a TV ministry that has a global audience.[16] It is not only these newer denominations and individuals that have seen a flourishing in this century, with African Indigenous/Initiated/Independent Churches (AICs) who trace their origins to the colonial era such as Kimbanguism[17] in the Bel-

---

11 A. Ukah, *The Redeemed Christian Church of God, Nigeria: Local Identities and Global Processes in African Pentecostalism* (PhD Thesis, University of Bayreuth, 2003).
12 Afe Adogame, *The African Christian Diaspora: New Trends and Emerging Currents in World Christianity* (London: Bloomsbury, 2013), 73.
13 Mark G. Gornik, *World Made Global: Stories of African Christianity in New York City.* (Grand Rapids: Eerdmans, 2011)
14 J. Kwabena Asamoah-Gyadu, "God is Big in Africa: Pentecostal Mega Churches and the Changing Religious Landscape," *Material Religion: The Journal of Objects, Art and Belief* 15:3 (2019): 390–92 doi.org/10.1080/17432200.2019.1590012.
15 Adogame, *The African Christian Diaspora*, 73–78.
16 Mark Cartledge et al *Megachurches and Social Engagement: Public Theology in Practice* (Leiden: Brill, 2019) ,190–212.
17 A.M. Gampiot, "Kimbanguism as a Migrants Religion in Europe," in *Christianity in Africa and the African Diaspora: The Appropriation of a Scattered Heritage*, ed. by Afe Adogame, Roswith Gerloff and Klaus Hoff (London: Continuum 2008) 304–13.

gian Congo, and the West African Aladura churches are following this pattern.[18] These have grown numerically and spread their wings geographically out of Africa and into the diaspora.

All the forms of Christianity described so far have traditionally been regarded as manifestations of Christianity derived from Africa or by Africans that were born on the continent. Here, the focus is on contemporary forms of Christianity, but it needs to be recognised that these forms emerge out of histories of Africans taking control of the faith, and utilising it to meet their spiritual, cultural, economic and political needs.[19] These groupings have been regarded as shaping the future of the faith, and giving it an African sensibility, distinct from versions of Christianity that came to Africa because of European missionary endeavour and colonial extraction. Those distinctions have been an important marker in labelling distinctive forms of faith emanating from Africa and outlining that Christianity was not solely the religion of the European transplanted to the continent.[20] In the twenty-first century, however, one might argue that these distinctions may increasingly become unnecessary or require rethinking. Anglicanism, Methodism, Presbyterianism, and even Catholicism were once European monoliths with Black and Brown outposts in the rest of the world, but are now experiencing seismic shifts in power and influence, where Africa and Africans play an increasingly important role on the global stage.[21] For some of these denominations, it is Africans on the continent and their brothers and sisters in the diaspora who are keeping these denominations alive. It can be asked whether these are still European religious expressions that Africans have embraced, or are they now African expressions? How long does a faith have to be present in the soil for it to be considered African? How many adherents or followers does it need? How do we characterise expressions of Christianity that have not arisen from the colonialism but have large numbers of African adherents both on the continent and the diaspora, such as Seventh Day Adventists, Jehovah's Witnesses, and Christian expressions emanating from Brazil and South Korea that are also attracting African descendants?[22] Do we need a broader conceptualisation of forms of African spiritual expressions one that recognises the changing shifts and contours of the Af-

---

18 Afe Adogame "Clearing New Paths into an Old Forest: Aladura Christianity in Europe" in *Orisa Devotion as World Religion* ed Olupona et al (Madison: University of Wisconsin Press, 2008) 247–62.
19 Graham Duncan and Ogbu U. Kalu, "Bakuzufu: Revival Movements and Indigenous Appropriation in African Christianity," in *African Christianity: An African Story*, ed. by Ogbu U. Kalu (Trenton: Africa World Press, 2007) 245–270.
20 Lamin Sanneh, *Disciples of all Nations: Pillars of World Christianity* (Oxford: Oxford University Press, 2008), 185–216.
21 Philip Jenkins, *The Next Christendom: The Coming of Global Christianity* (Oxford, Oxford University Press) 2007 edition.
22 See Laura Premack for a discussion of Nigerian Pentecostalism in Brazil and Brazilian Pentecostalism in Africa. Laura Premack, "The Coca-Cola of Churches' Arrives: Nigeria's Redeemed Christian Church of God in Brazil" in *The Public Face of African New Religious Movements in Diaspora: Imagining the Religious Other*, ed. by Afe Adogame (London: Routledge), 215–32.

rican lived experience? Perhaps we need one that recognises that global African spirituality has many points of origin.

The changing nature of Christian expression overtime leads me to believe that this does need to be the direction for future research. The need for this becomes more apparent when one considers the experiences of those African descendants who survived the middle passage and have developed a myriad of expressions of Christianity in the diaspora.[23] In the twenty-first century, African-descendant Christians in the diasporic space are still wrestling with the legacies of enslavement and ongoing struggles against white supremacy. In the United States, contemporary Christianity as practiced by African Americans has a range of political shades that vary from championing Black Lives Matter at one end of the political spectrum to supporting Donald Trump at the other. These are threads of resistance to and accommodations of systems of power that have long histories and speak to the continuity of African descendant's experiences out of which these contemporary contestations emerge.[24]

In an overview of this kind, one is always conscious that one cannot cover all the themes or give justice to all the expressions of African-descendant Christianity, and the places and spaces where it has been influential. To close this section, I do want to reiterate the importance of the Africa and the African experience in its multi-dimensional unfolding to understanding contemporary African Christianity, and moving us beyond it. Two examples will suffice:. Malcolm X, the Black nationalist/internationalist religious revolutionary was a Black Muslim and, latterly before his death, a Sunni Muslim.[25] It is his activism and searing analysis of white supremacy that paved the way for Black Power, and influenced a generation of Black Theologians. Starting with James H. Cone in the contemporary era, Black Theology emerged to move beyond a pietistic Christianity to one which was much more radical and critical of white society and white Christianity.[26] It is due to Malcolm X, a Muslim, that we have Christian Black Liberation Theology birthed in the twentieth century, and which provides support for Black political and social movements in the twenty-first century such as Black Lives Matter, and the decolonising of Eurocentric spaces. An approach that places the African descendant at the centre of analysis seeks to place Malcolm X and James Cone in relation to one another and seeing their spiritual similarities beyond the labels of Christian and Muslim that would seek to divide them. In the twenty-first century, as a normative position, we need to think about the connections and continuities of African spirituality and do much more compara-

---

[23] Noel Leo Erskine, *Plantation Church: How African-American Religion was Born in Caribbean Slavery* (Oxford: Oxford University, 2014).
[24] Gayraud S. Wilmore, *Black Religion and Black Radicalism: An Interpretation of the Religious History of African Americans* (New York: Orbis, 1998).
[25] Malcolm X, *The Autobiography of Malcolm X: with the assistance of Alex Haley* (London: Penguin, 1966).
[26] James H. Cone, *Black Theology and Black Power* (New York: Orbis, 2008, first edition 1969).

tive analysis across faith traditions that advance causes of justice for African descendant communities.

This leads to the second example, which is that of Womanist Theology,[27] a theological discourse that emerged on its own terms but also as a critique of Black Theology for its inability to incorporate Black women's experiences into its analysis of racism and white supremacy.[28] Women have been doing the labour that has kept the older and newer African descendant forms of Christianity alive, and is enabling it to flourish this century. Recognition, leadership positions, and equality, however have been slow in coming. The contemporary era has opened more spaces for African descendant women. Womanist, Black, African, and Post-Colonial theology are providing platforms to articulate the need for change and providing new ways to interpret African spirituality in light of African descendant experience. These are important trends, and this era is providing opportunities for African descendants around the world to make new connections and renew or reengage with old ones considered broken or lost.[29]

Will the twenty-first century lead to more forms of African Christian unity on the global stage, or are we destined for more multiplication, dynamism, and continual adaptation and development of African descendant Christian experience? Trends suggest both. The continued existence of one of the oldest denominations in the Ethiopian Orthodox Church speaks to a continuous heritage that has criss-crossed continents, and now in the twenty-first century is a Black and Brown majority faith expression with increasing African descendant spaces and places of influence.[30] How do other African expressions of religious practice and devotion compare? And what might this reveal about the future of African faith expressions overall in this century? We will turn to another of the Abrahamic traditions to engage with this question.

Twenty-first Century African Islam

Islam, in the contemporary era, has experienced a great deal of discrimination. As Christianity has loomed large in certain quarters of the African landscape, its cousin has not been given the respect and analysis it deserves in relation to its relevance and impact on the lives of people of African descent around the globe.[31] This lack

---

27 Stephanie Y. Mitchem, *Introducing Womanist Theology* (New York: Orbis, 2002).
28 Katie G. Cannon, *Katie's Cannon: Womanism and the Soul of the Black Community* (New York: Continuum, 1995).
29 Mercy Oduyoye, *Introducing African Women's Theology* (Sheffield: Sheffield Academic Press), 2001.
30 Ebenezer Obadare, *Pentecostal Republic Religion and the Struggle for State Power in Nigeria* (London: Zed, 2018).
31 Curtis IV, *The Call of Bilal*.

of attention relates to broader issues of language, culture, and power. Most of the texts written on African descendant religion are in English, from scholars (including myself) who have been in raised in Christian traditions that give very little credence to other faith traditions. The result is an undervaluing and misreading of the rich Islamic traditions that exist in African descendent communities.[32]

As stated in the introduction, Africans played a vital role in the founding of Islam and the religion throughout the centuries has played an important role in the cultural, economic, and intellectual life of the continent alongside its religious role. The world-renowned intellectual centers of Mali and Songhai speak to the significance of the Islamic tradition on the continent in the centuries preceding European colonisation.[33] African Muslims were also significant in the diaspora, being part of the Moorish conquest of Spain and the cultural renaissance of the Iberian Peninsula from the tenth to the fifteenth century.[34] Arabic leaders were engaged in the enslavement of African descendants resulting in the movement and conversion of people across the continent and into Asia and the Middle East. This resulted in African descendant communities settling in Jordan, Iraq, India, and Pakistan, as well as in Saudi Arabia and other countries[35] that comprise the region.[36] As well as African Muslims coming into being via this process, African descendent Muslims were also transported across the Atlantic to North America, the Caribbean, and South America as part of transatlantic enslavement. It is estimated that up to one million Muslims, were forcibly removed from their homelands and taken to the Americas.[37] We know less of their experience as discourses of Christian religion have tended to dominate the narratives concerning the enslaved, but Islamic traditions did survive the middle passage and varieties of Islamic expression have emerged and developed in the Americas, informing traditions such as Santería and Vodun.[38] In the United States, aspects of Islamic tradition have been woven into discourses of Black Nationalism to create specific Black Muslim expressions of faith,[39] most notably in the form of the Moorish Science Temple and the Nation of Islam.[40] Migration from Africa, and

---

[32] Zain Abdullah, "African 'Soul Brothers' in the Hood: Immigration, Islam and the Black Encounter," *Anthropological Quarterly* 82, 1 (2009): 37–62.
[33] I. Hbrek, *General History of Africa III Africa from the Seventh to the Eleventh Century* (London: James Currey, 1992) 38–43.
[34] Brian Catlos *Kingdoms of Faith: A New History of Islamic Spain.* (London, Hurst & Company, 2018).
[35] John Hunwick and Eve T. Powell, *The African Diaspora in the Mediterranean Lands of Islam* (Princeton: Markus Wiener, 2002).
[36] Joseph E. Harris, *The African Presence in Asia* (Evanston: Northwestern University Press, 1971)
[37] Sylviane A. Diouf, "Sadaqa Amongst African Muslims Enslaved in the Americas," *Journal of Islamic Studies* 10, 1 (1999): 22–32.
[38] Diouf Sadaqa, "Amongst African Muslims," 24.
[39] Aminah B. McCloud, *African American Islam* (New York: Routledge, 1995) 9–94.
[40] Herbert Berg, "Mythmaking in the African American Muslim Context: The Moorish Science Temple, The Nation of Islam and the American Society of Muslims," *Journal of the American Academy of Religion* 73, 3 (2005): 685–703.

connections between African Americans and Muslims from other countries has also resulted in more universal forms of the faith, primarily Sunni, but also Shia and Sufi.[41] The Islam derived from the culture and faith expression of the formerly enslaved has been joined by that of more recent migrants from different parts of Africa to North America,[42] who brought their Islamic traditions with them.[43] In Europe, migrants from Algeria, Tunisia, and Morocco have been joined by their Muslim brothers and sisters from Nigeria, Senegal, Ghana, Gambia, Somalia, the Sudan, and, in fact, right across Africa, to bring about a renewal of Islam as a global religion with a diverse array of African adherents and converts. This has made for interesting intersections of gender, race, and religious identification in the twenty-first century. One notable intersection has been the way in which African Caribbean youth in Britain, generally raised as Christian, have turned to Islam as a way of foregrounding a Black identity with a faith identity. Their movement across generations in time and geographical space from Africa, to the Caribbean, then to Europe has also resulted in a change of formal religious identification in a quest to find an authentic African identity.[44] The changing nature of identity is not just a diasporic phenomenon, Islam on the continent is a multi-faceted dynamic religion that throughout its history on the continent has been a complex unfolding faith with many facets that cannot be examined here. Regional variations, rural and urban dynamics, migrations and trade, education and political, economic and social change have all marked the diverse trajectories of Islam across the continent into the 21st Century.[45]

Religion is not independent of the historical divisions arising from the colonial era, economic scarcity, and globalisation. Centuries of movement, trade, cultural, and spiritual exchanges also create conditions for the flourishing of spiritual renewals. Looking beyond the religious labels, and instead following people and communities, opens the door to analysing these situations in a more nuanced way.

Islam in Africa in the twenty-first century is a space of art and culture, where centuries-old traditions have been combined with contemporary trends to create sounds and styles that are world renowned. The musical and storytelling traditions of West African griots, which have passed down over generations in which Islam and local spiritual traditions have combined and are reproduced and contemporised around the globe by noted musicians like Youssou N'Dour. The novels and films of Ousmane Sembène are another case in point, as Islam, traditional African reli-

---

41 Curtis IV, *The Call of Bilal*, 135–37.
42 Monica Salzbruhn, "The Occupation of Public Space Through Religious and Political Events: How Senegalese Migrants Became a Part of Harlem, New York *Journal of Religion in Africa* 33, 4 (2004): 469–92.
43 Curtis IV, *The Call of Bilal*.
44 Richard Reddie, *Black Muslims in Britain: Why are a growing number of young black men converting to Islam* (London: Lion Books, 2009).
45 Nehemia Levtzion and Randall L. Pouwels, eds., *The History of Islam in Africa* (Athens, Ohio University Press, 2000) 1–16.

gion, local and global confluences all find their way into the work of this Pan-African cultural giant. I have highlighted well-known individuals here, but it is important to note that they come from communities where these traditions are lived spiritual practices that move as the people move.

In the diaspora there is also a plethora of African Muslim identities on display and on the move. From West African migrants who have travelled to Europe in the post-colonial period such as the Mourid community of Senegal, Sufis who have a specific identity related to their physical and spiritual home of Touba,[46] to Somalis in the United Kingdom who first came as seamen in the latter part of the nineteenth century, and who today have established transnational Muslim communities, but do not define themselves as belonging to a wider African diaspora.[47] Continental African Muslims to varying degrees have tended to regard their religious and national identities as primary, and their racialised Black identities as secondary if they acknowledge them at all.[48] African Caribbean Muslim converts, on the other hand, link Muslim identification to issues of race and injustice, both on a local and global scale. Some of these people converted to the faith while in prison, others rejecting the faiths of their parents and looking for a faith expression that aligned with their cultural identity.[49]

The racialisation of Islam as an alternative way to conceptualise blackness or African identity also parallels facets of Islam in North America, where the descendants of enslaved Africans developed a version of Islam where issues of race were centralised in the expression of the faith.[50] The Nation of Islam founded by Wallace Fard Muhammed but made famous by Malcolm X and latterly by Louis Farrakhan are the prime examples of this facet of Islamic identification.[51] From the vantage point of the twenty-first century although not huge in terms of numbers, its importance in relation to the development of cultural and political ideas of Black nationalism cannot be underestimated.

As a result of recent African migrations in the post-colonial period and also African Americans who have converted, there are in the US more Sunni Muslims who although interested in social justice would not prioritise 'race' or notions of a Black identity over and above their faith identity. The interplay between race, religious, and cultural identity in the Muslim world is a complex one, with African descendants facing discrimination because of their blackness in Muslim majority countries such as Pakistan, United Arab Emirates, and Saudi Arabia, but also in Europe and the Amer-

---

46 Curtis IV, *The Call of Bilal* 65–72.
47 Peter Aspinall and Lavinia Mitton, *The Migration History, Demography, and Socioeconomic position of the Somali community in Britain* (New York: Nova Science Publishers, 2011).
48 Curtis IV, *The Call of Bilal*, 78.
49 Reddie, *Black Muslims in Britain*.
50 C.E. Lincoln, *The Black Muslims in America*, (Grand Rapids: William B Eerdmans, 1994 first published 1961).
51 Manning Marable, *Malcolm X A Life of Reinvention* (London: Allen Lane, 2011).

icas. Some African-descendent Muslims do not recognise themselves as having a racialised identity, even though they experience racialised and religious discrimination. African descendent Muslims practice a variety of Islamic traditions, from Sunni to Sufi to Shia, but in some contexts, they have married Islamic traditions to African traditional spiritual practices to create distinctive forms of Islamic practice. Issues of geographic location, historical and contemporary context, numbers, host country reception are changing the nature of what it means to be an African Muslim across time and space.[52]

We need to better understand how African descendants respond and adapt to these processes to maintain their religious identities. Are African descendant Muslims any different from their Christian cousins in this respect? Identities that are multi-dimensional and multicultural but discernibly African in relation to rituals and practices in some spaces, are also culturally Arabic or North American or Asian in other spaces. Are these Islamic conceptions of culturally-constituted faith also too narrow as Africans are practising both inside and outside of preconceived cultural norms? It may be that these questions of culture, identity, and authenticity come to the fore with Islam because it has also been viewed as a religious import, but we will see whether cultural and religious stability does exist in the African global context in our exploration of.

Twenty-first Century African Traditional Religions

From the vantage point of the twenty-first century, African traditional religion has survived the onslaught of European Christian and Arabic/Asiatic Islamic expansion on the African continent with their quests to wipe out what was considered to be the 'heathen' or 'devilish' practices that were perceived as holding African communities back. In a meaningful sense the multitude of traditions that are housed under this umbrella have developed and flourished, influencing the so-called mainstream faiths and spreading across the continent and the diaspora.[53]

To do this has meant change, adaptation, and innovation, suggesting that the term 'traditional' is not adequate to describe autochthonous African religious expression in the contemporary era. Africa is a vast continent, with a myriad of cultures, ethnicities, and identities and within these cultures and ethnic groupings are complex expressions of lived experience that seek to explore, explain, and make sense of life, death, nature, birth, marriage and the past, present, and future. We attempt to categorise these complex explanatory frameworks of modes of being in diverse African contexts as African traditional 'religion', but there is a danger that we, or I, in

---

[52] Michael A. Gomez, *Black Crescent: The Experience and Legacy of African Muslims in the Americas* (New York: Cambridge University Press, 2005).
[53] Olupona and Rey, *Òrìṣà Devotion as World Religion*, 6–8.

this case, can impose a Eurocentric, monotheistic framing on practices, rituals and experiences that are beyond these conceptualisations.[54] Do the cultures and traditions of the Yoruba, for example, out of which their stories, traditions and practices developed, have the same cultural and spiritual DNA as the traditions of the Xhosa of Southern Africa? They may have similarities traced through the lineage of Pan-African spirituality, but they are complex religious eco-systems in their own right, that speak to the specificities of the myths of their own origins, their gods, ancestors and cycles of life and death, and these need to be acknowledged and studied on their own terms and not merely reduced to wholesale labels.

The case of the Òrìṣà spiritual tradition of the Yoruba is a global tradition in its own right, which is alive and well on the continent and which travelled in the hearts of and minds of enslaved Africans and survived and revived in Cuba in the form of Santería, Candomblé in Brazil, and Shango in Trinidad.[55] Not a Yoruba-specific tradition, vodun in Haiti is also in the category of faiths that survived the horrors of European enslavement and which have adapted and continue to express Africanity in the diaspora.[56] In the twentieth and now twenty-first century, new technology, migration, and a renewed interest in African cultures by diasporic descendants has resulted in crossflows between Yoruba practitioners in Nigeria and leaders and adherents of their sister faiths in the Americas and other places where Africans have migrated.[57] The movement of people and their interactions in diasporic environments has meant that both the diasporic faith and the continental faith has undergone changes overtime and continues to change as result of dialogue and interactions between adherents. One example of this has been the role of women in the Òrìṣà tradition. In the US, African American women have played a leading role in reviving the tradition[58] and bringing it to new adherents, in so doing they have also become leaders/priestesses.[59] The traditions more generally on the continent were oral traditions, passed down from generation to generation, as a result of diasporic engagement, traditions are now taught and to a wider range of persons, turning distinctively African reten-

---

[54] Kofi Asare Opoku, "The Blacksmith's Razor and the Vulture's Head: African Spirituality and the Emancipation of Africa," in *Religion, Culture and Spirituality in Africa and the African Diaspora* (New York: Routledge, 2018) 33–35.
[55] See chapters in section "Yoruba Religious Cultures Beyond Africa" in Olopuna and Rey Òrìṣà Devotion as World Religion.
[56] Margarite Fernández Olmos and Lizabeth Paravisini-Gebert, *Creole Religions of the Caribbean: An Introduction from Vodou and Santeria to Obeah and Espiritismo*, (New York: New York University Press, 2011), Chapter 4.
[57] N. Fadeke Castor, *Spiritual Citizenship: Transitional Pathways from Black Power to Ifá in Trinidad* (Durham: Duke University Press, 2017).
[58] Tracey E. Hucks, *Yoruba Traditions and African American Religious Nationalism*, (Albuquerque: University of New Mexico Press, 2012).
[59] Rachel Harding, "'What Part of the River You're In': African American Women in Devotion to Oshun" in *Osun Across the Waters: A Yoruba Goddess in Africa and the Americas*, ed. by Joseph Murphy and Mei-Mei Sanford (Bloomington: Indiana University Press, 2001).

tions into multi-ethnic African diasporic expressions of faith.⁶⁰ In the earlier discussion of Islam and Christianity in Africa, the question was posed as to how long a faith and how many adherents it required to be considered an African, as opposed to imported, faith. In relation to traditions such as Candomblé, Santería, and Shango one can ask whether they are African indigenous transplanted faiths or given how long they have been transplanted (three hundred years and counting), should they be considered as indigenous diasporic faiths, with ways of being and knowing that stem from being in the diaspora? In this exploration of religious traditions in the contemporary era, what is evident is distinctions between the diaspora and the continent are of less importance as these faiths become global. This becomes more evident when we consider the emergence of contemporary religious expressions that have been birthed out of Africa by African descendants.

Twenty-first Century New Diasporic African Religions

An important feature of twentieth-century African descendant religious expression has been the ability of people in the diaspora to create new religious forms that have responded to their predicament as people living in a hemisphere built on white supremacy, where the legacy of enslavement and the oppression of Black bodies still looms large. Rastafarianism, birthed in Jamaica in the 1920s, is a case in point. Utilising aspects of the Hebrew scriptures, drawing on ideas of Ethiopianism and the sacredness of Africa, African-descendant Jamaicans fashioned a faith that spoke directly to their experience as descendants of enslaved Africans and their spiritual and physical yearning for redemption in the homeland.⁶¹ At its start, it was regarded as a socially undesirable expression in its birth place, but over time, even though its numerical growth has been small, it has become globally recognised due to the popularity of reggae and its global superstar adherent Bob Marley.⁶² Its socially and politically conscious message gained recognition in the United Kingdom in the 1970s, where Rastafarianism became synonymous with Black youth culture and youth struggles against police brutality.⁶³ In the twenty-first century that movement has become a global phenomenon, with adherents across the African continent and even attracting non-African descendants in Europe and Asia.⁶⁴ Ethiopia looms

---

60 Mercedes Cros Sandoval, "Santería in the Twenty-First Century" in *Òrìṣà Devotion as World Religion* (Madison: University of Wisconsin Press, 2008) 355–71.
61 Barry Chevannes, *Rastafari: Roots and Ideology* (Syracuse: University of Syracuse Press, 1994).
62 Steve Barrow and Peter Dalton, *The Rough Guide to Reggae* (London: Penguin Books, 2004).
63 Ernest Cashmore, *Rastaman: The Rastafari Movement in Britain* (London: George, Allen and Unwin, 1980).
64 Michael Barnett ed., *Rastafari in the new Millennium: A Rastafari Reader.*(Syracuse: University of Syracuse Press, 2014).

large in Rastafarianism and is part of a tradition of diasporic expressions, including versions of Christianity where African descendants have regarded that country as special.

The other nation that has been a source for the creation of diasporic religious or spiritual devotion has been Egypt, often referred to as 'kemet' by African descendants who have drawn on its Gods, iconography, and mythologies to fashion Afrocentric or African-centred spirituality.[65] The US as the global power at the beginning of the century has been the birthplace of these new religious expressions that draw on older forms of religious expression but are not necessarily tied to them.[66] The Nation of Islam is an example related to Islam, but quite unique in its adaptation, which came to global prominence due to having famous adherents such as Malcolm X and Mohammed Ali. A new cluster of African American faith expressions, which mix elements of different religious traditions and combine them with an African emphasis have been fashioned in the latter part of the twentieth century, including the Hebrew Israelites and the Nuwaubian Nation, small groups but which gain traction in diasporic African spaces around the world by having influential followers from the realms of African American music and sport.[67]

The development of these new spiritual traditions in the Western hemisphere in the twenty-first century and indeed new variants of Christianity, Islam and African Traditional Religions springing up all over the globe, speaks both to the continued importance of spirituality to the lived experience of African descendants and to their/our capacity to innovate, adapt and create, traditions, organisations and movements that bring this spirituality into new spaces and places.

One of the key places where we see the emergence of these spiritualities in the twenty-first century is in the fields of arts and culture. As stated in the introduction and worth repeating here African spirituality is on a continuum so what is being outlined here is only 'new' in the sense of time. African art, music, theatre, dance, sculpture, painting has always carried within it the spirit of the African. For traditional societies those stories, songs, costumes, objects and paintings that we now describe as art, were practical manifestations of their connections to the world of the spirits, the ancestors and of those yet to come. In the contemporary era, these spiritual creations are being re-created in art galleries, theatres, and cinemas.

Oral traditions are becoming written traditions and communal rituals are being repurposed as global rites of passage.[68] There are many manifestations of this phenomenon far too many to highlight and showcase in an overview of this kind. One

---

[65] Molefi Kete Asante, *Kemet, Afrocentricity and Knowledge* (Trenton: Africa World Press, 1990).
[66] Edward E. Curtis IV and Danielle Brune Sigler, eds., *The New Black Gods: Arthur Huff Fauset and the Study of African American Religions* (Bloomington: University of Indiana Press, 2009).
[67] Eugene B. Gallagher, *The New Religious Movements Experience in America* (Westport: Greenwood Press, 2004) 130–61.
[68] Anthony Pinn, ed., *Black Religion and Aesthetics: Religious Thought and Life in Africa and the African Diaspora* (New York: Palgrave Macmillan, 2009).

thinks of the centrality of spiritual themes in Nollywood productions, and how traditional African spirituality intersects with Christian piety or Islamic prayers to portray family relationships.[69] It is not only in traditional family settings that African spirituality is being utilised to tell stories, it is being portrayed in a futuristic fashion in Science Fiction through the work of writers such as Tomi Adeyemi and Nnedi Okorafor, who have both written best-selling works that retool the West African spiritual traditions and posit them into future worlds.[70] The work of Chigozie Obioma who weaves Igbo Cosmology right into the heart of his tragic global tale of love, racism, class and migration, *An Orchestra of Minorities*.[71] As stated, there are more and more examples of this interweaving of spirituality into contemporary arts. It was most notable in the 2018 global hit movie *Black Panther*,[72] which weaved African spirituality into a fast-paced science fiction narrative where the mythical Wakanda (in the heart of Africa) is a technology advanced civilisation. Black Panther Director Ryan Coogler drew on traditions from all over the continent in his incorporation of African spirituality into the African future.[73] He and the film were criticised in some quarters for not portraying traditions accurately, and for mixing them up together into a Pan-African blend. Yet, in essence, what the film demonstrated that one can create new mythologies based on past source material. In so doing, Coogler traces the path taken by the enslaved ancestors making the local global in the contemporary era. Just as African descendants in Trinidad added Shango to Baptism to create a new tradition, and diasporic Africans in the US added African to Methodism to form a new denomination in their image, so in the twenty-first century, African descendants are weaving the spirituality of the ancestors into new spaces, combining it with other forms of spirituality, aesthetics, and diverse cultures to reimagine themselves into the future and to understand the reality of their lives in this century. These forms are restless, they go in cycles which are not easy to track, and, as has been outlined in this chapter, are difficult to categorise with surety and accuracy. Hence the call for scholarship on African spirituality to move with the people locally, transnationally and globally.

---

[69] Toyin Falola, *The African Diaspora: Slavery, Modernity and Globalization* (Rochester: University of Rochester Press, 2013) 282–312.
[70] Nnedi Okorafor *Binti* (New York: Tor Books, 2016); Tomi Adeyemi *Children of Blood and Bone* (London, Macmillan, 2018).
[71] Chigozie Obioma, *An Orchestra of Minorities* (New York: Little Brown and Company, 2019).
[72] Ryan Coogler, *Black Panther* (Marvel Studios, 2018).
[73] Yolanda Pierce, "African cosmologies: spiritual reflections on the 'Black Panther' movie," accessed 6th December 2020, https://religionnews.com/2018/02/19/african-cosmologies-spiritual-reflections-on-the-black-panther-movie/

Reviving African Personality in the study of African Spirituality

It was E. W. Blyden, an African descendant born in the Danish colony of St. Thomas, who coined the term 'African Personality'.[74] It was both an analytical term to describe the African temperament, and an aspirational term to chart a destiny whereby Africans could flourish in the world, out of the wretched grasp of European enslavement and colonialism. Kwame Nkrumah also utilised the term, viewing it as a third way between the rampant capitalism of the West and the austere communism of the East. Africa could chart its own way in the world, based on its culture with its deep well of spirituality that put the human above the machine and sought harmony with the world rather than conquest and control.[75] At its heart, the African personality is trusting of the African capability in the world. Africans, the people maligned, exploited and mistreated by East, West, and Asiatic regions are always capable of creating, developing, and changing their circumstances for the good of their communities and the wider world. In an analytical and normative sense, scholars and students of religion need to prioritise the African in their focus.

Rather than focusing on the distinctive traditions, analytically we need to think about the people: where, why, and how they have moved to particular places, why have they adopted particular traditions? What have they done with these traditions? To what extent has the adoption of particular spiritual traditions aided the development of the African personality in a given place and space. By following the people rather than the tradition *per se*, we acknowledge that Africans are authentic in and of themselves, they are sacred human beings, belonging to special important communities that need to be studied, but also nurtured, protected and enabled to thrive and flourish. This is an essential consideration given the attempts at denigration and dehumanisation that have been wrought on us from the fifteenth up to the twenty-first century

This is also why the study of African spirituality cannot just be analytical project it also requires normative emphasis. A conscious attempt to understand who and what Africans are becoming in the world to enable our twenty-first century experience to be better than that of our nineteenth century and twentieth century.

---

[74] M. Yu. Frenkel, "Edward Blyden and the Concept of African Personality," *African Affairs* 73, 292 (1974): 277–89.
[75] Kwame Nkrumah, *Consciencism Philosophy and Ideology for Decolonisation* (London: Panaf, 1964).

Conclusion

In this chapter I have attempted to chart a course for twenty-first century African Spirituality, by outlining themes that currently exist in the major components of religions that African descendants currently adhere to. In looking at current religious practices across Christianity, Islam, African Traditional Religion and new diasporic religions, it is evident that across time and space African descendants have always been engaged in processes of adoption, adaptation, and innovation when it comes to spirituality and that in the twenty-first century Africans are conversing and connecting transnationally more than ever before. Students and scholars of African religion need to move and engage with these processes and conduct more comparative religious research. Through analysis and engagement with the lived experiences of African people we can better see where there is scope to outline processes, trends and conjunctures to make the African and the African Personality more visible and respected in the world.

Evelyn Onwaniban
Chapter 15
Africa and the Cold War

Abstract: The Cold War era marked a watershed in the history of Africa in international relations. African states enjoyed a new independence in dealing with other powers of the world, contrary to the past where they related as vassals under different colonial regimes. The economy of the continent became properly submerged into the global economy, a process that began over four centuries earlier. Africa and other Third World countries joined the Non-Aligned Movement in their bid to assert their independence and improve their political economy. This became a tool for national leaders to play in international politics with the two ideological blocs of the Cold War. The assistance rendered by the superpowers in support of ideologically aligned factions generated intense violence and crises. These Cold War divides destabilized the continent and lasted for decades after the Cold War. While the Cold War facilitated decolonization in Africa and provided avenues for Africa states to express their views internationally, it also created opportunity for the western superpowers to become intrinsically involved in the affairs of Africa. Today Africa remains underdeveloped, and external influence continues to hinder effective independence. The Non-Aligned movement did not succeed in the neutrality it envisaged. However, it continues to serve as a unique voice of the Third World Countries on the world stage.

Keywords: Cold War, Global capitalist economy, Non-Aligned Movement, foreign aid and independence.

Introduction

The Cold War marked an intense battle for ideological supremacy between the capitalist bloc, led by the United States, and socialist bloc, led by the Soviet Union. Ideologically, the capitalist bloc favored a free-market system while the socialist bloc advocated for a communist system. Both of the leading superpowers worked to undermine the interests of their rivals, including using propaganda, leveraging the Security Council of the United Nations to serve their interests, and providing economic and military aids to countries that were ideologically sympathetic. The mutual suspicion and distrust between the rival blocs led to an arms race that put the world on the brink of war in the 1960s. Africa was not isolated from the capitalist world system during the Cold War. However, unlike in the First and Second World Wars where African countries participated under their colonial masters, in the Cold War, especially after the 1960s, most participated as independent countries. Many African forces or states received financial and material support from one or the other of the leading superpowers. Most, however, also joined an international organization known as the Non-Alignment Movement, which they used as a platform for advancing their interest. The material and financial support received from the major Cold War actors, the efforts of Non-Aligned Movement, and the anti-colonial attitude of the two superpowers helped to quicken the independence process in Africa. Nevertheless, the Cold War had a deleterious impact on Africa.

Africa's Integration into the Global Capitalist Economy

Africa and the world capitalist economy have a long history. This history could be classified into four phases: the age of the Trans-Atlantic slave trade, the age of European colonial rule, the age of decolonization and anti-apartheid struggle, and the unipolar age.[1] It was within the context of the third phase that the Cold War took place.

African political and social-economic developments have been shaped not only by centuries of interactions among the peoples of the continent, but also by interactions with the external world through trade and migrations. Africa participated in the early Arab trade and Trans-Saharan trade which spanned across North Africa through the Sahara Desert to West Africa. In the early period, it also witnessed a series of conquest and re-conquests of territories by competing internal and external forces. Examples of such conquests include the reconquest of the Hyskos defeat of Ancient Egypt in about 1638 B.C., the Moroccan conquest of Songhay in 1591, and the Almoravid conquest of Ancient Ghana in 1076, However, whatever the impact of such conquests and reconquests, Africa's incorporation into the world capitalist economy first occurred through the continent's engagement with the Trans-Atlantic slave trade, which had a significant impact on the development of Africa.[2]

Following the abolition of the slave trade, European powers divided Africa into colonies in the late nineteenth century. This division of Africa marked the beginning of the second phase of Africa's incorporation into the world capitalist economy. Within this second phase, the whole continent, with the exemption of Ethiopia and Liberia, came under the rule of either Britain, France, Portugal, Germany, Belgium, Spain, or Italy. These European powers created different systems of colonial administration, encouraged cash crop production, introduced new currencies, and carried out other

---

[1] For more details on this period, see, for instance, Charles Krauthammer, "The Unipolar Moment," *Foreign Affairs* 70, 1 (1990/1991): 23–33.

[2] For more details on the impact of the slave trade on Africa, see Stanley Engerman and Joseph Inikori eds., *The Atlantic Slave Trade: Effects on Economies, Societies and Peoples of Africa, the Americas and Europe* (Durham, NC: Duke University Press, 1992); Paul E. Lovejoy, *Transformations in Slavery: A History of Slavery in Africa* (Cambridge: Cambridge University Press, 1983); and Patrick Manning, *Slavery and African Life: Occidental, Oriental and African Slave Trades*(Cambridge: Cambridge University Press, 1990).

reforms that ensured that Africa became more incorporated into the global economy. In intensifying the incorporation into the global economy, colonial rule brought dislocation in the sense that it ensured that African societies were unable to follow their own natural growth and development paths. Indeed, one of the enduring legacies of colonial rule is the cash crop export-oriented economy it created. This cash crop export-oriented economy is a phenomenon which has persisted over six decades of independence up until the present. Although colonial rule was largely disruptive and exploitative, it brought new ideas and other benefits for many African societies. For instance, even though the railways, roads, and bridges built by European powers in Africa were meant to facilitate colonial rule and ensure the smooth transportation of the raw materials from the point of extraction to the coast, they also offered many ancillary benefits such as easy and cheap mobility for the indigenous people and urban development in the long run.[3]

In a major study, Walter Rodney examined the historical relationship between Europe and Africa. He demonstrated that during the colonial era Europeans did not invest much in Africa and that the gains accrued from the continent were invested back into Europe. In other words, Rodney argues that the human and material resources of Africa were used to develop Europe during the colonial era.[4]

Right from the start, many Africans resisted European expansion. During the colonial era, attacks on colonial infrastructure, subversion of colonial policies and other strategies were used by Africans to express their grievances against colonial exploitation. By the 1930s, educated Africans across the continent had formed political organizations that demanded their inclusion in governance. Subsequently, what began as mere demands for inclusion of educated Africans in governance and moderate reforms transformed into demands for outright independence by the 1950s. The whole continent was in disarray over quest for independence. The roles played by Africa's nationalists in the struggle for independence are well documented in the literature.[5] Ghana was made independent in 1957, Somalia and other countries like Nigeria gained theirs in the 1960s and 1970s, and apartheid rule was ended in South Africa in 1994.

The late 1950s and early 1960s in which European powers began to transfer power to Africans marked the beginning of the third phase of Africa's incorporation into the world capitalist economy. It must be emphasized though, that while power was transferred to Africans, certain features and agents of the colonial era survived.

---

[3] For more details on the impact of colonial rule on Africa see, for instance, Crawford Young, *The African Colonial State in Comparative Perspectives* (New Haven: Yale University Press, 1994); and Richard Reid, *A History of Modern Africa: 1800 to the Present* (West Sussex: John Wiley and Sons Ltd., 2012).
[4] Walter Rodney, *How Europe Underdeveloped Africa* (Washington, Howard University Press, 1981).
[5] See, for instance, Frederick Cooper, *Decolonization and African Society: The Labor Question in French and British Africa* (Cambridge: Cambridge University Press, 1996); and John D. Hargreaves, *Decolonization in Africa* (London: Routledge, 2014).

Indeed, even after African countries achieved independence, European powers like Britain and France continued to maintain indirect forms of domination over their former colonies through foreign aid and foreign direct investment. This subtler form of domination started to emerge in the 1950s and helped to deepen Africa's subordination to the global capitalist system.[6] Indeed, by the 1980s, the economic recovery strategies that African countries were forced to adopt such as the Structural Adjustment Policies suggested by the World Bank and the International Monetary Fund, have helped to deepen the marginalization of Africa. Nevertheless, by the 1990s all African countries had achieved independence and apartheid rule in South Africa had ended.

The fourth and current phase of African global integration began in about the 1990s. This phase is characterized by the spread of information, technology, products, and jobs within an integrated world economy as well as by the dominance of the associated principles of economic freedom.[7] In this fourth phase, Africa has been exposed to more private enterprises that know neither national boundaries nor local allegiances. Since private enterprises are largely profit driven, it not surprising that the conditions of many Africans have worsened during the current phase of Africa's incorporation into the global capitalist system.

The third phase of African global integration, in which decolonization took place coincided with the Cold War. This Cold War was not African in origin. Although its origin is tied to the emergence of the United States and the Soviet Union as the dominant power after the Second World War, the Cold War had significant impact on Africa. In trying to consolidate their independence, the newly independent countries in Africa joined the United Nations and formed regional and sub-regional organizations such as the Organization of African Unity (OAU) now African Union, the Economic Community of West African States (ECOWAS), and the Economic Community of Central African States (ECCAS). However, of vital interest to this chapter is the fact that independent African states joined the Non-Aligned Movement, which was an international organization that advanced the views of Third World countries, including the views of the newly independent African countries, during the Cold War. Before considering the nature of the impact of the Cold War on Africa and highlighting attention to such issues as the Non-Aligned Movement, it is permissible to consider different views on the origins of the Cold War and to highlight some major developments that took place outside of the Africa.

---

[6] For further details see, for instance, Kwame Nkrumah, *Neo-Colonialism: The Last Stage of Imperialism* (New York: International Publishers, 1966); and Mark Langan ed., *Neo-Colonialism and the Poverty of Development in Africa* (Basingstoke: Palgrave Macmillan, 2018).

[7] For more information about this fourth phase see, for instance, Claude Ake, "The New World Order: A View from Africa," in Hans-Henrik Holm and Georg Sorensen, eds., *Whose World Order? Uneven Globalization and the End of the Cold War* (Boulder: Westview Press, 1995), 19–42; and James Petras and Henry Veltmeyer, *Globalization Unmasked: Imperialism in the Twenty-First century* (Halifax: Fernwood/Zed, 2001).

The Origins and Development of the Cold War

According to some, the Cold War began prior to the Second World War. Some advocates of this interpretation tie the origins of the Cold War specifically to the 1917 Bolshevik revolution in Russia. This revolution was led by communist forces who disagreed with the old capitalist system of the Tsarist regime. After seizing power in 1917, the Bolsheviks withdrew Russia from the World War I and took other actions that the former allies of their country such as Britain and France found to be in favor of Germany. In this context, Russia's former allies launched economic and military warfare against the Bolsheviks. In essence, for most of those who hold the view that the Cold War began prior to the Second World War, it was fears of communist threats that became evident after the Bolshevik revolution that led the great capitalist powers to embrace aggression towards Soviet communism even before the Second World War.[8] However, it is interesting to note that while most of those who hold the view that the Cold War began before the Second World War identify 1917 as the start date of the conflict, others argue that the origins of the Cold War could even be dated to earlier periods such as to the nineteenth century Crimean War or to the 1848 period in which the Communist Manifesto, which calls for the violent overthrow of the bourgeoisie, emerged.[9] Another interpretation stresses that the Cold War began after the Second World War, and it blames the United States for starting the conflict. According to this interpretation, the United States, encouraged by its possession of atomic bomb, abandoned its wartime policy of collaboration and consciously sought to undermine Russian influence in Eastern Europe by establishing democratic-capitalist states around the borders of the Soviet Union. In the context of this new postwar American policy, advocated of this interpretation further argue that the Soviet Union had no option but to protect its borders and security thereby resulting in the Cold War.[10]

Whether or not the Cold War began after the Second World War, it is evident that activities emanating from the policies of the two superpowers that emerged after the Second World War and those of their allies in Europe and other parts of the world led to ideological antagonism in every part of the world, and that put the world on the brink of war. Indeed, even though the Second World War was won by the allied powers (consisting of the United States, Britain, the Soviet Union and France among others) collaboration between the Soviet Union and capitalist nations deteriorated soon

---

8 Roger E. Kent. "The Supreme Quest for Empire: The Cold War and Soviet Support for Wars of National Liberation" *Cold War History* 6, 3 (2006): 331–352.
9 Good examples of works that offer such conventional interpretation include Martin F. Herz, Beginnings of the Cold War (Bloomington: Indiana University Press, 1966); and Louis J. Halle, *The Cold War as History* (London: Harper and Row, 1967).
10 For such revisionist interpretation see, for instance, D. F. Fleming, *The Cold War and its Origins 1917–1960* (New York: Doubleday and Company, 1961) and David Horowitz, *The Free World Colossus: A Critique of the American Foreign Policy in the Cold War* (New York: Hill and Wang, 1965).

afterwards. There was mutual suspicion among the allied powers by the end of the war. Britain and the United States harbored distrust of the aims of the Soviet Union's foreign policies goals. Namely, the issue of the postwar status of Poland caused mistrust between the United States and the Soviet Union; the United States was suspicious of Britain's policy of practicing socialism at home and being imperialistic abroad; and Britain distrusted the American economic power. The refusal to share information and the secret building of atomic bombs by the United States during the war later led to further distrust even amongst the former allies. Ultimately, such suspicions, mistrust, and the ensuing nuclear armament race did not lead to another physical world war but a cold war, an *ideological* war fought through proxies around the world, as both superpowers feared the consequences of direct nuclear warfare. The actions of the superpowers ensured that the whole world stood on the brink of war from the 1940s through the 1980s.

The Cold War became aggravated after 1948 due to several factors including the Soviets' blockade of West Berlin in1948, the establishment of the North Atlantic Treaty Organization (NATO) by the United States and its allies in 1949, the rise of Chinese Communists to power in China in 1949, the development of atomic warhead by the Soviet Union in 1949, and the Korean War that lasted from 1950 to 1953.[11] Even though the death of Joseph Stalin, the leader of the Soviet Union, in 1953, helped to lessen Cold War tensions, there were other notable Cold War developments in the 1950s. These included the establishment of the Warsaw Pact in 1955 by the Soviet Union and its allies; and the development of intercontinental ballistic missiles by both the United States and the Soviet Union from the late 1950s.

The Cold War competition and arms race reached its climax in the 1960s. This was the decade in which the Cuban Missile Crisis took place. The crisis was tied to the discovery by the United States that the Soviet Union was moving missiles to Cuba with the aim of launching attacks on major cities in the United States. Although this discovery almost led to war, the superpowers reached an agreement that ensured a peaceful resolution of the conflict. Following the end of the Cuban Missile Crisis, there was increasing conviction that peaceful coexistence was possible. Yet, the arm race persisted, and yet again, strategic and economic interests continued to encourage the superpowers to form alliances in Europe, the Middle East, Asia, and Africa. Scholars generally characterize the period after the Cuban Missile Crisis or the period of increasing conviction that peaceful coexistence was possible, and the easing of tensions between the superpowers as the era of *detente*. It was within this particular era that the Soviet Union ultimately collapsed, and the Cold War ended. However, the era was also characterized by continued proxy conflicts in Afghanistan, Vietnam, Ethiopia and elsewhere, which marred the prospects for peace and the end of the Cold War prior to 1991.

---

11 Peter Weiler, "British Labour and the Cold War: The Foreign Policy of the Labour Government, 1945–1951," *Journal of British Studies* 26, 1, *England Foreign Relations* (January 1987): 58–74.

Africa and the Cold War

The involvement of Africa in global conflicts dates back to the period before the Cold War. Prior to the Cold War, most African countries were under European rule when they participated in the two world wars. However, most African nations became independent shortly after the Cold War began. For most of the Cold War, therefore, the newly independent African countries sought to take sovereign decisions based on a consideration of their conditions. Largely based on such consideration, many of them joined the Non-Aligned Movement (NAM), an international organization that consisted largely of independent countries of Asia, Middle East, and Africa. The movement which began in 1961 called for refraining from the arrangement of collective defense agreements or alliances with the superpowers, and instead unite in support of national self-determination against all forms of colonialism, imperialism, racism ,and apartheid in the Third World countries. The Heads of States/Governments of the Non Aligned Movement also resolved to pursue peaceful resolution of conflict and peaceful coexistence, and considered disarmament as very crucial to include the elimination of all forms of military armament occupation in foreign bases except for peace-keeping purposes, and total prohibition of the production, possession and use of nuclear weapons, and other weapons of mass destruction on national territory, among others.[12] During the Arab-Israeli war of the 1970s, the organization influenced the international policy and continued to condemn Israeli's occupation of Palestinian land, Syrian Golan and other Arab territorials as well as the humanitarian issues that arose as a result of these occupation while advocating peace in the region.[13] At the Havana Declaration of 1979, the movement reinstated their purpose to help the newly independent countries to maintain their national independence, sovereignty, territorial integrity, and security, and to back them in their support against colonialism and neocolonialism among others. Subsequent conferences of NAM assessed and re-echoed this position.[14] In other words, the Non-Aligned Movement attempted to maintain neutrality in the Cold War and not involve themselves in the superpower politics and reaffirming their position for the respect of the sovereignty and territorial integrity of independent states among others. At the 9th and 10th Summit of NAM, held in Serbia in 1989 and Indonesia in 1992, which marked

---

[12] Final Document-Section on Nuclear Disarmament and Related Issues, 1st Summit Conference of Heads of State or Government of the Non-Aligned Movement Belgrade, Serbia 6 September 1961. http://cns.miis.edu/nam/documents/Official_Document/1st_Summit_FD_Belgrade_Declaration_1961.pdf

[13] Final Document of the 16th Summit of the Heads of States or Governments of the Non-Aligned Movement, Teheran, Islamic Republic of Iran, 26–31 August, 2012. http://cns.miis.edu/nam/documents/Official_Document/16thSummitFinalDocument(NAM2012-Doc.1-Rev.2).pdf. NAM 2012/Doc.1/Rev.2. Accessed 16 July 2020.

[14] André Munro, "Non-Aligned Movement," *Encyclopedia Britannica*, 13 July 2020, https://www.britannica.com/topic/Non-Aligned-Movement.

the end of Non Aligned Movement's Cold War posture and the beginning of a new dawn, these positions were reaffirmed but their focus drifted to other issues of grave global concern such as natural disaster, climate change, eradication of poverty and improvement of the living standards of their people, drug abuse and illicit trafficking, small arms proliferation, terrorism and human rights concern among others making it equally relevant even after the cold war.[15] While the movement aided many Third World countries to gain independence, the commitment of its members to maintain neutrality was not completely actualized as individual state's policies and interests worked against this goal. Hence, the Movement did not succeed in its neutrality posture during the Cold War as many members of the movement, including African leaders, tilted towards either the capitalist or communist blocs but they were united in pushing for the independence of the colonized peoples and maintaining one voice in protecting the sovereignty of the developing world, although in the end, the policies of these African countries, as they struggled to maintain their independence during the Cold War era, were influenced by those of other external powers.

Even though Africa's adherence to the policy of non-alignment was fraught with a number of contradictions, African Heads of State included non-alignment as one of the cardinal principles of the OAU Charter, and the number of African states participating in the NAM rose gradually until it peaked in the 1980s. In terms of membership of the NAM, only 11 or 44 percent of the total membership were African countries at the first Summit Conference of the Non-aligned Countries, which met in Belgrade (Yugoslavia) from 1–6 September 1961. At the Third Non-Aligned Summit held in in Lusaka, Zambia, on 8–10 September 1970, 62 per cent (or 33 out of 53) of the participants were African, and by 1986 when the 8th Summit of NAM took place in Harare (Zimbabwe) all the then 51 African countries were members of the NAM. Partly based on their growing numbers in the NAM, African states succeeded in giving the movement in question an African outlook. For instance, at the 8th Summit of the NAM, African countries ensured that the focus was on crucial African problems such as the critical economic situation in Africa and the apartheid situation in Southern Africa. In addition to ensuring a focus on such issues, African countries helped ensured that four (out of eight) Summit Conferences of the Non-Aligned Movement were held on the continent of Africa (Cairo 1964 ; Lusaka 1970 ; Algiers 1973 and Harare 1986) by the 1980s.[16]

The Non-Aligned Movement proved effective in lending one voice to issues of deterrents, disarmaments and other major issues that affect peaceful global relations. During the Arab-Israeli war of the 1970s, the organization influenced the relevant international policy and continued to condemn Israeli's occupation of Palestinian

---

[15] For information on the declarations of Non Aligned Movement documents visit http://cns.miis.edu/nam/documents/Official_Document/.
[16] For further discussion on Africa's role in the NAM see K. Mathew, "Africa and Non-Alignment," *India Quarterly* 43, 1 (1987): 40–51.

land, Syrian Golan and other Arab territories. It also drew attention to the humanitarian issues that arose as a result of these occupations and advocated for peace in the region.[17] This stand of the Non-Aligned Movement in the Middle East was upheld even after the cold war. At the sixteenth Summit of Heads of States or Governments in 2012, the Heads of State or Government of the Non-Aligned Movement reiterated the necessity and urgency of ending the prolonged, unlawful Israeli occupation of all of the Arab territories occupied since 1967. Additionally, while pledging their solidarity with the Palestinian cause, they stressed the need for intensified international and regional efforts to promote the resumption of substantial and accelerated negotiations between the parties of the Middle East crises for lasting peaceful settlement.[18] Similarly, the organization is known to have influenced the international policy agenda, the ending of apartheid in South Africa and the ending of colonial rule in Namibia among others and continues to emphasize the respect for the sovereignty of states.[19]

At the Havana Declaration of 1979, the movement reinstated their purpose to help the newly independent countries to maintain their national independence, sovereignty, territorial integrity, and security, and to back them in their support against colonialism and neocolonialism among others. Subsequent conferences of NAM assessed and re-echoed this position.[20] In other words, the Non-Aligned Movement attempted to maintain neutrality and not involve themselves in the superpower politics and reaffirming their position for the respect of the sovereignty and territorial integrity of independent states among others during the Cold War. However, the neutrality it envisaged was not embraced in the sense of the word 'nonaligned', as internal dynamics of individual states determined their foreign posture at different times.

Following the establishment of the NAM, a nonaligned caucus was established at the United Nations. By 1960, this caucus pressured the United Nations to increase its membership. Following this pressure, sixteen newly independent African states were admitted into the United Nations in 1960 alone. By the end of this same year, the decolonizing world became ascendant in the United Nation's General As-

---

17 Final Document of the 16th Summit of the Heads of States or Governments of the Non-Aligned Movement, Teharan, Islamic Republic of Iran, 26–31 August, 2012. http://cns.miis.edu/nam/documents/Official_Document/16thSummitFinalDocument(NAM2012-Doc.1-Rev.2).pdf. NAM 2012/Doc.1/Rev.2. Accessed 16 July 2020.
18 Final Document of the 16th Summit of the Heads of States or Governments of the Non-Aligned Movement, Teharan, Islamic Republic of Iran, 26–31 August, 2012. http://cns.miis.edu/nam/documents/Official_Document/16thSummitFinalDocument(NAM2012-Doc.1-Rev.2).pdf. NAM 2012/Doc.1/Rev.2. Accessed 16 July 2020.
19 Declaration of the 9th Summit Conference of Heads of State or Government of the Non-Aligned Movement. "Final Document- International Security and Disarmament" Belgrade, Serbia 4–7 September 1989, http://cns.miis.edu/nam/documents/Official_Document/9th_Summit_FD_Belgrade_Declaration_1989_Whole.pdf accessed 21 July 2020.
20 André Munro, "Non-Aligned Movement," *Encyclopedia Britannica*, 13 July 2020, https://www.britannica.com/topic/Non-Aligned-Movement.

sembly. Given the increasing influence of the nonaligned caucus in the United Nations, it is unsurprising that the UN's involvement in Africa also grew. In the context of its growing involvement in sub-Saharan Africa, the United Nations faced some of its greatest Cold War-era challenges and endured several stunning failures.[21] It struggled with the consequences of colonial maladministration, underdevelopment, and exploitation in the former Belgian Congo. Here, beginning in 1960, "the United Nations embarked upon a massive, unprecedented, undertaking of peacekeeping in the midst of heightened Cold War tensions, amidst weak state institutions, in the face of a violent, unforgiving, secessionist crisis, and a predatory former colonial overseer."[22] Similarly, in South Africa, Southern Rhodesia, and South West Africa (currently known as Namibia), the United Nations dealt with problems associated with white minority rule and Cold War geopolitics while in Angola and Mozambique, it confronted the problem of restoring peace and reconstituting societies shattered by the Cold War.[23]

The Cold War superpowers shared anti-colonial tradition and pursued policies that seemed to offer greater racial equality. From the onset of the Cold War, the Soviet Union had presented itself as anti-colonial to its very core. It was convinced that capitalism was the highest form of imperialism, and it encouraged the development of communist revolutionary movements as a means of undermining the spread of capitalist ideology. In its attempt to undermine the spread of the capitalist ideology or to ensure that the USA did not have an upper hand, the USSR initially focused on promoting revolution in Asia before turning its focus to Africa.

The USSR focused on Africa especially after Stalin's death in 1953. By the time of Stalin's death, anti-colonial sentiments had gathered momentum in Africa and agitations for independence had intensified owning to diverse factors including: the oppressive policies of colonial administrators, the influence of the superpowers, the influence of World War II veterans, and the influence of Pan-Africanists many of whom were based abroad.[24] By the 1960s, many African states had gained independence. By this same period, the Soviet Union offered different forms of *support* to African leaders who were viewed as sympathetic to communist ideas.

In North Africa, Soviet Union offered patronage and material assistance to Algeria and Egypt. For instance, in the former country it supported not only nationalist like Ahmed Ben Bella, but also the prominent nationalist organization known as the FLN. Similarly, in Egypt, the USSR supported Abdel Nasser's attempt to nationalize the Suez Canal and condemned Anglo-French action in Suez in 1956. The USSR's support for Abdel Nasser is interesting because at that time Nasser had no

---

21 For further details see Chistopher O'Sullivan, "The United Nations, Decolonization, and Self Determination in Cold War Sub-Saharan Africa, 1960–1994", *Journal of Third World Studies* 22, 2 (2005): 103–120.
22 O'Sullivan, "The United Nations, Decolonization, and Self Determination", 103.
23 O'Sullivan, "The United Nations, Decolonization, and Self Determination", 109–112.
24 Richard J. Reid, *A History of Modern Africa*, 131–61.

significant leaning towards socialism. In east and northeast Africa, the USSR supported Julius Nyerere and Mengistu Haile Mariam. Nyerere, a Tanzanian nationalist, cultivated friendly relations with the USSR and China in the 1960s-70s, when he was pursuing a villagization agricultural self-sufficiency project. Although the project was not without disastrous effects for Tanzania's economy, Nyerere's relationship with the communist bloc brought many benefits. For instance, it was as a result of such relationship that the Chinese funded the building of a railway linking Tanzania and Zambia. In the case of Mengistu Haile Mariam, an Ethiopian Marxist military leader who abandoned his country's long-time alliance with the United States, the USSR supported many of his aggressive socialist programs including one that involved the relocation of entire communities. In Southern Africa, the Soviet Union and Cuba supported the popular Movement for the Liberation of Angola (MPLA) against the Portuguese during the civil war of 1975–76.[25] Apart from these cases, there are other examples of communist support for African nationalist leaders in other parts of Africa like Congo, Kenya, Mali, Mozambique, Ghana, and Guinea.

In offering support to African countries, the Soviets hoped that African nations would implement socialism and that the implementation of the relevant model of socio-economic development would foster closer geopolitical alliance. However, unhappily for the soviets, African nations often embraced independent pragmatic objectives. While embracing such objectives, African nations, including those that formally committed to socialism, used ideology and exploited Cold War rivalries and superpower sensibilities for their own political advantage. In the end, therefore, African nations defied soviet expectations during the Cold War era.[26]

In pursing their own objectives, the United States and its allies, like the Soviet Union and other members of the communist bloc, provided material and financial support to many African countries and nationalist leaders. For instance, the capitalist bloc supported Ethiopia before they embraced the Soviet bloc. Similarly, they supported Kenya, Zaire, and South Africa. It is notable that in Zaire Mobutu Sese Seko received Western support in spite of massive corruption and mismanagement during his regime in the 1960s to 1970s.[27] It is also notable that the capitalist bloc supported South Africa even though the nation enforced a policy of apartheid since 1948, and in spite of its marked divergent ideas regarding democracy. It is evident that, in spite of their different ideas regarding democracy, United States backed South Africa and Congo partly because it wanted to gain access to their raw materials, especially ura-

---

[25] Robert G. Patman, "The Soviet Union in the Horn of Africa: The Diplomacy of Interventional and Disengagement", in *Soviet and East European Studies,* ed. by Ronald Hill *et. al.* (New York: Cambridge University Press, 1990), 6–14.
[26] Maxim Matusevich, "Revisiting the Soviet Movement in Sub-Saharan Africa," *History Compass* 7, 5 (2009): 1259–1268.
[27] Reid, *A History of Modern Africa,* 161–62.

nium.[28] However, in the Cold War context, other capitalist bloc countries like Britain also had interest in gaining access to uranium produced in South Africa, and in pursing their own interests in Africa. In recognition of this fact, the anti-communist apartheid regime in South Africa agreed to produce large quantity of uranium ore exclusively for the United States and Britain in the 1950s. This agreement brought many gains to South Africa. For instance, it made South Africa central to American national security policy.[29] Apart from having interest in gaining access to uranium, Britain cultivated friendly relationship with South Africa in order to secure the Cape Sea route, to safeguard British investment, and to gain access to other key minerals. Based on such complex interests of the capitalist bloc members, it is not surprising that even in the 1980s when the United Nations General Assembly placed an international economic embargo on the apartheid regime due to its racist and oppressive policies, the United States, Britain, and France boycotted the international sanctions and continued economic relations with the country.[30]

The material and financial support that African nationalists received from the competing capitalist and communist blocs initially had little impact on Africa's politics and nationalist movements, but it ultimately facilitated Africa's decolonization. In the early Cold War years, there were few communist parties in Africa, and the USSR's interest in this continent was minimal. In addition, even though the USSR viewed imperialism as evil, it did not favor a world revolution and provided little support to Africans during the early Cold War era. In the case of the United States and Western powers, the self-determination ideology which the United States and Britain propounded was underplayed after the Second World War. Thus, in the early stage of the Cold War, these western powers provided justification for the strengthening and retention of African colonies rather than their dissolution. For instance, the United States provided tacit support of Britain retention of her colonies partly on the justification that the African societies in question would serve as a bulwark against the spread of communism. Indeed, it is evident that the capitalist bloc did not only consider a strong ideological friendly imperial bloc as the best defense against communism, but was also convinced that hasty decolonization would "expose the swathes of the globe to Soviet's threat."[31] Despite the inclination of the cap-

---

28 Thomas Borstelmann, *Apartheid Reluctant Uncle: The United States and Southern Africa in the Early Cold War.* (New York: Oxford University Press, 1993), vii.
29 Borstelmann, *Apartheid Reluctant Uncle*, 4.
30 For details, see Weiler, "British Labour and the Cold War," 70. Richard Knight, "Oil Embargo against Apartheid South Africa" American Committee on Africa available at http://richardknight.homestead.com/files/oilembargo.htm, accessed 24 July 2020. See also, Overseas Development Institute (ODI) Briefing Paper December 1986, "Sanctions and the South African Economy"; and Anti-Apartheid Movement (AAM) archives, "Boycott South African Goods," *Forward to Freedom: The history of the British Anti-Apartheid Movement 1959–1994. https://www/aamarchives.org/campaigns/boycott.html* and "The Anti-Apartheid Movement in the 1980s" https://www/aamarchives.org/1980s.html assessed 15 June 2020.
31 Reid, *A History of Modern Africa*, 161.

italist bloc to not hasten decolonization and the initial little interest of the USSR in Africa, the financial, material and organizational support that African nationalists increasingly received made them more effective at home. In the end, the increasing efficiency of the nationalists made the European powers aware that they had very little choice but to end colonial rule in Africa.

Although some activities of the Cold War facilitated decolonization in Africa, other activities of the superpowers, especially the supply of arms and the provision of military training to African countries, resulted in intensified violence. Examples of the arms or military items supplied to African countries during this era include tanks, planes, ships, helicopters, and napalm. Such supplies ensured that African countries became militarized, and this in turn resulted in the institutionalization of a violent political culture. It is clear that in the context of the violence experienced in many parts of Africa during the Cold War, both the capitalist and communist blocs provided either arms or other forms of military support to state and non-state actors. For instance, in the Congo crises of 1960–65, internal crises and struggles for the control of natural resources found the superpowers supporting different factions by providing military support to them. Similarly, in the prolonged Angolan crises of 1975–2002 saw the United States and the Soviet Union backing different factions. In the case of Nigeria in the late 1960s during the civil war, the USSR supply of arms to Nigerian faction influenced the United States and Britain to intervene in by supplying arms to Nigerian government was presumed to be their natural ally by virtue of her colonial history.[32]

More so, to foster the supply of arms or to foster military collaboration, the Cold War actors often signed defense agreements with African forces. For instance, the United States signed such an agreement with Kenya, Zaire, Ghana, Liberia, and Senegal; Britain, a nation with military missions in many West African states signed training and supply agreements with many of its former colonies with the exemption of Tanzania; and France signed defense and cooperation pacts with her former colonies, excluding Guinea. As with the United States and its allies, the USSR signed treaties of friendship, which involved the provision of military assistance with newly Marxist Ethiopia, Angola, and Mozambique; China signed military aid agreement with Cameroon, Guinea, Mali and Tanzania; and Cuba entered similar agreements with Congo (Brazzaville), Guinea, Angola, Mozambique, and Ethiopia. These agreements led to an intense arms race with a range of weaponry being channeled

---

[32] *Nigerian News Thursday and Oriental Times October 24, 2019.* "How Russia Helped Nigeria Defeat Biafra During the Civil War- Buhari" https://www.pmnewsnigeria.com/2019/10/24/how-russia-helped-nigeria-defeat-biafra-during-civil-war-buhari/; and https://orientaltimes.co/2019/10/24/russia-helped-nigeria-defeat-biafra-civil-war-buhari/; and Atomic Heritage Foundation and National Museum of Nuclear Science and History, 2019, *Cold War History Friday August 24, 2018.* "Proxy Wars During the Cold War: Africa", *https://www.atomicheritage.org/history/proxy-wars-during-cold-war-africa* accessed 24 July, 2020.

towards many African governments.³³ Nevertheless, while arms supply by the Cold War actors favored different forces involved in conflicts in Africa, the unstable environment it created did not favor sustained political and economic development in the continent. As one scholar rightly summed up:

> By providing arms as well as direct military interventions, the Cold War actors militarized African countries. For emerging nations suffering from series of exploitations, weak foundations and exclusionary politics, one can imagine the damage caused by militarization of the political space at that early stage of Africa's attempt at self-government. Like colonial administration which created extractive and antidevelopment institutions in African colonies, the Cold War actors institutionalized a violent political culture that became a prelude to dictatorship, persistent crises and civil wars.³⁴

Conclusion

The Cold War helped to raise even higher the global roles of the United States and the Soviet, overthrowing the former imperial powers whose activities dominated global politics before the 1940s. The period coincided with birth of the United Nations and the decolonization process of the Third World countries, ushering the need for socio-economic development which not just the superpowers but Third World countries exploited to their advantages. While it was the case that some African countries aligned with their former colonial masters and the United States, some others drifted outrightly adopting the Soviet ideology at certain period. Inconsistencies in the foreign policy of countries, especially following the change of leadership, ensured that countries pursued the foreign policy objectives of their states regardless of the international political climate like the case of Ethiopia. No doubt Cold War politics destabilized the economic and political stability of African states, pervasive issues which emanated from these internal conflicts during the Cold War era remain till the twenty-first century. The alliances and interventions envisaged in Southern Africa, Angola, Mozambique, and Zaire now the Democratic Republic of Congo among others had devastating impact for their economies and politics. The Non-Aligned Movement, which African leaders and other leaders in Third World countries utilized as an avenue to assert their voice and opinions in the in the international system, did not succeed in achieving its major goal of maintaining neutrality and fostering economic independence of Third World states; especially as their former colonial masters continue to exert indirect influence on them and most have remained underdeveloped. Even though the Non-Aligned Movement has been criticized as having not achieved its goals of neutrality, and without formal constitution and permanent secretariat like other international organizations, it gave African countries the opportu-

---

33 Patman, "The Soviet Union in the Horn of Africa," See also Reid, *A History of Modern Africa*, 165.
34 K. Kalu, "The Cold War and Africa's Political Culture," *International Relations* 20, 1 (2020), 17.

nity to develop socio-economic and political connections with other countries that had experienced colonialism as well as a platform that they used to express their views internationally. The Non-Aligned Movement has also shaped many global events since its establishment and has striven to remain relevant in the face of increasing global challenges in the twenty-first century. For instance, the organization influenced the international policy during the Arab-Israeli war of the 1970s and has continued to condemn Israeli's occupation of Palestinian land, Syrian Golan, and other Arab territorials, as well as the humanitarian issues that arose as a result of these occupations while advocating peace in the region. At the sixteenth Summit of Heads of States or Governments in 2012, the Heads of State or Government of the Non-Aligned Movement reiterated the necessity and urgency of ending the prolonged, unlawful Israeli occupation of all of the Arab territories occupied since 1967, including East Jerusalem, among others. While pledging their solidarity with the Palestinian cause, they stressed the need for intensified international and regional efforts to promote the resumption of substantial and accelerated negotiations between the parties of the Middle East crises for lasting peaceful settlement.[35] Similarly, the organization is known to have influenced the international policy agenda, the ending of apartheid in South Africa and the ending of colonial rule in Namibia among others and continues to emphasize the respect for the sovereignty of states.[36] Most importantly, the Non-Aligned continues to advance the position of Third World countries in international affairs and inform reforms in the United Nations in the areas of transparency, inclusivity and balance with regard to the opinion of every members regardless of their contribution to the organization. In more recent Summits of the Non-Aligned Movement, the Heads of States/Governors reinstated their commitment to address problems of the world and advance the interests of Third World countries in the international system especially with regard to relations with the developed world; in the area of trade, development and international cooperation among others. They also lent their voice to the United Nations Security Council Resolution 1325 on the equality and participation of women in global crises management and conflict resolution and at the last (at time of writing) virtual summit held on May 4, 2020, called for a global collaborative efforts towards addressing the challenges of Covid-19, while setting up a taskforce to manage its member states with regard to the impact of the pandemic and finding lasting solution to addressing

---

[35] Final Document of the 16th Summit of the Heads of States or Governments of the Non-Aligned Movement, Teharan, Islamic Republic of Iran, 26–31 August, 2012. http://cns.miis.edu/nam/documents/Official_Document/16thSummitFinalDocument(NAM2012-Doc.1-Rev.2).pdf. NAM 2012/Doc.1/Rev.2. Accessed 16 July 2020.

[36] Declaration of the 9th Summit Conference of Heads of State or Government of the Non-Aligned Movement. "Final Document- International Security and Disarmament" Belgrade, Serbia 4–7 September 1989, http://cns.miis.edu/nam/documents/Official_Document/9th_Summit_FD_Belgrade_Declaration_1989_Whole.pdf, accessed 21 July 2020.

same.[37] The Cold War helped in shaping the unity of the African continent's where issues of international concern forced them to come together to identify their common goals and project same under the auspices of different regional, sub-regional and international organizations that were formed during this period and these organizations has continued to be relevant in the twenty-first century. However, many African countries continue to adopt the non-aligned posture in this same century, even in the context in which they grapple with several daunting challenges, such as climate change and environmental issues, poverty, disease, insurgencies, terrorism, banditry, and ethnic self-determination. This raises the question as to what should drive the foreign policy of a state. Should the foreign policy of African states remain static? Should not the ongoing domestic dynamics and international development affect the foreign policy of such states? Addressing such questions is outside the scope of this chapter.

---

[37] For further details see the official documents of all the Non-Aligned Movement Heads of State or Governments Summits available at http://cns.miis.edu/nam/documents/Official_Document/ accessed 20 June, 2020. see also Rifki Dermawan. 2020 "Non- Aligned Movement: New Role Amid a Pandemic?" in the *Asian Post, 8 June, 2020.* https://theaseanpost.com/article/non-aligned-movement-new-role-amid-pandemic Accessed 16 July, 2020

Flavia Gasbarri
Chapter 16
Africa and the USA

Abstract: This chapter investigates the relations between Africa and the United States since the decolonization of the African continent in the mid-1950s/early 1960s, in order to analyze Africa's relation to the "American Century" and the role that the continent played in US foreign policy. The encounters between the United States and independent Africa happened in the shadow of the emerging Cold War, and this defined the nature and the future of US-Africa relations. Consequently, the end of the Cold War offered an important turning point in US foreign policy in Africa and in the stance of the continent during the American "unipolar moment".

Keywords: Southern Africa, Horn of Africa, Cold War, United States, Decolonization.

Introduction

The postcolonial history of Africa coincides with the rise of the United States as superpower after the end of World War II. This chapter investigate how Africa fits within the "American Century" and the role that the continent played in US foreign policy. It is divided in two sections covering the period from the 1950s to the 1990s: the first section is on the Cold War period, the second one on the end of the Cold War and on the so-called "unipolar moment".[1]

The encounter between the United States and independent Africa happened in the shadow of the emerging Cold War, and this inevitably defined the nature and the future of US-Africa relations. Consequently, the end of the Cold War offered an important turning point in US foreign policy in Africa and in the stance of the continent during the American unipolar moment. In order to grasp this turning point, the chapter focuses on the two regions of the continent that became the principal theatres of the Cold War in Africa, hosting direct and indirect American intervention: Southern Africa and the Horn of Africa.[2]

---

[1] Charles Krauthammer, "The Unipolar Moment," *Foreign Affairs* 70, 1 (1990/1991).
[2] This chapter embraces the division commonly made between North Africa and sub-Saharan Africa and is founded on the assumption that the Cold War assumed a very different nature in the two regions, with the superpowers' relations with the North African countries strictly linked to political and military developments in the Middle East. Hereafter, the term "Africa" will refer only to sub-Saharan Africa. Furthermore, as stated above, the focus of the chapter is on two specific regions: Southern Africa and the Horn of Africa.

US-Africa Relations and the Cold War

Decolonization paralleled the rise of the United States as superpower after the end of World War II. Being born from a struggle against British colonial rule, American history was inevitably rooted in a longstanding tradition of professed anti-colonialism.[3] However, African decolonization also happened right at the beginning of the US competition with the USSR in the Cold War. When claims for independence arose in the colonies of European empires after World War II, the United States had to reconcile that longstanding tradition of professed anti-colonialism with the more urgent need to keep a strong alliance with the European empires (Great Britain and France, in particular) against the rising Soviet threat. The Soviet argument that colonialism was an intrinsic component of the capitalistic system promoted by the Western bloc served as a powerful incentive for radical and revolutionary changes that could open the doors to pro-Soviet regimes in the Third World. Consequently, Washington's position on decolonization "grew more conservative"[4] and the United States often displayed a controversial status quo attitude, intended to carefully encourage national independence in the colonies without fundamentally subverting the structure of relations between the new countries and the Western powers.[5]

Among the Third World regions, Africa became a US concern comparatively late. After World War II, despite signs of imminent decolonization, the continent was still considered under the responsibility of the Western colonial empires, and its affiliation to the Western sphere of influence was not really questioned. Furthermore, the American priority of reconstructing its European allies after the devastation of the war led Washington to focus on the "European side"[6] of African affairs, namely, maintaining access to Africa's raw materials for reconstruction. The same priority led the United States to develop ties with the white-minority government in South Africa. At the end of the 1950s, the first wave of decolonization and the independence of the first African countries started to draw US attention to the continent. The concurrent rise of the African Americans' civil rights movement at home, and its ideal connection with the cause of decolonization contributed to that process.[7] In 1958, the Eisen-

---

3 The professed American anticolonialism was not always applied in practice, such in the case of the US colonialization of the Philippines at the end of the 19th century. For more information see: Walter LaFeber, "The American View of Decolonization, 1776–1920: an Ironic Legacy" in *The United States and Decolonization: Power and Freedom*, ed. by David Ryan and Victor Pungong (Basingstoke: Macmillan, 2000), 24–40.
4 Thomas Noer, *Cold War and Black Liberation: The United States and White Rule in Africa, 1948–1968* (Columbia: University of Missouri Press, 1985), 64.
5 Odd Arne Westad, *The Global Cold War: Third World Interventions and the Making of Our Times* (Cambridge: Cambridge University Press, 2007), 110.
6 Westad, *The Global Cold War*, 131–132.
7 Elizabeth Schmidt, *Foreign intervention in Africa: from the Cold War to the War on Terror* (Cambridge: Cambridge University Press, 2013), 25; Brenda Gayle Plummer, *In Search of Power: African*

hower Administration established the Bureau for African Affairs within the US Department of States.[8] In 1960, during the so-called "year of Africa", the election of John F. Kennedy raised the hopes among Africans that they had finally secured Washington's attention.[9] During his mandate as Senator of the Massachusetts, and during his electoral campaign, Kennedy was often critical of French and British imperialism. He also engaged in a more direct and personal diplomacy through several trips to Africa and meetings with African leaders.[10] At the turn of the decade, therefore, it seemed that the United States had shifted from an "Eurocentric Africa policy to an Afrocentric policy."[11]

At the same time, many of the new independent African countries, most notably Kwame Nkrumah's Ghana, moved towards non-aligned positions and started to promote the idea of Pan-Africanism and emancipation from Cold War influences. Consequently, as stressed by Odd Arne Westad, in Washington's view, freedom for Africans carried the risk that they could move towards an "incorrect" form of modernity.[12] Despite Kennedy's rhetoric, Cold War imperatives were stronger. As it happened for the other regions of the emerging "Third World", radical nationalism and non-alignment in Africa were often confused with communism. Therefore, freedom for Africans "meant that the United States had to open up a new offensive in the Cold War"[13] and the African continent progressively became part of the all-embracing US containment strategy.

The major involvements of the United States in Africa took place in conjunction with the turbulent process of dismantling the weaker European colonial empires, namely Belgium and Portugal. The end of Belgian control over Congo in 1960 opened the doors to the first African crisis with an East–West connotation. Congo attracted American attention for its strategic position in Central Africa and for its wealth of natural resources, in particular the uranium deposits that were used for the building of the atomic bomb during World War II. In May 1960, the first democratic election in Congo brought to power Prime Minister Patrice Lumumba, who endorsed a strong nationalist, anti-colonialist, and non-aligned agenda. While there were different views within the Kennedy administration on whether or not the Congolese Prime Minister

---

Americans in the Era of Decolonization, 1956–1974 (Cambridge: Cambridge University Press, 2013), 59–60; David Newsom, *The Imperial Mantle: The United States, Decolonization, and the Third World* (Bloomington: Indiana University Press, 2001), 159–160.

8 See Philip Muehlenbeck, *Betting on the Africans: John F. Kennedy's Courting of African Nationalist Leaders* (Oxford: Oxford University Press, 2014).
9 Muehlenbeck, *Betting on the Africans*, 56.
10 Ibid., 34–57; David Newsom, *The Imperial Mantle: The United States, Decolonization, and the Third World* (Bloomington: Indiana University Press, 2001), 160–161.
11 Steven Metz, "American Attitudes Toward Decolonization in Africa," *Political Science Quarterly* 99, 3 (1984): 516.
12 Westad, *The Global Cold War*, 134.
13 Ibid., 135. See also: Schmidt, *Foreign intervention in Africa*, 24.

was also openly a "communist" or a "communist sympathiser",[14] Lumumba became progressively unpopular in Washington due to his political positions.[15] A few days after the independence, a mutiny among Congolese soldiers caused the intervention of the Belgian army without the previous approval of Lumumba, who then appealed for the UN intervention and, later, for the Soviet assistance. This was the beginning of five years of turmoil and civil war in Congo, which also marked the first US involvement in Africa, in order to prevent Congolese mineral resources from falling under the control of the Eastern bloc. Indeed, the United States feared a vacuum of power in Central Africa that could be exploited by the USSR, which after the death of Joseph Stalin, had taken a more active interest in the Third World.[16] During the five years of crisis and civil war that affected Congo, Washington, through the involvement of the CIA, backed General Joseph-Désiré Mobutu (later Mobutu Sese Seko) who in 1965 emerged as the undisputed ruler of Congo after the assassination of Lumumba in 1961.[17] Once in power, Mobutu renamed the country "Republic of Zaire" and established a one-party authoritarian regime. Notwithstanding the flagrant violation of democracy and human rights perpetrated by Mobutu, Zaire became one of the most important Western allies in Africa during the Cold War. The widespread "Mobutu or chaos" argument summarises the rationale of US–Zairian ties well: in order to safeguard American interests in the area, Zaire needed a strongman and Washington saw no alternative to Mobutu. His regime was considered the only way to maintain stability in the country, to counter rebellions and secessionist pushes, and keep communist influence out of Central Africa.[18] Throughout his thirty-two years in power, Mobutu exploited the same argument to maintain US economic

---

[14] CIA Director Allen Dulles compared Lumumba to Castro, while the reports of the Bureau of Intelligence and Research in the Department of State stated that there was not clear evidence of Lumumba's direct involvement with communist forces. See: John Kent, *America, the UN and Decolonisation: Cold War Conflict in the Congo* (London: Routledge, 2010), 22.

[15] Schmidt, *Foreign intervention in Africa*. 59; Westad, *The Global Cold War*, 138.

[16] Waldemar Nielsen, *The Great Powers and Africa*, (New York: Published for the Council on Foreign Relations by Praeger Publishers, 1969), 191–201; Geoffrey Roberts, *The Soviet Union in World Politics: Coexistence, Revolution, and Cold War, 1945–1991*, (New York: Routledge, 1999), 43–47.

[17] For an account of the 1960 Congo crisis, as well as of the US and CIA involvement see: Stephen Weissman, *American Foreign Policy in the Congo, 1960–1964* (Ithaca: Cornell University Press, 1974); Madeleine Kalb, *The Congo Cables: the Cold War in Africa from Eisenhower to Kennedy*, (New York: Macmillan, 1982), Kelly Sean, *America's Tyrant: the CIA and Mobutu of Zaire* (Washington: American University Press, 1993); Lise Namikas, *Battleground Africa: Cold War in the Congo, 1960–1965* (Washington, DC: Woodrow Wilson Center Press ; Stanford, California: Stanford University Press, 2013); Sergeĭ Vasilevich Mazov, *A Distant Front in the Cold War: The USSR in West Africa and the Congo, 1956–1964* (Stanford: Stanford University Press, 2010); Alanna O'Malley, *The Diplomacy of Decolonisation: America, Britain and the United Nations during the Congo crisis 1960–64* (Manchester : Manchester University Press, 2018).

[18] David Schmitz, *The United States and Right-Wing Dictatorships, 1965–1989* (Cambridge: Cambridge University Press, 2006), 9–35.

and military support to his regime, by presenting himself as the indispensable ally in the Cold War chessboard of Africa.[19]

Despite the significance of the Congo crisis, as well as of the American involvement, the 1960s did not yet see the beginning of a systematic American Cold War strategy in Africa. Already by the end of the 1960s – when the wave of decolonization was losing its early momentum – the general impression in Washington was that the Soviet threat in Africa had been exaggerated.[20] The global scenario, in fact, kept the American attention focused on some more sensitive issues, such as the Cuban missile crisis, the war in Vietnam, and the nuclear arms race, so that Africa still ranked low in Washington's priorities.[21]

The real turning point came during the 1970s, which was a very important decade for US-Africa relations. A series of events that happened from the mid-1970s in Southern Africa and in the Horn of Africa raised dramatically the relevance of the continent for the US Cold War strategy, which, in those same years, was going through the complex phase of *détente* between the two superpowers.

The first of these events happened in Southern Africa, when the last remnant of colonialism in the continent, the Portuguese empire, rapidly broke up after the Lisbon Carnation Revolution of 1974, causing a violent upheaval in the equilibrium of the region.[22] After World War II, Washington's main interests in the Southern Africa region had revolved almost exclusively around its relationship with South Africa. The economic and strategic relevance of this country, particularly rich in uranium deposits, as well as its government's strident anticommunism, made South Africa an important ally for the Western bloc in the first post-war decade.[23] On the other hand,

---

19 Michael Schatzberg, *Mobutu or Chaos? The United States and Zaire, 1960–1990* (Lanham: University Press of America, 1991).
20 Adrian Guelke, "Southern Africa and the Superpowers," in *Exporting Apartheid: Foreign Policies in Southern Africa, 1978–1988*, ed. Steve Chan (New York: St. Martin's Press, 1990), 224–27; Michael Clough, *Free at Last?: US Policy Toward Africa and the End of the Cold War* (New York: Council on Foreign Relations Press, 1992), 7–9; Piero Gleijeses, *Conflicting Missions: Havana, Washington, and Africa, 1959–1976* (Chapel Hill: University of North Carolina Press, 2002), 276–77.
21 See Paul Rich, "US containment policy, South Africa and the Apartheid dilemma," in *Exporting Apartheid*, ed. Chan, 309–10; Anthony Lake, *The "Tar Baby" Option: American Policy Toward Southern Rhodesia*, (New York: Columbia University Press, 1976), 74–76; Nielsen, *The Great Powers and Africa*, 305–09.
22 Since 1961, Lisbon had been involved in the so-called "Portuguese Colonial War" in its three African colonies: Angola, Guinea-Bissau and Mozambique. In the early 1960s, Kennedy provided moderate support to the anti-colonial movements in Angola and Mozambique and pressured Portugal to implement reforms in order to prevent the spread of radical nationalism that could attract communist influences. The following Johnson and Nixon administrations, however, progressively cut-off that support to avoid damaging the relations with Portugal, whose role within NATO was considered too important. See: Schmidt, *Foreign intervention in Africa*, 83–89
23 On the close economic and trade relationships between the United States and South Africa in the 1940s see: Thomas Borstelmann, *Apartheid's Reluctant Uncle* (New York: Oxford University Press, 1993), 38–55.

the growing racial discrimination of the apartheid system also created embarrassment in Washington. Furthermore, after WWII, South Africa refused to renounce to the League of Nations' Mandate for the administration of Namibia and started to administrate the territory as a "de facto" South African colony.[24] Through different policies and alternative outcomes, all US administrations from Harry Truman to Ronald Reagan tried to balance the dilemma between two opposing needs: encouraging Pretoria to move away from the apartheid system and from its intransigence on the Namibian issue, and protecting American interests in the area.[25]

The end of the Portuguese colonial rule in Angola and Mozambique in 1974 was particularly relevant for the equilibrium in this dilemma. The turmoil caused by the collapse of the Portuguese empire led, directly and indirectly, the white minority-dominated countries on the South African borders – Angola, Mozambique and, later, Zimbabwe – to move towards black majority rule. These new governments were hostile to Pretoria's racist policy and provided wide support to the anti-apartheid organizations in South Africa and to the groups fighting for independence in Namibia.[26] What was more relevant for US policy towards the region, however, was the political orientation of the parties that took power in Angola, Mozambique and Zimbabwe. The Movimento Popular de Libertação de Angola (MPLA), the Frente de Libertaçao de Moçambique (FRELIMO) and the Zimbabwe African National Union (ZANU) were all Marxist-inspired and received wide support from the Eastern bloc and China.[27] The USSR also backed the African National Congress and the South African Communist Party, which led domestic opposition to the apartheid system.[28] Furthermore, in 1975 a civil war broke out between the MPLA government in Angola and its two main opponent groups: the Frente Nacional de Libertação de Angola (FNLA) and the União Nacional para a Independência Total de Angola (UNITA). The civil war rapidly assumed the features of a proxy war, with the two blocs helping the opposing sides.[29] In 1975, Washington supported UNITA against the Soviet-backed MPLA

---

[24] In 1971, the International Court of Justice declared the South African occupation of Namibia illegal. See: Advisory Opinion, International Court of Justice, Legal Consequences for States of the Continued Presence of South Africa in Namibia (South West Africa) notwithstanding Security Council Resolution 276 (1970), June 21, 1971 – International Court of Justice, http://www.icj-cij.org/files/case-related/53/5597.pdf

[25] Alex Thomson, *US Foreign Policy Towards Apartheid South Africa, 1948–1994: Conflict of Interests* (New York: Palgrave Macmillan, 2008).

[26] For South Africa's response to the turmoil of the 1970s see: Jamie Miller, *An African Volk: The apartheid Regime and Its Search for Survival* (New York: Oxford University Press, 2016).

[27] Shubin Vladimir, *The Hot "Cold War": the USSR in Southern Africa* (London: Pluto Press, 2008).

[28] Vladimir, *The Hot "Cold War"*, 239–263.

[29] On the Angolan Civil War see: Fernando Andresen Guimaraes, *The Origins of the Angolan Civil War: Foreign Intervention and Domestic Political Conflict, 1961–76* (London: Palgrave, 2001).

with a covert CIA operation,[30] while the South African Defence Force (SADF) began a military invasion of Angola to also assist UNITA.[31] The South African invasion, however, led to an increase in the Soviet military aid and precipitated a massive deployment of Cuban troops in Angola to support the MPLA's military efforts against its enemies.[32] These developments complicated Washington's policy in the region. The collusion between the United States and the apartheid government, in fact, poisoned relations with other African countries.[33] At the same time, Pretoria emphasized the need for the American support to its policy, by portraying the turmoil in the region as an international conspiracy orchestrated by Moscow, and itself as the only remaining bastion against the spread of communism in the area. From the mid-1970s, therefore, the Southern Africa region became the theatre of a complex convergence and overlap between two distinct dynamics: on the one hand, a dramatic exacerbation of the century-old racial issue that had contraposed black majorities and white minorities, on the other, the US struggle against the communist expansion.[34]

The beginning of the Angolan civil war also caused another disorder in Zaire. In fact, the MPLA opened up the Angolan territory to the bases of the Front de Libération Nationale Congolais (FLNC) – a separatist movement that had its roots in the rich, southern Zairian province of Katanga. The FLNC formed one of the main opposition movements to Mobutu and from 1974–75 its militia was trained, along with MPLA troops, by the Cubans.[35] In March 1977, the FLNC crossed the Zairian border from its bases in north Angola and started an invasion of Katanga (renamed Shaba under Mobutu). This invasion was known as "Shaba I" and led to an immediate reaction from Zaire's allies. The United States provided Zaire with non-lethal military equipment. France, Belgium and Morocco intervened to help Mobutu counter the invasion and, within a month, the FLNC withdrew. In May 1978 however – only a little more than one year after Shaba I – the FLNC began a second invasion of Zaire and within a few days it captured the city of Kolwezi, the economic heart

---

30 Gleijeses, *Conflicting Missions*, 273–300, Stockwell John, *In Search of Enemies: a CIA Story* (London: Futura Publications, 1979) 40–57, Chester Crocker, *High Noon in Southern Africa: Making Peace in a Rough Neighbourhood* (New York: W.W. Norton, 1992), 48–50.
31 George Edward, *The Cuban intervention in Angola, 1965–1991: from Che Guevara to Cuito Cuanavale* (London: Frank Cass, 2005), 68–81; Gleijeses, *Conflicting Missions*, 270–300.
32 Ibid., 300–328; Westad, *The Global Cold War*, 234.
33 Thomson, *U.S. Foreign Policy*, 84.
34 Daniel John, "Racism, the Cold War and South Africa's Regional Security Strategies 1948–1990" in *Cold War in Southern Africa: White Power, Black Liberation*, ed. Onslow Sue (London: Routledge, 2009), 35.
35 On the FLNC see: Raymond Garthoff, *Détente and Confrontation: American-Soviet Relations from Nixon to Reagan* (Washington, DC: Brookings Institution, 1994), 688–94; Peter Schraeder, *United States Foreign Policy Toward Africa: Incrementalism, Crisis and Change* (Cambridge University Press, 1994), 87–88; Georges Nzongola-Ntalaja, *The Congo: From Leopold to Kabila, A People's History* (New York: Zed Books, 2003), 183–84; Miles Larmer, "Local Conflicts in a Transnational War: the Katangese Gendarmes and the Shaba wars of 1977–78", *Cold War History*, 13:1 (2013), 89–108.

of Katanga/Shaba. The so-called "Shaba II" thus represented a threat not only to Mobutu's rule, but also to Western economic investments in the region and to a few thousand US and European citizens living in the area under FLNC control. This time the United States intervened much more actively, together with its Western allies, offering transport and logistical support for both Belgian and French troops and forcing the invaders to withdraw.[36] The then Carter Administration also assumed a more confrontational stance *vis-à-vis* the Soviet Union and Cuba, directly accusing Moscow and Havana of involvement in the Shab II invasion.[37]

While these events were unfolding, another conflict broke out in another region of the continent, the Horn of Africa, creating another major upheaval of US political alignments in Africa. The 1974 *coup d'état* in Ethiopia and the establishment of a Marxist-inspired regime led by Mengistu Haile Mariam pushed Washington to end its long-lasting alliance with Addis Ababa and to resume ties with Somalia, Ethiopia's main regional antagonist. Similarly, the USSR, which had supported the Somali regime of Siad Barre since 1969, began to develop closer ties with the new socialist Ethiopia. The deep-rooted territorial disputes and ethnic rivalries between the two African countries, as well as their attempts to play one superpower off against the other eventually forced Washington and Moscow to take sides in the Ethiopian–Somali confrontation. By 1977 the overturning of alliances in the Horn of Africa was complete.[38] Existing US–Ethiopian agreements were terminated and Washington agreed to provide Mogadishu with military aid in July 1977.[39] A few days after this decision, Somali forces entered the Ogaden, a Somali-populated region on the eastern border of Ethiopia claimed by Mogadishu. The Somali invasion was an act of international aggression and caused quite some embarrassment in Washington. The USSR and Cuba intervened with money, equipment, and troops to support the Marxist Ethiopian regime.[40] The consequent defeat of US-backed Somalia in the war strengthened the Soviet position in the region, and it was perceived in the Carter Administration as another setback for the US stance in Africa *vis-à-vis* the communist bloc.

---

36 David Mets, *Land-Based Airpower in Third World Crises* (Air University, Maxwell Air Force Base, Alabama: Air University Press, 1986), 133–36.
37 Garthoff, *Détente and Confrontation*, 690–91; Schraeder, *United States Foreign Policy Toward Africa*, 92; Piero Gleijeses, "Truth or Credibility: Castro, Carter, and the Invasions of Shaba," *The International History Review*, 18: 1, (1996), 70–103; Larmer, "Local Conflicts in a Transnational War," 89–108.
38 For an overview of the shift of alliances see: Schraeder, *United States Foreign Policy toward Africa*, 141; Peter Woodward, *US Foreign Policy and the Horn of Africa* (Aldershot: Ashgate, 2006), 21; Donna Jackson, *Jimmy Carter and the Horn of Africa: Cold War policy in Ethiopia and Somalia* (Jefferson, N.C.: McFarland & Co., 2007, 36–47; Nancy Mitchell, *Jimmy Carter in Africa: Race and the Cold War* (Washington, DC: Woodrow Wilson Center Press, 2016), 253–303.
39 Garthoff, *Détente and Confrontation*, 700.
40 For an overview of the Soviet/Cuban involvement see Robert Patman, *The Soviet Union in the Horn of Africa: The Diplomacy of Intervention and Disengagement* (Cambridge: Cambridge University Press, 1990).

The 1970s was thus a decade of radical changes for Africa and for US policy towards the continent. Compared to the Congo Crisis in the early 1960s, the conflicts in Southern and Central Africa and in the Horn of Africa during the 1970s took place within a quite different international scenario. The United States was in fact involved in the détente with the USSR and the two superpowers were holding a delicate negotiation concerning the problem of arms control. This complex process, plus the memories of the recent American debacle in Vietnam, made the opportunities for Soviet expansionism in Africa appear much more threatening to Washington. The Americans saw the USSR's increasing willingness to intervene and, no less important, similar tendencies on the part of Cuba with respect to the Angolan civil war and the Ogaden war as unacceptable Soviet attempts to exploit détente in order to expand communist influence.[41] The recurrent clashes between the two superpowers in Africa was one of those factors that contributed to the decision of the United States not to ratify the Strategic Arms Limitation Talks (SALT) II and to end the détente policy in 1979. The then National Security Adviser Zbigniew Brzezinski famously stated that the SALT agreement – possibly the greatest accomplishment of the US–Soviet dialogue on arms control during the 1970s – was buried "in the sands of Ogaden",[42] stressing the strong influence that the Somali-Ethiopian war had on US decisions.

As stated by Christopher Clapham, the years from the mid-1970s to the mid-1980s was a period when it appeared not only that the Cold War might become critically important to Africa, but even that Africa might affect the Cold War and US foreign policy.[43] Consequently, from the mid-1970s, Africa became a fully integral part of the American containment strategy until the end of the Cold War in the late 1980s.

---

[41] Memo, Zbigniew Brezezinski to the President, 3 March 1978, "Meetings – SCC 61, 3/2/78," Box 28, Zbigniew Brezinski Collection, Jimmy Carter Presidential Library (JCPL); Zbigniew Brzezinski, *Power and Principle: Memoirs of the National Security Adviser 1977–1981* (London: Weidenfeld & Nicolson, 1983), 186–88. On the interaction between the African wars and détente and the USSR's rationale for intervention, see Arthur Klinghoffer, "The Soviet Union and Angola" in *The Soviet Union in the Third World: Successes and Failures*, ed. by Robert Donaldson, (Boulder; London: Westview Press, 1981); Garthoff, *Détente and Confrontation*, 574–93; Westad, *The Global Cold War*, 194–97; Peter Rodman, *More Precious Than Peace: The Cold War and the Struggle for the Third World* (New York: Scribner's, 1994), 178–79; Warren Cohen, *The Cambridge History of American Foreign Relations Volume 4: America in the Age of Soviet Power, 1945–1991* (Cambridge: Cambridge University Press, 2008), 182–218.
[42] Brzezinski, *Power and Principle*, 188.
[43] Christopher Clapham, "International Relations in Africa after the Cold War," in *After the Cold War: Security and Democracy in Africa and Asia*, ed. Hale William and Kienle Eberhard (London: Tauris Academic Studies, 1997), 101–102.

US-Africa relations, the End of the Cold War and the Unipolar Moment

The winding down of the Cold War from 1985 to the collapse of the USSR in 1991 was another crucial turning point for US-Africa relations. The dramatic changes of the international system and the progressive disappearance of the imperatives linked to the containment of communism affected the role of Africa within US foreign policy. In this process, 1988 was a particular important year for the disappearance of that Cold War mindset that had guided US action in the continent since the 1950s.[44]

After the exacerbation of the regional conflict at the end of the 1970s, throughout the 1980s the United States sought a solution to the increasingly complicated situation in Southern Africa. The Reagan administration developed a policy called "constructive engagement" which had a twofold aim: addressing the relations with apartheid South Africa and solving the regional war. As for the first point, recognizing that the nature of the South African political system prevented the United States from pursuing its interests without constraints and political damage, Washington applied a policy of both pressure and support for change. Rather than promoting economic sanctions and political isolation against South Africa, the Reagan administration opted for a constructive dialogue with Pretoria, in order to progressively "persuade" the apartheid regime to move towards democracy. In those same years however, the persistent intransigence of the South Africa government was giving momentum to a growing international movement against the apartheid, which invested several parts of civil society in Europe and in the United States and which became very critical of the Reagan administration's "soft" approach.[45]

As for the broader regional situation, Washington became progressively involved as mediator in a long negotiation process among Angola, Cuba, and South Africa in order to solve the regional war and ensure the containment of the Cuban and Soviet presence in Africa. In 1988, the three countries signed the US-brokered Tripartite Agreement, which committed South Africa to give independence to Namibia, and Cuba to withdraw its troops from Angola. The first measure solved the last colonial problem in Southern Africa; the second one removed the main US Cold War-related concern in the region. The 1988 agreement thus marked the beginning of the decoupling of that overlap between the regional issues and the US Cold War strategies that

---

[44] On this point see also: Flavia Gasbarri, *US Foreign Policy and the End of the Cold War in Africa: A Bridge between Global Conflict and the New World Order, 1988–1994* (Abingdon, Oxon; New York, NY: Routledge, 2020: Routledge, 2020).

[45] See: Hakan Thörn, *Anti-Apartheid and the Emergence of a Global Civil Society* (Springer: Palgrave, 2006); Anna Konieczna and Rob Skinner, *A Global History of Anti-Apartheid: 'Forward to Freedom' in South Africa* (Springer, 2019). In the United States, particularly relevant was the campaign implemented by the African-American lobby "TransAfrica" and the Free South Africa Movement. Crocker, *High Noon in Southern Africa*, 257–58; Schraeder, *United States Foreign Policy Toward Africa*, 217–18.

had developed in the mid-1970s. As such, it significantly changed the directives of US foreign policy in the region. After the withdrawal of the Cubans, the American support to UNITA in the Angolan civil war became increasingly difficult to justify and it stopped completely in 1992. At the same time, Washington actively supported the beginning of the negotiations between the parties of the conflict in Angola. While these negotiations were ultimately unsuccessful, in May 1993 the United States recognized the MPLA government, which emerged after the first democratic election in the country. Other actors in the regions experienced a similar change in US attitude. South Africa could not claim anymore to be the last bastion against the communist spread in the region and, consequently, it lost one of the main justifications for maintaining its regime of racial discrimination. With a global anti-apartheid movement going on since the 1980s, the US policy of "constructive engagement" and leniency toward racist South Africa became outdated and unjustifiable. In February 1990, the United States welcomed the historical announcement of the new South African President Frederik Willem de Klerk, who released the ANC's leader Nelson Mandela and opened the door for negotiations with the anti-apartheid organizations. During the four years of negotiations that led South Africa to the first democratic elections in 1994, Washington progressively changed its suspicious attitude towards the ANC, which had long been considered by Washington to be heavily infiltrated by communists.[46] Washington also started to focus its attention on how to manage economic assistance to Pretoria in order to build a solid market economy in the country. Between 1993 and 1994, South Africa was designated one of "ten emerging markets" that would receive "top American priority."[47] Washington also provided training and information to the ANC and other parties on various aspects of free market economics[48] and, in the aftermath of the South African elections, provided and leveraged about $600 million in funds to South Africa.[49]

---

[46] Memo, Herman Cohen to Vadm Donald S. Jones, 20 January 1987, folder "South Africa: ANC [2 of 4]," RAC box 16, African Affairs Directorate, NSC: Records, Ronald Reagan Presidential Library (RRPL).

[47] Clinton William, "Remarks on Signing the South African Democratic Transition Support Act," 23 November 1993 – The American Presidency Project, http://www.presidency.ucsb.edu/ws/?pid=46167; See also Talking Points for National Security Advisor Lake, 28 June 1995, "South Africa 1995 [4] [OA/ID 872]," Rice, Susan/Steinberg, Donald/Deshazer, MacArthur, African Affairs, White House Staff and Office Files, Clinton Presidential Records, Box 5, William J. Clinton Presidential Library and Museum (CPL)

[48] US House, Committee on Foreign Affairs, Subcommittee on Africa, *United States' Policy Toward the Transition in South Africa*, Hearings, 30 September 1993, 103rd Cong., 1st Sess. (Washington DC: GPO, 1994), 7

[49] William Clinton, Al Gore, "US Pledge to South Africa: Building Upon a Newfound Freedom", Statement at Event following South African Elections, Washington DC, 5 May 1994, *US Department of State Dispatch*, 5:19, (1993), 1. See also: Fact Sheet, US Assistance to the New South Africa, ND, "Visit of President Mandela of South Africa, October 4–6, 1994 [1] [OA/ID 2663]," Jett, Dennis/Steinberg, Donald/Deshazer, MacArthur et al, African Affairs, White House Staff and Office Files, Clinton Presidential Records, Box 1, CPL.

The political reassessment of the regional picture brought about by the 1988 Tripartite Agreement also affected the longstanding US relationship with Mobutu's Zaire. As already mentioned, the "Mobutu or chaos" argument had been at the core of US policy toward Zaire since the 1960s. During the 1980s Zaire was still a key ally in the region, as Mobutu allowed US supplies to UNITA to go through Zairian territory. In the aftermath of the 1988 Tripartite Agreement Mobutu's strategy was to show Washington that Zaire would continue to be an indispensable actor for the success of American policy in Southern Africa and to use it as leverage to keep asking for economic and military aid. In this regard, at least until 1991–1992, the US maintained an ambivalent position. On the one hand, it appreciated the importance of its relationship with Zaire and in June 1989, Mobutu was the first African head of state to be invited by the newly elected President George H. W. Bush to the White House. On the other hand, since the end of the 1980s Washington was aware that the regional changes were bound to affect long-term US policy toward Zaire. When the Bush administration took charge in 1989, a memorandum within the White House noted that there had not been a review of US policy toward Zaire through the last four administrations. The recent events, however, indicated profound changes in the situation in the region that may have begun to undermine President Mobutu's position, though not to the extent that his government was threatened or that the US should consider alternatives to that regime.[50] As this "change in the situation in the region" went on, however, the shift in US policy became more evident and Washington's ability to support Mobutu began to vanish. After the end of the US support to UNITA in 1992, the political and strategic relevance of Mobutu's regime declined inevitably. In this situation, two additional elements added weight to making US support for Mobutu no longer politically sustainable: the collapsing economic situation and the issue of human rights in Zaire. Washington started to show concern about Mobutu's "apparent unwillingness to distinguish between state finances and his own," which according to the Bureau of African Affairs, was at the heart of Zaire's dismal economic record.[51] In addition, the record on human rights abuses in Zaire began to raise criticisms from within Congress, which barred any transfer of funds to the Zairian government and triggered a cut-off of all military assistance beginning in late 1990. With a broad democratization process underway in Eastern Europe after the fall of the Berlin Wall, Mobutu began to be seen in Washington as another old, discredited dictator.[52] In

---

[50] Memo for the Vice President, ND, folder "Zaire (1)," OA/ID CF00213, David Passage Files, National Security Council, Bush Presidential Records, George Bush Presidential Library (GBPL)
[51] Herman Cohen, "US Policy and the Crisis in Zaire", Statement before the Subcommittee on Africa of the Senate Foreign Relations Committee, Washington DC, 6 November 1991, *US Department of State Dispatch*, 2:45, (1991), 828–29.
[52] Schraeder, *United States Foreign Policy Toward Africa*, 102–03.

June 1991, Zairian inability to repay debt led to the termination of all development assistance.[53]

Within this context, in April 1990 the US welcomed Mobutu's "momentous speech"[54] promising political and constitutional reforms. When only two years later he suspended the national conference and the democratic process reached a deadlock, the United States unsuccessfully tried for several years to use its influence to urge Mobutu to put Zaire back on the road to democracy. The civil war that broke out in Zaire in 1996 eventually led, one year later, to the removal of Mobutu and the end of its regime.

Since the mid-1980s, the winding down of the Cold War also had its effects on US policy in the Horn of Africa. The relaxation of tensions with the USSR and the progressive withdrawal of the Soviet support to Ethiopia dampened US Cold War-related interests in the Horn of Africa, as well as the rationale for a solid alliance with Somalia. In this context, critics of the despotic regime of Siad Barre and its increasing violations of human rights began to raise their voices in Congress, particularly within the subcommittee on Africa of the House Foreign Affairs Committee.[55] Under pressure from Congress, between 1986 and 1988 Washington reduced military assistance to Somalia.[56]

Simultaneously, both the regimes in Ethiopia and Somalia experienced a dramatic worsening of their internal situations, which rapidly deteriorated into civil wars. In order to turn their attention and resources to the domestic insurgencies, Mengistu and Barre tried to ease the external pressures by re-establishing diplomatic ties with each other. In April 1988 they signed an agreement in Mogadishu, which opened for a disengagement of forces along the Ethiopian–Somali border and ended ten

---

[53] US Senate, Committee on Foreign Relations, Subcommittee on African Affairs, *The Situation in Zaire*, Hearings, 6 November 1991, 102nd Cong., 1st Sess. (Washington DC: GPO, 1992), 3; US Department of State Daily Press Briefing #134, Friday, 9/13/91, http://dosfan.lib.uic.edu/ERC/briefing/daily_briefings/1991/9109/134.html.

[54] Telegram, Secretary of State to US Embassy in Kinshasa, 1 May 1990, folder "Zaire," OA/ID CF01300, John Ordway Files, Subject Files, National Security Council, Bush Presidential Records, GBPL.

[55] See US House of Representatives, Committee on Foreign Affairs, Subcommittee on Human Rights and International Organizations, Subcommittee on Africa, *The Human Rights Situation in South Africa, Zaire, the Horn of Africa, and Uganda*, Hearings, June 21; August 9, 1984, 98th Cong., 2nd Sess. (Washington DC: Government Printing Office, 1985); US House, Committee on Foreign Affairs, Subcommittee on Africa, *Reported Massacres and Indiscriminate Killings in Somalia*, Hearings, July 14, 1988, 100th Cong., 2nd Sess. (Washington DC: GPO, 1989); *Somalia: Observations Regarding the Northern Conflict and Resulting Conditions* – US General Accounting Office (GAO), http://www.gao.gov/assets/220/211267.pdf

[56] Herman Cohen, *Intervening in Africa: Superpower Peacemaking in a Troubled Continent* (Basingstoke: Macmillan, 2000), 202; Peter Schraeder, "The Horn of Africa: US Foreign Policy in an Altered Cold War Environment," *Middle East Journal* 46, no. 4, (1992), 574–577; Ottaway David, "Congress Blocking Aid to Somalia; Alleged Rights Abuses, Refusal to Talk Tie Up $55 Million", *The Washington Post*, October 26, 1988.

years of hostile disputes over the control of the Ogaden region. As it happened in Southern Africa, therefore, 1988 represents a turning point for US foreign policy in the Horn of Africa too, as the end of the Somali–Ethiopian disputes put in motion a series of important changes. The agreement was followed, in 1989–1990, by the final withdrawal of Cuban and Soviet troops and advisors from Ethiopia. Furthermore, the relaxation of the external tension did not help either Siad Barre or Mengistu to regain control over their domestic rebellions; in 1991, just a few years after the agreement, both dictators were overthrown by guerrilla insurgencies, causing ongoing destabilization of both countries.

With Moscow's progressive disengagement from the Horn of Africa, in 1989 the United States resumed its relations with Ethiopia after fifteen years. Washington then became increasingly involved as mediator in the Ethiopian civil war and, after the overthrown of Mengistu, it maintained its involvement as advisor, and supported the establishment of a transitional government. The new government, led by Meles Zenawi, opened a transition process that eventually ended with the drafting of a new constitution in 1994 and the first democratic multi-party elections in May 1995. During the transitional period in Ethiopia, the United States upgraded diplomatic relations to ambassadorial level in June 1992[57], and established a strong working relationship with Meles Zenawi in order to support the democratic transition. Ethiopia became one of the principal recipients of US foreign assistance[58] and relations with Washington strengthened during the Clinton Administration. Indeed, Ethiopia was considered a central player and an 'inescapable factor'[59] in the Horn of Africa. One of the US objectives became to enlist Addis Ababa in its efforts to address problems in neighbouring countries, most notably in Somalia where the US involvement would become particularly important.

The overthrow of Siad Barre in Somalia, in fact, did not mark the end of the civil war but opened the doors to a new dramatic conflict between and within the insurgent groups. The persistent state of war between the 'warlords' in Somalia caused a grave humanitarian and refugee crisis, while the situation of anarchy in the country severely constrained the delivery of international aid.[60] The risk of mass starvation in Somalia eventually drew the attention of the UN Security Council, which between 1992 and 1993 deployed two missions (UNOSOM I and II) in the country. It was in this context that the Horn of Africa became the theatre of the first American military

---

57 Office of Public Communication, Bureau of Public Affairs, "New Ambassadors," July 2, 1992, *US Department of State Dispatch* 3, no. 30, (1992): 593.
58 Private correspondence with George Moose (Assistant Secretary for African Affairs during the Clinton administration), 05/05/2013; US House, Committee on Foreign Affairs, Subcommittees on Africa, *Ethiopia: The Challenges Ahead*, Hearings, July 27, 1994, 103rd Cong., 2nd Sess. (Washington DC: GPO, 1993), 3.
59 Private correspondence with George Moose.
60 Somalia, UNOSOM I, Background – United Nations Peacekeeping, http://www.un.org/en/peace keeping/missions/past/unosom1backgr2.html (accessed October 29, 2016).

intervention on the continent since the end of the Cold War. In order to face the difficulties experienced by the first UNOSOM mission, Washington offered to lead a multinational operation (Operation Restore Hope) with the aim of restabilising the security conditions for a re-deployment of the UN troops of UNOSOM II. The deployment of 28,000 American soldiers in Somalia in 1992 was unprecedented in the history of the US involvement in the region. Furthermore, even after the withdrawal of Restore Hope, the United States sent the Delta Force and the Army Rangers in Somalia to support the UN effort to capture one of the most important Somali warlords, Mohamed Aidid, who was presumably responsible for a mortal attack on the Pakistani contingent of UNOSOM in June 1993. The so-called 'hunt for Aidid' was at the origin of the famous "Black Hawk Down" incident. In October 1993, the Rangers and the Delta Force undertook an airstrike against a suspected refuge of Aidid in Mogadishu. During the attack two Black Hawk helicopters were shot down by Aidid's militia, sparking a violent battle in which eighteen US soldiers were killed.[61] Images of one of the corpses dragged along the streets of the city by a jubilant crowd were broadcast on television all over the world, causing huge shock among the American public and spurring a decision by President Clinton to withdraw US troops by May 1994, marking the end of the American humanitarian venture in the Horn of Africa.

Conclusion

In the mid-1950s, the African continent started the process of decolonization, which led to the final disintegration of the Western colonial empires and was one of the most epochal events of the last century. In those same years, the United States had consolidated its role of superpower after WWII, and it had embarked in a global ideological, military and political confrontation with the USSR. This chapter has investigated the encounter between those two main processes and the way in which their interaction has affected the development of US-Africa relations up to the end of the twentieth century.

From the mid-1950s to the end of the 1980s, the global Cold War dynamics and the strategic imperative of fighting the USSR were very influential in defining US-Africa relations and Washington's approach to the continent. Africa became part of the containment strategy of the United States and it was instrumental to the US struggle with the communist bloc. This became evident in particular in the 1970s, when during the détente the United States engaged significantly in the continent and became involved in many conflicts, which assumed the features of proxy wars and had sig-

---

[61] John Hirsch and Robert Oakley, *Somalia and Operation Restore Hope: Reflections on Peacemaking and Peacekeeping* (Washington DC: United States Institute of Peace Press, 1995), 127; Tom Kenworthy and John Lancaster, "At Least 5 Americans Killed in Somali Attack; Two Army Helicopters Shot Down During UN Operation Against Warlord Aideed", *The Washington Post*, October 4, 1993; John Cushman, "5 G.I.'s are killed as Somalis down 2 US helicopters", *New York Times*, October 4, 1993.

nificant influence in US policy. At the same time, several African actors, like Zaire and South Africa, also played with the Cold War game in order to maintain a solid and beneficial alliance with the United States.

The Cold War also had the effect of creating an overarching and unifying strategic imperative for US foreign policy in Africa. Indeed, the global character of the struggle with the Soviet Union, helped to keep Africa on Washington's radar screen, by linking what was originally a marginal area to the central directives of the American foreign policy in a way that, otherwise, would have been quite unlikely. As a consequence, the end of the Cold War was bound to have the deepest influence in US policy in Africa. This happened in particular after 1988 when, as explained above, the main Cold War related conflicts in Southern Africa and in the Horn of Africa found their solution with the signature of the Tripartite Agreement and the Somali-Ethiopian agreement, which put in motion a series of important changes in the political and military dynamics in those regions.

From the end of the 1980s, US involvement was characterised by a growing focus on the domestic roots of the problems in Southern Africa and in the Horn. Ideological labels became outdated as the Cold War logic drained away. The recognition of the MPLA as a legitimate force in Angola and the resumption of relations with Mengistu clearly testify to this trend. Similarly, the concern about the "communist influence" within the ANC and on the economic agenda of the new post-apartheid South Africa, evaporated by the early 1990s. Consequently, in those years the issues of promotion of democracy and human rights began to play a bigger role in US policy toward Africa, especially in deciding economic and military assistance to the regional allies. The "freedom fighters" or the "need to contain communism in Africa" arguments, were no longer credible justifications to counter the growing criticism from Congress and public opinion of apartheid in South Africa, the dictatorial regimes of Mobutu and Siad Barre, and UNITA's violation of human rights. In some cases, the United States also implemented a quite active policy of mediation and conflict resolution – such as in the Ethiopian and the Angolan civil wars – or significant humanitarian intervention, as it happened in Somalia in 1991. This approach was overall coherent with the rhetoric that characterized the first conception of a post-Cold War "New World Order", envisaged by the Bush Administration and based on the expansion of peace, freedom and democracy.[62]

However, it soon became clear how the directives of this New World Order were not strong enough to play the same role that the containment strategy had had during the Cold War. In fact, the new focus on democracy and human rights, as well as the humanitarian rationale as justifications for involvement in Africa turned out to be contradictory and, ultimately, insufficient to justify and support American intervention. In this sense, the tragic end of the US military intervention in Somalia is

---

[62] George H.W. Bush, "Toward a New World Order," Address before the joint session of Congress, Washington DC, September 11, 1990, *US Department of State Dispatch*, vol. 1, n. 3; 91–94.

probably the most illustrative example. The intervention was badly conceived, and implemented with poor understanding of the complexity of the roots of the civil war and the humanitarian emergency in Somalia. The rapid withdrawal of all the US troops from Somalia after the Black Hawk Down incident clearly showed the inconsistencies in defining the boundaries of the humanitarian commitment, and, more generally, of the difficulties in finding a clear guideline for involvement in crises in Africa. The records of the dismissive attitude struck by Washington towards the genocide in Rwanda in 1994, and the progressive US disengagement from the mediation effort in the Angolan Civil War – which then lasted until 2002 – further confirmed these difficulties.

Throughout the 1990s, therefore, Africa experienced a downgrading in Washington's priorities,[63] and the US relations with Africa were often characterized by an uncoherent policy, which was the results of the difficulties in finding new general rules of conduct in an area where the end of the Cold War had removed an important, overarching strategic imperative.

---

[63] On this point see: Rüland Jürgen, Hanf Theodor, Manske Eva (eds), *US Foreign Policy Toward the Third World: a Post-Cold War Assessment* (Armonk, NY: M. E. Sharpe, 2006); Karl Magyar (ed.), *United States Interests and Policies in Africa: Transition to a New Era* (Basingstoke: Macmillan Press, 2000); Abbas Grammy, Kaye Bragg (eds.), *United States–Third World Relations in the New World Order* (New York: Nova Science, 1996).

Jodie Yuzhou Sun
Chapter 17
Africa and China

Abstract: An investigation into what Julia Strauss called "historical and rhetorical lineages in China['s] relations with Africa," is of historiographical importance and great contemporary significance. In particular, the ways in which this older Afro-Asian solidarity discourse is used to legitimise more recent political, economic, and cultural connections between former "Third World" allies remains under-researched and underappreciated. The uniqueness of China-Africa relations in the socialist and post-socialist periods is reflected in its challenge to the "East/West" and the "North/South" divides. Therefore, an examination of China-Africa relations beyond the Cold War enables an understanding of the extent to which the Cold War itself was the key influence on the evolution of these enduring and complex relationships.

This chapter provides an overview of post-colonial Africa's relations with the People's Republic of China. The comparative approach of studying countries' engagements with China reveals the structural differences in their domestic and foreign politics that were informed and shaped by the Cold War. The resulting contestation of power should not simply translate into foreign manipulation. Facing similar challenges of state-building and economic development, newly independent African nations approached, deepened, and negotiated their relations with China as they searched for ideological and material support. In this way, it hopes to contribute to the much-cited, but little explained concept of "African agency".

Keywords: China, Cold War, foreign policy, decolonization, African agency.

> Everyone knows that Africa is very far from us. But emotionally, it is so close to us. We all want to learn more about Africa, but we did not know much in the past. ...... We met many people for the first time, but the friendship of shared struggle had already united us together.[1]
>
> Han Beiping, 1964

Han Beiping's comment captures the paradox of how Chinese feel towards Africa and its people. A journalist and member of the China Writers Association, Han had visited Africa twice in the early 1960s, making him a rare Chinese observer of the newly independent African countries. He vividly recalled the moment he stepped down the airplane in Cairo, "with cold wind blowing my face, I got a cold shiver. Do you think Africa is hot everywhere?" But he was equally impressed by the warm reception he received from the locals, making him feel at home and not strange. The bond be-

---

[1] Han Beiping 韩北屏, *Feizhou Yehui* 非洲夜会 (Nights in Africa) (Tianjin: Baihua Edition, 1964), 239–241.

tween the Chinese and Africans was said to be their shared struggle against imperialism and colonialism, as well as the courageous efforts to build their nations. Such claims, which tend to pass over as mere propagandist slogans by today's media, in fact reflect the historical baggage that contemporary actors of China-Africa relations need to bear when engaging with each other.

Few topics about China's remarkable ascension to global superpower have captured the interest and imagination of both popular and academic audiences more than its renewed engagement with the African continent. Africa has become a major platform from which to analyse and understand China's growing influence in the global South. Since the mid-2000s, research on 'China in Africa' has generated scholarship from a range of disciplinary backgrounds, mainly political sciences, international relations, economics, anthropology, and sociology.[2] Nevertheless, the history of Chinese relations with Africa has been largely underrepresented. Considered either too recent to constitute historical facts, or insignificant in the formation of contemporary metanarratives, historical relations between China and Africa during the period are often discussed briefly and in reductionist ways before referring to their ongoing dynamics.[3] Western scholars like David Shinn, Joshua Eisenman, and Donovan Chau have recently used English-language newspapers and US government documents to revisit Chinese policy-making in Africa during the Mao Zedong era, but little effort has been made for their selected African nations.[4]

In order to overcome this limitation, it is necessary to address the "two-sided" epistemological challenge of writing on China-Africa relations: on the one hand, there is a problematic tendency towards an oversimplified "dragon in the bush" narrative; on the other hand, this China-Africa literature carries strong moral baggage shaped by Africa's colonial past and racialised discourse.[5] According to Large, this scholarship risks characterising China's rise in Africa in terms of "a monolithic Chinese dragon in an un-variegated African bush stripped of historical and political con-

---

[2] For a summary of the vast literature on this topic, see: May Tan-Mullins, "China and Africa," *Oxford Bibliographies* (Oxford University Press, 2016), http://www.oxfordbibliographies.com/view/document/obo-9780199920082/obo-9780199920082-0137.xml; Meine Pieter van Dijk, "China in Africa," *Oxford Bibliographies* (Oxford University Press, 2017), http://www.oxfordbibliographies.com/view/document/obo-9780199846733/obo-9780199846733-0192.xml; "Course Outlines & Bibliographies," China-Africa Knowledge Project Resource Hub, http://china-africa.ssrc.org/teaching-research-resources/course-outlines-reading-lists-bibliographies/.

[3] Ian Taylor, *China and Africa: Engagement and Compromise* (London: Routledge, 2006); Chris Alden, *China in Africa* (London: Zed Books, 2007); Robert Rotberg, ed., *China into Africa: Trade, Aid, and Influence* (Washington, DC: Brookings Institution, 2008).

[4] David H. Shinn and Joshua Eisenman, *China and Africa: A Century of Engagement* (Philadelphia: University of Pennsylvania Press, 2012); Donovan C. Chau, *Exploiting Africa: the influence of Maoist China in Algeria, Ghana, and Tanzania* (Naval Institute Press, 2014).

[5] Yuzhou Sun, "The Two Challenges of Writing China-Africa Relations," Oxford University China Africa Network, 3 February 2016, https://oucan.politics.ox.ac.uk/index.php/blog/14178-the-two-challenges-of-writing-china-africa-relations, accessed February 2019.

tent."⁶ For contemporary observers, there are two dominant but contrasting images of China. In the first three decades since its independence, the Chinese Communist Party (CCP) remained in the shadow of its Marxist-Leninist roots, its worldview rooted in its absolute domination of power, a command and control economy, and a vehemently anti-imperialist revolutionary agenda. Since Deng Xiaoping's "Opening-Up" in 1978, however, China has embraced a market economy and a pragmatic foreign policy. This "new" China, dominated by economic imperatives, has increasingly sought out natural resources and the sale of its goods to global market, particularly in the global South. The changes (and continuities) in China's positions mean that parallels with Europe's historical experiences in Africa are not particularly revealing. Two ends of the analytical spectrum tend to monopolise the discourse: critics highlight the more exploitative aspects of Chinese engagement with Africa, while more sympathetic observers emphasise the opportunities presented by a supposed alternative approach to Western capitalist relations.⁷

The second epistemological challenge concerns the moral disposition of this China-Africa literature, shaped as it has been both by Africa's troubled colonial past and equally historically significant Western fear of the "Yellow Peril" and communism. Because both China and Africa were subject to (albeit distinct) histories of Western dominance and racism, their historical connection in a framework of anti-imperialist and South-South cooperation exemplified a major challenge to the global order dominated first by Europe and subsequently, the United States. Their multifaced and disaggregated engagements contribute to our understanding of human encounters across geographical landscapes to embrace a more encompassing cosmopolitanism. This Sino-African relationship was fuelled by their respective understandings of modernity, which did not necessarily correspond to the Western ideal. These had the potential to challenge the boundaries of the long-held view of the global trajectory of human evolution, beyond Fukuyama's "end of history".⁸ With only a few exceptions, such as Jamie Monson, the linguistic challenge for African historians to explore Chinese sources is nonetheless formidable.⁹

A comprehensive investigation into what Strauss called "historical and rhetorical lineages in China['s] relations with Africa," is therefore of both historiographical im-

---

6 Daniel Large, "Beyond 'Dragon in the Bush': The Study of China–Africa Relations," *African Affairs* 107, 426 (2008), 45–61.
7 For examples of critics, see: Pádraig Carmody, *The New Scramble for Africa* (Cambridge: Polity, 2011); Howard W. French, *China's Second Continent: How a Million Migrants Are Building a New Empire in Africa* (New York: Knopf, 2014). For examples of positive views, see: Deborah Brautigam, *The Dragon's Gift: The Real Story of China in Africa* (Oxford: Oxford University Press, 2009); Dambisa Moyo, *Winner Take All: China's Race for Resources and What It Means for Us* (London: Penguin, 2013); Deborah Brautigam, *Will Africa Feed China?* (Oxford: Oxford University Press, 2016).
8 Francis Fukuyama, *The End of History and the Last Man* (London: Hamish Hamilton, 1992).
9 Jamie Monson, *Africa's Freedom Railway: How a Chinese Development Project Changed Lives and Livelihoods in Tanzania* (Bloomington: Indiana University Press, 2009).

portance and great contemporary significance.¹⁰ In particular, the ways in which this older Afro-Asian solidarity discourse is used to legitimise more recent political, economic and cultural connections between former "Third World" allies remains both under-researched and underappreciated. The uniqueness of China-Africa relations in both the socialist and post-socialist periods is reflected in its challenge to both the "East/West" and the "North/South" divides. Therefore, an examination of China-Africa relations beyond the Cold War timeframe enables an understanding of the extent to which the Cold War itself was the key influence on these enduring and complex relationships and how these relationships evolved following its conclusion.

Early Encounter and Overseas Chinese in Africa prior to 1949

"China and Africa" is a very old story. African goods such as ivory and incense were arriving in China from at least the seventh century CE. If the year 1492 is central to the 'rise of the West', the earlier part of the fifteenth century marked the start of China-Africa relations. However, writing the history of premodern China's encounter with Africa suffers from inherent methodological constraints. On the one hand, China's imperial archive of the Tang, Song, Yuan, and Ming dynasties is vulnerable to "distortion by secondary handlers";¹¹ on the other hand, "no written records other than the tangible archaeological finds" could be identified in contemporary Africa.¹² It is generally believed that Admiral Zheng He's fleet reached as far as Mombasa, Malindi, and Lamu in today's Kenya, which marks the first third of the fifteenth century as the "height of premodern Sino-African relations."¹³ In 1967, the secretary of the Royal Anthropological Institute in London confirmed that "Indian and Chinese contacts with Africa began many centuries before the first Europeans rounded the Cape of Good Hope," as pieces of Chinese porcelain more than 1,000-years-old have been excavated on the Kenyan coast.¹⁴ A record from the Tang dynasty (618–907) mentions the port of Malindi, and in 1225 a guide from a superintendent of foreign trade to East Africa described "Zangibar" as the Land of the Black People, probably

---

10 Julia C. Strauss, "The Past in the Present: Historical and Rhetorical Lineages in China's Relations with Africa," *The China Quarterly* 199 (2009), 777–95.
11 John Shen, "Foreword: Thoughts on the Use of Chinese Documents in the Reconstruction of East African History," in *A History of Overseas Chinese in Africa to 1911*, ed. by Li Anshan (New York: Diasporic Africa Press, 2012), ii–iii.
12 Karen L. Harris, "Contested Encounters (遭遇和竞争: 古代中非历史文献综述)," *Journal of Chinese Overseas* 13, 2 (2017), 249.
13 J. L. L. Duyvendak, *China's Discovery of Africa* (London: Arthur Probsthain, 1949).
14 "Historians gather the threads which link us with Asia," *Times of Zambia*, 14 April 1967.

a reference to today's Zanzibar.¹⁵ In addition to the official records of oriental traders, there were also tales of Chinese sailors who were shipwrecked on an island called Pate. They probably brought porcelains with them to local villages. As these Chinese sailors settled down and married locally, the village was named Shange, to resemble the pronunciation of Shanghai.¹⁶ In 2005, a nineteen-year-old girl originally from the village of Siyu in the Lamu islands received a scholarship to pursue further studies in a Chinese college. This was based on her account that her forefathers were among those Chinese sailors.¹⁷

The idea of "China" or "Chinese-ness" is not only about the state itself. As important as state-to-state relations between China and Africa are interpersonal ties. In this sense, it is essential to draw attention to the existence of a Chinese community in Africa even before the establishment of the People's Republic of China (PRC). "Overseas Chinese" is the common English translation of *huaqiao*. The epitome of such individual was "a sojourner who enjoyed the protection of the Chinese government (throughout its embassies or consulates), and who lived in spirit in China, politically, culturally and emotionally attached to his mother country."¹⁸ It was reported in 1955 that there were 36,000 Chinese overseas in Africa, mostly resident in four African countries: Mauritius, South Africa, Madagascar and Reunion.¹⁹ Between 1904 and 1910, a total of 63,695 Chinese indentured laborers were transported to South Africa to work on the Witwatersrand mines.²⁰ The labor scheme had an enduring impact on the political future of South Africa and beyond – forming part of "a new politics of empire, race, and citizenship."²¹ In contrast to the forced use of Chinese labor in South Africa, the first generation of overseas Chinese settled in East Africa of their free will. Mostly from Hong Kong and Guangzhou, some were skilled laborers, and some worked in restaurants.²²

---

15 Melanie Yap and Dianne Leong Man, *Colour, Confusion and Concessions: The History of the Chinese in South Africa* (Hong Kong: Hong Kong University Press, 1996), 1.
16 Xia Chunping 夏春平 (ed.), *Shijie huawen chuanmei nianjian* 世界华文传媒年鉴 (Yearbook of Global Chinese Language Media), (Beijing: China News Service, 2011), 526.
17 "Feature: Kenyan girl with Chinese blood steals limelight," *Xinhua*, 30 June 2005, http://ke.china-embassy.org/eng/sbgx/t202741.htm, accessed November 2017.
18 Lynn Pan, *Sons of the Yellow Emperor* (London: Secker&Warbug, 1990), quoted in Yap and Man, *Colour, Confusion and* Concessions, 405.
19 Society for the Studies of Chinese Overseas 华侨问题研究会, *Yafei diqu Huaqiao qingkuang jieshao* 亚非地区华侨情况介绍 (Introduction of Overseas Chinese in Asia and Africa), (1955).
20 Thomas Ellis Naylor, *Yellow Labour: The Truth about the Chinese in the Transvaal* (London: Daily Chronicle Office, 1904); Peter Richardson, *Chinese Mine Labour in the Transvaal* (London: Macmillan Press, 1982).
21 Rachel K. Bright, *Chinese Labour in South Africa, 1902–10: Race, Violence, and Global Spectacle* (New York: Palgrave Macmillan, 2013); Jamie Monson, "Review of *Chinese Labour in South Africa, 1902–10: Race, Violence, and Global Spectacle*," *The American Historical Review* 119, 5 (2014): 1829.
22 Interview with Han Jun, the President of the Overseas Chinese Association in Kenya, Nairobi, 10 November 2016.

The construction of overseas Chinese identity in Africa is, of course, a historical process. For example, Park's studies of Chinese in contemporary South Africa revealed the historical tensions among three waves of Chinese migrants, i.e. Chinese South Africans; Taiwanese and more settled Chinese from the PRC; and the newest migrants from Fujian Province.[23] South Africa is a peculiar case here, as race was of paramount importance in the apartheid regime. According to Yap and Man, the small numbers of these Chinese made it difficult to accommodate them in terms of "apartheid" divisions:

> They lived and traded on the fringes of all race groups, having established good working relationships with their customers. Being neither 'White' nor 'Black', and variously categorized as either 'Asiatic' and 'Colored', the Chinese felt compelled to safeguard their own culture and identity by obtaining classification as a group in their own right.[24]

The limited available data creates difficulty in constructing a comprehensive history of overseas Chinese in Africa. But it is at least crucial to point out the existence of such communities whose more local scale of interaction existed alongside the realm of international relations. The newly established country under the Communist leadership would engage more formally with the continent on the basis of 'Third World' solidarity.

Defining China's Foreign Policy towards Africa, 1949–1954

In the first years of the PRC, its revolutionary leaders adopted the "Leaning to One Side" foreign policy based on the belief that China naturally belonged to the Soviet camp, representing the advanced side of the principal contradiction i.e. proletarian regimes against capitalist imperialists, the latter led by the United States. The contestation of power on the Korean peninsula reinforced China's binary view of the world, according to which the clash of ideologies would deteriorate into the worst form of conflict, i.e. war. The Communist government also faced the challenge of Taiwan, whose Chinese Nationalist Party regime was still considered by many Western countries as the only legitimate Chinese regime.[25] The issue of China's representation in the United Nations was the central focus of China's foreign policy until 1971. The diplomatic slogan "sweep the house before inviting guests" reflected Beijing's determination to reject any foreign affiliations with Taiwan. Eager to break the economic

---

23 Yoon Jung Park, "Boundaries, Borders and Borderland Constructions: Chinese in Contemporary South Africa and the Region," *African Studies* 69, 3 (2010): 457–79.
24 Yap and Man, *Colour, Confusion and Concessions*, 317–18.
25 Note that except for direct quotations, all references to China in this chapter mean the People's Republic of China.

embargo and diplomatic isolation of China by the US and its allies in Asia in the 1950s, Mao Zedong developed the concept of an 'intermediate zone' to describe the vast majority of Asia, Africa, and Latin America that belonged to neither the communist nor capitalist bloc.[26] "Apart from the question of geographical distance" from Africa, Beijing was not yet "strong enough to adopt any meaningful policy towards Africa."[27] In September 1954, however, China's annual Government Work Report declared that developing de facto relations with Africa was essential to enhance mutual understanding and create the conditions to establish de jure relations.[28]

The Sino-Soviet split between 1956–1966 was driven by opposing interpretations of Orthodox Marxism. China and the Soviet Union diverged on the means to achieve socialism domestically and on the direction of the global socialist camp against the capitalist world. China's support for independence struggles in Africa throughout the Cold War can be partly explained by its own historical trajectory. While the Russian Revolution primarily aimed to remove class inequalities and build socialism within Russia, debates on the Chinese revolutionary path were at the outset focused on a nationalist impetus to defeat foreign invaders who had bestowed on the country "a century of humiliation."[29] At the time when China was subject to Japanese occupation during the Second World War, Mao criticised the Italian invasion of Ethiopia in 1935.[30] China's revolutionary outlook was thus inherently anti-imperialist.

However, there were obvious difficulties in Chinese practice of direct involvement with African decolonisation. Not unlike the US or the Soviet Union, the PRC had to build up its contacts from nowhere. Sporadic contacts and communications with African delegates were enabled through organising and attending international conferences. Among them, events for youth groups, student unions, women's organisations, and labor unions were crucial. For instance, against the background of the Korean War, the Third World Festival of Youth and Students was held in 1951 in East Berlin. At this conference, Chinese youth delegates met their counterparts from Nigeria, Ghana (then the Gold Coast), Tunisia, and Algeria[31] Since decolonization occurred earlier in North Africa, Algeria and Tunisia were among the earliest countries to send formal delegations to China.

---

26 Mao Zedong, "Talks with Anna Louis Strong," in *Selected Works of Mao Zedong*, volume 4 (Beijing: Foreign Languages Press, 1967), 1191–92.
27 Alaba Ogunsanwo, *China's Policy in Africa, 1958–1971* (Cambridge: Cambridge University Press, 1974), 4.
28 Ai Zhouchang 艾周昌, and Mu Tao 沐涛, *Zhongfei Guanxi Shi* 中非关系史 (History of Sino-African Relations), (Shanghai: East China Normal University Press, 1996), 218.
29 Jeremy Scott Friedman, *Shadow Cold War: The Sino-Soviet Competition for the Third World* (Chapel Hill: University of North Carolina Press, 2015), 1–2.
30 Wang Qinmei 汪勤梅, "Maozedong yu Zhongfei Guanxi" 毛泽东与中非关系 (Mao Zedong and China-Africa relations), *Foreign Affairs Review* 4 (1996): 4–8.
31 LuTing'en 陆庭恩, *Feizhou Wenti Lunji* 非洲问题论集 (Treatises on Africa), (Beijing: World Knowledge Press, 2005), 554.

Particular distinctions were drawn between social class and nationalism in Africa. Inhabited by a largely illiterate and rural population, Africa was not an ideal location for a Soviet-style working-class revolution. In 1946, Stalin personally denounced indigenous political elites in the colonies, claiming "these leaders in their majority are corrupt and care not so much about the independence of their territories, as about the preservation of their privileges regarding to the population of these territories."[32] It was only during the Khrushchev era that the Soviet Union formed a meaningful policy on Africa, whose underpinning was the socialist model of development. This was based on the belief that "a faster and better modernity would allow for the final victory of Soviet socialism over Western capitalism."[33] In contrast, Maoism was attractive to many African leaders who were eager to mobilise their large rural population in their nation-building process.

From the mid-1950s, the following "Five Principles of Peaceful Coexistence" became the underlying basis of Chinese foreign policy: mutual respect for each other's territorial integrity and sovereignty; mutual non-aggression; mutual non-interference in each other's internal affairs; equality and cooperation for mutual benefit; peaceful co-existence.[34] Its promulgation can be seen to have taken place at a pivotal moment. Western European powers in the process of decolonisation created the potential for nationalist advancement in most former colonies. Yet such decolonising processes brought the threat of new foreign intervention in the context of the Cold War. Non-alignment was therefore favoured by many leaders of newly independent countries, both to avoid being dragged into proxy wars and to take advantage of funds and resources from both blocs.[35]

China-Africa Relations in the Bandung Era, 1955 – 1965

The five principles were incorporated in modified form in a statement at the historic first Afro-Asian Conference held in Indonesia, later known as the Bandung Conference. Attended by twenty-nine countries including the PRC, the conference took place on 18 – 24 April 1955. It sought to enhance the solidarity among Asian and Af-

---

32 Stalin to Molotov, 20 November 1946, quoted in Odd Arne Westad, *The Global Cold War. Third World Interventions and the Makings of Our Times* (Cambridge: Cambridge University Press, 2005), 60.
33 Alessandro Iandolo, "The Rise and Fall of the 'Soviet Model of Development' in West Africa, 1957–64," *Cold War History* 12, 4 (2012), 683–704.
34 "China's initiation of the Five Principles of Peaceful Co-Existence," Ministry of Foreign Affairs of People's Republic of China, http://www.fmprc.gov.cn/mfa_eng/ziliao_665539/3602_665543/3604_665547/t18053.shtml, accessed January 2016.
35 John W. Burton (ed.), *Non-Alignment* (London: Ander Deutsch Limited, 1966), 11–27; Mark Atwood Lawrence, "The Rise and Fall of Nonalignment," in *The Cold War in the Third World,* ed. by Robert J. McMahon (Oxford: Oxford University Press, 2013), 139–55.

rican countries in their struggle against imperialism and colonialism, to achieve and maintain national independence, and to secure world peace. Divisions of political orientation, race, colour, class, education, and national identity among delegates nevertheless made it difficult to achieve agreement. Due to its close ties with the Soviet Union, Communist China was widely viewed as a proxy for the former's interests.[36] Premier Zhou Enlai however demonstrated his charisma and diplomatic acumen in advancing Beijing's autonomous position through his message of "seeking common ground while reserving differences." Through the invented narrative of a shared history with Africa of colonial subordination, China succeeded in presenting itself as an autonomous Third World leader.

China's "modern debut onto the world stage," however, would not have been possible without intellectual support to its political leadership.[37] In early 1960 the Ministry of Foreign Affairs established a separate department to deal with African affairs. The year 1960, dubbed the "Year of Africa," was a turning point in which seventeen countries became independent. China had by then established diplomatic relations with eight African countries: Egypt, Sudan, Algeria, Morocco, Ghana, Guinea, Mali, and Somalia. Among the "Africa hands" in the Ministry, He Ying (ambassador to Tanzania) and Huang Hua (ambassador to Ghana) were among the most capable.[38] Chinese diplomats not only dealt with political affairs in their host country but also made initial visits to establish links with numerous nationalist movements in still colonised countries. The embassy staff were also responsible for recruiting about 500 African students to enrol in courses at the Institute of Foreign Languages in Beijing by the end of 1960.[39]

Back home, Chinese communist leaders were keen to publicly celebrate "revolutionary" progress in colonial Africa, and invited nationalists and other African representatives to Beijing on various occasions. China's "revolutionary friendship" with Africa is best illustrated by the case of Algeria.[40] China was the first non-Arab country to recognise the Algerian Provisional Government in 1958 led by the National Liberation Front (FLN), whose political orientation was strongly influenced by Maoism. Non-state actors from Algeria, such as football teams, labor unions, journalists, and women's delegations, also paid frequent visits to China between 1958 and early 1960. They were warmly received in Shanghai by various Chinese civil groups led by the

---

[36] Christopher J. Lee (ed.), *Making a World after Empire: the Bandung Moment and Its Political Afterlives* (Athens: Ohio University Press, 2010), 13.
[37] John K. Cooley, *East Wind over Africa: Red China's African Offensive* (New York: Walker and Company, 1965), 11.
[38] Philip Snow, *The Star Raft: China's Encounter with Africa* (New York: Cornell University Press, 1988), 89.
[39] Compiling Group of China Africa Education Cooperation and Communication 中非教育合作与交流编写组, *Zhongguo yu Feizhou Guoji Jiaoyu Hezuo yu Jiaoliu* 中国与非洲国家教育合作与交流 (China Africa Education Cooperation), (Beijing: Peking University Press, 2005).
[40] Kyle Haddad-Fonda, "An Illusory Alliance: Revolutionary Legitimacy and Sino-Algerian Relations, 1958–1962," *The Journal of North African Studies* (2014): 1–20.

municipal government. China's adeptness in social mobilisation was illustrated in these visits. Although it is hard to assess the degree of success of Chinese propaganda in winning the hearts and minds of Africans, it was certainly believed to be influential by the British, whose intelligence operations sought to be a "real and perceived bulwark against communism."[41] In its report on communist activities in Africa in 1961, the British Foreign Office's African Section of Research Department concluded:

> While the Chinese effort in Africa is on a smaller scale than that of the Russians, particularly in regard to technical assistance, it is nevertheless formidably efficient and well-directed, and appears to be making considerable progress.[42]

What worried Britain most were Chinese and Soviet "subversive" activities in Africa including "supplying material, moral and in some cases military, support to selected African regimes and most fiercely anti-colonialist in attitude, or most radical in their domestic policies."[43] Labelled as "terrorists" by the British, such African radicals would pose a great threat to colonial or apartheid rule; and without doubt, the Chinese were great teachers on such matters.

In parallel to the increasing number of visits by African delegations to China, Beijing also actively approached many newly independent African countries from the start of the 1960s. From 13 December 1963 to 5 February 1964, Premier Zhou and Vice-Premier Chen Yi toured ten African countries. The greatest legacy of these visits was the publication of the following "eight principles for economic aid and technical assistance to other countries": mutual benefit; no conditions attached; the no-interest or low-interest loans that would not create a debt burden for the recipient country; to help the recipient nation develop its economy, not to create its dependence on China; to help the recipient country with project that needs less capital and quick returns; the aid in kind must be of high quality at the world market price; to ensure that the technology can be learned and mastered by the locals; the Chinese experts and technicians working for the aid recipient country are treated equally as the local ones with no extra benefits for them.[44] In essence, these eight principles provided the basis for Communist China's economic and cultural cooperation with the newly-emerged countries of Asia, Africa and Latin America throughout the decolonisation period.

---

[41] Caroline Elkins, "Archives, Intelligence and Secrecy: The Cold War and the End of the British Empire," in *Decolonization and the Cold War: Negotiating Independence*, ed. by Leslie James and Elisabeth Leake (London: Bloomsbury, 2015), 269.
[42] The National Archives of UK (hereafter TNA), FCO 141/7090, "Chinese activities and influence in Africa," December 1961.
[43] TNA, FCO 141/7090, "Memorandum: Sino-Soviet propaganda in Africa," 1961.
[44] "The Chinese Government's Eight Principles for Economic Aid and Technical Assistance to Other Countries," January 15, 1964, History and Public Policy Program Digital Archive, *Zhou Enlai waijiao wenxuan* 周恩来外交文选 (Selected Diplomatic Papers of Zhou Enlai) (Beijing: Central Party Literature Press, 1990), 388.

One of the major motivations of this grand tour was to gather support for the upcoming Second Afro-Asian Conference. As China had severed its relations with the Soviet Union in the late 1950s, the question of where and when the Conference would be held became a battle between the two communist superpowers. By the time Zhou's delegation completed its official mission, six out of ten of the African countries visited had expressed open support for China's position with regard to the Second Afro-Asian conference. This led to the "tactical success" for China in excluding the Soviet delegation from the Preparatory Meeting for an Asian-African Conference to take place in Algiers in April 1964.[45] On 19 June, a coup took place in Algeria that overthrew Ben Bella's government. Most African representatives thus decided to postpone the meeting. This showed that African countries were politically sensitive to domestic turmoil and retained significant agency on issues concerning global ideological confrontations. China made a difficult compromise to indefinitely delay the conference in order to avoid being isolated in international politics.[46] China, as the weakest of the Cold War superpowers, had the most complicated relationship to non-alignment. Its alleged "grand" policy in Africa was, in practice, far from coherent, and had to be continually negotiated with African counterparts in a fast-changing international environment.

Sino-African Relations amidst the Cultural Revolution, 1966–1976

In May 1966, an unprecedented revolution swept over Mao's China. The "spill-over" of the Cultural Revolution on Chinese foreign policy was powerful. Reflecting Marshal Lin Biao's description of Maoist thoughts as "a powerful ideological atomic bomb," it sought to universalise China's revolutionary trajectory "in the age of complete breakdown of imperialism and victory of socialism in the whole world."[47] In less than a year, more than three quarters of the approximately forty countries with which China had diplomatic relations experienced degradation or deterioration in diplomatic relations, including six African countries.[48] Chinese embassies in African countries were either controlled by Red Guards who intentionally distributed Mao's published works and badges, or in a state of *laissez-faire* in which diplomats disengaged from local affairs in the host countries. Long points out that exporting

---

45 Ogunsanwo, *China's Policy in Africa, 1958–1971*, 126.
46 Li Qianyu 李潜虞, "Shilun Zhongguo dui Dierci Yafeihuiyi Zhengce de Yanbian" 试论中国对第二次亚非会议政策的演变 (China's Policy towards the Second Afro-Asian Conference), *International Politics Quarterly* 4 (2010): 115–33.
47 Lin Biao, "Preface to the Reprint of Quotations from Chairman Mao," in Mao Zedong, *Chairman Mao on World Revolution* (Nanjing: Nanjing Revolutionary Committee, 1970).
48 Barbara Barnouin and Changgen Yu, *Chinese Foreign Policy during the Cultural Revolution* (London: Kegan Paul International, 1988), 66.

revolution in the post-colonial African context not only went against the protocol of international relations, but also challenged the legitimacy of new African leaders who desired political independence and economic development above anything else.[49] The ways in which African countries and their leaders approached, deepened and negotiated their relations with China as they searched for both ideological and material support in achieving these goals reveals the structural differences in their domestic and foreign politics that were informed but were also shaped by the global ideological confrontation of the Cold War.

Take Kenya and Zambia for contrasting examples. In the mid-1960s, both Kenya and Zambia officially adopted socialism as their national philosophies, which became known as "African socialism" and "African Humanism" respectively.[50] As Askew and Pitcher point out, "no fewer than thirty-five countries out of fifty-three proclaimed themselves 'socialist' at one or another point in their history" between the 1950s and 1980s.[51] The socialism advanced by these countries' leaders acted neither as "a mechanistic instrument of Pan-Africanist efforts to achieve transnational unity" nor as "rhetorical instruments" to "explain, rationalize, and justify governmental involvement."[52] This is not to deny the temptation for authoritarian regimes to consolidate their power over citizens through a socialist doctrine. For example, Jomo Kenyatta arguably articulated a moderate version of socialism as a way of deflecting domestic criticism of his close relations with former colonial powers like Britain. For those who were considered conservative and capitalist by Marxist standards, international ideological confrontations offered them a degree of leverage that could counterbalance domestic criticism of potential foreign interference in their domestic regimes. The increasingly aggressive activities of a "culturally revolutionary" China between 1966 and 1969 had diverging impacts on Kenyan and Zambian politics, which cannot be explained by recourse to realist theories. In August 1967, at a time when the Tanzanian and Zambian governments had dispatched a joint ministerial team to Beijing to negotiate the construction of the 1,042-mile cross-border TAZARA rail link, KANU officials and members were marching in protest to the Chinese Embassy in Nairobi.[53] The mid-to-late 1967 was thus a critical moment in both Chi-

---

[49] Long Xiangyang 龙向阳, "1966–1969 Nian Zhongguo yu Feizhou Guanxi Chutan" 1966–1969 年中国与非洲关系初探 (An Initial Investigation of Sino-African Relations, 1966–1969), in *Peking University African Studies Series*, 79.
[50] For African socialism, see Jodie Yuzhou Sun, "Historicizing African Socialisms: Kenyan African Socialism, Zambian Humanism, and Communist China's Entanglements," *International Journal of African Historical Studies* 52, 3 (2019), 349–374.
[51] M. Anne Pitcher and Kelly M. Askew, "African Socialisms and Postsocialisms," *Africa* 76, 1 (2006), 1.
[52] Priya Lal, *African Socialism in Postcolonial Tanzania: Between the Village and the World* (New York: Cambridge University Press, 2015), 39.
[53] For Sino-Kenyan relations, see Jodie Yuzhou Sun, "'Now the Cry Was Communism': The Cold War and Kenya's Relations with China (1964–1970)," *Cold War History* 20, 1 (2020): 39–58.

nese history and China's relations with African countries: While some deepened ties with Beijing, China's presence in others was increasingly unpopular.

Another region that attracted China's attention was southern Africa. China's support of liberation movements derived largely from its own analysis of African revolution. The Chinese believed that successful national revolutions would "multiply and speed the continental revolution," and that the Chinese revolutionary experience could provide useful lessons for Africans.[54] Guided by Mao's theory of consolidating the "intermediate zone," China dispatched military advisers to African countries alongside arms supplies. In military camps based in Tanzania, Chinese advisers trained freedom fighters exiled from Mozambique, Angola and Rhodesia from 1964 onwards. China's support for Angolan liberation was atypically stronger and more complex. Initially lacking a clear preference among the competing nationalist movements in Angola, Beijing's material commitment to the struggle was relatively low. Jackson finds that the Popular Movement for the Liberation of Angola (MPLA) was the main Angolan movement featured in the Chinese press up to 1973, but thereafter, attention turned to the National Liberation Front of Angola (FNLA) which developed a patron-client relationship with China in late 1973.[55] The application of the "Three Worlds theory" in Beijing's foreign policy decisions became increasingly confusing and contradictory from the mid-1970s onwards.[56] In Angola, China worked with National Union for the Total Independence of Angola (UNITA) – alongside the USA and South Africa – fighting against the Moscow-backed MPLA party, which had Soviet support and decisive Cuban military intervention.[57] The latter's military victory and seizure of power in November 1975 created a difficult legacy for Beijing: a supportive actor in the course of Angolan independence, China had however supported the "wrong friends" in utilitarian terms, and its supposed best friend from the victorious party – Viriato da Cruz – had been expelled by the party's leadership and later became embroiled in China's internal political tribulations.[58]

---

[54] Bruce Larkin, *China and Africa, 1949–1970: The Foreign Policy of the People's Republic of China* (Berkley: University of California Press, 1971), 167–68.
[55] Steven F. Jackson, "China's Third World Foreign Policy: The Case of Angola and Mozambique, 1961–1993," *China Quarterly* 142 (1995): 401.
[56] Stephen Chan, "China's Foreign Policy and Africa: The Rise and Fall of China's Three World Theory," *The Round Table: The Commonwealth Journal of International Affairs*, 74, 296 (1985): 378.
[57] Stephan Chan (ed.), *The Morality of China in Africa* (London, Zed Books, 2013), 12–13.
[58] For Viriato da Cruz, see Jodie Yuzhou Sun, "Viriato da Cruz and His Chinese Exile: A Biographical Approach," *Journal of Southern African Studies* 46, 5, forthcoming in 2020.

China's Political Transition and its Multifaceted Engagements with Africa, 1977–1989

In September 1976, Chairman Mao Zedong died in Beijing. With the death of the once all-powerful leader of the PRC, the country experienced fierce power struggles between the so-called "Gang of Four" and Hua Guofeng. Backed by the People's Liberation Army, Hua Guofeng managed to supress the Gang and seized the party leadership along with Ye Jianying, Chen Yun, and Li Xiannian. Having been rehabilitated from previous prosecutions, Deng Xiaoping launched the country's economic reform programme in 1978. Due to the decreasing priority of Communist ideology in the party, the CCP progressively developed direct relations with political parties beyond the communist bloc. In autumn 1977, an unidentified "senior African politician" proposed to visit China on behalf of his party, but was rejected by the Chinese authorities. Prompted by negative implications of this event, Beijing issued an official decree that approved Sino-African party-to-party exchanges. It declared that such relations should be based on the principles of "self-independence, complete equality, and non-interference of domestic politics".[59]

According to Strauss, a key feature of China's official rhetoric about its relations with Africa is its "substantial continuities with the Maoist past."[60] This was a result of CCP's constant self-reflection. According to the Deputy Head of the International Liaison Department of the CCP:

> ... the history of Socialism is young and since it is young, it is engaged in learning. Like a child who learns to walk, in the process, it makes mistakes. Since learning is not subject to a fixed pattern, Socialism is far from being perfect, that's why there is need to sum-up the past experiences and to build anew each socialist country, basing its revolutionary struggles on the local conditions prevailing.[61]

The China 'model' to be introduced to its African guests necessarily reflected these changes, and sometimes even the contradictions between the past and present. For example, the ways in which Zambia and Kenya perceived China's post-revolutionary foreign agenda strikingly reversed the pattern of the Mao era. Kenneth Kaunda and his United National Independence Party (UNIP), influenced by radical socialist movements and ideas, and experiencing unprecedented military destabilisation by its racist southern neighbours, anxiously rejected China's deepening political and economic relations with the West. During a 1979 visit to Beijing, the UNIP delegates

---

59 Zheng Kejun 郑克军, "八十年代初期中国对非洲政策的调整" (Adjustments of China's Policy towards Africa in the Early 1980s"), in *Zhongguo yu Feizhou* 中国与非洲 (China and Africa) (Beijing: Peking University Press, 2000), 90–91.
60 Strauss, "The Past in the Present," 777.
61 United National Independence Party Archives at The British Library (hereafter UNIP BL), EAP121_2_5_4_32pt1, "Analyse conditions objectively," 23 January 1980.

viewed the new Chinese senior leadership with "a sense of uncertainty": "China is now bent on modernisation," they noted, and was "courting western countries and doing away with a few traditional encumbrances."[62] In contrast, Kenyatta and Daniel arap Moi took advantage of the normalisation of China-US relations to renew political and economic cooperation with the PRC. China's post-Mao leadership was described as "significantly pragmatic and forward looking." Kenya had rediscovered this "great country's importance in world affairs."[63]

China's changing foreign policy in the reform era also had fundamental implications for its economic relations with Africa. As mentioned above, Communist China's official aid policy was set out in the Eight Principles laid down by Premier Zhou Enlai during his Africa tour in 1963–1964. These eight points urged the self-reliance of African countries in developing mutual interests with China, especially when other donors refused to offer assistance. According to Larkin, Beijing's efforts to expand markets and economic advantage rested on the assumption that those countries which received Chinese aid would "take public stands friendly to China."[64] Occasionally, economic interests might be sacrificed for political reasons. This changed dramatically after 1982. During his 1982–1983 tour of eleven African countries, Premier Zhao Ziyang launched the new Four Principles of Chinese aid policy towards Africa. Although the Maoist virtue of self-reliance was re-asserted, it was now adapted to the prevailing international status quo. Zhao made it clear that aid would be limited as "China is also readjusting its economy and we have our own difficulties … we must not strain to do what is beyond our country's capabilities." [65] Compared to Chinese aid policy during Mao's era, aid and technical assistance would now be offered based on the practical considerations of both sides and implemented in more diverse forms.

In addition to economic and technical aid, there were also changes to the terms of Sino-African trade. For instance, China's total copper imports from Zambia rose from 10,000 metric tons per year in the early 1970s to 20,000 metric tons in 1976.[66] Meanwhile, Zambia restructured its imports by removing "unpopular" Chinese goods, which mainly consisted of tinned beans, beef, and pork. Other cheaper and more durable exports, such as white cotton sheets and bicycles were, however, welcomed by Zambian consumers. Having suffered from a severe drop in the global copper price, Zambia's volume of trade with China reached an estimated 40 percent of

---

[62] UNIP BL, EAP121_2_5_1_10, 1979, "Visit to the People's Republic of China by a UNIP delegation 22nd July – 10th August 1979," August 1979.
[63] Note that the *East African Standard* changed its name into *The Standard* in 1977. "Editorial: Kenya and China," *The Standard*, 23 August 1980.
[64] Larkin, *China and Africa, 1949–1970*, 107.
[65] Zheng, "Adjustments of China's Policy towards Africa in the Early 1980s," 93–94.
[66] UNIP BL, EAP121_2_5_1_9pt6, Correspondence by Ministry of Commerce & Report on the visit to the PRC, 1976, 'Report on the visit to the PRC', 22 October 1976.

its total trade by 1978.[67] China also pledged to increase its imports of coffee, tea and soda ash from Kenya, and both countries agreed to implement their new international development strategy.[68] Nigeria even became China's eighth largest trading partner in 1980. By 1980 the total trade between China and Africa had risen by 70 percent to a total value of $1.1 billion, of which $600 million consisted of Chinese exports.[69]

Dual Liberalisation and China's 'Return' to Africa from 1990 onwards

From the late 1970s, China experienced a structural change in its economy, which resulted in a diverse mix of state-owned, collective, private, foreign-funded, and shareholding economic entities. To the surprise of contemporaneous domestic dissidents and external observers, China did not democratise in the same way as Central and Eastern Europe did in 1989. It is exactly China's "abnormal" experience of dual liberalisation that characterises its "return" to Africa. China's engagement with Africa is, according to Alden, Large, and Soares de Oliveira, occurring under new circumstances "in which a more developed China operates under conditions of growing interdependence and plays an increasingly important role in the global economy."[70] China's increasing overseas investments should be understood as a direct result of domestic economic decentralisation since the mid-1980s. In the name of the "Go out" policy introduced in 1999, the Chinese government sought to reduce red tape as well as to provide fiscal and non-fiscal incentives for Chinese enterprises to develop activities beyond the national border.[71] The intensified competition provided by multinational companies in China's partly liberalised domestic market also forced Chinese companies to globalise. China has been Africa's largest economic partner since the turn of the millennium. China-Africa trade has grown at approximately 20 per cent per year since 2000. It is estimated that Chinese foreign direct investment in Africa has grown from nearly zero to approximately $50 billion in a decade.[72] Africa's construction sector has been the largest recipient of financing from China in recent years.

---

67 "Zambia may drop food imports from China," *Times of Zambia*, 13 October 1978.
68 "China to buy more from Kenya," *The Standard*, 18 January 1983.
69 Snow, *The Star Raft*, 178.
70 Chris Alden, Daniel Large, and Ricardo Soares de Oliveira (eds.), *China Returns to Africa: A Rising Power and A Continent Embrace* (London: Hurst and Co., 2008), 6.
71 Peter Kragelund and Godfrey Hampwaye, "Seeking Markets and Resources: State-Driven Chinese and Indian Investments in Zambia," *International Journal of Technology and Globalisation* 6, 4 (2012), 357.
72 Irene Yuan Sun, Kartik Jayaram, and Omid Kassiri, "Dance of the Lions and Dragons: How Are Africa and China Engaging, and How Will the Partnership Evolve?" McKenzie&Company, June 2017.

These fast-growing economic relations were accompanied by powerful endorsement at the state level. In 2000 China established a multilateral platform for exchanges and cooperation with African countries that have formal diplomatic relationships with China. The Forum of China-Africa Cooperation (FOCAC) has the stated aims of strengthening friendly relations and cooperation, dealing with the challenges of economic globalisation, and seeking mutual development.[73] FOCAC ministerial conferences, held every three years, and alternating between China and Africa, have, along with their follow-up actions, facilitated Sino-African collaboration across different sectors. It is clear that China-Africa cooperation has both dramatically expanded and deepened in less than two decades. While bilateral economic and trade relations have been stressed in the media and public discourse, cooperation in other fields has been gradually expanding. Therefore, FOCAC should be understood as a multi-level and comprehensive mechanism critical to the historical trajectory of China- Africa relations.

In retrospect, the years surrounding 1990 marked a watershed in the history of these relations. The world was preoccupied with a strong sense of historical determinism resulting from the Western victory at the end of the Cold War. According to Francis Fukuyama, the advent of Western liberal democracy signalled the endpoint of humanity's sociocultural evolution and the final form of human government.[74] African intellectuals equally acknowledged the significance of this historical watershed, but with a different answer. According to Ogot:

> In East Asia, a new type of history was in the making which showed that just as cultural nationalism helped end the era of formal colonialism, it might still play a part in resisting dominant global orders. They chose to build the present on the foundations of the past. They argued that unlike the West, where the individual is the centrepiece of a democracy that is intended to disempower government, in East Asia the tradition is one of respect for authority with the individual under strong obligation to the group.[75]

If there were a choice to be "between the past and the present," Ogot considers that the East Asian model promoted above all by China, is probably more suitable for Africa. China's ability to achieve economic success while maintaining its "supposed" political tradition in the past few decades has effectively challenged the Western norm, therefore, providing an "alternative" path of governance and development for the post-Cold War Global South. The focus of recent studies on Chinese politics has also shifted from the potential for democratic transition to authoritarian resil-

---

73 "Forum on China-Africa Cooperation," FOCAC Official Website, https://www.focac.org/chn/ltjj/ltjz/, accessed June 2018.
74 Francis Fukuyama, "The End of History?" *The National Interest* 16 (1989), 3–18.
75 Bethwell Allan Ogot, *Who, If Anyone, Owns the Past? Reflections on the Meaning of 'Public History'* (Kisumu: Anyange Press Ltd, 2010), 227.

ience.⁷⁶ While it is impossible to review all relevant literature in this respect, it is at least critical to highlight the various attempts to challenge the political dichotomies and linear models of change in modern China.

The Discourse of Anti-imperialist Nostalgia beyond the Cold War Timeframe

Just as China's unique historical trajectory from a Third World leader to a leading global economy means that it poses an attractive model for many African leaders to follow, its hybridity of socialist and capitalist features is best exemplified in the discourse of anti-imperialist nostalgia in China-Africa relations. While most colonial states "mourn the passing of what they themselves have transformed" based on "imperialist nostalgia,"⁷⁷ this anti-imperialist nostalgia does exactly the opposite: it "holds in mind hope for changes that have yet to be realized, changes that were always yet to be realized."⁷⁸ This on-going process, in which the limitations of what has been achieved are acknowledged, whilst at the same time an imagined better future is pursued, dominated the development discourse in many newly independent countries. In the context of the Cold War, the two Communist giants envisaged contrasting revolutionary programmes: while the CPSU claimed its legitimacy of rule by building a superior economic system, the mandate of the CCP, itself a product of anti-imperialist revolution, was to "build a strong, united, independent, prosperous, and modern China".⁷⁹

In this sense, the terminology of the "Third World" was a powerful imaginary. Dissatisfied with the new world order divided between West and East, people on the fringes of this binary division envisioned alternative possibilities, which should ideally have come into reality yet could only arrive in a (perpetually delayed) future. By acknowledging "the past's vision of the future" while at the same time recognising "the distance and the difference between that vision and the realities of the present," this anti-imperialist nostalgia prompted discussions of "historicity, the nation-state, and utopian projection and promise."⁸⁰ Instead of being a *fait accompli*, anti-imperialism, loosely (re)interpreted as struggles against global inequality and injustice, continues regardless of the collapse of both the European empires and later the USSR, encapsulated in the continuity of the slogan *"a luta continua"* long after its specific deployment in anti-liberation struggles ceased to be directly relevant.

---

76 Vivienne Shue and Patricia Thornton (eds.), *To Govern China: Evolving Practices of Power* (Cambridge: Cambridge University Press, 2018).
77 Renato Rosaldo, "Imperialist Nostalgia," *Representations* 26, 1 (1989), 107–22.
78 Jennifer Wenzel, "Remembering the Past's Future: Anti-Imperialist Nostalgia and Some Versions of the Third World," *Cultural Critique* 62 (2006), 2.
79 Friedman, *Shadow Cold War*, 215–24.
80 Wenzel, "Remembering the Past's Future," 7–8.

Conclusion

The phenomenon of "China in Africa" has undoubtedly captured the on-going popular imagination. But most contemporaneous observations of China's renewed interest in Africa have failed to seriously and critically engage with the historical aspects of this complex relationship. This chapter has provided an overview of post-colonial Africa's relations with the People's Republic of China from ideological, political, economic and social perspectives. While it makes no attempt to provide an analysis that is representative of the African continent as a whole, the comparative approach of studying countries such as Kenya and Zambia's engagements with China nonetheless reveals the structural differences in their domestic and foreign politics that were informed but are also shaped by the global ideological confrontation of the Cold War period. The resulting contestation of power should not simply translate into foreign manipulation. Facing similar challenges of state-building and economic development, newly independent African nations approached, deepened, and negotiated their relations with China as they searched for both ideological and material support in achieving these goals. In this way, it hopes to contribute to the much-cited, but little explained concept of "African agency".

Nnaoma Hyacinth Iwu
Chapter 18
Foreign Aid to Africa Since 1940

Abstract: African states have continued to grapple with humanitarian emergencies six decades after independence from colonial rule. The capacity to respond to humanitarian emergencies is critical if a state is to be classified as underdeveloped, developing, or developed. Foreign aid is given as a response to excruciating poverty, hunger, diseases, natural or manmade disasters, killings, destruction arising from war and holocaust of any type, challenges on educational institutions, girls' education, poverty, and infrastructural decay. Trillions of dollars of foreign aid from multilateral agencies, America, Europe, and Asia, international non-governmental organizations to Africa have not been able to contain these challenges. Broadly, aid to Africa could be classified into developmental and humanitarian aid. The former targets long-run projections that could prevent the emergence of a humanitarian crisis that would warrant the latter. This paper examined foreign aid as a phenomenon and interrogated the two contending debates on why Africa has continued to demand aid. The first blames exogenous factors that find an excuse for the stringent conditionality of the donor agencies; the second blames the failure on endogenous factors that find African leaders culpable and then argues that aid to Africa should stop. This argument highlights African leaders' inabilities to understand the logic of capitalism that ensues prudent management of their economy, hence corruption and the absence of horizontal accountability pervade government business. This paper shows that aid to Africa is largely given under specific titles as an aid for infrastructure, extraction of solid minerals, disaster problems, control of migrants to Europe, erosion control, peacebuilding, a war against terrorism, disease control or eradication, and general budget support (GBS), etc., however, combined discussion was made of them. Relying on secondary data sources and big push theory, the findings support the culpability of African leaders for problems necessitating consistent demand for humanitarian aid.

Keywords: Foreign aid, humanitarian aid, underdevelopment, poverty, corruption, conflicts.

> After several decades of large international aid flows to Africa, approaching or exceeding an estimated 1-trillion dollars in total, simply "more" is clearly not the answer. (Larry Diamond)[1]

---

[1] Larry Diamond, "Forward" in *Smart aid for African Development,* ed. By Richard Joseph and Alexandra Gillies (Boulder London: Lynne Rienner Publishers, 2009), vii.

Introduction

This statement by Larry Diamond remains relevant after a decade. The African continent is richly endowed with natural resources, but the resources have not been effectively utilized. While receiving foreign aid seems to translate to acceptance of incapacitation on the part of the recipient, the idealist might view such aid as the generosity of the giver. Whatever the receiving of foreign aid translates to, the emergence of Africa as a foreign aid receiving continent was because of the United States (US) strategic national interest to curtail the communist global onslaught during the Cold War. After the end of the Cold War, the major capitalist countries mounted pressure for democratization in Africa, and as part of such pressure, they provided financial aid to the relevant countries. Indeed, after the Cold War ended, major capitalist actors demanded open and purposeful governance in Africa or pressured sit-tight political leaders in the continent to open up the political space for competition and inclusive governance. In terms of aid provision, they often gave priority to those who were more willing to run inclusive governance. However, for many African political forces, opening up political space for competition and inclusive governance brought new challenges that undermined their efforts to cater to the needs of people. To enhance their ability to cater to the needs of their citizens, therefore, many African leaders were often forced to seek more aid, and in the end, Africa remains a major aid-receiving continent today. This chapter explores some aspects of the history of foreign aid to Africa.

Foreign aid is often a difficult concept to define, but it broadly refers to financial grants, loans, materials, labor, or expertise given to a needy nation. This is classified into two broad groups: humanitarian aid and developmental aid. Humanitarian aid targets immediate outcome or short-term results, such as when aid is given to managing disaster situations like the Ebola disease, the COVID-19 pandemic, the civil war-based refugee problems, and the drought-based malnutrition problems. The main target of this form of aid is saving lives under immediate threat. Developmental aid, on the other hand, has a long-term target. Aid meant to respond to systemic problems, for economic, social, and political development is considered developmental aid because the result might be expected in the long term. Humanitarian aid is used interchangeably with humanitarian assistance or emergency aid, especially when developed countries are offering immediate assistance in response to disaster emergencies or problems emanating from conflicts.[2] Aid is given for humanitarian assistance and usually comes in the form of grants, which do not necessarily attract interest rates, but aid given for developmental projects attracts low-interest

---

[2] Lawson, Marian L., and Emily M. Morgenstern, "Foreign aid: An introduction to US programs and policy", *Congressional Research Service (R40213)* (2019). Also, Immanuel Fillemon Wise, B. Econs, and German Berlin, "Is Western Aid to Africa the Solution to the Embattled Continental Economy?, *The International Symposium on Cultural Diplomacy in Africa* 4 (2011), 11–17.

rates repayable over a long period. It is worth noting that the definition of aid offered by the US Foreign Assistance Act of 1961 (FAA) captures the whole gamut of foreign aid. According to the Act, foreign aid is;

> "any tangible or intangible item provided by the United States Government (including through a gift, loan, sale, credit, or guaranty), to a foreign country or international organization under this or any other Act, including but not limited to any training, service, or technical advice, any item of real, personal, or mixed property, any agricultural commodity, United States dollars, and any currencies of any foreign country which are owned by the United States Government."[3]

Even though this definition captures the gamut of foreign aid, we must bear in mind that the United States is not the only country that offers foreign aid to Africa. Indeed, in addition to other developed countries, private organizations and multilateral financial institutions (such as the World Bank and the United Nations) often provide humanitarian and other forms of aid to countries in Africa.

In their contributions to the expanding literature on foreign aid, some scholars have focused on the issue of the emergence and motive of foreign aid. Some scholars who emphasized these issues employ a realist paradigm to explain foreign aid. In this regard, they portray foreign aid as an instrument for fostering the national interest of the donor countries on recipient nations. They claim, for example, that although under the Marshall Plan of 1948–1951 executed by the US, foreign aid was initially meant to protect recipient nations from the perceived threat posed by the communist ideology.[4] In contrast to the realists, idealists view foreign aid as a humanitarian act motivated by compassion to help nations in need of assistance. Idealists stress the liberalism that favors interdependence among nations, and some of them expect that foreign aid given to Africa will lead to modernization and other positive changes.[5] Among the idealists, some stress a theory known as "The Big Push Model".[6] According to this model, Africa is poor because it is stuck in a "poverty trap," and to get out of this trap, it needs a significant amount of aid to give local investment a "Big Push". For those who embrace this model, if saving is too low to keep up with population growth and the depreciation of capital, then per capita growth will be zero or negative, resulting in a poverty trap. Therefore, according to

---

[3] Marian L. Lawson, and Emily M. Morgenstern, "Foreign aid: An introduction to US programs and policy", 1.

[4] Craig A Snyder,""Contemporary Security and Strategy", in *Contemporary security and strategy* (London: Palgrave, 1999), 1–12; see also John Baylis, James Wirtz, and Colin Gray eds., *Strategy in the Contemporary World* (New York: Oxford University Press, 2018).

[5] Richard Jackson, Georg Sørensen, and Jørgen Møller, *Introduction to International Relations: Theories and Approaches* (New York: Oxford University Press, 2019).

[6] Walt Whitman Rostow, *The Stages of Economic Growth: A Non-Communist Manifesto* (Cambridge: Cambridge University Press, 1990); see also Hollis B. Chenery and Alan M. Strout, "Foreign Assistance and Economic Development: Reply", *The American Economic Review* 58, 4 (1968), 912–16; William Easterly, "Can Foreign Aid Save Africa?"Clemens Lecture Series, 13(2005), https://digitalcommons.csbsju.edu/clemens_lectures/13.

them, the role of aid is to fill the financing gap caused by the distance between the low domestic saving rate and the investment requirement.

In their contributions to the expanding literature of foreign aid, other scholars have concentrated on examining why Africa has continued to demand such aid despite huge assistance, including debt relief received from donors. Among those who have examined this question, some blame the conditionalities attached to aid by donor countries. For instance, Hudson in his book *Killing the Host: How Financial Parasites and Debt Destroy Global Economy* argues that "the financial sector has the same objective as military conquest: to gain control of land and basic infrastructure and collect tribute….as long as debt-strapped nations permit bankers and bondholders to dictate their laws and control their planning and politics."[7] Hudson's position conforms to what Okonjo-Iweala refers to as "hawking of loans by creditor nations" that entice African governments to take loans on the condition of accepting the Structural Adjustment Programs (SAP).[8] SAP intensified Africa's integration into the global capitalist economy. Before accepting to implement the SAP, many African states were at a different level of economic development, but common to them was poverty and infrastructural decay. Thus, despite the oil boom of 1971–81, some countries like Nigeria had to approach the IMF/World Bank for funds that they would use for state projects. Rapley argues that the IMF forced Nigeria and other African states into accepting neoclassical economic policies in return for aid.[9] However, Okonjo-Iweala[10] and Rapley[11] also show that some African countries did not fully adopt the neoclassical prescription. Okonjo-Iweala in particular notes that Nigerians were skeptical about the IMF recipe; therefore, they came up with a new program called National Economic Empowerment and Development Strategy (NEEDS) to prove to the international body that Nigeria can tackle a number of her economic problems if granted debt relief.

Some scholars argue that SAP is ineffective because it is based on a rational economic theorem that does not take into consideration the ecology of the African sociopolitical environment. They further suggest that for it to be effective, the IMF, World Bank, and other donor agencies should drop ideas that optimize profits and create conditions that favor or leverages needy nations. To scholars such as Käkönen,[12]

---

[7] Michael Hudson, *Killing the Host: How Financial Parasites and Debt Bondage Destroy the Global Economy* (Baskerville: Institute for the Study of Long-Term Economic Trends (ISLET): CounterPunch,2015), 37.

[8] Ngozi Okonjo-Iweala, *Reforming the Unreformable: Lessons from Nigeria* (Cambridge: MIT Press, 2014), 96.

[9] John Rapley, *Understanding Development: Theory and Practice in the Third World* (London: UCL Press, 1997), 96.

[10] Ngozi Okonjo-Iweala*Reforming the Unreformable*, 99.

[11] Rapley. *Understanding Development*, 69.

[12] JyrkiKäkönen, "The World Bank: A Bridgehead of Imperialism", *Instant Research on Peace and Violence* 5, 3 (1975):150–64.

Isbister,[13] Griffith-Jones,[14] Ismi,[15] Bond,[16] Stiglitz and Tsuda,[17] Moyo,[18] and Muhumed and Gas,[19] the economic relations between developing nations and developed nations is only parasitic (and beneficial to the former). However, it is significant to note that one problem with these scholars' interpretation is that it is not guided by the logic of capitalism, a logic that will never tolerate that aid should be given to a wasteful government which may result that the giver may, at the long run, also become poor and a receiver.

In contrast to those who blame the conditionalities attached to aid by donor countries, other scholars blame African countries for their continuing demand for foreign aid and developmental assistance. It is evident that the scholars who blame African countries often tied the inability of such societies to provide a rule of law and sound economic policies to their continuing demand for foreign aid and developmental assistance. It is also evident that many African countries have been unable to provide a rule of law and sound economic policies since they achieved independence from European rule. Isbister refers to the poor economic policies of the immediate post-independence era as a "false start".[20] Other scholars, like Castles,[21] Banaji,[22] Empson,[23] and Wood,[24] note that, rather than emphasizing institutions that build up human capacity that spurs research on technology, African governments went into the consumption of imported luxury goods from developed countries immediately after achieving independence. Such governments obtained foreign loans to pay for the luxury goods consumed by the emerging middle-classes, who were often strong supporters of the ruling political parties. Over time, the continuing reliance on imported goods dominated the economy, and it resulted in Africa's entrepreneurs devoting their ingenuity to obtaining official privileges rather than to increasing production. For many critics of African governments, therefore, it was

---

[13] John Isbister, *Promises not Kept: The Betrayal of Social Change in the Third World* (West Hartford, Connecticut: Kumarian Press Inc., 1991).
[14] Stephan Griffith-Jones, "Governance of the World Bank", *Report prepared for DFID, Institute for* (2002).
[15] Asad Ismi, *Impoverishing a continent: The World Bank and the IMF in Africa* (Ottawa: Canadian Centre for Policy Alternatives), 2004.
[16] Patrick Bond, *Looting Africa: The Economics of Exploitation* (London: Zed Books, 2006).
[17] Joseph E. Stiglitz and Tsuda Kenta, "Democratizing the World Bank", *The Brown Journal of World Affairs* 13, 2 (2007), 79–86.
[18] Dambisa Moyo, *Dead Aid: Why Aid is not Working and How There is a Better Way for Africa* (London: Macmillan, 2009).
[19] Muhumed Mohamed,and Sayid Aden Gas, "The World Bank and IMF in Developing Countries: Helping or Hindering?" *World* 28 (2016).
[20] Isbister, *Promises not Kept*, 150.
[21] Francis G. Castles, *The Disappearing State?* (London: Edward Elgar Publishing, 2007).
[22] Jairus Banaji, *Theory as History: Essays on Modes of Production and Exploitation* (Chicago: Brill, 2010).
[23] Martin Empson, *Food, Agriculture, and Climate Change* (London: International Socialism, 2016).
[24] Ellen M. Wood, *The Origin of Capitalism* (London: Verso, 2017).

the rent-seeking society that they were based on that resulted in economic stagnation, continuing demand for foreign aid, and such other problems, according to Isbister,[25] and Kitschelt, and Wilkinson.[26]

Without attempting to refute any of the theories discussed above, the task of the next section of this chapter is to draw on diverse sources such as journal articles, newspapers, magazines, and online World Bank/IMF papers. This is to provide a brief survey of the origin and growth of the foreign aid to Africa and essentially to: identify the agencies providing aid to Africa; appropriate discursively the different types of aid that donors provide to Africa; and lastly, to identify foreign aid disbursement hurdles. In addressing these issues, the next section seeks to establish that, since the 1940s, Africa has remained a major aid-receiving continent. It also seeks to demonstrate that local corruption, the conflicting agendas of external forces, and African leaders undermine the aim of foreign aid disbursements in Africa.

Aid to Africa as a Phenomenon

Foreign aid in its modern form began in the 1940s. This became more pronounced after World War II when America deployed the Marshall Plan of 1948–1951 to rebuild an economically devastated Europe. Under the Marshall Plan, (which was also known as the European Recovery Program), the USA transferred 2–3 percent of its national income to help restore Europe.[27] In its commitment to contain the spread of communism in Africa, the United States also started providing financial and material support to African countries shortly after it introduced the Marshall Plan. By the 1960s, the European economies had recovered thanks to the Marshall Plan, and this recovery contributed to encouraging erstwhile colonial powers to provide aid to Africa.

Today, aid is considered the biggest part of the world's development cooperation, and it involves the flow of money from developed to developing countries. Aid is also known as Official Development Assistance (ODA) when it comes from any Development Assistance Committee member government. Staicu and Barbulescu[28] show that, since 1961, twenty-nine developed countries (including those that constitute the European Union) decided to work with Development Assistance Committee (DAC) and the broader Organization for Economic Cooperation and Development

---

25 Wood, *The Origin of Capitalism*, 165.
26 Herbert Kitschelt and Steven I. Wilkinson, eds., *Patrons, Clients and Policies: Patterns of Democratic Accountability and Political Competition* (Cambridge: Cambridge University Press, 2007).
27 Finn Tarp *etal.*, "Aid Effectiveness", A Note Prepared Based Both on Joint Work with Channing Arndt and Sam Jones Including an Unpublished Report for NORAD and 2009 UNU-WIDER Research Paper Entitled *"Aid and Growth: Have We Come Full Circle?"* (Dated September 2009), 1–22.
28 Gabriel Staicu and Razvan Barbulescu, "A Study of the Relationship Between Foreign Aid and Human Development in Africa", *International Development* (2017), 135–51.

(OECD) to provide official assistance to developing countries. ODA has three key elements: (1) it targets improving living conditions and the welfare of poor countries. (2) OECD assists their governments or their national agencies. (3) The assistance could take the form of a grant or a loan at an interest rate lower than the market rate.

While African and non-African countries receive aid from various donors, countries outside of Africa like South Korea, Malaysia, Singapore, Hong Kong, and Taiwan have been able to develop technology that enabled them to produce manufactured goods that spread relevant benefits to the poor. Thus, it is mainly in Africa that one finds serious problems in the areas of life expectancy, education, infant mortality, hunger, diseases, wars, and infrastructure. According to Tarp, since poor African countries lack physical capital, human capital, technology, and well-functioning institutions, their demand for foreign aid becomes a matter of necessity.[29] In the same vein, Derryck argues that "the continent has virtually every development paradox confronting aid workers and donors: periodic famine, endemic disease, persistent illiteracy, decaying infrastructure, and underperforming economies."[30] By 2005, in recognition of the serious problems in Africa, British Prime Minister Tony Blair rallied G8 members to support the creation of a Commission for Africa, as a measure for strengthening African capacity through expanded investments in human capacity building, poverty reduction, growth, and increased trade.[31] By that year, therefore, G8 members of the Commission for Africa planned to provide twenty-five billion dollars per year in development assistance to Africa to 2010. It also planned to provide an additional $25 billion by 2015 after careful consideration of the outcome of the first disbursement made in 2005.[32]

As De Laat and Gorin note, in the period after 2015, "for better or worse, humanitarianism is more closely associated with sub-Saharan Africa than anywhere else."[33] In many ways, most of the African continent has "been the crucible and proving ground for modern humanitarian action: the site of hideous famines, diseases and conflicts, and the arena in which some of the formative moments of contemporary humanitarian history have been played out."[34] More recent research conducted after the publication of the work of De Laat and Gorin, stresses that humanitarian assistance, unlike development aid, is devoted largely to the immediate alleviation of human suffering in emergencies, both natural and man-made. Such studies identify the refugee, hunger, and other problems related to such events like the Nigerian civil war of 1967–1970, the Rwandan genocide of 1994, the 1997 massacres in Zaire

---

[29] Staicu and Barbulescu, "A Study of the Relationship between Foreign," 2.
[30] Vivian Lowery Derryck, "The Commission for Africa: Assessing the Approach", *Smart Aid for African development* (2009), 49–64.
[31] Derryck, "The Commission for Africa", 50.
[32] Commission for Africa, *Our Common Interest: An Argument* (Penguin UK, 2005), 16.
[33] Sonya De Laatand Valérie Gorin,"3 Iconographies of Humanitarian Aid in Africa", *HPG* 15 (2016): 1.
[34] Sonya De Laat and Valérie Gorin,"3 Iconographies of Humanitarian Aid in Africa", 2.

and South Sudan, the ongoing massacre in Somalia, and the Boko Haram insurgency in the Northern Nigeria, as man-made humanitarian emergencies. Relief materials, food, technical assistance including the outright transfer of cash are provided to African governments that experience such humanitarian emergencies. Besides, such aid is used to finance international non-governmental organizations (INGOs) or their national counterparts (NGOs) called to provide assistance where government forces cannot do that.[35]

In the last two decades, many African countries have received considerable aid from the United States Agency for International Development (USAID). For example, between 2010–2019 USAID disaster response funding for West Africa shows that Nigeria got $1,104,409,859, Chad $793,002,048, Niger $552,388,871 and Mali $408,402,195. Even in April 2020, the African Development Bank AfDB announced the creation of a new COVID-19 Response Facility to assist regional member countries in fighting the pandemic. The facility is designed to provide up to $10 billion in financial support, including $5.5 billion in market-based financial assistance to governments, $3.1 billion in concessional financial assistance to governments, and $1.35 billion in market-based financial assistance to the private sector. Other financial institutions have responded to the problems caused by COVID-19. Nelson and Weiss[36] show that amid the pandemic more than half of the IMF's membership has requested IMF support, and the IMF announced taping into its total lending capacity of about $1 trillion, to support governments in Africa and elsewhere responding to COVID-19. The World Bank has committed to mobilizing $160 billion over the next fifteen months, and other multilateral development banks have committed to providing $80 billion during that period. A US Fact Sheet shows that the US is the leading donor in response to COVID-19 to Africa amounting to several billions of dollars, which means Africa will continue to service its debt and will continue to borrow as it struggles to manage a humanitarian crisis.

In addition to USAID, aid to Africa is provided by several agencies, including bilateral donors like governments of developed nations, multilateral donors like the World Bank and IMF, non-governmental organizations, corporate business bodies like multinational companies, and individual industrialists. These multiple donors create problems for coordination among recipient nations in Africa. Multiple donors raise the problem of harmonization. For example, the figure below shows bilateral donors as contained in the Lawson and Morganstern2019 report.

On the other hand, the table below shows the top 10 recipients of ODA in Africa.

---

[35] Marc Lindenberg and Bryant Coralie, *Going Global: Transforming Relief and Development NGOs* (Bloomfield, CT: Kumarian Press, 2001).
[36] Rebecca M. Nelson and Martin A.Weiss,"COVID-19: Role of International Financial Institutions," https://crsreports.congress.gov R46342. *Congressional Research Service* (2020), accessed 4th May 2020.

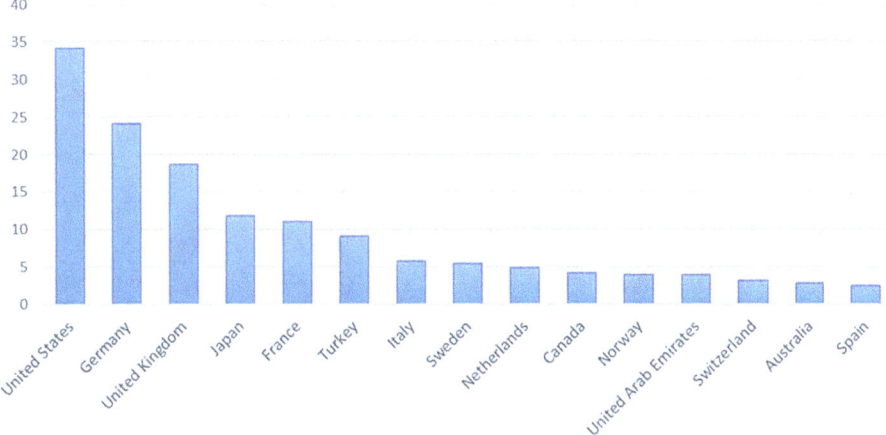

Figure 1. Top 15 Bilateral Donors of Official Development Assistance, 2017. (In billions of dollars)
Source: Marian L. Lawson, and Emily M. Morgenstern. "Foreign aid: An introduction to US programs and policy." *Congressional Research Service (R40213)* (2019).

Table 1. Top 10 ODA receipts by the recipient. USD million, net disbursements in 2017

Top 10 ODA receipts by the recipient.	USD million, net disbursements in 2017	
1	Ethiopia 4 117	8%
2	Nigeria 3 359	6%
3	Tanzania 2 584	5%
4	Kenya 2 475	5%
5	The Democratic Republic of the Congo 2 280	4%
6	South Sudan 2 183	4%
7	Uganda 2 008	4%
8	Morocco 1 885	4%
9	Mozambique 1 776	3%
10	Somalia 1 760	3%
11	Other recipients 28 373	54%
TOTAL	52 800	100%

Source: Development aid at a glance: Statistics by region. 2. Africa 2019 edition.
Development Aid at a Glance: Statistics by Region: Official Development Assistance (ODA). http://www.oecd.org/dac/financing-sustainable-development. Accessed 5/30/2020

Equally, the figure below shows US-specific aid to 11 recipient countries in Africa. The figure shows that request for aid is already available for the 2021 financial year.

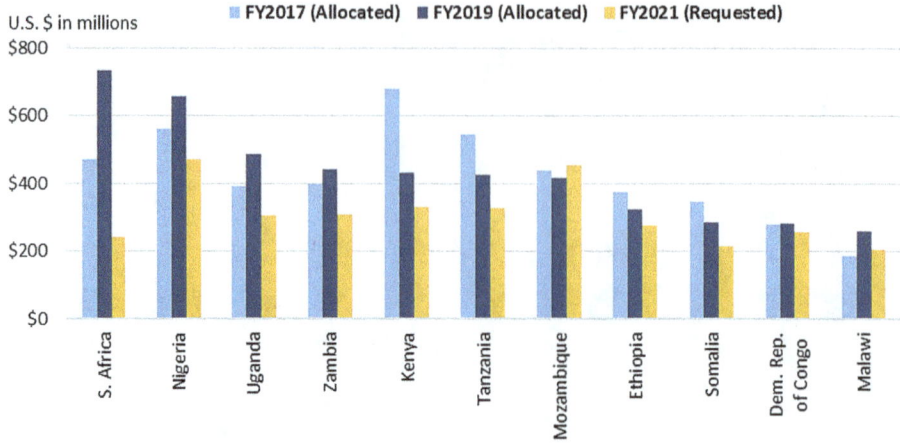

Figure 2. U.S. Aid to Africa, Top Recipients, Recent Allocations vs. FY2021 Request[37]
Source: Nicolas Cook, Alexis Arieff, Lauren Ploch Blanchard, B. Williams, and T. Husted. "Sub-Saharan Africa: Key issues, challenges, and US responses." *Washington, DC. Congressional Research Service* (2017). Updated May 2020.

In a major study, Lancaster[38] highlights the challenge of carrying out aid under different titles through different institutions. In so doing, he even stresses that the involvement of several US-based agencies like the USAID, the Department of State, Millennium Challenge Corporation (MCC), the US Treasury, and the Department of Defence (DOD), raises the problem of coordination and coherence. In the latter regard, such involvement of diverse institutions is known to have produced incoherency in program execution and operations, which, in turn, sometimes put transaction costs on both recipient and donor countries. For example, in the context in which the World Bank and IMF fund a project in Africa with money derived from Canada and in which Canada funds the same project in the continent, the recipient country is expected to coordinate and pay multiple interests, which goes to one donor through several sources.

Multilateral financial institutions are established to provide financial assistance to developing countries in the form of loans and grants for investment projects and policy-based loans. They target large infrastructural projects, such as highways, power plants, port facilities, and dams, as well as social projects, including health

---

[37] For a list containing US aid to all states in Africa, see Nicolas Cook, Alexis Arieff, Lauren Ploch Blanchard, B. Williams, and T. Husted, "Sub-Saharan Africa: Key Issues, Challenges, and US Responses", *Washington D.C. Congressional Research Service* (2017). Updated May 20, 2020. https://crsreports.congress.govR46368.

[38] Carol Lancaster, "How Smart are Aid Donors? The Case of the United States", *Smart Aid for African Development*(Boulder: Lynne Rienner Publishers,2009), 31–48.

and education initiatives,[39] and The World Bank/IMF[40] the oldest of these institutions. The World Bank's active record shows that Africa received the aid of 77.7 billion Dollars in 2019.[41] I show in table 2 below the bilateral debt owed by some African countries to the US alone. In the same vein, figure 3 shows US assistance to Africa in FY2019, by Program Area. The aid, including the debt, excludes aid disbursed to contain COVID-19.

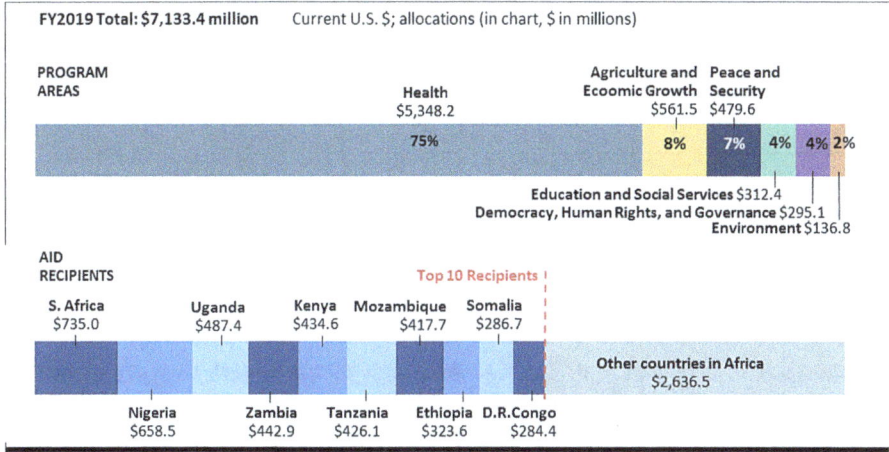

Figure 3. US Assistance to Africa in FY2019, by Program Area.
Source: Nicolas Cook, Alexis Arieff, Lauren Ploch Blanchard, B. Williams, and T. Husted, "Sub-Saharan Africa: Key issues, challenges, and US responses", *Washington D. C. Congressional Research Service* (2017). Updated May 20, 2020.https://crsreports.congress.gov R46368.

---

39 Rebecca M. Nelson, "Multilateral Development Banks: Overview and Issues for Congress", Library of Congress, *Congressional Research Service*, 2012. Updated 11February 2020.
40 NewAfrican, Cover Story: The case against IMF, World Bank, (2007: 18–20). World Bank was established in 1944, when 44 countries gathered in a conference after the Second World War in the New Hampshire resort town of Bretton Woods to deliberate on global economic rules that would promote stability, prevent another great depression and devise strategy that would rebuild Europe once the war ends. Intended to serve as International Clearing Union (ICU) as suggested by John Maynard Keynes (a world-renowned economist who represented the United Kingdom (UK), was rejected by US who instead proposed a creation of international monetary fund that will aim at lending money to countries with financial deficits. That saw to establishment of International Monetary Fund (IMF). Lending money to countries with financial deficits contrast with the intention of ICU which was to provide funds to balance government experiencing trade and other payments deficits with those in surplus.
41 Nelsonand Weiss,"COVID-19: Role of International," 1.

Table 2. shows the bilateral debt owed by the US by low-income countries in December 2019. Amounts expressed in US dollars.

Sudan	2986.3
Somali	1101.8
Zimbabwe	300.9
Ghana	284.4
Cameroon	100.7
Zambia	69.1
Eritrea	34.6
Kenya	21.6
Mozambique	3.5
Nigeria	3.0
Côte d'Ivoire	2.1

Source: Rebecca M. Nelson and Martin A. Weiss, "COVID-19: Role of International Financial Institutions". https://crsreports.congress.gov R46342. Congressional Research Service (2020). Accessed 4th May 2020.

The World Bank has three sub institutions: the International Bank for Reconstruction and Development (IBRD), the International Development Association (IDA), and the International Finance Corporation (IFC) that make loans and grants to developing countries. The United States has the largest financial commitment to the IBRD, accounting for 16.57 percent of total IBRD resources. The U.S. paid-in capital is $2.9 billion and U.S. callable capital is $43.5 billion. The IBRD earns income on its equity investments and the interest it charges on loans, which it uses to pay for World Bank operating expenses. Furthermore, World Bank has two other specialized institutions that are not involved in giving loans or grants to developing countries but are involved in helping to raise confidence levels for donor agencies giving grants or loans to developing countries. Examples of specialized institutions that help to raise confidence levels for donors include the Multilateral Investment Guarantee Agency (MIGA) that provides political risk insurance to foreign investors, the International Centre for Settlement of Investment Disputes (ICSID) that provides facilities for conciliation and arbitration of disputes between governments and private foreign investors.[42]

---

[42] One critique against World Bank is that it provides loans to corrupt or authoritarian governments in Africa, ignoring that such loans may not be paid back or not utilized for public interest (I will return to this debate later). Therefore, it is important to note that MIGA and ICSID serves as insurance or safety valve incase of default from recipient governments.

Nelson shows that across the 18 replenishments of resources since IDA's creation, donor countries have contributed $258 billion to IDA.[43] The IBRD can borrow from international capital markets because it is backed by the guarantees of member governments. IBRD's total capital is $280 billion. Most of the capital ($263 billion) is guarantees from donor countries ("callable" capital) and a small portion ($17 billion, about 6 percent) has been paid to the IBRD by donor countries ("paid-in" capital). Because the funds come from different donors, it is not given free and without conditionality, as some critics may expect.[44] The IMF and World Bank have a set condition that must be met by African countries before they can access the loans.[45] The IMF lending conditionality as argued by Wood[46] differs in some countries, but the fundamental thrust is that the borrowing nation must enact policy reform that will encourage private sector investment, decentralization of public service provisioning, private sector provision of basic infrastructure, liberalization of trade, privatization of state-owned agricultural enterprise, reform of public financial management and accountability procedures. The reform known as the Structural Adjustment Program (SAP) is heavily criticized by African nations because they are unable to repay their loan.[47] However, the IMF and World Bank argue that debtor countries are not able to repay their loans due to failures in the structure of their economies and so they need to stabilize and adjust to overcome their structural problems.[48] Besides the World Bank and IMF, the African Development Bank (AFDB) lends money to African nations. The AFDB was founded in 1974. The US joined in 1976, and to date is the second-largest contributor to the bank. In 1982, the concession was opened to other countries, and it and now has eighty states as shareholders, fifty-four of which are Africans, and the rest are from the Americas, Asia, and Europe. It gives loans to private sector firms through its non-concessional window, with a special focus on development in the region.[49]

Aid to Africa is of various types. The table below shows the various types of aid and the amount in the US dollar to Africa in 2017.

---

[43] Rebecca M. Nelson, "Multilateral Development Banks: US Contributions FY2000-FY2020", (2020).
[44] Muhumed and Gas, p. 4. The authors argued that both institutions are used to protect the interest of the West and are imperialists tools, arguing that they replicate the dominance and dependency system that enable foreign capital to get easy and safe access to the market and investment fields of developing countries.
[45] Martin Knoll, *Budget Support: A Reformed Approach or Old Wine in New Skins?* No. 190. United Nations Conference on Trade and Development, 2008;Alexandra Gillies and Joseph Richard Joseph, "Smart Aid: The Search for Transformative Strategies", *Smart Aid for African Development* (2009): 1–14; Ngozi Okonjo-Iweala, *Reforming the Unreformable: Lessons from Nigeria* (MIT Press, 2014).
[46] A. Wood, "World Bank's Poverty Reduction Support Credit—Continuity or Change?"(Dublin: Debt and Development Coalition Ireland2005), 7.
[47] I will return to this argument later.
[48] *New African Magazine*, "The case against IMF and World Bank: How IMF, World Bank Failed Africa", January 2007, No. 458,www.Africasia.com, 21.
[49] Nelson, "Multilateral Development Banks: Overview and Issues for Congress".

Table 3. ODA to Africa by sector and recipient in 2017 US Million Dollar Commitments

Social	Economic	Production	Multi-Sector	General Program Aid	Debt	Humanitarian	Others	Total
28 212	13 618	8 174	4 114	3 372	159	8 256	1 454	67 359

Source: Development aid at a glance: Statistics by region. 2. Africa 2019 edition. http://www.oecd.org/dac/financing-sustainable-development/

As table 3 shows, humanitarian aid is in a separate role like others. Unlike humanitarian aid, other titles including general program aid, social aid, and production aid may encompass other titles not specified. Regardless of this fact, aid allocation generally follows the law of comparative advantage championed by the World Trade Organization's (WTO) international economic order.[50] For example, even though the European Development Fund (EDF) disburses aid to Africa for the export of agricultural products and solid minerals through its STABEX and SYSMIN funds respectively, some countries are qualified to receive aid to export only agricultural products based on their ability to cultivate crops more efficiently than mining solid mineral.

Available evidence indicates that even though individual donor countries have followed different strategies in aid disbursement to Africa, their approach often included conditionality similar to those evident in World Bank/IMF aid disbursements. For instance, conditionalities are evident in the aid offered by China to Nigeria following the failure of the 340 million dollars (₦50.3 billion). This project is titled the NIGCOMSAT-1 project (a fifteen-year project started in 2007 in which China agreed to build a telecommunications satellite for Nigeria that will provide broadband multimedia services, telecommunications, and broadcastings).[51] Lucas reveals that the aid China offered to Nigeria to build another telecommunication satellite after the failure of the NIGCOMSAT-1 project was designed to prevent "competitive bidding" or that it was tied to at least one condition that did not benefit Nigeria: that a Chinese engineering company including its personnel who must execute the project.[52]

As part of its strategy of maintaining control over some African societies or of protecting its interests in Africa, China also uses aid or investment to threaten the former. For instance, Majirioghene shows that China threatened to withdraw its investment from South Africa when the latter invited the Dalai Lama, the Tibetan spi-

---

[50] Humphrey Orjiako, *Killing Sub-Saharan Africa with Aid* (New York: Nova Publishers, 2001);Joseph E. Stiglitz and Andrew Charlton, *The Development Round of Trade Negotiations in the Aftermath of Cancun* (Commonwealth Secretariat, 2004).

[51] *The Business Eye Magazine*, "China to replace NIGCOMSAT-1 for free", 30 March. www.businesseyeng.com. (2009), 24. See also Lucas Muyiwa, "China: The new bride on the runway", *Tell Magazine*, October 21, No. 42. (2013), 18.

[52] Zhao Yingjie, "Chinese NGOs' Humanitarian and Development Aid in Africa: The Case of the China Foundation for Poverty Alleviation" (2018) https://ihsa.info/content/uploads/sites/2/papers/215/20180712111352/Conference%20article.docx.

ritual leader, to attend a peace conference in South Africa in 2009.[53] The threat worked as the Dalai Lama was denied a South African visa. It should be mentioned that the Dalai Lama got into trouble with China when, in 2009, or on the fifteenth anniversary of his failed Tibetan uprising, he complained about the maltreatment of his people by the Chinese government. It should also be stressed that China also used aid to threaten Nigeria when it invited the Dalai Lama to attend the tenth session of the Emmanuel Onyechere Osigwe-Anyiam-Osigwe lecture series at the Nigeria Institute of International Affairs (NIIA), Lagos, in November 2008. As part of this Nigerian incident, China threatened to close its investment up to the tune of $2.8 billion, mostly in the oil and gas sector of the Nigerian economy. However, unlike the case of South Africa, Nigeria granted the Dalai Lama a visa to attend the lecture series, even though invited key Nigerian figures like the President, vice president, governor of Lagos, and the Sultan of Sokoto did not show up to the event.

That aid is channeled through major financial institutions like the World Bank and IMF is indisputable. However, largely from the 1990s, the donor countries have coalesced their aid strategy to Africa under what is referred to as General Budget Support (GBS).[54] Budget support is an aid modality that involves making a direct money transfer to the treasuries of the recipient government contrary. This aid modality is remarkable partly because even though it is an idea developed by OECD countries, it seeks to empower Heavily Indebted Poor Countries (HIPC) to devise their strategic plans for poverty reduction and reform. With the notable exception of the US, other major bilateral donors like Britain, the Netherlands, and the Scandinavian countries provide a quarter of their aid through Budget Support.

Another effort aimed at allowing Africans to devise their plans for poverty reduction is known as the Poverty Reduction Strategy. Countries that have embraced the Poverty Reduction strategy like Uganda and Tanzania have produced Poverty Reduction Strategy Papers. The World Bank and IMF's Board of Governors have adopted the strategic plans articulated under such Poverty Reduction Strategy Papers (PRSP). Ultimately, these world financial bodies require low-income countries that qualify for IDA to develop their own PRSP.[55] As Barkan notes, the adoption of the strategy that requires recipient countries to devise their plans for poverty reduction rather than being pressured to implement a list of donor conditions is a response to the demand for ownership of reform programs by recipient governments.[56]

---

53 Bob Majiriogehene, "Derailing the Rails,"*Tell Magazine*, June 1, No. 22. (2009), 44–45.
54 Joel Barkan, "Rethinking Budget Support for Africa: A Political Economy Perspective", in *Smart Aid for African Development*, ed. by Richard Joseph and Alexandra Gillies (Boulder, Colorado: Lynne Rienner Publishers, 2009); Knoll, *Budget Support: A Reformed Approach or Old Wine in New Skins?*,p. 12.
55 World Bank. *Partners in Transforming Development: New Approaches to Developing Country-owned Poverty Reduction Strategies*, http://www.imf.org/external/np/prsp/pdf/[rspbroc.pdf. (2000), 3.
56 Barkan, "Rethinking Budget Support for Africa," 71.

The New Partnership for Africa's Development (NEPAD), noted by Adesina, *et al.*, was another effort aimed at reducing poverty and at promoting growth and development in Africa.[57] NEPAD is the brainchild of African leaders like Abdelaziz Bouteflika (Algeria), Thabo Mbeki (South Africa), Olusegun Obasanjo (Nigeria), and Abdoulaye Wade (Senegal), who wanted to take "ownership" of political and economic reforms or who wanted to demonstrate that Africans were serious about economic and political reforms. To foster the achievement of its diverse goals, NEPAD introduced the African Peer Review Mechanism (APRM) in 2005. This mechanism was specifically designed to monitor and evaluate each countries performance. APRM is a good initiative but the workability is in question since it did not overrule African Union (AU) Charter on the principle of non-interference in the internal affairs of Member States. Moreover, although African governments articulated their "wishes" or wanted to take "ownership" of reforms under NEPAD and PRSP, the creation of the Poverty Reduction Strategy Credit (PRSC) by the World Bank in 2001 raises doubt over the "ownership" of reforms or of the implementation process by the aid recipient governments.

Another instrument that undermines the usefulness of NEPAD and PRSP is known as the Poverty Reduction and Growth Facility (PRGF). The EC budget support, according to Knoll,[58] a study conducted by the Independent Evaluation Office of the IMF in 2004 and 2007 on aid delivery to sub-Saharan Africa indicated that PRSP policy did not provide the basis on which aid to recipient countries in Africa was based. Rather, it was based on macroeconomic policy recommendations in the PRGF. For African governments, the inconsistent application of either PRSP or PRSC documents by the bilateral donors complicates their efforts to shape poverty reduction in their societies. In terms of their aid to Africa, Knoll and other scholars demonstrated that the Norwegian Agency for Development Cooperation (NORAD) did not tie its disbursal decisions on the IMF or the World Bank's appraisal rather, she strives for consistency in conditionality among the NORAD donor groups.[59] The Swedish Agency for International Development Cooperation (SIDA), directly or indirectly through the EC, attached its decisions to the recipient(s) in compliance with PRDF conditionality on a case-by-case basis.[60] The Belgian budget-support scheme for Burkina Faso was attached to PRSC conditionality; the UK Department of International Development

---

[57] Jimi O. Adesina, Graham Yao and Adebayo Olukoshi (eds.), *Africa and Development Challenges in the New Millennium: The NEPAD Debate*. No. 5. (London: Zed Books, 2006).

[58] "E C. Budget Support: An Innovative Approach to Conditionality. Directorate General Development," February. http://spa.synisys.com/resources/2005/EC_GBS_VT_Review.pdf, (2005);Martin Knoll, *Budget Support: A Reformed Approach or Old Wine in New Skins?* (No. 190. United Nations Conference on Trade and Development, 2008), 9.

[59] NORAD, *Norway's Provision of Budget Support to Developing Countries: Guidelines*. (Oslo, 2006), 20.http://www.norad.no/default.asp?V_ITEM_ID=8208.

[60] SIDA, "Thirteen Questions and Answers About Swedish Budget Support"(2007), p. 35. Http://www.sida.se./sida/jsp/sida.jsp?d=1357&a=25107&language=en_US.

(DFID) draws it disbursal conditions from the PRSP, or PRGF if the aspect of the provision is consistent with the British approach, and the Danish International Development Agency (DANIDA) in dealing with Tanzania partly draws from PRSC and PRSP for prior actions. None of these show that PRSP as originally conceived is operational; therefore, recipient nations are tied up to IMF and World Bank conditionalities despite shifting towards GBS as well as despite forming NEPAD and allowing PRSP.

Two strands of debate emerge regarding how to balance the effectiveness of aid to African governments and societies. One strand of the debate places non-governmental organizations (NGOs) as a critical segment of the society that can liberate African states from the wastefulness and corruption that result in demand for foreign aid. The other strand of the debate interrogates the capacity of the non-governmental organizations to engage the states in question given the undemocratic structures of some of the civil societies, poor financial base, and outright usurpation of their independence in decision making by donor agencies. Gregory Mann and Benedetta Rossi's works highlight how the weak state structures of the Sahel region called for the intervention of NGOs.[61] Mann, for instance, presents the Sahel region as a 'political assemblage, a zone of intervention' characterized by open and masked military intervention.[62] According to him, the effect of military rule in the Sahel region of Niger and Mali resulted in the weakening of the state economy and relapse to authoritarian measures that abrogated civil rights and liberties in order to foster development by the military juntas. The problem in the region led to questions that interrogated the basis of government.[63] Rossi and Mann show that the civil society in the provision and service delivery in the Sahel region reshaped the power fields of governmentality through intense negotiation and collaboration between states and international organizations. Mann employed the term 'nongovernmentality' not just to invoke some form of state paralysis, but rather the outcome of the interplay between state and non-state actors in the field of political sovereignty in Mali and Niger. The interplay could raise some questions in the context of neutrality expected of the international NGOs' involvement in African development.[64]

Donor countries and agencies have brilliant ideas on how to help Africa escape poverty and other humanitarian calamities, but how the financial aid is utilized by western middlemen organizations often raises some questions about whether aid is meeting its objectives. Some of the western middlemen NGOs are known as the implementing partners (IP). Often from the donor countries, such IPs typically acted as

---

61 Gregory Mann, *From Empires to NGOs in the West African Sahel. The Road to Nongovernmentality* (Cambridge, Cambridge University Press, 2014); and Benedetta Rossi, "From Slavery to Aid. Politics, Labour, and Ecology in the Nigerien Sahel, 1800–2000," *The Journal of the International African Institute* 87, 1 (2017), 211–212.
62 Mann, *From Empires to NGOs*, 244.
63 *Ibid.*, 8.
64 Anderson M, African Report, NGOs: Blessing or Curse? https://www.theafricareport 2017. Accessed 6/30/2020

go-between African NGOs and the donor countries or agencies. One of the criticisms is that the funds meant for developing Africa are utilized by the IPs as operational costs. Kew argues that the western IP typically consumes much of the budget of the project since they need new office structures, expatriate staff, Western-standard facilities as well as the time acclimate to the African political landscape.[65] IPs have also been accused of setting the terms of the contract to replicate key features of neo-patrimonialism, and of furthering corruption among civil societies.

While the involvement of IPs often worsens the accountability problem among NGOs in Africa, the civil society groups yield to manipulation by the political class through funding and incorporation into ethnic politics that erodes any cross-cutting agenda. Politicization, therefore, becomes a major problem when countering the power of the state, checking its abuses, and exposing corruption. Where civil society is weak, political leaders initiate policies without restrain. For example, countries like Nigeria started playing the "big brother role" after independence after that was tied to oil export that is highly susceptible to international politics. After it survived all these foreign operational games to aid, a major internal conflict or civil war that caused a drain on the resources Nigeria quickly started playing the big brother role that undermined the economic principle of cost-efficiency. Fawole noted that Gowon's regime offered economic aid, technical assistance, interest-free loans, even sold petroleum at reduced prices to some countries as the Republic of Benin and the Niger Republic.[66] There is also evidence that in some instances, salaries of black people in Grenada and other parts of the world were even paid up by Nigeria. The evidence of corruption, which has reduced African governments to aid dependency, is well documented by the works of Reno,[67] Nyong'o,[68] Enweremadu,[69] Joseph,[70] and Pierce.[71] Nyong'o presents corruption in Africa as reflecting a way of life and notes, "Kenyans seem to adopt the time-honored philosophy of hearing nothing, seeing nothing, and saying nothing about corruption in public life."[72] Reporting on the Liberian case, Reno highlights a meeting held in Copenhagen in 2005 between donors and the Liberian government to address the issue of more

---

[65] Darren Kew, "Democratizing Donor-Civil Society Relations: Evidenced from Governance Programs in Nigeria" *Smart Aid for African Development*, 215,221.
[66] Alade W. Fawole, *Nigeria's External Relations and Foreign Policy Under Military Rule 1966 1999* (Ile-Ife: Obafemi Awolowo University Press Ltd., 2003),68.
[67] William Reno, "Rethinking Anticorruption Efforts in Liberia", in *Smart Aid for African Development*, 147–162.
[68] Peter Anyang Nyong'o, "Beyond the Political Economy of Corruption: The Kenyan Challenge," in *Smart Aid for African Development*, 163–180.
[69] David U. Enweremadu, "Anti-Corruption Campaign in Nigeria (1999–2007): The Politics of a Failed Reform", African Studies Centre, Leiden (2012).
[70] Joseph, Richard A. *Democracy and prebendal politics in Nigeria*. Vol. 56. Cambridge University Press, 2014.
[71] Steven Pierce, *Moral Economies of Corruption* (Duke University Press, 2016).
[72] Anyang, "Beyond the Political Economy of Corruption,"164.

than $520 million mismanaged aid given to Liberia after the end of almost fourteen years of war in 2003.[73] It is commonly believed that the "fight against corruption" in Africa is a plummet policy from the beginning because the people waiting to get the opportunity to loot the public treasury are more than those already looting the public treasury.

O'Donnell's account of the role of the legislature in keeping up with horizontal accountability is largely absent in Africa.[74] Clientelist or patronage relations have weakened the legislative role of representing the interest of ordinary citizens in the government. The instrument of oversight over what the executive arm does has turned out to be an instrument through which the legislatures threaten and bargain with the executive arm of government for a share of the public treasury. In this case, horizontal accountability becomes a mirage, and the civil society is made to "shut up"[75] because they have also been compromised through incorporation into the game of clientelism and patronage politics. Bratton and Logan argue that what emerges under such corrupt circumstances is "voters but not yet citizens".[76] Citizens cast votes on election day but there is no consensus among them that the purpose of government is to serve collective as against sectional interest. The end-result is fleecing of money into private hands, poverty, wars, and construction of extremist groups by the ruling parties to backup holding to power. As more monies are borrowed and wasted on frivolous things, responding to humanitarian emergencies becomes an insurmountable task. Africa, therefore, emerges as a continent riddled with humanitarian challenges as Ebola, HIV/AIDS, COVID-19 pandemic, erosion disasters, and refugee problems. With common news of internally displaced persons (IDPs), river blindness, an infestation of worms among children, hunger, poverty, migration, famine, children learning under the rain and scorching sun, drop out of children from school, girl child out of school, overpopulation, and such other problems African continent projects itself as the arena of hawking foreign aid with inevitable scorching conditionality. The scorching conditionalities probably could not have occurred if the resources wasted through corruption and financing intractable wars are available.

---

[73] Reno, "Rethinking Anticorruption Efforts", 147–162.
[74] Guillermo A. O'Donell, "Delegative Democracy", *Journal of Democracy* 5, 1 (1994), 55–69.
[75] Because civil societies in Africa lack fund for most their activities; they have become easy prey in the hands of both national politicians and donor agencies. Championing the interest of political leaders from the same ethnic groups by leaders of civil societies is common in Africa. Most scholars whose works have focused on civil societies in Africa (Makumbe 1998, Nwabueze 1993, Iwu 2010, Obadare 2011) raise these problems as well. J. Mw Makumbe, "Is There Civil a Society in Africa?"*International Affairs* 74, 2 (1998), 305–317; B. O Nwabueze, "A Virile Civil Society," in *Democratization*, ed. By B. O. Nwabueze (Spectrum Law Publishing, 1993), 84–91; H. N. Iwu, "Leadership and Good Governance: Civil Society Perspective" *Africa: Journal of Contemporary Issues*, 8, .8 (2010), 32–44; and E. Obadare, "Civil society in Sub-Saharan Africa," in *The Oxford Handbook of Civil Society*, ed. by Michael Edwards (Oxford: Oxford University Press, 2011), 183–196.
[76] Michael Brattonand Carolyn Logan, "Voters But not Yet Citizens: Democratization and Development Aid", *Smart Aid for African Development*, 181–206.

Conclusion

Africa has continued to receive foreign aid since 1940 from the US, Europe, Japan, and in recent times, China and India have joined as aid donors. Consistent aid to Africa raises worry over how the previous aid has been used. Repayment of the aid and interests upon it has continued to put a strain on the resources available to address other challenges, including humanitarian emergencies. Some African countries that have received debt relief continue to make further demands, showing a lack of prudent management of their resources. Failure to utilize aid by the African government is blamed on the conditionalities attached to the aid, but a contrary view blames it on their political leaders, with glaring evidence of institutional failure and corruption. This chapter shares the view that the logic of capitalism does not support wasteful spending, else, the donor will, in the long run, become a receiver of aid. Therefore, blaming aid conditionalities for the failure by African leaders to use the aid effectively cannot be sustained. Worrisomely, a continent enmeshed in ethnic politics that overrides the use of excellent minds cannot build strong institutions for research and innovation that can spur the technology needed to produce goods and services for global and domestic markets' needs.

Idom T. Inyabri
Chapter 19
Globalization, African Popular Culture and Hip Hop: An Embedded History

Abstract: This essay examines Nigerian hip hop exponents from the early 1990s who have taken advantage of the resources of globalization as cultural equipment to speak to their existential realities and empower themselves. Locating the study in the context of the socio-economic, political, and technological circumstances that define globalization, I posit that hip hop in Africa has offered Nigerian youth, like their peers all over Africa, the cultural handle to engage forces of global capitalism and articulate a liberal identity that confronts the conservative structures of their nations. Ultimately, I perceive hip hop as a popular culture practice that has creatively connected the African youth and Africa generally to a new global reality.

Keywords: Globalization, Popular Culture, hip hop, African Youth, Nigeria.

Introduction

> Though much has been written about 'globalization', more attention could be paid to the specific ways it works through local African scenes of cultural production and consumption, and the question of what African audiences actually do with, or make of, imported cultural products.[1]

Globalization has facilitated a seamless flow of economies around the world. However, it has inaugurated a cycle of activity that has ushered in a dimension of life that is determined by the same ideational, institutional, and technological infrastructure that were meant to facilitate a new world economy. Infrastructure such as the internet, the adoption of regional/confederate currency and financial systems, an open border, and a redefinition of nationality, have facilitated the movement of people and communication across the world in an unprecedented manner. Globalization, therefore, has collapsed distances and challenged time, radicalized the interconnection of the world and made it into what is now known as a global village.

The fluidity that now characterises the interconnectivity of the world has inadvertently transformed the everyday cultural expressions of people in Africa.[2] This

---

[1] Karin Barber, "Introduction," in *Readings in African Popular Culture*, ed. by Karin Barber (Bloomington: Indiana University press, 1997), 7.
[2] It is important to state here that I am indeed conscious of the limits of generalization with such terms as "Africa", "African", and "Nigerian" in this chapter. Hence, in my discussion I proceed by conditioning the terms with plural modifiers to acknowledge obvious multiplicities/accents with re-

is due to the digital linkages of Africa to the rest of the world. It is within the intricacies of this global flow that I propose that the pressures of globalization on popular culture in Africa can be seen most clearly through the example of hip hop. This will also help us to come to terms with the layered history that comes with engaging that phenomenon of every day expression referred to as popular culture.

Even if the term 'popular culture' calls for a definition, scholars today are generally agreed to the fact that a strict definition of the term is fraught with contradictions that make the exercise almost futile. This is because the general materialist understanding of what constitutes the "popular" in the west collapses in many African contexts, where they is a subtle connection between such concepts as the proletariats, masses, vernacular, traditional and oral on the one hand and the elitist, bourgeois, royalty and written on the other hand. It is exactly this reality that Karin Barber acknowledges when she notes that even in the west, where there is a more established history of class, the boundaries and categories that are implied by the term, "popular", have become problematic and inadequate, "slippery and elusive".[3] In Africa, as she asserts, the term is "highly porous and shifting".[4] But, for the purpose of our discussion, I shall adopt an understanding of popular culture to designate those cultural expressions that arise from collective aesthetics, a history of shared practice or as linguists will have it "a community of practice"[5] that speaks to a collective consciousness. But again I must stress that this conception of popular culture should not necessarily be equated, exclusively, with "low class" or the "masses".

In pre-colonial Africa, popular culture included all those aspects of cultural expressions which today have been unfortunately tagged vernacular culture. These cultural expressions manifest as birth songs, work songs, riddles, panegyrics, all forms of folk theatre, tattoos, wrestling etc. These forms are still practised today in many African societies along with popular culture genres that have evolved as a result of Africa's contact with the west and east through trade, religious interactions, education, and the colonial enterprise. These forms include dance, sports, photography, western/eastern music which have in turn given birth to musical genres such as Sukus, High life, Makosa among many others. Particularly, photography, music, and film became Africa's modes of apprehending and expressing a form of modernity which arose as a result of new technologies introduced to Africa from the west. However, hip hop, which is of particular interest to us, along with video film, is one of the latest genres of popular culture expression in Africa that displays a new form of (post)modernity that emerged as a result of pressures from globalization

---

gard to the nuanced formations of hip hop in the continent and even, within a country like Nigeria. The use of the term is in no way to invent or re-invent any sense of a mono-cultural zone.
3 Barber, "Introduction", 3.
4 Barber, "Introduction", 4.
5 P. Eckert and S. McConnell-Ginet, "Think Practically and Look Locally: Language and Gender as Community-Based Practice", *Annual Review of Anthropology* 21 (1992), 464.

and the diasporic antecedents that have conditioned it. To properly appreciate the emergence of hip hop in Africa it is important to place it within the historical, economic and socio-political influences that birthed it. This will aid us to speak to the challenge which Barber seems to have posed to scholars.[6]

The Birth of a Popular Culture Genre

As a complex youth-based subculture, hip hop is a mode of expression and a practice that includes dance, rap, dress code, hairstyle, beats, graffiti, MCing, DJing and speech patterns that have deep African American influences.[7] The humble beginnings of hip hop have been traced to the interactions of Afro-Caribbean and African American youths in the post-industrial city of the Bronx.[8] Since its emergence in the 1970s, hip hop has characteristically spread across cultural spaces so much that there is, arguably, no part of the world that this youth subculture cannot be found. Its ubiquity derives from its malleability and syncretism,[9] which are testimonies of its adaptability. In this manner, hip hop, through its complex capillaries functions as cultural equipment for youth expressiveness and identity all over the African continent. Although this youth culture is easily identifiable by its African American origins, what is now known as the Global Hip Hop Nation (GHHN) is a polyglot, heterogeneous style community replicated in its multiple homes.[10] Hip hop in Africa may best be understood through an outline of its emergence among Nigerian youths in the early '90s, which, incidentally, is the period when the hip hop wave began to catch up with youths in other parts of Africa, especially the West African region.[11]

As a postcolonial art, the hybridity of Nigerian hip hop is defined by the creative fusion of sound bites from indigenous traditional melodies and modern precursor local music such as High life and other urban musical genres such as Fela's Afro-

---

6 Barber, "Introduction," 7.
7 H. Samy Alim, "Introduction: Straight Outta Compton, Straight *aus Munchen*: Global Linguistic Flows, Identities and the Politics of Language in a Global Hip Hop Nation," in *Global Linguistic flows: Hip Hop Cultures, Youth Identities and the Politics of Language*, ed. by H. Samy Alim, Awad Ibrahim, and Alistair Pennycook (New York: Routledge, 2009), 2; Tope Omoniyi. "'So I choose do am Naija Style': Hip Hop Language and Postcolonial Identities," in *Global Linguistic Flows: Hip Hop Cultures, Youth Identities and the Politics of Language,* ed. by H. Samy Alim, Awad Ibrahim and Alistair Pennycook (New York: Routledge, 2009), 116.
8 Paul Gilroy, *The Black Atlantic: Modernity and Double Consciousness* (London: Verso, 1993), 103; Tricia Rose, *Black Noise: Rap Music and Culture in contemporary America* (London: Wesleyan University Press, 1994), 3; and Eric Charry, "A Capsule History of African Rap," in *Hip Hop Africa: New African Music in a Globalizing World,* ed. by Eric Charry (Indiana: Indian University Press, 2012). 1–25.
9 Gilroy, *The Black Atlantic*, 108.
10 Omoniyi. "'So I choose do am Naija Style,'" 121.
11 Charry, "A Capsule History of African Rap", 16; Jesse Weaver Shipley, *Living the Hiplife: Celebrity and Entrepreneurship in Ghanaian Popular Music* (Durham: Duke University Press, 2013), 16.

beats, Apala, Fuji, Sukus and Makosa have also been blended with Caribbean reggae, Dance Hall, and Calypso to produce the lyrical mosaic of hip hop music in Nigeria. Without attempting to name all the originators in the industry of Nigerian hip hop, let me state that the pioneer vocalists are young men such as the group Junior and Pretty, Baba Fryo, Dady Showkey, Zaky Azees, among other DJs and MCs. These young people filled a gap of a popular youth music tradition in Nigeria that had been practiced by the likes of Chris Okotie (now a famous Pentecostal pastor), Felix Liberty, and Chris Mba in the 1980s.

However, it is important to specify that Nigerian hip hop bears the tensions of a deeply egregious post-independent socio-political and economic history, and the auspicious digital media technological revolution which was budding in the 1990s, and which rapidly blossomed in the millennium. It is also important to underscore these socio-political and technological co-ordinates because they facilitate a deeper understanding of its phenomenon and especially its peculiar music content. Taking a trajectory from Nigeria's independence, therefore, the newly independent nation in the 1960s had the promise of economic prosperity and national development. But all that promise and self-confidence soon burst as the nation degenerated into a tragic civil war that was defined by ethnicity, vain ego, and a desperate attempt to come to terms with the idea of a nation state bequeathed by British colonialism. However, the end of the war witnessed a revamped economy which rested squarely on the newly found crude oil, and the astronomical foreign exchange that accrued to the nation from it.

Thus, the 1970s ushered in a decade of national bounty from petrol dollars to the extent that General Yakubu Gowon, the Nigerian military dictator at the time, was reported to have said, the problem of the country was not lack of money but how to spend that accumulated wealth.[12] It was perhaps within this context of uncontrollable wealth and the lack of informed economic vision that the government spent extravagantly. The consequences of this extravagance manifested in the early 1980s, when the world was plunged into an economic crunch. With a weak economic system arising from the inability of the military government to build economic structures that would have cushioned the hardships, Nigeria, like several other Third World countries, implemented a Structural Adjustment Programme (SAP) on the advice of the International Monetary Fund (IMF) and the World Bank. One of the implications of the SAP policy was widespread retrenchment of public/civil servants, the bulk of whom were in the middle class. Coupled with the high level of inflation into which the country had been inadvertently dragged, retrenchment and salary cuts deepened the austerity measures and engendered a psychology of desperation among the citizenry. This desperation became the impulse that drove many Nigerians to adopt several "social short-circuits" to contend with and earn a manner of living

---

12 Yinka Odunmakin, "Nigeria: Tackle Issues with common sense", *Vanguard Nigeria* (2017) https://www.vanguardngr.com/2017/01/nigeria-tackle-issues-common-sense/ Accessed 13/07/2020

which they thought had been denied them.¹³ It planted the seeds for the advance fee fraud, or "419" as it is popularly named, after the penal code in Nigeria. That psychology is also the root of the bizarre attraction to ritual and other levels of superstition adopted as means of wealth creation and affluent living, what Ihaenyi M. Enwerem refers to as "money magic" practiced in Nigerian urban centres.¹⁴ The culture and consequences of this "occult economy", as the Camaroffs refer to it, became a major theme in Nollywood films.¹⁵ In the midst of this desperation, the educational sector began to feel the pinch of the economic downturn as succeeding generations of military government implemented a budget cut on education, while the militarization of the Nigerian socio-political space forced the cream of Nigerian intellectuals and professionals abroad – a situation which came to be known as brain drain in the country.

Thus, the generation born after the civil war in Nigeria were bequeathed a heritage of lack, superstition, ignorance, vanity, and anxiety. It is this situation that created a 'lost generation' among many other African youths of their time.¹⁶ In a deeply contemplative lecture, Stanley Macebuh uses the case study of Igbo youth to exquisitely describe this generation as "the authentic children of the war and all its dislocations."¹⁷ This is because the young people born after the Nigerian civil war truly began to personify the socio-political consequences of that war. Macebuh goes further to describe them as the "anger-ridden, money-driven avengers of a collective grievance…"¹⁸ His characterization encapsulates the anxieties and cravings of these youths to move beyond the bad condition that is palpable around them and which seems to be consuming their parents. Here, Macebuh consolidates our appreciation of the historical antecedences and the social space into which the generation, who control the complex industry of Nigerian hip hop, was born.

However, it needs to be added that beyond the negativity that the SAP crisis engendered, part of the creative impulses of young Nigerians from the 1990s were directed towards harnessing the new digital technologies of portable cameras, audio-visual recorders, computers, software packages and the mobile phone to

---

13 Idom T. Inyabri, "Youth and Postcolonial Subjectivity in Contemporary Nigerian Pop Music," *Postcolonial Text* 8, 3 & 4 (2013), 9.
14 Iheanyi M.Enwerem, "'Money-Magic' and Ritual Killing in Contemporary Nigeria", in *Money Struggles and City Life: Devaluation in Ibadan and Other Urban Centers in Southern Nigeria 1986–1996*, ed. by Jane I. Guyer, LaRay Denzer & Adigun Agbaje (Ibadan: BookBuilders, 2003), 189.
15 Jean Comaroff and John Comaroff, "Occult Economies and the Violence of Abstraction: Notes from the South African Postcolony", *American Ethnologist* 26, 2 (1999).
16 Deborah Durham, "Youth and the Social Imagination in Africa: Introduction to Parts 1 and 2", *Anthropological Quarterly* 73, 3 (2000), 113.
17 Stanley N. Macebuh, "Humanism in Chains: an Applied Example", 17th Alumni Annual Lecture Delivered at Trenchard Hall University of Ibadan (2002), 13.
18 Macebuh, "Humanism in Chains", 14

begin to re-imagine and represent themselves.[19] Within the angst of the neoliberal regime into which their parents have been forced and in a (third) world that has bequeathed them very little social structures upon which to build their destinies, digital devices became agencies for the Nigerian hip hop exponents we are engaging here to negotiate spaces and exploit the facilities of globalization for survival. This indeed is what Adam Haupt has metaphorically captured as "stealing empire", an ideological and creative enterprise through which young people from the margins exploit the possibilities of the digital infrastructure to negotiate spaces and make meaning of the global hegemony in their time.[20]

In Nigeria, the rise of hip hop also coincided with the rise of Nollywood, Nigeria's booming film industry, now the third biggest video film industry in the world after United States' Hollywood and India's Bollywood.[21] Scholars have ably accounted for how the portable digital devices from Japan, China, and other Asian countries equipped young Nigerians to create alternatives to American, Indian, and Mexican films for the teeming Nigerian audience from the early 1990s.[22] Hip hop artists in Nigeria, like their counterparts in other parts of Africa, also latched onto the opportunities available to their Nollywood counterparts to create indigenous entertainment for the emerging private radio and television stations that arose as part of the neoliberal privatization policy of the Ibrahim Babangida junta in the early 1990s.[23]

Although media culture critics like Liwhu Betiang seem to suggest that media privatization in Nigeria gave room for imported "pure-entertainment programs" like hip hop to dominate Nigeria's media industry, I think hip hop as a subculture in Nigeria has been indigenized and, like Nollywood, opened the space for young people to playfully foreground themselves.[24] DJ Jimi Jatt, arguably Nigeria's foremost celebrity disc jockey, affirms the liberating force of the new digital technology and the privatization of the media, when he eloquently stated that privatization of the media "opened the space for us and broke open all the gates that used to be shut on us. And in a space where only the likes of Premier Records used to function, Ni-

---

[19] Paul Ugor, "Small Media, Popular Culture, and New Youth Spaces in Nigeria," *The Review of Education Pedagogy & Cultural Studies* 31.4, (2009), 393.
[20] Adam Haupt, *Stealing Empire: P2P, Intellectual Property and hip-hop Subversion* (Cape Town: HSRC Press, 2008), xxiii.
[21] Ugor, "Small Media, Popular Culture, and New Youth Spaces in Nigeria," 394.
[22] Onookome Okome and Jonathan Haynes, *Cinema and Social Change in West Africa*, (Jos: Nigerian Film Corporation, 1997); and Onookome Okome, "Nollywood: West African Cinema", *Postcolonial Text* 3, 2 (2007).
[23] Paul Ugor and Giovanna Santanera, "Media Globalization, African Popular Culture and the History form Below: Nigerian Video Films", in *The Third Wave of Historical Scholarship on Nigeria*, ed. by Saheed Aderinto and Paul Osifodunrin (Newcastle upon Tyne: Cambridge Scholars Publishing, 2012); Liwhu Betiang, "Global Drums and Local Masquerades: Fifty Years of Television Broadcasting in Nigeria: 1959–2009", *SAGE Open* (2013).
[24] Betiang, "Global Drums and Local Masquerades", 7.

gerian youths have come to dominate."[25] In this testimony, Jimi not only specified the power and centrality of new digital media in the imagination of young people in Nigeria, he has also indicated the dynamics of the power shift from one generation to another. More so, he paid tribute to the empowerment that comes with new media technologies even in throes of a late modern world.

From the foregoing, what becomes palpable about Nigerian hip hop as a popular culture expression is an affirmation of the theoretical postulations of Arjun Appadurai[26] on the character and implication of the imagination in a globalised world or what he would call the "postelectronic" world.[27] In this new world popular culture arises from an imagination that has been liberated from the cocoon of the elite / bourgeois, it is much more defined by collective action and, as the discussion of Nigerian hip hop here will show, that collective imagination becomes a staging ground for (collective) action.[28] But as Appadurai himself would have it, two elements, the media and migration, have become the major "constitutive" propellers through which that imagination is accessed and realized.[29] Some of the major exponents of hip hop in Nigeria like in many African countries are either children of migrants to the west or are themselves young people who had come back from studies abroad. But further to this, they have come to form a creative mass with their peers at home, who were already experiencing North America through video and audio cassettes, and are appropriating the prevalent small electronic devices at their disposal in a project to re-imagine themselves as stars, entrepreneurs, and creators of a new modernity.

Reconstructing Social Angst Through Hip Hop

Indeed, in a circumstance where digital apparatus and the entire virtual infrastructure of the web has become platforms for creativity and dissemination, consumption, and interaction, Nigerian hip hop has also become a "deterritorialized"[30] and "transnational"[31] agency. In the sections that follow, I shall engage the manner in which Nigerian hip hop, through selected examples, metonymically signify the layered socio-economic and cultural history of much of the African postcolony. Through these examples, I also hope to show how Africa and its youths have now become part of a historical transformation of the world.

---

25 D J Jimi Jatt, Interviewed by author July 2016.
26 Arjun Appadurai, *Modernity at Large: Cultural Dimensions of Globalization* (Minneapolis: University of Minneapolis Press, 1996).
27 Appadurai, *Modernity at Large*, 5.
28 Appadurai, *Modernity at Large*, 7.
29 Appadurai, *Modernity at Large*, 3.
30 Appadurai, *Modernity at Large*, 4.
31 Homi Bhabha, *The Location of Culture*. (London: Routledge, 1994), 303.

Narrating the rise from a bad condition

As I have noted above, part of what Nigerian youth strive for today arises from consequences of the economic policies in the 1980s implemented at the behest of the Bretton Woods' institutions namely, the World Bank and International Monetary Fund (IMF). These institutions, which are purveyors of globalization have been generally perceived as capitalist institutions that are projecting neo-liberal, western imperialist agenda that are targeted at keeping African and Third World countries generally in servitude and subjected to the whims and caprices of their major financiers in the West. It is for the reason of their neo-colonialist, exploitative tendencies and the new form of imperialism which they allegedly implement through globalization that Haupt,[32] taking after Antonio Negri, sees them as a new empire. Hip hop music in Africa performatively projects the practical ways in which everyday people respond to the complex economic and social pressures initiated by these new empires and implemented by self-seeking African dictators and political elites. All through sub-Saharan Africa, hip hop artists give accents to the painful life that is linked to the economic situation described above. This fate can be perceived in stories of their rise from an austere, painful life to stardom.[33] Much of these stories of the "rags-to-riches fantasies" theme are cathartic tales of ordinary family struggles in post-Structural Adjustment times.[34]

In Nigerian hip hop, we have examples of these lyric narratives in Timaya, Waconzy, Duncan Mighty, Mad Mellon and Mountain Black, Wizkid, and Don Tom. In "Plantain Boy" for instance, Timaya narrativizes his personal ordeal in his struggle to stardom.[35] The title of the song is indeed a socio-linguistic marker of his family's status at his childhood. To be a plantain boy in the Nigerian setting is to be a retailer of the ware (plantain), spending time in the marketplace among the poor. It is in this condition that the young Timaya found himself eking out life with his mother, shown in the music video as a pensive, agitated, and poorly dressed market woman. The lyric tells of the stereotypes and stigma that Timaya himself had to endure because of his penurious existence. In a society where poverty is erroneously a marker for social ills, the young Timaya could only be seen as a rough-neck or as his music persona would put it: "many people see me as a useless boy". But in the midst of their life struggles Timaya tells us that he and his poor mother were members of one Nigeria's most spirited Pentecostal churches, Mountain of Fire Ministries (MFM), where he was praying for relief from their hardship:

---

32 Haupt, *Stealing Empire*, xv
33 Inyabri, "Youth and Postcolonial Subjectivity", 10.
34 Shipley, *Living the Hiplife*, 23.
35 Timaya, "Plantain seller", Director of video. Jay Will, 2014, Accessed: 13/7/2020 https://www.youtube.com/watch?v=15gzJf8_P3Y.

I dey for choir [I was in the choir],
back in the days of Mountain of Fire
Na so I just dey hala! God come answer my mama prayer
[That's how I was shouting! God answered my mother's prayer]

You ride *Okada*, e no mean say you no go get Hummer
[If you're riding an *Okada*, it doesn't mean you can't drive a Hummer (SUV)]
Even if you sell *pure-water*, e no mean say your life dey for gutter
[If you sell *pure-water*, it doesn't mean that your life is in gutters]
From nobody, God you make me a somebody
Oh my God I'm so happy ye

....

I dey my own ye
[I was to myself]
Jehovah just bless me ye

A cursory look at Timaya's lyrics will reveal much about the social context that he comes from and the collective impulse that defines the people and especially the youth of his time. There is resilience in the words of the musician, which indexes the resoluteness of the Nigerian youth in egregious conditions. That spirit can be seen in his advice to the Nigerian youth to rise above present poverty by sheer determination to convert limitations to building blocks for upward social mobility. That is what is contained in the admonition well articulated in Nigerian pidgin (NP):

> "If you dey sell *pure-water* e no mean say your life dey for gutter
> [If you sell *pure-water*, it doesn't mean that your life is in gutters]
>
> If you dey ride *Okada*, e no mean say you no feel drive Hummer
> [If you're riding an *Okada*, it doesn't mean you can't drive a Hummer (SUV)]

In the advice above, we find the binary of social opposites namely, the *pure-water* which is cheap water source for urban dwellers, usually produced and packaged in unreliable sanitation. There is also the *Okada* (slang for motorbike), a quick intra-city transportation in Nigeria, which is also very precarious and vulnerable. On the other hand, there is the Hummer, a sport utility vehicle (SUV), which is a symbol of affluence. For Timaya, the Nigerian youth should strive to move above the pure-water / Okada level to the opulence of the Hummer SUV. But it is also important to identify the centrality of the hand-of-God, which Timaya claims is the means through which he could be lifted from his hard condition.

In a postcolony, where political systems have hopelessly failed the people in providing social security and the good life, recourse to supernatural help becomes a predominant social grammar. In fact, intricately linked to the confidence in God and the supernatural is the phenomenon of the scapegoat. That is, the propensity to identify a cause, remote or temporal, as the impediment to one's progress. This sentiment that is expressed in Timaya's song has become capital for many dubious Nigerian religious leaders, who have often exploited it for their own aggrandizements. The condition and psychology expressed in Timaya's lyric is truly collective. We can also find it articulated in Wizkid's "Ojuelegba", where the musician tells of his personal hustles to make it as an artist in the street of Ojulegba, Lagos Nigeria.[36] In telling his story of struggle, he also links it to the angst of his people who obviously share in his pain of survival:

> Ni Ojuelegba oooo!
> [At Ojuelegba!]
> My People dey dier, my people suffer
> [my people're there, my people're suffering]
> Dem dey pray for blessing
> [they're praying for blessings]
> Ni Ojuelegba ooo! My people dey dier, dem dey pray for blessing
> [At Ojuelebga! My people 're there, they're praying for blessings]
> For better living.

The search for "better living" that we find in Wizkid's song is, indeed, the preoccupation of Duncan Mighty's "The Hand of Jesus" and Waconzy's "I Celebrate," which are also thick in the expression of the anxieties and supernatural interventions in the young musicians' struggles and their rise to stardom.[37] The life of the persona in Duncan Mighty's song is made more unbearable because of prolonged haemorrhage of his mother and the misery which the illness engenders on the family. In this song we also have the presence of perceived enemies and the betrayal of extended relatives who abandon the impoverished family in the time of challenge. Again, out of fervent prayers, the young Duncan mighty and his poor family in the ghetto experienced a miraculous relief and a reversal in their situation:

> When God come, God heal my mother
> [When God showed up, God healed my mother]
> Safe my mother, bless my talent and make my mother happy

As a celebrity, Duncan Mighty tells his listeners that he is now being guarded by the military – "But now army stand for my gate [But now my gate is guarded by a soldier]". The whole narrative of Duncan Mighty like that of Wizkid in "Ojuelegba" also speaks to the general failure of the state and the collective misery of the people in a raped polity. When Mighty says that he, who was harassed by the police, is now guarded by the army at his gate, he is only stating the unfortunate reality in the odd Nigerian state; a situation where the military and security apparatus of the state can be bought by private citizens. This abuse and privatization of state security is one of the many contradictions that have contributed to making security inadequate and corrupt in the country. Yet, it is important to state that Mighty's boast is only an ex-

---

[36] Wizkid, "Ojuelegba", https://www.youtube.com/watch?v=Q7QiLceJSLQ. 2014, Accessed 13/7/2020.
[37] Duncan Mighty, "Hand of Jesus" 2011, https://www.youtube.com/watch?v=qMniU5-9c0I; accessed 13/7/2020; Waconzy, "I celeberate", 2010, https://www.youtube.com/watch?v=IfO1-JYD2UA. accessed 13/07/20.

pression of the situation in Nigeria, where politicians move in convoys of armed policemen, while the masses remain utterly unguarded.

Duncan Mighty's grass to grace tale connects with Waconzy's in his hit single "I Celebrate". Here also, we have another youth telling a slant of a grand narrative of a generation's striving. In waconzy's song there is the plot of a suffering child, who was "born with a silver spoon" but who lost that spoon, because of the failure of his parents' marriage. Thus, the musician tells us that he was brought up by his "poor single mother", another suffering mother figure like Timaya's mother in "Plantain Boy" and Duncan Mighty's sick mother in "Hand of God". Perhaps these young people seem to assert that in dispossessed times women and youths are the worst hit. But it is also the recurrence of the hand-of-God theme in Waconzy's lyric that may interest us in characterising the making of music and coming of age in the late modern era, where globalization has come to mean the dispossession and intensification of strive for many in the global south. As it is for his peers, Timaya, Duncan Mighty, and many other hip hop musicians in sub-Saharan Africa, the pain of Waconzy is only taken away by God or by sheer luck.

Self-reliance, Enterprise and Social-short circuits

It is obvious from the lyrics of the young Nigerian hip hop stars discussed here that the circumstance of the global economic crunch that predates or defines their incarnation has become part of the psycho-social propellers that motivate them to seek alternative means of survival. The catharsis that arises from the songs ends up in the supernatural rise of hip hop artists and in the fact that their musical talents have led to financial empowerment or "hammer" as a popular Nigerian pidgin term would have it. In this sense, for this generation of music makers, hip hop and its associated arts (graffiti, pose, dance, drama, etc.) also becomes an entrepreneurial handle. This is evident in the digital music production studios, night clubs, boutiques, malls, movie sign-ups, branding companies, million Naira advertisements / brand deals, corporate promotion and shows that come with their music career. In a sense, this is one instance where one popular culture genre becomes a solution to global socio-economic challenges. The capacity for hip hop artists to make economic fortunes from music confirms Shipley's notion that "the entrepreneurial potential to earn wealth from musical products relies on the practitioners' abilities not only to make music but also to make their own authority as purveyors of popular taste." [38] In this regard, African hip hop artists and their teeming associates in the industry now make capital from their iconicity as artists and the enchantment that their image and sound ascribe to them in a neo-liberal world. The idea of the street as an open space of struggle and prosperity is a recurrent motif in Nigerian hip hop. To this ex-

---

38 Shipley, *Living the Hiplife*, 24.

tent, I find the song of 9ice (pronounced "Nice"), "Street Credibility",[39] featuring Tu-Face (or 2face) quite expressive of the positive values of hard work and creativity in the Nigerian youth:

> With my brain brain working all day
> Like say I no be manmade
> [As if I'm not born of a human]
> The streets keep urging me to do more
> ... ...
> I'm made from the street
> why I no go Blow!
> [why won't I make it big!]
> Originality work for me
> Why I no go show
> [why won't I show off]
> To the street I belong

From the stanzas above, one can decipher a work ethic that is associated with the youth in Nigeria. In the song the artist seems to promote dignity in resilience and importantly the element of originality, which in global hip hop is signified as "keeping it real," the pursuit of uniqueness and an identity marker. Yet the street, a metaphor of enterprise, self-reliance and resilience rather than government employment and bureaucracy remains the lifeline and confidence of the young artist in a country where government has failed in providing the needed assurances for the future.

On the other hand, we also witness ambivalence to Nigerian hip hop artists' self-reliance. Scholars have drawn attention to the fact that some Nigerian hip hop artists have been associated with cyber-fraud or the internet scam that is popular called "Yahoo-Yahoo" in Nigerian pidgin.[40] Without legitimizing this opportunistic form of self-empowerment, it seems that this form "social short circuit," as I have referred to this cybercrime somewhere else, arises from the dire economic circumstances, amongst which are unemployment and poverty in the midst of immoral and unexplainable wealth displayed by neo-colonial political elites.[41] Many Nigerian hip hop artists have exploited these reasons in their lyrics to legitimise or explain this path to wealth. Apart from Mode 9's "419 State of mind", I find Olu Maintain's "Yahoozee" and Wizboy's "Owusagi" quite interesting in glamorizing and subtly authen-

---

[39] 9ice, "Street Credibility", 2008, https://www.youtube.com/watch?v=BEymsiBpceQ&app=desktop. Accessed 13/7/2020

[40] Sandra Shonekan, "Nigerian Hip Hop: Exploring a Black World Hybrid", *Hip Hop Africa: New African Music in a Globalized World*, ed. by Eric Charry (Bloomington: Indiana University Press, 2012); Inyabri, "Youth and Postcolonial Subjectivity"; Suleman Lazarus, "Birds of a Feather Flock Together: The Nigerian Cyber Fraudsters (Yahoo Boys) and Hip Hop Artists", *Criminology, Criminal Justice, Law and Society* 19.2 (2018).

[41] Inyabri, "Youth and Postcolonial Subjectivity", 9.

ticating this criminal tendency.⁴² In Olu Maintains hit song "Yahoozee" we have an unreserved celebration of the spoils that come from yahoo-yahoo (cybercrime). The video of this song shows a spree, where young men portray a sense of masculinity that is obviously the result of mischievous control of the cyberspace. In the lines below we see how they legitimate the yahoo-yahoo crime by reconstructing it as hard work all through the week:

> Monday Tuesday Wednesday Thursday!
> Boys dey hustle!
> [Boys are working hard]
> Friday, Saturday, Sunday...

The reward of their hard work is the excess cash that comes with their crockery. The music video of "Yahoozee" also shows young men basking in a hedonistic celebration amidst champagne, vintage cars, confetti of dollar bills, and as the lead vocalist would have it in American parlance – "It's all about the Benjamins babe".

Like Olu Maintain's "Yahoozee", Wizboy's "Owusagi" seems to also legitimise cyber-fraud by suggesting that extreme lack is an eye-opener for youths to devise means of survival. This is what is implied when the vocalist says in Igbo: "Owsagi, ima 'ife [when hunger strikes you'll be wise]". Part of the lyrics articulated in a code mix of Nigerian pidgin and Igbo asserts that making big money is not an easy engagement:

> "To hammer money no be small t'ing o!
> [To make money is not easy]
> Brother, sister, Poverty ajoka nu onweya
> [Brother, sister poverty is bad / ugly]
> From Monday to Friday I dey on top of my system o
> [From Monday to Friday I've been on my (computer) system
> dey tidy sequence
> [working hard on sequence]
> Ko di kwa k'ane me
> [to show that I'm working]
> Now I don make My money
> [Now I've made my money]
> From busy to efizzy
> [from busy to showing off]
> Ony welu obi
> [One who has the heart/courage]
> eji eli ego
> [to spend]

---

42 Olu maintain, "Yahooze", 2007, Dir, DJ Tee https://www.youtube.com/watch?v=OMW7kcZnaiA; Accessed 12/7/2020; Wizboy, "Owusagi", 2010, https://www.youtube.com/watch?v=y6oB52-pb7Y. Accessed 13/7/2020

make you carry dey go!
[Go on with it!]

Beyond the premise of lack with which the lyric legitimizes the option taken, there is a sense in which Wizboy seems to speak the same language of Olu Mountain by stating that his wealth comes by dint of hard work "from Monday to Friday". In a previous study I suggest that the word *sequence* as used above has two possible implications: one could imply hard work at the music studio where the musician could be fine-tuning the art of mixing his beats.[43] But it is also plausible that the slang, as it is used in reference to cyber-fraud in Nigeria, is used here to gloss over cyber-crime or the yahoo-yahoo scam. Again there is glamorization of this fraud as in Olu Mountain's "Yahoozee," when the young musician justifies the means of his wealth by stating that he has moved from hard work (busy) to enjoyment (effizzy). This "effizzy", the pursuit of good life, especially in a context where they (the youths) are daily exposed to the outlandish life style of their North American hip hop icons and the display of vain politicians at home, keeps hip hop artist close to cybercrime and peers who are associated with internet scam. Although some other hip hop artists such as Simisola have been unequivocal in rejecting the stereotype of criminality associated with Nigerian hip hop artists, musical lyric such as the ones cited here and especially the allegations against now popular Nigerian hip hop artist, Naira Marley and his subsequent arrest have continued to make cyber-fraud part of the identity of Nigerian hip hop.[44]

Political Consciousness

All over the world hip hop is known for its political content. This is a factor that keeps it relevant across time. In Africa, its birth is incidental on the dire political situation of the continent in the late twentieth century; a situation where the youth have been systematically emasculated by generations of dictatorship and vain politics that disempower women and youths and narrow the political space of their homeland. In fact, deriving from decades of youth emasculation in sub-Saharan Africa, the youth have justifiably developed the psychology of otherness by seeing themselves as removed from the politics of their countries. The lack of social systems and infrastructures such as a tradition of formidable mentorship, education, and smooth political transition among many others that should ensure an enviable political culture have made it difficult for young people to participate in politics and take up leadership roles. To this end, hip hop artists in Africa have lived up to their bid-

---

[43] Idom T. Inyabri, "Youth and Linguistic Stylization in Naija Afro Hip Hop", *Sociolinguistic Studies* 10, 1 & 2 (2016), 100.
[44] Simisola, BOI G TV, 2019 "Simi Reply Naira Marley on Yahoo Boys", https://www.youtube.com/watch?v=w-YAIYDCXWw. Accessed 13/7/2020

ding by remaining conscious of the politics in their home countries in diverse ways. While some have continued to produce unequivocal lyrics that question the double standards of moribund political elites, in Nigeria for instance, artists such as the Lagos-based Banky W have moved a step further by contesting elections to take their political conviction to the next level of political engagement. This way, hip hop in Africa has been a proven committed art.

The example of Eedris Abdulkareem is relevant in this context. His famous track "Nigeria Jaga Jaga [Nigeria is hopelessly bad or Nigeria is spoilt]"[45] is a music that troubled the political establishment during the administration of General Olusegun Obasanjo, a Nigerian civil war veteran (1967–1970), military president (1976–1979) and years after, democratically elected President of Nigeria (1999–2007). Responding directly to a culture of impunity, dictatorship, failed policies, embezzlement, strife and insecurity Eedris Abdulkareem's music speaks truth to power. It has been said that the President Obasanjo had answered back at the young musician the year the music was released by saying "na him papa and mama Jaga jaga! [it is his father and mother who have gone mad/bad!]".[46] But, in a bid to justify his critical position on the insufferable condition of the Nigerian state over a decade after, the musician who has remained in a troubled relationship with Obasanjo and indeed the Nigerian establishment, recently reminded an audience in a show that the Obasanjo government unjustly stereotyped him and denied his criticism without bases.[47]

However, before the Eedris Abdulkareem's "Jaga Jaga sensation," Timaya had used his music to speak of the jungle justice meted on his people in Nigeria's oil rich Bayelsa state during the same administration of General Obasanjo. Reacting against what may be said to be a case of homicide in the oil-rich Odi in the year 1999, the military moved in a platoon of soldiers who wreaked havoc on defenceless citizens. Coming on the heels of the extra-judicial murder of Ken Saro-Wiwa and the Ogoni nine from the same region, this savagery became one more level of injustice against a people who have been dispossessed of the crude oil wealth, their natural resource which has remained the mainstay of the Nigerian economy. It is this injustice and the collective tragedy of his people, even in a democracy, that Timaya performs in his "Dem don Kill dem Mama [They have killed (our) Mothers]."[48] The video of this song shows a hoard of armed military men invading a hapless population in a

---

[45] Eedris Abdulkareem, "Jaga jaga", 2004, https://www.youtube.com/watch?v=UO4qhDthUAU. Accessed 13/7/2020

[46] Abisola Alawode, 2018, "How Eedris Abdulkareem and Ex-President Obasanjo 'Fought in Public'", *Nigeria Entertainment News*,
https://www.legit.ng/1171767-how-eedris-abdulkareem-president-olusegun-obasanjo-fought-public.html. Accessed 14/07/2020

[47] Eedris Abdulkareem,, 31/7/2018 Siderz Entertainment TV, "Eedris Abdulkareem Rips Obasanjo",. https://www.youtube.com/watch?v=hbuGc33tQME. Accessed 13/07/2020

[48] Timaya, "Dem Mama", 2011, https://www.youtube.com/watch?v=kqC-6YdZVL8. Accessed 12/7/2020

place that is boldly identified as Odi. In the video, Timaya, as the people's leader and spokesman, angrily addresses the press on the injustice meted on his people.

In Abdulkareem's "Jaga Jaga" and Timaya's "Dem don kill dem Mama" we see the image of the hip hop artist as spokesman for the dispossessed people. That image also comes through in Falz's "This is Nigeria"[49], a song which takes after Childish Gambino's "This is America". Re-contextualizing Gambino's American lyric, Falz uses his own song to foreground and satirize a plethora of socio-political malaise that bedevil the Nigerian society. Indeed, the video of "This is Nigeria" is a kaleidoscope of the failings and complete tragedy that has become of the Nigerian state. From the re-cycling of failed and corrupt political oligarchs, brazen embezzlements, misappropriation of funds, and police brutality to religious hypocrisy, crockery, bigotry, the menace of Fulani herdsmen, cybercrime or "yahoo-yahoo," and drug abuse, Falz's performance becomes a palimpsest of contemporary Nigerian woes. Perhaps more important for the character of popular culture in Africa in the twenty-first century is the fact that Falz, like his peers, is using hip hop as a cultural instrument to speak of the scapegoat they are made of and the socio-economic strife that his generation encounters. There is, therefore, a formidable youth politics underlying Falz's "This is Nigeria". In the midst of myriad of problems faced by the Nigerian youth, the persona in "This is Nigeria" uncouples the hypocrisy of the Nigerian government when the President (General Mohamadu Buhari) blames the youth for being lazy:

> This is Nigeria,
> No electricity failure,
> Your people are still working multiple jobs,
> You talk say we lazy o!
> [You say we are lazy]

Reflecting on the lines above, one can say that the music draws attention to the perennial marginalization and dispossession that the youth are facing in the Nigerian state[50] and the victimhood, which also makes them "Nigeria's mid-night's children" to use Niyi Osundare's words.[51] But as Akingbe and Onanuga would further affirm, "This is Nigeria" is indeed a lyrical accent of the anxieties of youths all over the world vis-a-vis the oppressive structures of the state.[52] That accent is an expression

---

[49] Falz, "This is Nigeria", 2018, Dir Prodigeezy, https://www.youtube.com/watch?v=UW_xEqCWrm0. Accessed 12/7/2020

[50] Niyi Akingbe and Paul Onanuga, "'Voicing Protest': Performing Cross-Cultural Revolt in Gambino's 'This is America' and Falz's 'This is Nigeria'", *Contemporary Music Review* (2020), 3. Accessed 14/7/2020. DOI: 10.1080/07494467.2020.1753473.

[51] Niyi Osundare, "Singers of a New Dawn: Nigerian Literature from the Second Generation on," in *Thread in the Loom: Essays on African Literature & Culture* ed. by Niyi Osundare (Trenton: AWP, 2002), 73.

[52] Akingbe and Onanuga, "'Voicing Protest'", 21.

of a collective global youth cultural practice that has been instantiated in different cultural spaces through appropriation or "re-appropriation".[53] This way, African hip hop artists are connected in a global popular culture kinship with their peers all over the world through the vortex of performance.

Conclusion

The scholarship on hip hop has always touched on the layers of history that have fallen in place to make this genre of popular culture what it has become at different times and places. This layered experience, from its African oral roots, to the 'vernacular' traditions in the New world, the convergence of afro-Caribbean / American and Hispanic youths to birth the culture in America and its return to Africa is a vibrant history that we find in the work of Gilroy,[54] Rose,[55] Ojo-Ade,[56] and Shipley,[57] among many other scholars. It is, therefore, how hip hop is informed by and responds to globalization in Africa, an aspect of its multi-layered character that I have been concerned with in this study. Through the instrumentality of hip hop as heterogeneous global culture I have looked at the peculiar history of its incarnation in Africa and its implication on the socio-cultural life of the continent through the struggles of the Nigerian youths, who are truly a reflection of the dynamics of a society as Colette Daiute would have it. [58] Here in lies the "embedded" history of hip hop and popular culture in this discourse. My approach here has been to show how the technological, financial, and cultural agents of globalization have been catalyst for the African youths in the twenty-first century. In responding to the pressures of globalization these youths at the margins of global markets and techno-life have created a brand of popular culture that has given them voice in an asphyxiating environment. That voice helps them to playfully re-invent and sustain themselves in spite of the odds in their societies. But, perhaps, more significant is the fact that through the serendipitous connection of new media technology and popular culture in the globalized world, African youths and Africa as a whole are in turn connected in a rhythm of cultural flow to the rest of the world.

---

53 Omoniyi, "'So I choose do am Naija Style'", 118.
54 Gilroy, *The Black Atlantic*.
55 Tricia, *Black Noise*.
56 Femi Ojo-Ade, "Reflections on Pan-Africanism, Black Aesthetics and the Black Condition," in Being *Black Being Humane*, ed. by Femi Ojo-Ade (Ile-Ife: OAU Press, 1996).
57 Shipley, *Living the Hiplife*.
58 Colette Daiute, "General Introduction: The Problem of Youth Conflict," in *International Perspectives on Youth Conflict and Development*, ed. by Colette Daiute, *et al.* (New York: OUP, 2006), 10.

Toyin Falola
Chapter 20
Contemporary Globalization and Africa

Abstract: The chapter begins by examining the links between colonization, capitalism, and globalization. It then discusses the nature of the current fourth industrial revolution, as well as how technology is at the forefront of this revolution. Indeed, technology has created a global village of sorts, through which one major, online culture dominates. The chapter then considers how Africa has been affected by globalization–for better or worse–and how Africa can see and position itself in an increasingly globalized world.

Keywords: World-as-global-village, Fourth industrial revolution, African personality, Economics, Globalization.

Introduction

Globalization emerged as cultures and peoples created more grounds for relations and integrations by inventing technologies and advancing science.[1] As a concept, it collapses the barriers of closer human relations and cultural integration, just as it tends to enhance individuality and competition. This paradoxical idea, in other words, simultaneously promotes the centralization of humanity and human consciousness into a global village while also facilitating the individuality of humans within this village. Therefore, rather than the global village to enhance the communal spirit of humanity through the transnationality of borders and peoples, it stiffens this space and worsens the social relations among the productive forces in this village.

The technologies that have enabled globalization initially eased transportation, communication, documentation, production, and transactions but would later create another problem for humanity—climate change and its attendant disasters.[2] Indeed, the intensive capitalist orientation that underlays globalization, which began during the first industrial revolution in Britain in the eighteenth century, characterizes the paradoxical nature of the phenomenon.[3] By integrating markets, creating transna-

---

[1] Henry Kissinger, *World Order: Reflections on the Character of Nations and the Course of History* (New York: Penguin Press, 2014).
[2] Thomas J. Crowley, "Causes of Climate Change Over the Past 1000 Years," *Science* 289, no. 5477 (2000): 270–277.
[3] This revolution provided the basis for the modern technological advancements, innovations and societal form that are shaping, producing, reproducing, and animating the globalization process. Atul Kohli, *State-Directed Development: Political Power and Industrialization in the Global Periphery* (New York: Cambridge University Press, 2004).

tional citizens and boundaries, internationalizing productions, universalizing governance, and defining humanity based on capital, globalization created a global community of humankind with widening inequality, social (dis)integration, inadequate resources, increasing competition, injustice, and intensive power play, particularly in Africa.[4]

The phenomenon, which created a global elite capable of shaping the social evolution of societies and global consciousness of peoples,[5] should also be seen as one of the inevitable evolutions in human history, given the continued dependence of sovereign entities and their peoples, century after century.[6] Therefore, the task would be to examine the trajectory of the interdependence of cultures, how this has evolved into the contemporary morphology anchored by fourth-generation technologies, and the place of Africa in all of this. Whereas Africa has been at the periphery of the operationalization of globalization, its people have benefitted from it tremendously, particularly from the transnationality of their being and skills in recent times.

This chapter examines what all of this portends for Africa in the twenty-first century and the possible role of the continent in salvaging the cancerous effects of globalization on Africans and all of humanity, especially in the face of climate change.

Globalization: So Far, So Good?

The history of humans is full of volumes of accounts of reproduction and migration, with their multiplier effects on the human environment and societal formation.[7] From the time humans evolved into a sedentary species, the bricks of globalization had begun to be laid by the "primitive" peoples. Through the relations among the forces of production, relations of production, and technological innovations across cultures—even in varying degrees—the earliest process leading to what is today conceptualized as globalization was birthed.[8] Further, wars, invasions, and other incidences leading to the incapacitation of a society or individual were also instrumental in shaping the maturation and existence of a global village. Globalization today is nothing more than the struggle for economic sustenance by states and their peoples alike and scramble for political influence and prowess by states. This might have ex-

---

[4] Hilary E. Kahn and Saskia Sassen, *Framing the Global* (Bloomington: Indiana University Press, 2014).
[5] John E. Flint, "Nigeria: The Colonial Experience from 1800 to 1914," in *Colonialism in Africa 1870–1960* Vol. 1, eds. L. H. Gann and Peter Duignan (Cambridge: Cambridge University Press, 1977), 220.
[6] Kissinger, *World Order*.
[7] John Burrow, *A History of Histories: Epics, Chronicles, Romances and Inquiries from Herodotus and Thucydides to the Twentieth Century* (London: Penguin Books, 2009).
[8] B. A. Ogot, ed., *General History of Africa- V: Africa from the Sixteenth to the Eighteenth Century* (Paris: UNESCO Publishing, 2000).

panded in scope and limitations, as seen, for instance, in the coming and preponderance of non-state actors on the scene. Technically, this is in no way different from what it was during the age of the "primitive men."

Trade and politics drove migrating groups back to one another.[9] Sociocultural exchanges and relations were established in this process as individuals acted as the ambassador of their civilization. As social forces of change, politically inclined to pursue material gains through the production and reproduction of material needs, the morphology and paradigm of relations among peoples of different languages and cultures have evolved, changing the nomenclature of the society itself.[10]

The continuity of the globalization process is further brought to light in recent times with the current preoccupation of China with her Belt and Road Initiative. This project is aimed at building "connectivity and co-operation across six main economic corridors encompassing China and: Mongolia and Russia; Eurasian countries; Central and West Asia; Pakistan; other countries of the Indian sub-continent; and Indochina."[11] It entails resuscitating and rehabilitating the old trading routes, primarily for more effective modern trading relations, than creating new routes.[12]

As early as the seventh century, Islam emerged as a major force in Africa, particularly in the Maghreb region. Like the later European imperialist incursions into Africa, the Arabs came with their religion and socio-political institutions during the trans-Saharan slave trade era in Sub-Saharan Africa. Before and after the incursion of these two into this region, several centuries of economic, sociocultural, and political relations had existed among African groups. Although reconstructing the past of preliterate societies has proven to be difficult in the past, the introduction of transdisciplinary bearing to the study of these societies has come to assuage the difficulties. If anything is true of the archeological and linguistical findings of the transdisciplinary approach across Africa, it is the evidence they evince that speaks to the above.[13] In this way, the form of homogeneity that contemporary globalization envisages is well-rooted in the sociocultural mixtures and economic relations long-established among social forces in the society during the preindustrial age. The two major drivers of globalization, market, and innovations (technology and culture), have consistently determined who gets what, when this is obtained, and how. Or, in other words, the politics of globalization.

---

9 Ogot, ed., *General History of Africa*.
10 A. I. Yandaki, *The State in Africa: A Critical Study in Historiography and Political Philosophy* (Zaria: Gaskiya Corporation, 2015).
11 OECD Business and Finance Outlook, "China's Belt and Road Initiative in the Global Trade, Investment and Finance Landscape," OECD. Accessed September 2, 2020, https://www.oecd.org/finance/Chinas-Belt-and-Road-Initiative-in-the-global-trade-investment-and-finance-landscape.pdf
12 Joshua J. Mark, "Silk Road," World History Encylopedia. Accessed September 2, 2020, https://www.ancient.eu/Silk_Road/.
13 J. F. A. Ajayi, "Africa at the Beginning of the Nineteenth Century: Issues and Prospects," in *General History of Africa- VI: Africa in the Nineteenth Century until the 1880s*, ed., J. F. Ade Ajayi (Oxford: Heinemann Educational Publishers, 1995), 18.

During the trans-Saharan trade, the Arabs, through their trading relations with Africans, engineered the first cultural imperialism in Africa by imposing hierarchical relations between the two groups, in which the Arabs were at the core and Africans at the periphery. African slaves were bought and transported with lots of other material goods from different parts of Africa.[14] The slaves, together with camels, served as the means of transporting these goods to the Middle East. Thus, the trans-Saharan trade opened the first path that linked Sub-Saharan Africa to the outside world. The systemic infusion of Arab cultural innovations into Africa was a great catalyst to the language and ideological barrier in their relations with the latter. This changed the face of many societies and relations among the forces of production, as these societies began to look Arab and cultivate Arabic institutions and practices. Through this, African dressing, marriage traditions, language, burial rites, political system, social formations, and others were tilted towards the Middle East. However, globalization cannot be said to have been fully attained, nor would it be dictated by the Arabs.

Centuries later, the Europeans came along the coast in the late fifteenth century to usurp this project from the Arabs. Meanwhile, Africans were neither idle nor onlookers in the evolving scheme of things. It was in the bid by different cultural groups in Africa to expand their territories, build stronger polities, and break the barrier of people and market connectivity—all with the potential to spur further changes—that the European colonization of Africa took form.[15] Although many novel inventions had been made in the maritime history of the world before the late fifteenth-century European voyages to Africa, led by the Spanish and the Portuguese, this period signals a fundamental bend in the history of the evolution of a "planetary age."[16] This was mainly due to mastering the waters and maritime skills that had evolved in Europe at this time. The trading routes patterned along this line would later prove to be more profitable and efficient for state growth, compared to the one that required less technological input along the Sahara. Events shifted along the coasts of Africa, and new cities emerged with a pseudo-image of the West.

Therefore, by the late 1880s, when the rush to colonize Africa by European imperialists began earnestly, along the Sahara were the states heavily linked to Arab civilization and those along the coast to the West. Britain and France assumed the mantle of European imperial leadership from Portugal and Spain at this time, with the two holding the largest and most profitable colonies in Africa. This power transition cannot be isolated from the technological advancement and cultural innova-

---

[14] Toyin Falola and Matthew M. Heaton, eds., *A History of Nigeria* (Cambridge: Cambridge University Press, 2008), 11–12.
[15] A. Adu Boahen, ed., *General History of Africa: VII Africa Under Colonial Domination 1880–1935*. Abridged Edition (Paris: UNESCO, 1990).
[16] Mahmood Mamdani, Thandika Mkandawire, and Wamba-dia-Wamba, "Social Movements, Social Transformation and Struggle for Democracy in Africa," *Economic and Political Weekly* 23, no. 19 (1988): 974.

tions that Britain and France championed during the industrial revolution. They brought these technologies and innovations along with them to their colonies across the world. Both Arab- and early European-influenced areas before colonization experienced the gradual imposition of Western structures and values. The extent to which this was formed often depended on how deep Islamic institutions were entrenched in these areas. Yet, this could not stand as an impediment to Western universality. By the decade of African independence, which was in the 1960s, modern African states emerged with what Mazrui referred to as a triple identity heritage, with an overwhelming presence of Western modernity through government bureaucracy and social configuration of the society.[17]

More than at any time in the history of the world, the colonization project of Western European states melted cultures and structures as it collapsed boundaries and hitherto conceived limitations. Events in Europe in the preceding century—the industrial revolution in the main—made the colonial project a reality. The industrial revolution transformed the society from an analog form of production to a mechanical one. Large industries emerged in Europe, overshadowing the artisan productions of previous ages, thereby reducing human labor in production (one of the reasons for the abolition of the slave trade) and increasing productivity and efficiency of time. The revolution spawned telecommunications, transportation systems, power supply, typewriters, and other inventions that facilitated colonial projects around the world.

More so, the simple financial system of the society was reformed by the creation of a banking system and organized financial structures in Europe. This introduced European currencies and currency boards in Africa. Colonization exacerbated the globalization process with forms and structures that various colonial powers left in their colonies, all of which many post-independent states have been reproducing ever since.[18] This metamorphosed into the democratization of modern states and the creation of liberal societies as the yardstick for good governance.[19] Altogether, these structures became the instruments of modern governance, social relations, and market engagements. The idea of colonization now forms the basis of a global community where, among other things, the whole world gravitates towards advancing a single culture. It bears telling that, generally, the twentieth century was a vital turning point in the evolution of a world-as-global-village.

From colonization to the world wars, the Cold War to the rise of independence movements, the formation of a new template of an international community to the emergence of new actors in the international community (the new world order), the rise and collapse of new powerful states to the triumph of capitalism and emergence of what some have referred to as a unipolar world under the tutelage of the United States together with her European allies. There was also the birth of a new

---

[17] Ali A. Mazrui, *The Africans: A Triple Heritage: A Commentary* (Washington, DC: WETA, 1986).
[18] Kohli, *State-Directed Development*.
[19] Amartya Sen, "Democracy as a Universal Value," *Journal of Democracy* 10, no. 3 (1999): 3–17.

industrial revolution marked by enhanced efficiency in communication, transportation, production, consumption, and business transaction. This also includes the emergence and proliferation of regional and trans-regional communities, among other things, fundamentally the twentieth century consolidated events of the previous centuries. The twentieth century saw to it that the local was linked to the global in terms of events and implications. Eventually, globalization came to replace colonization as the same actors anchored the two projects. However, unlike colonization, globalization gave modern states the liberty to form alliances, make agreements, sign treaties, conceive of national goals, and play an active role as a major actor in the international community.

As earlier mentioned, these fundamentals, when placed side-by-side with the precolonial engagements of Africans with one another and the outside world, what comes up is a similitude of consciousness and drive of the social forces fueling these paradigms. As in the old, the extent to which a modern state exercises this liberty in the (international) community depends heavily on its status as a duly independent state. The yardstick for this in the world political system is predominantly based on the financial and military muscle of the state. Invariably, these two are products of the technological advancement of the state. Wherever technology and trade go, a favorable globalization train follows, putting the western countries in charge of this train for long; until recently, with the rise of the likes of China and the United Arab Emirates. As found in Africa and others elsewhere, the aid-dependent states cannot reflect the above opportunities offered by globalization, all of which adumbrate its departure from colonization.

Africa in the Globalization Discourse

Today, the world is moving through the fourth industrial revolution characterized by data and the Internet of Doing Things. The convergence of (human) science and technology is producing results that promise to alter not only the social formation of man but the very nature of humanity. More and more, technology is amending the roles of humans in their environment. From reducing the need for human-to-human and human-to-machine contact to integrating the world more efficiently through the clouds, among many other things, the fourth industrial revolution remains the current force driving contemporary globalization around the world. This new revolution is building on the third that was characterized by the transformation of the second industrial revolution inventions into smart and more efficient components and now serves as a bridge between the digital and the physical world.

However, this convergence has not only shaped customers' experience and engagements; it has equally changed the whole paradigm of doing business. Businesses in the new era of digitization, from infrastructural setup to executing transactions and taking business decisions, can now be done online with little to no physical contact between buyer and seller. The best strategy for today's businesses is not to have a permanent address or infrastructure but to build a vast online presence. This has not only changed the forces of production and the role of land in this; more importantly, it has altered the relations among these forces. No better term fits this evolution succinctly than the digital economy. Africans have benefitted from this to some extent with online stores like Jumia, Afrikart, Kikuu, Konga, Jiji, Planet54, Zando, and many more in Nigeria, South Africa, and Mozambique, for instance, and other online businesses that have succeeded in breaking the jinx of physical facility and contact before transactions could be made.

In the same vein, platforms like Amazon, eBay, AliExpress, ASOS, and other international brands allow many Africans with the means and access to purchase products outside of their physical geographical space and reach. WhatsApp, Instagram, Tiktok, Facebook, and other social media platforms have created another set of entrepreneurs. No matter how absurd the preoccupation might appear, "followers" on these platforms constitute another community of people influenced by the same culture, a culture beyond the web of a single civilization. This is instructive in light of the region's Hyphenate unemployment, underemployment, and poverty.

The twenty-first century offers opportunities for the pluriversal world and epistemologies that many Africanist scholars have subscribed to for long.[20] Within the space of about two decades, the number of African populations with access to the internet bourgeoned from a mere 4,514,400 to 526,710,313 in 2020.[21] Although this number represents merely half of the total African population, which currently stands around 1.5 billion (62.9 percent penetration rate). When compared to the 397,988,114, which represents 89.4 percent access in Europe[22] or 90 percent of the total 331,319,877 in America,[23] the community still provides an alternative as well as a major avenue for engaging the emerging market. In the overall analysis of the internet penetration worldwide, the same *Internet World Stats* recorded a 100 percent internet penetration, implying a new community of peoples around the globe with access to the exact content of information and likely to be influenced by a similar culture.

To own a media house is not necessarily linked to building a physical structure anymore, unlike in the previous industrial regime. The real community that exists

---

20 Toyin Falola, *The Toyin Falola Reader on African Culture, Nationalism, Development and Epistemology* (Austin: Pan-African University Press, 2018), 889–910.
21 IWS, "Internet Users Statistics for Africa (Africa Internet Usage, 2020 Population Stats and Facebook Subscribers)," Internet World Stats. Accessed August 31, 2020, https://www.internetworldstats.com/stats1.htm.
22 IWS, "Internet Usage in the European Union (Internet User Statistics, Facebook Subscribers and 2020 Population for the 27 European Union Member States)," Internet World Stats. Accessed August 31, 2020, https://www.internetworldstats.com/stats9.htm.
23 Monica Anderson, Andrew Perrin, Jingjing Jiang and Madhumitha Kumar, "10% OF Americans Don't Use the internet. Who are they?" *Pew Research Center*, April 22, 2019, Accessed August 31, 2020, www.pewresearch.org/fact-tank/2019/04/22/some-americans-dont-use-the-internet-who-are-they/%3famp=1.

today is online. To this extent, as mentioned earlier, globalization collapsed national boundaries and created a transnational community but erected another synthetic form of social boundaries. The global village now exists online, and this is where the new community of persons is formed. This community incubates modern civilization and not states. At the same time, it influences popular culture. In the age of globalization, popular culture is beyond national boundaries or control as it concentrates more on the social configuration of humanity, which has proven to be essential in the political and economic culture of every society. The transnationality of the globalized world and peoples has created a kind of relief, if not complacency, on the part of modern African states in their bid to provide employment opportunities and a conducive environment to explore an acquired skill to the latter by their citizens. Significantly, from the 1980s, when many African states were faced with the consequences of policy inconsistency and failures, leading to widespread economic hardship and increasing poverty, the rate of Africans migrating abroad, to Europe and America in particular, has grown more than ten times over, compared with the previous decades. This period marked the time the Bretton Woods Institutions were making inroads into the newly independent African states to launch neoliberal economies in this region as part of the Cold War ideological struggle for dominance and influence around the world.

The austerity measures of the Structural Adjustment project of these institutions, led at this time by the World Bank, spelled out doom for these states' economies. From hyper-inflation to skyrocketing unemployment rates, and other financial instabilities that became telling on the foreign reserves, exchange strength, and ability of the states to defend their economies or maintain a sustainable political ambiance, post-independent Africa became a paradox of expectation on the part of the people of the region.[24] The human capital flight soon became the trend by African professionals and skilled workers whose services were needed elsewhere. In more recent times, the list of countries with the need for professional and skilled labor, which many unemployed and underemployed Africans perfectly fit in, are increasing at different rates across states and regions. Hence, the job market for Africans has expanded beyond their conventional boundaries to OECD countries, including Turkey, Australia, Canada, and others like the United States and Europe earlier mentioned. Other places include China, Cuba, Saudi Arabia, the United Arab Emirates, and many more of the so-called greener pastures. This post-independent set of African migrants now form a new wave and a new community of African diaspora, especially in the Americas and parts of Europe.[25]

Through this medium of transnationality, foreign remittance and other immaterial assistance provided by this diaspora population occupy a significant space in the

---

[24] Ali Mazrui and C. Wondji, *General History of Africa Vol. VIII: Africa Since 1935* (Berkley: University of California Press, 1993).
[25] Toyin Falola and Adebayo Oyebade, eds., *The New African Diaspora in the United States* (London: Routledge, 2017).

evolution of post-independent African states. Transnationality opens another means for (struggling) states to generate revenue and assuage the pains of their population. In its 2018 foreign remittance ratings based on the officially captured flows, the World Bank reports that "Excluding China, remittances to low- and middle-income countries ($462 billion) were significantly larger than foreign direct investment flows in 2018 ($344 billion)."[26] Out of this capture, foreign remittance to Africa "grew almost 10 percent to $46 billion," all because of the chain effects of events across boundaries, which is characterized by economic growth and the emergence of strong economies around the world.[27] Ironically, this was when African economies were dragging with the two economic powers in the region, Nigeria and South Africa, battling with economic challenges stemming from mismanagement and failed policies that punctured the economic fortunes of these states. Revenues generated from the diaspora population have always gone a long way in assuaging the economic situation in these countries, sometimes more than foreign aids and assistance. The rise of African studies in Europe, the United States, and parts of Asia, like China and Japan, is another aspect of the dimension in which the "collapse of boundaries" and creation of a planetary age have impacted Africa.[28]

Globalization in the twenty-first century offers opportunities to states and their peoples alike to engage the space, increasingly created and modified for more efficiency, to their advantage. African studies in institutions based in these countries give the African narrative that has been so battered a facelift. African narrative has begun to trend, implicitly seeing to it that the process that repressed it in the first place is bringing it back to life.[29] However, these are just at the margins of the gains of globalization that there are, for Africa, considering her enormous potentials in human and natural resources. This is more so as they all appear to primarily be in service of other regions' drive for an advantageous place in the globalization race. At the same time, Africa is left with secondary gains. Indeed, the human capital flight from Africa could be regarded as an African way of engaging the global village in similitude with the medical diplomacy of Cuba, which serves the purpose of transferring medical labor to other countries, but neither the pattern nor the drive for the raging human capital flights from Africa is palatable.

Virtually all of these flights are aimed at escaping the debilitating working environment, abusive relationship with the state, and professional retrogression/stagna-

---

26 The World Bank, "Record High Remittances Sent Globally in 2018," The World Bank. Accessed August 31, 2020, https://www.worldbank.org/en/news/press-release/2019/04/08/record-high-remittances-sent-globally-in-2018.
27 The World Bank, "Record High Remittances."
28 Paul Tiyambe Zeleza, ed., *The Study of Africa, Volume 2: Global and Transnational Engagements* (Dakar: CODESRIA, 2007).
29 Zeleza ed., *The Study of Africa*.

tion.[30] Consequently, whatever the states get in turn substantially from this community are from the financial assistance they offer to their relatives back home and personal projects, while their skills and intellects are put in the service of producing what these remittances would be used to consume so that these revenues find their ways back to various European capitals, America, and/or China.

In addressing the place of Africa in contemporary globalization discourse entirely, it is a matter of necessity for one to understand two things: the social relations among production forces in the region and the morphology of her external relations. Whereas the latter is a phantom built on the reality of the former, the former gives a complex representation of the societal culture, without which the latter can hardly be adequately understood. As Zeleza and other scholars have rightly contended, one of the most problematic aspects of globalization is in the area of establishing the "intersections between the local and the global, the external and the internal, the inside and the outside."[31] This notwithstanding, James is of the view that:

> It is not the world systems that beget change in social relations, but rather social forces that emerged and extended their activities that produce the world market. The transformation wrought within the societies by the insertion in the world market must be seen as an ongoing reciprocal relationship between the forces and relations of production within a social formation and those that incorporate through the world market.[32]

In a way, James gives a perceptive interpretation of the relationship between the local and the global reality of things in a way that mirrors the preponderance of social formation of a state on its external relations and how these relations produce changes in the social formation and processes of the society through the agency of the production forces. In light of this, the other side of the place of Africa in the global setting exists in the realm of consumers and not producers of the globalization process and trends. As James rightly pointed out, this structure came in place due to the reaction of the social forces in Africa to the unraveling of a planetary age that reached a decisive stage with the eighteenth-century events in Europe—most telling of which was the French Revolution and the Industrial Revolution. Because of the path of governance the French Revolution ushered, albeit in principle, to the rest of the world,

---

30 Kenneth Kalu and Toyin Falola, *Exploitation and Misrule in Colonial and Post-colonial Africa* (New York: Palgrave Macmillan, 2019); Wale Adebanwi and Ebenezer Obadare, eds., *Encountering the Nigerian State* (New York: Palgrave Macmillan, 2010); Ali Mazrui, "Mega-Nigeria from Lugard to Gowon: Between Exceptionalism and Typicality," in *Brain Gain for the African Renaissance*, eds. Okello Oculi and Yakubu Nasidi (Zaria: Ahmadu Bello University Press, 2007), 12; Eniola Akinkuotu, "Doctors' Exodus Looms as International Flights Resume," Punch News, August 26, 2020, https://punchng.com/doctors-exodus-looms-as-international-flights-resume-this-week/, accessed on August 30, 2020.
31 Zeleza, ed., *The Study of Africa*, 9.
32 Petras James, "Dependency and World System Theory: A Critique and New Directions," *Latin American Perspectives* 8, no. 3–4 (1981): 150.

Fukuyama referred to this period as the end of history.[33] To date, this has become the template for social movements in every part of the world.[34] On the other hand, the industrial revolution extended and consolidated the material taste, which the precolonial African noble and royal classes have developed over time since their centuries of relations with European merchants from the late fifteenth century.[35]

The colonial enterprise of the various western European capitals in Africa, as noted earlier, incorporated the entire region directly into the European economy, which at the time serves as a euphemism for the world economy. The structure of relations this project configured for these colonies epitomized their subordinate status and allowed them to play the peripheral role in the evolving scheme, ground, or petty. Industries were supported by the colonial governments insofar as they were extractive for the production of minerals for the service of European industries who send the finished products back at huge prices. Meanwhile, indigenous productions and initiatives still endured during the colonial period through the early independence period, albeit under a life-support machine; the post-independence government removed the life-support machine as it did to all other colonial infrastructures that helped in the systemic exploitation of the colonies.[36]

So, while it is true that the cocoa farmer in Cote d'Ivoire gains from the global cocoa trade, like his ancestors, his fate in the business is anchored on the price manipulation that is beyond him. At the same time, his labor is not commensurate with his earnings because his European and Chinese buyers take the lion's share of the profits, not only through price manipulation but extensively through the production of several products from his cocoa seed. The farmer, like his forefathers, hardly knows anything about the value of the seed, the products gained from it, or how to transform his role in these relations.

The relations between the land and industry and the full exploitation of the environment have largely lagged in post-independent Africa. By the second decade of independence, the parochial formation of African economies has fully grown, and it was based on this template and its consequences that they began to engage the emerging global village. Among other things, the cacophony of the post-independent states in Africa—as reflected in inter-ethnic rivalries and rise of secessionist movements, religious crises, resource control conflicts, and others which the United Nations Resident Coordinator in Nigeria Edward Kallon recently put it identity, political,

---

33 Francis Fukuyama, "The End of History," *The National Interest* 16 (1989): 3–18.
34 Ron Eyerman, "Social Movements and Social Theory," *Sociology* 18, no. 1 (1984): 71–82; Tim Gee, *Counterpower: Making Change Happen* (Oxford: New International Publications Ltd., 2011).
35 R. Olufemi Ekundare, *An Economic History of Nigeria 1860–1960* (London: Methuen & Co Ltd, 1973).
36 Crawford Young, "Africa's Colonial Legacy," in *Strategies for African Development*, eds. Berg. R. J. and J. S. Whitaker (Berkeley: University of California Press, 1986), 25.

and resource caused instabilities[37]—derailed the wheel of a consciously defined role in the evolving planetary age.[38] All of these have their histories dating back to the immediate past epoch in Africa and its divisive tendencies.

Central to the operationalization and functionality of the global system are two actors: state and non-state actors. The state actors who play the leading role in molding this transformation, as constituted in Africa, represent fragmented geographical entities carved by European colonial powers and inherited from the same upon independence. Despite their cultural similarities and centuries of relations and exchanges before the colonial experience, these fragmented entities lack a shared vision. The sculptors of globalization carved Africa into their design as colonized and primitive peoples to be redeemed by the European Blood.

The territories upon which the emerging states would govern upon independence and through which their global relations would be coined and maintained were designed out of pure exploitative concerns of the colonial powers. Despite the fusion of hitherto fragmented cultures and communities into a more significant state, emotional attachment to primordial identities still prevailed in the colonies. As this continued bad blood and rivalries in the polities were good for the colonial government, so was it for post-independent governments in Africa. Feeding on the divisions among the population is useful for creating an estate of exploitation to benefit a section of the estate and their foreign counterparts in their drive at engaging the ever-evolving global market and the community, but not for gainful engagement of the estate as a whole.[39]

In the grand scheme of things, as it has been experienced in Africa and the other so-called Third World countries, such formation creates a space for mutual suspicion that gives no room for a coherent engagement with the outside world.[40] Nonetheless, as Nwadawere once opined, many Africanist scholars have joined in cautioning that it is not for us to pretend as if there is no division amongst us in terms of culture, history, and trajectory. Still, the most important thing is for us to realize that, in all the differences, there abound a plethora of similarities that can be built on.[41] With the increasing role of non-state actors in the global relations of things, it re-

---

[37] Olalekan Adetayo, "Insecurity: UN Urges Buhari to Consider Dialogue, Political Approach," Punch News, August 24, 2020. Accessed Augist 30, 2020, https://punchng.com/insecurity-un-urges-buhari-to-consider-dialogue-political-approach/.

[38] Thandika Mkandawire, "Shifting Commitments and National Cohesion in African Countries," in *Common Security and Civil Society in Africa*. ed. Lennart Wohlgemuth, Samantha Gibson, et al. (Sweden: Nordiska Afrikainstitutet, 1999), 23.

[39] Emmanuel Mayah, et al., "Inequality in Nigeria: Exploring the Drivers, Even It Up," *Oxfam International* (2017): 9–10.

[40] Toyin Falola, *Violence in Nigeria: The Crisis of Religious Politics and Secular Ideologies* (Rochester: University of Rochester Press, 1998).

[41] Thandika Nwadawere, ed., *African Intellectuals: Rethinking Political, Language, Gender and Development* (Dakar and London/New York: CODESRIA Books and Zed Books, 2005), 12–14.

mained to be seen the extent to which the state would continue to matter in the future of globalization.[42]

The African Personality and the Future of Globalization

It is taken into consideration here that, according to Marxist theory, Africa remained at the primitive communalism stage before the colonial period, and for the fact that it had no tendency to move beyond this stage, the colonization of the people was imperative. The argument on the entirety of this truth needs not to delay us here, as many Africanist scholars have shown otherwise with impeccable evidence from this past.[43] Nonetheless, it is important to reiterate that the different cultures that made up the modern states today played various roles in the formation of transnational humanity and were incorporated into the global system in tandem with these roles. And as earlier mentioned, these roles were guided by the cultural sophistication and innovation of the people.

To be sure, this was a major point of departure between the so-called Third World countries and their counterparts at the top of the globalization ladder. From the late 1400s, when trading relations were opened between Africans and their European contacts, these areas of departure have been long designed and established. This was the same way the Arab drive was imprinted in its relations with the people of Africa. Simply put, these cultures were relatively above Africa in terms of cultural sophistication and innovation at the point of contact and in the process of relations.[44]

China is putting on this toga in recent times, and the rise of its influence and dominance in Africa, as elsewhere around the world, has become the source of major concern for the West. Tellingly, in his study of Development-from-Above theory (the top-down model of development), Abass opined that "the disparities between the industrialized and under-developed countries will continue to widen remarkably, as long as the latter continues to adopt innovations or strategies that originates from the former."[45] This understanding could be seen in the recalibration of the relations

---

42 Already, the emerging culture in the current century, as earlier mentioned, is beyond the dictate of a single civilization or the reach of a state, even though this is predominantly western in form because of their leaning towards a liberal world.
43 See, for example, Monday Yakiban Mangvwat, *A History of Class Formation in the Plateau Province of Nigeria, 1902–1960: The Genesis of a Ruling Class* (Durham: Carolina Academic Press, 2013).
44 This clearly explains the preponderance of foreign religious and social forms on the African personality and society as well as the constant transfer of technology to Africa from the west, starting with the likes of guns and luxury products.
45 Isah Mohammed Abass, *The Political Economy of Rural Development in Nigeria* (Zaria: Ahmadu Bello University Press, 2014), 35.

between the colonial powers in Europe and China, countries in Southeast Asia, and their former settler colony of America, whose fight for independence set a precedence for the violent war of independence in other colonies.

Quite revealingly, the United States, in the shadows of World War II, emerged as a superpower, but its superpower signature would not follow the European template. The emergence of the United States in the world as a superpower altered the established form of state domination and influence significantly from what the Egyptians, Ethiopians, Persians, Greeks, Romans, Spanish, Portuguese, Japanese, British, French, and the rest conceived it to be during their reigns. In the same light, the British, French, Spanish, Portuguese, and other European imperial powers modified this structure away from the Babylonian age. All of these were attempts at creating a system that could help serve the purpose of cultural and economic imperialism over the ages by creating a shared community of humanity. The United States succeeded in creating this through the establishment of a global body, the United Nations, which inspired further closer relations among modern states and by advancing science and technology. Its domination of the new world order is anchored on vague entities that it has almost total control over.

By the end of World War II, industrial advancement and technological innovations had reached a stage where there was no need for the emerging powers to maintain the colonial form of influence and power. Already, these colonies existed on a web of structures woven to different European capitals, which was itself under the mercy of the United States to survive. Hence, the campaign for decolonization and globalization by the United States. It has been noted earlier how the Cold War played a major role in this campaign.[46] China is tapping into this current structure of state relations, dominance, and influence today, but with a different model from its history, culture, social formation, and contemporary global relations. Therefore, if the western ideological approach of engagement with Africa and the rest of the world is humanitarian, as it is often touted, that of the Chinese is developmental. Although, in the practical sense, both are less concerned about the humanitarian implications of their actions in Africa. Their official policy paths dictate what is expected of them and their relations with states in the region.

Still following the Abass submission, Singapore and other South-East Asian countries have modified their involvement in this evolving structure in their unique ways, giving birth to what has been described as the Asian Miracle.[47] Accordingly, there are a plethora of instances that suggest the validity of the Abass submission, which now resonates with the debate for the decolonization of Africa by many Afri-

---

[46] Gilbert M. Khadiagala, "Thoughts on Africa and the New World Order," *The Round Table: The Commonwealth Journal of International Affairs* 81, no. 324 (1992): 431–450.

[47] Issa Aremu, "Reflection on Asian Crisis," in *Reflections on Africa and the Global Affairs*, ed. Issa Aremu (Lagos: Malthouse Press, 2015), 12–15.

canist scholars around the world.[48] Replicating this miracle in Africa has been tasking, expectedly. This is more so in light of the reproduction of the bourgeois or would-be bourgeois of the nationalist period in post-independence Africa.[49] These actors sabotaged the reinvention of Africa as well as its relations with the outside world.

Generally, the region has surmounted many economic difficulties, but not by confronting them boldly, but by the "fortunate" emergence of new sources,[50] among which has been the foreign remittances. Africa has never been short of advice, indeed receiving more from external bodies than any other continent. Nevertheless, it has remained the poorest due to its disadvantaged place in the global relations of peoples, institutions, and markets. To this extent, Felix followed other scholars of Third World economies to warn that "Because of the 'leaps' that a later industrializer must make, their investments will tend to violate market wisdom and so they "must find some of their rationale and political support in prophetic, ideological visions of the long-run national interest."[51] This has become even more imperative when one considers that, as Edward Jaycox, a former vice president of the World Bank in the early 1990s, once noted: "After 30 years of technical assistance and so much money spent, Africa's weak institutions, lack of expertise, and current need for more—rather than less—assistance tells us we have failed badly in our efforts.... The donors have done a disservice to Africa, and many African governments have participated blindly."[52]

From the preceding are the positions of two institutions integral to the debated globalization trend on Africa, with the two implicitly speaking to the need for the decolonization of African economies and peoples, since the conventional template has proven to be inadequate. In the face of the evolving implications of the principal drivers of the global village— science and technologies—Africa can only position itself in a way in which it could lead the drive towards saving humanity by championing the green energy pursuit of the world, advancing "naturalogy" instead of tech-

---

[48] Linda Tuhiwai Smith, *Decolonizing Methodologies: Research and Indigenous Peoples (Second Edition)* (London: Zed Books, 2012); Achille Mbembe, *On the Post-Colony* (Berkeley: University of California Press, 2001); Ngugi wa Thiong'o, *Decolonising the Mind The Politics of Language in African Literature* (Harare: Zimbabwe Publishing House, 1981); Toyin Falola and Christian Jennings, eds., *Africanizing Knowledge: African Studies Across Disciplines* (New Jersey: Transaction Publishers, 2002).
[49] Jean Suret-Canale and A. Adu Boahen, "West Africa 1945–60," in *Africa Since 1935*, ed. Ali A. Mazrui (Paris: UNESCO Publishing, 1999), 162.
[50] A. I. Pogoson, *Nigeria Since Independence: The First 25 years: Launching Addresses, Speeches, and Reviews* (Ibadan: The Presidential Panel on Nigeria Since independence History Project, 1991).
[51] David Felix, "The Technological Factor in Socio-Economic Dualism Toward an Economy of Scale Paradigm for Development Theory," in *Essays on Economic Development and Cultural Change in Honour of Bert Hoselitz*, ed. M. Nash (Chicago: University of Chicago Press, 1977), 163.
[52] Edward Jaycox quoted in Thandika Mkandawire, "Shifting Commitments and National Cohesion," 31.

nology to protect the ecosystem.⁵³ It is pertinent to add that not everyone sees globalization from the perspective of positivity. For instance, scholars such as Cooper believe globalization as a concept has inadequacies, especially when mirroring it from his Afro-historical perspective.⁵⁴ In his work, he concisely argues the overemphasis on the influence and direction of globalization, much as modernization.

As a historian in assessing the causes, processes, and perhaps even more succinctly, the foundation of globalization, it does not portend a good narrative for Africa, while it might have been great for Europe and North America, and in recent times, China and other Asian powers. In his argument on contemporaneity, he asserts that the foundation of the reality of interconnectedness is missing in the concept of globalization.⁵⁵ In his strong critique of globalization, he exposed the unevenness which characterizes the continents and players within the concept. Indeed, globalization has been examined within the framework of universalism; uniformity of cultural practices, relative ease of cross-bordering, futuristic examination of limitations and resolving them, and the likes.

However, what has often been missing is that globalization has not changed the structure and position of the world, and neither has it relatively benefitted the continent of Africa, which remains at the bottom of the structure ladder. His argument found a valid premise in how internalization (which he prefers to globalization) doomed Africa's finances with the introduction of the Structural Adjustment Program to hapless African countries in the last two decades of the twentieth century. The result was all the same, a case of how globalization could also be viewed from the perspective of how foreign domination has continued the trend of inequality, with Africa being at the receiving end of foreign importation of ideas and not parity in production power.

Conclusion

Africans have been engaging the emerging world market for long, and in their terms, before they were arm-twisted by western imperial-turned-colonial powers through a capitalist proclivity that has lost its nuts, leaving the wheels in a constituted menace. However, aside from the technological advancement of Europe, which was ahead of Africa at the time, as it still is, the standard front formed by the modern states now referred to as the western imperial powers, was, and is still, fundamental to the dominance of western culture and these modern states in the contemporary globalization discourse.

---

53 More than anything, the naturalogy is concerned about the human and environmental cost of innovations and inventions.
54 Frederick Cooper, "What is the Concept of Globalization Good For? An African Historian's Perspective," *African Affairs* 100, no. 399 (2001): 189–213.
55 Cooper, "Concept of Globalization?"

As seen in the case of China, which is also taking the lead in this grand scheme in the twenty-first century, as the rise of nationalism continued to spread in the West, a clear national vision and ideology enhance the global vision and engagement of a state. As earlier mentioned, globalization and nationalism are two antithetical notions, and this explains why China stands as the carrier of the global village vision in more recent times.[56]

However, African states are not even faced with the challenge of any ideological leaning like nationalism, conservatism, liberalism, and others, but with a primitive preoccupation with their linguistic, cultural, and religious differences, which they frantically make an effort to protect. As the above has shown, this has neither transformed their role in the periphery of the global system nor allow for a coherent national vision that could have reflected any hope of nationalism as seen the Trump's America, for instance. If anything, this tendency sealed the place of Africa in this peripheral condition that started even when the states were living their different polities. This implies that the present stage in the societal evolution of Africa might not be viable for the transformation of role and place in the evolving global scheme. Therefore, it is vital that the relations among the forces of production and the relations of production are attentively seen in Africa through an entire social revitalization process of the society. The world is moving at an unprecedented pace of innovations and inventions. Africa is currently nowhere in these productions, but its peoples and resources have consistently played integral roles.

Annexing these opportunities for regional growth, reinforcing an African personality, and creating a pluriversal world where epistemologies, ontologies, and methodologies are attached to their relative significance and inclusion, should be unnegotiable in the task of creating a better future for all Africans in Africa and a proud heritage for those in the diaspora. As the world keeps connecting and the barriers of all real and imagined boundaries are collapsing—as it is expected regardless of the turn of events in the West which championed and modeled this project in the first place more than any other civilization—Africa, as Gumede once noted, can position itself in a place of advantage for the next century from the current one, or waste it on its current form.[57] Whatever the case, the time for Africa to reconstitute her engagement with this space is now, and this will tell of its place in the twenty-second century.

---

[56] Among other instances, we see the United Kingdom breaking loose from an age-long union that serves as a template to other regional bodies across the world; the United States turning the tide against free market and threatening the global order, and the rise of populist parties in different parts of Europe, all within the last decade.

[57] Vusi Gumede, "Exploring Thought Leadership, Thought Liberation and Critical Consciousness for Africa's Development," *Africa Development / Afrique et Développement* 40, no. 4 (2015): 91–111.

Select Bibliography

Abass, Isah Mohammed. *The Political Economy of Rural Development in Nigeria* (Zaria: Ahmadu Bello University Press, 2014).
Abdulkadir, M.S., *An Economic History of Igalaland Central Nigeria 1896 1939* (Zaria: Ahmadu Bello University Press, 2014).
Abiola, E. Ola, *A Textbook of West African History A.D. 1000 to the Present* (Ado Ekiti: Omotayo Standard Press and Bookshops, 1975).
Adebanwi, Wale and Obadare Ebenezer, Eds., *Encountering the Nigerian State* (New York: Palgrave Macmillan, 2010).
Adesina, J. O., Graham and Yao Olukoshi, A., *Africa and Development Challenges in the New Millennium: The NEPAD Debate* (London: Zed Books, 2006).
Adi, H., *Pan Africanism A History* (London: Bloomsbury Academic, 2018).
Adams, John, *Remarks on the Country Extending from Cape, Palmas to the River Congo* (London: Frank Cass, 1966).
Abbink, Jon, Mirjam de Bruijn, and Klaas van Walraven, Eds., *Rethinking Resistance: Revolt and Violence in African History* (Leiden: Brill, 2003).
Afigbo, Adiele E., "Africa and the Abolition of the Slave Trade" *William and Mary Quarterly* LXVI, 4 (2009): 705–714.
Ai, Zhouchang 艾周昌, and Mu, Tao 沐涛, *Zhongfei Guanxi Shi* 中非关系史 (History of Sino-African Relations), (Shanghai: Huadong shifan daxue chubanshe, 1996).
Ajayi, J. F. A., "Africa at the Beginning of the Nineteenth Century: Issues and Prospects," in *General History of Africa- VI: Africa in the Nineteenth Century until the 1880s* ed. Ajayi J.F.A (Oxford: Heinemann Educational Publishers, 1995).
Ajayi, J. F. A., and Michael Crowder, Eds., *History of West Africa Vol. 1: The Nineteenth Century to the Partition* (London, Longman, 1968).
Ajayi, J. F. A. and Ian Espie, Eds., *A Thousand Years of West African History* (Nairobi, Ibadan and University Progress and Nelson, 1965).
Ajayi, S. Ademola, Ed., *African Culture and Civilization* (Ibadan, Atlantis Books, 2005).
Ake, C., *African Political Economy* (New York: Longman Ltd, 1981).
Albright, D., *South Africa's Secret Nuclear Weapons* (Washington: Institute for Science and International Security, 1994).
Alden, Chris, Daniel Large, and Ricardo Soares de Oliveira, Eds., *China Returns to Africa: A Rising Power and A Continent Embrace* (London: Hurst and Co., 2008).
Alilio, M.S., et al., "Are Multilateral Malaria Research and Control Programs the Most Successful? Lessons from the Past 100 Years in Africa," *The American Journal of Tropical Medicine and Hygiene* 71, 2 (2004): 268–278.
Alim, H. Samy, "Introduction: Straight outta Compton, Straight *aus Munchen*: Global Linguistic flows, Identities and the Politics of Language in a Global Hip Hop Nation," in *Global Linguistic flows: Hip Hop Cultures, Youth Identities and the Politics of Language,* eds. H. Sami Alim, Awad Ibrahim & Alistair Pennycook (New York: Routledge, 2009), 1–22.
Alkalimat, Abdul A., "The Contribution of African-Americans to the Development of the United States of America," in *African Today* ed. Ralph Uwechue (London: African Books, 2000).
Allen, Richard B., "Human Trafficking in Asia before 1900: A Preliminary Census," *International Institute for Asian Studies Newsletter* 87 (October 2020): 32–33.
Almond, D., and B. Mazumder, "The 1918 Influenza Pandemic and Subsequent Health Outcomes: An Analysis of SIPP Data," *American Economic Review* 95, 2 (2005), 258–262.
Alpers, Edward A., *The Indian Ocean in World History* (New York: Oxford University Press, 2014).

Alpers, Edward A., "East Central Africa," in *The History of Islam in Africa* eds. Nehemia Levtzion and Randall L. Pouwels (Athens, OH/Oxford/Cape Town: Ohio University Pres/James Currey/David Philip, 2000).

Alpers, Edward A., "Recollecting Africa: Diasporic Memory in the Indian Ocean World," *African Studies Review* 43, 1 (April 2000): 83–99.

Amanfu W., "Contagious Bovine Pleuropneumonia (Lung Sickness) in Africa," *Onderstepoort Journal of Veterinary Research* 76, 1 (2009),13–17.

Anene, Joseph C., *Essays in African History: 19th and 20th Centuries* (Ibadan: Onibonoje Press, 1977).

Anene, Joseph C., and G. N. Brown, *Africa in the 19th and 20th Centuries* (Ibadan: Ibadan University Press, 1966).

Anywar, G., E. Kakudidi, R. Byamukama, J. Mukonzo, A. Schubert, and H. Oryem-Origa, "Indigenous Traditional Knowledge of Medicinal Plants used by Herbalists in Treating Opportunistic Infections Among People Living with HIV/AIDS in Uganda," *Journal of Ethnopharmacology* 246 (2020), 112–20.

Appadurai, Arjun, *Modernity at Large: Cultural Dimensions of Globalization* (Minneapolis: University of Minneapolis Press, 1996).

Appiah, Kwame Anthony, "Europe Upside Down: Fallacies of the New Afrocentrism," in *Perspectives on Africa: A Reader in Culture, History, and Representation,* ed. by Roy Richard Grinker and Christopher B. Steiner (Oxford: Blackwell, 1999), 728–731.

Aremu, Issa., "Reflection on Asian Crisis" in *Reflections on Africa and the Global Affairs* ed. Issa Aremu (Lagos: Malthouse Press, 2015), 12–15.

Asante, Molefi Kete., *Kemet, Afrocentricity and Knowledge* (Trenton, Africa World Press, 1990).

Aspinall, Peter and Lavinia Mitton., *The Migration History, Demography, and Socioeconomic Position of the Somali community in Britain* (New York, Nova Science Publishers, 2011).

Attaran, A., and L. Gillespie-White, "Do Patents for Antiretroviral Drugs Constrain Access to AIDS Treatment in Africa?" *Jama* 286, 15 (2001), 1886–1892.

Babalola, E. O., *The Advent and Growth of Islam in West Africa* (Lagos: Publication and International, 1973).

Baird, J. K., Resurgent Malaria at the Millennium, *Drugs*, 59, 4 (2000), 719–743.

Ballester-Arnal, R., and M.D. Gil-Llario, "The Virus That Changed Spain: Impact of COVID-19 on People with HIV," *AIDS and Behavior* 24, 8 (2020): 2253–2257.

Banaji, Jairus, *Theory as History: Essays on Modes of Production and Exploitation.* (Chicago: Haymarket Books, 2010).

Bang, Anne, *Sufis and Scholars of the Sea: Family Networks in East Africa, 1860–1925* (Abingdon/New York: Routledge, 2003).

Barber, Karin, "Introduction," *Readings in African Popular Culture*, ed. by Karin Barber (Bloomington and Indianapolis: Indiana University press, 1997), 1–12.

Barham, Lawrence S., and Peter J. Mitchell, *The First Africans: African Archaeology from Earliest Toolmakers to Most Recent Foragers* (Cambridge: Cambridge University Press, 2008).

Barkan, Joel, "Rethinking Budget Support for Africa: A Political Economy Perspective," in *Smart Aid for African Development,* eds. Richard Joseph and Alexandra Gillies Boulder (London: Lynne Rienner Publishers, 2009), 67–85.

Barnett, Michael, Ed., *Rastafari in the New Millennium: A Rastafari Reader* (Syracuse, University of Syracuse Press 2014).

Barnouin, Barbara, and Changgen Yu, *Chinese Foreign Policy during the Cultural Revolution* (London: Kegan Paul International, 1988).

Barraclough, Geoffrey, *Turning Points in World History* (London: Thames and Hudson, 1979).

Barrow, Steve and Peter Dalton, *The Rough Guide to Reggae* (London, Penguin Books, 2004).

Barton, Nick, and Abdeljalil Bouzouggar, "Hunter-gatherers of the Maghreb 25,000–6,000 Years Ago," in *The Oxford Handbook of African Archaeology* ed. by Peter J. Mitchell and Paul J. Lane (Oxford: Oxford University Press, 2013), 431–444.

Bastide, Roger, *African Civilizations in the New World* (London: C. Hurst & Company, 1967).

Basu, Helene "Drumming and Praying: Sidi at the Interface of Spirit Possession and Islam," in *Struggling with History: Islam and Cosmopolitanism in the Western Indian Ocean,* ed. by Edward Simpson and Kai Kresse (New York: Columbia University Press, 2008), 291–322.

Basu, Helene "Redefining Boundaries: Twenty Years at the Shrine of Gori Pir," in *Sidis and Scholars: Essays on African Indians* eds. Amy Catlin-Jairazbhoy and Edward Alpers (Trenton, NJ: Rainbow Publishers, 2004), 62–85.

Bauer, Peter T., *Dissent on Development* (Boston: Harvard University Press, 1972).

Bayart, Jean Francois, and Stephen Ellis, "Africa in the World: A History of Extraversion," *African Affairs* 99, 395 (2000): 217–267.

Baylis, J., J. J. Wirtz, and C. S. Gray, Eds., *Strategy in the Contemporary World* (Oxford: Oxford University Press, 2010).

Behrendt, Stephen, A. J. H. Latham, and David Northrup, *The Diary of Antera Duke, an Eighteenth-Century African Slave Trader* (Oxford and New York: Oxford University Press, 2010).

Berg, Herbert., "Mythmaking in the African American Muslim Context: The Moorish Science Temple, The Nation of Islam and the American Society of Muslims," *Journal of the American Academy of Religion* 73, 3 (2005), 685–703.

Berger, Iris, *South Africa in World History* (Oxford: Oxford University Press, 2009).

Bhabha, Homi, *The Location of Culture* (London: Routledge, 1994).

Bishaw, M., (1991), "Promoting Traditional Medicine in Ethiopia: A Brief Historical Review of Government Policy," *Social Science and Medicine* 33, 2 (1991): 193–200.

Blackburn, Robin, *The Overthrow of Colonial Slavery: 1776–1848* (London, 1988).

Boahen, A. Adu, Ed., *UNESCO General History of Africa, Vol. VII, Abridged Edition: Africa Under Colonial Domination 1880–1935* (Berkeley, California: University of California Press, 1990).

Bodomo, Adam, "The African Trading Community in Guangzhou: An Emerging Bridge for Africa-China Relations," *The China Quarterly* 203 (2010): 693–707.

Bond, Patrick, *Looting Africa: The Economics of Exploitation* (London: Zed Books, 2006).

Borstelmann, Thomas, *Apartheid Reluctant Uncle: The United States and Southern Africa in the Early Cold War* (New York: Oxford University Press, 1993).

Boston, J., "Medicines and Fetishes in Igala," *Africa: Journal of the International African Institute* 41, 3 (1971), 200–207.

Bouzouggar, Abdeljalil, et al., "82,000-Year-old Shell Beads from North Africa and Implications for the Origins of Modern Human Behavior," *Proceedings of the National Academy of Sciences (USA)* 104 (2007): 9964–9969.

Bratton, Michael and Carolyn Logan, "Voters but Not Yet Citizens: Democratization and Development Aid," in *Smart Aid for African Development* eds. Richard Joseph and Alexandra Gillies Boulder (London: Lynne Rienner Publishers, 2009), 181–206.

Braudel, F., *The Mediterranean and the Mediterranean World in the Age of Philip II,* (London: Collins, 1972).

Brautigam, Deborah, *The Dragon's Gift: The Real Story of China in Africa* (Oxford: Oxford University Press, 2009).

Brautigam, Deborah, *Will Africa Feed China?* (Oxford: Oxford University Press, 2016).

Bremond, Laurent, et al., "Past Tree Cover of the Congo Basin Recovered by Phytoliths and $\delta^{13}C$ along Soil Profiles," *Quaternary International* 434 (2017): 91–101.

Breunig, Peter, Ed., *Nok: African Sculpture in Archaeological Context* (Frankfurt am Main: Africa Magna Verlag, 2014).

Bright, Rachel K., *Chinese Labour in South Africa, 1902–10: Race, Violence, and Global Spectacle* (New York: Palgrave Macmillan, 2013).

Broodbank, Cyprian, *The Making of the Middle Sea: A History of the Mediterranean from the Beginning to the Emergence of the Classical World* (London: Thames and Hudson, 2013).

Brooke-Smith, Robin, Ed., *The Scramble for Africa* (London: Macmillan, 1987).

Brown, Christopher L., *Moral Capital: Foundations of British Abolitionism* (Chapel Hill: University of North Carolina Press, 2006).

Bruder, Edith and Tudor Parfitt, Ed., *African Zion: Studies in Black Judaism* (Newcastle upon Tyne, Cambridge Scholars, 2012).

Brzezinski, Zbigniew, *Power and Principle: Memoirs of the National Security Adviser 1977–1981* (London: Weidenfeld & Nicolson, 1983).

Burrough, Sallie L., "Late Quaternary Environmental Change and Human Occupation of the Southern African Interior," in *Africa from MIS 6–2: Population Dynamics and Paleoenvironments* ed. by Sacha C. Jones and Brian A. Stewart (Dordrecht: Springer, 2016), 161–174.

Burrow, John, *A History of Histories: Epics, Chronicles, Romances and Inquiries from Herodotus and Thucydides to the Twentieth Century* (London: Penguin Books, 2009).

Burto, John W. ed., *Non-Alignment* (London: Ander Deutsch Limited, 1966).

Byfield, Judith, and Carolyn Brown, eds., *Africa and World War II* (New York: Cambridge University Press, 2015).

Caini, S., et al., "Distribution of Influenza Virus Types by Age using Case-Based Global Surveillance Data from Twenty-Nine Countries, 1999–2014," *BMC Infectious Diseases* 18, 1 (2018): 1–10.

Campbell, C., Y. Nair, S. Maimane, and J. Nicholson, "'Dying Twice' A Multi-Level Model of the Roots of AIDS Stigma in Two South African Communities," *Journal of Health Psychology* 12, 3 (2007): 403–416.

Campbell, G., K. A. Roberts, and N. Sarkaria, "Witchcraft, Spirit Possession and Belief Based Abuse," in *Harmful Traditional Practices* (London, Palgrave Macmillan, 2020):101–117.

Campbell, Gwyn, ed., *The Structure of Slavery in Indian Ocean Africa and Asia* (London: Frank Cass/Routledge, 2004).

Campbell, Gwyn, "Slavery in the Indian Ocean World," in *The Routledge History of Slavery*, ed. by Gad Heuman and Trevor Burnard (London: Routledge, 2011), 52–63.

Campbell, Gwyn, *Africa and the Indian Ocean World from Early Times to circa 1900* (Cambridge, UK: Cambridge University Press, 2019).

Cann, Rebecca L., Mark, Stoneking, and Allan C. Wilson, "Mitochondrial DNA and Human Evolution," *Nature* 325 (1987): 31–36.

Cannon, Katie G., *Katie's Cannon: Womanism and the Soul of the Black Community* (New York, Continuum, 1995).

Carmody, Pádraig, *The New Scramble for Africa* (Cambridge: Polity, 2011).

Cartledge, Mark, Sarah Dunlop, Heather Buckingham, and Sophie Bremmer, *Megachurches and Social Engagement: Public Theology in Practice* (Leiden: Brill, 2019).

Casey, Joanna, "The Stone to Metal Age in West Africa" in *The Oxford Handbook of African Archaeology* ed. Peter J. Mitchell and Paul J. Lane (Oxford: Oxford University Press, 2013), 603–614.

Cashmore, Ernest, *Rastaman: The Rastafari Movement in Britain* (London, George, Allen and Unwin, 1980).

Casson, Lionel, *The Periplus Maris Erythraei* (Princeton, NJ: Princeton University Press, 1989).

Castor, N. Fadeke., *Spiritual Citizenship: Transitional Pathways from Black Power to Ifá in Trinidad* (Durham: Duke University Press, 2017).

Catlos, Brian., *Kingdoms of Faith: A New History of Islamic Spain* (London: Hurst & Company, 2018).
Chan, Steve, *Exporting Apartheid: Foreign Policies in Southern Africa, 1978–1988* (New York: St. Martin's Press, 1990).
Charry, Eric, "A Capsule History of African Rap," in *Hip Hop Africa: New African Music in a Globalizing World,* ed. Eric Charry (Indiana: Indian University Press, 2012), 1–25.
Chenery, H. and A. M. Strout, "Foreign Assistance and Economic Development," *The American Economic Review* 56, 4 (1966), 679–731.
Chevannes, Barry., *Rastafari: Roots and Ideology* (Syracuse, University of Syracuse Press, 1994).
Chan, Stephen, "China's Foreign Policy and Africa: The Rise and Fall of China's Three World Theory," *The Round Table: The Commonwealth Journal of International Affairs* 74, 296 (1985): 376–384.
Chan, Stephen, ed., *The Morality of China in Africa* (London, Zed Books, 2013).
Childs, S. Terry, and Eugenia W. Herbert, "Metallurgy and its Consequences," in *African Archaeology: A Critical Introduction* ed. Ann B. Stahl (Oxford: Blackwells, 2005), 276–300.
Chinweizu, *The West and the Rest of Us; Black Slaves and the African Elite* (U.S.A: Random House, 1975).
Chirikure, Shadreck, *Metals in Past Societies: A Global Perspective on Indigenous African Metallurgy* (Cham: Springer, 2015).
Chittick, Neville, *Kilwa: An Islamic Trading City on the East African Coast* (Nairobi: British Institute in Eastern Africa, 1974).
Chouin, Gérard and Chris R. DeCorse, "Prelude to the Atlantic Trade: New Perspectives on Southern Ghana's Pre-Atlantic History (800–1500)," *Journal of African History* 51 (2010): 123–145.
Chorev N., "Changing Global Norms Through Reactive Diffusion: The Case of Intellectual Property Protection of AIDS Drugs," *American Sociological Review* 77, 5 (2012): 831–853.
Clark, J. Desmond, *Kalambo Falls Prehistoric Site, Volume III* (Cambridge: Cambridge University Press, 2001).
Cline, Eric H., *1177 B.C.: The Year Civilization Collapsed* (Princeton: Princeton University Press, 2014).
Cline, Lawrence E., *The Lord's Resistance Army* (Santa Barbara, Praeger, 2013).
Close, Angela E., "*Plus ça change:* The Pleistocene-Holocene Transition in Northeast Africa," in *Humans at the End of the Ice Age: The Archaeology of the Pleistocene-Holocene Transition* ed. by Lawrence G. Straus, Berit V. Eriksen, Jon M. Erlandson, and David R. Yesner (New York: Plenum Press, 1996), 43–60.
Close, Angela E. and Fred Wendorf, "North Africa at 18,000 BP," in *The World at 18,000 BP, Volume II, Low Latitudes* ed. by Clive S. Gamble and Olga Soffer (London: Unwin Hyman, 1990), 41–57.
Clough, Michael, *Free at Last?:US Policy Toward Africa and the End of the Cold War* (New York: Council on Foreign Relations Press, 1992).
Cohen, Herman, *Intervening in Africa: Superpower Peacemaking in a Troubled Continent* (Basingstoke: Macmillan, 2000).
Cohen, Warren, *The Cambridge History of American Foreign Relations Volume 4: America in the Age of Soviet Power,* 1945–1991 (Cambridge: Cambridge University Press, 2008).
Cone, James H., *Black Theology and Black Power* (New York, Orbis 2008, first edition 1969).
Comaroff, Jean and John Comaroff, "Occult Economies and the Violence of Abstraction: Notes from the South African Postcolony," *American Ethnologist* 26, 2 (1999): 297–303.
Compiling Group of China Africa Education Cooperation and Communication 中非育合作与交流编写组, *Zhongguo yu Feizhou Guoji Jiaoyu Hezuo yu Jiaoliu* 中国非洲国家教育合作与交流 (China Africa Education Cooperation), (Beijing: Beijing

daxue chubanshe, 2005).
Cooley, John K., *East Wind over Africa: Red China's African Offensive* (New York: Walker and Company, 1965).
Cooper, Frederick, *Colonialism in Question Theory, Knowledge, History* (Berkeley: University of California Press, 2005).
Craddock, Paul T., "New paradigms for Old Iron: Thoughts on E. Zangato & A.F.C. Holl's 'On the Iron Front,'" *Journal of African Archaeology* 8 (2010): 29–36.
Craig, A. M. et al, *The Heritage of World Civilization* (New Jersey, Pearson, 2005).
Creel, Margaret W., *A Peculiar People: Slave Religion and Community-Culture among the Gullahs* (New York: University Press, 1988).
Crocker, C., *High Noon in Southern Africa: Making Peace in a Rough Neighbourhood* (Johannesburg: Jonathan Ball, 1992).
Crocker, Chester, *High Noon in Southern Africa: Making Peace in a Rough Neighbourhood* (New York: W.W. Norton, 1992).
Crowther, Alison, et al, "Coastal Subsistence, Maritime Trade, and the Colonization of Small Offshore Islands in Eastern African Prehistory," *Journal of Island and Coastal Archaeology* 11 (2016a): 211–237.
Crowther, Alison, et al, "Ancient Crops Provide First Archaeological Signature of the Westward Austronesian Expansion," *Proceedings of the National Academy of Sciences (USA)* 113 (2016b): 6635–6640.
Crowder, Michael, *The Story of Nigeria* (London: Faber and Faber, 1975).
Curtin, Philip, *Cross-Cultural Trade in World History* (Cambridge: Cambridge University Press, 1984).
Curtis IV, Edward E., and Danielle Brune Sigler, eds., *The New Black Gods: Arthur Huff Fauset and the Study of African American Religions* (Bloomington, University of Indiana Press, 2009).
Daiute, Colette, "General Introduction: The Problem of Youth Conflict," *International Perspectives on Youth Conflict and Development*, ed. by Colette Daiute, Zeynep Beykont, Craig Higson-Smith & Larry Nucci (New York: OUP, 2006): 3–20.
Donaldson, Robert, *The Soviet Union in the Third World: Successes and Failures* (Boulder; London: Westview Press, 1981).
David, Noy, *Foreigners at Rome: Citizens and Strangers* (UK: Classical Press of Wales, 2000).
Davidson, Basil, *Africa in History* (New York: Macmillan, 1969).
Davidson, Basil, *A History of West Africa 1000–1800* (London, Longman, 1965).
Davies, J. E., *Constructive Engagement? Chester Crocker and the American Policy in South Africa, Namibia and Angola*, (Athens: Ohio University Press, 2007).
de Maret, Pierre, "Archaeologies of the Bantu Expansion," in *The Oxford Handbook of African Archaeology* ed. by Peter J. Mitchell and Paul J. Lane (Oxford: Oxford University Press, 2013), 627–643.
Derryck, Vivian Lowery, "The Commission for Africa: Assessing the Approach," in *Smart Aid for African Development*, ed. by Richard Joseph and Alexandra Gillies (Boulder London: Lynne Rienner Publishers 2009), 49–64.
Diamond, Larry, "Forward," *Smart Aid for African Development* eds. Richard Joseph and Alexandra Gillies (Boulder London: Lynne Rienner Publishers, 2009), vii-xi.
Diara, B. C., J. C. Diara, and N. G. Christian, "The 19th Century European Missionaries and the Fight Against Malaria in Africa," *Mediterranean Journal of Social Sciences* 4, 16 (2013), 89–89.
di Lernia, Savino, "The Emergence and Spread of Herding in Northern Africa: A Critical Reappraisal," in *The Oxford Handbook of African Archaeology*, ed. by Peter J. Mitchell and Paul J. Lane (Oxford: Oxford University Press, 2013), 527–540.

Diouf, Sylviane A., ed., *Fighting the Slave Trade: West African Strategies* (Athens: Ohio University Press, 2003).
Diouf, Sylvanie, A., "Sadaqa Amongst African Muslims Enslaved in the Americas," *Journal of Islamic Studies* 10, 1 (1999): 22–32.
Diop, Cheikh Anta, *The African Origin of Civilization: Myth or Reality,* ed. by Mercer Cook (Chicago: Chicago Review, 1989).
Dobson, M., *Murderous Contagion: A Human History of Disease* (Quercus Publishing, 2015).
Domínguez-Rodrigo, Manuel, et al, "Cutmarked Bones from Pliocene Archaeological Sites at Gona, Afar, Ethiopia: Implications for the Functions of the World's Oldest Stone Tools," *Journal of Human Evolution* 48 (2005): 109–121.
Drake, Nick, and Paul Breeze, "Climate Change and Modern Human Occupation of the Sahara from MIS 6–2," in *Africa from MIS 6–2: Population Dynamics and Paleoenvironments* ed. by Sacha C. Jones and Brian A. Stewart (Dordrecht: Springer, 2016), 103–122.
Drake, St Clair., *Black Folk Here and There: An Essay in History and Anthropology Volume 2* (Los Angeles, Center for Afro-American Studies, University of California, 1990).
Dubois, W. E. B., *The World and Africa: An Inquiry into the Part Which Africa Has played in World History* (New York: Viking, 1946).
Duiker, William J., and Jackson J. Spielvogel, *The Essential World History*. 9th ed. (Boston: Cengage, 2019).
Dunn, Ross E., *The Adventures of Ibn Battuta: A Muslim Traveler of the Fourteenth Century*, 3rd edition (Berkeley/Los Angeles: University of California Press, 2012).
Dunne, Julie, et al, "First Dairying in Green Saharan Africa in the 5th millennium BC," *Nature* 486 (2012): 390–394.
Dupuy, Trevor Nevitt, *Land Battles, North Africa, Sicily, And Italy: Military History of World War II V3* (Kila, Kessinger Publishing, L.L.C., 2007).
Durham, Deborah, "Youth and the Social Imagination in Africa: Introduction to Parts 1 and 2," *Anthropological Quarterly* 73, 3 (2000): 113–120.
Duyvendak, J. L. L., *China's Discovery of Africa* (London: Arthur Probsthain, 1949).
Dvorkin-Camiel, L., and Whelan, J. S., "Tropical American Plants in the Treatment of Infectious Diseases," *Journal of Dietary Supplements* 5, 4 (2008), 349–372.
Eaton, Richard, *A Social History of the Deccan, 1300–1761: Eight Indian Lives* (Cambridge, UK: Cambridge University Press, 2005).
Eckert, Penelope, and Sally McConnell-Ginet, "Think Practically and Look Locally: Language and Gender as Community-Based Practice," *Annual Review of Anthropology* 21 (1992): 461–490.
Edwards, David N., *The Nubian Past: An Archaeology of the Sudan* (London: Routledge, 2004).
Edward, George, *The Cuban intervention in Angola, 1965–1991: from Che Guevara to Cuito Cuanavale* (London: Frank Cass, 2005).
Ekundare, R. Olufemi, *An Economic History of Nigeria 1860–1960* (London: Methuen & Co Ltd, 1973).
El-Khawas ,M. and B. Cohen, eds., *National Security Memorandum 39: The Kissinger Study of Southern Africa (Secret)* (Westport: Lawrence Hill, 1976).
Elkins, Caroline, "Archives, Intelligence and Secrecy: The Cold War and the End of the British Empire," in *Decolonization and the Cold War: Negotiating Independence* ed. by Leslie James and Elisabeth Leake (London: Bloomsbury, 2015), 257–283.
Elsayid, E., *"The Hidden Role of World Bank and IMF in Developing Countries. Egypt, Malaysia and Turkey.* (Saarbrucken: AV Akademikerverlag, 2016).
Eltis, David, "Europeans and the Rise and Fall of African Slavery in the Americas: An Interpretation," *The American Historical Review* 98, 5 (1993): 1399–1423.
Empson, Martin, *Food, Agriculture and Climate Change.* (London: International Socialism, 2016).

Englebert, Pierre, "Pre-colonial Institutions, Post-colonial States, and Economic Development in Tropical Africa," *Political Research Quarterly,* 53 (2000), 7–35.

Engerman, David C., "The Cold War," in *Blackwell Companion to World History: A Companion to Russian History,* ed. by Abbot Gleason (United Kingdom; Wiley Blackwell, 2008), 414–423.

Enwerem, Iheanyi M., "'Money-Magic' and Ritual Killing in Contemporary Nigeria,. *Money Struggles and City Life: Devaluation in Ibadan and Other Urban Centers in Southern Nigeria 1986–1996,* ed. by Jane I. Guyer, LaRay Denzer & Adigun Agbaje (Ibadan: BookBuilders, 2003), 189–217.

Enweremadu, D. U., *Anti-Corruption Campaign in Nigeria (1999–2007): The Politics of a Failed Reform.* (Leiden, African Studies Centre, 2012).

Erskine, Noel Leo., *Plantation Church: How African-American Religion was Born in Caribbean Slavery* (Oxford, Oxford University, 2014).

Eyerman, Ron, "Social Movements and Social Theory," *Sociology* 18, 1 (1984): 71–82.

Falola, Toyin, *Violence in Nigeria: The Crisis of Religious Politics and Secular Ideologies* (Rochester: University of Rochester Press, 1998).

Falola, Toyin, *The Toyin Falola Reader on African Culture, Nationalism, Development and Epistemology* (Austin: Pan-African University Press, 2018), 889–910.

Falola, Toyin, and Adebayo Oyebade, eds. *The New African Diaspora in the United States* (London and New York: Routledge, 2017).

Falola, Toyin, and Matthew M. Heaton, eds., *A History of Nigeria* (Cambridge: Cambridge University Press, 2008).

Falola, Toyin, and A. Adediran, *A New History of Nigeria for Colleges Book I* (Lagos: John West Publication, 1986).

Farajalle, Samaan Boutros, "Non-Alignment: Ideological Pluralism," *Indian Quarterly* 2 (1989):198–206.

Fawole Alade, W., *Nigeria's External Relations and Foreign Policy under Military Rule 1966–1999.* (Ile-Ife: Obafemi Awolowo University Press Ltd, 2003).

Fee, Sarah, "Filling Hearts with Joy: Handcrafted 'Indian Textiles' Exports to Central Eastern Africa in the Nineteenth Century," in *Transregional Trade and Traders: Situating Gujarat in the Indian Ocean from Early Times to 1900,* ed. by Edward A. Alpers and Chaya Goswami (New Delhi: Oxford University Press, 2019), 163–217.

Feierman, "Therapy as a System-in-Action in Northeastern Tanzania," *Social Science & Medicine. Part B: Medical Anthropology* 15, 3 (1981), 353–360.

Fenner, F., (1993). "Smallpox: Emergence, Global Spread, and Eradication," *History and Philosophy of the Life Sciences,* 397–420.

Foley, Robert A., "Hominin Evolution as the Context for African Prehistory," in *The Oxford Handbook of African Archaeology* ed. by Peter J. Mitchell and Paul J. Lane (Oxford: Oxford University Press, 2013), 269–288.

Fomin, E. S. D., *A Comparative Study of Societal Influence on Indigenous Slavery in Two Types of Societies in Africa.* (New York: The Edwin Mellen Press, 2002).

Ford, N., et al, "Sustaining Access to Antiretroviral Therapy in the Less-Developed World: Lessons from Brazil and Thailand," *AIDS* 21 (2007), 21–29.

Förster, Frank, "Beyond Dakhla: The Abu Ballas Trail in the Libyan Desert (SW Egypt)," in *Desert Road Archaeology in Ancient Egypt and Beyond* ed. by Frank Förster and Heiko Riemer (Köln: Heinrich-Barth Institut, 2013), 297–338.

Franke, Gabrielle, "A Chronology of the Central Nigerian Nok Culture – 1500 BC to the Beginning of the Common Era," *Journal of African Archaeology* 14 (2016): 257–289.

Freeman-Grenville, G. S. P., *A Modern Atlas of African History* (London, Rex Collings, 1976).

French, Howard W., *China's Second Continent: How a Million Migrants Are Building a New Empire in Africa* (New York: Knopf, 2014).

Frenkel, M. Yu., "Edward Blyden and the Concept of African Personality," *African Affairs* 73, 292 (1974): 277–289.
Friedman, Jeremy Scott, *Shadow Cold War: The Sino-Soviet Competition for the Third World* (Chapel Hill: University of North Carolina Press, 2015).
Fukuyama, Francis, "The End of History?" *The National Interest* 16 (1989): 3–18.
Fukuyama, Francis, *The End of History and the Last Man* (London: Hamish Hamilton, 1992).
Fuller, Dorian Q., and Elisabeth Hildebrand, "Domesticating Plants in Africa," in *The Oxford Handbook of African Archaeology* ed. by Peter J. Mitchell and Paul J. Lane, (Oxford: Oxford University Press, 2013), 507–525.
Gbadamosi, G. T. O., *The Growth of Islam Among the Yorubas 1841–1908* (London, Longman Group Limited, 1978).
Gallagher, Eugene B., *The New Religious Movements Experience in America* (Westport, Greenwood Press, 2004).
Gallego, Llorente, et al, "Ancient Ethiopian Genome Reveals Extensive Eurasian Admixture Throughout the African Continent," *Science* 350 (2015): 820–822.
Gallup, J. L., and J. D. Sachs, "The Economic Burden of Malaria," *The American Journal of Tropical Medicine and Hygiene* 64, 1 (2001), 85–96.
Gamble, Clive S., *Settling the Earth: The Archaeology of Deep Human History* (Cambridge: Cambridge University Press, 2013).
Gampiot, A. M., "Kimbanguism as a Migrants Religion in Europe," in *Christianity in Africa and the African Diaspora: The Appropriation of a Scattered Heritage*, ed. by Afe Adogame, Roswith Gerloff and Klaus Hoff (London, Continuum, 2008), 304–313.
Gann, L. H., and Peter Duignan, eds., *Colonialism in Africa, 1870–1960* (Cambridge: Cambridge University Press, 1970).
Garthoff, Raymond, *Détente and Confrontation: American-Soviet Relations from Nixon to Reagan* (Washington, DC: Brookings Institution, 1994).
Gasbarri, Flavia, *US Foreign Policy and the End of the Cold War in Africa: A Bridge between Global Conflict and the New World Order, 1988–1994* (Abingdon, Oxon; New York, NY: Routledge, 2020: Routledge, 2020).
Gee, Tim, *Counterpower: Making Change Happen* (Oxford: New International Publications, 2011).
Gerber J., (2014), *International economics (6th ed.)* (Boston: Pearson 2014).
Gifford-Gonzalez, Diane and Olivier Hanotte, "Domesticating Animals in Africa," in *The Oxford Handbook of African Archaeology* ed. by Peter J. Mitchell and Paul J. Lane (Oxford: Oxford University Press, 2013), 491–505.
Gilbert, Erik, and Reynolds Jonathan T., *Africa in World History: From Prehistory to the Present* (Upper Saddle River, NJ: Pearson, 2004).
Gillies, Alexandra, and Richard Joseph, "Smart Aid: The Search for Transformative Strategies," in *Smart Aid for African Development* eds. Richard Joseph and Alexandra Gillies Boulder (London: Lynne Rienner Publishers, 2009), 1–14.
Gilroy, Paul, *The Black Atlantic: Modernity and Double Consciousness* (London: Verso, 1993).
Glassman, Jonathon, *Feasts and Riot: Revelry, Rebellion, and Popular Consciousness on the Swahili Coast, 1856–1888* (Portsmouth, NH: Heinemann, 1995).
Gleason, Abbot ed., *Blackwell Companion to World History: A Companion to Russian History* (United Kingdom: Wiley Blackwell, 2008).
Gleijeses, Piero, *Conflicting Missions: Havana, Washington, and Africa, 1959–1976* (Chapel Hill: University of North Carolina Press, 2002).
Goba, A., S. Humarr Khan, et al, "An Outbreak of Ebola Virus Disease in the Lassa Fever Zone," *The Journal of Infectious Diseases* 214, 3 (2016): 110–121.
Goldie, Hugh, *Calabar and its Mission* (Edinburgh and London: Oliphant Anderson & Ferrier, 1901).

Gomez, Michael A., *Black Crescent: The Experience and Legacy of African Muslims in the Americas* (New York, Cambridge University Press, 2005).

Gomez, Michael A., *Reversing Sail: A History of the African Diaspora* (Cambridge, UK: Cambridge University Press, 2005).

Gornik, Mark G., *World Made Global: Stories of African Christianity in New York City* (Grand Rapids, Eerdmans, 2011).

Gowlett, John, and Richard W. Wrangham, "Earliest Fire in Africa: Towards the Convergence of Archaeological Evidence and the Cooking Hypothesis," *Azania: Archaeological Research in Africa* 48 (2013): 5–30.

Grammy, Abbas, and Kaye Bragg, eds., *United States-Third World Relations in the New World Order* (New York: Nova Science, 1996).

Graves, Jazmin, "Mai Misra's Khicari: Remembrance and Ritual, Re-Presentation in the Sidi (African-Indian) Sufi Tradition of Western India," *Symposia*, 9 (2018): 1–13.

Grenville, J. A. S., *A History of the World in the Twentieth Century* (Great Britain; The Belinap Press of Harvard University Press, 1994).

Grier, Robin M., "Colonial Legacies and Economic Growth," *Public Choice,* 98 (1999), 317–335.

Güldemann, Tom, "A Linguist's View: Khoe-Kwadi Speakers as the Earliest Food-Producers of Southern Africa," *Southern African Humanities* 20, 1 (2008): 93–132.

Gumede, Vusi, "Exploring Thought Leadership, Thought Liberation and Critical Consciousness for Africa's Development," *Africa Development / Afrique et Développement* 40, 4 (2015): 91–111.

Haaland, Randi, "Porridge and Pot, Bread and Oven: Food Ways and Symbolism in Africa and the Near East from the Neolithic to the Present," *Cambridge Archaeological Journal* 17 (2002): 165–182.

Haber, Marc, et al, "A Rare Deep-Rooting D0 African Y-Chromosomal Haplogroup and its Implications for the Expansion of Modern Humans out of Africa," *Genetics* 212 (2019): 1421–1428.

Haddad-Fonda, Kyle, "An Illusory Alliance: Revolutionary Legitimacy and Sino Algerian Relations, 1958–1962," *The Journal of North African Studies* (2014): 1–20.

Hair, P. E. H., and Robin Law, "The English in Western Africa to 1700," in *The Oxford History of the British Empire, vol. 1. The Origins of Empire: British Overseas Enterprise to the Close of the Seventeenth Century* ed. by Nicholas Canny (Oxford: Oxford University Press, 1998), 241–263.

Hale, William and Eberhard Kienle, eds., *After the Cold War: Security and Democracy in Africa and Asia* (London: Tauris Academic Studies, 1997).

Hallet, Robin, ed., *Records of the African Association: 1788–1831* (London: Thomas Nelson and Sons, 1904).

Halloway, Joseph, *Africanisms in American Culture* (Bloomington: Indiana University, 1991).

Han, Beiping, 韩北屏, *Feizhou Yehui* 非洲夜会 [Encounter with Africa] (Tianjin: Baihua Edition, 1964).

Hargreaves, J. D., *Decolonization in Africa* (New York: Addison Wesley Longman Limited, 1996).

Harmand, Sonia, et al, "3.3-Million-Year-Old Stone Tools from Lomekwi 3, West Turkana, Kenya," *Nature* 521 (2015): 310–315.

Harms, Robert, *Africa in Global History With Sources* (New York and London: W. W. Norton and Company, 2018).

Harris, Joseph, E., *The African Presence in Asia* (Evanston: Northwestern University Press 1971).

Harries, Patrick, "Mozambique Island, Cape Town and the Organization of the Slave Trade in the South-West Indian Ocean, c. 1797–1807," *Journal of Southern African Studies* 42, 3 (2016): 409–27.

Harrison, Robert T., *Gladstone imperialism in Egypt: Techniques of Domination* (Westport, CT: Greenwood Press, 1995).

Hassan, Fekri A., "Palaeoclimate, Food and Culture Change in Africa: An Overview," in *Droughts, Food and Culture: Ecological Change and Food Security in Africa's Later Prehistory* ed. by Fekri A. Hassan (New York: Kluwer Academic/Plenum Publishers, 2002), 11–26.
Hastings, Adrian, *The Church in Africa 1450–1950* (Oxford: Clarendon Press, 1994).
Haupt, Adam, *Stealing Empire: P2P, Intellectual Property and hip-hop Subversion* (Cape Town: HSRC Press, 2008).
Hbrek, I., *General History of Africa III Africa from the Seventh to the Eleventh Century* (London, James Currey 1992).
Heaton, M. and T. Falola, "Global Explanations versus Local Interpretations: The Historiography of the Influenza Pandemic of 1918–19 in Africa," *History in Africa* 33, (2006): 205–230.
Herbert, E. W., "Smallpox Inoculation in Africa," *Journal of African History* 16, 4 (1975): 539–559.
Hegel, Georg W. F., *Lectures on the Philosophy of World* (Cambridge: Cambridge University Press, 1975).
Hirsch, John, and Robert Oakley, *Somalia and Operation Restore Hope: Reflections on Peacemaking and Peacekeeping* (Washington DC: United States Institute of Peace Press, 1995).
Hodgson, Marshall G. S., *Rethinking World History: Essays on Europe, Islam and World History* ed. by Edmund Burke III (Cambridge and New York, Cambridge University Press, 1993).
Hopkins, A. G., *An Economic History of West Africa* (London: Longman, 1973).
Hopper, Matthew S., *Slaves of One Master: Globalization and Slavery in Arabia in the Age of Empire* (New Haven/London: Yale University Press, 2015).
Horton, Mark, and John Middleton, *The Swahili: The Social Landscape of a Mercantile Society* (Oxford, UK/Malden, MA: Blackwell, 2000).
Hounam, P. and McQuillan, S., *The Mini-Nuke Conspiracy: Mandela's Nuclear Nightmare* (London: Faber & Faber, 1995).
Hovers, Erella, Shimon Ilani, Ofer Bar-Yosef, and Bernard Vandermeersch, "An Early Case of Color Symbolism: Ochre use by Modern Humans in Qafzeh Cave," *Current Anthropology* 44 (2003): 491–522.
Hucks, Tracey E., *Yoruba Traditions and African American Religious Nationalism* (Albuquerque: University of New Mexico Press, 2012).
Hume, David, *Essays and Treatises on Several Subjects in Two Volumes, Volume 1* (London: T. Cadell, 1777).
Hudson, Michael, *Killing the Host: How Financial Parasites and Debt Destroy the Global Economy*. (Baskerville: ISLET-Verlag, 2015).
Hunwick, John and Eve. T. Powell, *The African Diaspora in the Mediterranean Lands of Islam* (Princeton, Markus Wiener, 2002).
Iandolo, Alessandro, "The Rise and Fall of the 'Soviet Model of Development' in West Africa, 1957–64," *Cold War History* 12, 4 (2012): 683–704.
Iliffe, John, *The African AIDS Epidemic: A History* (Ohio: Ohio University Press, 2005).
Imbua, David L., *Slavery, Slave Trade and the African Diaspora* (Makurdi: Aboki Publishers, 2018).
Inyabri Idom T., "Youth and Linguistic Stylization in Naija Afro Hip Hop," *Sociolinguistic Studies* 10. 1 & 2. (2016): 90–108.
Inyabri Idom T., "Youth and Postcolonial Subjectivity in Contemporary Nigerian Pop Music," *Postcolonial Text*. 8.3 & 4. (2013): 1–17.
Isaacman, Allen F., and Barbara S. Isaacman, *Slavery and Beyond: The Making of Men and Chikunda Ethnic Identities in the Unstable World of South-Central Africa, 1750–1920* (Portsmouth, NH: Heinemann, 2004).
Isbister, John, *Promises not Kept: The Betrayal of Social Change in the Third World* (West Hartford, Connecticut: Kumarin Press, 1988).

Isichei, Elizabeth, *History of West Africa since 1800* (London and Basingstoke: Macmillan Education Limited, 1977).

Van Sertima, Ivan, *The Golden Age of the Moors* (USA: Transaction Publishers, 1992).

Jackson, Donna, *Jimmy Carter and the Horn of Africa: Cold War policy in Ethiopia and Somalia* (Jefferson, N.C.: McFarland & Co., 2007).

Jackson, Robert and Georg Sørensen, *Introduction to International Relations: Theories and Approaches* (Oxford: Oxford University Press, 2010).

Jackson, Steven F., "China's Third World Foreign Policy: The Case of Angola and Mozambique, 1961–1993", *China Quarterly* 142 (1995): 388–422.

James, Leslie, and Elisabeth Leak, eds., *Decolonization and the Cold War: Negotiating Independence* (London: Bloomsbury, 2015).

Jaspers, Karl, *The Origin and Goal of History*, translated by M. Bullock (London, Routlege and Paul, 1953).

Jayasuriya, Shihan de Silva, and Richard Pankhurst, eds., *The African Diaspora in the Indian Ocean* (Trenton, NJ: Africa World Press, 2003).

Jayasuriya, Shihan de Silva, and Jean-Pierre Angenot, eds., *Uncovering the History of Africans in Asia* (Leiden/Boston: Brill, 2008).

Jenkins, Philip., *The Next Christendom: The Coming of Global Christianity* (Oxford, Oxford University Press, 2007).

Jiménez-Vicario, P. M., García-Martínez, P. & Ródenas-López, M. A., "The Influence of North African and Middle Eastern Architectures in the Birth and Development of Modern Architecture in Central Europe (1898–1937)," *Mediterranean Historical Review* 33, 2 (2018): 179–198.

Johannes, Leo Africanus, *A History and Description of Africa* (Whitefish, USA: Kessinger Publishing, LLC, 2007).

Johnson, N. P., and Mueller, J., "Updating the Accounts: Global Mortality of the 1918–1920 'Spanish' influenza pandemic," *Bulletin of the History of Medicine* (2002): 105–115.

Jones, Sacha C., and Stewart, Brian A., eds., *Africa from MIS 6–2: Population Dynamics and Paleoenvironments* (Dordrecht: Springer, 2016).

Joseph, Richard, A., *Democracy and Prebendal Politics in Nigeria* (Cambridge: Cambridge University press, 1987).

Kahlheber, Stefanie, Koen Bostoen, and Katharina Neumann, "Early Plant Cultivation in the Central African Rain Forest: First Millennium BC Pearl Millet from South Cameroon," *Journal of African Archaeology* 7 (2009): 253–272.

Kahn, E. Hilary, and Saskia Sassen, *Framing the Global* (Bloomington: Indiana University Press, 2014).

Kalu, Ogbu, ed., *African Christianity: An African Story* (Trenton, Africa World Press 2007).

Kalb, Madeleine, *The Congo Cables: The Cold War in Africa from Eisenhower to Kennedy*, (New York: Macmillan, 1982).

Kalu, Kenneth, and Falola Toyin, *Exploitation and Misrule in Colonial and Post-colonial Africa* (New York: Palgrave Macmillan, 2019).

Katz, David Brock, *South Africans versus Rommel: The Untold Story of the Desert War in World War II*. Illustrated Edition (Guilford, Connecticut: Stackpole Books, 2017).

Kay, Andrea U. et al., "Diversification, Intensification and Specialization: Changing Land use in Western Africa from 1800 BC to AD 1500," *Journal of World Prehistory* 32 (2019): 179–228.

Keeley, Lawrence H. and Nicholas Toth, "Microwear Polishes on Early Stone Tools from Koobi Fora, Kenya," *Nature* 293 (1981): 464–465.

Kelly, Sean, *America's Tyrant: the CIA and Mobutu of Zaire* (Washington: American University Press, 1993).

Kemp, Barry, *The City of Akhenaten and Nefertiti: Amarna and its People* (London: Thames and Hudson, 2012).

Khadiagala, M. Gilbert, "Thoughts on Africa and the New World Order," *The Round Table: The Commonwealth Journal of International Affairs* 81, 324 (1992): 431-50.

Killingray, David, and Martin Plaut, *Fighting for Britain: African Soldiers in the Second World War* (Woodbridge, James Currey, 2012).

Kimble, David, *A Political History of Ghana: The Rise of Gold Coast Nationalism, 1850–1928* (Oxford, Oxford University Press, 1997).

Kissinger, Henry, *World Order: Reflections on the Character of Nations and the Course of History* (New York: Penguin Press, 2014).

Kitchen, Kenneth A., "The land of Punt," in *The Archaeology of Africa: Food, Metals and Towns* ed. by Thurstan Shaw et al, (London: Routledge, 1993), 586–608.

Kitschelt, Herbert, and, Steven I. Wilkinson, eds., *Patrons, Clients and Policies: Patterns of Democratic Accountability and Political Competition* (Cambridge: Cambridge University Press, 2007).

Kohli, Atul, *State-Directed Development: Political Power and Industrialization in the Global Periphery* (New York: Cambridge University Press, 2004).

Kragelund, Peter, and Godfrey Hampwaye, , "Seeking Markets and Resources: State-Driven Chinese and Indian Investments in Zambia," *International Journal of Technology and Globalisation* 6, 4 (2012): 352–368.

Kusimba, Sibel B., "The Early Later Stone Age in East Africa: Excavations and Lithic Assemblages from Lukenya Hill," *African Archaeological Review* 18 (2001): 77–123.

Lake, Anthony, *The "Tar Baby" Option: American Policy Toward Southern Rhodesia*, (New York; Guildford: Columbia University Press, 1976).

Lal, Priya, *African Socialism in Postcolonial Tanzania: Between the Village and the World* (New York: Cambridge University Press, 2015).

Lambo, T.A., "Psychotherapy in Africa," *Human Nature* 1, 3, (1978): 32–39.

Lane, Paul J., "The Archaeology of Pastoralism and Stock-Keeping in East Africa," in *The Oxford Handbook of African Archaeology,* ed. by Peter J. Mitchell and Paul J. Lane, (Oxford: Oxford University Press, 2013), 585–601.

Lane-Poole, Stanley, *The Story of the Moors in Spain* (South Carolina: CreateSpace Independent Publishing Platform, 2016).

Large, Daniel, "Beyond 'Dragon in the Bush': The Study of China–Africa Relations," *African Affairs* 107, 426 (2008): 45–61.

Larkin, Bruce, *China and Africa, 1949–1970: The Foreign Policy of the People's Republic of China* (Berkley: University of California Press, 1971).

Larson, Pier M., *Ocean of Letters: Language and Creolization in an Indian Ocean Diaspora* (New York: Cambridge University Press, 2009).

Larson, Pier M., "Horrid Journeying: Narratives of Enslavement and the Global African Diaspora," *Journal of World History* 19, 4 (December 2008): 431–464.

Larson, Pier M., "African Slave Trades in Global Perspective," in *The Oxford Handbook of Modern African History,* ed. by John Parker and Richard Reid (Oxford, UK: Oxford University Press, 2013).

Laumann, Dennis, *Colonial Africa: 1884–1994* (New York, Oxford University Press, 2012).

Launay, Robert, and Benjamin F. Soares, "The Formation of an 'Islamic Sphere' in French Colonial West Africa," *Economy and Society* 28 (1999): 497–519.

Law, Robin, and Kristin Mann, "West Africa in the Atlantic Community: The Case of the Slave Coast." *William and Mary Quarterly* LVI, 2 (1999): 307–334.

Lawrence, Mark Atwood, "The Rise and Fall of Nonalignment," in *The Cold War in the Third World* ed. by Robert J. McMahon (Oxford: Oxford University Press, 2013), 139–155.

Lazarus, Suleman, "Birds of a Feather flock Together: The Nigerian Cyber Fraudsters (YahooBoys) and Hip Hop Artists," *Criminology, Criminal Justice, Law and Society* 19, 2 (2018): 63–80.

Lee, Christopher J., ed., *Making a World after Empire: the Bandung Moment and Its Political Afterlives* (Athens: Ohio University Press, 2010).

Lee, Richard B., *The !Kung San: Men, Women and Work in a Foraging Society.* (Cambridge: Cambridge University Press, 1979).

Levtzion, N. and J. F. P. Hopkins, *Corpus of Early Arabic Sources for West African History* (New Jersey: Markus Wiener, 2000).

Levtzion, Nehemia, and Randall L. Pouwels, eds. *The History of Islam in Africa* (Athens: Ohio University Press, 2000).

Li, Anshan, ed., *A History of Overseas Chinese in Africa to 1911* (New York: Diasporic Africa Press, 2012).

Lincoln, C.E., *The Black Muslims in America* (Grand Rapids, William B Eerdmans, 1994 first published 1961).

Linderberg, Marc, and Coralie Bryant, *Going Global: Transforming Relief and Development NGOs* (New York: Kumarian Press Inc, 2001).

Li, Qianyu 李潜虞, "Shilun Zhongguo dui Dierci Yafeihuiyi Zhengce de Yanbian" 试论中 对第二次亚非会议政策的演变 [China's Policy towards the Second Afro-Asian Conference], *International Politics Quarterly* 4 (2010): 115–133.

Lobato, Alexandre, *A expansão portuguêsa em Moçambique de 1498 a 1530,* I (Lisbon: Agência Geral do Ultramar, 1960).

Lombard, Marlize, "Hunter-gatherers in Southern Africa Before 20,000 Years Ago," in *The Oxford Handbook of African Archaeology,* ed. Peter J. Mitchell and Paul J. Lane, (Oxford: Oxford University Press, 2013), 367–386.

Long, Xiangyang 龙向阳, "1966–1969 Nian Zhongguo yu Feizhou Guanxi Chutan" 1966–1969 年中国与非洲关系初探 [An Initial Investigation of Sino-African Relations, 1966–1969], in *Peking University African Studies Series: China and Africa* (Beijing: Peking University Press, 2000), 72–86.

Lovejoy, Paul, *Jihad in West Africa During the Age of Revolutions (*Athens, Ohio University Press, 2016*).*

Lovejoy, Paul, "Miller's Vision of Meillassoux," *The International Journal of African Historical Studies* 24.1 (1991): 133–145.

Lovejoy Paul E., and J. S. Hogendorn, "Revolutionary Mahdism and Resistance to Colonial Rule in the Sokoto Caliphate, 1905–6," *Journal of African History* 31, 2

(1990): 217–44.

Lugard, Frederick, *The Political Memoranda: Revision of Instructions to Political Officers on Subjects Chiefly Political and Administrative* (London, Frank Cass and Co. Ltd, 1970).

Lu, Ting'en 陆庭恩, *Feizhou Wenti Lunji* 非洲问题论集 (Treatises on Africa), (Beijing: Shijiezhishi chubanshe, 2005).

Lyons, M., *The Colonial Disease: A social History of Sleeping Sickness in Northern Zaire, 1900–1940* (Cambridge: Cambridge University Press, 2002).

Machado, Pedro, "Memory, Memorialization, and 'Heritage' in the Indian Ocean," in *Reimagining Indian Ocean Worlds* eds. Smriti Srinivas, Bettina Ng'weno and Neelima Jeychandran (London & New York: Routledge, 2020), 149–164.

Machado, Pedro, "Slavery and Histories of Unfreedom in the Indian Ocean," in *Indian Ocean Current: Six Artistic Narratives.* ed. Prasannan Parthasarathi (Boston/Chicago: McMullen Museum of Art & University of Chicago Press, 2020).

Magyar, Karl, ed., *United States Interests and Policies in Africa: Transition to a New Era* (Basingstoke: Macmillan Press, 2000).

Mazov, Sergeĭ Vasilevich, *A Distant Front in the Cold War: The USSR in West Africa and the Congo, 1956–1964* (Stanford: Stanford University Press 2010).

Maley, Jean, et al, "Late Holocene Forest Contraction and Fragmentation in Central Africa," *Quaternary Research* 89 (2018): 43–59.

Malinowski, B., *The Dynamics of Culture Change: An Inquiry into Race Relations in Africa*, ed. by Phyllis M. Kaberry (New Haven: Yale University Press, 1946).

Malowany, M., "Unfinished Agendas: Writing the History of Medicine of Sub-Saharan Africa," *African Affairs*, 99, 395 (2000): 325–349.

Mandela, Nelson, *Long Walk to Freedom: The Autobiography of Nelson Mandela* (Boston: Little, Brown, 1994).

Mangvwat, Monday Yakiban, *A History of Class Formation in the Plateau Province of Nigeria, 1902–1960: The Genesis of a Ruling Class* (Durham, North Carolina: Carolina Academic Press, 2013).

Manning, Katie, et al., "4500-Year-Old Domesticated Pearl Millet (*Pennisetum glaucum*) from the Tilemsi Valley, Mali: New Insights into an Alternative Cereal Domestication Pathway," *Journal of Archaeological Science* 38 (2011): 312–322.

Mann, Kristin, *Slavery and the Birth of an African City. Lagos, 1760–1900* (Bloomington: Indiana University Press, 2007).

Manning Patrick, *Navigating World History: Historians Create a Global Past* (New York, Palgrave Macmillan, 2003).

Manning Patrick, *Slavery and African Life* (Cambridge, Cambridge University Press, 1990).

Mao, Zedong, *Chairman Mao on World Revolution* (Nanjing: Nanjing Revolutionary Committee, 1970).

Mao, Zedong, *Selected Works of Mao Zedong* (Beijing: Foreign Languages Press, 1967).

Marable, Manning., *Malcolm X A Life of Reinvention* (London, Allen Lane, 2011).

Marean, Curtis W., "Implications of Late Quaternary Mammalian Fauna from Lukenya Hill (South-Central Kenya) for Palaeoenvironmental Change and Faunal Extinction," *Quaternary Research* 10 (1992): 65–128.

Margoliouth, David Samuel, *Mohammed and the Rise of Islam* (Wood Dale, IL: Alpha Editions, 2019).

Marshall, Fiona B., and Hildebrand, Elisabeth, "Cattle Before Crops: The Beginning of Food Production in Africa," *Journal of World Prehistory* 16 (2002): 99–143.

Mathew, Johan, *Margins of the Market: Trafficking and Capitalism across the Arabian Sea* (Oakland: University of California Press, 2016).

Mazrui, Ali, and C. Wondji, eds., *General History of Africa Vol. VIII: Africa Since 1935* (California: University of California Press, 1993).

Mbajekwe, Patrick U., "East and Central Africa in the Nineteenth Century," in *Africa: African History Before 1885* ed. Toyin Falola (Durham: Carolina Academic Press, 2000), 335–358.

Mbembe, Achille, *On the Post-Colony* (London: University of California Press, 2001).

Mbida, Christophe, et al, "The Initial History of Bananas in Africa. A reply to Jan Vansina," *Azania* 40 (2003): 128–135.

McBrearty, Sally, and Alison S. Brooks, "The Revolution that wasn't: A New Interpretation of the Origin of Modern Human Behavior," *Journal of Human Evolution* 39 (2000): 453–563.

McCloud, Amina B., *African American Islam* (New York, Routledge, 1995).

Mitchem, Stephanie Y., *Introducing Womanist Theology* (New York, Orbis, 2002).

McDow, Thomas F., *Buying Time: Debt and Mobility in the Western Indian Ocean* (Athens, OH: Ohio University Press, 2018).

McGrew, Bill, *Chimpanzee Material Culture: Implications for Human Evolution.* (Cambridge: Cambridge University Press, 1992).

McInnes, C., "Conflict, HIV and AIDS: A New Dynamic in Warfare?" *Global Change, Peace & Security* 2, 1 (2009): 99–114.

McIntosh, Roderick J., *The Peoples of the Middle Niger: The Island of Gold* (Oxford: Blackwells, 1998).

McIntosh, Susan K., "Modeling Political Organization in Large-Scale Settlement Clusters: A Case Study from the Inland Niger Delta," in *Beyond Chiefdoms: Pathways to Complexity in Africa* ed. Susan K. McIntosh (Cambridge: Cambridge University Press, 1999), 66–79.

McMahon, Robert J., ed., *The Cold War in the Third World* (Oxford: Oxford University Press, 2013).

McNeill, William, "A Defence of World History (The Prothero Lecture)," *Transactions of the Royal Historical Society* 32 (1982), 75–89.

Meli, F., *South Africa Belongs to Us: A History of the African National Congress* (Harare: Zimbabwean Publishing House, 1987).

Mellars, Paul A. "Why did Modern Human Populations Disperse from Africa ca. 60,000 years ago? A new Model," *Proceedings of the National Academy of Sciences (USA)* 103 (2006): 9381–9386.

Menocal María Rosa,, *Ornament of the World: How Muslims, Jews, and Christians Created a Culture of Tolerance in Medieval Spain* (New York: Back Bay Books, 2002).

Merkyte, Inga, Søren Albek, and Klavs Randsborg, "Urbanizing Forest: Archaeological Evidence from Southern Bénin," *Journal of African Archaeology* 17 (2019): 95–120.

Mets, David, *Land-Based Airpower in Third World Crises* (Alabama: Air University Press, 1986).

Mgumia, J. H., "*Chuma Ulete*: Business and Discourses of Witchcraft in Neoliberal Tanzania," *Journal for the Study of Religion* 33, 1 (2020),1–26.

Michael, Barry, *Homage to Al-Andalus: The Rise and Fall of Islamic Spain* (Dublin, Ireland: Andalus Press, 2016).

Miller, Jamie, *An African Volk: The Apartheid Regime and Its Search for Survival* (New York: Oxford University Press, 2016).

Min, H. (2012). "Mapping the Supply Chain of Anti-Malarial Drugs in Sub-Saharan African Countries," *International Journal of Logistics Systems and Management* 11, 1 (2012): 1–23.

Mitchell Nancy, *Jimmy Carter in Africa: Race and the Cold War* (Washington, DC: Woodrow Wilson Center Press, 2016).

Mitchell Peter J., *The Archaeology of Southern Africa* (Cambridge: Cambridge University Press, 2002).

Mitchell Peter J., "Why the Donkey Didn't go South: Constraints on the Spread of *Equus asinus* into Southern Africa," *African Archaeological Review* 34 (2017): 21–41.

Mitchell Peter J., *The Donkey in Human History: An Archaeological Perspective* (Oxford: Oxford University Press, 2018).

Mohammed, A. R., *History of the Spread of Islam in the Niger-Benue Confluence Area: Igalaland, Ebiraland and Lokoja c.1900–1960* (Ibadan: University Press, 2014).

Mohamed, Kyari, "The Message and Methods of Boko Haram," in *Boko Haram: Islamism, Politics, Security and the State in Nigeria,* ed. by Marc-Antoine Pérouse de Montclos (Leiden, African Studies Centre, 2014), 9–32.

Monson, Jamie, "Review of *Chinese Labour in South Africa, 1902–10: Race, Violence, and Global Spectacle,*" *The American Historical Review* 119, 5 (2014): 1829–1830.

Montalvo, J. G., and M. Reynal-Querol, "Fighting Against Malaria: Prevent Wars while waiting for the "Miraculous" Vaccine," *The Review of Economics and Statistics*, 89, 1(2007): 165–177.

Moorjani, Priya, *et al*, "Variation in the Molecular Clock of Primates," *Proceedings of the National Academy of Sciences* 113 (2016): 10607–10612.

Mora, Rafael, and Ignacio de la Torre, "Percussion Tools in Olduvai Bed I and II (Tanzania): Implications for Early Human Activities," *Journal of Anthropological Archaeology* 24 (2005): 179–192.

Morgan, Philip D., "Africa and the Atlantic, C.1450 to C. 1820," in *Atlantic History: A Critical Appraisal* ed. Jack P. Green and Philip D. Morgan (Oxford: Oxford University Press, 2009), 223–248.

Morrell, R., "Silence, Sexuality and HIV/AIDS in South African Schools," *The Australian Educational Researcher* 30, 1 (2003): 41–62.

Moyo, Dambisa, *Winner Take All: China's Race for Resources and What It Means for Us* (London: Penguin, 2013).

Moyo, Dambisa, *Dead Aid: Why Aid is not Working and How There is a Better Way for Africa* (New York: Farrar, Strauss and Giroux, 2009).

Mtika, M. M., "Political Economy, Labor Migration, and the AIDS Epidemic in Rural Malawi," *Social Science & Medicine* 64, 12 (2007), 2454–2463.

Muehlenbeck, Philip, *Betting on the Africans: John F. Kennedy's Courting of African Nationalist Leaders* (Oxford: OUP, 2014).

Murray, Martin J., "'The Natives Are Always Stealing': White Vigilantes and the 'Reign of Terror' in the Orange Free State, 1918–1924," *Journal of African History* 30, 1 (1989): 107–23.

Namikas, Lise, *Battleground Africa: Cold War in the Congo, 1960–1965* (Washington, DC: Woodrow Wilson Center Press ; Stanford, California: Stanford University Press, 2013).

Naylor, Thomas Ellis, *Yellow Labour: The Truth about the Chinese in the Transvaal* (London: Daily Chronicle Office, 1904).

Ndege, G. O., *Health, State, and Society in Kenya* (Rochester, University Rochester Press, 2001).

Newsom, David, *The Imperial Mantle: The United States, Decolonization, and the Third World* (Bloomington: Indiana University Press, 2001).

Nguyen-Van-Tam, J. S., and A. W. Hampson, "The Epidemiology and Clinical Impact of Pandemic Influenza," *Vaccine*, 21, 16 (2003), 1762–1768.

Nielsen, Waldemar, *The Great Powers and Africa*, (New York: Published for the Council on Foreign Relations by Praeger Publishers, 1969).

Nimtz, A. H., *Islam and Politics in East Africa: The Sufi Order in Tanzania* (Minneapolis: University of Minnesota Press, 1980).

Nkrumah, Kwame, *Consciencism Philosophy and Ideology for Decolonisation* (London, Panaf, 1964).

Noah, Monday, *Old Calabar: The City States and the Europeans, 1800–1885* (Uyo: Scholar Press, 1980).

Noer, Thomas, *Cold War and Black Liberation: The United States and White Rule in Africa, 1948–1968* (Columbia: University of Missouri Press, 1985).

Norman, Kasih, *et al,* "An Early Colonisation Pathway into Northwest Australia 70–60,000 years Ago," *Quaternary Science Reviews* 180 (2018): 229–239.

Northrup, David, *Africa's Discovery of Europe, 1450–1850* (New York and Oxford: Oxford Press, 2009).

Nunn, Nathan, "The Long Term Effects of Africa's Slave Trades," *Quarterly Journal of Economics* (2008), 139–176.

Nuno, R. R,. *et al,* "The Early Spread and Epidemic Ignition of HIV-1 in Human Populations," *Science* 346, 6205 (2014): 56–61.

Nwadawere, Thandika, ed., *African Intellectuals: Rethinking Political, Language, Gender and Development* (Dakar and London/New York: CODESRIA Books and Zed Books, 2005).

Nzongola-Ntalaja, Georges, *The Congo: From Leopold to Kabila, A People's History* (New York: Zed Books, 2003).

Oas, Sarah E., *et al*, "10,000 Year History of Plant use at Bosumpra Rockshelter, Central Ghana," *Vegetation History and Archaeobotany* 24 (2015): 635–653.

Obadare, Ebenezer, *Pentecostal Republic Religion and the Struggle for State Power in Nigeria* (London, Zed, 2018).

Obeng, Pashington, *Shaping Membership, Defining Nation: The Cultural Politics of African Indians in South Asia* (Plymouth, UK: Lexington Books, 2007).

Obioma, Chigozie, *An Orchestra of Minorities* (New York, Little Brown and Company, 2019).

O'Brien, Donal Cruise, "Towards an 'Islamic Policy' in French West Africa, 1854–1914," *Journal of African History* 8, 2 (1967): 303–16.

O'Donnell, Guillermo, "Delegative Democracy," *Journal of Democracy* 5, 1 (1994). 55–69.

Oduyoye, Mercy., *Introducing African Women's Theology* (Sheffield, Sheffield Academic Press 2001).

Offiong, D. A., "Traditional Healers in the Nigerian Health Care Delivery System and the Debate over Integrating Traditional and Scientific Medicine," *Anthropological Quarterly,* (1999):118–130.

Ogot Bethwell Allan., *Who, If Anyone, Owns the Past? Reflections on the Meaning of 'Public History'* (Kisumu: Anyange Press Ltd, 2010).

Ogundiran, Akinwumi, "Towns and States of the West African Forest Belt," in *The Oxford Handbook of African Archaeology* ed. Peter J. Mitchell and Paul J. Lane (Oxford: Oxford University Press, 2013), 859–873.

Ogunsanwo, Alaba, *China's Policy in Africa, 1958–1971* (Cambridge: Cambridge University Press, 1974).

Ojo-Ade, Femi, "Reflections on Pan-Africanism, Black Aesthetics and the Black Condition," *Being Black Being Human* ed. by Femi Ojo-Ade (Ile-Ife: OAU Press. 1996), 1–31.

Okome, Onookome, and Jonathan Haynes, *Cinema and Social Change in West Africa* (Jos: Nigerian Film Corporation, 1997).

Okonjo-Iweala, Ngozi, *Reforming the Unreformable: Lessons From Nigeria.* (Cambridge: MIT Press, 2012).

Oku, Ekei E., *The Kings and Chiefs of Old Calabar, 1785–1925* (Calabar: Glad Tidings, 1989).

Okwo-Bele, J. and T. Cherian, "The Expanded Programme on Immunization: A Lasting Legacy of Smallpox Eradication," *Vaccine* 29 (2011),74–79.

Olaoye, R. A., and N.E. Attah, "Orthopaedics in the Traditional Medical System of Igala," in *Africa's Indigenous Science and Knowledge System,* ed. by D. O. Akinwumi et al (Abuja, Roots Books, 2007), 368–377.

Oliver, Roland and Anthony Atmore, *Africa since 1800* (Cambridge, Cambridge University Press, 1972).

Olmos, Margarite Fernández, and Lizabeth Paravisini-Gebert, *Creole Religions of the Caribbean: An Introduction from Vodou and Santeria to Obeah and Espiritismo* (New York, New York University Press, 2011).

O'Meara, D., *Volkskapitalisme: Class, Capital and Ideology in the Development of Afrikaner Nationalism, 1934–1948* (Johannesburg: Ravan Press, 1983).

Omer-Cooper, J. D., E. A. Alayandre, R. J. Gaven, and E. A. Afigo, *The Growth of Modern Africa Vol. 1: The Nineteenth Century to the Partition* (London, Longman, 1968).

Omoniyi, T., "'So I choose do am Naija Style': Hip Hop Language and Postcolonial Identities," *Global Linguistic Flows: Hip Hop Cultures, Youth Identities and the Politics of Language,* ed. by H. S. Alim, A. Ibrahim and A. Pennycook (New York: Routledge, 2009) 25–42.

Onselen, Charles van, *Chibaro: African Mine Labour in Southern Rhodesia, 1900–1933* (London: Pluto Press, 1976).

Onslow, Sue, ed., *Cold War in Southern Africa: White Power, Black Liberation* (London: Routledge, 2009).

Orjiako, Humphrey, *Killing Sub-Saharan Africa with Aid* (New York: Nova Science Publishers, 2000).

Oster, E., "Sexually Transmitted Infections, Sexual Behavior, and the HIV/AIDS Epidemic," *The Quarterly Journal of Economics* 120, 2 (2005): 467–515.

Page, Melvin E., *Africa, and the First World War* (New York, St. Martin's Press, 1987).
Pakenham, Thomas, *The Scramble for Africa, 1876–1912* (New York: Random House, 1991).
Park, Yoon Jung, "Boundaries, Borders and Borderland Constructions: Chinese in Contemporary South Africa and the Region." *African Studies* 69, 3 (2010): 457–479.
Patman, Robert G. ed., *Soviet and East European Studies* (New York: Cambridge University Press, 1990).
Patman, Robert, *The Soviet Union in the Horn of Africa: The Diplomacy of Intervention and Disengagement* (Cambridge: Cambridge University Press, 1990).
Patterson, K. D., "The Influenza Epidemic of 1918–19 in the Gold Coast" *Journal of African History* 24, 4 (1983), 485–502.
Patterson, Orlando, *Slavery and Social Death: A Comparative Study* (Cambridge: Harvard University Press, 1982).
Pearson, M. N., *Port Cities and Intruders: The Swahili Coast, India, and Portugal in the Early Modern Era* (Baltimore: Johns Hopkins University Press, 1998).
Pettigrew, William A., "Free to Enslave: Politics and the Escalation of Britain's Transatlantic Slave Trade, 1688–1714," *William and Mary Quarterly* LXIV. 1 (2007): 3–38.
Phillipson, David W., *African Archaeology* (Cambridge: Cambridge University Press, 1995).
Pitcher, M. Anne, and Kelly M. Askew, "African Socialisms and Postsocialisms," *Africa* 76, 1 (2006): 1–14.
Pinn, Anthony, ed., *Black Religion and Aesthetics: Religious Thought and Life in Africa and the African Diaspora* (New York, Palgrave Macmillan, 2009).
Pipes, Daniel, *Slave Soldiers and Islam* (New Haven: Yale University Press, 1981).
Pliny the Elder, *The Natural History*, ed. by John Bostock and H.T. Riley (London: Taylor and Francis, 1855).
Plummer, Brenda Gayle, *In Search of Power: African Americans in the Era of Decolonization, 1956–1974* (Cambridge: Cambridge University Press, 2013).
Pomeroy, William J. *Apartheid, Imperialism and African Freedom* (New York: International Publishers, 1986).
Popescu, Monica, "On the Margins of the Black Atlantic: Angola, the Eastern Bloc and the Cold War," *Research in African Literature* 45, 3 (2014): 91–109.
Power, Robert C., Tom Güldemann, Alison Crowther, and Nicole Boivin, "Asian Crop Dispersal in Africa and Late Holocene Human Adaptation to Tropical Environments," *Journal of World Prehistory* 32 (2019): 353–392.
Prestholdt, Jeremy, *Domesticating the World: African Consumerism and the Genealogies of Globalization* (Berkeley: University of California Press, 2008).
Purkitt, H., and S. Burgess, *South Africa's Weapons of Mass Destruction* (Bloomington: Indiana University Press, 2005).
Rangan, Haripriya, Edward A. Alpers, Tim Denham, Christian Arthur Kull, and Judith Carney, "Food Traditions and Landscape Histories of the Indian Ocean World: Theoretical and Methodological Reflections," *Environment and History*, 21, 1 (2015): 135–157.
Ranger, Terrence O., *Peasant Consciousness and Guerrilla War in Zimbabwe: A Comparative Study* (Berkeley: University of California Press, 1985).
Rapley, John, *Understanding Development: Theory and Practice in the Third World* (London: UCL Press, 1996).
Rathbone, Richard. "World War I and Africa: Introduction," *Journal of African History* 19, 1 (1978): 1–9.
Ravallion, M., "The World Bank: Why it is Still Needed and Why it Still Disappoints," *The Journal of Economic Perspectives* 30, 1 (2016): 77–94.
Reddie, Richard., *Black Muslims in Britain: Why are a Growing Number of Young Black Men Converting to Islam* (London, Lion Books, 2009).

Reid, Richard J., *A History of Modern Africa 1800 to the Present* (West Sussex: John Wiley and Son Limited, 2012).
Richards, P., *Ebola: How a People's Science Helped End an Epidemic* (Zed Books Ltd., 2016).
Richardson, Peter, *Chinese Mine Labour in the Transvaal* (London: Macmillan Press, 1982).
Richter, Daniel, et al, "The Age of the Hominin Fossils from Jebel Irhoud, Morocco, and the Origins of the Middle Stone Age," *Nature* 546 (2017): 293–296.
Roberts, Geoffrey, *The Soviet Union in World Politics: Coexistence, Revolution, and Cold War, 1945–1991,* (New York: Routledge, 1999).
Roberts, Patrick, *Tropical Forests in Prehistory, History, and Modernity* (Oxford: Oxford University Press, 2019).
Roberts, Patrick, and Brian A. Stewart, "Defining the 'Generalist Specialist' Niche for Pleistocene Homo Sapiens," *Nature Human Behaviour* 2 (2018): 542–550.
Robinson, David, *Paths of Accommodation: Muslim Societies and French Colonial Authorities in Senegal and Mauritania, 1880–1920* (Athens, Ohio University Press, 2000).
Robinson, Ronald, and John Gallagher, *Africa and the Victorians: The Climax of Imperialism in the Dark Continent* (New York: St. Martin's Press, 1961).
Robbins, Kenneth X., and John McLeod, eds., *African Elites in India: Habshi Amarat* (Ahmedabad: Mapin Publishing, 2006).
Rockel, Stephen J., *Carriers of Culture: Labor on the Road in Nineteenth-Century East Africa* (Portsmouth, NH: Heinemann, 2006).
Rodman, Peter, *More Precious Than Peace: The Cold War and the Struggle for the Third World* (New York: Scribner's, 1994).
Rodney, Walter, *How Europe Underdeveloped Africa* (London: Bogle-L'ouverture Publications 1972).
Rodrik, Dani, *The Globalization Paradox: Why Global Markets, States, and Democracy Can't Coexist* (Oxford: Oxford University Press, 2011).
Roebroeks, Wil, and Marie Soressi, "Neandertals Revised," *Proceedings of the National Academy of Sciences (USA)* 113 (2016): 6372–6379.
Rosaldo, Renato, "Imperialist Nostalgia," *Representations* 26, 1 (1989): 107–122.
Rose, Tricia, *Black Noise: Rap Music and Culture in contemporary America* (London: Wesleyan University Press, 1994).
Rüland, Jürgen, Theodor Hanf, Eva Manske, eds., *US Foreign Policy Toward the Third World: A Post-Cold War Assessment* (Armonk, NY: M.E. Sharpe, 2006).
Russell, Thembi, and Faye Lander, "'What is Consumed is Wasted': From Foraging to Herding in the Southern African Later Stone Age," *Azania: Archaeological Research in Africa* 50 (2015): 267–317.
Ryan, David, and Victor Pungong, eds., *The United States and Decolonization: Power and Freedom* (Basingstoke: Macmillan, 2000).
Ryder, A. F. C., "Portuguese and Dutch in West Africa before 1800," in *A Thousand Years of West African History,* ed. by J. F. Ade Ajayi and Ian Espie (Ibadan: Ibadan University Press, 1965), 216–236.
Sachs, Jeffery, *The End of Poverty: Economic Possibilities for our Times* (New York: Penguin Press, 2005).
Sadr, Karim, "An Ageless View of First Millennium AD Southern African Ceramics," *Journal of African Archaeology* 6 (2008): 103–130.
Sadr, Karim, "The Archaeology of Herding in Southernmost Africa," in *The Oxford Handbook of African Archaeology* eds. Peter J. Mitchell and Paul J. Lane (Oxford: Oxford University Press, 2013), 645–655.
Safran, Janina, *Defining Boundaries in al-Andalus: Muslims, Christians, and Jews in Islamic Iberia* (Ithaca, USA: Cornell University Press, 2013).

Sahnouni, Mohamed, Sileshi Semaw, and Michael Rogers, "The African Acheulean: an Archaeological Summary," in *The Oxford Handbook of African Archaeology,* eds. Peter J. Mitchell and Paul J. Lane (Oxford: Oxford University Press, 2013), 307–324.

Salau, Mohammed Bashir, *Plantation Slavery in the Sokoto Caliphate: A Historical and Comparative Study* (Rochester, University of Rochester Press, 2018).

Salzbruhn, Monica., "The Occupation of Public Space Through Religious and Political Events: How Senegalese Migrants Became a Part of Harlem," *New York Journal of Religion in Africa* 33, 4 (2004): 469–492.

Sandoval, Mercedes Cros., "Santería in the Twenty-First Century," in *Òrìṣà Devotion as World Religion: The Globalisation of Yoruba Religious Culture,* eds. Jacob K. Olupona and Terry Rey Madison (University of Wisconsin Press, 2008), 355–371.

Sanneh, Lamin, *Disciples of all Nations: Pillars of World Christianity* (Oxford, Oxford University Press, 2008).

Şaul, Mahir, and Patrick Royer, *West African Challenge to Empire: Culture and History in the Volta-Bani Anticolonial War* (Athens: Ohio University Press, 2001).

Scerri, Eleanor, "The North African Middle Stone Age and its Place in Recent Human Evolution," *Evolutionary Anthropology* 26 (2017): 119–135.

Scheel, Bernd, *Egyptian Metalworking and Tools* (Oxford: Shire Publications, 1989).

Schatzberg, Michael, *Mobutu or Chaos: The United States and Zaire, 1960–1990* (Lanham: University Press of America, 1991).

Schmidt, Elizabeth, *Foreign Intervention in Africa: From the Cold War to the War on Terror* (Cambridge: Cambridge University Press, 2013).

Schraeder, Peter, *United States Foreign Policy Toward Africa: Incrementalism, Crisis and Change* (Cambridge University Press, 1994).

Seesemann, Rüdiger, *The Divine Flood Ibrahim Niasse and the Roots of a Twentieth-Century Sufi Revival* (Oxford: Oxford University Press, 2011).

Seijas, Tatiana, *Asian Slaves in Colonial Mexico: From Chinos to Indians* (Cambridge, UK: Cambridge University Press, 2014).

Sen, Amartya, "Democracy as a Universal Value," *Journal of Democracy* 10, 3 (1999): 3–17.

Shaw, Ian, ed., *The Oxford Illustrated History of Ancient Egypt* (London: Thames and Hudson, 2000).

Shaw, Ian, "Egypt and the Outside World," in *The Oxford Illustrated History of Ancient Egypt* ed. Ian Shaw (Oxford: Oxford University Press, 2000), 308–323.

Shell, Robert, *Children of Bondage: A Social History of Slave Society at the Cape of Good Hope, 1652–1838* (Hanover/London: Wesleyan University Press, 1994).

Shen, John, "Foreword: Thoughts on the Use of Chinese Documents in the Reconstruction of East African History," in *A History of Overseas Chinese in Africa to 1911,* ed. by Li Anshan (New York: Diasporic Africa Press, 2012), i–x.

Shepperson, George, "The Centennial of the West African Conference of Berlin, 1884–1885," *Phylon* 46, 1 (1985): 37–48.

Sheriff, Abdul, *Dhow Cultures of the Indian Ocean: Cosmopolitanism, Commerce and Islam* (London: C. Hurst & Co, 2010).

Shillington, K., *Encyclopedia of African History* Vol. A-G (New York; Taylor and Francis, 2005).

Shipley, Jesse Weaver, *Living the Hiplife: Celebrity and Entrepreneurship in Ghanaian Popular Music* (Durham: Duke University Press, 2013).

Shonekan, Sandra, "Nigerian Hip Hop: Exploring a Black World Hybrid," in *Hip Hop Africa: New African Music in a Globalized world ed.* Eric Charry (Bloomington: Indiana University Press, 2012),147–167.

Shue, Vivienne and Patricia Thornton, eds., *To Govern China: Evolving Practices of Power* (Cambridge: Cambridge University Press, 2018).

Shubin, Vladimir, *The Hot "Cold War": the USSR in Southern Africa* (London: Pluto Press, 2008).
Sidebotha, Steven, *Berenike and the Ancient Maritime Spice Route* (Berkeley: University of California Press, 2011).
Skinner, D., and Mfecane, S., "Stigma, Discrimination and the Implications for People Living with HIV/AIDS in South Africa," *Sahara-j: Journal of Social Aspects of HIV/AIDS* 1, 3 (2004): 157–164.
Skoglund, Pontus, et al, "Reconstructing Prehistoric African Population Structure," *Cell* 171 (2017): 59–71.
Smith, Andrew B., *African Herders: Emergence of Pastoral Traditions* (Walnut Creek: AltaMira Press, 2005).
Smith, G. L., and McFadden, G., "Smallpox: Anything to Declare?" *Nature Reviews Immunology* 2, 7 (2002): 521–527.
Smith, Linda Tuhiwai, *Decolonizing Methodologies: Research and Indigenous Peoples* (London: Zed Books, 2012).
Snow, Philip, *The Star Raft: China's Encounter with Africa* (New York: Cornell University Press, 1988).
Soderbaum, Fredrik, *Handbook of Regional Organizations in Africa* (Nordiska Afrikainstitutrt, 1996).
South African Democracy Education Trust, *The Road to Democracy in South Africa: South Africans Telling their Stories* (Houghton: Mutloatse Arts Heritage, 2008).
Spengler, Oswald, *The Decline of the West,* 2 vols. (New York, Knopf, 1934).
Stammers, Rhiannon C., Matthew V. Caruana, and Andy I. R. Herries, "The First Bone Tools from Kromdraai and Stone Tools from Drimolen, and the Place of Bone Tools in the South African Earlier Stone Age," *Quaternary International* 495 (2018): 87–101.
Stewart, Brian A., et al, "Ostrich Eggshell Bead Strontium Isotopes Reveal Persistent Macroscale Social Networking Across Late Quaternary Southern Africa," *Proceedings of the National Academy of Sciences* 117: (2020): 6453–6462.
Stewart, Katherine M., *Fishing Sites of North and East Africa in the Late Pleistocene and Holocene: Environmental Change and Human Adaptation* (Oxford: British Archaeological Reports, 1989).
Stiglitz, J. E., and K. Tsuda, "Democratizing the World Bank," *The Brown Journal of World Affairs,* 13, 2 (2007): 79–86.
Stillwell, Sean, *Slavery and Slaving in African History* (Cambridge, UK: Cambridge University Press, 2014).
Stockwell, John, *In Search of Enemies: A CIA Story* (London: Futura Publications, 1979).
Strachan, Hew, *The First World War: A New History* (London, Simon & Schuster, 2014).
Strandes, Justus, *The Portuguese Period in East Africa* (Nairobi: East African Literature Bureau, 1961).
Strauss, Julia C., "The Past in the Present: Historical and Rhetorical Lineages in China's Relations with Africa," *The China Quarterly* 199 (2009): 777–795.
Stride, G. T. and C. Ifeka, *Peoples and Empires of West Africa 1000–1800* (Nairobi Kenya, Thomas Nelson, 1971).
Stringer, Chris B., "Modern Human Origins – Distinguishing the Models," *African Archaeological Review* 18 (2001): 67–75.
Subrahmanyam, Sanjay, "Between Eastern Africa and Western India, 1500–1650: Slavery, Commerce and Elite Formation," *Comparative Studies in Society and History*, 61, 4 (2019): 805–834.
Sun, Jodie Yuzhou, "'Now the Cry Was Communism': The Cold War and Kenya's Relations with China (1964–1970)," *Cold War History* 20, 1 (2020): 39–58.
Sundkler, B., and C. Steed, *A History of the Church in Africa* (Cambridge, Cambridge University press, 2004).

Tatem, A. J., D. J. Rogers, and S.I. Hay, "Global Transport Networks and Infectious Disease Spread," *Advances in Parasitology* 62 (2006), 293–343.
Thiong'o, Ngugi wa, *Decolonising the Mind The Politics of Language in African Literature* (Harare: Zimbabwe Publishing House, 1981).
Thomson, Alex, *An Introduction to African Politics* (London and New York; Routledge Taylor and Francis Group, 2016).
Thompson, Leonard, *A History of South Africa* (New Haven, CT: Yale University Press, 2001).
Thörn, Hakan, *Anti-Apartheid and the Emergence of a Global Civil Society* (Springer: Palgrave, 2006).
Tishkoff, Sarah A., et al, "Convergent Adaptation of Human Lactase Persistence in Africa and Europe," *Nature Genetics* 39 (2007): 31–40.
Toynbee, Arnold J., *A Study of World History,* 12 vols. (Oxford, Oxford University Press, 1934–1961).
Touval, Saadia, "Treaties, Borders, and the Partition of Africa," *Journal of African History* 7, 2 (1966): 279–93.
Triaud, Jean-Louis, "Islam in Africa under French Colonial Rule," in *The History of Islam in Africa* ed. by Nehemia Levtzion and Randall L. Pouwels (Athens: Ohio University Press, 2000), 169–188.
Ugor, Paul, and Giovanna Santanera, "Media Globalization, African Popular Culture and the History from Below: Nigerian Video Films," *The Third Wave of Historical Scholarship on Nigeria* eds. Saheed Aderinto and Paul Osifodunrin (New Castle upon Tyne: Cambridge Scholars Publishing, 2012), 1–33.
Ugor, Paul, "Small Media, Popular Culture, and New Youth Spaces in Nigeria," *The Review of Education Pedagogy& Cultural Studies* 31, 4 (2009): 387–408.
Ukah, A., *The Redeemed Christian Church of God, Nigeria: Local Identities and Global Processes in African Pentecostalism* (Doctoral dissertation, University of Bayreuth, 2003).
Umar, Muhammad Sani, "The Tijâniyya and British Colonial Authorities in Northern Nigeria," in *La Tijâniyya* ed. by Jean-Louis Triaud and David Robinson (Paris: Editions Karthala, 2000), 327–355.
UNDP, *Human Development Report* (New York: United Nations, 1992).
Ushie, Joseph A., and David L. Imbua, *Essays on the History, Language and Culture of Bendi* (Ibadan: Kraft Books Limited, 2011).
Uya, Okon, *African Diaspora and the Black Experience in New World Slavery* (Calabar: Clear Lines Publishers, 2010).
van de Loosdrecht, Marieke, et al, "Pleistocene North African Genomes Link Near Eastern and Sub-Saharan African Human Populations," *Science* 360 (2018): 548–552.
Van Donk, M., "'Positive, Urban Futures in Sub-Saharan Africa: HIV/AIDS and the Need for ABC (A Broader Conceptualization)," *Environment and Urbanization* 18, 1 (2006):155–175.
Vansina, Jan, "A Slow Revolution: Farming in Subequatorial Africa," *Azania* 29/30 (1994/95): 15–26.
Vecchiato, N.L., "Illness, Therapy, and Change in Ethiopian Possession Cults," *Africa* 63, 2 (1993):176–196.
Venter, A. J., *How South Africa Built Six Atom Bombs: And then Abandoned its Nuclear Weapons Program* (Johannesburg: Ashanti Publishing, 2008).
Verdu, Paul, et al, "Origins and Genetic Diversity of Pygmy Hunter-Gatherers from Western Central Africa," *Current Biology* 19 (2009): 312–318.
Vernet, Thomas, "Slave Trade and Slavery on the Swahili Coast (1500–1750)," in *Slavery, Islam and Diaspora,* ed. by B.A. Mirzai, I.M. Montana, and P. Lovejoy (Trenton, NJ: African World Press, 2009),

Vink, Markus, "World's Oldest Trade: Dutch Slavery and Slave Trade in the Indian Ocean in the Seventeenth Century," *Journal of World History* 14, 2 (2003): 131–177.
Virmani, K. K., *Nelson Mandela and Apartheid in South Africa* (Delhi: Kalinga Publications, 1991).
Wadley, Lyn, "Those Marvellous Millennia: The Middle Stone Age of Southern Africa," *Azania: Archaeological Research in Africa* 50 (2014): 155–226.
Waddell, Hope M., *Twenty-Nine Years in the West Indies and Central Africa: A Review of Missionary Work and Adventure, 1829–1858* (London: T. Nelson & Sons, 1963).
Wang, Qinmei 汪勤梅, "Maozedong yu Zhongfei Guanxi" 毛泽东与中非关系 (Mao Zedong and China-Africa relations), *Waijiao Pinglun* 4 (1996): 3–8.
Ward, Cheryl, "Building Pharaoh's Ships: Cedar, Incense and Sailing the Great Green," *British Museum Studies in Ancient Egypt and Sudan* 18 (2012): 217–232.
Ward, Kerry, "Southeast Asian Migrants," in *Cape Town Between East and West: Social Identities in a Dutch Colonial Town* ed. by Nigel Worden (Johannesburg/Hilversum: Jacana and Verloren, 2012).
Wasylikowa, Krystyna, Józef Mitra, Fred Wendorf, and Romuald Schild, "Exploitation of Wild Plants by the Early Neolithic Hunter-Gatherers of the Western Desert, Egypt: Nabta Playa as a Case Study," *Antiquity* 71 (1997): 923–941.
Weiler, Peter, "British Labour and the Cold War: The Foreign Policy of the Labour Government, 1945–1951," *Journal of British Studies* 26, 1 (1987): 58–82.
Weiskel, Timothy C., *French Colonial Rule and the Baule Peoples: Resistance and Collaboration, 1889–1911* (Oxford: Clarendon Press, 1980).
Wells ,Julia C. *We Now Demand! The History of Women's Resistance to Pass Laws in South Africa* (Johannesburg: Witwatersrand University Press, 1993).
Weinberg, Gerhard L., *A World at Arms: A Global History of World War II* (Cambridge, Cambridge University Press, 2005).
Weissman, Stephen, *American Foreign Policy in the Congo, 1960–1964* (Ithaca: Cornell University Press, 1974).
Welsby, Derek A., *The Kingdom of Kush. The Napatan and Meroitic Empires* (Princeton: Markus Wiener Publishers, 1996).
Wengrow, David. *The Archaeology of Early Egypt: Social Transformations in North-East Africa* Cambridge: Cambridge University Press, 2006).
Wenzel, Jennifer, "Remembering the Past's Future: Anti-Imperialist Nostalgia and Some Versions of the Third World," *Cultural Critique* 62 (2006): 1–32.
Westad, Odd Arne, *The Global Cold War. Third World Interventions and the Makings of Our Times* (Cambridge: Cambridge University Press, 2005).
Wilmore, Gayraud S., *Black Religion and Black Radicalism: An Interpretation of the Religious History. of African Americans* (New York, Orbis, 1998).
Winchell, Frank, *et al*, "On the Origins and Dissemination of Domesticated Sorghum and Pearl Millet Across Africa and into India: A View from the Butana Group of the Far Eastern Sahel," *African Archaeological Review* 35 (2018): 483–503.
Wood, Ellen Meiksins, *The Origin of Capitalism* (London: Verso, 2017).
Woodson, Carter G., *African Heroes and Heroines* (Washington, Associated Publishers, 1939).
Woodward, Peter, *US Foreign Policy and the Horn of Africa* (Aldershot: Ashgate, 2006).
Worden, Nigel, "Indian Ocean Slaves in Cape Town, 1695–1807," *Journal of Southern African Studies* 42, 3 (2016): 389–408.
Wright, Donald R., *The World and a Very Small Place in Africa* (Armonk, NY: M. E. Sharpe, 1997).
Wynne-Jones, Stephanie and Adria LaViolette, eds., *The Swahili World* (London/New York: Routledge, 2018).
X, Malcolm, *The Autobiography of Malcolm X: with the assistance of Alex Haley* (London, Penguin, 1966).

Xia, Chunping 夏春平, ed., *Shijie huawen chuanmei nianjian* 世界华文传媒年鉴 (Yearbook of Global Chinese Language Media), (Beijing: China News Service, 2011).
Yandaki, A.I., *The State in Africa: A Critical Study in Historiography and Political Philosophy* (Zaria: Gaskiya Corporation, 2015).
Yap, Melanie and Dianne Leong Man, *Colour, Confusion and Concessions: The History of the Chinese in South Africa* (Hong Kong: Hong Kong University Press, 1996).
Yener, K. Aslihan *et al*, "New Tin Mines and Production Sites Near Kültepe in Turkey: a Third-Millennium BC Highland Production Model," *Antiquity* 89 (2015): 596–612.
Zangato, Etienne, and Augustin F. C. Holl, "On the Iron Front: New Evidence from North-Central Africa," *Journal of African Archaeology* 8 (2010): 7–23.
Zeleza, Paul Tiyambe ed., *The Study of Africa, Volume 2: Global and Transnational Engagement* (Dakar: CODESRA, 2007).
Zeleza, Paul T., "Rewriting the African Diaspora: Beyond the Black Atlantic," *African Affairs* 104, 414 (2005): 58–62.
Zhaoyu, Zhu, *et al*, "Hominin Occupation of the Chinese Loess Plateau Since about 2.1 Million Years Ago," *Nature* 559 (2018): 608–612.
Zheng, Kejun 郑克军, "八十年代初期中国对非洲政策的调整" [Adjustments of China's Policy towards Africa in the Early 1980s"], in *Zhongguo yu Feizhou* 中国与非洲 (China and Africa) (Beijing: Peking University Press, 2000), 87–99.

Newspapers and Periodicals

"Africa's Role in WWI a Forgotten Chapter," *The Washington Times*, Wednesday, 28 July 2004.
Crocker, C., 'South Africa: Strategy for Change', *Foreign Affairs,* Winter, 1980/81.
Crocker, C., 'The United States and Africa', *Africa Report*, September–October 1981.
Jackson, H.F., 'Reagan's Policy Rupture', *Africa Report*, September–October 1981
Marder, M., and Oberdorfer, D., 'How the West, Soviets Acted to Defuse South African A-Test', *Washington Post*, 28 August 1977.
Meli, F., 'South Africa Joins Imperialist Bloc in Indian Ocean Offensive', *The African Communist*, Second Quarter, 1975.
"United Nations and Apartheid: Special Committee Holds Sessions in Europe," *Sechaba,* Vol. 8/9 Aug/September 1974.
"The Nuclear Conspiracy: FRG collaborates to strengthen Apartheid," *Sechaba,* No. 9, November–December 1975.
"NATO and South Africa," *Sechaba*, Vol. 9, No. 3, 1975.
"The Simonstown Agreement," *Sechaba*, Vol. 4, No. 10, 1970.
"Zambia may drop food imports from China", *Times of Zambia*, 13 October 1978.
"China to buy more from Kenya", *The Standard*, 18 January 1983.
"Editorial: Kenya and China", *The Standard*, 23 August 1980.
"Historians gather the threads which link us with Asia", *Times of Zambia*, 14 April 1967.

Dissertations

Alabi, A. S., Transmission of Learning in Modern Ilorin: A History of Islamic Education 1897–2012 (Doctoral dissertation, Universiteit Leiden, 2015).

Mabvurira, V., Influence of African Traditional Religion and Spirituality in Understanding Chronic Illnesses and its Implications for Social Work Practice: A case of Chiweshe Communal Lands in Zimbabwe (Doctoral dissertation, University of Limpopo, 2016).

Rhamie Gifford, C.A., Whiteness, Conviviality and Agency: The Ethiopian Eunuch (Acts 8:26–40) and Conceptuality in the Imperial Imagination of Biblical Studies (Doctoral dissertation, Canterbury Christchurch University, 2019).

Sunday, M.M., Organization Structure and Participation of the Evangelical Church of West Africa in the Delivery of Primary Health Care Services in Kafanchan and Kaduna Districts in Kaduna State, Nigeria (Doctoral dissertation, Mzumbe University, 2011).

Oral Data

Han Jun, interviewed by Sun Jodie Yuzhou, Nairobi, 10 November 2016.

Jakkie Celliers, interviewed by Du Preez conducted by Max du Preez, Pretoria, October 2007, SADET Oral History Project (SOHP).

Joe Gaobakwe Matthews, interviewed by S.M. Ndlovu and B.M. Magubane, 18 July 2001, SOHP.

'Pik' Botha, interviewed by S.M. Ndlovu and Bernard Magubane, Johannesburg, 3 August 2001, SOHP.

Salim Salim, interviewed by S.M. Ndlovu and Miranda Strydom, Dar es Salaam, August 2015.

Stoffel van der Merwe, interviewed by Max du Preez, Pretoria, July 2007, SOHP.

Thabo Mbeki, interviewed by S.M. Ndlovu, Pretoria, 23 February 2011 and 23 March 2020. SOHP.

Internet materials

9ice, "Street Credibility," https://www.youtube.com/watch?v=BEymsiBpceQ&app=desktop. Accessed 14/7/2020.

Abdulkareem, Eedris, "Free Sowore," https://www.youtube.com/watch?v=xtOMuCzbR70&list=RDEMhPAdgX9jRsmblx8EvFiYCw&start_radio=1. Accessed 13/7/2020.

Abdulkareem, Eedris, "Jaga jaga," https://www.youtube.com/watch?v=UO4qhDthUAU. Accessed 13/7/2020.

Abdulkareem, Eedris, Siderz Entertainment TV. "Eedris Abdulkareem rips Obasanjo". https://www.youtube.com/watch?v=hbuGc33tQME. Accessed 13/7/2020.

Alawode, Abisola, "How Eedris Abdulkareem and ex-President Obasanjo 'fought in Public'" https://www.legit.ng/1171767-how-eedris-abdulkareem-president-olusegun-obasanjo-fought-public.html. Accessed 14/7/2020.

Anderson, Monica, Andrew Perrin, Jingjing Jiang and Madhumitha Kumar, "10% of Americans Don't Use the internet. Who are they?" *Pew Research Center*. April 22, 2019, www.pewresearch.org/fact-tank/2019/04/22/some-americans-dont-use-the-internet-who-are-they/%3famp=1. Accessed on August 31, 2020.

"China's initiation of the Five Principles of Peaceful Co-Existence", Ministry of Foreign Affairs of People's Republic of China, http://www.fmprc.gov.cn/mfa_eng/ziliao_665539/3602_665543/3604_665547/t1805 Shtml. Accessed January 2016.

Congressional Research Service (2019). *Foreign aid: an introduction to U.S. programs and policy*. Updated 2019. https//crsreports.congress.gov R40213. Accessed 20/5/2020.

Congressional Research Service (2020). COVID-19: Role of the international financial institutions Nelson. May 4. Summary by Rebecca M. Nelson and Martin A. Weiss. https://crsreports.congress.gov R46342. Accessed 4/6/2020.

De Laat, Sonya, and Valerie Gorin (2016). Iconographies of Humanitarian Aid Africa. Humanitarian Policy Group Overseas Development Institute. http://www.odi.org/hpg. Accessed 3/5/2020.

Development Aid at a Glance (2019). *Development aid at a glance: statistics by region. Africa.* 2019 edition. http://www.oecd.org/dac/financing-sustainable-development/. Accessed 20/5/2020.

Duncan Mighty, "Hand of Jesus," https://www.youtube.com/watch?v=ZpASxidgcwo. Accessed 13/7/2020.

Easterly, William (2005). *Can foreign aid save Africa?* Clemens Lecture Series, 13. https://digitalcommons.csbsju.edu/clemens_lectures/13. Accessed 19/5/2020

Falz. "This is Nigeria". Vevo. Accessed 14/7/2020 https://www.youtube.com/watch?v=UW_xEqCWrm0

"Feature: Kenyan girl with Chinese blood steals limelight", *Xinhua*, 30 June 2005, http://ke.china-embassy.org/eng/sbgx/t202741.htm. Accessed November 2017.

"Forum on China-Africa Cooperation", FOCAC Official Website, https://www.focac.org/chn/ltjj/ltjz/. Accessed June 2018.

Immanuel Fillemon Wise (2011). *Are Western aid to Africa the Solution to the embattled continental economy.* Paper presented at the International Symposium on Cultural Diplomacy in Africa, 11th – 17th July 2011, Institute for Cultural Diplomacy, Berlin, German. culturaldiplomacy.org/academy/content/pdf/participant-papers/africa/Fillemon-Wise-Immanuel-Are-Western-Aids-To-Africa-The-Solution-To-The-Embattled-Continental-Economy. Accessed 21/5/2020.

"Internet Users for Africa (Africa Internet Usage, 2020 Population Stats and Facebook Subscribers)." *Internet World Stats.* https://www.internetworldstats.com/stats1.htm, accessed on August 31, 2020.

"Internet Usage in the European Union (Internet User Statistics, Facebook Subscribers and 2020 Population for the 27 European Union member States)." *Internet World Stats.* https://www.internetworldstats.com/stats9.htm. Accessed on August 31, 2020.

Jarus, O., (2020), "20 of the Worst Epidemics and Pandemics in History". *LiveScience*. https://www.livescience.com/worst-epidemics-and-pandemics-in-history.html. Accessed on 14th July, 2020 at 10:09 pm.

Knoll Martin (2008). Budget support: a reformed approach or old wine in new skins?. UN Conference on Trade and Development. Discussion Paper. UNCTAD/OSG/DP/2008/5, No. 190 October. Accessed 23/5/2020.

Mark, J. Joshua. "Silk Road," *An Ancient History Encyclopedia,* May 1, 2018, https://www.ancient.eu/Silk_Road/. Accessed on September 2, 2020.

Mighty Duncan, "Hand of Jesus," https://www.youtube.com/watch?v=qMniU5-9c0I. Accessed 14/7/2020.

Olu maintain, "Yahooze," https://www.youtube.com/watch?v=0MW7kcZnaiA. Accessed 13/7/2020.

Pierce Yolanda "African Cosmologies: Spiritual Reflections on the 'Black Panther' movie," (Religious News Service 2018 https://religionnews.com/2018/02/19/african-cosmologies-spiritual-reflections-on-the-black-panther-movie/. Accessed 6th December 2020.

Press Release: "Record High Remittances Sent Globally in 2018." *The World Bank.* April 8, 2019, https://www.worldbank.org/en/news/press-release/2019/04/08/record-high-remittances-sent-globally-in-2018. Accessed on August 31, 2020.

Simisola, BOI G TV. "Simi reply Naira Marley on Yahoo boys," https://www.youtube.com/watch?v=w-YAIYDCXWw. Accessed 13/7/2020.

Statement on Behalf of the Non-Aligned Movement (NAM), on the Occasion of the Special Meeting in Observance of the International Day of Solidarity with the Palestinian People. Vienna, 29 November, 2019. https://www.namazerbaijan.org/pdf/Statement15.pdf. Accessed 13 July, 2020.

Timaya, "Dem Mama," https://www.youtube.com/watch?v=kqC-6YdZVL8. Accessed 13/7/2020.
Timaya, "Plantain Seller," https://www.youtube.com/watch?v=15gzJf8_P3Y. Accessed 13/7/2020.
Waconzy, "I celeberate," https://www.youtube.com/watch?v=IfO1-JYD2UA. Accessed 14/7/2020.
Wizboy, "Owusagi," https://www.youtube.com/watch?v=y6oB52-pb7Y. Accessed 14/7/2020.
Wizkid, "Ojuelegba," https://www.youtube.com/watch?v=Q7QiLceJSLQ. Accessed 13/7/2020.
Wood, A. (2005). World Bank's PRSC: Continuity or Change: DDCI, Dublin. Available at: http://siteresources.worldbank.org/PROVECTS/578280-1119562936151/20576770. Accessed 23/5/2020.
World Bank (2000). Partners in Transforming Development: New Approaches to Developing Country-owned Poverty Reduction Strategies. http://www.imf.org/external/np/prsp/pdf/[rspbroc.pdf. Accessed 3/6/2020.
World Health Organisation, (WHO) (2020) *African Countries Move from COVID 19 Readiness to Response as Many Confirm Cases.* WHO Africa. https://www.afro.who.int/health-topics/coronavirus-covid-19. Accessed on 14th July, 2020 at 10:11 pm.

Archival materials

The National Archives of UK, FCO 141/7090, "Chinese activities and influence in Africa", December 1961.
The National Archives of UK, FCO 141/7090, "Memorandum: Sino-Soviet propaganda in Africa", 1961.
United National Independence Party Archives at The British Library, EAP121_2_5_1_9pt6, Correspondence by Ministry of Commerce & Report on the visit to the PRC, 1976, 'Report on the visit to the PRC', 22 October 1976.
United National Independence Party Archives at The British Library, EAP121_2_5_1_10, 1979, "Visit to the People's Republic of China by a UNIP delegation 22nd July – 10th August 1979", August 1979.
United National Independence Party Archives at The British Library, EAP121_2_5_4_32pt1, "Analyse conditions objectively", 23 January 1980.

Notes on Contributors

William Ackah is a Senior Lecturer in Black and Community Geographies in the Department of Geography at Birkbeck University of London. He is current chair of the Transatlantic Roundtable on Religion and Race an international organization that brings together academics, community activists and church leaders with the aim of tackling injustices faced by people of African descent around the world. He is the co-editor with Jualynne Dodson and R. Drew Smith of *Religion, Culture and Spirituality in Africa and the African Diaspora* (Routledge, 2018). He is a Fulbright Research Scholar and is doing ongoing research on gentrification and its impact on African American Communities in Pittsburgh and Black communities in London.

Abdulwasiu Ajibola Abdulrahman is a PhD candidate in History at the University of Mississippi. His areas of interest include slavery, labor, and colonial rule in Africa. His PhD research focuses on the history of the Freed Slaves' Homes in Northern Nigeria during the colonial period. Abdulrahman's research interests also include African diaspora history. He has done some research on James Meredith, the first African American to enroll and graduate from the University of Mississippi and his involvement in the Nigerian Civil War.

Sakariyau Aliyu Alabi is a Senior Lecturer at Bayero University, Kano, Nigeria. He studied for his PhD at Universiteit Leiden, The Netherlands, working on the thesis "Transmission of Learning in Modern Ilorin: A History of Islamic Education 1897–2012." He is interested in the dynamics of Islamic education, particularly in the Nigerian context. In 2016 he was a Cadbury Fellow of the 'Knowing Each Other' Program at the University of Birmingham, United Kingdom, leading to the publication of 'The Modernisation of Islamic Education in Ilorin: A Study of the Adabiyya and Markaziyya Educational Systems' in the journal *Islamic Africa.*

Pedro Machado is Associate Professor of History at Indiana University, Bloomington. He is the author of several works, among them *Ocean of Trade: South Asian Merchants, Africa and the Indian Ocean, c. 1750–1850* (Cambridge University Press, 2014); "Views from Other Boats: On Amitav Ghosh's Indian Ocean 'Worlds,'" *American Historical Review*, Vol. 121, No. 5 (December 2016); *Textile Trades, Consumer Cultures and the Material Worlds of the Indian Ocean* (Palgrave Macmillan, 2018); and *Pearls, People and Power: Pearling and Indian Ocean Worlds* (Ohio University Press, 2020). He is currently at work on a global history of pearl shell collection and exchange while also developing research on eucalyptus and colonial forestry in the Portuguese empire in the nineteenth and twentieth centuries.

Noah Echa Attah is a Professor in the Department of History and Diplomatic Studies, Federal University of Kashere, Gombe State. He received his PhD in History from University of Ibadan and his BA in History from Lagos State University, Ojo. He is a recipient the African Humanities Programme Postdoctoral Fellowship from the American Council of Learned Societies, the Otto Bennemann Fellowship by the Georg Eckert Institute, Brauschweig, Germany and the African Peacebuilding Network of the Social Science Research Council, New York. He has authored several peer reviewed book chapters and journal articles. He co-edited a book on *Critical Perspectives on Peace, Conflict and Warfare in Africa* in 2012.

Toyin Falola is the Jacob and Frances Sanger Mossiker Chair in the Humanities and University Distinguished Teaching Professor at the University of Texas at Austin. He has served as the President of the African Studies Association, and he is currently the President of Pan-African

University Press. He has published almost 200 books and received over 30 lifetime awards, including 13 honorary doctorates.

Flavia Gasbarri is a lecturer in the War Studies Department at King's College London, co-chair of the KCL Africa Research Group and member of the KCL Centre for Grand Strategy. She completed her PhD in War Studies at KCL in 2014, and she then worked as Teaching Fellow in the War Studies Department for four years. In 2015, she was also appointed Teaching Fellow in the Defence Studies Department at the Joint Services Command and Staff College (JSCSC) in Shrivenham, where she worked as Academic Tutor for the British Armed Forces (both at junior and senior level). In 2018–2019, she was Academic Tutor at The Royal College of Defence Studies. Flavia Gasbarri's research and main publications focus on the study of the Cold War in the Third World, the development of post-Cold War US foreign policy and US-Africa relations. She has also extensively researched and published on US policy in the Rwandan genocide and in the Great Lakes region.

Moses I. Olatunde Ilo teaches history at the Department of History, Tai Solarin College of Education, Omu Ijebu, Ogun State, Nigeria. He was a former head of the Department and currently a senior lecturer at the College. He is also a doctoral student at University of Ibadan. Moses has conducted extensive research on diverse topics including economic history, gender, urbanization, international relations, and Nigerian history. He has attended significant academic seminars, workshops, and conferences in various parts of Nigeria, and he is a research fellow at the French Institute for Research in Nigeria (IFRA). In 2017, Moses was awarded a fellowship by the Lagos Studies Association. His works have appeared in scholarly journals and edited books. Between 2011 and 2017, Moses served as chairman of two committees in his department: the Examination Committee and the Seminar Committee. At present, he is the head of the men's wing of Covenant Christians Ministries, secretary of Adio Fasina Desendancy, secretary of Ilo Abioro's Family as well as one of the Special Marshals of the Federal Road Safety Corps in Nigeria. Moses is married to Edith and both are blessed with children.

David L. Imbua is an award-winning Lecturer at the Department of History and International Studies, University of Calabar, Nigeria. He researches the Atlantic world and the institution of pawnship and slavery in precolonial and colonial Southeastern Nigeria. He has been quite prolific in scholarly output and in participation in academic conferences, seminars, and symposia around the world. Dr. Imbua is the author of several books, which traverse history and historical fiction, book chapters and articles in learned national and international journals. He is the author of *Intercourse and Crosscurrents in the Atlantic World: Calabar-British Experience, 17th–20th Centuries* (Carolina Academic Press, 2012) which won the Lapai Book Prize for Outstanding Historical Text in International History in 2015. Among his works in progress is *The Notorious Massacre at Calabar in 1767*, with Paul E. Lovejoy and Randy J. Sparks.

Idom T. Inyabri obtained MA and PhD from the Universities of Ibadan and Calabar, Nigeria. He is Associate Professor at the Department of English and Literary Studies, University of Calabar, where he teaches courses in African literature (oral and written), ecocriticism and popular culture. Dr. Inyabri is a fellow of the African Humanities Program with generous support from the American Council of Learned Societies.

Nnaoma Hyacinth Iwu is a senior lecturer in the Department of Political Science and Public Administration, Adekunle Ajasin University, Akungba-Akoko Ondo State, Nigeria. He graduated with a BSc, MSc, and PhD from University of Ibadan, Ibadan, Nigeria, with a specialization in comparative politics. His research interests span across civil society, conflict resolution, political economy, and strategic studies. His works have been published in international and national journals. One of his recent works titled "Football theory of scientific development: a theory for the end of Africa's underdevelopment" provides a paradigm for Africa to engage with other continents in globally competitive markets.

Abdul Kuba is a PhD student at the University of Mississippi. He studies African history with special interest in African economic history, African diasporic studies, and slavery and emancipation. Kuba holds a BA in history from the University of Cape Coast and an MA in history from the University of Texas at San Antonio and the University of Cape Coast. He has also served as a teaching and a research assistant at both the University of Cape Coast (Ghana) and the University of Texas at San Antonio. Kuba has presented papers in various conferences in the United States and published articles in different academic journals. Some of his works include; "Migration and wage labor: a case study of Ghanaians in New York City, 1957–2010," "Women nationalists in nineteenth and twentieth-century Ghana and Zimbabwe: Case studies of Charwe Nehanda Nyakasikana and Yaa Asentewaa," and "The clash of two cultures: A historical analysis of social changes in the Gold Coast in the twentieth century."

Peter Mitchell read Archaeology & Anthropology at Cambridge and then completed his doctorate in Oxford in 1987. After working in Cape Town and Wales, he returned to Oxford to take up his current post as Professor of African Archaeology and Tutor and Fellow in Archaeology at St Hugh's College in 1995. He is also a Research Associate of the Rock Art Research Institute, University of the Witwatersrand, South Africa. Mitchell combines a longstanding interest in the archaeology of southern African hunter-gatherers (including fieldwork in Lesotho) with broader themes in African archaeology as a whole and has more recently tackled aspects of the history of human relations with animals. Co-editor of *Azania: Archaeological Research in Africa*, he is author of *The Archaeology of Southern Africa* (2002), *African Connections: Archaeological Perspectives on Africa and the Wider World* (2005), *The First Africans: African Archaeology from the Earliest Toolmakers to Most Recent Foragers* (2008, with Larry Barham), *Horse Nations: The Worldwide Impact of the Horse on Indigenous Societies Post-1492* (2015), and *The Donkey in Human History* (2018), as well as co-editor with Paul Lane of the *Oxford Handbook of African Archaeology*.

Sifiso Mxolisi Ndlovu is a Professor of History at University of South Africa and executive director at the South African Democracy Education Trust. He has an MA in History from the University of Natal, Pietermaritzburg and a PhD in History from the University of the Witwatersrand. His book publications include *The Soweto Uprisings: Counter-Memories of June 1976* (Picador Africa, 2017) and *King Dingane ka Senzangakhona: The Second Monarch of the Zulu Kingdom* (Palgrave Macmillan). He is co-author of *The Thabo Mbeki I Know* (Picador Africa, 2016) and also co-author of *Public History and Culture in South Africa: Memorialisation and Liberation Heritage Sites in Johannesburg and the Township Space* (Palgrave Macmillan, 2019). He is the editor-in-chief of *The Road to Democracy in South Africa*, a multi-volume series.

J. Akinyele Oluyitan is an Associate Professor and the Acting Head of Department of History and International Studies at Ajayi Crowther University, Oyo. Formerly, he was the Sub-Dean of Postgraduate School. Oluyitan has a passion and an abiding interest in the history of public hygiene, colonial history of medicine, the environment and urbanization. He has also published articles in social history. He is a member of the Historical Society of Nigeria, West African Research Association, and the Nigerian Health Historians Network.

Onwaniban Evelyn is a doctoral student at the Department of History, University of Ibadan, Nigeria. She obtained her master's degree in 2015 and graduated as one of the best students in her set. She attended the University of Benin, Nigeria and obtained her B. A. International Studies and Diplomacy in 2010 with a Second Class Upper Division. Onwaniban is a prolific researcher, writer, and author. She has publications in peer-reviewed journal and books. Some of her books include Nigerian history texts for primary and junior secondary schools. Her research areas include African studies, women and military studies. Onwaniban won the University of Ibadan Post Graduate Teaching and Research Assistant Award 2018/2019 session and the Lagos Studies Association Women Mentoring Programme Award in 2019. She has lectured as a Teaching and Research Assistant in the University of Ibadan, Assistant Lecturer in Admiralty University of Nigeria and currently a Research Fellow in Nigerian Army Resource Centre, Abuja.

Bukola Oyeniyi is historian of African history, with specialization in Africa's social and cultural history in the early nineteenth and twentieth centuries. His current research focuses on the place of Africa's expressive culture, especially dress, in the construction of individual and group identity. In his book, *Dress in the Making of African Identity: A Social and Cultural History of the Yoruba People* (Cambria Press, 2015), he examines the history of Yorubaland as seen through dress and the history of Yorùbá dress, especially its place in the construction of Yorùbá ethno-national identity. Other works of Oyeniyi include *The History of Libya*, (Greenwood, 2019); *Nigeria: Africa In Focus*, co-authored with Toyin Falola, (ABC-CLIO, 2015). Oyeniyi currently teaches African history at the Department of History, Missouri State University, Springfield, Missouri, USA.

Bala Saho received his PhD in African history from Michigan State University in 2012 and his MA in African studies from the University of Illinoi, Urbana-Champaign in 2007. He is a historian of nineteenth and twentieth century West Africa (religious, legal, cultural, and social, women and gender history). His book, *Contours of Change: Muslim Courts, Women, and Islamic Society in Colonial Bathurst, the Gambia, 1905–1965* (Michigan State University, 2018), explores the place of women in the formation of colonial Bathurst, the evolution of women's understanding of the importance of law in securing their rights, as well as the ways in which women utilized the new qadi court system to fight for growing rights within the domestic sphere. He is currently working on a second book titled, *Ritualizing the Womb: Kañeleŋyaa, Infertility, and Motherhood in The Gambia*

Mohammed Bashir Salau is Professor of history at the University of Mississippi. He has authored two books on slavery and Islam.

Jodie Yuzhou Sun is Senior Lecturer at the Department of History, Fudan University, China and a Research Fellow at the International Studies Group, University of the Free State, South Africa. Her primary research interests are the history of China-Africa relations, with particular foci on Kenya and Zambia, the history of the Cold War in the global South and global history of socialist ideas. She has published in the *Cold War History*, *International Journal of African Historical Studies*, and *Journal of Southern African Studies*. She obtained her DPhil in History and Msc in African Studies from the University of Oxford in 2019 and 2014

Index

A. A. Y. Kyerematen 166
Abbas Ibn Firnas 57
Abd al-Muttalib 50
Abdoulaye Wade 350
Abeokuta Ladies Club (ALC) 188
Abu Anjashah al-Ha-bashi 50
Abu Ishaq Ibrahim al-Kanemi 58
Abu Kamil Shuja ibn Aslam 57
Adrian Hastings 104
African Bushmen (San) 28
African Development Bank (AFDB) 342, 347
African Independence 185, 377
African Indigenous/Initiated/Independent Churches (AICs) 266
African Mineworkers Union (AMWU) 182
African nationalism 14, 176, 185–191, 194, 200, 203, 208
Afrikaner nationalism 203, 206, 211
Afrocentrism 3
Ajayi Crowther 136f., 139, 421
Akan 101, 112, 118, 173
Alexander the Great 34
Alexandria 46, 54, 57, 81, 143
Alfred Nzo 236
Algeria 29, 45, 53f., 56, 68, 73, 143, 156, 178, 195, 210, 260, 271, 290, 316, 321, 323, 325, 350
Algiers 178, 288, 325
al-Hasan ibn Muhammad al-Wazzan al-Fasi 57
al-Hassar 57
Al-Idrisi 57
Al-Jahiz 57
Al Ksar–al-Kabir 73
All African Convention (AAC) 207
Allied forces 169, 171, 174, 177–180
Al-Qarawiyyin 57
Al-Qayrawan 57
al-Qurashi 57
Alvin Aileyi 120
Anastasius I 53
ANC (African National Congress) 14, 205, 207–209, 213–218, 220, 224–233, 236f., 307, 312
Anglo-Zulu War 148
Angola 26, 104, 118, 123, 135, 195, 199, 212, 214f., 224, 226–229, 236f., 290f., 293f., 301–303, 305–307, 312, 327

Angolan army (FAPLA) 212
Angolan Civil War 302f., 305, 307, 312f.
Anne Samson 169f.
Antera Duke 121
anti-communism 204, 219
AOU 198
apartheid 14f., 146, 148, 187, 203–208, 210–231, 233, 282–284, 287–289, 291f., 295, 301–303, 306f., 312, 320, 324
Arabia 32, 44, 67, 71, 80–82, 84, 86f., 89, 91f.
Arabian Peninsula 87, 89, 91, 96
Arab invasion 56
Arab-Israeli war 287f., 295
Arab Muslims 11, 43, 46, 50f., 62
Archibald Dalzel 122
Aristide Zolberg 195
Arjun Appadurai 361
Armah An-Najashi 45
Arnold Tonybee 1
Arthur Mitchel 120
Askia Dawud 73
Aswan High Dam 34
Atlantic Charter 191f.
Atlantic world 5, 99f., 102, 104, 108f., 113, 115, 117, 119, 124, 420
Australasia 23
Australia 23–25, 255, 380
Australopithecus anamensis 21
Axis powers 169, 180, 182f.

Baba Fryo 358
Bafour 49
Bahia 92
Bantu 6, 11, 38–40, 81, 231
Barakah Um Ayman 49
Battle of Cuito Cuanavale 212
Bay of Bengal 87
Belgian Congo 160, 171, 189, 221, 246, 267, 290
Belgium 143f., 151, 155, 169, 174, 282, 299, 303
Benedetta Rossi 351
Bénin 37f.
Berber people 49
Berber traders 48
Berlin Conference 13, 141, 143f., 147, 169

Berlin Wall 308
Bernard Bailyn 99
Bibi Titi Muhammed 196
Bight of Benin 111, 128, 130, 134
Bight of Biafra 111, 128
Bilal Ibn Rabah 50, 264
Bishop Henry 103
Black Catholics 118
Black Consciousness Movement (BCM) 209, 230
Black Hawk Down 311, 313
Black Panther 277
Blombos 24
Blues 119
Blyden 278
Boers 145, 171
Bollywood 360
Bolshevik revolution 285
Bolshoi Theatre 234
Bosumpra Cave 33
Brazil 117–119, 234, 256, 259, 267, 274
Bretton Woods 345, 362, 380
Britain 53, 94, 111, 123, 125, 127–129, 131, 133, 141–145, 151, 155, 163–165, 169–171, 173f., 176, 179, 188, 191f., 195f., 198, 209, 221, 225, 252, 271f., 275, 282, 284–286, 292f., 298, 300, 324, 326, 349, 373, 376f.
British Somaliland 178
British Togoland 197, 200
Broederbond 205, 216
Bronislaw Malinowski 165f.
Bulgaria 210, 232
Bumi Jeleen 102
Burundi 39
Busaidi sultanate 87
Byzantium 62

Calabar 104f., 111, 114f., 117, 120–123, 127, 131, 134, 136, 138, 420
Caliph Muawiyah I 45
Caliph Umar ibn al-Khattab 45
Caliph Uthman Ibn Affan 45
Calvinism 203
Calypso 119, 358
Cameroon 33, 37–39, 41, 143, 171, 173, 176, 195, 260, 293, 346
Canada 234, 344, 380
Cape Verde 106f., 109
Captain Hugh Crow 131

Caribbean 109f., 116, 119, 124, 165f., 190, 192, 268, 270–272, 274, 357f., 371
Carolyn Brown 170, 180, 183
Carter G. Woodson 2
Carthage 36f., 53f., 70
Casablanca 178
Cassius Make 237
Charles II 111
Charles van Onselen 149f.
Cheikh Anta Diop 2f.
Chen Yi 324
Chifumbaze complex 40
Childish Gambino 370
China 7, 11, 16, 22, 25, 87, 92, 95, 141, 209, 226, 252, 259, 286, 291, 293, 302, 315–333, 348f., 354, 360, 375, 378, 380–382, 385f., 388f., 422
Chinese Communist Party (CCP) 317
Chris Mba 358
Chris Okotie 358
Christianity 6, 11f., 15, 45–47, 54–56, 99–104, 118, 126, 135, 137, 139, 143, 153, 160, 162, 167, 263–269, 275f., 279
Christian missionaries 12f., 15, 101, 125, 135–139, 160–162
Cold War 14–16, 193, 198, 210, 219f., 222f., 226, 231, 281f., 284–294, 296–306, 309, 311–313, 315, 318, 321f., 324–326, 331–333, 336, 377, 380, 386, 420, 422
Colette Daiute 371
Colonialism 4, 13, 71, 77, 138, 141f., 144f., 147–149, 151, 153–155, 158, 163–166, 185f., 190, 193, 198f., 204, 235, 250, 267, 278, 284, 287, 289, 295, 298, 301, 316, 323, 331, 358, 374
Comores 83
Comoros 80f., 85f., 91, 95, 130
Congo Basin 22, 28, 39, 245
Convention of Democratic South Africa (CODESA) 218
coronavirus (COVID-19) epidemic 252, 259
Cote d'Ivoire 197, 383
Council of Non-European Trade Unions (CNETU) 182
Council on African Affairs (CAA) 192
Cross River 121, 134, 136
Cuba 109, 117–119, 212f., 226, 274, 286, 291, 293, 301, 303–306, 310, 327, 380f.
Czechoslovakia 232

Dady Showkey 358
Dahomey 128, 133, 171, 253
Damascus 46, 52, 57
Daniel F. Malan 204
Danish International Development Agency (DANIDA) 351
Darfur 47
David Eltis 113
David Hume 1
David Killingray 149, 155, 170, 174, 179–182, 252
David Livingstone 137, 143
David Northrup 101f., 115, 120f.
David Noy 52
David Robinson 150
David Shinn 316
David Welsh 206
decolonization 9, 13, 15, 155, 185–187, 189, 191–198, 200f., 281–284, 290, 292–294, 297–299, 301, 311, 315, 321, 324, 386f.
Defence Manpower Committee (DMPC) 212
Democratic Republic of Congo 177, 254, 294
Development Assistance Committee (DAC) 340
Diaspora 1f., 58, 87–92, 95, 99f., 102, 114, 116, 118, 124, 182, 190, 192f., 263–268, 270, 272–277, 380f., 389, 419
Dick Van Galen 170, 173, 182
Diepkloof 24
Diogo Cao 103
Dizzy Gillespie 119
Djibouti 25, 88
Djinguereber 58
Dom Joao 102
Donald R. Wright 4
Donovan Chau 316
Don Tom 362
Dr. James. S. Moroka 207
Dr. J.B. Danquah 193
Duncan Mighty 362, 364f.

East Africa 4f., 26–28, 34, 39–41, 44, 49, 51, 62, 79, 81–87, 89, 91f., 94f., 128–130, 137, 146, 149f., 171f., 174–177, 179, 189, 227, 245, 248f., 253, 255, 260, 318f., 329
East Asia 23, 92, 331, 386
Ebola 252, 257f., 260f., 336, 353
Edward Alpers 4, 87, 95
Eedris Abdulkareem 369
Egbe ECWA Hospital 250

Egypt 1f., 11, 27, 30, 32, 34–36, 45–47, 49–52, 54, 56–62, 71, 73, 79–82, 84, 86, 88, 100, 143, 175–177, 179, 260, 264, 276, 282, 290, 323
Ekpene Obom 251
Eleoi Pomare 120
Elijah 55
Emmanuel Onyechere Osigwe-Anyiam-Osigwe 349
Emperor Marcus Aurelius 53f.
Emperor Septimius Severus 53
England 51, 60, 84, 122f., 126f., 130f., 136, 143, 207, 233, 251, 253, 286
Eric Williams 109, 165
Erik Gilbert 5, 142
Eritrea 25, 32, 35, 44, 80, 88, 346
Ernie Pyle 178
Ethiopia 19, 21f., 32, 41, 44–46, 50, 59, 61f., 82, 88f., 101, 147, 169, 178f., 190f., 242f., 251, 264, 275, 282, 286, 291, 293f., 304f., 309f., 312, 321, 343
Ethiopianism 275
Ethiopian Orthodox Church 269
Ethiopian Progressive Association (EPA) 190
Ethiopian–Somali confrontation 304
Eurocentric 3, 5, 184, 268, 274, 299
European Development Fund (EDF) 348
European Recovery Plan (ERP) 220

Federation of Nigerian Women's Societies (FNWS] 188
Felix Houphouet-Boigny 195
Felix Liberty 358
Ferdinand V 109
foreign aid 10, 16, 281, 284, 335–341, 343, 351, 353f., 381
Forum of China-Africa Cooperation (FOCAC) 331
Fourth industrial revolution 373, 378
France 51, 60, 93, 111, 142–144, 149, 151, 155, 159f., 163, 169, 171, 179, 191, 196, 198, 209f., 221, 225, 252, 257, 282, 284f., 292f., 298, 303, 376f., 419
Franklin Frazier 117
Frantz Fanon 186
Frederick Cooper 4, 92, 142, 153, 186, 195, 198, 283, 388
Frederick Lugard 145, 159
Fredrick Cooper 154, 186f., 196f.
FRELIMO 200, 302

Frente Nacional de Libertação de Angola (FNLA)   302
Front de Libéra tion Nationale Congolais (FLNC)   303
Fulani   145, 173, 370

Gambia   47, 101, 106 f., 147, 245, 271, 422
Gambia River   4, 106
Garamantes   48, 60 f.
Garveyism   163 f., 189
Gaur Radebe   207
General Yakubu Gowon   358
Geoffrey Barraclough   3
geopolitics   45, 219–221, 290
George Mackenzie   129
Germany   60, 142–146, 151, 155 f., 171, 175 f., 192, 210, 225, 282, 285, 419
Ghana   33, 38, 47 f., 70, 73 f., 101, 118, 145, 157, 174, 194 f., 197 f., 247, 249, 260, 266, 271, 282 f., 291, 293, 299, 316, 321, 323, 346, 421
Global Hip Hop Nation (GHHN)   357
Globalization   3 f., 9, 11, 15–17, 84, 92, 252, 263, 277, 284, 355 f., 360–362, 365, 371, 373–378, 380–382, 384–389
Global North   266
Godfrey M. Pitje   207
Gold Coast   105–108, 111, 122 f., 134, 138 f., 143, 157, 171, 173 f., 183, 193, 195, 247, 254, 321, 421
Graeco-Roman   43, 46
Great Depression   13, 153, 187 f., 345
Gregory Mann   351
Guinea   47, 106, 127, 186, 195, 197–200, 257 f., 291, 293, 323
Guinea-Bissau   199, 301

Hadrami   86, 91
Hannah Kudjoe   197
Hans Sloane   119
Hausa   68 f., 161, 173
Havana Declaration of 1979   287, 289
Hendrik F. Verwoerd   206
Henry Morton Stanley   13, 143
Henry Sylvester-Williams   190
Henry Venn   136
Herbert Macaulay   188
HIV/AIDS   244 f., 251, 254–256, 261, 353
Homo sapiens   19, 24, 60
Hope Waddell   136

Horn of Africa   90, 177 f., 291, 294, 297, 301, 304 f., 309–312
Houphouet-Boigny   197
Human evolution   19–24, 317
Human origins   5 f., 11, 19, 21, 23
Hungary   232

Ibadi Muslims   49
Iberian Peninsula   51, 270
Ibn al-Yasamin and Ibn Mun'im   57
Ibn Hawqal   58
India   14, 32, 62, 66, 80–84, 87–90, 92–96, 103, 106, 108, 116, 127, 129, 147, 164, 204, 210, 219 f., 229, 234, 241, 253, 270, 288, 318, 330, 354, 357, 360, 375
Indian Ocean   4, 8, 12, 41, 76, 79–84, 86–89, 91–97, 127, 220–222, 419
International Atomic Energy Agency (IAEA)   223 f.
International Monetary Fund (IMF)   16, 284, 345, 358, 362
Internet of Doing Things   378
Iran   53, 287, 289, 295
Islam   3, 5, 11, 15, 44–46, 48–52, 56–60, 62, 65, 67 f., 71, 74–76, 79, 81, 84–87, 89, 91, 93, 102, 142, 153, 160–162, 167, 263–265, 269–273, 275 f., 279, 375, 422
Israel   24 f., 80, 225
Italy   13, 25, 151, 155, 162 f., 169, 178, 257, 282
Ivory Coast   70, 108, 149, 195, 253, 260

Jamaica   110, 117, 119, 275
James Cone   268
James H. Cone   268
James Stevenson   137
Japan   92, 164, 179, 354, 360, 381
Jazz   119
Jean Francois Bayart   4
Jebel Irhoud   23, 60
J. E. Casely Hayford   174
Jerry Bentley   3
Jerusalem   55, 264, 295
Jesuit Missionaries   250
Jesus Christ   55
J.G. Strijdom   204
jihād   142
Jingereber   58
Johann Krapf   137
John Chilembwe   160
John F. Kennedy   299

John Hawkins 106 f.
Johnny Makathini 237
Jolof 101–103
Jonathan T. Reynolds 5, 142
Joseph Stalin 286, 300
Joshua Eisenman 316
Josiah Akindayomi 265
Josiah Crowther 136
J. S. Hogendorn 150
Judaism 264
Judith Byfield 170, 183
Julius Nyerere 160, 194, 196, 199, 201, 291
Junior and Pretty 358

Kabwe Conference 232
Kalahari 26, 29 f.
Kalambo Falls 23
Karl Jaspers 1
Katanga/Shaba 304
Kazakhstan 234
Kenneth Kaunda 328
Ken Saro-Wiwa 369
Kenya 21 f., 27, 31, 145, 156, 165, 174, 176–178, 189, 194 f., 197, 200 f., 253 f., 256, 260, 291, 293, 318 f., 326, 328–330, 333, 343, 346, 352, 422
Kharijite 49
Khartoum 36
Kimbanguism 189, 266
King Afonso 103, 147
Kingdom of Aksum 45
Kingdom of Alodia 47
King Joao 102 f.
King Joao II 102
King Opobo Pepple 131
King Solomon 80
Klasies River 24
Kongo 101, 103 f., 115, 118 f., 122 f., 147
Kordofan 47
Kufra 68
Kwame Nkrumah 192, 194 f., 198 f., 278, 284, 299

Labana of Cordoba 57
Lake Victoria 39
Laptis 70
Last Glacial Maximum (LGM) 26
League of Coloured People (LCP) 165
Lenin School 14, 232–235
Leopold Senghor 166, 195

Leptis Magna 53
Lesotho 27 f., 41, 421
Levant 35
Liberia 106, 133, 147, 169, 255, 257 f., 282, 293, 352 f.
Libya 35, 37, 45 f., 48 f., 53, 60, 153, 163, 174, 179, 422
Liwhu Betiang 360
Lomekwi 21
Lt. Col. R. A. De B. Rose 173

Madagascar 41, 81, 83, 85 f., 91–96, 106, 128–130, 179, 319
Mad Mellon 362
Mafia Island 40, 83
Maghreb 11, 19, 27, 29 f., 33, 36, 46, 49–51, 57, 68, 100, 252, 375
Mahdist resistance 150
Mahir Şaul 149
Maji Maji uprising 146, 150
Major General Dobell 173
Makuria 46 f., 59, 62
Malawi 28, 40, 95, 129 f., 132, 146, 148, 159, 253–256
Malcolm X 268, 272, 276
Mali 19, 30 f., 37, 47, 49, 56, 58, 67, 70, 74, 143, 257, 270, 291, 293, 323, 342, 351
Malik 'Ambar 90
Malla 25
Mansa Musa 49, 70
Mao Zedong 316, 321, 325, 328
Marcus Garvey 166, 190
Mario Greznes 228
Marion Islands 226
Marqosi Danghe 251
Marshall Hodgson 3
Marxist/Marxism 185, 233, 236, 291, 293, 302, 304, 317, 321, 326, 385
Masalik al-Absar 58
Mascarenes 94 f.
Mauretania 47, 49, 68
Mauris/Moors 51, 52, 59, 60
Mauritius 93 f., 96, 319
Mecca 45, 50, 71
Mediterranean 5, 7, 11, 25, 27, 33, 35, 43 f., 46, 54, 56 f., 59–63, 65, 69, 73 f., 78, 81, 91, 100, 107, 162, 177–179, 250, 270
Mediterranean Sea 43 f., 46, 52, 65, 178
Mekatilili wa Menza 177
Meles Zenawi 310

Melvin E. Page   170, 173
Mengistu Haile Mariam   291, 304
Merina empire   128 f.
Michael Colin   198
Middle East   7, 45, 72, 90 f., 162, 175, 222, 228, 270, 286 f., 289, 295, 297, 309, 376
Middle Stone Age   23 f., 29
MK fighters   232, 236
Modibo Keita   195
Mohamadu Buhari   370
Mohammed Bashir Salau   1, 8, 192, 422
Monday Noah   122
Mongolia   375
Monophysitism   100
Morocco   5, 23 f., 29, 33, 45, 56 f., 60, 68, 73, 78, 107, 143, 178, 260, 271, 303, 323, 343
Moscow Red Square   234
Mountain Black   362
Mountain of Fire Ministries (MFM)   362
Mozambique   83, 86 f., 91–96, 119, 128–130, 148, 171, 177, 195, 198–200, 213, 236 f., 255, 290 f., 293 f., 301 f., 327, 343, 346, 379
Mr. W. C. F. Robertson   173
Muhammad Mani   58
Muhammed ibn Muhammed al-Fulani al-Kishnawi   57
Mulay Ahmed   73
Musa ibn Nusayr   51
Muslim-Swahili   87
Muslim troops   45

Namibia   143, 209, 212 f., 215, 219, 222, 227, 229, 256, 289 f., 295, 302, 306
National African Union of Independent Mozambique, (UNAMI)   199
National Association for the Advancement of Colored People (NAACP)   192
National Democratic Union of Mozambique (UDENAMO)   199
National Economic Empowerment and Development Strategy (NEEDS)   338
Nationalism   13 f., 49, 156, 165, 174, 176, 185–189, 191, 194–197, 199–201, 270, 272, 274, 299, 301, 322, 331, 379, 389
National Party   14, 206
Ndembu people   243
Nelson Mandela   146, 148, 212, 217, 307
New Guinea   41

New Partnership for Africa's Development (NEPAD)   350
Niger Basin   146
Niger-Basin   44
Niger Delta   38, 126, 130, 134, 136, 140
Nigeria   16, 19, 24 f., 33, 36–38, 48, 66, 115, 122, 130, 136, 145, 147, 157–159, 174, 176, 180 f., 187–189, 193–195, 197, 225, 241, 247, 249–251, 253, 256 f., 260, 265–267, 269, 271, 274, 283, 293, 321, 330, 338, 341–343, 346–350, 352, 355–366, 368–371, 374, 376, 379, 381–385, 387, 419–422
Nigeria Institute of International Affairs (NIIA)   349
Nigerian Hip Hop   16, 355, 357–362, 365 f., 368
Nigerian National Democratic Party (NNDP)   188
Nigerian pidgin   363, 365–367
Nigerian Progress Union (NPU)   190
Niger River   33, 46, 144
Nile Valley   19, 30, 34, 36, 44, 46, 178
Niyi Osundare   370
Nizam Shahi dynasty   90
Nnamdi Azikiwe   165, 189 f., 194 f.
Nnedi Okorafor   277
Nok Culture   33, 38
Nollywood   277, 359 f.
Non-Aligned Movement (NAM)   15, 210, 281 f., 284, 287–289, 294–296
North Africa   1, 6 f., 22, 24 f., 27, 29 f., 33, 36, 44–49, 51–53, 56, 59, 61 f., 65, 67–75, 78, 84, 107, 142 f., 162, 167, 177–179, 191, 210, 222, 260, 282, 290, 297, 321, 323
North Atlantic Trea- ty Organization (NATO)   221, 286, 301
Norwegian Agency for Development Cooperation (NORAD)   350
Nubia   32, 34–36, 46 f., 49, 59, 62
Nyamwezi   87, 131
Nyasaland   160, 253

OAU   198 f., 284, 288, 371
Obafemi Awolowo   160, 193 f., 352
OECD (Organization for Economic Cooperation and Development)   341, 349, 375, 380
Official Development Assistance (ODA)   340, 343
Ogoni nine   369

Old World 22 f., 47
Oliver R. Tambo 207
Olu Maintain 366 f.
Olu Mountain 368
Olusegun Obasanjo 350, 369
Oluyole 134
Operation Torch 178
Oregenes Adamantius 54
Orlando Patterson 113
Oromo name Chapu 90
Oswald Spengler 1
Ousmane Sembène 271
Out-of-Africa 22 f., 25

Pakistan 32, 49, 270, 272, 375
Palaeolithic 29
Palestine 100, 234
Pan-Africanism 153, 163, 165, 185, 189 f., 193, 299, 371
Patrick Manning 3 f., 8, 282
Patrick Royer 149
Paul Gilroy 100, 357
Paul Lovejoy 91, 112, 121, 150
Peari Primus 120
Pelindaba nuclear station 223
Pemba island 85
People's Republic of China (PRC) 315, 319 f., 322, 327, 329, 333
Perorsi 49
Persian Gulf 81, 89, 91, 221, 227
Pharusii 49
Pik Botha 212, 231
Pleistocene 19, 21 f., 24–29
Pope Gelasius I 53
Pope Miltiades 53
Popular Movement for Liberation of Angola / Movimento Popular de Libertação de Angola (MPLA) 199, 212, 291, 302, 303, 307, 312, 327, 430
Portugal 33, 52, 82, 102–104, 106, 122, 128 f., 144, 151, 155, 169, 198–200, 282, 299, 301, 376
Poverty Reduction and Growth Facility (PRGF) 350
Poverty Reduction Strategy Papers (PRSP) 349
Premier Zhou 323 f., 329
Prentice Hall 5, 89
President F.W. de Klerk 217
Prince Edward 226
Principe 106, 132

Professor Pieter de Lange 216
Professor Willie Esterhuysen 215
Progressive Federal Party (PFP) 215
Prophet Muhammed 44, 49 f.
Publius Terentius Afer 53
P. W. Botha 211 f., 214, 224, 226

Qasr Ibrim 62

racism 165 f., 181, 190, 193, 204, 230, 264, 269, 277, 287, 303, 317
Ras Mkumbuu 85
Rastafarianism 275 f.
Reagan administration 227, 306
Redeemed Christian Church of God (RCCG) 265–267
Red Sea 25, 32, 35, 44, 47, 51, 79–82, 84, 86, 89–91, 95
Reggae 119, 275, 358
Regional Security Councils (RSC) 212
Rev. J. F. Schon 135
Richard Rathbone 170 f., 180–182
Rio de Janeiro 92
Robert Herderson 228
Roman Empire 52 f., 55
Rosa Luxemburg 235 f.
Russia 14, 224, 234–236, 285, 293, 321, 375
Rwanda 39, 255 f., 313, 341, 420
Ryan Coogler 277

Sabratha 70
SADF 212 f., 215, 222–224, 303
Sahara Desert 22, 43 f., 47, 49, 61, 65, 75, 282
Salim Salim 231
Samuel Crowther 135
Santo Domingo 109 f.
Sao Tome 104, 106 f., 109, 123, 132
Saudi Arabia 45, 270, 272, 380
Sekou Toure 194 f.
Senegambia 71, 76, 110 f., 127
Serving in Mission (SIM) 250
Shango 117, 274 f., 277
Shia Muslims 85
Siad Barre 304, 309 f., 312
Sibudu 24
Sicily 54, 163, 178
Sierra Leone 106, 121, 133, 147, 255, 257 f.
Simon Kibangu 160
Slave Coast 100, 111, 130

slavery 5, 8f., 13, 49f., 65, 68f., 75, 79, 87–96, 104, 107, 109, 112–114, 116–120, 125–129, 132–135, 137–140, 148, 158, 268, 277, 282, 351, 419–422
slave trade 1, 6–9, 12f., 15, 66, 74, 88–91, 93–95, 99, 104, 107–118, 120–122, 124–135, 137–139, 141f., 148, 154, 282, 375, 377
Socialist Revolution 233, 236
Sokoto Caliphate 8, 133, 142, 150
Somalia 44f., 83, 88, 95, 256, 271, 283, 304, 309–313, 323, 342f.
Songhai 47, 70, 73–76, 270
Soninke Empire 47, 49, 56
Soul 119, 231, 269f.
South Africa 4, 14, 19, 21–24, 27, 40, 93, 145f., 148, 154, 171, 175, 179–182, 187, 203–234, 236, 248, 253, 255f., 260, 266, 283f., 289–292, 295, 298, 301–303, 306f., 309, 312, 319f., 327, 348–350, 359, 379, 381, 421f.
South African Institute of Race Relations (SAIRR) 214
Southeast Asia 25, 41, 88, 91–93, 386
Southern Negro Youth Congress (SNYC) 192
Soviet Komsomol 233
Soviet Union 14, 209, 213, 219–221, 226, 228, 231f., 234, 237, 281, 284–286, 290f., 293f., 300, 304f., 312, 321–323, 325
Spain 33, 49, 51f., 56, 60, 68, 151, 155, 169, 198, 223, 252, 257, 259, 270, 282, 376
Spanish influenza 252, 261
Sri Lanka 93
Stanley Macebuh 359
State Security Council (SCC) 211
St. Augustine 53–56, 100
Stephen Ellis 4
Steven Bantu Biko 231
St. John 55
Stoffel van der Merwe 213
St. Paul 54
Strait of Gibraltar 25
Strategic Arms Limitation Talks (SALT) 305
Structural Adjustment Programs (SAP) 16, 338
St. Thomas 278
Sudan 27, 30–32, 34–36, 43f., 47f., 56f., 67, 70f., 74–76, 80, 88f., 101, 147, 149f., 178, 181, 256, 260, 271, 323, 342f., 346
Sufi 85, 90, 162, 271, 272, 273, 392
Sultan Djata 245

Sultan of Sokoto 349
Sunni Muslims 272
Suppression of Communism Act 206
Swahili 56, 79, 81–87, 89, 91f., 95, 129f., 137
Swakopmund 171
Swedish Agency for International Development Cooperation (SIDA) 350
Syrian Golan 287, 289, 295

Tanganyika 95, 129, 147, 150, 189, 196, 209, 250
Tanzania 22, 28, 39f., 85, 143, 189, 194–197, 200f., 208f., 224, 232, 237, 241f., 291, 293, 316f., 323, 326f., 343, 349, 351
Tariq Ibn Ziyad 51f.
Terence. Apuleius 53
Terrence Ranger 13, 148
Tete Ansa 157
Thabo Mbeki 14, 203, 209, 214f., 231–235, 350, 421
the People's Movement for the Liberation of Angola (MPLA) 327
the Sahel 33, 41, 46–48, 62, 74, 351
Third World 281, 284, 287f., 290, 294f., 298–300, 304f., 313, 315, 318, 320–323, 327, 332, 338f., 358, 362, 384f., 387, 420
Thomas Clarkson 112
Thomas Clegg 136
Timaya 362f., 365, 369f.
Timbuktu 44, 46, 56–59, 70, 73f., 78, 102f.
Timothy Parsons 170, 180
Timothy Weiskel 13, 149
Tippu Tib 132
Titus Flavius Clemens 54
Togoland 171, 173, 176
Tomi Adeyemi 277
Tony Blair 341
Touba 272
Toucouleur 49
trade 4, 6–13, 16, 30f., 34, 36–38, 40f., 43, 46–49, 56, 59, 61f., 65–95, 99, 101f., 104–108, 111, 113–116, 120–142, 148, 154, 157, 161, 175, 181f., 186f., 194, 196, 245, 247, 254, 271, 282, 295, 301, 316, 318, 329–331, 341, 345, 347f., 350, 356, 375f., 378, 383, 419
Tretiakov Gallery 234
Trinidad 117, 274, 277
Tripartite Agreement 306, 308, 312
Tuareg bandits 76

Tunisia 25, 33, 45, 53 f., 56, 68, 73, 143, 176, 178 f., 271, 321
Turkey 36, 380

Uganda 39, 145, 159, 171, 174, 177, 189, 244 f., 251, 253 f., 256, 309, 343, 349
'Umar Taal 142
UNESCO 3, 58 f., 155, 159, 169, 175, 374, 376, 387
União Nacional para a Independência Total de Angola (UNITA) 302
Union of People of Angola (UPA) 199
United Arab Emirates 272, 378, 380
United Kingdom 59, 190, 193, 257, 272, 275, 345, 389, 419
United National Independence Party (UNIP) 328
United Nations 3, 14, 185, 192, 198, 230, 281, 284, 289 f., 292, 294 f., 300, 310, 320, 337, 347, 350, 383, 386
United States Agency for International Development (USAID) 342
United States of America 119 f., 127, 147, 185, 259
Universal Ethiopian Students Association (UESA) 190
Universal Negro Improvement Association (UNIA) 190
Upper Guinea 107, 121, 128
US Army 222

Visigothic Hispania 51 f., 60
Vladimir Lenin 236
VOC (Vereenigde Oostindische Compagnie or Dutch East India Company) 93
Volta-Bani 149, 177

Waconzy 362, 364, 365
Walter Rodney 4, 108 f., 114, 116, 154, 283
W. E. B. Dubois 2
West Africa 4, 6, 8, 22, 27, 30 f., 33, 36–38, 41, 44, 46–49, 51, 57–59, 66–78, 94, 100, 105–107, 111 f., 114, 122, 126–128, 130–133, 136, 138–140, 143–145, 148–150, 154–158, 160–162, 164–166, 169, 171, 173 f., 176, 181, 188–190, 193, 195, 198, 209, 219, 222, 229, 245, 249 f., 252, 254, 257 f., 260, 267, 271 f., 277, 282, 284, 290, 293, 300, 302, 322, 342, 351, 357, 360, 387, 421 f.
West African Frontier Force (WAFF) 145, 173 f.
West African Student Union (WASU) 164 f., 188, 190
white supremacy 176, 183, 204, 211, 219, 268 f., 275
Willen Bosman 105
William Ansah 123
William Davenant 105
William McNeill 3
William Pettigrew 111
Wizkid 362, 364
Wolof 47, 49
World Bank 255, 284, 337–340, 342, 344–351, 358, 362, 380 f., 387
World Health Organization (WHO) 241, 257, 259
World War I 13, 149, 155 f., 160, 163, 166 f., 169–172, 175, 177, 184, 189 f., 285
World War II 13, 166, 170, 177–183, 188 f., 191 f., 194–196, 220, 222, 290, 297–299, 301, 340, 386

Xhosa 274

Yemen 25, 86
Yemeni 91
Yoruba 112, 136, 138 f., 161 f., 173, 265, 274, 422
Youssou N'Dour 271
Yusuf Dadoo 231

Zaire 228, 245 f., 257, 291, 293 f., 300 f., 303, 308 f., 312, 341
Zaky Azees 358
Zambesia 129
Zambia 23, 40, 95, 208 f., 215, 221, 224, 232, 254, 288, 291, 318, 326, 328–330, 333, 346, 422
Zanzibar 83 f., 86 f., 92, 95, 130, 132, 137, 145, 174, 319
Zimbabwe 82, 85 f., 148 f., 158, 177, 221, 224–226, 244, 255, 288, 302, 346, 387, 421
Zimbabwe African National Union (ZANU) 302

www.ingramcontent.com/pod-product-compliance
Lightning Source LLC
Chambersburg PA
CBHW080405230426
43662CB00016B/2326